Air Rifles

Fourth Edition

Revised and enlarged

by

Dennis E. Hiller

ISBN 0 9507046 7 9
© Copyright September 1985

Published by Dennis E. Hiller

Dennis E. Hiller,
56 Princess Way,
Euxton,
Chorley,
Lancs PR7 6PJ

Hiller, Dennis E.
　　Air Rifles — — 4th ed.
　　1. Air guns — — collectors and collecting
　　1. Title
　　683.4'22　　　　TS537.5

　　ISBN 0 9507046 7 9

Printed by T. Snape & Co. Ltd., Boltons Court, Preston. Tel: (01772) 254553.

*To my mother,
who in 1984, joined my
father in making me
an
orphan.*

LONE PASSAGE

So much alone,
So on my own.
Who's there to see
stark misery?
Hidden away,
Day after day.
Clouded by dust,
Go on I must.
Rescuer — none,
burdens — alone.

I've wings to fly,
across the sky.
Across the sea,
to sanctuary.
I'll conquer yet,
I will not fret.
I'll not desert
this patch of dirt,
until the seeds,
fulfil our needs.
Until the air,
is fresh, and there
a Green Bay tree,
for you and me.

HELENA M. HILLER (1920—1984).

DENNIS E. HILLER
56 Princess Way, Euxton, Chorley,
Lancs PR7 6PJ, England.

Copyright © D. E. Hiller. 1978, 1979, 1980, 1982, 1985.

All rights reserved. No part of this publication may be reproduced, stored in a retrieval system, or transmitted in any or by any means, electronic, mechanical, photo-copying, recording, or otherwise, without the prior permission of the publishers.

Previous Editions and Publications

1978	"Air Rifles" First Edition
1979	"Air Pistols" First Edition
1980	"Air Rifles" Second Edition (Revised & enlarged)
1982	"Air Pistols" Second Edition (Revised & Enlarged)
1984	"Air Rifles" Third Edition (Revised & enlarged)
1984	"Complete Airgunner" (1907), R. B. Townshend B.A.
1992	"Complete Airgunner" (1907), R. B. Townshend B.A.
1993	"Air Pistols" Third Edition

ACKNOWLEDGEMENTS

I am grateful to the following for their help and assistance in the preparation of this publication and the many collectors and friends who the Author has met at arms fairs, auctions and antique fairs throughout the country and to the constant dribble of information that flows together to form the river of knowledge in the field of airguns.

Roughly speaking, in alphabetical order, the Author would like to thank the following; R. Beddoe Jnr of Ellesmere a constant companion and irritating competitor at many a local auction, and after almost six years having finally spelt his name correctly! B.S.A. Guns Limited of Birmingham, England. Dennis Commins, I'm deeply indebted to Dennis and he is living proof that most people named Dennis are great! J. Cross and Bill Eastwood, Bob Gulliford of Cardiff who turns out excellent stocks. The late Dr. J. S. E. Gilbart who shall be remembered by all airgun enthusiasts, also the late T. H. Kline of Preston. To Charlie Quinn, Tom Reid of Preston who has also helped at arms fairs and whose knowledge of car speeds and bends was proved the morning he correctly predicted that the Author was going too fast and with two ton of guns in the back we gently slid off the road and demolished a row of black and white road markers, we returned to the road with half the Derbyshire countryside clinging to the underside of the car and Tom still muttering "You're not going to make this bend, Dennis". The late and much admired S. J. Roche. Geoff Scarber of Hitchin, C. J. Romer of Harlebury, Viktor Søndergaard of Roskilde, Denmark, and to Webley & Scott Ltd., Birmingham. To A. A. Brown & Son for the information regarding the Abas airpistol. To Ray Czerkas (the Cat-man to Welham Green) and his charming Wife Maya who both accommodated the Author kindly on his London trips, and to Bob Gulliford and his wife Jackie, a black belt in both Judo and cooking, who have given the Author every assistance when on his Cardiff trips. My many thanks also go to John Poloczek of Whittle-le-Woods for his help in the shop and his brewing capabilities. Finally I would like to extend every gratitude to my wife Julie, who has continued to allow me to squander my life away on airguns, and then there is my son Jonathan who constantly reminds me that we are not so far removed from Neanderthal Man!

INTRODUCTION

It is a continuous process adding information to the original text of the Second Edition as it was with the First Edition so it is with the Second. So from the seeds of the First Edition has flourished the Second Edition and this has now matured into this the Third Edition.

The values have been very steady over the years and only two major changes have taken place due mainly to the acceptance of airguns as collectable items by the dealer's trade. Firstly the main bulk of airguns have remained static in value, prices of the run-of-the-mill airguns have remained the same over the last three to four years, rubbish, rough and cheap airguns have gone down in value, whilst the mint and rare examples have gone sky-high, particularly English airguns from the Webley and B.S.A. stables. The majority appear to collect Webley followed closely by B.S.A. airguns. Pellet tins and accessories are also collected and these can make interesting additions to the collection and give some idea of the way the hobby was taken so seriously in the 1920s and 1930s when many a father took great pride in coaching his son in the fine art of airgun shooting, unlike today when no doubt tomorrow's collectable item will be video games!

The air rifles appear in alphabetical order by manufacturer, or by its common model name, and lastly even by its importer if this alone is known. Within the category they are entered in chronological order and follow through any variations that may have taken place.

The page format follows the First Edition, the photographs are followed by the text made up of MODEL, MAKER, DATE, VALUATION, DETAILS, and finally SERIAL NUMBERS. These are better explained as follows:

MODEL Most air rifles are called by either a model number or name and this appears at the head of the page. The variations and minor changes I have tried to place in order as they appeared.

MAKER Usually this is known but some are just marked "FOREIGN" so these are entered under importer's name as are the Relum air rifles.

DATE These are usually only approximate and in some cases cannot even be guessed at. Old catalogues help and even talking to the original owners or the older generation. Have tried to be as accurate as possible.

VALUATION These are a guide only and cannot accept any responsibility for monies lost or gained in deals based on valuations given. They are a guide only and should be used as such bearing in mind that values change as often as the weather. If nobody wants your airgun then its not worth much. The valuations have been arrived at by watching advertisements and auction prices. Trends in values soon become apparent and average figures can usually be arrived at. Some airguns are very rare and appear infrequently in auctions etc, but usually these represent good investment pieces. There are usually three sets of figures under valuation, as an example: £54n, £25—£40, £22a—£33a.

£54n — The approximate new price. Even this will vary from supplier to supplier and only applies to current models, discontinued air rifles will not have a new valuation.

£25—£40 — represents the approximate limits of the secondhand value from average to very good condition. For rough and minty specimens then prices can be lower or higher if required.

£22a—£33a — from a list of recent auction prices I have taken the lowest and highest bids gained and used these to give some idea of the sort of value to be gained from putting in, or buying from, an auction. Where air rifles have not appeared in auctions then no value appears.

The dollar equivalents are equated by allowing one pound sterling to equal $1.50 and only relate to the values in the British market and DO NOT relate to American values or auction prices. Although values are roughly the same on each side of the Atlantic it must be realised that the Author has no actual knowledge of American values for air rifles featured in this edition. From observation it would appear that American values are often higher than English.

MUZZLE VELOCITIES These have been dropped and only appeared in "Air Rifles" First Edition. They proved to be of little value, time consuming in their measurement and dangerous, flying lead!

Not only were they time consuming, but of very little value as it is very easy to uprate the power of an airgun by just changing the mainspring and the piston washer for a start. A step further is made by polishing the air chamber and playing about with the transfer port diameter for optimum air flow. Even the choice of pellet has an effect on the muzzle velocity as does the lubricant you use and even whether you seat the pellet into the barrel bore.

One illusion that I wish to dispel is the belief that pre-war airguns are more powerful than present day models that are manufactured to a muzzle energy limit. Quite the reverse is the case, as before the limit was introduced manufacturers built airguns on the accepted design that Big was Powerful. Which in present designs is just not the case. The pre-limit airguns were manufactured with no limit in mind, power varied from gun to gun with the same model. When the muzzle energy limit was introduced the manufacturers had to start monitoring the energy produced and many airguns had to be modified to UPRATE the power in order to compete in what is now a very competitive market. So if you are shooting with a pre-war-limit airgun, this applies to spring weapons only, then except for the very small exception you have no need to worry about the muzzle energy level.

MUZZLE ENERGY Any airgun can be collected as long as the power output does not exceed 12 foot pounds. This does not apply to CO_2 or any other type of gas gun as by the 1968 Fire Arms Act they "are not propelled by air". It is quite safe to assume that all spring airguns fall below this limit. The power output is measured in terms of Kinetic energy of the pellet at the muzzle. Should any gun exceed this limit of 12 foot pounds then a firearms certificate is required. The formula for Kinetic energy, foot pounds, is $\frac{WV^2}{2g}$ where

W = weight of pellet in pounds,
V = velocity of pellets in feet per second.
g = acceleration due to gravity, 32.2 feet/second^2.

For .22 air pistols with a pellet weighing 14.7 grains (0.0021 lb) the maximum velocity would be about 428 feet per second, whilst for a .177 air pistol it is 560 feet per second. It has been proved that the .22 pellet is more efficient than the .177 in converting the energy of the spring into velocity, this could be why Webley's produced far more .22 airguns than .177. Webley's have also shown that using the same airgun with interchangeable barrels there is a 18 per cent drop in pellet energy when going from .22 to .177 even though there is an increase in velocity.

DETAILS As much information as possible entered here. Have used this section to build up as complete a picture as possible.

SERIAL NUMBERS The variation and dating can be made easier if the serial numbers and individual characteristics can be listed and hope that a pattern emerges. As more air rifles are seen then a more complete picture will evolve and help the student of airguns. The Gem air rifles pose many problems as there are so many variations and will need many a reshuffle to arrive at some order of manufacture and maker.

REFERENCE AND READING MATERIAL
"AIRGUN DIGEST", R. Beeman
"AIRGUN FROM TRIGGER TO MUZZLE", G. Cardew
"THE AMERICAN B.B. GUN", A. T. Dunothan
"AIRGUNS AND OTHER PNEUMATIC ARMS", Arne Hoff
"GAS, AIR & SPRING GUNS OF THE WORLD", W. H. B. Smith
"THE AIRGUN BOOK", John Walter
"AIRGUNS & AIRPISTOLS", L. Wesley
"AIRGUNS", E. G. Wolff

MONTHLY MAGAZINES
"GUNS REVIEW", Ravenhill Publishing Co. Ltd.
"AIRGUN WORLD", Romsey Publishing Co. Ltd.
"GUNS MAGAZINE", American publication
"SPORTING AIR RIFLE", Peterson Publishing Co. Ltd.
"AIRGUNNER", Romsey Publishing Co.

WEEKLY MAGAZINES
"EXCHANGE & MART", available each Thursday
"SHOOTING TIMES", available each Thursday

COLLECTING AIR RIFLES

When I pick up an air rifle with a view to purchasing I split it into three parts; barrel, air chamber, and stock.

BARREL: Always examine it for straightness, if break action look down the bore and rotate the end slowly and watch for any shadows that might appear down the inside. Usually a bent barrel is pretty obvious, but any persistent shadows in the bore are a good sign that the barrel is bent. Bending often occurs just after the barrel support block, if over strong cocking has taken place then barrel will bend downwards. If the action has been fired in cocked position and the barrel allowed to fly up then the bend in the barrel will be upwards, there may also be a build up of metal on the top of the barrel breech where it has struck the top of the transfer port. Have seen this on the B.S.A. Cadet and Cadet-Majors. Sideward bends can indicate a bad fall where the owner has fallen on top of the air rifle and there may also be signs of a broken stock. It is possible to re-straighten a barrel using a leather headed hammer and sandbag, but often a steel hammer is used so watch out for the obvious marks on the barrel. Sometimes the wrong barrel has been fitted, have seen an A.S.I. Sniper barrel fitted to a Diana Model 25. What people can do with air rifles is quite amazing at times. Next look at the sights. These should be complete and in full working order so always try them for adjustment. They should always be the correct type for the particular air rifle. Underlevers tend to have fewer barrel problems than breakactions, but are not so easily replaceable if something should go wrong. Have seen a Webley Service .22 barrel screwed into the action of a Gem and a pre-war B.S.A. "L" pattern underlever barrel turned down to form a replacement barrel for the Kynock "Swift". The Webley Service barrel should have a matching serial number to the air rifle unless it is an extra barrel. The German "Millita" air rifles had serial numbers stamped all over the place so make sure that all numbers match because to a collector these are important. Many air rifles from the same manufacturer have interchangeable parts, i.e. the pre-war B.S.A. underlevers, the trigger blocks can be swopped over at will and as these carry the serial numbers watch out for the many hybrids being hawked about.

AIR CHAMBER: Look for bulges near the air transfer port end which indicate savage dieselling. Have seen many Webley Mk. IIIs suffering from this. Check the telescopic sight grooves for excessive wear, if they are original and if not have they been well machined on. On the Webley Mk. III the ramp was fixed by three spot welds and is prone to lift and even come off altogether so look for repairs with solder or even araldite. On repeater air rifles ask if you can load and fire the action as only too often the reason for selling is that the owner has tampered with the action and it no longer functions properly. The early post-war Diana's had a removable scope ramp held in place by two small screws, should these be missing it will not effect the performance. With underlever action rifles some people cock the action with the tap closed then open the tap as if loading and then release the action and test if the tap will hold air. This test will only prove two things, whether the tap and/or piston washer is air-tight. Webley Mk. IIIs do quite well at this test, but it is not a test for performance. The Author has tried B.S.A. Airsporters that have not even given a hiss of air when tested, but when fired a different story is told. Look at the state of the screw heads, a careful owner uses a screwdriver whilst the opposite will use anything to tear the airgun apart. The state of the piston washer can only be guessed at, but if leather then look for fibres that may be left in the barrel after it has been fired. This indicates that the washer is beginning to break up and will need replacing. Always check the trigger action by cocking then releasing whilst holding either the barrel or underlever in the cocked position and allowing the mainspring to slowly return to unfired position, this test gives you some idea of the strength of the mainspring and degree of bite to the sear of the trigger action. A buckled mainspring will judder when the action is being cocked, but this can easily be replaced should the overall condition of the airgun be quite good.

STOCK: Now down to the woodwork. Always kill active woodworm! This will show itself by small piles of powdered wood on the floor after the old airgun has been left standing overnight. The only advantage in having woodworm is that it will lessen the weight of the airgun and make it barrel heavy and so aid balance and accuracy. Look over the stock and take notice of minor surface marks that should pose no problems, but very deep marks, or engravings of buffalos and other animals that previous owners have had a go at will devalue the airgun, unless of course the engraving has been expertly done, then it can add to the value. As can the excellent engraving to metal parts that is being done nowadays. Try and make sure that the stock is the correct one for the air rifle. Also look for breakages and repair jobs particularly to the pistol grip as this nearly always breaks if some heavy object falls on top of the airgun, such as a clumsy owner. Check the butt plate. Often the pre-war B.S.A. underlevers have the small wooden cap and spring metal plate missing from the base of the stock. The stocks are sometimes stamped with retailers marks and these can be of interest. Some shops even use these now. The chequering and style of stock can give some idea of the age if you know what to look for.

FINDING AIRGUNS: The Author has heard of Pope air pistols that have been dug up in back gardens and Gem air rifles found in dustbins, so where do you start looking for air rifles?

Try the following:

>Second-hand shops
>Gun shops
>Antique shops
>Auctions
>Arms Fairs
>Fellow collectors
>Magazine advertisements
>"Contacts".

Second-hand Shops: These sometimes produce surprises and are worth visiting regularly. They rarely know the true value of unusual airguns, but the rare pieces only turn up once in a blue moon. They are usually ready to haggle and may even take modern airguns in part exchange. When visiting shops, always take your time and be courteous, an ill-mannered and domineering approach will often get you nowhere. People often will not do business with those they do not like.

Gun Shops: The comments for Second-hand shops also apply to gun shops. Regular visits can pay dividends and it pays to keep in contact with the Gunsmith and let him know of your interests. He may also be able to help with information of airguns sold even before the Second World War, i.e. pre-1939.

Antique Shops: Have never had much success with these. Only rarely have airguns turned up, but keep on trying as you never know when one will appear in a house clearance or auction. Antique shops often either charge very low prices for choice items or put prices like £45 on Diana tinplate air rifles. Again, ask nicely and be courteous and you never know what turns up.

Auctions: Antique and household auctions sometimes feature air rifles, but the best are the arms and militaria auctions that regularly appear around the country. Airguns nearly always feature in these and can be obtained quite cheaply if the reserve price is low and no one else wants it. The reserve price is the lowest amount that the owner wants for the airgun when he enters it for the action. When you, the hopeful owner, starts bidding you may be bidding against someone else in the auction room, or a postal bidder, or if on our own then the auctioneer will be bidding against you until either you back out of bidding before it reaches its reserve price, or if you reach the reserve price, the auctioneer will ask for any further bids and if there are no more then down will come the hammer and you have gained another airgun for your collection. Postal bidding is where people who cannot attend send in their maximum bids for particular items in the auction catalogue. Occasionally postal bidders acquire items for less than their maximum bid. Always try and arrive early at auctions in order to thoroughly check over the airguns appearing for any faults and decide which ones you are interested in and to how much you are prepared to pay. Don't be shy when bidding starts, get in and bid for it's soon over and takes only seconds. The usual number of lots auctioned is about one hundred an hour.

Arms Fairs: Good hunting grounds. Surprising what turns up at an arms fair. If they occur in your area then try and attend. If you want the bargains then arrive early. Some stalls offer airguns only whilst others dabble in almost anything. The traders will haggle and take your unwanted air rifles in part exchange. Most arms fairs have a happy friendly atmosphere.

Fellow Collectors: For swapping information and airguns. See also "Contacts". Collectors in different parts of the country find different classes of airguns and different levels of prices, so it helps in having as many friends who collect or know of your interest.

Magazines: These can add up to quite a weekly bill. The Author takes the following:

"Exchange and Mart" weekly, Thursday, look under SHOOTING for various airguns. Also under ANTIQUES and the MILITARIA section for news regarding the antique fairs and militaria fairs. All good hunting grounds.

"Shooting Times". Rarely features any articles about airguns, but does give news of auctions of sporting guns and these often contain airguns. Thursday.

"Airgun World". A must for any airgun collector. Monthly.

"Guns Review". Again, a must for any collector. Monthly.

"Sporting Air Rifles". The Author writes articles for this magazine.

"Airgunner". A monthly magazine.

You can advertise your unwanted items in any of the above or even advertise your requirements. It is also worthwhile placing an advert in your local paper for airguns. Although some daily papers will not accept adverts if they mention such dirty words as GUN or AIRGUN etc. Such is public opinion at the moment.

Man is the hunter, so go ye and seek an airgun!!!

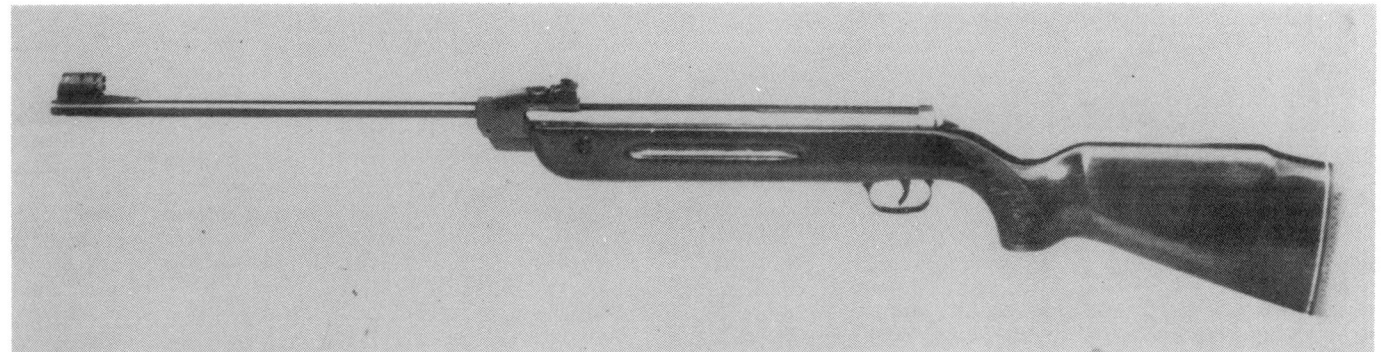

Airgunaid Model SP5

MODEL "Airgunaid SP5".

MAKER Basically a British Diana from Scotland fitted with a .200 calibre barrel by Airgunaid, 131 Springfield Road, Chelmsford, Essex. Due to a fire in the early 1980s this firm is no longer operating.

DATE From 1980 to 1982.

VALUATION Was £50 new when available.
£50n, £30—£80, £35a.
($75, $45—$90, $52a).

DETAILS As stated earlier this SP5 is a Diana Model 79/80 with a .200 calibre barrel. Many shooters consider this calibre to be the ultimate combination of the hitting energy of the .22 and the velocity of the .177. Underside of the stock fore-end bears the date stamp, in this case "80 1". Top of air chamber, between the scope rails, "CAL .200 — AIRGUNAID SP5 — MADE IN GREAT BRITAIN". From a collectors' point of view this must rank as quite a find as both Airgunaid and Diana have both gone out of business and the SP5 was only in production for about two years. Stock style may have changed, it was first advertised with a square fronted fore-end, but later appeared with a more rounded front and with a single parallel groove on each side of the fore-end, as how can a single groove be parallel? Advertised weight 7 lbs., 42 inches long with a 17⅜ inch barrel. Fully adjustable rearsight and a tunnel foresight with three interchangeable elements. Trigger unit was fully adjustable and can be removed very easily as one unit by removing the rear chamber cross pin.

A review of the SP5 appears in "Airgun World" June 1980, in which they tested various .200 calibre pellets and reached the following conclusions:

PELLET	WEIGHT (GNS)	VELOCITY (F.P.S.)	ENERGY
Blitz	9.8	685	10.21
Champion	10.5	663	10.25
Sheridan	15.2	542	9.9
Bimoco Torpedo	15.7	534	9.94
H&N Pointed	13.11	591	10.17
Norman May Viper	8.32	680	9.57

Note how the heavier and lighter the pellet the lower the muzzle energy, the optimum weight would appear to hover around the 10 grains.

Anschutz Model 275

MODEL 275.

MAKER Present day airguns made by J. G. Anschutz, GmbH Jagd — und Sportwaffenfabrik, 79, Ulm/Donau, West Germany, Daimlerstrabe 12.

DATE From the early 1950s to late 1970s, but were rarely advertised and sold in small numbers only. May even still be available but by special order only.

VALUATION £40—£90, £36a. ($60—$135).

DETAILS Measures 41 inches (104 cms) in length. Bolt action repeater using a twelve or six shot force fed magazine clip that plugged into the underside of the barrel. Similar action to the pre-war Haenel Model 33 and the target Model Haenel 311 of present day, also the Haenel Model 310. Safety catch at rear of action. Serial number stamped on barrel. Stamped on the barrel "Cal. 4.40 — Nr9" and above that "ANSCHUTZ ERZEUGNIS MODELL 275". Rearsight appears to be adjustable for elevation only. Advertised as having a finely rifled barrel, and weighing 6½ lbs. Should therebe any need to unblock the barrel there is a small grub screw on top of the breech just in front of the rearsight. Undo this and remove the small spring and steel ball bearing. Any barrel obstruction can then be pushed down to the breach and be pushed out from the top. Remove magazine and cock action in order to carry this out. When barrel is clear replace ball bearing, spring and grub screw. To operate action when removed from stock it is necessary to press a lever in front of the main pivot for the bolt action otherwise the bolt cannot be raised up into the vertical position for cocking. This lever normally rests against the front inside surface of the outer housing that hangs down below the airgun.

For details of Patents linked to the above action see Haenel air rifles. A very cheap supply of 4.4 mm calibre lead ball can be had by using BB size lead shot normally used for loading shotgun cartridges. A bag of this should last a lifetime.

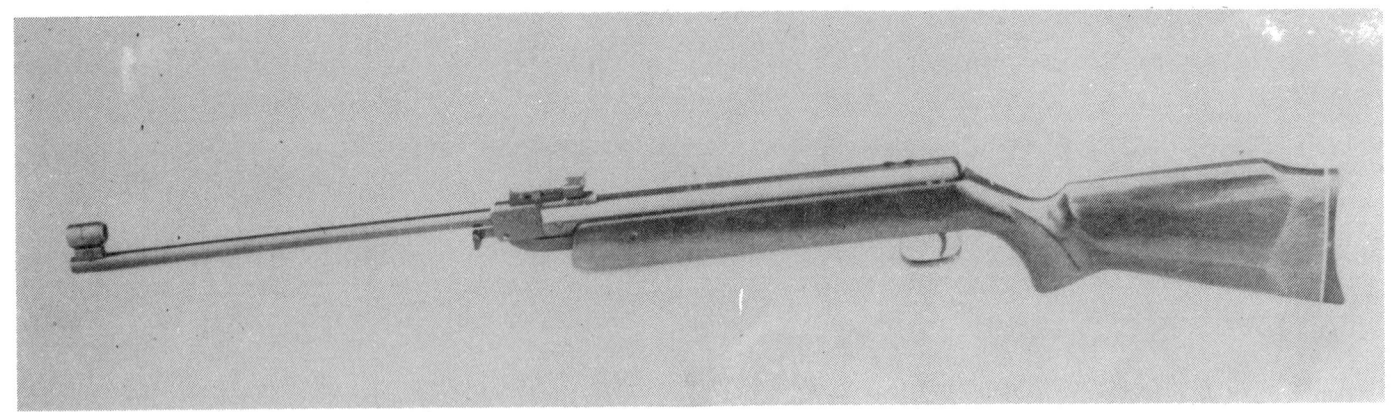

Anschutz Model 335

MODEL 335 for .22 and 335S for .177, but with spare barrels some deviation of the above rule may occur.

MAKER J. G. Anschutz GmbH, Jagd-und Sportwaffenfabrik, 79, Ulm/Donau, West Germany, Daimlerstrabe 12. Imported by Frank Dyke & Co., London.

DATE Introduced during the middle of 1971 and is till a current model.

VALUATION £40–£80, £30a–£34a. ($60–$120).

DETAILS Has the feel of quality. Almost all metal construction. 43¼ inches (110 cms) in length with an 18½ inch (47 cms) rifled barrel. Tunnel foresight mounted on dovetail, interchangeable foresight elements by way of spring loaded inner sleeve, push in to change elements. Calibre and serial number is stamped on L.H.S. of barrel near breach end. The under lever barrel latch is pulled forward on early models to release the barrel. Top of air chamber is stamped "ANSCHUTZ MOD.335", and has been machine dovetailed for telescopic and aperture sights. Piston fitted with leather washer. Weight almost 8 lbs. For review of above see "Gun Review" August 1971. The trigger block is a one piece unit so would ease the removal for main spring renewal. The Model 335 was available as follows:

   335 — .22 strong sporting mainspring.
   335 — .177 strong mainspring.
   335S — special target mainspring.
   For review see "Airgun World" November 1977.

Top of barrel stamped "J. G. Anschutz GmbH. Waffenfabrik Ulm/D GERMANY". During 1980 the barrel locking latch was changed to one that pressed up to release the barrel instead of the older type that was pulled out.

A review of the 335 appears in "Sporting Air Rifle" September 1984.

Lauflänge:	ca. 47 cm, fein gezogen	Barrel length:	18½ inches	Longueur du canon:	env. 47 cm
Kaliber:	4,5 mm (P 177)	Caliber:	4.5 mm (P 177)	Calibre:	4,5 mm (P 177)
Gesamtlänge:	ca. 111 cm	Length over-all:	43⅓ inches	Longueur totale:	env. 111 cm
Visierung:	Kurvenvisier	Sights:	Tangent rear-sight	Viseurs:	La hausse à curseur
Gewicht:	ca. 3,4 kg	Weight:	9.8 lbs	Poids:	env. 3,4 kg

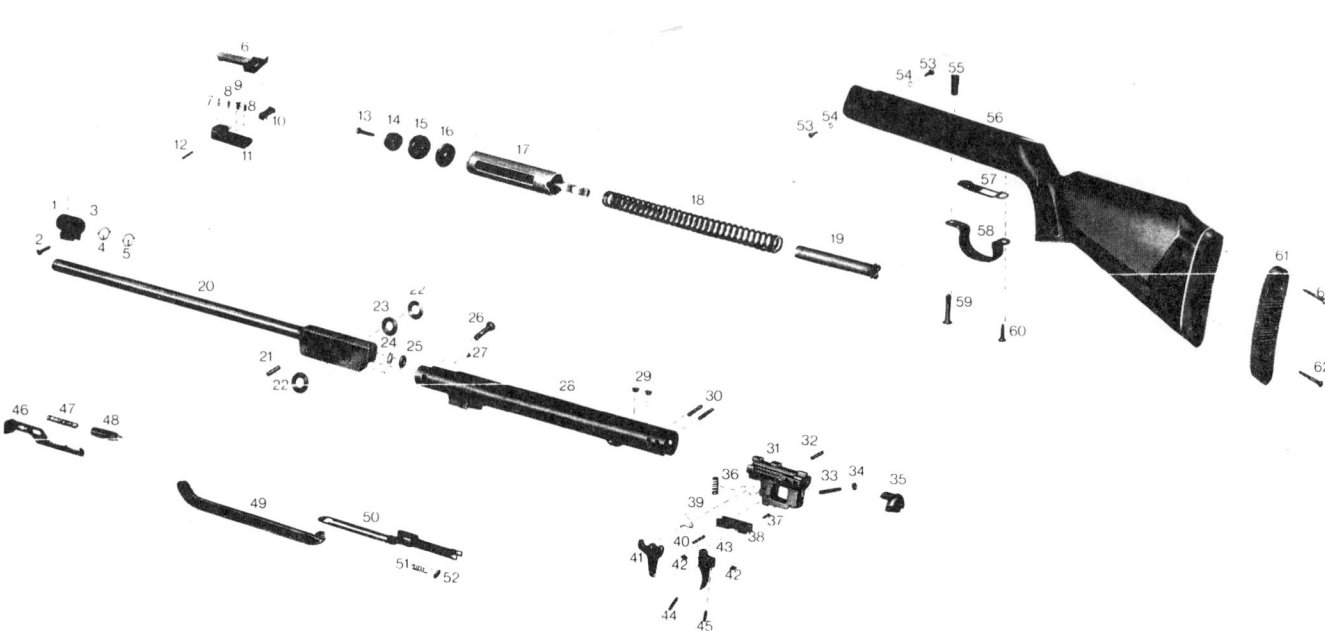

Anschutz 335 Parts Diagram

A.S.I. Paratrooper Repeater Mk. I 1969 to 1975. (Shooting Times)

MODEL Paratrooper Repeater. Model 68 (U.S.A.).

MAKER El Gemo, Spanish. A.S.I. Importers. Also manufactured in Brazil.

DATE Introduced 1969, Mk II model, 1975.

VALUATION £30—£60. ($45—$90).

DETAILS A very handy little air rifle. Magazine holds about 25—28 pellets and from then on you cock and fire. Have always found the action reliable unless it has been tampered with. The military style stock aids holding and it can be very steady when shooting. Trigger adjustment can be achieved by three screws at the rear of the trigger guard. The middle screw is the locking screw and must be loosened before adjustment and tightened after. The fore screw adjusts the length of trigger pull, whilst the hind screw is for pressure adjustment. 37 inches (94 cms) long with a 17¾ inch (45 cms) rifled barrel. Grips moulded plastic and action has black crackled finish. Blued air chamber and barrel. Stamped on top of air chamber "MADE IN SPAIN ELGAMO" with the deer's head trademark. Stamped on the L.H.S. of the barrel breech "CAL. 4.5 (.177) 'F' " the "F" being in a pentagon, also the serial number appears. Grooved for telescopic sight. In 1975 the Mk. II paratrooper repeater and single shot air rifles were introduced with improved style wood finish grips. The fore-end grips were extended along the action and the pistol grip was modified for either left or right handed use. The repeater was only available in .177 whilst the single shot in either .22 or .177.

For a review of the A.S.I. Paratrooper Repeater Mk. II see "Airgun World" August 1979. When it first appeared, magazine chargers were also advertised in packs of five, have yet to see one of these. Sold in America as the Model 68, could be named after the year of introduction. Very early models were marked "MOD GAMO 55" on the side of the barrel breech and on top of the air chamber "EL GAMO BARCELONA ESPANA".

Care should be taken when totally unscrewing the rearsight elevation adjuster wheel because underneath this are two very small ball bearings and they are kept in place by the tension of the sight arm pressing against the underside of the adjuster wheel. When replacing the wheel a small drop of oil in the two indentations for the ball bearings will hold them down as you replace the wheel. To save having to remove the loading tube each time you need to introduce more pellets just file a slot in one side of the tube just in front of the plunger in its drawn back and locked position. File the cut away so that it makes the groove for the plunger handle just wide enough for pellets to be dropped in when the plunger has been drawn back. In this way pellets can be added even when the magazine tube still contains some pellets. When inserting pellets hold air rifle in downward position so the pellets fall towards the breech.

Barrel removal can be quite dangerous if care is not taken. First unscrew the collar nut on the right hand side of the pivot bolt then tap out the barrel pivot pin from the same side. It can be quite a tight fit, but it will drift out. By this time the barrel should be in the broken position, there is an inner sleeve inside the barrel pivot hole that also needs to be drifted out, BUT BE CAREFUL, this holds the barrel plunger in place and when the inner sleeve has been removed the plunger can fly out with considerable force. As the barrel is being removed there will be two dished washers on either side of the barrel, these are placed so that the concave surface faces away from the sides of the barrel.

It can happen that when the magazine is empty and the action is broken for reloading the magazine plunger can be pushed into the loading gate and in fact jam the action open. If you try and force the action closed the only thing that might happen is to break off the metal strip that pushes the loading gate down. Should the action jam open in this state just pull back the magazine plunger and then gently close action as normal and reload with pellets and repeat cocking action to feed another pellet into the loading gate.

A.S.I. Paratrooper Repeater, Mk. II

The Sniper

MODEL The Sniper, and later the Rangemaster.

MAKER Elgamo, Spain. Imported by A.S.I., Alliance House, Snape, Saxmundham, Suffolk. Also manufactured in Brazil.

DATE Earliest advert seen is 1968 and still a current model.

VALUATION £20—£60, £9a—£17a, single shot.
($30—$60).
£25—£60, repeater.
($35—$75).

DETAILS 40¼ inches (120 cms) long with a 17¾ inch (45 cms) rifled barrel. Hooded foresight. L.H.S. of barrel breech stamped with the serial number and calibre. Rearsight adjustable for windage and elevation and is stamped with the deer's head trademark of Elgamo. Top of air chamber has small hole for lubrication and stamped at the rear "MADE IN SPAIN BY ELGAMO" with the deer's head trademark. Linked cocking lever. Advertised weight 6 lbs. Above model available in repeater form. Sold in either .22 or .177. Advertised velocity is 650 f.p.s., this must be for .177. Light coloured stock with plastic trigger guard. Double pull trigger. Black plastic butt plate with deer's head trademark. Have seen the above with stick-on label bearing the following message "HIGH POWER — A.S.I. SNIPER-MICRO ACCURACY". Later models were without the finger groove on the stock fore-end and butt plate lacking the deer's head trademark. Scope ramps on the air chamber measure 11 mm. Trigger adjustment is by use of screwdriver through the small hole in the rear trigger guard strut. A review of the Sniper appeared in "Airgun World" March 1981. At a later date they appeared as the Rangemaster with the following gold and black stick-on label on the air chamber "A.S.I. RANGEMASTER MICRO-ACCURACY". The stock lacked the two fore-end grooves. Trigger adjustment by way of tiny hole through rear pillar of trigger guard.

Sold in America as the Models "Expo" and 300. The only difference is the style of the stock. Also as a "Target" air rifle with a smooth stock and having a well formed fore-end.

The repeater version of the Sniper uses the same system as that fitted to the Paratrooper and is available in .177 only.

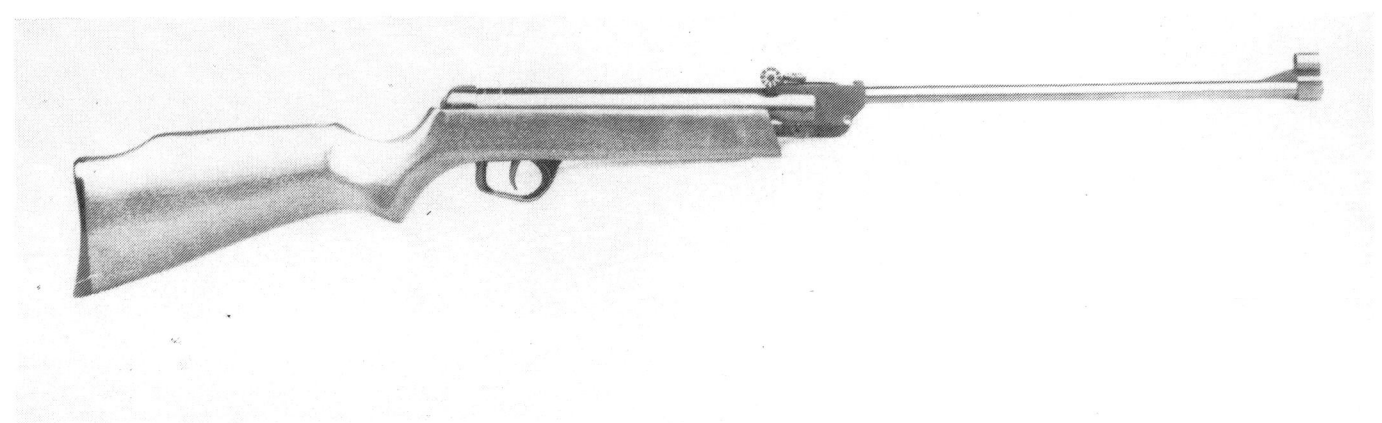

A.S.I. Rangemaster. Note improved foresight, lack of grooves in fore-end of stock, and improved styling

A.S.I. Apache

MODEL "Apache".

MAKER Industrias El Gamo SA, Carretera Sta Cruz de Calafell, Km.10, San Baudilio de Llobregat, Barcelona, Spain. Distributed by A.S.I., Alliance House, Snape, Saxmundham, Suffolk IP17 1SW.

DATE Appears to have been introduced as the "Cadet" during 1979, but very shortly afterwards the barrel length was increased by one inch and became the "Apache" during 1980.

VALUATION £20—£40. ($30—$60).

DETAILS A very well made junior sized air rifle. Follows the same pattern line as the Sniper. Available in .177 and single shot only. 37 inches long (94 cms) with a 16 inch (40.5 cms) barrel. The black plastic foresight appears to have a push-on fit, the rearsight is the same as that fitted to the rest of the excellent El Gamo range. Side of the barrel breech is stamped with the calibre and F-in pentagon denoting the lower lever of muzzle energy allowed in Europe, the serial number is also stamped in this position. The air chamber is grooved for scope mounts, 9 mm. The side of the chamber is stamped with the El Gamo deer's head trademark and "MADE IN SPAIN". The non-adjustable trigger action has a safety catch just in front of the trigger that drops down when the action is cocked, it cannot be pushed up until the barrel has been returned to the firing position. Quite a handy place to have a trigger safety if you're careful and don't suffer from fat fingers. Very well formed stock with grooved fore-end, has a hardwood look about it. The "Apache" is supposed to be aimed at the junior end of the market and the stock measurement from trigger to mid point of the butt is 13 inches (33 cms). Advertised weight 5 lbs 3 oz. Muzzle velocity 557 f.p.s. A review of the "Apache" appeared in "Airgun World" December 1980.

A.S.I. Statical Recoiless Air Rifle

MODEL "Statical".

MAKER El Gamo, Spain and imported by A.S.I., Alliance House, Snape, Saxmundham, Suffolk.

DATE Introduced during the late 1970s.

VALUATION £40—£80. ($60—$120).

DETAILS Recoiless .22 hunting air rifle. Works on similar principle to the Feinwerkbau in that the barrel and air chamber move back when fired. 41½ inches long with a 17¼ inch rifled barrel. Plastic ramp foresight with hood protector and all metal rearsight fully adjustable for windage and elevation. L.H.S. of barrel breech stamped with serial number and calibre, also has the "F" in pentagon which is the European level of muzzle energy, this being lower than ours, but could easily be overcome with a little tuning. Double linked cocking lever that has a small click when action is cocked. Top of air chamber stamped "MADE IN SPAIN" with the El Gamo trademark. Telescopic grooves being 9 mm apart. Small hole on top for oiling of piston etc. A stick-on label appears on top of air chamber. Trigger adjustment by way of small screw behind the trigger. High standard of finish. Barrel and air chamber blued, whilst body of action has black crackle finish. Small wooden fore-end screwed on to the action. The stock rather small in reach but suitable for either left or right handed use.

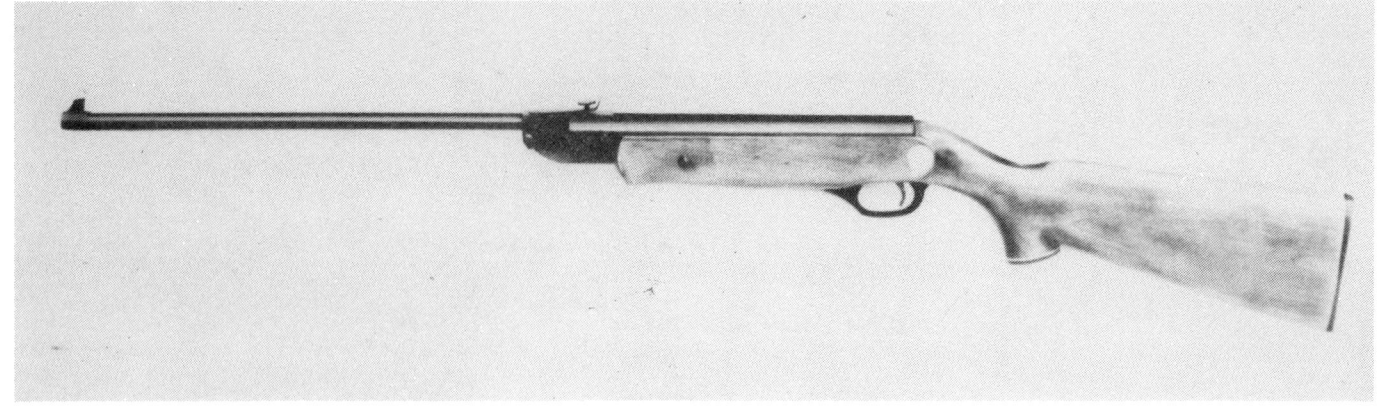

The Baikal Air Rifle

MODEL IJ-22, alias Model 2-55, alias "The Cossack", alias "Baikal", alias G530.

MAKER Baikal, U.S.S.R., and or Universal Firearms Corp., Hialech, Fla. No. 15, Mfg. Ijevsk, U.S.S.R.

DATE Introduced 1966 by A.E.S. Mathews Limited, importers of Russian target rifles and pistols.

VALUATION £10–£20, £9a–£20a.
($15–$30, $13.5a–$30a).

DETAILS 40¾ inches long with a 17¾ inch brass lined barrel in .177 only. Strong pillar foresight and rearsight adjustable for elevation only. Barrel latch on L.H.S. of breech. Push lever down to release barrel. Serial number stamped on L.H.S. of breech. Air chamber not grooved for telescopic sight. Birchwood stock with two white plastic medallions, "IJ-22 MADE IN U.S.S.R." on each and NX+22 on butt plate. A very well made air rifle for a modest price. The above was also advertised as having a beechwood stock. Was also imported by Rangemore Sports Ltd., 71 Watling Street, London EC4. Advertised muzzle velocity 500 f.p.s., at a later date this was increased to 725 f.p.s. when Sussex Armoury took over the distribution during the middle 1970s. Towards the late 1970s it would appear that Milbro imported the above and called it the Model G530. It was sold with spare spring, piston washer and cleaning rod. On other models seen the plastic stock medallions have been in black and stamped on the side of the air chamber "UNIVERSAL FIREARMS CORP., HIALEAH, FLA. No. 15, MFG., IJEVSK, U.S.S.R. AIR RIFLE MOD. IU-22, CAL .177". If you like looking at screw threads, just unscrew the butt plate and have a look at the threads on the above, they are the weirdest threads I've ever seen!

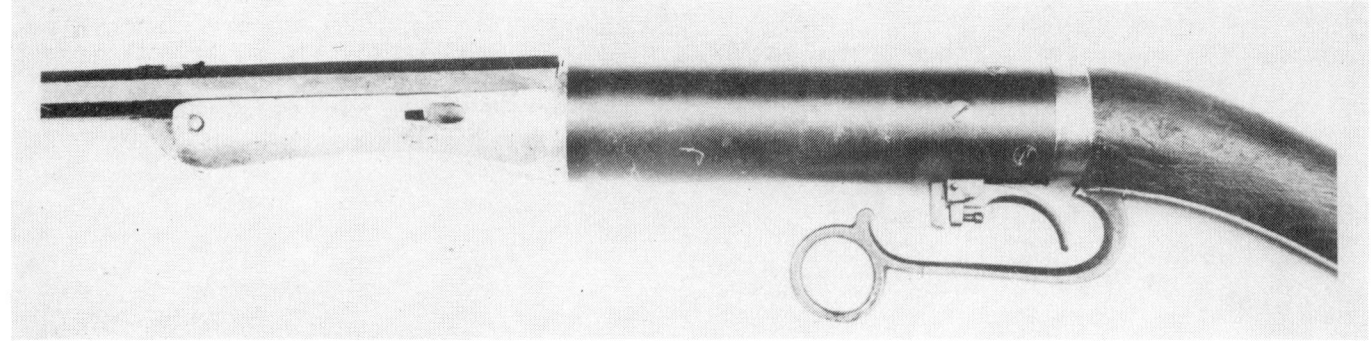

Blickensdoerfer and Schilling St. Louis Type Gallery Air Rifle

MODEL St. Louis Type Gallery Airgun.

MAKER Blickensdoerfer & Schilling, 7 South Street, between Market and Walnut, St. Louis, Missouri, U.S.A.
When Schilling took over the address became 12 South Third Street.

DATE From around 1865 to 1875, gallery airguns with Blickendoerfer's name only were made before Frederick Schilling joined the company. He joined the company in 1865 and Blick. appears to have dropped out of the airgun scene about 1875 with Schilling still working from the same address.

VALUATION These early American gallery guns are quite rare and have yet to make an appearance in auctions. They have been known to sell from between £200 and £500. ($300–$750).

DETAILS Extremely heavy for a target airgun. 44 inches long with a 22⅞ inch smoothbore barrel whose bore measures 7 mm. Dovetail mounted foresight with tipped blade, rearsight also dovetail mounted. Top of barrel "BLICKENSDOERFER & SCHILLING ST. LOUIS" and the serial number 130. Barrel lever is set in brass fore-end. Air chamber 7⅝ inches long. The sear is of the drop action variety that links directly with the trigger. Trigger adjustment is the small screw facing back towards the stock. Cocked by means of drawing back the trigger guard with "O" ring, this causes the sear to drop as it bears on the piston rod. Similar cocking action to the German Bugel spanner except for the external sear arrangement of the above. Examples of the above with Blick's name only were manufactured before 1865 and would assume from about 1860. During the late 1870s the hand-made gallery airguns were priced out of the market by the cheaper mass produced airguns of Quakenbush, as well as imports from Europe. For further details see "Airguns" by Eldon G. Wolff.
Only three are known to the Author, two are pre-1865 and bear the name "BLICKENSDOERFER" and have the serial numbers 28 and 66, whilst the other has both names and a serial number 130, this one being post-1865.

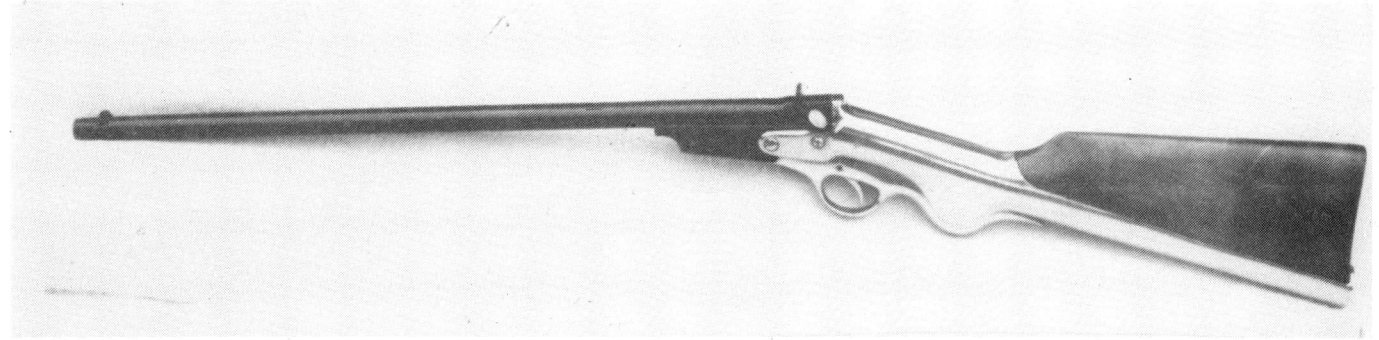

First Pattern Britannia Air Rifle

MODEL Britannia First Model.

MAKER Two examples noted were stamped "Made in Germany" see "Airgun World" April 1980.

DATE From around 1903 to 1905.

VALUATION Must be more rare than the next model, £150—£400, have yet to appear in auction. ($225—$600).

DETAILS All Britannia's are rare, but the first model must surely rank as the rarest. For sometime it was thought that these were not produced and even in 1977 D. H. Commins in his excellent series of airgun patents states that "the Britannia was not produced to this patent". This first model bears German characteristics in the way that the action is all nickel plated and the barrel is blued, typical Gem style rearsight blade which is dovetail mounted, as is the foresight. The serial number, in this case 169, is stamped in almost the same places as on Gem air rifles, including on the cocking link come trigger guard, and on the breech face appears a letter M which is very much like that in style to Gem serial number prefixes. British characteristics are the breech washer being on the barrel face and not on the transfer port face, and the use of screws, where as the Germans liked tapered pins during this period of manufacture.

36¼ inches long (92 cms) with a 21¾ inch (55.5 cms) .177 smoothbore barrel. The barrel appears to be mounted into the breech casting that acts as the pivot support and is pegged twice on the breech face. Apart from the barrel everything else has been nickel plated and from photographs this would appear to be the original type of finish. All screw heads are on one side of the action only in true British style. The stock appears to be walnut. Apart from the barrel latch, sights, and style of air chamber the model is the same as the second model as produced by Bonehill's.

The first design was patented by Frederick Stanley Cox of 6 Freef Road, Handsworth, Birmingham, England and listed as a gun maker, who also manufactured targets and his agent for the patent was Henry Skerret, 24 Temple Row, Birmingham. The patent 15712 was applied for on the 15th July 1902 and was accepted on the 7th May 1903. The design was for the air chamber forming part of the body, hollow plunger, inner spring guide fixed to rear chamber plug, cocking lever acting as trigger guard and containing the trigger, the action two or more sear engagements for varying degrees of power and finally having the stock perched on top of the air chamber.

The Britannia has been described as a variation of the Gem, but this connection is as near as that between a Mini and a Rolls Royce.

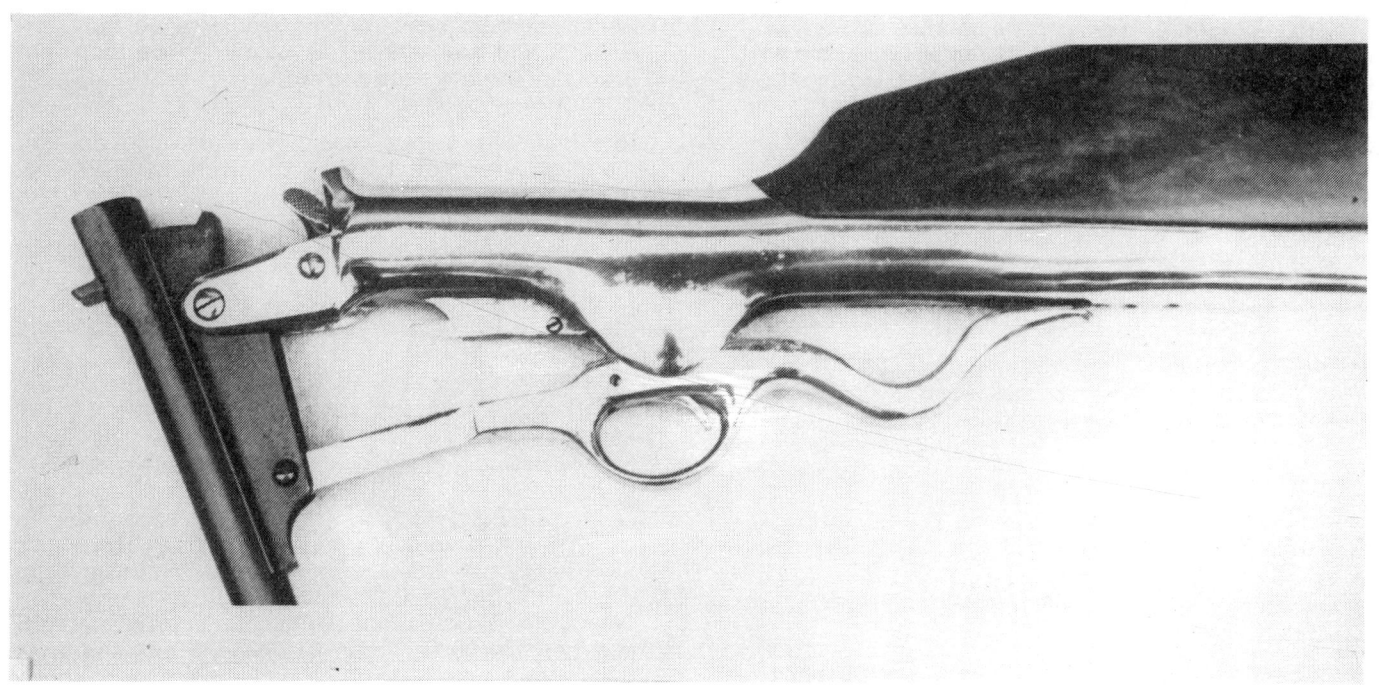

Britannia Action

11

The Britannia "Anglo Sure Shot Mk. I"

MODEL Britannia "Anglo-Sure Shot (Mk. I)".

MAKER C. G. Bonehill, Birmingham.

DATE 1905 to around 1908. Quite a rare air rifle.

VALUATION £200—£350, £90a—£215a.
($300—$525, $135a—$322.50a).

DETAILS 35½ inches long with a 21 inch .177 rifled barrel. Barley corn foresight set in dovetail, similar to pre-war B.S.A. but not so high. Rearsight set in dovetail as shown, the blade has elevation marks that correspond with the raised portion behind the sight, see photograph. Stamped just in front of the rearsight is "COX'S PATENT", stamped on the barrel breech part appears "ANGLO SURE-SHOT MARK 1" and on the other side "MADE ONLY FOR R. RAMSBOTTOM MANCHESTER". The Britannia trademark appears on the side of the barrel flat. Serial number stamped on all major parts, 1011. Barrel stirrup has "PAT" stamped on the side. Stamped on the side of the trigger and cocking lever "RD.394207". The action is as new and closes with a crispness that time cannot erase. When action is cocked there is an adjusting screw for the sear on the L.H.S. of the sear. Most of the above style have two stages of firing. There are two notches for the sear to engage and a stop screw on the underside of the air chamber just behind the cocking lever slot. Moving the screw to the forward hole only allows the first engagement to take place, whilst when the screw is removed to second hole this allows the second engagement to take place for more powerful shots. This giving a slightly longer piston stroke. On the above this did not work, can only assume it is spring bound. The stock is held in place by one screw through the metal semi-butt plate and two through the air chamber and can only be removed when the spring and piston have been removed. The end chamber plug is held by tension in a bayonet fitting, to remove first unscrew small screw, then press in with a screwdriver and rotate to the left. All in all a very powerful airgun and way ahead of its time, but far too costly to produce. The Britannia rearsights varied in design, one example, the "see-saw" type is shown in "Airgun World" February 1980.

The first review of the above appeared in "Arms & Explosives" 1905, for a copy see "Guns Review" May 1976. The above was sold with a descriptive leaflet. On other models it would appear that the adjuster screw for the sear can be approached through a small hole in the cocking lever. Advertised weight was 6¼ lbs. Cost £2 in 1905. The first model was made in Germany, see "Airgun World" April 1980. The first patent for the Britannia style air rifle was dated 1902 and the above style was produced, in Germany in very small numbers. See "Guns Review" April 1977. The barrel latch was patented in 1904/5, see "Guns Review" June 1978. This was an improvement on the 1902 model barrel latch and would date any made before this patent.

Serial numbers seen for this model range from 590 to 3209 and are detailed as below. These represent examples actually seen and noted.

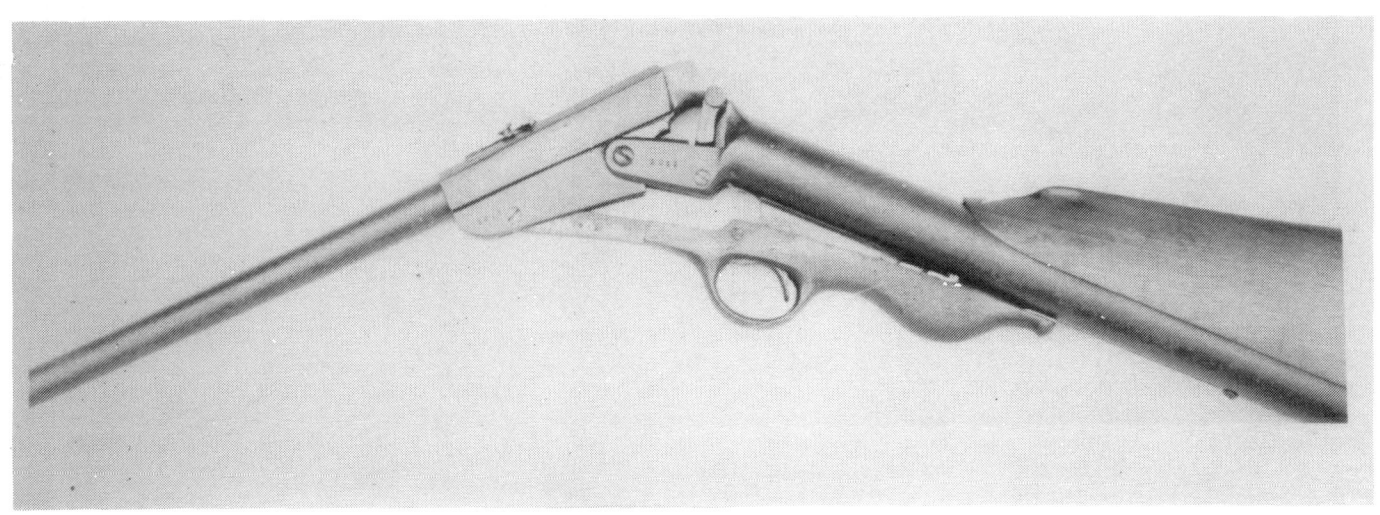

Britannia Action partially opened

SERIAL NUMBERS seen for the Britannia.

244 — .177 rifled, barrel flats stamped "COX'S PATENT, C. G. BONEHILL SOLE MANUFACTURER, BIRMINGHAM". Twin bladed pivoted rearsight. Side screw adjuster on sear.

590 — .177 rifled, barrel flats stamped "COX'S PATENT, C. G. BONEHILL SOLE MANUFACTURER, BIRMINGHAM". No hole in cocking for adjusting sear.

711 — .177, rearsight of breech block, "68" under rearsight dovetail. Barrel flat stamped "ANGLO SURE-SHOT MARK I" and on other side "MADE FOR R. RAMSBOTTOM, MANCHESTER". Top of breech block stamped "COX'S PATENT".

820 — .177, fitted with simple blade rearsight. Stamped with Cox's patent and Britannia trademark. See "Guns Review" June 1976.

1011 — Identical to text.

1032 — .177, rearsight similar to 1011, "PAT" stamped on the barrel latch. Cox's Patent and Britannia trademark stamped on barrel flats.

1129 — .177 rifled, barrel flats engraved —"ANGLO SURE-SHOT MARK I, MADE ONLY FOR R. RAMSBOTTOM, MANCHESTER" also stamped "COX'S PATENTS". Has Britannia trademark on side of action. Trigger adjustment on sear with no hole through cocking lever.

1203 — .177 rifled. 35¾ inches long with a 21 inch barrel. Rearsight set in dovetail on barrel. Top of barrel breech flat stamped "C. G. Bonehill Sole Manufacturer Cox's Patents". Has "BRITANNIA" trademark stamped on side. Stamped on trigger action "RD 394207". The rearsight is stamped "PATENT". Double cocking action with trigger adjustment through hole on underside of cocking link.

1222 — .177, seesaw rearsight. Barrel flats stamped "ANGLO SURE-SHOT MARK I COX'S PATENTS MADE ONLY FOR R. RAMSBOTTOM, MANCHESTER".

1237 — Stamped "ANGLO SURE-SHOT MARK I MADE ONLY FOR RAMSBOTTOM, MANCHESTER" and with Cox's Patent and Britannia trademark. See "Guns Review" June 1976.

1765 — .22 which is unusual. Fitted with folding peepsight and raised foresight. Has no normal rearsight. See "Airgun World" December 1980.

1873 — 36 inches long with 21 inch barrel. Stamped "C. G. BONEHILL SOLE MANUFACTURER".

1985 — .177 rifled, 35½ inches x 21 inch barrel. Seesaw rearsight, top flat stamped "COX'S PATENTS, ANGLO SURE-SHOT MARK I, MADE ONLY FOR R. RAMSBOTTOM, MANCHESTER".

2348 — rifled, seesaw rearsight, round section barrel all the way along, barrel stamped "COX'S PATENT, C. G. BONEHILL SOLE MANUFACTURER".

2524 — .25, stamped "Cox's Patent, C. G. Bonehill Sole manufacturer." Almost identical markings to 1011, but has "PATENT" on the stirrup. Top section of barrel is rounded whereas normally it has flats where the stampings occur. See "Airgun World" April 1980.

2928 — .177, round section barrel stamped "COX'S PATENT, C. G. BONEHILL SOLE MANUFACTURERS". Seesaw rearsight.

3209 — 38 inches long with 23 inch barrel. Stamped "C. G. BONEHILL SOLE MANUFACTURER". Calibre .25. Stamped "PATENT" on barrel latch.

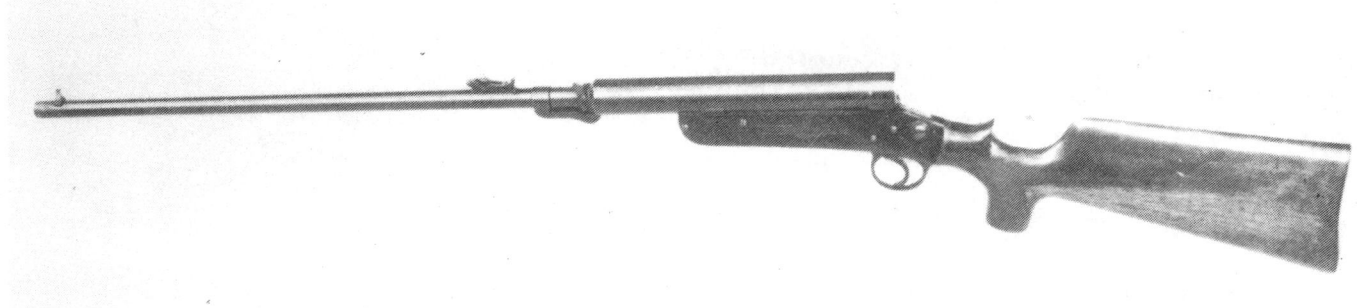

"Improved" Model Britannia

MODEL The "Improved" Model Air Rifle.

MAKER C. G. Bonehill, Belmont Firearms Works, Birmingham.

DATE Production of improved model began about 1908, assume cessation around 1910.

VALUATION £200—£450, £320a.
(\$300—\$675, \$480a).

DETAILS Serial number of above 1309. Serial number stamped on all components. Also has "LLH" stamped on underside of barrel. Stamped on top of air chamber "THE IMPROVED MODEL BRITTANIA AIR RIFLE PATANTEE & SOLE MANUFACTURER, C. G. BONEHILL, BELMONT FIREARMS WORKS, BIRMINGHAM" and on the L.H.S. of the trigger block is stamped "THE BRITTANIA AIR RIFLE" between the Brittania and Air is a typical lady Brittania trademark complete with sea in the background with lighthouse and sailing ship. Above measures 44½ inches in length.

13

Barrel and air chamber measures just over 29½ inches. The foresight looks like a B.S.A., whilst the rearsight is flip up on a ramp and is adjustable for elevation and windage, similar in design to the Webley air pistol rearsight. The action is broken by a side lever on the R.H.S. of the trigger block, this lever being pushed forward to release the barrel and air chamber. See "Guns Review" December 1978 for details of the patent granted for the above design.

Further details see "Gun Review" May and June 1976. A plunger device was patented for the introduction of pellets into the circular rotating breech. Details of above patent can be found in "Guns Review" February 1979.

To remove the barrel unscrew the small grub screw underneath the barrel support frame. The revolving collar tap rotates inside the frame. When the grub screw has been removed the barrel can be unscrewed as normal and removed leaving the rotating tap collar still in the frame. The collar can also be pulled out of the frame as it is a spring held under tension.

Have only seen two of these and they had serial numbers 729 and 1309.

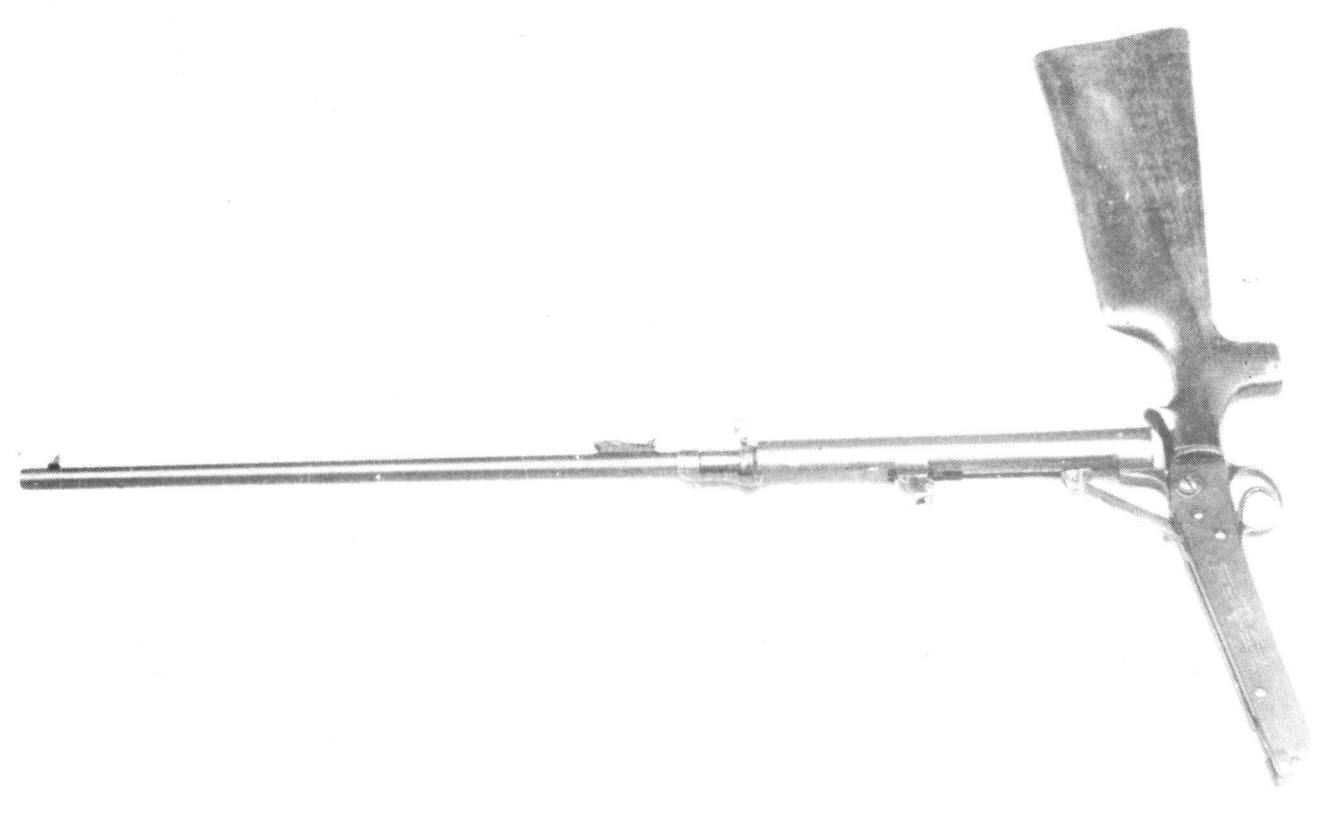

"Improved" Britannia in cocked position

Brno Air Rifle. Note push button barrel release on side of air chamber, similar action to 1906—1908 Model Millita Air Rifle.

MODEL

MAKER The "Z" trademark also appears on pistols marked "Ceska Zbrojovka-Narodni Strakonice" (Czech Arm Factory, National Co-operative, Strakonice", Bohemia.

DATE Could well be after 1948 as this was when the nationalisation of Czechoslovakian arms factories took place.

VALUATION £20—£40. ($30—$60).

DETAILS It is safe to assume that the above was never imported into Britain. Break barrel action with a barrel lock identical to the Millita air rifles of the early 1900s. 39½ inches long with a 16¼ inch .177 rifled barrel. Barrel and stock fitted with sling swivels. Blade foresight mounted in a dovetail and rearsight ramp appears to be spot welded. Serial number stamped on underside of barrel and across top of air chamber, 26269. The ramp rearsight is calibrated from 10 to 25. The top of the air chamber is stamped with "Z" inside a rifled barrel trademark. the interesting part is the barrel latch. This is identical to the pre-war Millita. You press in the button in order to release the barrel. Stock has a black vulcanite butt plate. Single pull non-adjustable trigger. The serial number may also appear stamped on the underside of the barrel breech near the cocking lever pivot screw.

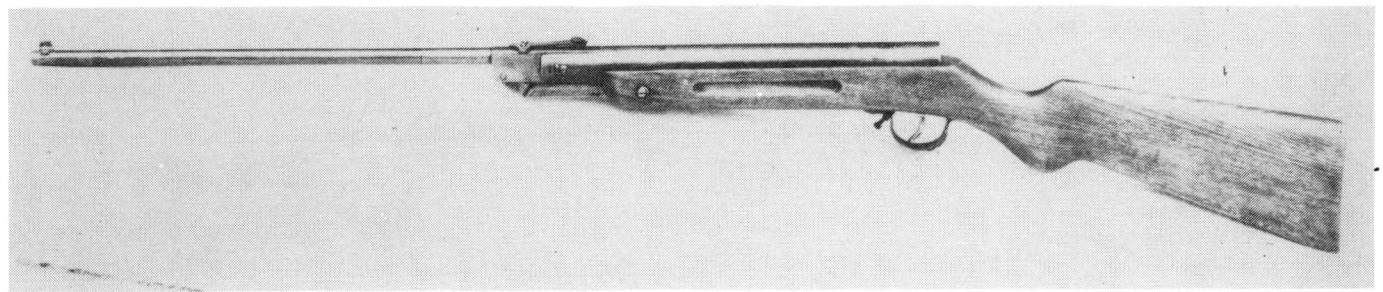

Brno Model 20

MODEL

MAKER "Z" trademark also appears on pistols stamped "Ceska Znrojovka-Narodni Strakonice", (Czech Arms Factory, National Co-operative, Strakonice, Bohemia.

DATE Would assume 1950s to 1960s.

VALUATION £20—£40. ($30—$60).

DETAILS Usual robust Eastern Block construction. 43¼ inches long with a 19¼ inch rifled barrel. Blade foresight set in dovetail and ramp rearsight similarly mounted. Underside of barrel stamped with serial number, in this case 012259. Number also appears on the underside of the air chamber near trigger block, which screws into the air chamber. Top of air chamber stamped with "Z" in rifled barrel trademark, "20 MADE IN CZECHOSLOVAKIA". Although printed in English no advertisements have been found for the above. Trigger adjustment by screw through front of trigger guard. One piece stock without any extras.

The "L" (Light) Pattern Lincoln Air Rifle

MODEL L The Lincoln Air Rifle. The "L" or Light Model. Also called the Junior, Juvenile, or Boy's Model. Not to be confused with the "L" model with push button cocking lever.

MAKER B.S.A. At first under licence for Lincoln Jeffries. In October 1905 B.S.A. took over the licencing rights and became the manufacturer and distributer of the Lincoln Jeffries air rifles marking them with both B.S.A. and Lincoln Jeffries trademarks.

DATE The light model is rare and appeared in 1906 carrying the following serial numbers:
2130 to 2727
4830 to 5829 Numbers allocated to Lincoln Jeffries and manufactured in 1906.
The example examined bears the number 22605 which lies in the series of numbers allocated to B.S.A.'s as follows.

1130—1905 to 2129—1906	28000—1909
2730—1906 to 4829—1906	34000—1910
5830—1906 to 7829—1906	45000—1911
8830—1906 to 10229—1907	51000—1912
11230—1907 to 13229—1908	60000—1913
14230—1908	78212—1914
19000—1908	

All sorts of models are included in the above serial numbers. Those with "S" prefix are fitted with a double sear arrangement. The earliest being about S64846. About 1,000 extra air rifles were manufactured with various numbers up to 86126 and spasmodic production carried on till 1917. See "Guns Review" March 1978. The date of the above example is 1908 to 1909.

VALUATION £70—£150, £47a—£55a.
($105—$225, $71a—$83a).

DETAILS A very elusive model. Have seen many cut down air rifles made to look like the Junior Model and even offered to the public for £150! The guiding points to look for are the following; very slender barrel the thickness of a man's little finger, the barrel should measure about 15 to 17 inches long. Very small cocking lever measuring 9 inches. Length of air chamber 7½ inches. Stock fitted to the above is 13¼ inches although the 11¼ inch stock was also available. The above model could be the first of the "L" pattern that appeared with a push button cocking lever during 1919. 38¼ inches long with the above dimensions. Stamped with the B.S.A. triple rifles trademark just behind the rearsight that is not original. Top of air chamber stamped "L THE 'LINCOLN' AIR RIFLE. PATENT.8761/04". This patent was taken out by Lincoln Jeffries in 1904 to cover a fixed barrel with a separate cocking lever that at the time of the patent was designed to open the breech as the action was being cocked. See "Guns Review" May 1978. Trigger adjustment by way of screw through trigger guard. Hand chequered stock. Nothing appears stamped on the cocking lever. Nothing appears stamped on the stock. All the above information applies to the example 22605 and variations abound within the overall model under discussion. The Light Pattern was available with either straight or pistol grip stocks, and were supplied with 13¼ inch stock "unless one measuring 13¾ inches or 14¼ inch were preferred". Advertised weight 5 lb 10 oz. The stock measurement was taken from the trigger to half way down the butt plate. The Light Model was sold in .177 only. Advertised effective range 50 yards. On airgun number 2635 the top of the air chamber is stamped "L THE 'LINCOLN' AIR RIFLE. PATENT., MANUFACTURED BY THE B.S.A. Co. Ltd., BIRMINGHAM", it had a straight hand stock stamped with the standing man trademark of Lincoln Jeffries and marked "LINCOLN JEFFRIES, INVENTOR & PATENTEE". Lincoln Jeffries also sold a tinplate sight protector that clipped on to the end of the barrel in order to protect the foresight bead. It was pushed forward and rotated to expose the sight for firing.
Only three Light Pattern Lincoln Jeffries have been seen and these had serial numbers 2635, 12175 and 22605.

B.S.A. Model "Lincoln" or "H. The Lincoln"

MODEL "Lincoln" Air Rifle. The "H" or Heavy Model.

MAKER B.S.A., Birmingham, England.

DATE Dating by serial number as follows:
Numbers allocated to Lincoln Jeffries 130—14229 and manufactured from 1905 to the middle of 1908.

   130(1905) — 1129(1906)
  2130(1906) — 2727(1906)
  4830(1906) — 5829(1906)
  7830(1906) — 8829(1906)
10230(1906) — 11229(1907)
13230(1907) — 14229(1908)

Serial numbers allocated to B.S.A. These also contain the "Improved" models with side lever release for the underlever.

  1130(1905) — 2129(1906)   28000(1909)
  2730(1906) — 4829(1906)   34000(1910)
  5830(1906) — 7829(1906)   45000(1911)
  8830(1906) — 10229(1907)   51000(1912)
11230(1907) — 13229(1908)   60000(1913)
14230(1908)   78212(1914)
19000(1908)   86126(1917)

Above also contain "S" prefix serial numbers which indicates a double bent piston rod and safety sears. For further details see "Guns Review" September 1972.

VALUATION £50—£150. ($75—$225).

DETAILS Serial number 22688, made around 1908/1909. 43¼ inches long. Stock stamped with Lincoln Jeffries trademark of standing man pointing gun with a dog at his feet, also stamped "REGISTERED INVENTOR & PATENTEE, LINCOLN JEFFRIES". Top of chamber stamped "H THE 'LINCOLN' AIR RIFLE PATENT 8761/04". R.H.S. of tap stamped "P.PAT." Bayonet underlever without strengthening fences. See "Guns Review" February and March 1978.

On "Lincoln" air rifle serial number 8518, a number allocated to Lincoln Jeffries, the top of air chamber is stamped "H. THE 'LINCOLN' AIR RIFLE PATENT". The B.S.A. triple rifle trademark appears between the rearsight and loading port. From the above it could be assumed that ALL Lincoln air rifles were produced by B.S.A. A foresight protector was available for the Lincoln air rifle. This was made of folded thin metal that slid on to the end of the barrel and when in position acted as a cover to the foresight, when firing the cover was pushed forward and rotated through 90° so as not to obstruct the line of sight. The sight was stamped "LINCOLN JEFFRIES PATENT".

It is safe to assume that all Lincoln Jeffries air rifles with serial numbers from 130 were made by B.S.A. A Mr Kenneth Davis, Secretary to B.S.A. accepted a contract from L.J.'s to produce 1,000 air rifles, but soon after Mr. Kirby, General Manager of B.S.A. obtained royalty arrangements with L.J.'s and started to sell L.J. air rifles under their own flag. This initial order for 1,000 started with serial number 130, if there are any air rifles with serial numbers less than 130 there could be some doubt as to where they were made.

When changing the mainspring the air chamber has to be unscrewed from the trigger block, this may appear to have jammed after removing the two trigger guard screws, what may be stopping the chamber from unscrewing is the trigger being pushed into a slot cut in the outer edge of the chamber, to release just pull the trigger and at the same time turn the chamber, and Hey Presto it should come free!

The following air rifles have been seen with "H THE LINCOLN AIR RIFLE" stamped on the air chamber: 728, 4883, 5102, 8610, 13348, 14153 and 14213.

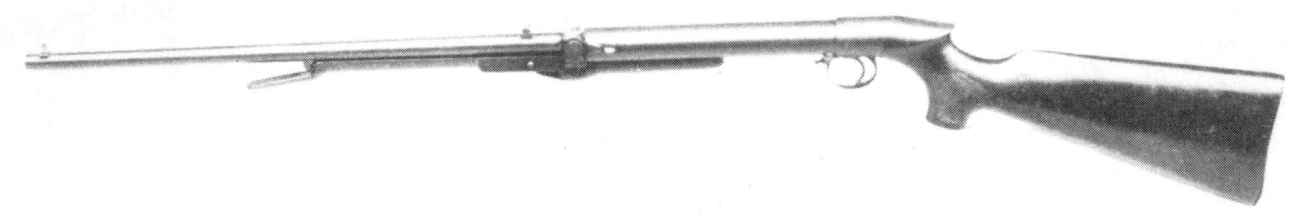

The "B.S.A. Air Rifle"

MODEL "B.S.A. Air Rifle".

MAKER B.S.A., Birmingham, England.

DATE Above example 1906—1907. Serial numbers used by B.S.A. 8830(1906) to 10229(1907), also from 14230(1908) to 19000(1908). More detailed serial numbers are listed under the "Lincoln" Air Rifle.

VALUATION £30—£80, £30a—£62a.
                ($45—$120, $45a—$93a).

DETAILS Serial number 9569 stamped on trigger block. 43¼ inches long. Bayonet style underlever without the side strengtheners. Pistol grip stock with hand chequering. Metal butt plate. Stock has trademark of three standing rifles. Trigger adjustment through the trigger guard. Top of air chamber stamped "B.S.A. AIR RIFLE ———— LINCOLN JEFFRIES' PATENT, MADE BY THE BIRMINGHAM SMALL ARMS COMPANY LTD." Stamped on tap cover plate and lever "P PAT". Between tap and rearsight is stamped "LOAD" and the stacked rifles trademark. The above was advertised as the "Improved B.S.A. Air Rifle". The tap plug was improved and no longer needed the seating pin to insert the pellet into the tap. There was a lighter model made of above with the bayonet underlever, this measured about 39 to 40 inches in length.

Sold with either the pistol grip stock or the straight hand stock and in three sizes 13¼ inches, 13¾ inches, or usually 14¼ inches. This being distance between trigger and centre of butt plate. Advertised weight 6 lb 14 oz to 7 lbs. See "Guns Review" February and March 1978. On air rifle serial number 15619 the lettering on the air chamber was "B.S.A. AIR RIFLE MADE BY THE BIRMINGHAM SMALL ARMS COMPANY LIMITED", otherwise the air rifle is identical. The serial number may also appear on the underside of the barrel. Stamped on the underside of the cocking lever "LINCOLN JEFFRIES' PATENT". The "B.S.A. AIR RIFLE" first appeared with the straight through tap with a locking screw and grub screw on the other side. These were the models with the serial number allocated to B.S.A.

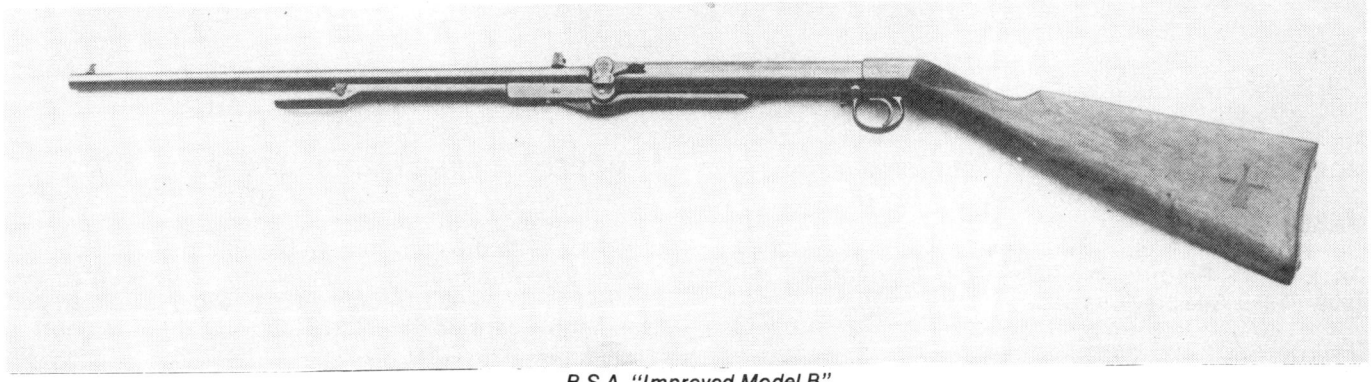

B.S.A. "Improved Model B"

MODEL "Improved Model B".

MAKER B.S.A., Birmingham, England.

DATE Serial numbers allocated to B.S.A. These also contain the "Improved" models with side lever release for the underlever.

1130(1905) — 2129(1906)	28000(1909)
2730(1906) — 4829(1906)	34000(1910)
5830(1906) — 7829(1906)	45000(1911)
8830(1906) — 10229(1907)	51000(1912)
11230(1907) — 13229(1908)	60000(1913)
14230(1907) — 13229(1908)	60000(1913)
14230(1908)	78212(1914)
19000(1908)	86126(1917)

Above also contain "S" prefix serial numbers which indicates bent piston rod and safety sears. For further details see "Guns Review", September 1972.

VALUATION Quite a rare model and considered more scarce than the "Improved Model D". £60—£180, only seen once in auction and it was in excellent condition and raised £180a. ($90—$270).

DETAILS 43 inches long. .177 has same stamps on top of air chamber except for "B" instead of the usual "D". Tap port plate and lever are stamped "P.PAT". Serial number of above 16512. Underside of underlever stamped "LINCOLN JEFFRIES PATENT". Bayonet underlever of the earlier pattern without strengthening side fences. Straight hand stock — hand chequered with B.S.A. triple rifle trademark. Stock has metal butt plate. One hole trigger block and trigger adjustment via trigger guard. See various models for comparison.

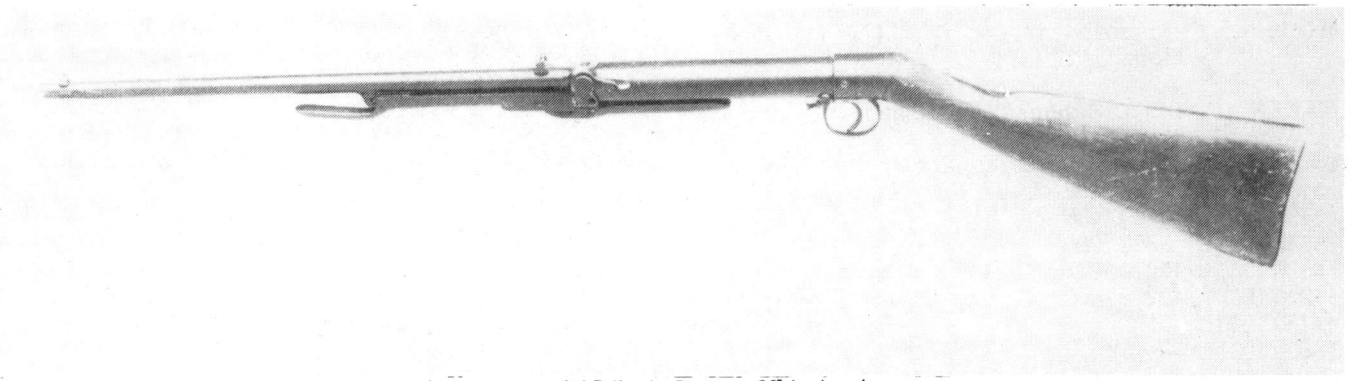

Improved Model D (Light Pattern) 38⅝ inches long

MODEL Improved Model D, Junior, or Boys Model.

MAKER B.S.A. Co. Ltd., Birmingham, England.

DATE Serial number of above example is 24847 so lies in the following series of numbers:

Serial Number	Date
19000	1908
28000	1909
34000	1910
45000	1911
51000	1912
60000	1913
78212	1914

VALUATION £50—£100. ($75—$150).

DETAILS Appears to be a progression of the Light Pattern Lincoln Jeffries, see other pages. Identical in all aspects except for the improved tap and plate. 38⅝ inches long with a 17 inch barrel, 7⅝ inch air chamber and fitted with a 13¾ inch straight hand stock with metal butt plate. Cocking lever stamped "LINCOLN JEFFRIES PATENT 8761/04" and tap plate marked "P. PAT. 8246/06". Top of air chamber stamped "THE B.S.A. AIR RIFLE (Improved Model D), THE BIRMINGHAM SMALL ARMS COMPANY LIMITED, SOLE MANUFACTURERS. Fitted with hand chequered stock and metal butt plate. Apart from the tap the above is identical to the "L" Pattern Lincoln Jeffries. Above also sold with the 13¾ inch pistol grip stock.

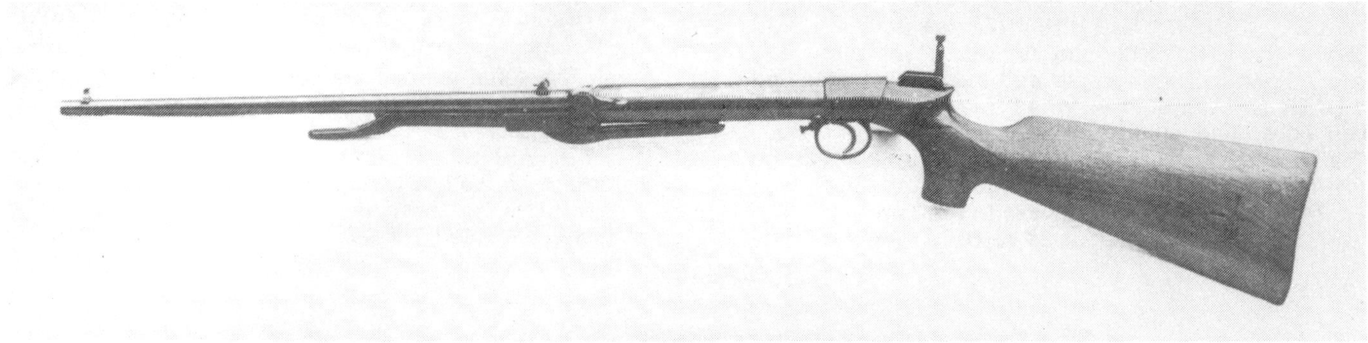

B.S.A. "Improved Model D"

MODEL "Improved Model D" (39 inch Model).

MAKER B.S.A.

DATE Production 1905—1914. Date of above 1909—1910. See previous page.

VALUATION £50—£125.
($75—$185).

DETAILS .177 model, 39¼ inches long with Alec Parker peepsight. Serial number 29706. Top of air chamber stamped "THE B.S.A. AIR RIFLE (IMPROVED MODEL D) — THE BIRMINGHAM SMALL ARMS LTD, ENGLAND, SOLE MANUFACTURERS". Bayonet underlever with improved pattern side fences as opposed to the early pattern bayonet that did not have the side strengtheners. Underside of barrel stamped "Pat 11817 — 05". Underside of cocking lever stamped "Lincoln Jeffries Patent 8761/04. on side of tap port is stamped "PATENT 8246/06". The B.S.A. triple rifle trademark is stamped into the wood of the stock. Two hole trigger block with trigger adjustment through the trigger guard. Later models were fitted with the side lever catch cocking lever. For further details see "Guns Review" February and March 1978.

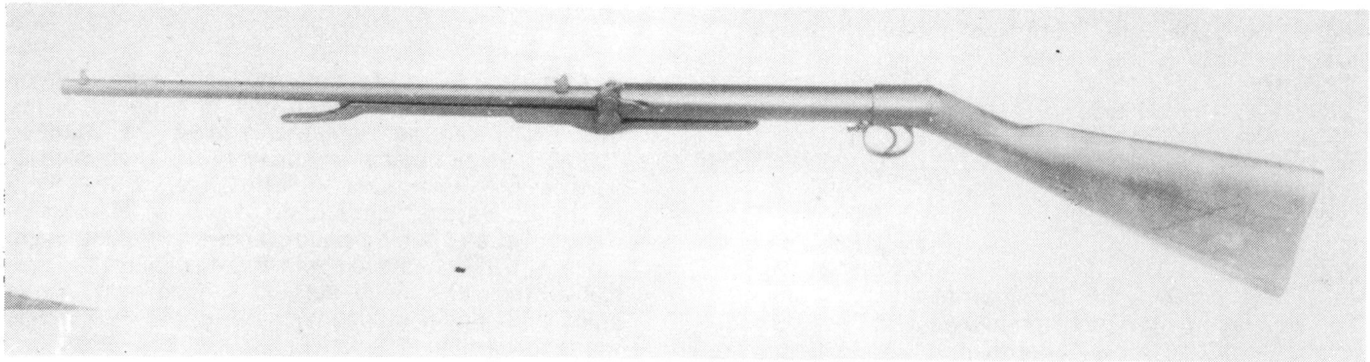

B.S.A. Improved Model D with straight hand stock

MODEL "Improved Model D". .177 (43 inch Model).

MAKER B.S.A., Birmingham, England.

DATE 1905—1914. Serial numbers as follows:

1130 1905 to 2129 1906	28000 1909
2730 1906 to 4829 1906	34000 1910
5830 1906 to 7829 1906	45000 1911
8830 1906 to 10229 1907	51000 1912
11230 1907 to 13229 1908	60000 1913
14230 1908	78212 1914
19000 1908	

Other models are included in the above.

VALUATION £50—£150.
($75—$225).

DETAILS Serial number 33473. 43¾ inches long. Stamped on top of air cylinder "THE B.S.A. AIR RIFLE (IMPROVED MODEL D), THE BIRMINGHAM SMALL ARMS COMPANY LIMITED, SOLE MANUFACTURERS. Metal butt plate, hand chequered, Bayonet underlever. "LOAD" and three rifles trademark in front of tap pellet hole. "LINCOLN JEFFRIES PATENT 8761/04" stamped underside of underlever, also a patent number on side of tap (8246/06). Underside of barrel stamped with the serial number and "11817-05" this applies to the manufacture of barrels solid with the breech and loading tap. See "Guns Review" June 1978 for details of the patent. The stock bears the trade stamp of "CROSS BROS. LTD., CARDIFF".

By 1913 the following models of B.S.A. air rifles were sold. They were all fitted with a bayonet underlever, so would assume them all to follow the general design of the "Improved Model D".

	Standard		Light	Junior
Bore	.177	.22	.177 only	.177 only
Weight	7¼ lbs.	7½ lbs	6¼ lbs	5½ lbs
Overall Length (14¼ inch stock)	43¾ inches	45¾ inches	39¼ inches	34¾ inches
Stock Length trigger to butt. All the above were fitted as standard.	14¼ inches	14¼ inches	13¼ inches	11¼ inches
Stocks Available	13¾ inches 13¼ inches	13¾ inches 13¼ inches	13¾ inches 14½ inches	Only fitted with 11¼ inch
Barrel Length	19¼ inches	19¼ inches	17 inches	15¼ inches
Range (Effective)	50 yards	50 yards	30 yards	20 yards

Interesting to note that in 1908 the "Improved Model" B.S.A. air rifle was advertised in two calibres, .177 and .25.

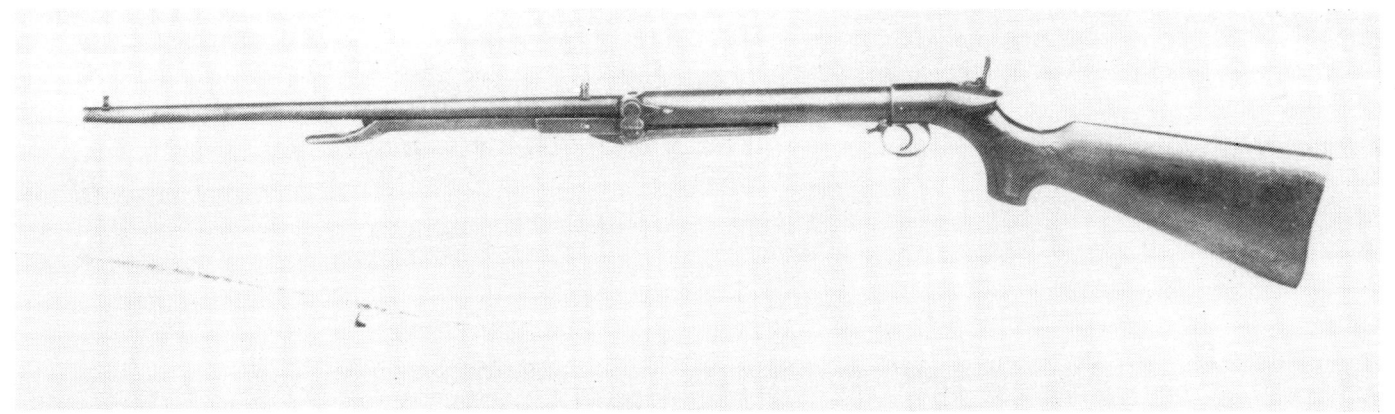

"Improved Model D", early pattern, Light Model, 39 inches long

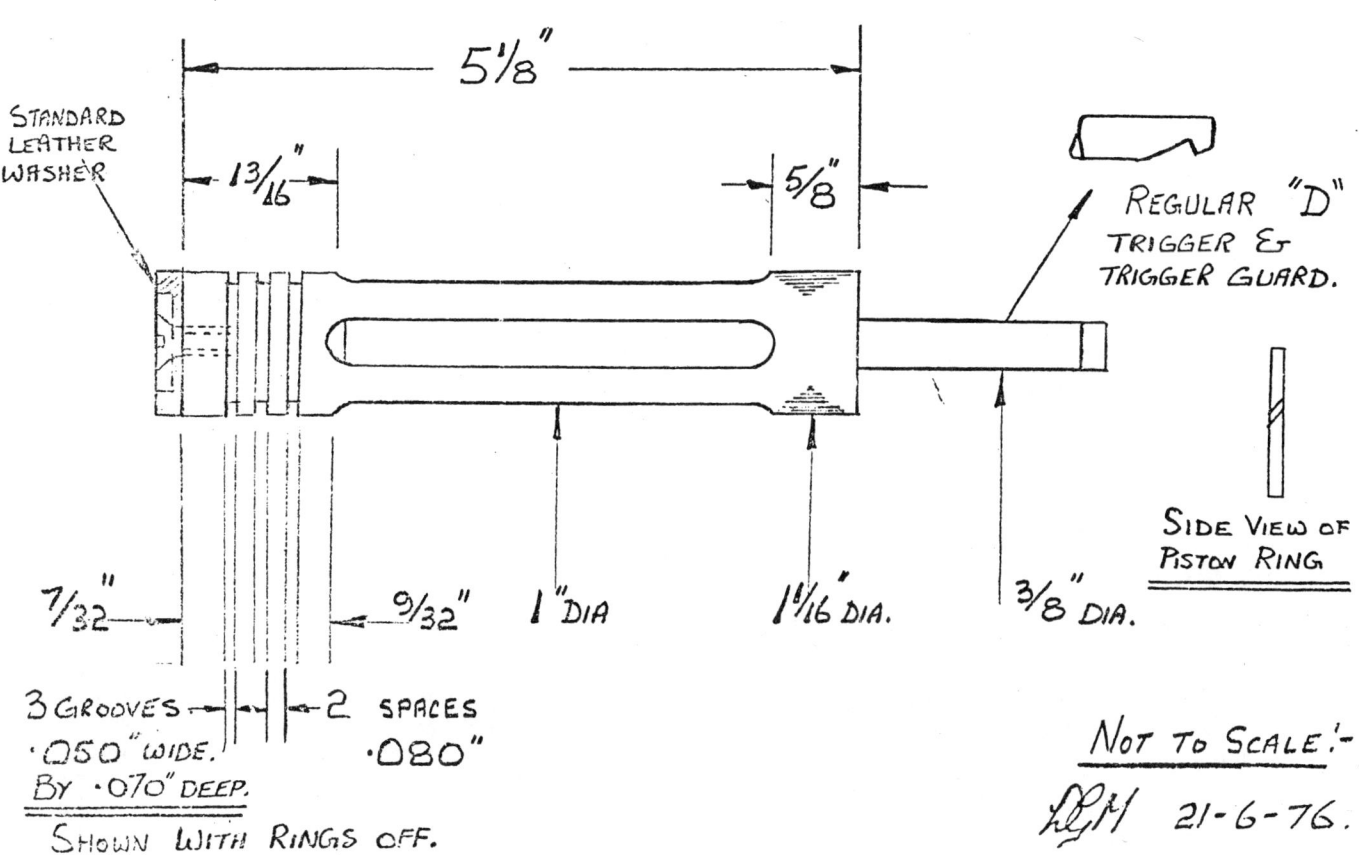

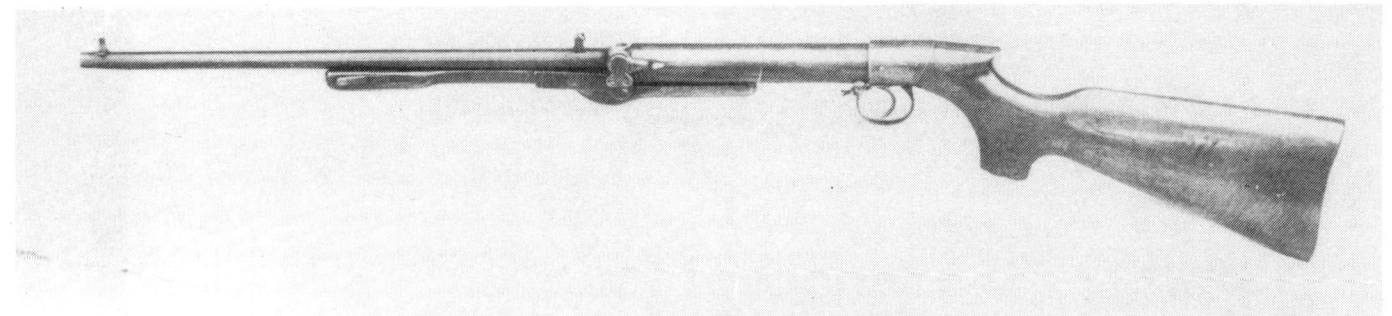

"Improved Model D" later pattern, Light Model 39 inches long

MODEL   Improved Model D. 39 inch model with single sear trigger.

MAKER   B.S.A., Birmingham, England.

DATE   The side lever cocking arm appeared sometime between serial number 42784 and 47290 so this was about 1910 and 1911. The above variation of the Improved Model D lies in the following group of serial numbers:

Serial Number	Year
34000	1910
45000	1911
51000	1912
60000	1913
78212	1914

VALUATION   £50—£125.
($75—$185).

DETAILS   The fore-runner of the Light Pattern underlever. About 39 inches long with a rifled .177 barrel. Underside of barrel stamped "Rd.No.479972". Underside of cocking lever stamped "B.S.A. PATENTS 8761-04, 25783--10, Rd.479972". These are explained on previous pages. Top of air chamber stamped "THE B.S.A. AIR RIFLE (IMPROVED MODEL D), THE BIRMINGHAM SMALL ARMS Co. Ltd., ENGLAND, SOLE MANUFACTURER". On air rifle number 58355 there was a metal butt plate. Fitted with one hole trigger block with trigger adjustment through the guard. Have a care when removing the trigger block that the trigger spring does not drop out when the trigger is allowed to travel forward beyond its normal allowance. A later variation is the fitting on a side catch cocking lever.

Some of the above will be found with "S" prefix serial numbers, this indicates that the trigger action fitted has two sears and is double pull with one of the sears being a safety device. The trigger block will also be stamped with the Patent number 30338-10, details of this are given elsewhere.

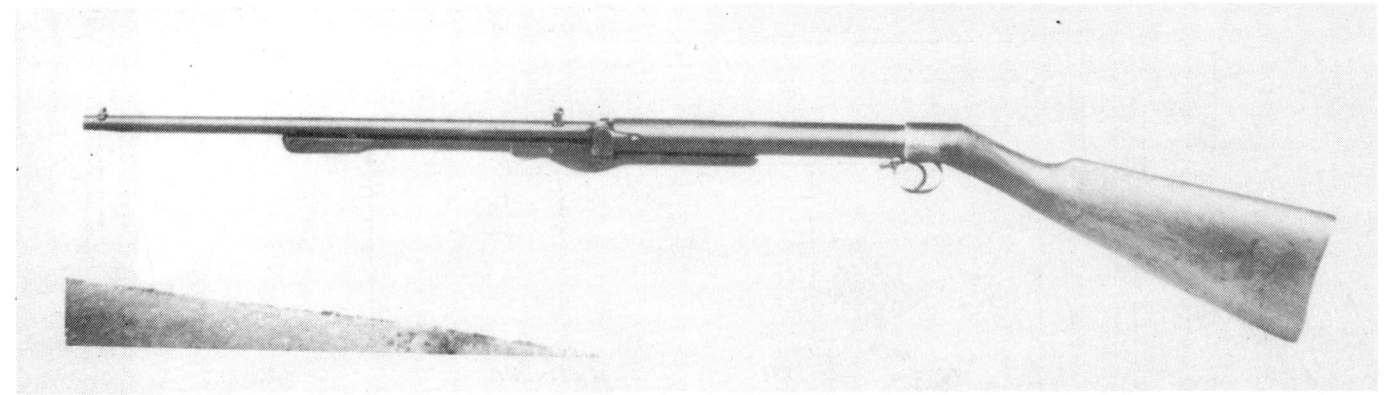

B.S.A. "Improved Model D" .22 and 45 inches long

MODEL   "Improved Model D" large 45 inch model. May have been called "Standard" by the late 70,000 serial numbers.

MAKER   B.S.A. Co. Ltd., Birmingham, England.

DATE   The side lever cocking lever catch was patented in 1910 and used on air rifles from about 1911 so any side lever catch air rifles lies in the following group of serial numbers:

Serial Number	Year
45000	1911
51000	1912
60000	1913
78212	1914

The lowest number seen for a side catch airgun is 47290. The above numbers apply to all the various lengths of "Improved" models made so the actual number of 45 inch models made is not known.

VALUATION   £60—£180.
($90—$270).

DETAILS   Quite a rare variation of the "Improved" Model, a much rarer type is the .25 calibre. The Author has a vague idea that this is the first introduction of the large or giant variety of pre-war B.S.A. air rifles. 45¼ inches long, 19½ inch barrel, 11 inch air chamber and fitted with a 14¼ inch straight hand stock, although pistol grip were also fitted. The above example had a pivoted foresight with two blades, angular pillar and smaller pillar with circular shroud. These are set at a 90° angle. Underside of barrel stamped "RD.No. 479972" and the cocking lever arm "B.S.A. PATENTS 8761-04, 25783-10, RD.479972". The first patent number 8761 refers to one made by Lincoln Jeffries for a fixed barrel with loading tap and cocking by a separate lever, and the second one, number 25783, was for the side lever cocking lever latch. Side of tap plate is stamped "PATENT 8246/06" another B.S.A. patent for the spring loaded breech plug and fitted into a blind hole in the action of the air rifle. It also covered the design of the tap retaining plate held into place by two screws. Top of air chamber is marked "THE B.S.A. AIR RIFLE (IMPROVED MODEL D), THE BIRMINGHAM SMALL ARMS Co. Ltd., ENGLAND, SOLE MANUFACTURER. Trigger adjustment is by way of screw through front of

trigger guard. Serial number stamped on trigger block as is usual for B.S.A. air rifles. Straight hand stock bears the triple rifle B.S.A. trademark, and fitted with metal butt plate. From a drawing of the piston it would appear that this might be fitted with piston rings.
These giant model .22s were sold with the double sear trigger arrangement and further details may be gained by looking under "Improved Model D" further on. These would have a "S" prefix serial number and the patent number 30338-10 would be stamped above it on the trigger block.

On air rifle number S77948 the "Improved Model D" appears to have been dropped and in its place etched on top of the air chamber "THE B.S.A. STANDARD — AIR RIFLE .22 BORE — THE BIRMINGHAM SMALL ARMS Co. Ltd., — SOLE MAKERS". This could be the first occasion when "Standard" was used as a model name.

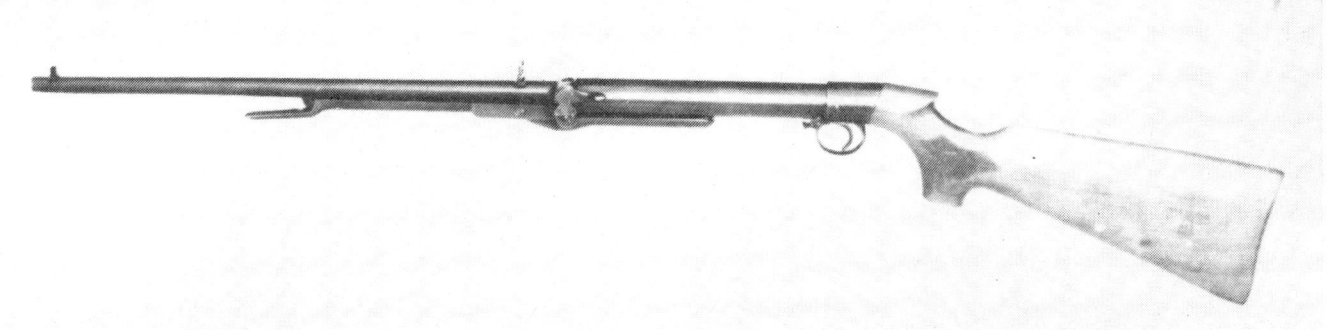

The .25 calibre B.S.A. "Improved Model D". Note rearsight design that differs from all other B.S.A. underlevers

MODEL "Improved Model D" .25 calibre.

MAKER The Birmingham Small Arms Company Ltd., Small Heath, Birmingham. Address at time of manufacture. London office, 6 Great Winchester Street, London E.C.

DATE 1908 to 1909. All .25 "Improved Model D's" appear to lie in the 21000's and this places them in the following range of serial numbers: 1908 started with number 19000 and by 1909 had reached 28000.

VALUATION A very rare air rifle, second-hand value from around £200 to £400 and in auction one recently (1982) realised £300a. ($300—$600, $450a).

DETAILS This model must surely rank with the Military Pattern in rarity. Specimen seen had serial number 21047. It might be safe to assume that if any .25 "Improved Model D" were to turn up with trigger block bearing a serial number NOT beginning with 21 then the block is not original. Measures 43½ inches (1.10m.) long with a 14¼ inch pistol grip stock. 19½ inch rifled barrel with dovetail mounted sights. The sights usually fitted are not those seen on other B.S.A. pre-war air rifles. The foresight is barleycorn and rearsight described as "Government wide V". The rearsight is a standing gate with a slider that rides up and down. On the example seen this does not fold down. Underside of cocking lever is stamped "LINCOLN JEFFRIES' PATENT 8761/04", this patent covered the use of a separate cocking lever to cock the action thus allowing the barrel to be fixed and thus do away with the air leakage often encountered by break action air rifles of the time. This patent lead to the Lincoln Jeffries air rifles and then on to the B.S.A. stable. Near the rearsight is stamped the triple rifle B.S.A. trademark and "LOAD", there may also appear the figure "3" which indicates the bore size. At the time Number 1 was .177, Number 2 stood for .22 and Number 3 was .25. Tap side plate is stamped "P.PAT.8246/06". This was for the improvement of the loading tap, spring loaded tension applied to one end to take up any wear with the tap being tapered, also having a wider loading hole with a possibly tapered loading hole so that a pellet pusher was no longer necessary. Early Lincoln Jeffries air rifles might suffer from this problem in that pellets needed to be pushed down into the loading tap. Hence the "Improved Model D". See "Guns Review" September 1978. Top of air chamber stamped "THE B.S.A. AIR RIFLE (IMPROVED MODEL D) — THE BIRMINGHAM SMALL ARMS COMPANY LIMITED — SOLE MANUFACTURER". Fitted with cast trigger guard with adjustment through front, hand chequered pistol grip, triple rifle trademark stamped on side of stock and fitted with metal butt plate. Serial numbers seen for the .25 are 21047, 21124, 21215, 21360 and 21465. Just as a point of interest the Author has seen more military pattern air rifles, so is the .25 even more rare? At a later date the "Company Limited" on the air chamber was abbreviated to "Co. Ltd.". In 1908 the 43 inch "Improved Model D" was advertised in either .177 or .25.

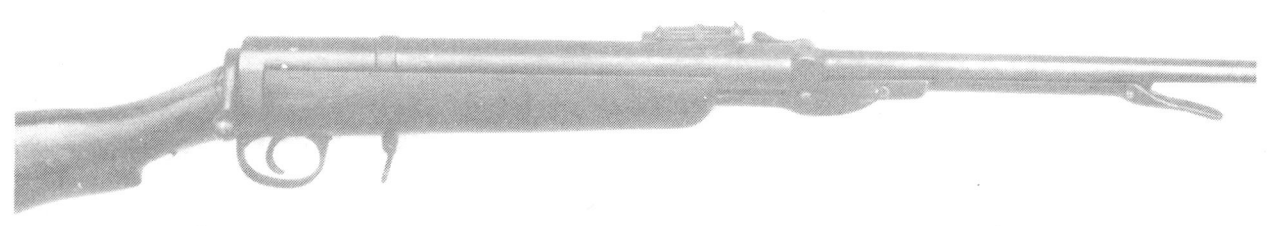

B.S.A. Military Pattern

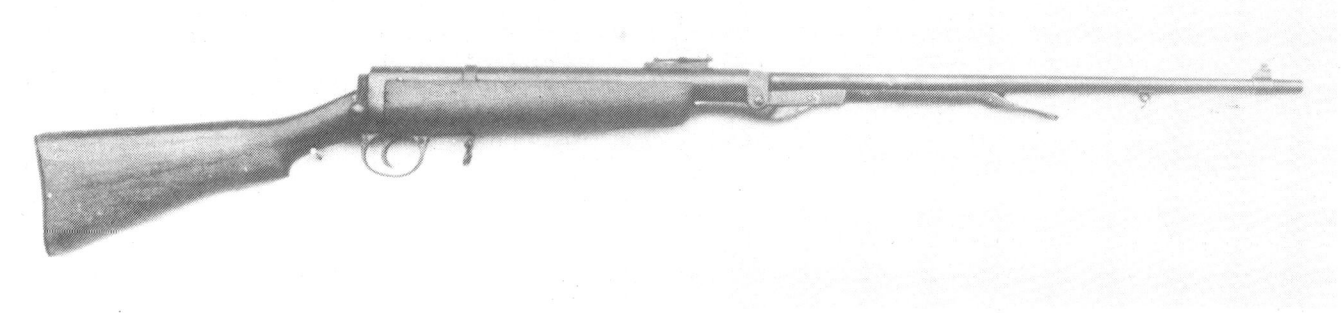

B.S.A. Military Pattern

MODEL Military Pattern. (Long Model).

MAKER B.S.A., Birmingham, England.

DATE Between 1906 to around 1914.

VALUATION Another very rare B.S.A. air rifle, second-hand value from £500 to in excess of £1,000 as one went through auction during 1982 and realised a selling price of £500. ($750–$1500, $750a).

DETAILS 48½ inches long. Pillar foresight set 1¼ inches from the end of barrel. Foresight adjustable for windage. Six inches in from end of barrel is an eyelet for a sling, this has been fixed on to the underside of the barrel. Bayonet underlever with side strengthening fences, underlever stamped "LINCOLN JEFFRIES PATENT 8761/04". This applies to the original patent for tap loading air rifles, see "Guns Review" May 1978. Underside of barrel stamped with the serial number, 246, and various other inspecton marks. Tap retaining plate stamped "PATENT 8246/06" see Gun's Review" September 1978. About five inches in front of the tap loading orifice is lightly stamped "ARMY & NAVY C.S.Ld, LONDON". Rearsight is a flip up military style ramp with a sliding cross piece for long range work. Stamped on top of air chamber "THE B.S.A. AIR RIFLE (MILITARY PATTERN) — THE BIRMINGHAM SMALL ARMS COMPANY LIMITED — SOLE MANUFACTURERS". Serial number 246 appears on the L.H.S. of the trigger block near dummy bolt. The number 53736 appears engraved on the trigger guard that also incorporates the rear sling swivel. The butt bears the triple rifle trademark and has a plain metal butt plate. Fitted with trigger adjustment via screw through the front of the trigger guard, this is secured by a locking screw. See "Guns Review" September 1978 for further details of the patent for converting air rifles for military use. Have seen the above with a side lever cocking lever. See "Airgun World" March 1979. Advertised weight 9 lb 4 oz the same as the Lee Enfield 303. For comparison between the above see "Guns Review" February 1978. Further details of the military style B.S.A.'s can be gleaned from "Guns Review" October 1972 and February 1976.

Some military style air rifles have been fitted with stocks with brass butt plates, I doubt if these are original as the Lee Enfield stock will interchange with the air rifle. There were two models of the above: Long Model after the Lee Enfield Territorial Service Long Rifle and a Short Model after the Lee Enfield Short Mk. III Military Rifle. It would appear that the Long version was available in either .177 or .22, whilst the Short model was only sold in .177. Weight of Long Model 9 lb 4 oz. A fully stock short military pattern is featured in "Airgun World" September 1981. An advert dated 1913 prices the Long Military Model at 80/- (£4.00) and the Short Model at 120/- (£6.00).

The following serial numbers have been seen in the Military Pattern B.S.A. air rifle, 41, 119, 222 all had the bayonet style cocking lever, whilst 246 and 388 were fitted with the improved style lever with side fances.

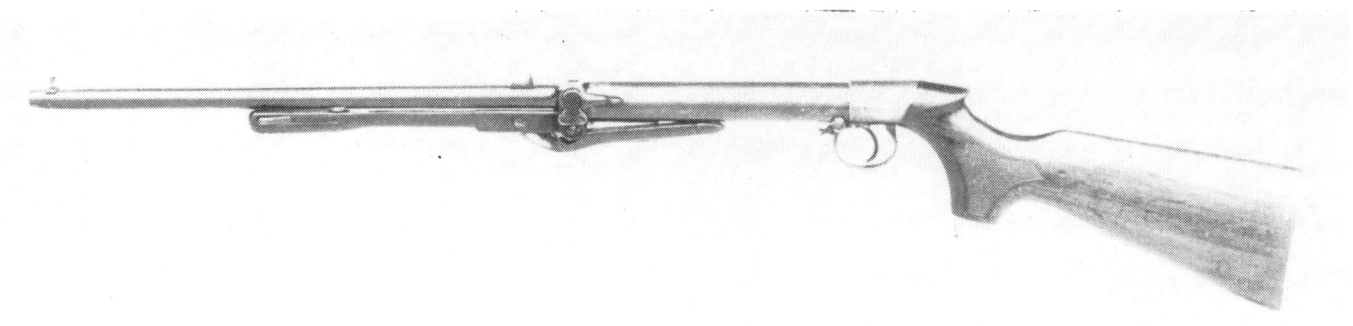

Improved Model D (Junior Model)

MODEL "Junior" Model of "Improved Model D".

MAKER The Birmingham Small Arms Company Ltd., (B.S.A.), Small Heath, Birmingham, England. Address at time of manufacture.

DATE Actual sample seen with serial number S5977, 1913 to 1914. The "Improved Model D's" are mixed up in the following serial numbers and dates; see other pages dealing with similar model.

VALUATION £50–£150. ($75–$225).

DETAILS This is the "Junior" and should not be confused with the "Light" or "Ladies" model that is longer. Barrel of Junior measures 15½ inches whilst the Light Model measures 17¼. The Junior is also a miniature of the Light Model in every respect. Once you've seen one you never forget it. 35½ inches long with a 15½ inch barrel. Blade foresight set in dovetail and twin blade rearsight, one of which folds down. Smaller one stamped 10 whilst other stamped 20, would assume these stand for yards. B.S.A. triple rifle trademark on barrel whilst on the underside "Rd. No. 479972". Side lever latch cocking lever stamped "B.S.A. PATENTS 8761-04, 25783-10, RD 479972" Patent 8761 was originally made by Lincoln Jeffries and dealt with having an airgun with a fixed barrel and a separate cocking lever, whilst Patent 25783 was again lodged by Lincoln Jeffries and covered the side latch cocking lever. It is a minor miracle that all these numbers are stamped on such a small cocking lever, only 9¼ inches long. Top of air chamber stamped "THE B.S.A. AIR RIFLE (IMPROVED MODEL D), THE BIRMINGHAM SMALL ARMS Co. Ltd., ENGLAND, SOLE MANUFACTURER". Serial number appears on the trigger block as well as "PAT.30338-10", another patent made by Lincoln Jeffries and covered the use of a second sear that engaged with safety notch on the piston plunger, all B.S.A. underlevers with this design were prefixed "S" when they were manufactured between 1913 and 1914, not to be confused with the "Standard" Large Model .22 underlever that appeared later. Further details of these patents can be seen in "Guns Review" March 1979. Fitted with very small and narrow stock with length 11¼ inches, the usual three sizes for early B.S.A. underlevers were 13¼, 13¾, and 14¼ inches, measured from the trigger to the centre of the butt face. It was pointed out that the 13¼ inch was the standard stock length for the British Service Rifle, 13¾ inch was the more common length used by airguns whilst the 14¼ inch was not recommended for prone firing, but more for firing in the standing position. The tap plate cover is stamped "PATENT 8246-06" and is the only patent lodged by B.S.A.'s marked on this airgun. It applies to the improved style of loading tap in that it is spring loaded so as to take up any wear due to constant usage. The tap being tapered and loading hole made oversize to do away with the loading tool necessary on the earlier models to push the pellet down into the tap. Details see "Guns Review" September 1978. All in all a rare model. The Junior "Improved Model D" was also sold with a 11¼ inch straight stock.

The following serial numbers have been seen for the Junior Model Improved Model D: 65650, S65850, S65977, S77070 and S80666.

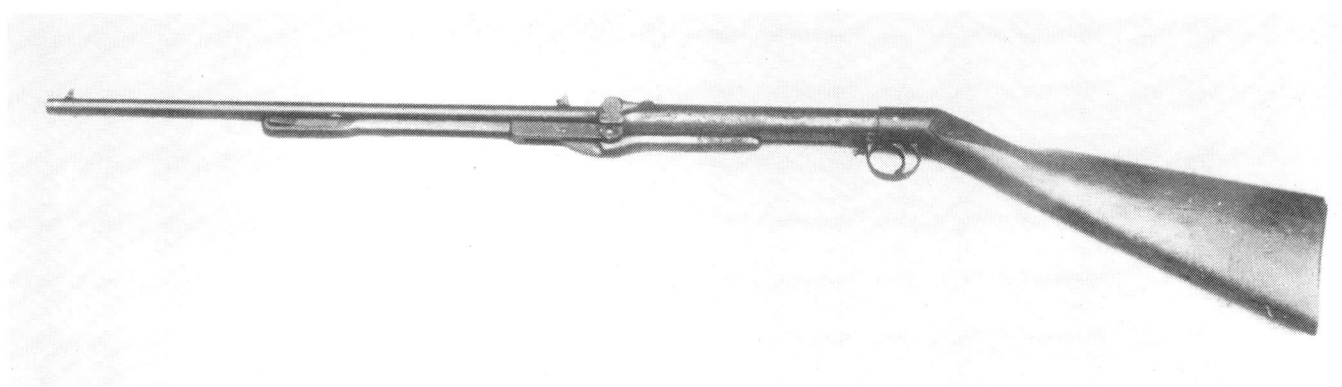

B.S.A. "Improved Model D" with straight-hand stock and double safety sear

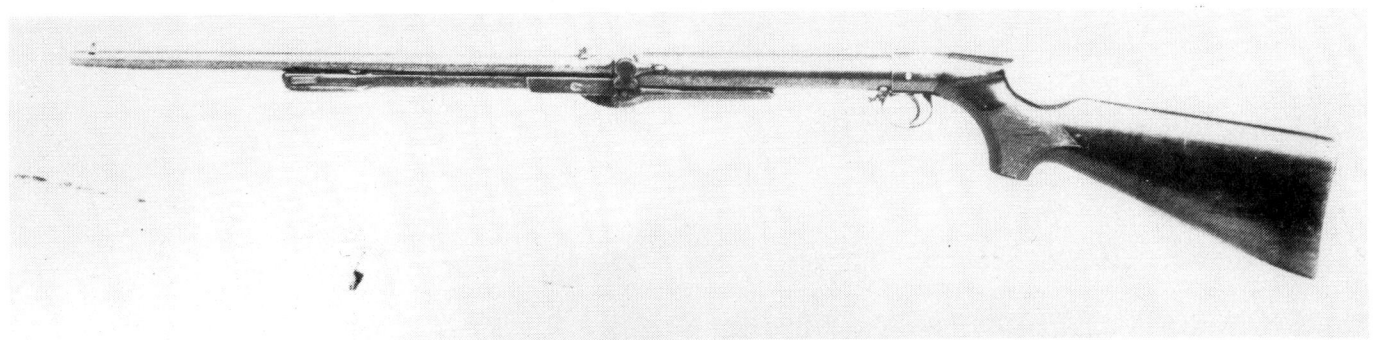

B.S.A. "Improved Model D" with Pistol Grip Stock. 43¼ inches long

MODEL "Improved Model D". 39 and 43 inch models with side lever cocking lever.

MAKER B.S.A.

DATE Serial numbers 60000—78212 with "S" prefix, 1913—1914.

VALUATION £50—£100 although have seen them advertised for as much as £150. £37a—£72a. ($75—$150, $56a—$108a).

DETAILS Serial number of above S68996. 39¼ inches or 43¼ inches long. One hole trigger block. Side lever catch underlever. "S" prefix denotes double sear arrangement. Stamped on top of air chamber "THE B.S.A. AIR RIFLE (IMPROVED MODEL D), THE BIRMINGHAM SMALL ARMS CO. LTD., ENGLAND, SOLE MANUFACTURERS". On the underside of the underlever "B.S.A. PATENTS 8761-04, 25783-10. RD 479972" and above the serial number on the trigger block "PAT. 30338-10". For further details of the patent 25783 see "Guns Review" March 1979. This applies to the side lever catch for the cocking lever. On underside of barrel is "RD NO 479972". The patent 30338 applies to the double notch sear arrangement, see "Guns Review" March 1979. The above two variations *in length* are more *commonly* found with the simpler type trigger mechanism with the adjuster screw through the front of the trigger guard, these models do not have the "S" prefix to the serial numbers.

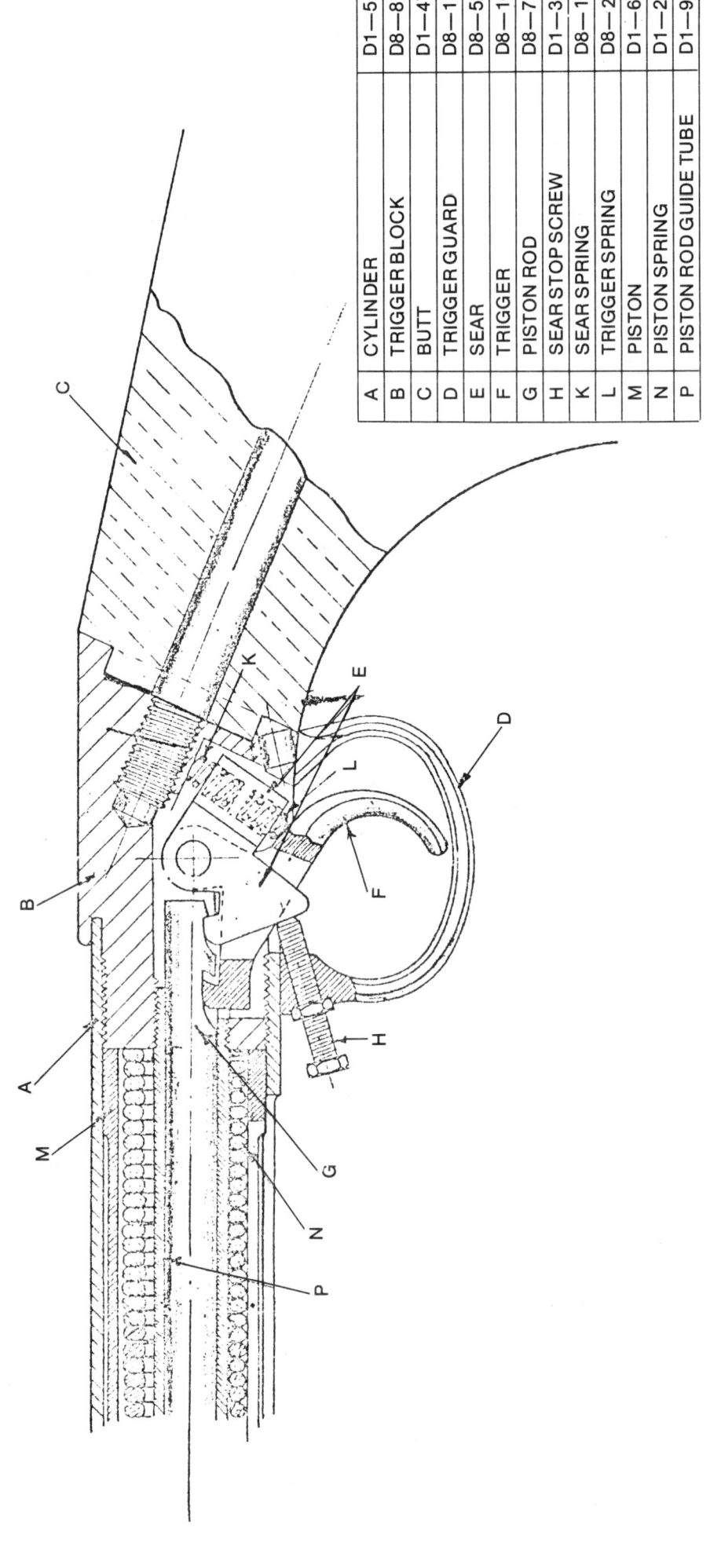

B.S.A. "L" Model

MODEL No. 1 Model or known as "Light" or "Ladies" model.

MAKER B.S.A., Birmingham, England.

DATE 1919—1935. By serial numbers as follows:
1—1919	33000—1928
4000—1920	35000—1929
12000—1920	38000—1932
16000—1921	39000—1934
17000—1922	40000—1935
18000—1923	40343—1935
22000—1924	
26000—1925	
30000—1927	

VALUATION £30—£82, £38a—£55a.
($45—$123, $57a—$83a).

DETAILS 39½ inches long. Serial number always on trigger block. Three hole trigger block. All the above serial numbers should have a "L" prefix. Chequering is pressed into the stock. All "L" prefix underlevers should be .177. Advertised with 12 groove rifling and weighing 6 lb 4 oz. The sear is almost identical to that fitted to the Webley Mk. III air rifle and they may interchange should a replacement be required. Early models of the Light Pattern were fitted with two hole trigger blocks. The early models were fitted with a two hole trigger block and between serial numbers L20710 and L28208 this was changed to a three hole trigger block.

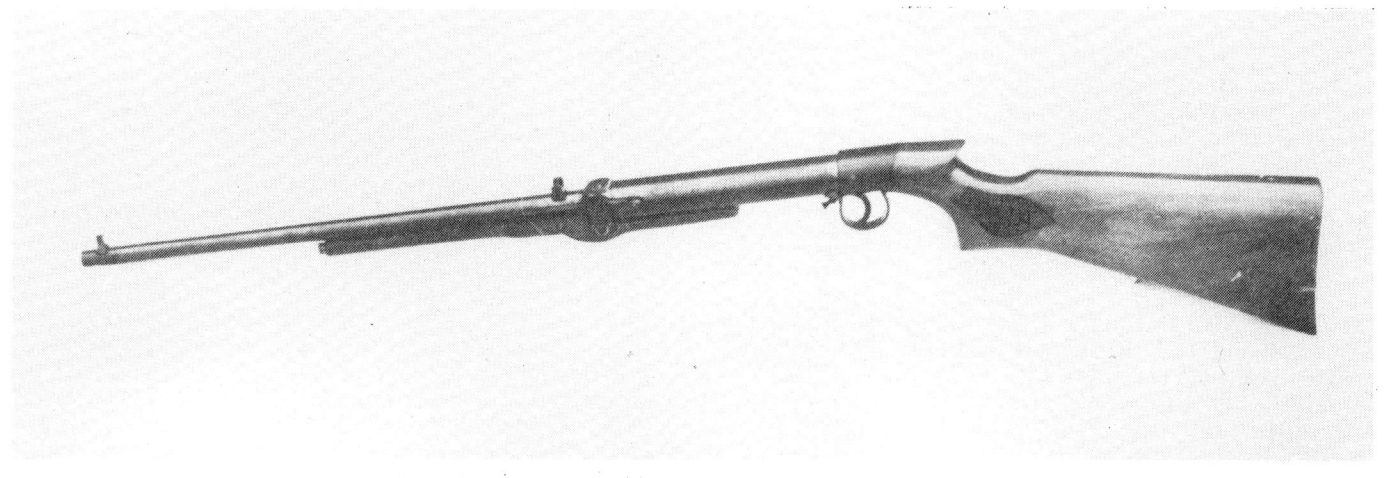

"A" Series B.S.A. underlever air rifle

MODEL "A" Series, a follow on from the "L" pattern.

MAKER B.S.A., Birmingham, England.

DATE Production started 7.5.1936 with number 1 and ceased with number 3939 dated 8.6.1939.
Dating by serial numbers as follows all with "A" prefix.
1	7.5.1936
1000	1936
2000	1937
3000	1938
3711	1939
3939	8.6.1939

As can be seen from production figures the above is quite a rare model. For further details see "Guns Review" March 1978.

VALUATION £30—£82, £38a—£55a.
($45—$123, $57a—$83).

DETAILS Similar to the "L" model. 39¾ inches long. Serial number stamped on block near trigger. One hole trigger block with sheet metal trigger guard that housed an adjustment screw. Stamped "1" between tap and rearsight denoting .177 calibre. Lightly etched on top of air chamber as follows:

THE B.S.A. STANDARD
AIR RIFLE .177 BORE (No. 1)
THE BIRMINGHAM SMALL ARMS Co. Ltd. ENGLAND.
© PATENTED SOLE MAKERS.

AUSTRALIA No. 7686 JAN. 2nd., 1907. CANADA 1906 No. 97984 1907. No. 108159. U.S.A. APRIL 3rd., 1906 AND JUNE 16th, 1908. FRANCE No. 358745. S.G.D.G. Gt. BRIT Rd. No. 479972.

See also markings for the B.S.A. "S" prefix pre-war .22 underlever. The above model was also known as the "No. 1 Model". Advertised weight 6¼ lbs. Chequering on stock has been pressed in complete with B.S.A. motif.

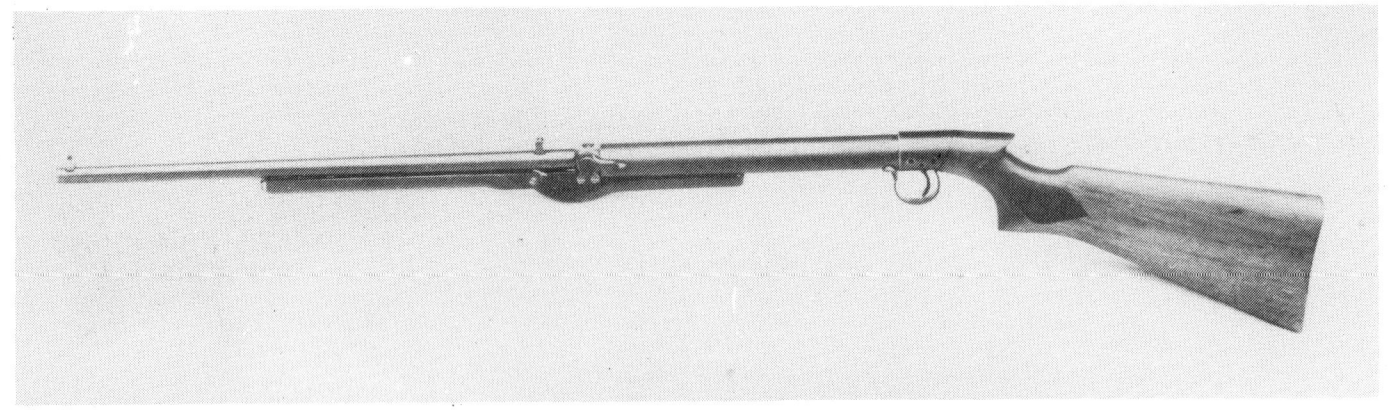

B.S.A. "Standard" pre-war underlever air rifle

MODEL "Standard" Model No. 2. .22 (S prefix).

MAKER B.S.A., Birmingham, England.

DATE 1919 to 1935 by serial numbers with "S" prefix for .22 or "CS" prefix for .177 as follows:

1—6000	1919/1920	35000	1928
10000	1921	42000	1929
14000	1922	46000	1930
17000	1923	47000	1931
19000	1924	49000	1932
24000	1925	51000	1933
29000	1926	52000	1934
30000	1927	55442	1935

VALUATION £60—£150, although minty examples have been sold from £150 to £210, and through auction, £190a. ($90—$225, mint $225—$315, $57a—$120a).

DETAILS Serial number of above "S7273". Two hole trigger block. Light etching not visible on top of air cylinder. "2 LOAD" in front of tap pellet hole. 45 inches long. Chequering on stock is pressed and not hand cut. Rifled barrel has 12 grooves. Advertised weight 7 lb 10 oz.

On a better example of the "Standard" the following etching can be seen on the top of the air chamber:

THE B.S.A. STANDARD
AIR RIFLE   .22 BORE (No.2)
THE BIRMINGHAM SMALL ARMS Co Ltd ENGLAND.
© PATENTED SOLE MANUFACTURERS.
AUSTRALIA No 7686 JAN 2nd 1907. CANADA 1906 No 97984 1907 No 108159. U.S.A. APRIL 3rd. 1906 AND JUNE 16th 1908. FRANCE No. 358745 S.G.D.G. Gt. BRIT. Rd No 479972.

Above read as accurately as possible, but some of the 8's, 6's and similar figures were faint and may have been misread. The above appeared on a B.S.A. Standard serial number S47529, dated 1932. The B.S.A. triple rifle trademark appeared between the "B.S.A." and "STANDARD" and continued downwards between "RIFLE" and ".22". On air rifle S54171 the piston is stamped "P.PAT.16982.29". This patent (No. 332346 of 1929—30) was for an improved method of mounting the cupped washer on to the end of the piston using a metal washer or disc lying within the leather washer and threaded on to a projecting threaded end of the piston. See "Guns Review" April 1980 for further details. The above example also had a three hole trigger block. One example, serial number S41735, when stripped and examined had anti-clockwise rifling. It has been suggested that the B.S.A. Airsporter mainspring will fit the above. If ever the cocking lever plunger should break or the catch lip shear off then the loading lever plunger from the Webley Mk. III, part number AR 30, will act as a replacement with no work fitting if required.

Somewhere between S13253 and S16893 the two hole block became a three hole trigger action. In the directions for use it was suggested that the action was cocked first before the pellet was introduced into the tap, because if done the other way around the pellet could be drawn into the air chamber as the action was being cocked and might jam the piston.

In order to examine the bore of this or any other underlever air rifle, remove the tap side plate and withdraw the tap and insert a piece of white paper into the vacant tap hole and this will reflect some light down into the bore, look through other end and see "What the Butler saw"! It is recommended that the sights are removed from left to right and replaced from right to left as looking down on top of the air rifle as it points away from you. The B.S.A. pre-war mainsprings were stamped with the triple rifle trademark on the end coils to indicate their authenticity.

On the three hole trigger block adjustment is by way of a tapered screw that engages with the top left rear of the trigger when the action is cocked. A locking screw with a flat head is positioned on the opposite of the trigger block for tightening down on to the adjuster screw and thus locking it into position. The Model "Standard" is adjusted at the factory for an average trigger pull of 5 lbs, but for a lighter pull turn adjuster screw towards "L" and for a heavier trigger pull turn towards "H", loosen locking screw before each adjustment and tighten down afterwards.

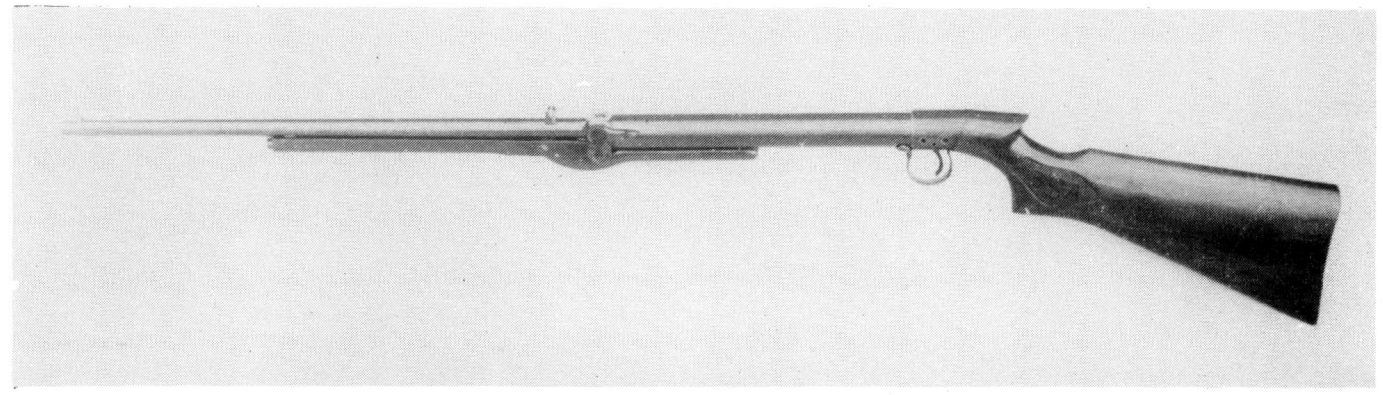

"T" prefix B.S.A. "Standard"

MODEL "Standard" Model No. 2 (.22). "T" prefix serial number.

MAKER B.S.A., Birmingham, England.

DATE The "T" series date from 1936 to 1939, serial numbers as follows:
T1 to T2100 — 1936
T2101 to T4300 — 1937
T4301 to T4800 — 1938
T5801 to T7660 — 1939
See "Guns Review" September 1972 for further details.

VALUATION Average from about £50 up to £150, but more for excellent specimens. Can be placed in the same value bracket as normal "S" serial numbered air rifles. ($75—$225).

DETAILS "T" series made from 1936 to 1939. About 8,000 made. Three hole trigger block. Number of about T2548. 45 inches long. All known "T" series are in .22 with trigger adjustment through trigger guard, although many with three hole trigger blocks have been seen. Chequering pressed into stock with letters "B.S.A." top of air chamber lightly etched:
THE B.S.A.   STANDARD
AIR RIFLE   .22 BORE (No.2)
AUSTRALIA No.7686 JAN 2nd 1907. CANADA 1906 No.97984 1907 No.108159. U.S.A. APRIL 3rd 1905 AND JUNE 16th 1908. FRANCE No.358745 S.G.D.G. Gt BRITAIN Rd No.479972.
Note that the above is identical to the etching on the previous Model "S". One specimen of the above was fitted with double round section mainsprings similar to the Lincoln air rifle, also the rifling was anti-clockwise. The B.S.A. Airsporter mainspring may fit the above.

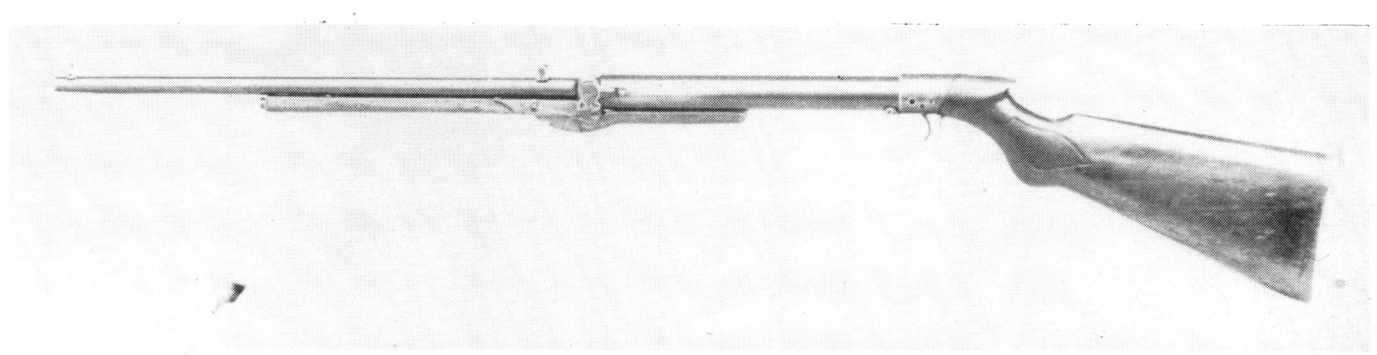

B.S.A. "Club Special"

MODEL "CS" or "Club" Special". Also referred to as the No. 4 Model.

MAKER B.S.A. Ltd., Birmingham, England.

DATE Manufactured at the same time as the "Standard" Model underlever and the serial numbers for the CS Model were mixed in with the serial numbers of the Standard. More .22 Standard Models were produced than the .177 Club Special.
Period of manufacture from about 1924 to 1935, when the "C" or "Club" Model appeared in 1936.
The "CS" series appears dotted throughout the following serial numbers as these also include the "S" or Standard Model.
18801—28000   1924/1926
28001—37700   1927/1928
37701—42300   1929
42301—46200   1930
46201—47600   1931
47601—49300   1932
49301—50900   1933
50901—52620   1934
52621—55442   1935

VALUATION £50—£150, although much more for excellent examples. ($75—$225).

DETAILS Large model in .177. 45 inches long. Serial number always stamped on the trigger block, but as these interchange don't be surprised if you see various models with mixed trigger blocks, i.e. .22 Club Specials? Fitted with sheet metal trigger guard and usually a three hole trigger block. Stamped on barrel near loading port "LOAD 1". Top of air chamber was etched with lettering, but this is not visible on example examined. Stock has pressed chequering. Earlier Models were fitted with trigger guards with the trigger adjustment screw through the front and a one hole trigger block. Advertised weight 7 lb 11 oz. 12 grooved rifling and advertised effective range of 50 yards. This model was advertised as the "Special Club".

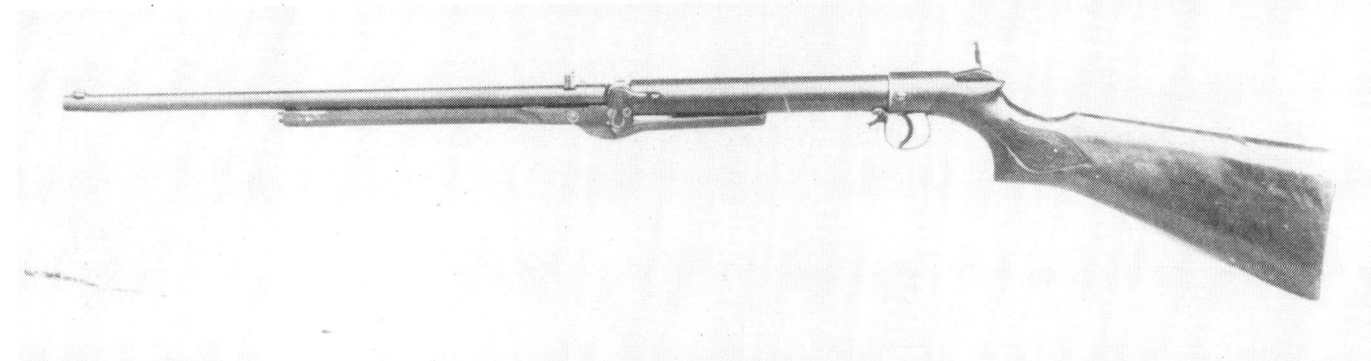

B.S.A. "Club" Underlever

MODEL "Club", also called the "No. 4 Club Model".

MAKER Birmingham Small Arms Co. Ltd., Birmingham, England.

DATE 1936 to 1939. All serial numbers have a "C" prefix.
C1 to C720	1936
C721 to C1500	1937
C1501 to C2435	1938
C2436 to C2500	1939
C2524 to C3530	1939, odd numbers only.

VALUATION £50–£150. ($75–$225).

DETAILS The follow-on of the Club Special, "CS". Quite a rare model as only about 3,000 were made. Available in .177 only, 43¼ inches long with a 19⅜ inch barrel. Almost identical to the "S" and "T" Series except for the calibre. Cocking lever pivot has now been altered to be just a free floating pin held in place by the tap cover plate. Another simplification is a one screw trigger block with the trigger adjustment by way of screw through the trigger guard. Stock has pressed chequering with B.S.A. motif in the centre. Advertised weight 7 lbs 6 ozs. They were all fitted with the standard stock length of 14¼ inches. At the same time that the above was being sold to the public B.S.A. also offered a booklet titled "There is money in this for your Club" such was the interest in shooting before the turn of public opinion. The advertised range was given as 50 yards, not as far as the 80 YARDS quoted for the Webley Mk. II Service! The advert also stated that B.S.A.'s had reverted to the original pre-war (First World War), weight and measurements in the production of the Club. An optional extra available for the above was the patent Sprawson-Parker traversing foresight with a guarded bead. It enabled the shooter to adjust his sight to get an exact dead-on-aim. Peepsights were also available and screwed on to the stock grip, and trigger block.

B.S.A. Pre-war "Break Action"

MODEL "Breakdown" Model .177 bore.

MAKER B.S.A., Birmingham, England.

DATE By serial numbers as follows:
Without "B" prefix.	101–1050	1932
	1051–2700	1933
	2701–4750	1934
	4751–6642	1935
With "B" prefix.	1–270	1935
	271–3200	1936
	3201–6800	1937/8
	6801–8562	1938/9

VALUATION £40–£80. ($60–$120).

DETAILS Serial number of above B5716. 41¼ inches long. Stamped with "BSA" and three rifles just in front of rearsight. Rifled, but could be supplied smoothbore to special order. Cost £2/10/0 in 1939. The B.S.A. Meteor mainspring should fit the above if some of the coils are cut off and the end ground flat. Sold in .177 only. Advertised weight 5¼ lb. Barrel rifled with 12 grooves. Top of air chamber etched:
THE B.S.A. AIR RIFLE.
BREAKDOWN PATTERN .177 BORE.
THE BIRMINGHAM SMALL ARMS Co. Ltd, ENGLAND
Rifling is unusual in that it runs anti-clockwise.

AIR RIFLES AND PISTOLS SPARES

Cadet Air Rifle

PRICES ON OPPOSITE PAGE

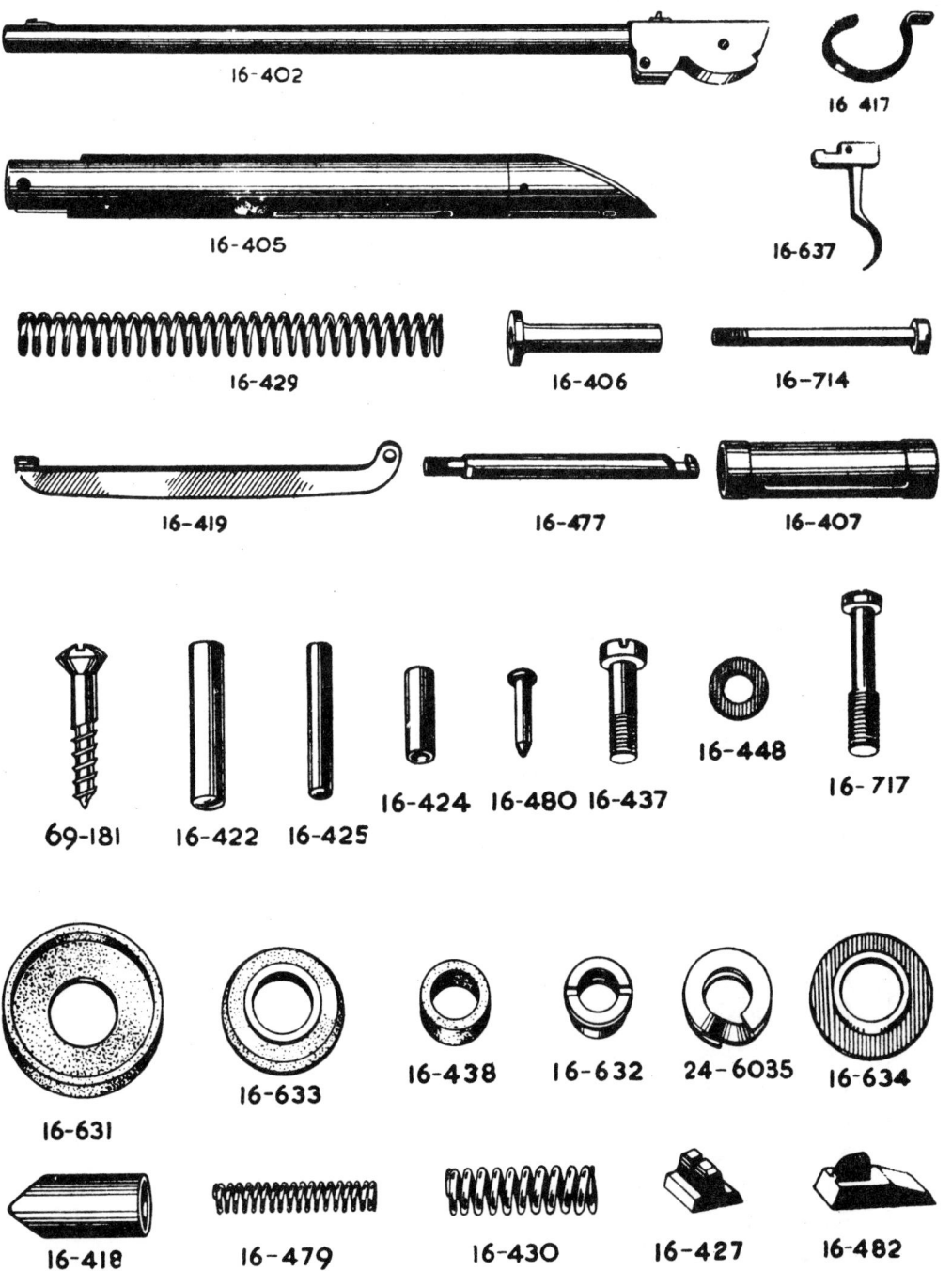

THOMAS BLAND & SONS, 4-5 WILLIAM IV STREET, LONDON, W.C.2

AIR RIFLES AND PISTOLS SPARES

Cadet Air Rifle

POSTAGE ON SMALL PARTS OFTEN EXCEEDS COST OF PART.
PRICES INCLUDE POSTAGE.

PART No.	DESCRIPTION	PRICE
16-402	Barrel assembly complete with sights and sealing washer	£3/1/0
16-405-715	Cylinder and Back Block	£1/11/6
16-406	Piston guide assembly	2/-
16-407	Piston body and end plug	10/6
16-417	Trigger guard	1/9
16-419	Cocking lever	9/6
16-429	Mainspring	3/-
16-708	Stock (complete) (not illustrated)	£2/7/9
16-709	Fore-end bush (not illustrated)	4d.
16-477	Piston rod	3/2
16-637	Trigger	7/-
16-714	Stock bolt	2/6
16-418	Barrel latch	1/3
16-422	Barrel hinge pin	6d.
16-424	Cocking lever axis pin	6d.
16-425	Sear axis pin	6d.
16-427	Back sight	3/-
16-430	Barrel latch spring	9d.
16-447	Trigger guard retaining screw	7d.
16-438	Barrel sealing washer	6d.
16-448	Trigger guard retaining screw washer	4d.
16-479	Sear spring	6d.
16-480	Sear spring guide	6d.
16-482	Foresight	
16-631	Piston washer leather (outer)	1/3
16-632	Piston washer nut	1/-
16-633	Piston washer rubber (buffer)	1/2
16-634	Piston washer (buffer)	10d.
16-717	Fore-end screw	8d.
24-6035	Stock bolt spring washer	6d.
69-181	Trigger guard screw (rear)	8d.
16-715	Back block	10/-
16-631/4	Washer set complete	3/6
16-630	Piston assembly complete	16/6

THOMAS BLAND & SONS, 4-5 WILLIAM IV STREET, LONDON, W.C.2

Care and Cleaning of the BSA "CADET" Air Rifle

Fig. 1.

1. SNAPPING.

The trigger should not be pulled to release the piston when the rifle is unloaded unless the barrel is held firmly in the break-down position and returned slowly. The unrestricted blow of the piston subjects the rifle to undue strain.

2. THE RENEWAL OF THE PISTON SPRING.

The removal of a broken or weakened spring and new replacement is a simple matter.

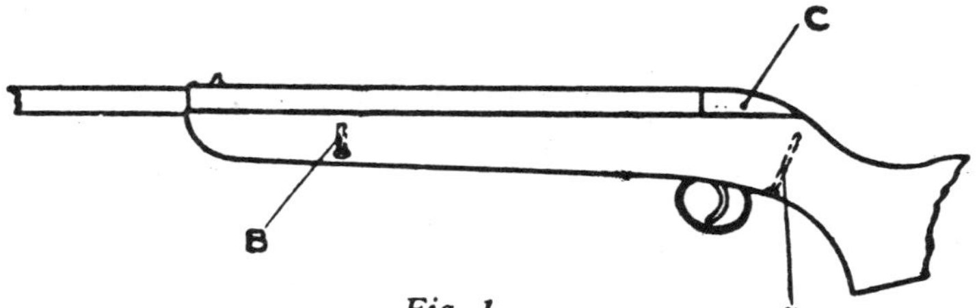

First of all make sure that the rifle is not cocked. The trigger guard screw A is then removed, also the two foreend screws B (see Fig 1). The whole action can then be lifted clear from the woodwork. Unscrew the rear block C, remove the old spring, insert replacement and reassemble. It is advisable that new springs should be lightly greased before insertion.

3. FITTING NEW PISTON WASHER.

Remove rear block C as previously described and, with the barrel in the breakdown position, disengage the cocking lever from the slot in the cylinder, when the piston may be withdrawn. Holding the latter firmly in a vice, the metal washer nut E (Fig. 2) should be forcibly unscrewed to break the securing clenches G.

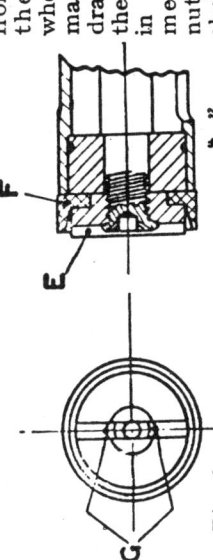

Fig. 2. HEAD OF PISTON UNIT "D"

After removal of the metal nut E, the old leather washer F can be lifted off and replaced by the new washer; this should be soaked in oil before assembly. After replacing the metal nut, the screwed end of the piston rod should be again punched over into the slots of the nut to secure, before replacing the piston unit in the cylinder.

4. HANDLING AND LOADING THE RIFLE.

The method of loading the rifle is by breaking down the barrel and inserting the pellet direct into the barrel breech round nose downwards. Return the barrel to its original position. The rifle is then ready for firing.

5. LUBRICATING THE PARTS.

The cylinder and piston should be oiled before the rifle is put away or after every 500 rounds of continuous firing. To oil the spring and piston pour a little oil through the slot in the cylinder. To oil the barrel hold the rifle in an upright position and drop a little oil into the muzzle. Allow the rifle to remain upright for a few minutes to enable the oil to run down to the breech.

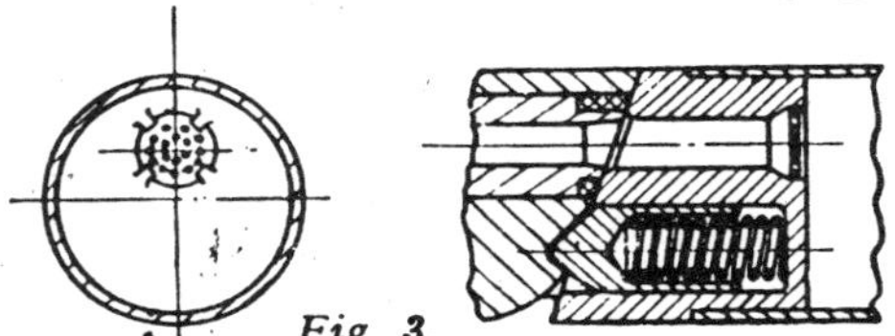

Do not attempt to remove the small perforated disc (Fig. 3) permanently fixed at the rear of the cylinder air outlet. It prevents foreign matter falling into the cylinder.

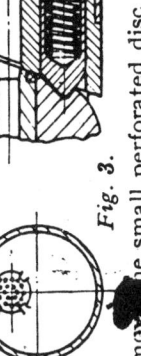

Fig. 3.

B.S.A. PELLETS.

To obtain the best results it is imperative that you should use only B.S.A. Air Rifle Pellets, which are specially designed and carefully manufactured for use with B.S.A. Air Rifles.

B.S.A. Guns Limited, Birmingham, 11.

Directors: Sir Bernard Docker, K.B.E., J.P. Sir Patrick Hannon, M.P.
J. Leek, C.B.E.

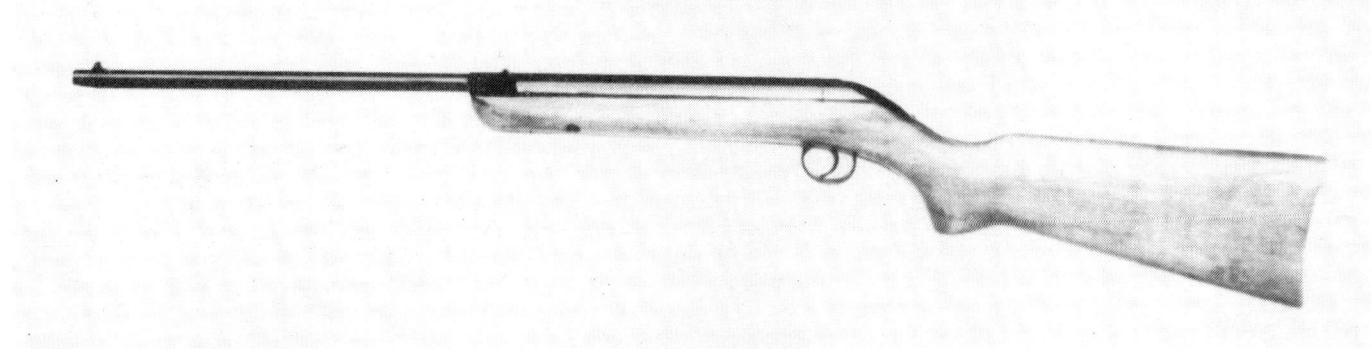

B.S.A. "Cadet"

Cadet stock with insertion of cross-grain strengthener. Introduced early 1946, and lack of stock bolt to hold action to butt. Rear trigger guard screw held action to stock. Stock bolt introduced May 1948

MODEL   Cadet — .177.

MAKER   B.S.A., Birmingham, England.

DATE   By serial number as follows:
"A" prefix 1945—1946
"B" prefix 1946—1949
"BA" & "W" prefix 1949—1951
"BC" prefix 1951—1959

VALUATION £15—£35, although mint examples have been known to sell for £60, £8a—£30a. ($23—$53, mint examples $90, $12a—$45a).

DETAILS Serial number of above BC14202. 37½ inches long. Fixed sights. Compact design and should still give years of good service. Serial number stamped on side of trigger block. Was a firm fairground favourite. Top of air chamber etched "THE BIRMINGHAM SMALL ARMS Co Ltd — "CADET" .177 AIR RIFLE — MADE IN ENGLAND" the BSA triple rifle trademark appears between the "CADET" and ".177". Advertised weight 4¾ lbs.

Have seen two B.S.A. Cadet smoothbores, they are distinguishable by "S.B." stamped on the side of the barrel breech and SB in an oval stamped next to the serial number on the trigger block. Serial number of one that I know of is BC18081(SB) dated 1951—1959. Have seen B.S.A. Cadet with the filter that is associated with the Cadet Major. Number of above Cadet BC16192. The filter appears to be inserted from the air chamber side. Holes in filter are wide, seven holes appear in the transfer port, although filter is larger. An advertisement dated December 1952 stated that both the Cadet and Cadet Major were fitted with the "B.S.A. patent filter disc, which prevents dust or other injurious matter entering the cylinder bore". The B.S.A. Meteor mainspring should fit the above if some of the coils are cut off and the end ground flat.

Early examples of the Cadet were fitted with three piece stocks similar to those fitted to the Airsporter Mark I. As seen on B17453. The two fore-ends were glued onto the butt part near the trigger action. This caused a weakness in construction as the glue tended to fail after a time or in any damp environment. This example also had the rear stock screw going through the trigger guard and not through the stock pistol grip. These early examples are quite rare.

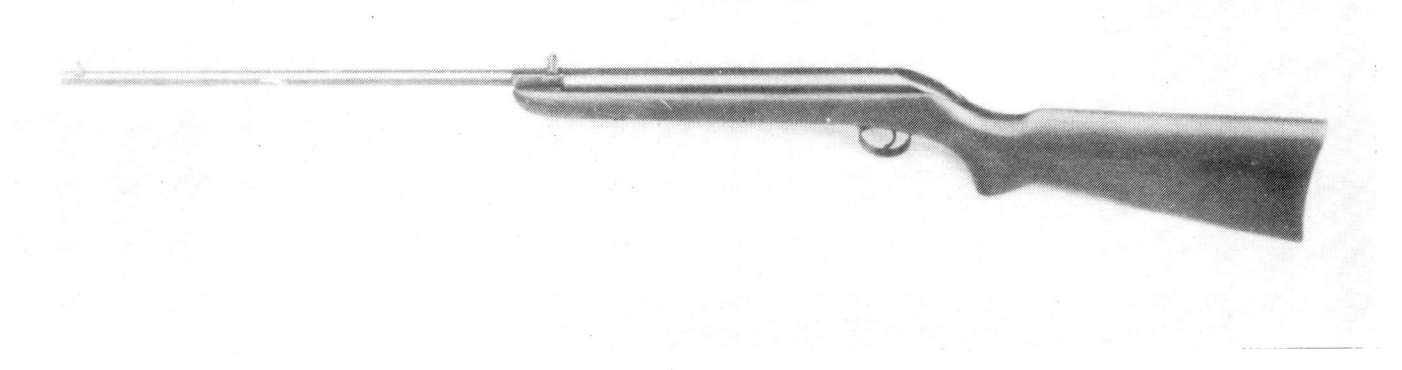

B.S.A. "Cadet-Major"

MODEL Cadet Major.

MAKER B.S.A., Birmingham, England.

DATE By prefix letters as follows:
"M" 1947—1948
"C" 1948
"Y" 1949
"CA" 1949—1955
"CC" 1955—1957

VALUATION £20—£70.
($30—$105).

DETAILS Larger version of the Cadet. Measures almost 42 inches long, trigger adjustment screw on top in trigger block, adjustable rearsight, and has an air filter gauze in the transfer port. Model name and maker was lightly etched on top of the air chamber, but on the above is not visible. Serial number CC19890 and is stamped on side of trigger block. Some had "B.S.A." stamped in the side of the stock. Very well made. Advertised weight 5½ lbs. From another Cadet Major the following appears etched on top of the air chamber, "THE BIRMINGHAM SMALL ARMS Co Ltd — CADET — MAJOR trademark" .177 AIR RIFLE — MADE IN ENGLAND". It has been suggested that the Webley Osprey mainspring could fit the Cadet Major. The smoothbore version was similary marked as for the Cadet, i.e. "SB" in an oval logo near the serial number and "SB" stamped on the side of the barrel breech near the rearsight. In Britain these are quite rare.

CARE and CLEANING of the BSA "CADET-MAJOR"

1. SNAPPING.
The trigger should not be pulled to release the piston when the rifle is unloaded unless the barrel is held firmly in the break-down position and returned slowly. The unrestricted blow of the piston subjects the rifle to undue strain.

2. THE RENEWAL OF THE PISTON SPRING.
The removal of a broken or weakened spring and new replacement is a simple matter

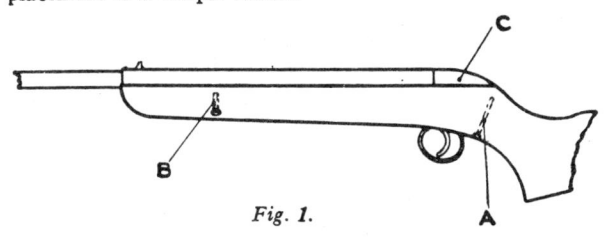

Fig. 1.

First of all make sure that the rifle is not cocked.
The trigger guard screw A is then removed, also the two fore-end screws B (see Fig. 1). The whole action can then be lifted clear from the woodwork. Unscrew the rear block C, remove the old spring, insert replacement and reassemble. It is advisable that new springs should be lightly greased before insertion.

3. FITTING NEW PISTON WASHER.
Remove rear block C as previously described and, with the barrel in the breakdown position, disengage the cocking lever from the slot in the cylinder after having removed the axis pin. The piston may now be withdrawn. Holding the latter firmly in a vice, metal washer nut E (Fig. 2) should be forcibly unscrewed to break

Fig. 2.

the securing clenches G. After removal of the metal nut E, the old leather washer F and the buffer H can be lifted off and replaced. The washer F should be soaked in oil before assembly. After replacing the metal nut, the screwed end of the piston rod should be again punched over into the slots of the nut to secure, before replacing the piston unit in the cylinder.

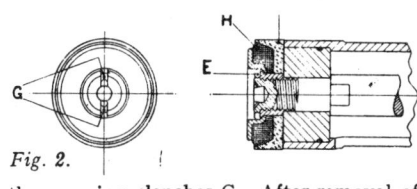

4. HANDLING AND LOADING THE RIFLE.
The method of loading the rifle is by breaking down the barrel and inserting the pellet direct into the barrel breech round nose downwards. Return the barrel to its original position. The rifle is then ready for firing.

5. LUBRICATING THE PARTS.
The cylinder and piston should be oiled before the rifle is put away or after every 500 rounds of continuous firing. To oil the spring and piston pour a little oil through the slot in the cylinder. To oil the barrel hold the rifle in an upright position and drop a little oil into the muzzle. Allow the rifle to remain upright for a few minutes to enable the oil to run down to the breech.

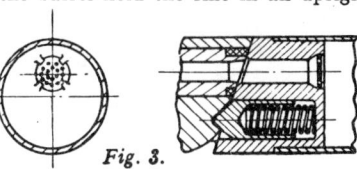

Fig. 3.

AIR RIFLES AND PISTOLS SPARES
Cadet Major Air Rifle

PRICES ON NEXT PAGE

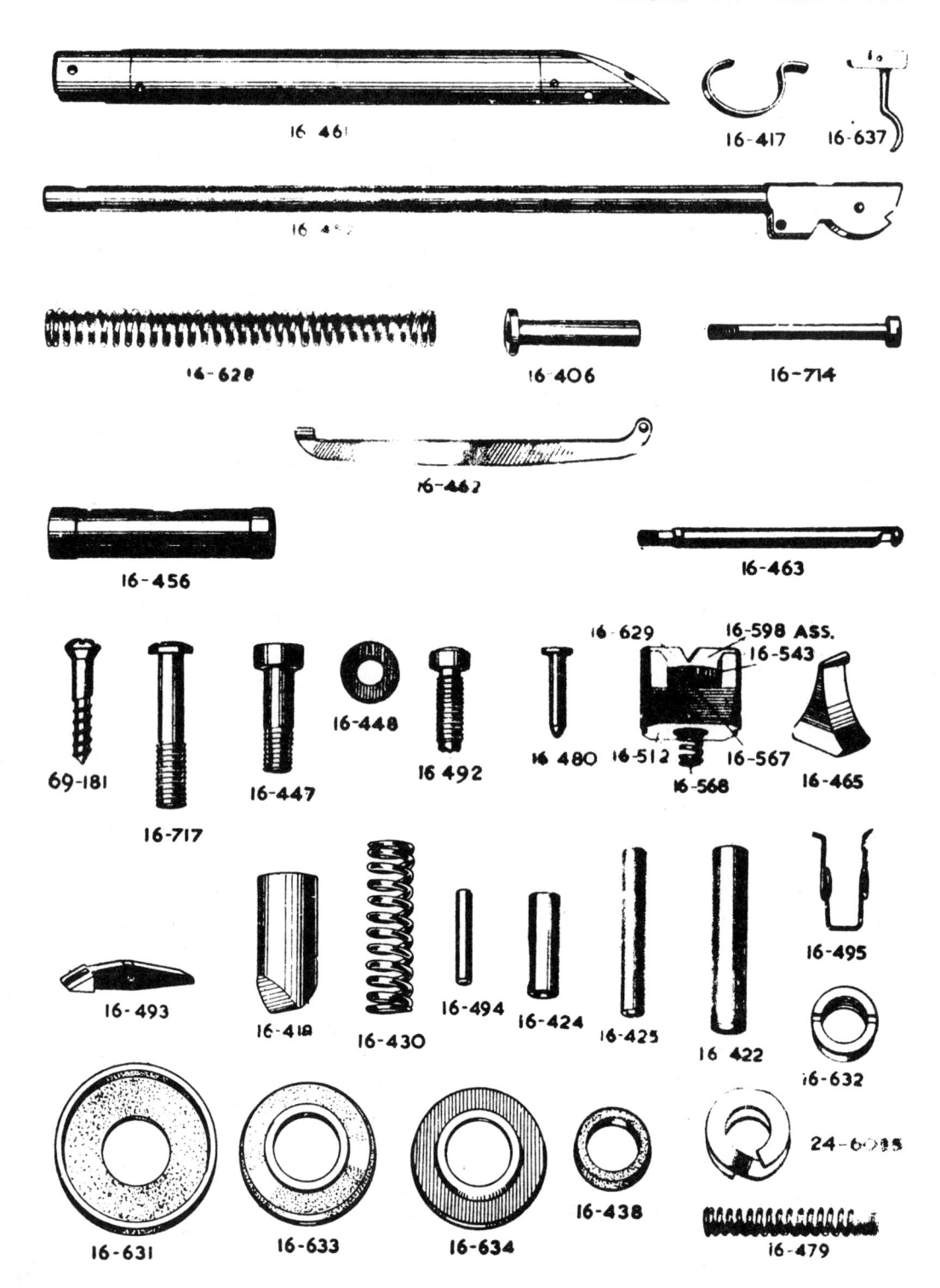

16-461
16-417
16-637
16-462
16-628
16-406
16-714
16-462
16-456
16-463
69-181
16-717
16-447
16-448
16-492
16-480
16-629
16-598 ASS.
16-543
16-512
16-567
16-568
16-465
16-493
16-418
16-430
16-494
16-424
16-425
16-422
16-495
16-632
16-631
16-633
16-634
16-438
24-6?5
16-479

THOMAS BLAND & SONS, 4-5 WILLIAM IV STREET, LONDON, W.C.2

AIR RIFLES AND PISTOLS SPARES

Cadet Major Air Rifle

POSTAGE ON SMALL PARTS OFTEN EXCEEDS COST OF PART.
PRICES INCLUDE POSTAGE.

PART No.	DESCRIPTION	PRICE
16-406	Piston guide assembly	5/6
16-417	Trigger guard	3/-
16-709	Fore-end bush (not illustrated)	6d.
16-452	Barrel assembly complete with sights and sealing washer	£6/18/8
16-456	Piston body and end plug	£1/2/0
16-461-730	Cylinder and back block	£4/13/3
16-462	Cocking lever	£1/1/0
16-463	Piston rod	9/-
16-731	Stock (complete) (not illustrated)	£3/10/0
16-628	Mainspring	5/9
16-637	Trigger	15/6
16-714	Stock bolt	3/-
16-418	Barrel latch	3/-
16-422	Barrel hinge pin	1/3
16-424	Cocking lever axis pin	1/3
16-425	Sear axis pin	9d.
16-430	Barrel latch spring	1/3
16-438	Barrel sealing washer	9d.
16-447	Trigger guard retaining screw	1/3
16-448	Trigger guard retaining screw washer	9d.
16-465	Foresight (bead)	7/-
16-479	Sear spring	9d.
16-480	Sear spring guide	9d.
16-492	Sear adjusting screw	2/3
16-494	Sear adjusting pawl	5/6
16-489	Sear adjusting axis pin	9d.
16-495	Sear adjusting spring	2/9
16-512	Backsight bed	10/3
16-543	Backsight screw	1/3
16-567	Backsight plunger	9d.
16-568	Backsight spring	9d.
16-593	Backsight complete	£1/1/0
16-629	Backsight leaf	8/3
16-631	Piston washer leather (outer)	1/6
16-632	Piston washer nut	1/3
16-633	Piston washer rubber (buffer)	1/9
16-634	Piston washer (buffer)	9d.
16-717	Fore-end screws (2)	2/6
24-6035	Stock bolt spring washer	9d.
69-181	Trigger guard screw rear	9d.
16-635	Piston assembly complete	£1/17/6

THOMAS BLAND & SONS, 4-5 WILLIAM IV STREET, LONDON, W.C.2

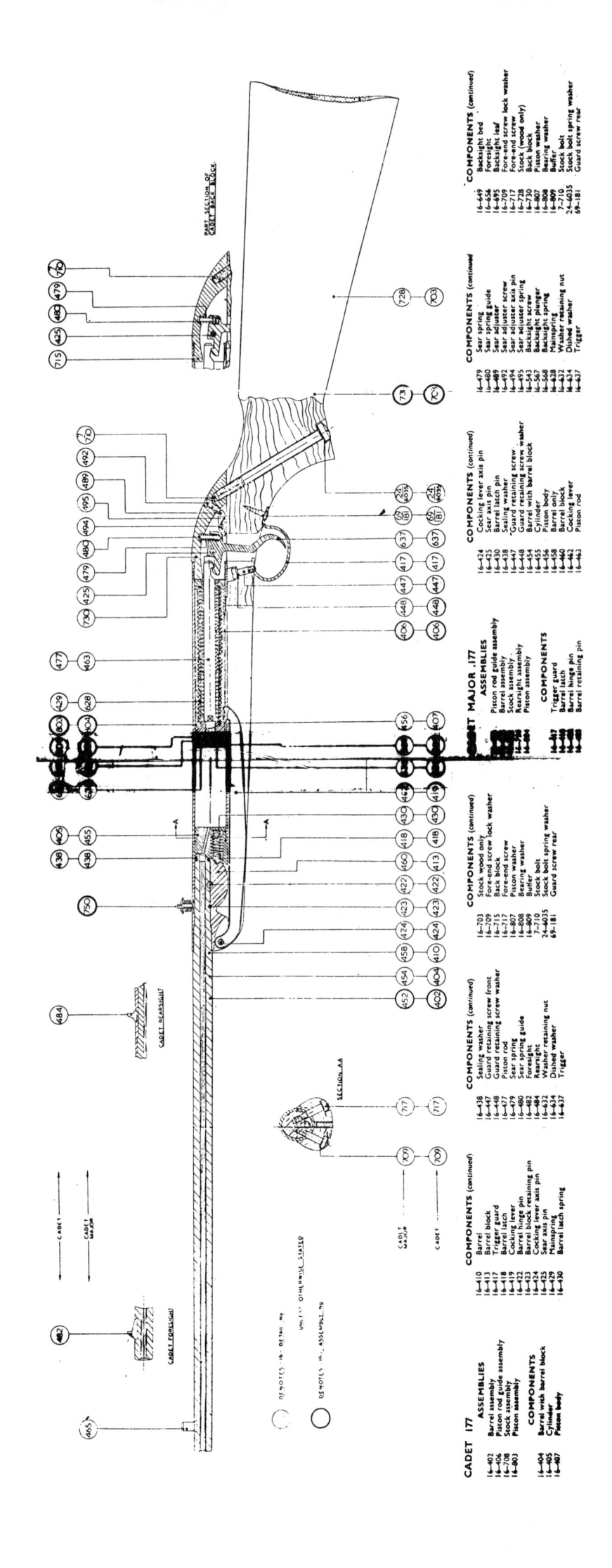

CADET .177

ASSEMBLIES
16-402	Barrel assembly
16-706	Piston rod guide assembly
16-708	Stock assembly
16-803	Piston assembly

COMPONENTS
16-404	Barrel with barrel block
16-405	Cylinder
16-407	Piston body

COMPONENTS (continued)
16-410	Barrel block
16-413	Barrel latch
16-417	Trigger guard
16-418	Barrel latch pin
16-419	Cocking lever
16-422	Barrel hinge pin
16-423	Barrel block retaining pin
16-424	Cocking lever axis pin
16-425	Sear axis pin
16-429	Mainspring
16-430	Barrel latch spring

COMPONENTS (continued)
16-438	Sealing washer
16-447	Guard retaining screw front
16-448	Guard retaining screw washer
16-477	Piston rod
16-479	Sear spring
16-480	Sear spring guide
16-482	Foresight
16-484	Rearsight
16-632	Washer retaining nut
16-634	Dished washer
16-637	Trigger

COMPONENTS (continued)
16-703	Stock wood only
16-709	Fore-end screw lock washer
16-715	Back block
16-717	Fore-end screw
16-807	Piston washer
16-808	Bearing washer
16-809	Buffer
7-710	Stock bolt
24-4035	Stock bolt spring washer
69-181	Guard screw rear

CADET MAJOR .177

ASSEMBLIES
16-403	Piston rod guide assembly
16-406	Barrel assembly
16-710	Stock assembly
16-804	Rearsight assembly
16-805	Piston assembly

COMPONENTS
16-411	Trigger guard
16-414	Barrel latch
16-420	Barrel hinge pin
16-421	Barrel retaining pin

COMPONENTS (continued)
16-426	Cocking lever axis pin
16-427	Sear axis pin
16-428	Barrel latch pin
16-431	Sealing washer
16-447	Guard retaining screw
16-448	Guard retaining screw washer
16-454	Barrel with barrel block
16-455	Cylinder
16-458	Piston body
16-460	Barrel block
16-462	Cocking lever
16-463	Piston rod

COMPONENTS (continued)
16-479	Sear spring
16-480	Sear spring guide
16-489	Sear adjuster
16-492	Sear adjuster screw
16-494	Sear adjuster axis pin
16-495	Sear adjuster spring
16-543	Backsight screw
16-567	Backsight plunger
16-568	Backsight spring
16-628	Mainspring
16-632	Washer retaining nut
16-634	Dished washer
16-637	Trigger

COMPONENTS (continued)
16-649	Backsight bed
16-656	Foresight
16-695	Backsight leaf
16-709	Fore-end screw lock washer
16-717	Fore-end screw
16-728	Stock (wood only)
16-730	Piston washer
16-808	Bearing washer
16-809	Buffer
7-710	Stock bolt
24-4035	Stock bolt spring washer
69-181	Guard screw rear

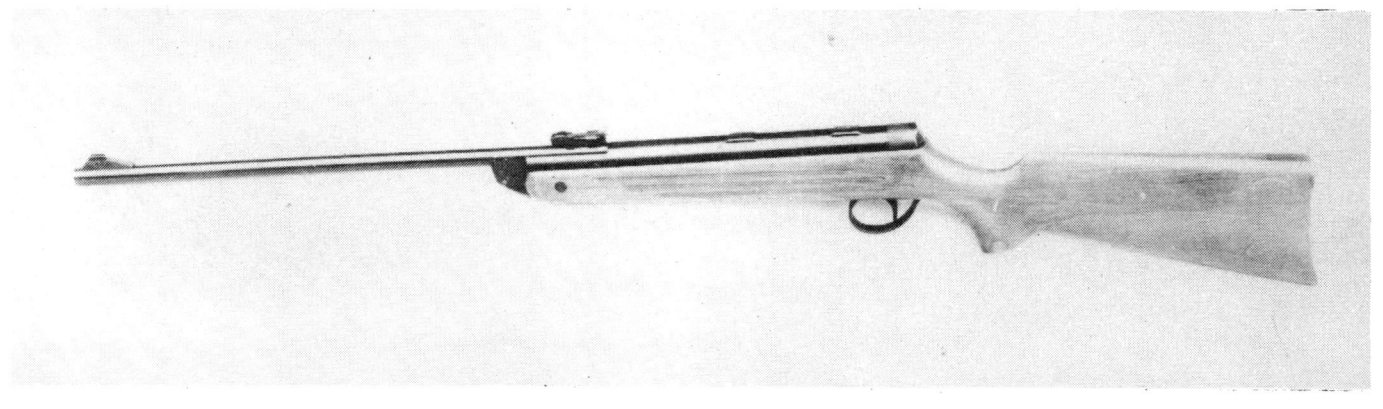

B.S.A. Meteor (T7738) Mk. I

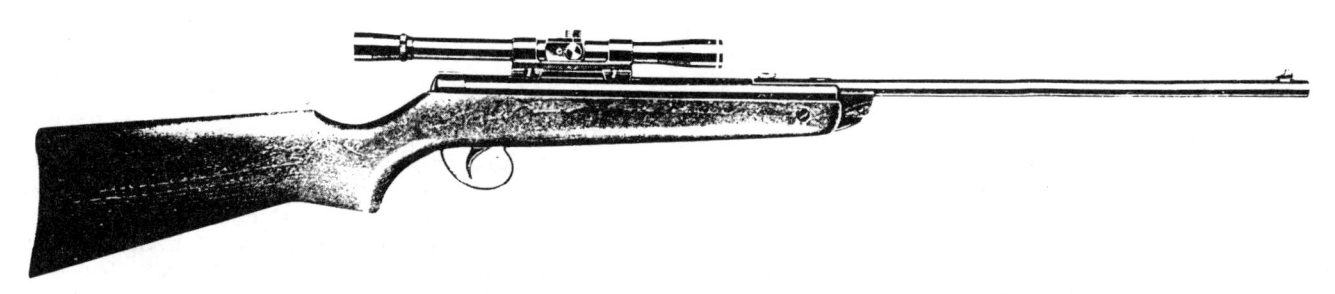

B.S.A. Meteor Mk. II
May 1962 to June 1966
Prefix letters "NA" for .177
Prefix letters "TA" for .22

June 1966 to January 1968
Prefix letters "NB" for .177
Prefix letters "TB" for .22

Dovetail mounted fore and rearsights. Trigger adjustment by way of screws actually in trigger

MODEL Meteor Mk. I.

MAKER B.S.A.

DATE Mk. I Meteor made from February 1959 to June 1962.
"N" prefix for .177 air rifles of which serial numbers ran from 1000 to 47000.
"T" prefix for .22 air rifles of which serial numbers ran from 1000 to 54000.
Further dating can be made from the following changes in design.
End of 1960 — air chamber end cap changed to plastic from metal.
End of 1961 — Rear trigger guard screw changed to screw into the action rather than the stock and rearsight changed to screw adjustable blade instead of the earlier ramp type rearsight.

VALUATION £20—£60.
($30—$90).

DETAILS First model Meteor after introduction to take the place of the Cadet and Cadet Major. 41 inches long with an 18 inch rifled barrel. Serial number appears stamped under the barrel near cocking lever pivot. Serial number of above T7409. Foresight appears to be fixed whilst rear ramp sight set in dovetail and is adjustable for elevation and windage. Top of barrel stamped "B.S.A. GUNS LTD. ENGLAND .22 CAL". The barrel of above is stamped with a small "T" on the L.H.S. of the breech near pivot for cocking lever. Air chamber has two raised portions of metal for telescopic sight. Lightly etched on top appears "B.S.A." in an arrow design followed by the word "METEOR". Stamped on the rear raised portion for sight mounting the triple B.S.A. trademark. Air chamber has metal end cap. Well shaped stock has three deep grooves cut into the fore-end on each side. Advertised weight 5¼ lbs. Was also available in rifled or smoothbore versions. Interesting to note that the Cadet and Cadet Major were still being advertised well into the very early 1960s. The smoothbore barrels are stamped "SB" on the opposite side of the serial number on the under side of the barrel near the cocking lever pivot pin.

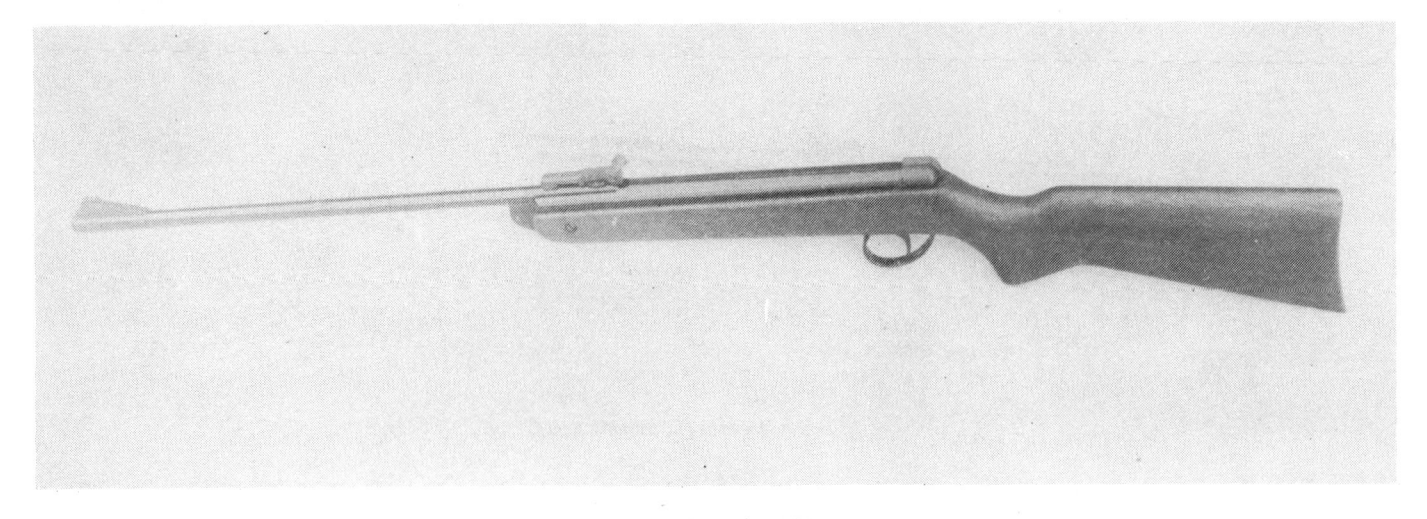

B.S.A. Meteor Mk. IV

MODEL   Meteor. Mk. IV Standard.

MAKER   B.S.A. Guns Ltd., Shirley, Solihull, Warwickshire.

DATE   Mk. IV Meteor introduced February 1973. Prefix letters used "NG" for .177 and "TG" for .22. After May 1974 the rearsight was altered to the Bridge style.

VALUATION   £20—£60.
($30—$90).

DETAIL   41 inches long with 18½ inch barrel. Black finish with blued trigger guard and cocking lever. Serial number TG90572 and appears on the underside of the barrel breech near the cocking lever pivot pin. Top of barrel stamped "B.S.A. GUNS LTD, ENGLAND .22 CAL." with the triple rifle trademark. Top of air chamber stamped "BSA METEOR" and lined with gold paint. Plain stock with no chequering or butt plate. Advertised weight 6 lbs.

For details on how to strip the B.S.A. Meteor see "Airgun World" December 1979. A "Cadet Meteor Air Rifle" was sold for Cadet training, this was a standard Meteor fitted with a 303 military rearsight. They were supplied in .177 only.

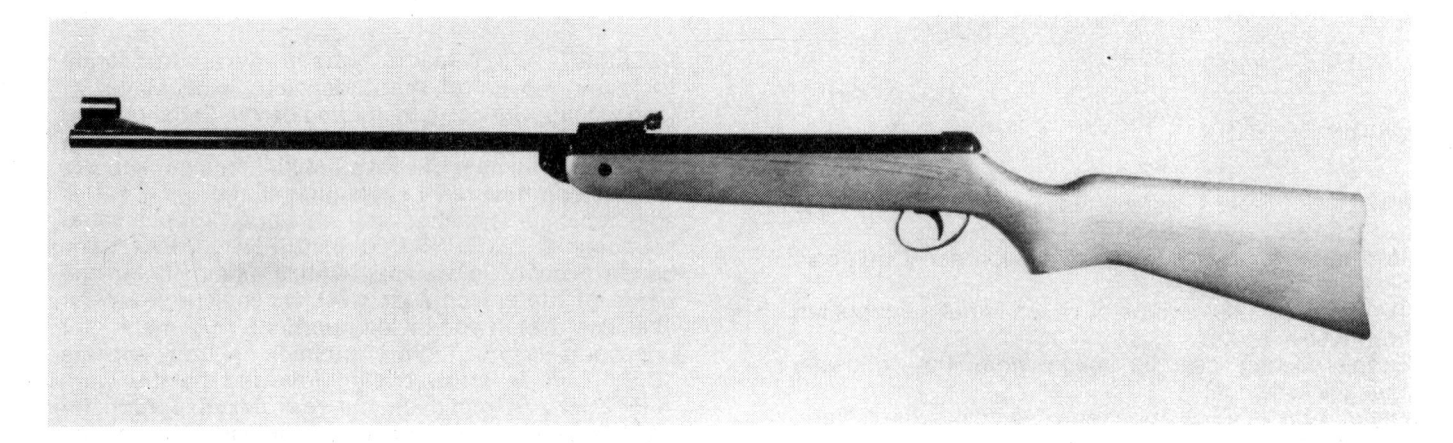

METEOR SUPER AND METEOR STANDARD AIR RIFLE

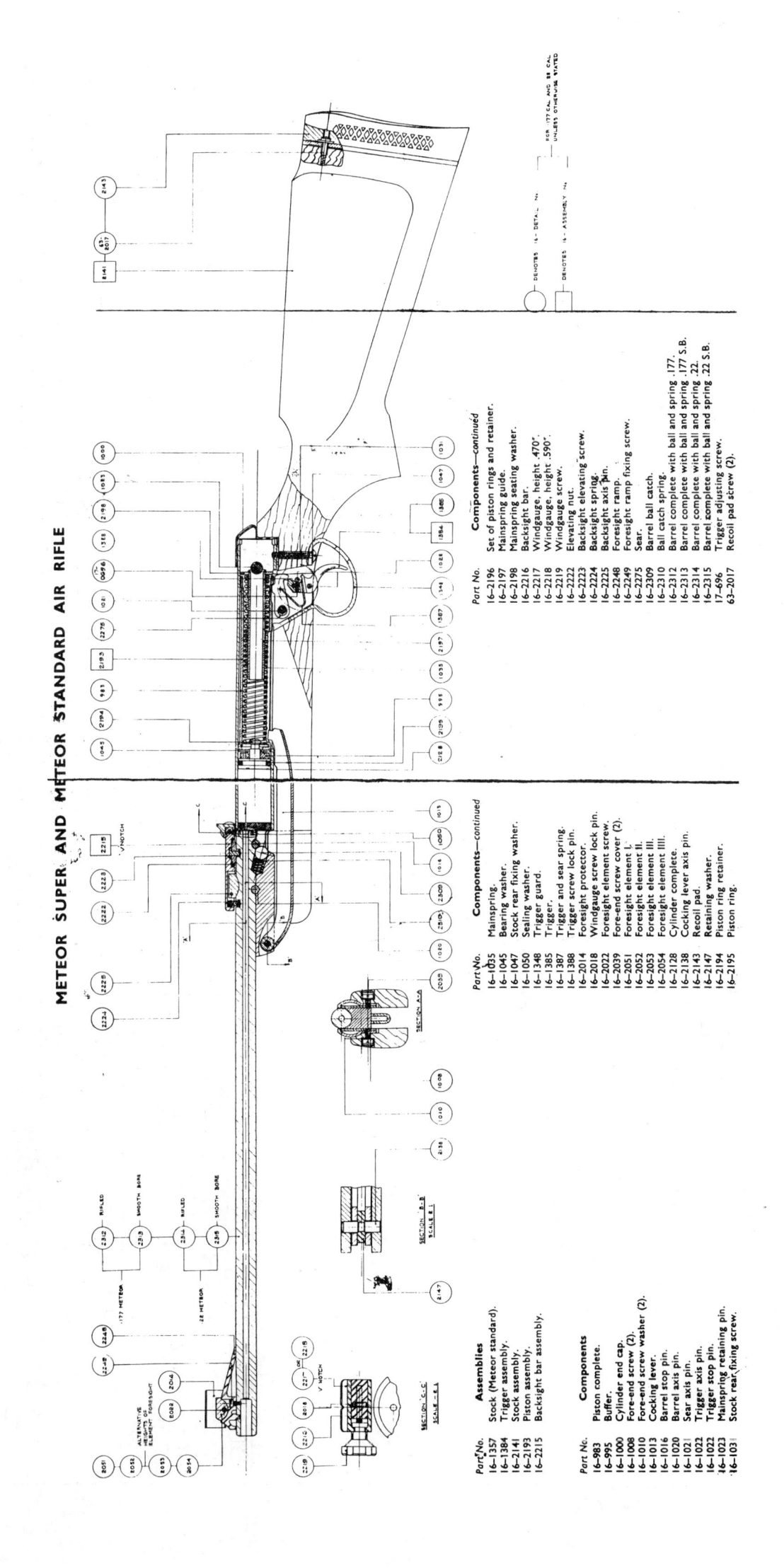

Part No.	Assemblies
16-1357	Stock (Meteor standard).
16-1384	Trigger assembly.
16-2141	Stock assembly.
16-2193	Piston assembly.
16-2215	Backsight bar assembly.

Part No.	Components
16-983	Piston complete.
16-995	Buffer.
16-1000	Cylinder end cap.
16-1008	Fore-end screw (2).
16-1010	Fore-end screw washer (2).
16-1013	Cocking lever.
16-1016	Barrel stop pin.
16-1020	Barrel axis pin.
16-1021	Sear axis pin.
16-1022	Trigger axis pin.
16-1022	Trigger stop pin.
16-1023	Mainspring retaining pin.
16-1031	Stock rear fixing screw.

Part No.	Components—continued
16-1035	Mainspring.
16-1045	Bearing washer.
16-1047	Stock rear fixing washer.
16-1050	Sealing washer.
16-1348	Trigger guard.
16-1385	Trigger.
16-1387	Trigger and sear spring.
16-1388	Trigger screw lock pin.
16-2014	Foresight protector.
16-2018	Windgauge screw lock pin.
16-2022	Foresight element screw.
16-2039	Fore-end screw cover (2).
16-2051	Foresight element I.
16-2052	Foresight element II.
16-2053	Foresight element III.
16-2054	Foresight element IIII.
16-2128	Cylinder complete.
16-2138	Cocking lever axis pin.
16-2143	Recoil pad.
16-2147	Retaining washer.
16-2194	Piston ring retainer.
16-2195	Piston ring.

Part No.	Components—continued
16-2196	Set of piston rings and retainer.
16-2197	Mainspring guide.
16-2198	Mainspring seating washer.
16-2216	Backsight bar.
16-2217	Windgauge, height .470″.
16-2218	Windgauge, height .590″.
16-2219	Windgauge screw.
16-2222	Elevating nut.
16-2223	Backsight elevating screw.
16-2224	Backsight spring.
16-2225	Backsight axis pin.
16-2248	Foresight ramp.
16-2249	Foresight ramp fixing screw.
16-2275	Sear.
16-2309	Barrel ball catch.
16-2310	Ball catch spring.
16-2312	Barrel complete with ball and spring .177.
16-2313	Barrel complete with ball and spring .177 S.B.
16-2314	Barrel complete with ball and spring .22.
16-2315	Barrel complete with ball and spring .22 S.B.
17-696	Trigger adjusting screw.
63-2017	Recoil pad screw (2).

BSA METEOR
MODEL PREFIX TG & NG

ITEM	DESCRIPTION	COMPT No.	No I	No II	No III
A(1-4)	FORESIGHT UNIT	16-2419	*16-2051	16-2052	16-2053
1	RAMP FORESIGHT	16-2248			16-2054
2	SCREW FIXING FORESIGHT RAMP	16-2244	D(14-16)	BARREL UNIT .177	
3	ELEMENT FORESIGHT	16-2051		BARREL UNIT .22	
4	PIN TENSION FORESIGHT RAMP	16-2346	14	BARREL .177	16-2470
				BARREL .22	16-2471
			15	LATCH BARREL	16-1012
B(6-13)	BACKSIGHT UNIT	16-2745	16	SPRING LATCH BARREL	16-1034
C(6-9)	BAR BACKSIGHT ASSY	16-2740	17	WASHER SEALING	16-1050
6	BAR BACKSIGHT INC 7	16-2741	18	LEVER COCKING	16-1013
7	PIN LOCKING WINDGAUGE SCREW	16-2018	19	PIN AXIS COCKING LEVER	16-2138
8	WINDGAUGE	16-2218	20	WASHER RETAINING AXIS PIN	16-2147
9	WINDGAUGE SCREW	16-2219	21	PIN AXIS BARREL	16-1020
10	SCREW FIXING BACKSIGHT	16-2249	E(22-24)	CYLINDER UNIT	16-2425
11	NUT ELEVATING BACKSIGHT	16-2222	22	CYLINDER	16-2128
12	SCREW ELEVATING BACKSIGHT	16-2223	23	END CAP CYLINDER	16-1000
			24	PIN RETAINING MAIN SPRING	16-1023

F(25-30)	PISTON UNIT	16-2193	37	SCREW ADJUSTING TRIGGER	17-0696
25	PISTON	16-0983	38	SEAR	16-1386
26	PISTON WASHERS & RETAINER (27-30)	16-2196	39	TRIGGER & SEAR SPRING	16-1387
27	RETAINER SEALING RING	16-2194	40	PIN AXIS TRIGGER	16-1022
28	BEARING WASHER	16-1045	41	PIN STOP TRIGGER	16-1022
29	SEALING RING	16-2195	42	PIN AXIS SEAR	16-1021
30	BUFFER	16-2347	43	TRIGGER GUARD	16-1348
G(31-33)	MAIN SPRING UNIT	16-2427	44A	STOCK	16-1357
31	MAIN SPRING	16-1035	45	SCREW FIXING STOCK REAR	16-1031
32	MAIN SPRING GUIDE	16-2197	46	WASHER SCREW FIXING REAR	16-047
33	MAIN SPRING SEATING WASHER	16-2198	47	SCREW FIXING STOCK FRONT	16-1008
H(34-39)	TRIGGER MEC UNIT	16-2398	48	WASHER FRONT FIXING SCREW	16-1010
34	TRIGGER ASSY (35-37)	16-1384			
35	TRIGGER	16-1385			
36	PIN LOCKING ADJ SCREW	16-1388			

JAN 1975   ISSUE No. 4

BSA METEOR Mk5
MODEL PREFIX NH & TH

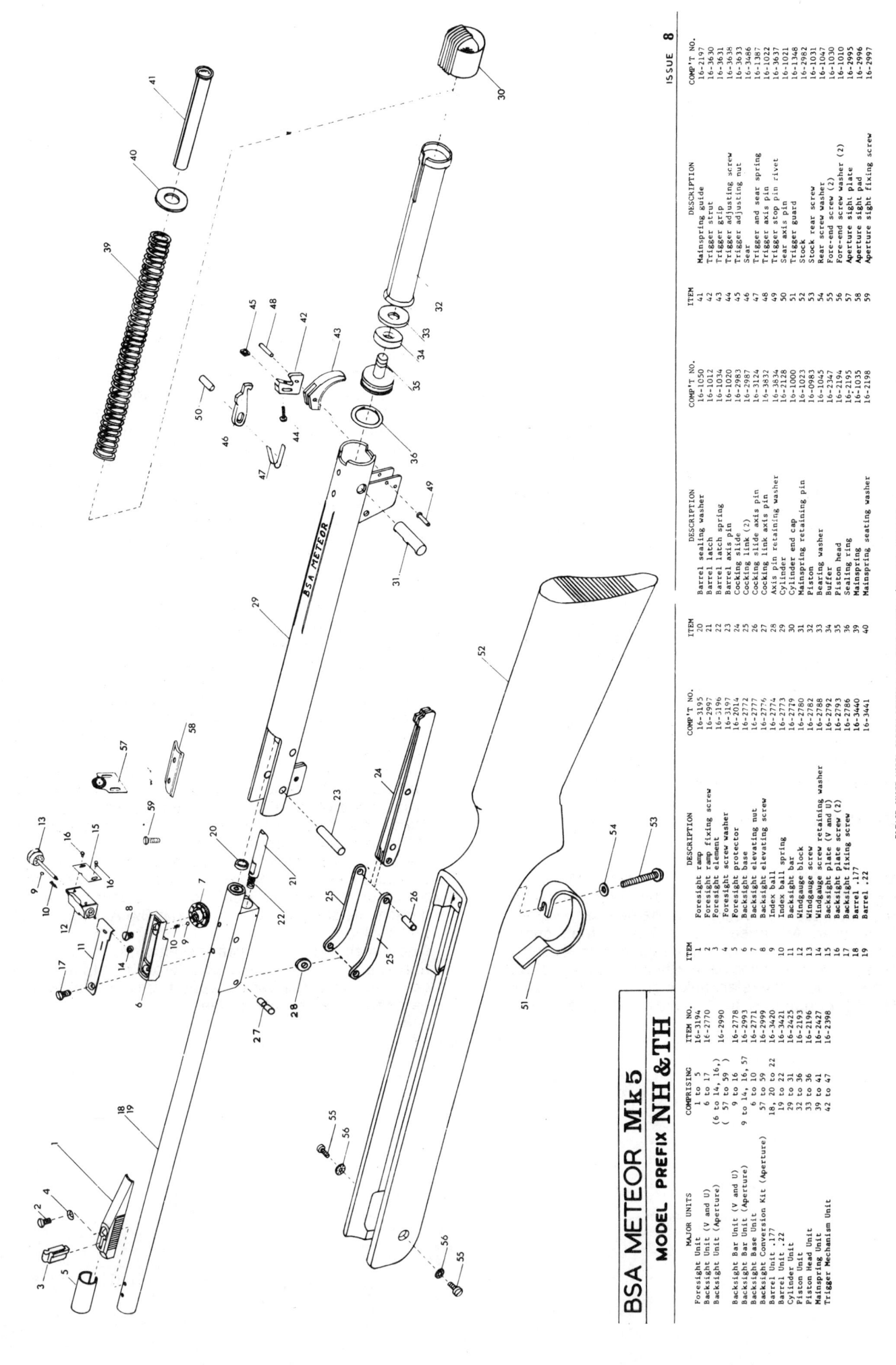

MAJOR UNITS	COMPRISING	ITEM NO.
Foresight Unit	1 to 5	16-3194
Backsight Unit (V and U)	6 to 17	16-2770
Backsight Unit (Aperture)	(6 to 14, 16,) (57 to 59)	16-2990
Backsight Bar Unit (V and U)	9 to 16	16-3197
Backsight Bar Unit (Aperture)	9 to 14, 16, 57	16-2778
Backsight Base Unit	6 to 10	16-2993
Backsight Conversion Kit (Aperture)	57 to 59	16-2999
Barrel Unit .177	18, 20 to 22	16-3420
Barrel Unit .22	19 to 22	16-3421
Cylinder Unit	29 to 31	16-2425
Piston Unit	32 to 36	16-2193
Mainspring Unit	33 to 41	16-2427
Trigger Mechanism Unit	42 to 47	16-2398

ITEM	DESCRIPTION	COMP'T NO.
1	Foresight ramp	16-3195
2	Foresight ramp fixing screw	16-2997
3	Foresight element	16-3196
4	Foresight screw washer	16-3197
5	Foresight protector	16-2014
6	Backsight base	16-2772
7	Backsight elevating nut	16-2771
8	Backsight elevating screw	16-2777
9	Index ball	16-2776
10	Index ball spring	16-2774
11	Backsight bar	16-2773
12	Windgauge block	16-2779
13	Windgauge screw	16-2780
14	Windgauge screw retaining washer	16-2788
15	Backsight plate (V and U)	16-0983
16	Backsight plate screw (2)	16-2792
17	Backsight fixing screw	16-2793
18	Barrel .177	16-2786
19	Barrel .22	16-3441

ITEM	DESCRIPTION	COMP'T NO.
20	Barrel sealing washer	16-3195
21	Barrel latch	16-2997
22	Barrel latch spring	16-3196
23	Barrel axis pin	16-3197
24	Cocking slide	16-2014
25	Cocking link (2)	16-2772
26	Cocking slide axis pin	16-2771
27	Cocking link axis pin	16-2777
28	Axis pin retaining washer	16-2776
29	Cylinder end cap	16-2774
30	Mainspring retaining pin	16-2773
31	Piston	16-2779
32	Bearing washer	16-2780
33	Buffer	16-2788
34	Piston head	16-2792
35	Sealing ring	16-2793
36	Mainspring	16-3440
39	Mainspring seating washer	16-3441
40		

ITEM	DESCRIPTION	COMP'T NO.
41	Mainspring guide	16-1050
42	Trigger strut	16-1012
43	Trigger grip	16-1034
44	Trigger adjusting screw	16-1020
45	Trigger adjusting nut	16-2983
46	Sear	16-2987
47	Trigger and sear spring	16-3124
48	Trigger axis pin	16-3832
49	Trigger stop pin rivet	16-3834
50	Sear axis pin	16-2128
51	Trigger guard	16-1000
52	Stock	16-1023
53	Rear screw	16-2982
54	Rear screw washer	16-1031
55	Fore-end screw (2)	16-1045
56	Fore-end screw washer (2)	16-1047
57	Aperture sight plate	16-2194
58	Aperture sight pad	16-1035
59	Aperture sight fixing screw	16-2198

ISSUE 8

PLEASE QUOTE MODEL PREFIX LETTERS AND PART NUMBERS (NOT ITEM NUMBERS).

41

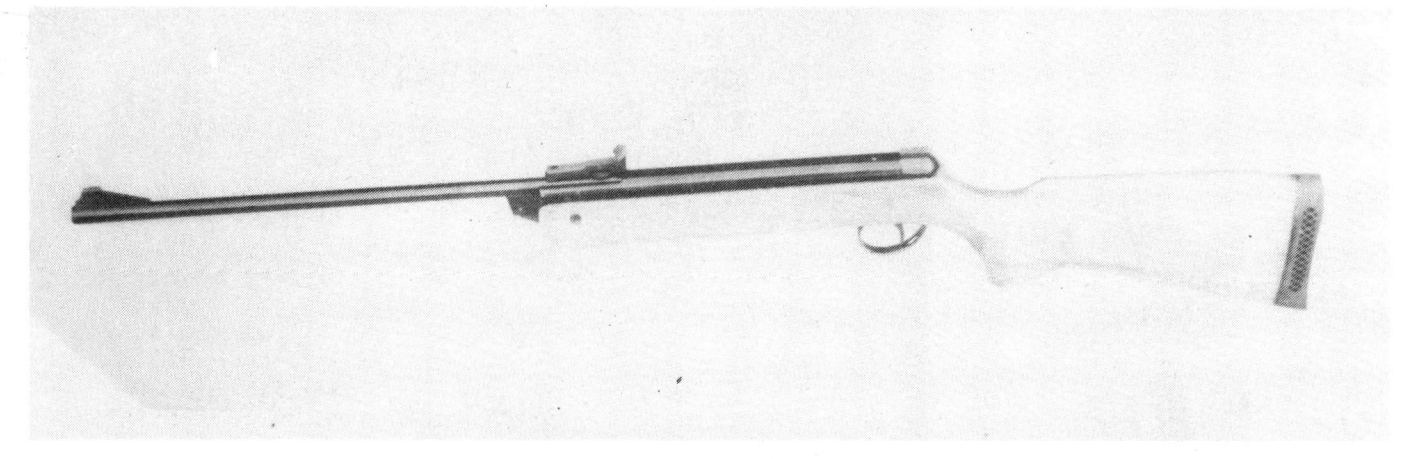

B.S.A. Super Meteor

MODEL Meteor (Super).

MAKER B.S.A.

DATE Introduced in 1966/67 to replace the standard Meteor and was produced on its own until 1969 when the Standard Meteor was re-introduced and both are now current models.

Mk. III Meteor (Super)	Prefix "ND" for .177
December 1967—1969.	Prefix "TD" for .22
July 1969—February 1973.	Prefix "NE" for .177
	Prefix "TE" for .22
Mk. IV Meteor introduced February 1973	
	Prefix "NG" for .177
	Prefix "TG" for .22
Mk. V Meteor	Prefix "NH" for .177
	Prefix "TH" for .22

Further datings of Meteors can be made from the following changes:
1960 — Cylinder end cap made of plastic.
1961 — Rear trigger guard screw to screw into cylinder and rearsight changed to a screw adjustable blade.
1968 (December) — Piston "O" ring fitted.
1974 (May) — Rearsight changed to pivot bridge type.

VALUATION £30—£70.
($45—$105).

DETAILS Differed from the "Standard" Meteor in having a superior stock and a hooded foresight. Serial number stamped on underside of barrel near pivot for cocking lever. Advertised as having a "high comb Monte Carlo cheek stock of Scandinavian Beech". Foresight tunnel is removable. Stamped on top of air chamber between the telescopic sight grooves is "BSA METEOR" as opposed to the arrow design on other Meteors. 41½ inches long with 19 inch barrel. See "Airgun World" February 1979, also "Airgun World" March 1979. Advertised weight 6 lbs.

On introduction of the Mk. V during July/August 1977 the rearsight could be relocated at the rear of the air chamber and blade changed for a peepsight element. Two small holes were drilled and tapped for the interchange. Other improvements were a double linkage cocking lever, common to many Continental air rifles, the Standard stock was made slightly broader whilst the Super stock remained unaltered. The trigger action was much improved and so was the width of the trigger. For a review of the Mk. V Meteor see "Guns Review" July 1977.

The first "TD" Series were fitted with an all metal rearsight and foresight, whereas the later models had plastic sights. The Meteor was also available smoothbore in either .22 or .177. The only distinguishing feature appears to be a "S" stamped on the underside of the barrel near the cocking lever pivot. Have seen one .22 smoothbore, serial number TG21191. It has been suggested that these were exported to Ireland and overseas where rifled airguns are prohibited.

During the summer of 1981 the millioneth Meteor to be manufactured was donated by B.S.A. as a prize in a raffle in aid of the Gun and Allied Trades Benevolent Fund. This Meteor was on show at the 1981 Game Fair at Stowe School, Buckinghamshire, and was fitted with a walnut stock, the lettering were inlaid with gold, and was supplied with a special full shooting kit comprising of a super deluxe gun cover, telescopic sight, detachable sling swivels, sling, and B.S.A. badges and belt buckle.

One small fault that can develop is in the over tightening of the fore-end screws on the stock, these can draw open the barrel support arms and allow the barrel to slop from side to side.

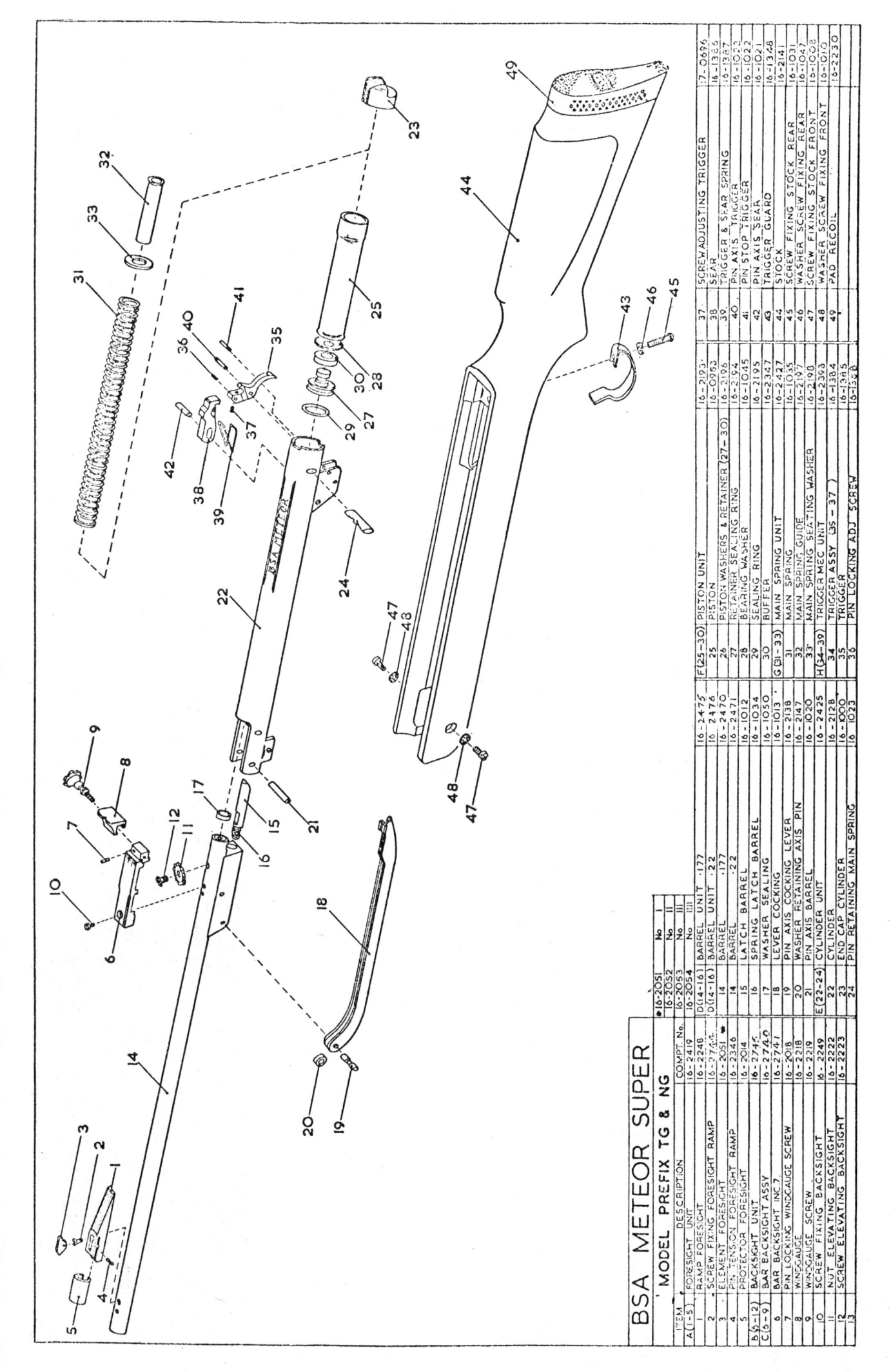

BSA METEOR SUPER
MODEL PREFIX TG & NG

ITEM	COMPT. No.	DESCRIPTION
A(1-5)		FORESIGHT UNIT
	*16-2051	No I
	16-2052	No II
	16-2053	No III
1	16-2419	RAMP FORESIGHT
2	16-2248	SCREW FIXING FORESIGHT RAMP
3	16-2744	ELEMENT FORESIGHT
4	16-2051	PIN TENSION FORESIGHT RAMP
5	16-2346	PROTECTOR FORESIGHT
B(6-12)	16-2014	BACKSIGHT UNIT
6	16-2745	BAR BACKSIGHT ASSY
	16-2740	BAR BACKSIGHT INC.7
7	16-2741	PIN LOCKING WINDGAUGE SCREW
8	16-2018	WINDGAUGE
9	16-2218	WINDGAUGE SCREW
10	16-2219	SCREW FIXING BACKSIGHT
C(5-9)	16-2249	
11	16-2222	NUT ELEVATING BACKSIGHT
12	16-2223	SCREW ELEVATING BACKSIGHT
13		
14	D(14-16)	BARREL UNIT .177
	D(14-16)	BARREL UNIT .22
	16-2475	BARREL .177
	16-2476	BARREL .22
14	16-2470	
15	16-2471	LATCH BARREL
16	16-1012	SPRING LATCH BARREL
17	16-1034	WASHER SEALING
18	16-1050	LEVER COCKING
19	16-1013	PIN AXIS COCKING LEVER
20	16-2138	WASHER RETAINING AXIS PIN
21	16-2147	PIN AXIS BARREL
E(22-24)	16-1020	CYLINDER UNIT
22	16-2425	CYLINDER
23	16-212B	END CAP CYLINDER
24	16-1000	TRIGGER
	16-1023	PIN RETAINING MAIN SPRING
F(25-30)		PISTON UNIT
25	16-2475	PISTON
26	16-2476	PISTON WASHERS & RETAINER (27-30)
27	16-2470	RETAINER SEALING RING
28	16-2471	BEARING WASHER
29	16-1012	SEALING RING
30	16-1034	BUFFER
G(31-33)	16-1050	MAIN SPRING UNIT
31	16-1013	MAIN SPRING
32	16-2147	MAIN SPRING GUIDE
33	16-1020	MAIN SPRING SEATING WASHER
H(34-39)	16-2425	TRIGGER MEC UNIT
34	16-212B	TRIGGER ASSY (35-37)
35	16-1000	TRIGGER
36	16-1023	PIN LOCKING ADJ SCREW
37	16-2193	SCREW ADJUSTING TRIGGER
38	16-0953	SEAR
39	16-2196	TRIGGER & SEAR SPRING
40	16-2194	PIN AXIS TRIGGER
41	16-1045	PIN STOP TRIGGER
42	16-2195	PIN AXIS SEAR
43	16-2367	TRIGGER GUARD
44	16-2427	STOCK
45	16-1055	SCREW FIXING STOCK REAR
46	16-2197	WASHER SCREW FIXING REAR
47	16-2190	SCREW FIXING STOCK FRONT
48	16-010	WASHER SCREW FIXING FRONT
49	16-2230	PAD RECOIL

JAN 1975   ISSUE No. 4

METEOR & METEOR SUPER PREFIX TE&NE

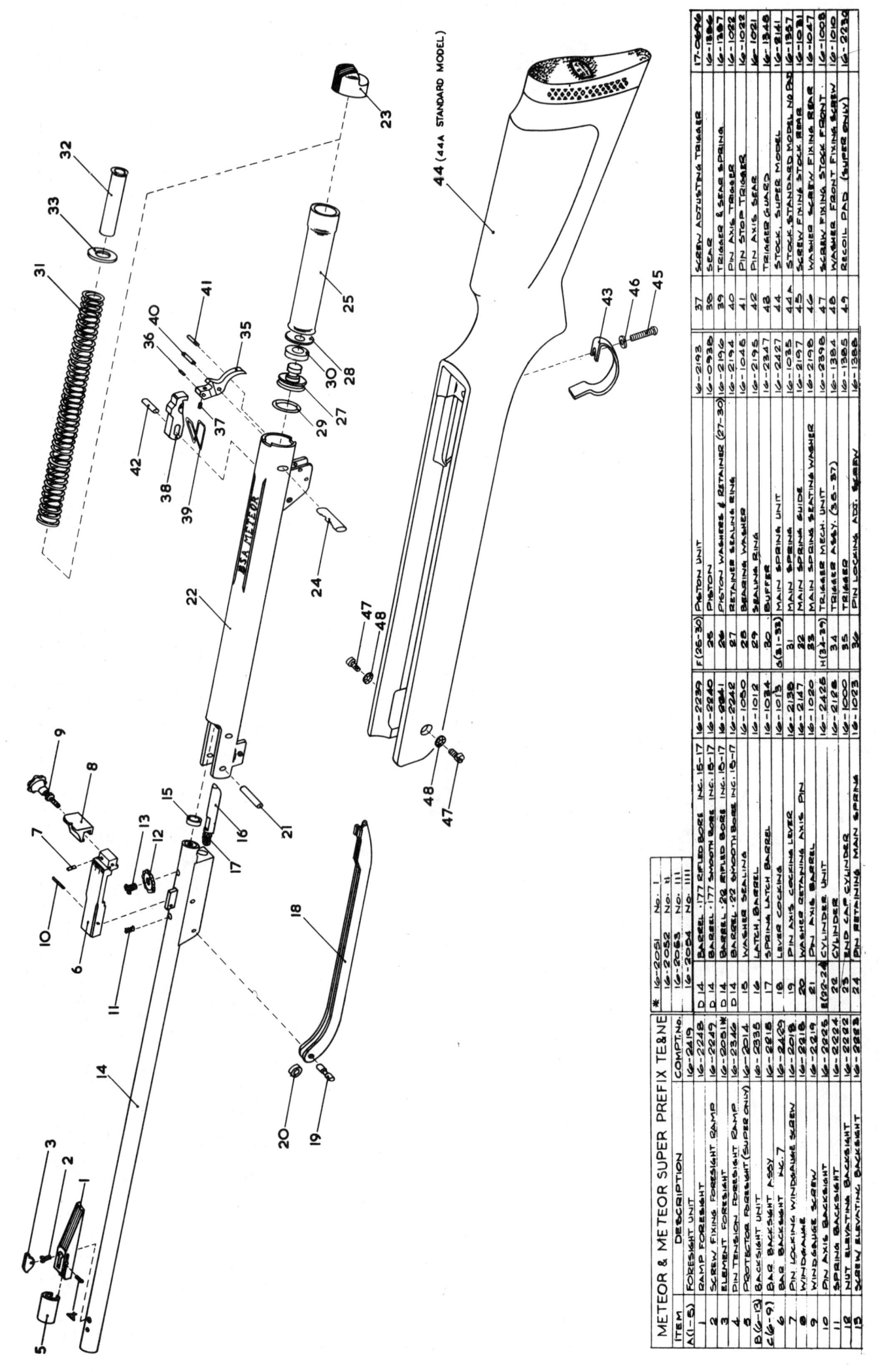

*	16-2051	No. I
	16-2052	No. II
	16-2063	No. III
	16-2064	No. IIII

ITEM	DESCRIPTION	COMPT. No.
A(1-5)	FORESIGHT UNIT	16-2419
1	RAMP FORESIGHT	16-2248
2	SCREW FIXING FORESIGHT RAMP	16-2249
3	ELEMENT FORESIGHT	16-2251*
4	PIN TENSION FORESIGHT RAMP	16-2346
5	PROTECTOR FORESIGHT (SUPER ONLY)	16-2214
B(6-13)	BACKSIGHT UNIT	16-2235
6(6-9)	BAR BACKSIGHT ASSY	16-2415
6	BAR BACKSIGHT Mk.7	16-2429
7	PIN LOCKING WINDGAUGE SCREW	16-2218
8	WINDGAUGE	16-2219
9	WINDGAUGE SCREW	16-2224
10	PIN AXIS BACKSIGHT	16-2222
11	SPRING BACKSIGHT	16-2100
12	NUT ELEVATING BACKSIGHT	16-2223
13	SCREW ELEVATING BACKSIGHT	16-1388

D 14	BARREL .177 RIFLED BORE INC. 15-17	16-2239
D 14	BARREL .177 SMOOTH BORE INC. 15-17	16-2240
D 14	BARREL .22 RIFLED BORE INC. 15-17	16-2241
D 14	BARREL .22 SMOOTH BORE INC. 15-17	16-2242
15	WASHER SEALING	16-1050
16	LATCH BARREL	16-1012
17	SPRING LATCH BARREL	16-1024
18	LEVER COCKING	16-1015
19	PIN AXIS COCKING LEVER	16-2138
20	WASHER RETAINING AXIS PIN	16-2147
21	PIN AXIS BARREL	16-1020
E(22-24)	CYLINDER UNIT	16-2425
22	CYLINDER	16-2128
23	END CAP CYLINDER	16-1000
24	PIN RETAINING MAIN SPRING	16-1023

F(26-30)	PISTON UNIT	16-2193
25	PISTON	16-2240
26	PISTON WASHERS & RETAINER (27-30)	16-0936
27	RETAINER SEALING RING	16-2196
28	BEARING WASHER	16-2194
29	SEALING RING	16-1045
30	BUFFER	16-2195
G(31-33)	MAIN SPRING UNIT	16-1034
31	MAIN SPRING	16-2347
32	MAIN SPRING GUIDE	16-2427
33	WASHER SPRING SEATING WASHER	16-2398
H(34-39)	TRIGGER MECH. UNIT	16-2426
34	TRIGGER ASSY (36-37)	16-1384
35	TRIGGER	16-1325
36	PIN LOCKING ADJ. SCREW	16-1388
37	SCREW ADJUSTING TRIGGER	17-0846
38	SEAR	16-1366
39	TRIGGER & SEAR SPRING	16-1367
40	PIN AXIS TRIGGER	16-1022
41	PIN STOP TRIGGER	16-1022
42	PIN AXIS SEAR	16-1021
43	TRIGGER GUARD	16-1348
44	STOCK SUPER MODEL	16-2141
44A	STOCK STANDARD MODEL No PAD	16-1035
45	SCREW FIXING STOCK REAR	16-1357
46	WASHER SCREW FIXING REAR	16-1047
47	SCREW FIXING STOCK FRONT	16-1103
48	WASHER FRONT FIXING SCREW	16-1100
49	RECOIL PAD (SUPER ONLY)	16-2230

BSA SUPERSPORT AIR RIFLE
MODEL PREFIX AR and DS

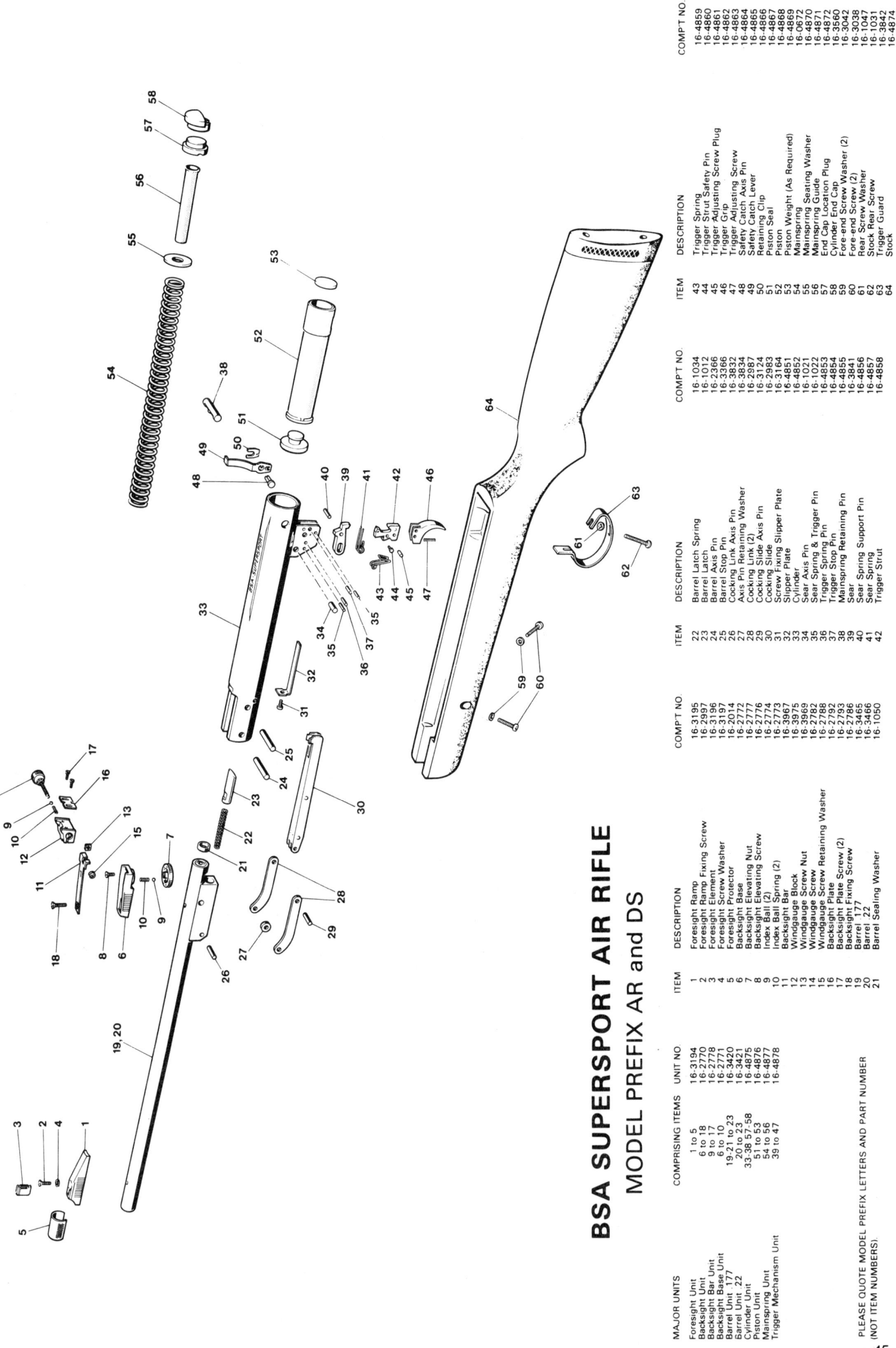

MAJOR UNITS	COMPRISING ITEMS	UNIT NO
Foresight Unit	1 to 5	16-3194
Backsight Unit	6 to 18	16-2770
Backsight Bar Unit	9 to 17	16-2778
Backsight Base Unit	6 to 10	16-2771
Barrel Unit .177	19,21 to 23	16-3420
Barrel Unit .22	20 to 23	16-3421
Cylinder Unit	33-38, 57-58	16-4875
Piston Unit	51 to 53	16-4876
Mainspring Unit	54 to 56	16-4877
Trigger Mechanism Unit	39 to 47	16-4878

PLEASE QUOTE MODEL PREFIX LETTERS AND PART NUMBER (NOT ITEM NUMBERS).

ITEM	DESCRIPTION	COMPT NO
1	Foresight Ramp	16-3195
2	Foresight Ramp Fixing Screw	16-2997
3	Foresight Screw Washer	16-3196
4	Foresight Element	16-3197
5	Foresight Protector	16-2014
6	Backsight Base	16-2772
7	Backsight Elevating Nut	16-2777
8	Backsight Elevating Screw	16-2776
9	Index Ball (2)	16-2774
10	Index Ball Spring (2)	16-2773
11	Backsight Bar	16-3967
12	Windgauge Block	16-3975
13	Windgauge Screw Nut	16-3969
14	Windgauge Screw	16-2782
15	Windgauge Screw Retaining Washer	16-1022
16	Backsight Plate	16-2788
17	Backsight Plate Screw (2)	16-2792
18	Backsight Fixing Screw	16-2793
19	Barrel .177	16-2786
20	Barrel .22	16-3465
21	Barrel Sealing Washer	16-1050

ITEM	DESCRIPTION	COMPT NO
22	Barrel Latch Spring	16-1034
23	Barrel Latch	16-2997
24	Barrel Axis Pin	16-2366
25	Barrel Stop Pin	16-3197
26	Cocking Link Axis Pin	16-3832
27	Axis Pin Retaining Washer	16-3834
28	Cocking Link (2)	16-2987
29	Cocking Slide Axis Pin	16-3124
30	Cocking Slide	16-2983
31	Screw Fixing Slipper Plate	16-3164
32	Slipper Plate	16-4851
33	Cylinder	16-4852
34	Sear Axis Pin	16-1021
35	Sear Spring & Trigger Pin	16-1022
36	Trigger Spring Pin	16-4853
37	Trigger Stop Pin	16-4854
38	Mainspring Retaining Pin	16-4855
39	Sear	16-3841
40	Sear Spring Support Pin	16-4856
41	Sear Spring	16-4857
42	Trigger Strut	16-4858

ITEM	DESCRIPTION	COMPT NO
43	Trigger Spring	16-4859
44	Trigger Strut Safety Pin	16-4860
45	Trigger Adjusting Screw Plug	16-4861
46	Trigger Grip	16-4862
47	Trigger Adjusting Screw	16-4863
48	Safety Catch Axis Pin	16-4864
49	Safety Catch Lever	16-4865
50	Retaining Clip	16-4866
51	Piston Seal	16-4867
52	Piston	16-4868
53	Piston Weight (As Required)	16-4869
54	Mainspring	16-0672
55	Mainspring Seating Washer	16-4870
56	Mainspring Guide	16-4871
57	End Cap Location Plug	16-4872
58	Cylinder End Cap	16-3560
59	Fore-end Screw Washer (2)	16-3042
60	Fore-end Screw (2)	16-3038
61	Rear Screw Washer	16-1047
62	Stock Rear Screw	16-1031
63	Trigger Guard	16-3842
64	Stock	16-4874

45

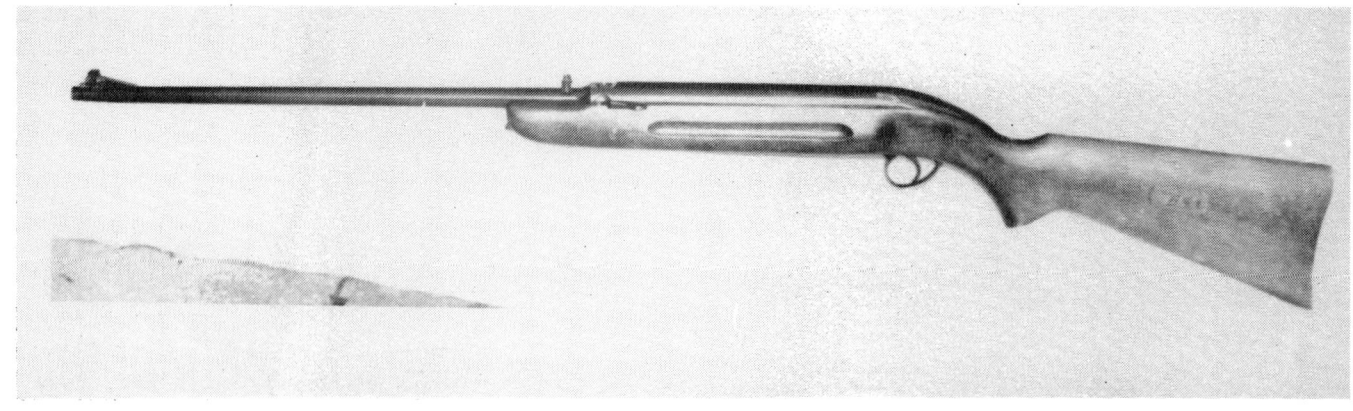

The B.S.A. "Club" Airsporter

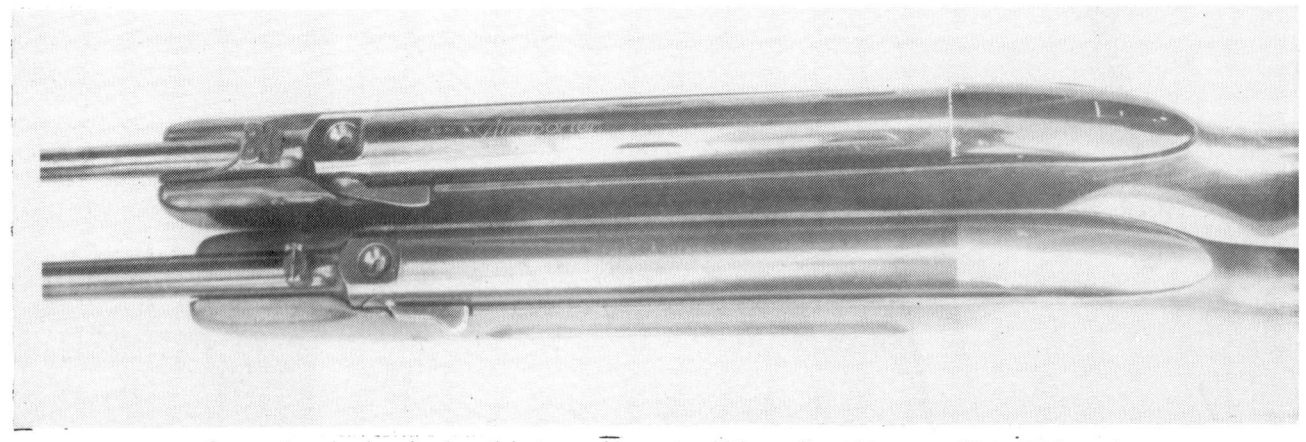

Comparison in chamber length between Airsporter .22 (upper) and Airsporter Club .177 (lower)

MODEL "Club".

MAKER B.S.A.

DATE Dating by the prefix letters as follows:
"E" Late 1948 — December 1950
"EA" December 1950 — October 1954
"EB" Late 1955 — October 1957
"EC" March 1956 — May 1956
"ED" March 1959 — December 1959. Identical to Airsporter but .177 model called "CLUB MK II".
"EE" Name "CLUB" not used, either "CLUB MK II" or just "AIRSPORTER".

VALUATION £50–£150. The above is quite rare as only about 14,500 were produced. £40a, very few appear in auctions. Mint examples have been known to be sold for £200. ($75–$225).

DETAILS Serial number E12720 appears underside of trigger block just in front of trigger guard. Also stamped is the patent number 607045. Measures 44 inches long. Etched on top of air chamber appears "THE BIRMINGHAM SMALL ARMS Co Ltd — "CLUB" .177 AIR RIFLE — MADE IN ENGLAND". The triple rifle trademark is between the "CLUB" and ".177". Stock is made from three pieces laminated together and has a winged B.S.A. stamped into the wood. The "Club" had a 2.4 inch piston stroke as opposed to the "Airsporter" which had a 2.8 inch stroke. See "Airgun World" February 1979. By the time of the "EC" series the patent number stamped on the underside of the trigger block appears to have been dropped. The patent number 607045 was applied for 1946 and accepted 1947. It referred to the cone-shaped piston head and matching head to the air chamber. For further details see "Guns Review" October 1980.

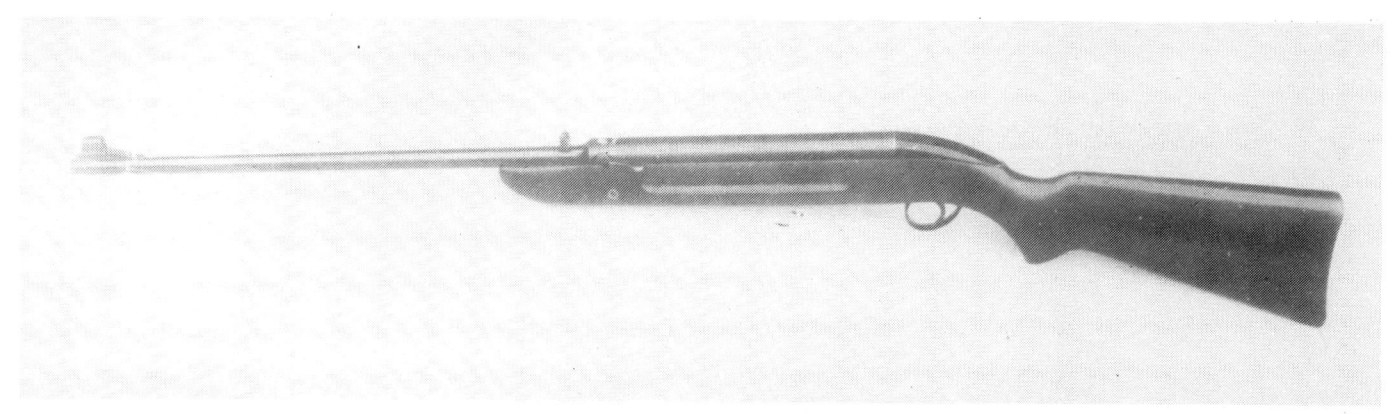

B.S.A. "Airsporter" Mk. I

MODEL "Airsporter" Mk. I.

MAKER B.S.A., Birmingham, England.

DATE Dating by serial numbers as follows:
"G" prefix 1948—1954
"GA" prefix 1955—1956
"GB" prefix 1956—1958
"GC" prefix 1958—1959

VALUATION £40—£80, £26a—£35a.
($60—$120, $39a—$53a).

DETAILS First model of the Airsporters. Not grooved for telescopic sight. Automatic tap port opening as underlever is pulled down. On top of air cylinder was a light etching as follows: "THE BIRMINGHAM SMALL ARMS Co Ltd" "'AIRSPORTER' .22 AIR RIFLE" and then "MADE IN ENGLAND". Serial number is in front of trigger. In my day it was THE airgun to have as well as the Webley Mk. III. Serial number of above GB6921.
Have seen two of the above with black powder-proof marks stamped on the underside of the barrel at the tap port end. Marks being the calibre, "BP" with a crown then "BV" with a crown. The marks cannot be seen unless underlever is pulled right back into cocked position. It has been suggested that these were for Australia and the purpose of the proof marks was either because of import restrictions on unproofed weapons, or there was no import tax imposed on proofed guns. Another reason given was that the Aussies regarded airguns as toys so to counter this belief and custom difficulties airguns generally were proofed.
According to a 1958 Parker-Hale catalogue the loss of equipment and essential tools during the war lead to the complete re-design of the range of B.S.A. airguns, hence the introduction of the Airsporter in 1945. Advertised weight of the MK. I Airsporter was 8 lbs, and could be supplied with a Sportarget aperature sight which was fitted to the duralumin trigger block. A replacement piston washer can be easily made from a Webley Mk. III washer. Have seen a one piece stock stamped SILE, this was apparently made in Italy at Sile Spa, Brescia. B.S.A. contracted out the manufacture of some of their stocks for the Airsporter Mk. I.

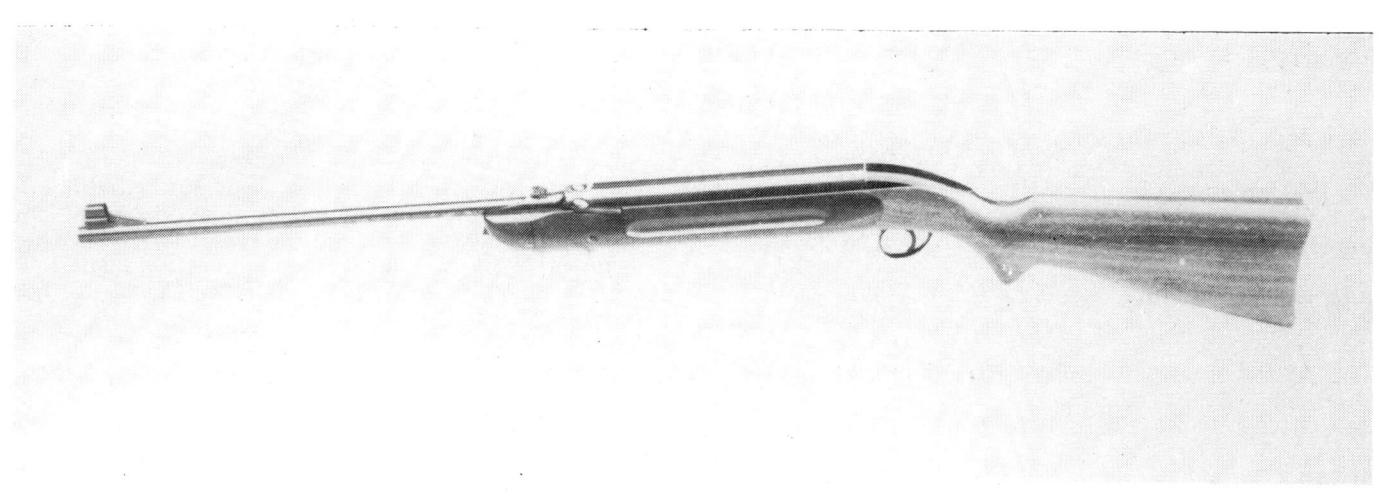

B.S.A. Airsporter Mk. II

MODEL Airsporter.

MAKER B.S.A. Guns Ltd., Birmingham B11 2PZ, England.

DATE Serial number prefix letters are "GC" hence manufactured between December 1958 and September 1959. Only about 3,000 were produced in this series.

VALUATION £50—£80, £26a—£35a.
($60—$120, $39a—$53a).

DETAILS The above model falls between the production of the Mk. I and Mk. II Airporters. 43½ inches long. Flip up rearsight, but barrel is NOT stamped with the usual marks for maker and calibre. Braised barrel, but air chamber is NOT grooved for telescopic sight. Automatic loading tap opening. Duralumin alloy trigger block with trigger adjustment at rear of trigger guard. Stock fitted is one piece, as opposed to the usual three piece pattern. Serial number stamped on underside of the trigger block just in front of the trigger guard.

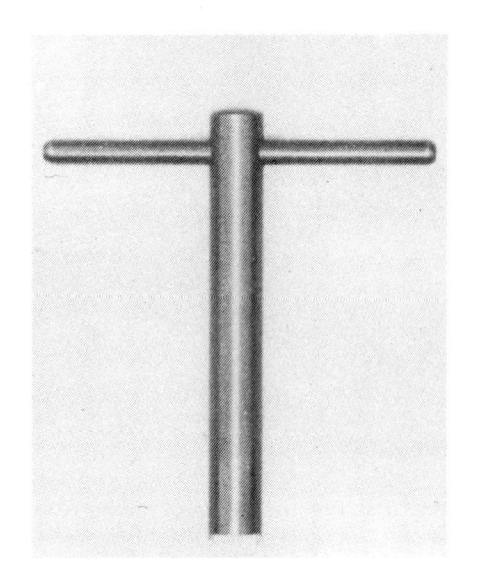

"T" BAR TOOL FOR STOCK BOLT
The cap is unscrewed and the above tool is inserted into the underside of the stock. The two protruding pins engage with the bolt and the stock can either be tightened up or taken off.

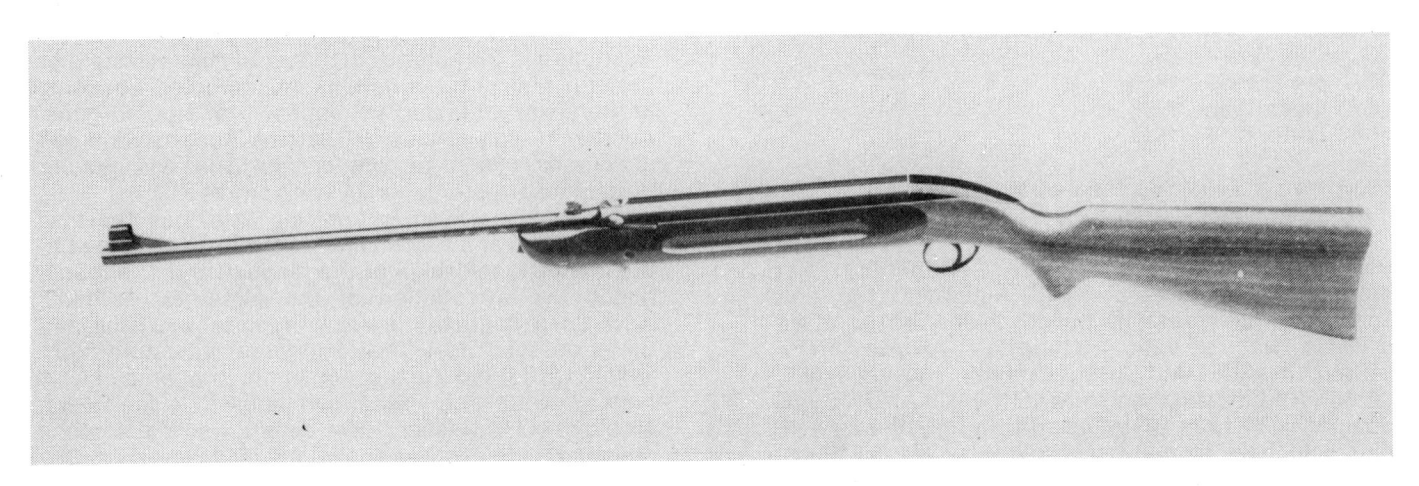

MODEL "Airsporter" Mk. II.

MAKER B.S.A., Birmingham, England.

DATE Mk. II introduced September 1959.
Dating by prefix letters:

September 1959 to December 1965.	"EE" for .177
	"GD" for .22
December 1965 to mid 1967.	"EF" for .177
	"GE" for .22
Mid 1967 to June 1968.	"EG" for .177
	"GF" for .22
June 1968 to mid 1969.	.177 not produced
	"GG" for .22
June 1969 to June 1971.	"EK" for .177
	"GI" for .22

VALUATION £40—£80, £40a—£80a, mint examples often sell for £100 or even more.
($60—$120, $60a—$120a, mint examples $150 or more.

DETAILS 43¾ inches long. Serial number of above GD19946 always appears on the underside of the alloy trigger block just in front of the trigger. Has two separate pairs of grooves for telescopic sight, but are rather wide apart. Etched on top of air chamber is B.S.A. in an arrow followed by the word "AIRSPORTER". Flip up rearsight that usually folds forwards. Top of barrel stamped "B.S.A. GUNS LTD, ENGLAND, .22 CAL" also the triple gun trade stamp. Has the automatic tap opening as the underlever is drawn back. The stock is three piece laminated at the trigger block, although have seen one piece stocks. Often referred to as the "Braized barrel model" as opposed to the Mk. I Airsporter that is often called the "Taper-barrelled model". The stock does not have the plastic plug for the stock bolt as that which appears on the Mk. I.
Advertised weight 8 lb, and muzzle velocities for .177 600 f.p.s. and for .22 550 f.p.s., also the penetration of aluminium plates 0.006 inches thick placed ½ inch apart were 20 for .177 and 24 for .22. It could be assumed from the above figures that although the .177 is faster it does not penetrate as well as the heavier .22 pellet. Have seen a "GE" series Airsporter with two continuous grooves for telescopic sight machined on top of air chamber. These were ½ inch apart. Have seen some "GD" series with no stampings on top of the barrel.
A variation of the above is the "GF" series. Only about 2,800 were made. Similar to the usual model but had two parallel telescopic sight grooves 11 mm apart. Have seen many of the above with one piece stocks. Barrel stamped as for the usual pattern and the air chamber etched with "B.S.A." in an arrow motif with "AIRSPORTER" following after. Serial number stamped just in front of the trigger guard.

ASSEMBLIES

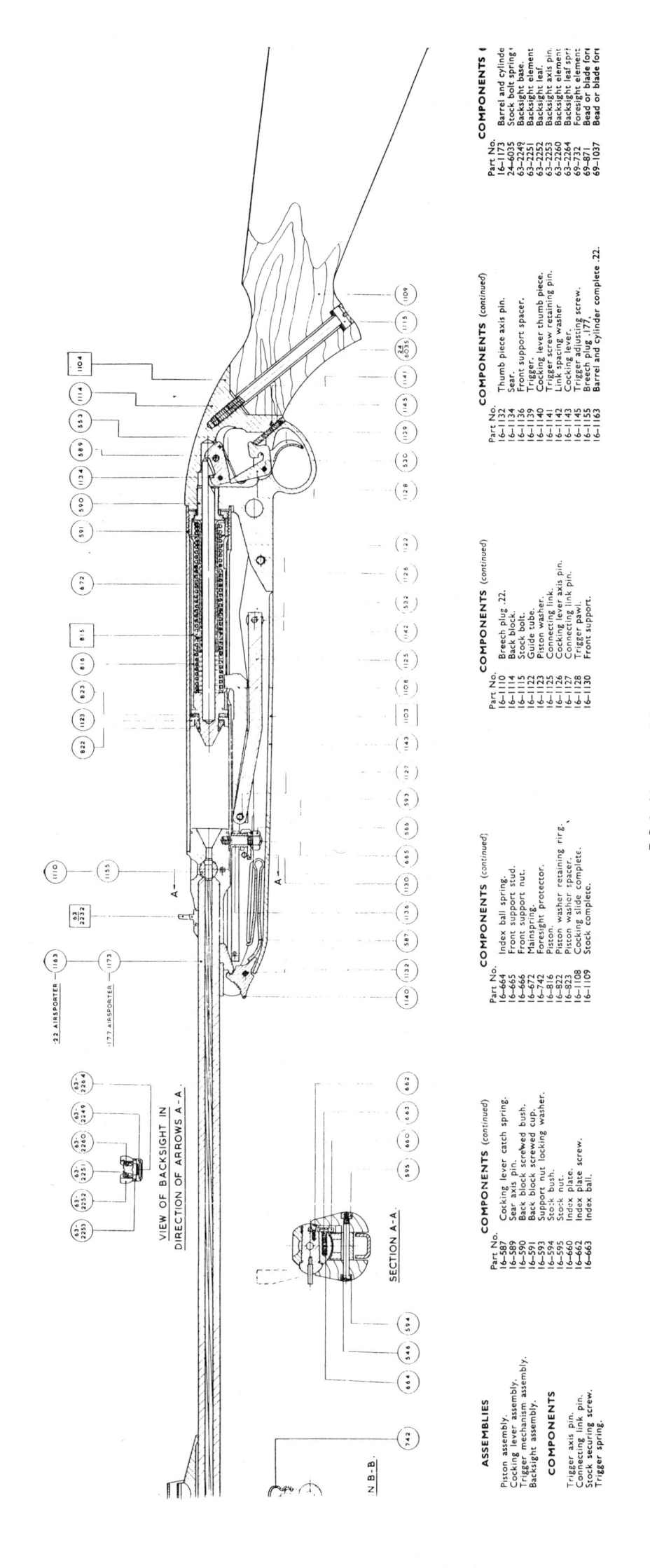

Piston assembly.
Cocking lever assembly.
Trigger mechanism assembly.
Backsight assembly.

COMPONENTS

Part No.	
16-587	Cocking lever catch spring.
16-589	Sear axis pin.
16-590	Back block screwed bush.
16-591	Back block screwed cup.
16-593	Support nut locking washer.
16-594	Stock bush.
16-595	Stock nut.
16-660	Index plate.
16-662	Index plate screw.
16-663	Index ball.

COMPONENTS (continued)

Part No.	
16-664	Index ball spring.
16-665	Front support stud.
16-666	Front support nut.
16-672	Mainspring.
16-742	Foresight protector.
16-816	Piston.
16-822	Piston washer retaining ring.
16-823	Piston washer spacer.
16-1108	Cocking slide complete.
16-1109	Stock complete.

COMPONENTS (continued)

Part No.	
16-1110	Breech plug .22.
16-1114	Back block.
16-1115	Stock bolt.
16-1122	Guide tube.
16-1123	Piston washer.
16-1125	Connecting link.
16-1126	Cocking lever axis pin.
16-1127	Connecting link pin.
16-1128	Trigger pawl.
16-1130	Front support.

COMPONENTS (continued)

Part No.	
16-1132	Thumb piece axis pin.
16-1134	Sear.
16-1136	Front support spacer.
16-1139	Trigger.
16-1140	Cocking lever thumb piece.
16-1141	Trigger screw retaining pin.
16-1142	Link spacing washer
16-1143	Cocking lever.
16-1145	Trigger adjusting screw.
16-1155	Breech plug .177.
16-1163	Barrel and cylinder complete .22.

COMPONENTS

Part No.	
16-1173	Barrel and cylinder
24-6035	Stock bolt spring
63-2249	Backsight base.
63-2251	Backsight element
63-2252	Backsight leaf.
63-2253	Backsight axis pin.
63-2260	Backsight element
63-2264	Backsight leaf spr
69-732	Foresight element
69-871	Bead or blade for
69-1037	Bead or blade for

B.S.A. Airsporter Mk. II

49

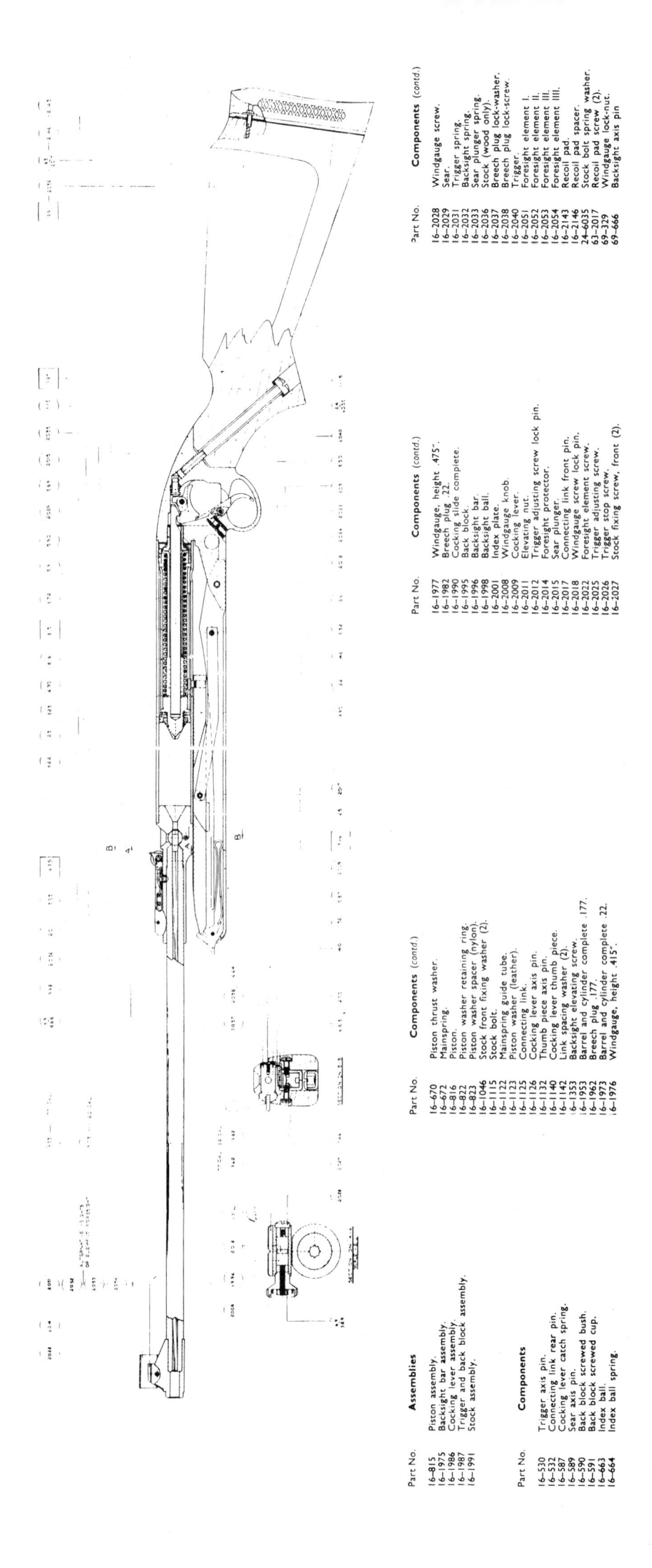

Part No.	Assemblies
16-815	Piston assembly.
16-1975	Backsight bar assembly.
16-1986	Cocking lever assembly.
16-1987	Trigger and back block assembly.
16-1991	Stock assembly.

Part No.	Components
16-530	Trigger axis pin.
16-532	Connecting link rear pin.
16-587	Cocking lever catch spring.
16-589	Sear axis pin.
16-590	Back block screwed bush.
16-591	Back block screwed cup.
16-663	Index ball.
16-664	Index ball spring.

Part No.	Components (contd.)
16-670	Piston thrust washer.
16-672	Mainspring.
16-816	Piston.
16-822	Piston washer retaining ring.
16-823	Piston washer spacer (nylon).
16-1046	Stock front fixing washer (2).
16-1115	Stock bolt.
16-1122	Mainspring guide tube.
16-1123	Piston washer (leather).
16-1125	Connecting link.
16-1126	Cocking lever axis pin.
16-1132	Thumb piece axis pin.
16-1140	Cocking lever thumb piece.
16-1142	Link spacing washer (2).
16-1353	Backsight elevating screw.
16-1953	Barrel and cylinder complete .177.
16-1962	Breech plug .177.
16-1973	Barrel and cylinder complete .22.
16-1976	Windgauge, height .415″.

Part No.	Components (contd.)
16-1977	Windgauge, height .475″.
16-1982	Breech plug .22.
16-1990	Cocking slide complete.
16-1995	Back block.
16-1996	Backsight bar.
16-1998	Backsight ball.
16-2001	Index plate.
16-2008	Windgauge knob.
16-2009	Cocking lever.
16-2011	Elevating nut.
16-2012	Trigger adjusting screw lock pin.
16-2014	Foresight protector.
16-2015	Sear plunger.
16-2017	Connecting link front pin.
16-2018	Windgauge screw lock pin.
16-2022	Foresight element screw.
16-2025	Trigger adjusting screw.
16-2026	Trigger stop screw.
16-2027	Stock fixing screw, front (2).

Part No.	Components (contd.)
16-2028	Windgauge screw.
16-2029	Sear.
16-2031	Trigger spring.
16-2032	Backsight spring.
16-2033	Sear plunger spring.
16-2036	Stock (wood only).
16-2037	Breech plug lock-washer.
16-2038	Breech plug lock-screw.
16-2040	Trigger.
16-2051	Foresight element I.
16-2052	Foresight element II.
16-2053	Foresight element III.
16-2054	Foresight element IIII.
16-2143	Recoil pad.
16-2146	Recoil pad spacer.
24-6035	Stock bolt spring washer.
63-2017	Recoil pad screw (2).
69-329	Windgauge lock-nut.
69-666	Backsight axis pin.

B.S.A. Airsporter Mk. III (pre May 1970) (or late Mk. II)

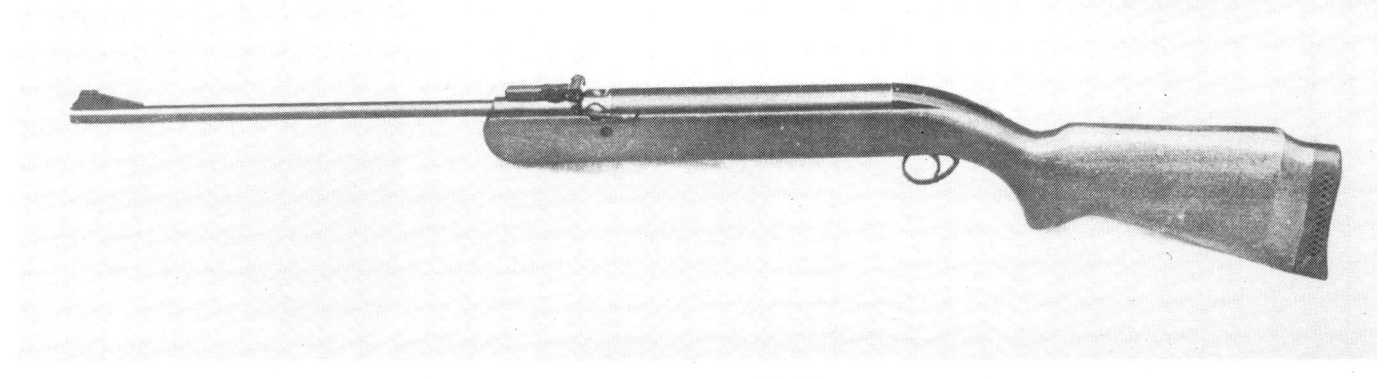

B.S.A. Airsporter Mk. IV

MODEL Airsporter Mk. IV.

MAKER B.S.A. Guns Ltd., Armoury Road, Birmingham 11. Address at time of manufacture.

DATE Airsporter Mk. IV introduced in 1969 and used the following serial numbers "EK" for .177 and "GI" for .22 air rifles. Produced until 1971, when the Mk. V Airsporter appeared.

VALUATION £40—£80.
($60—$120).

DETAILS 44 inches (120 cm) in length. One piece stock with rubber recoil pad. Trigger adjustment by way of Allen key just in front of the trigger guard. Metal loading tap. Top of air chamber stamped between the telscopic sight grooves "BSA AIRSPORTER". Plastic rearsight. Serial number of above GI15028 and is stamped on the underside of the barrel and cannot be seen unless the action is cocked. Stamped along upper edge of barrel "B.S.A. GUNS LTD. ENGLAND .22 CAL". The triple trademark appears after "ENGLAND". See "Airgun World" February 1979. For a review of the above see "Guns Review" November 1971.

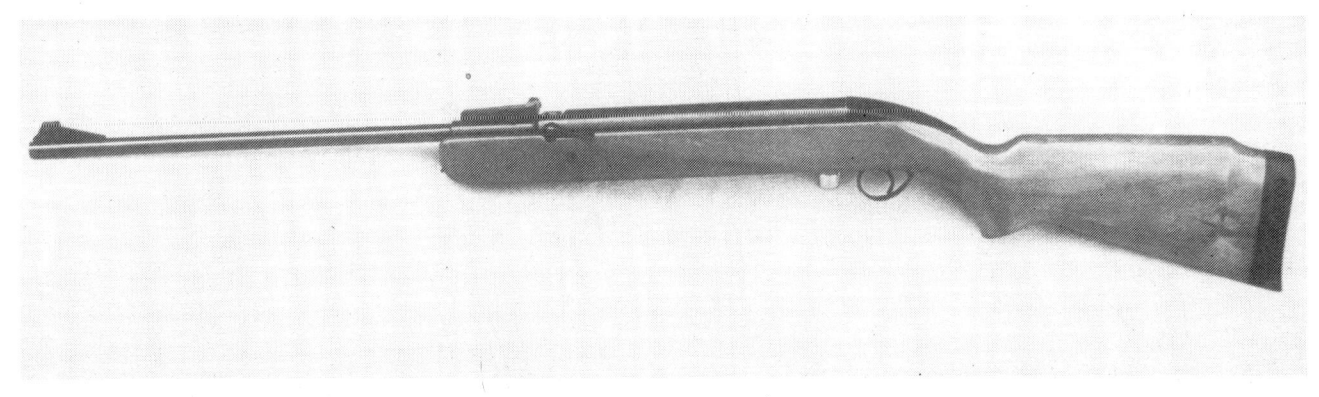

B.S.A. Airporter Mk. V

MODEL "Airsporter". (Mk. V).

MAKER B.S.A.

DATE .22 "GJ" prefix   1971—1974
.177 "EL" prefix   1971—1974

VALUATION £40—£80.
($60—$120).

DETAILS Serial number of above GJ7682 and is stamped on underside of barrel at breech end, can only be seen when underlever is cocked. Tap does not open automatically when cocked and some people do not like the use of plastics, i.e. the rearsight and tap port lever, although with normal use they should be strong enough. 44 inches long. At the Air Rifle Club's Association Third Annual National Championship finals held at Smethwick on Sunday, 3 June 1973 a prototype Airsporter was exhibited with target aperature sights. It is doubtful if this variation ever went into production.

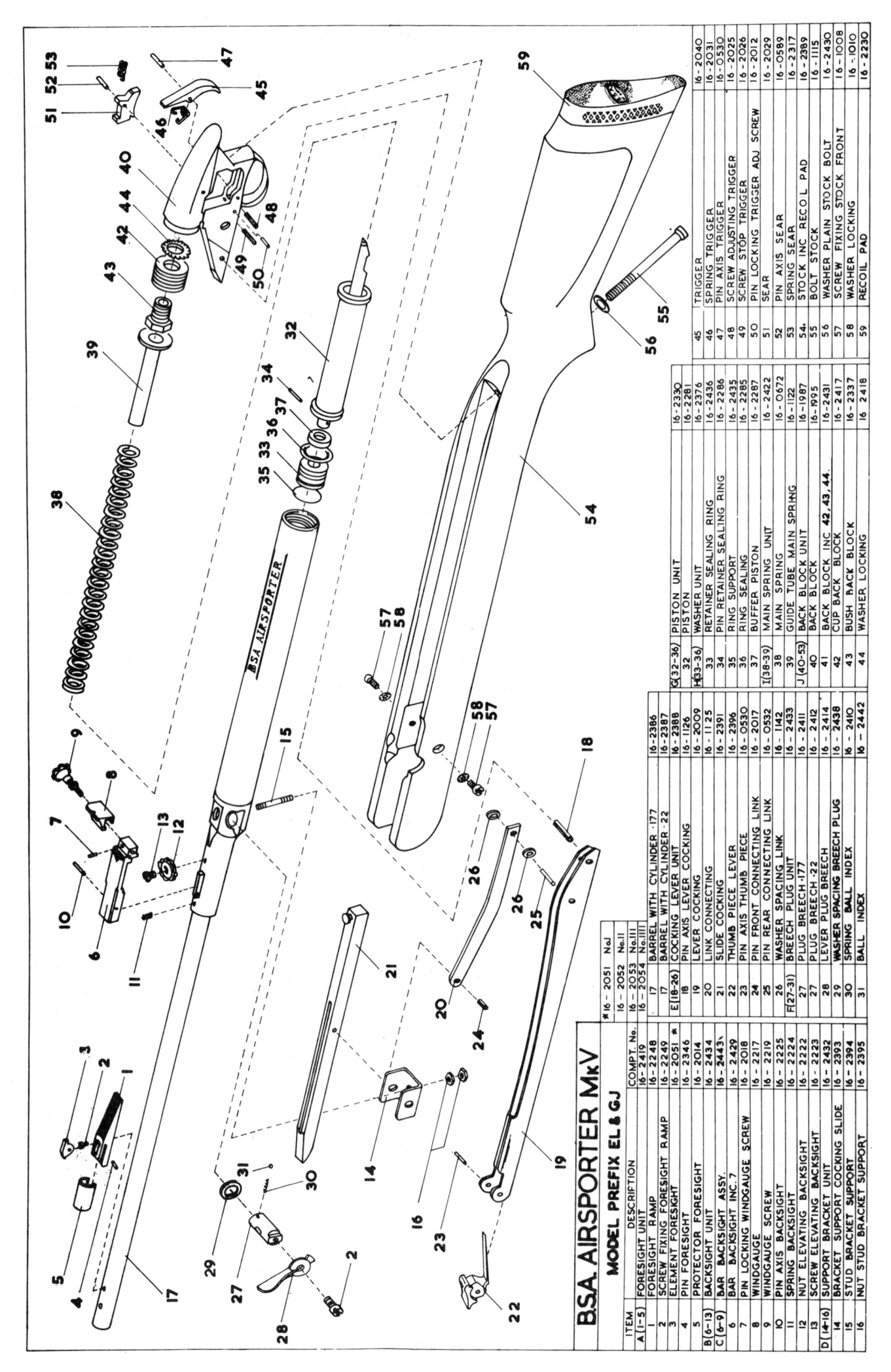

BSA AIRSPORTER MkV
MODEL PREFIX EL & GJ

ITEM	DESCRIPTION	COMPT. No.
A (1-5)	FORESIGHT UNIT	16-2419
1	FORESIGHT RAMP	16-2248
2	SCREW FIXING FORESIGHT RAMP	16-2249
3	ELEMENT FORESIGHT	16-2051 *
4	PIN FORESIGHT	16-2346
5	PROTECTOR FORESIGHT	16-2014
B (6-13)	BACKSIGHT UNIT	16-2434
C (6-9)	BAR BACKSIGHT ASSY.	16-2443
6	BAR BACKSIGHT INC. 7	16-2429
7	PIN LOCKING WINDGAUGE SCREW	16-2018
8	WINDGAUGE	16-2217
9	WINDGAUGE SCREW	16-2219
10	PIN AXIS BACKSIGHT	16-2225
11	SPRING BACKSIGHT	16-2224
12	NUT ELEVATING BACKSIGHT	16-2222
13	SCREW ELEVATING BACKSIGHT	16-2223
D (14-16)	SUPPORT BRACKET BACKSIGHT	16-2432
14	BRACKET SUPPORT COCKING SLIDE	16-2393
15	STUD BRACKET SUPPORT	16-2394
16	NUT STUD BRACKET SUPPORT	16-2395

*16-2051	No.I	
16-2052	No.II	
16-2053	No.III	
16-2054	No.IIII	
17	BARREL WITH CYLINDER .177	16-2386
17	BARREL WITH CYLINDER .22	16-2387
E (18-26)	COCKING LEVER UNIT	16-2388
18	PIN AXIS LEVER COCKING	16-1126
19	LEVER CONNECTING	16-2009
20	LINK CONNECTING	16-1125
21	SLIDE COCKING	16-2391
22	THUMB PIECE LEVER	16-2396
23	PIN AXIS THUMB PIECE	16-0530
24	PIN FRONT CONNECTING LINK	16-2017
25	PIN REAR CONNECTING LINK	16-2219
26	WASHER SPACING LINK	16-2225
F (27-31)	BREECH PLUG UNIT	16-1142
27	PLUG BREECH .177	16-2411
27	PLUG BREECH .22	16-2412
28	LEVER PLUG BREECH	16-2414
29	WASHER SPACING BREECH PLUG	16-2393
30	SPRING BALL INDEX	16-2410
31	BALL INDEX	16-2442

G (32-36)	PISTON UNIT	16-2330
32	PISTON	16-2281
H (33-36)	WASHER UNIT	16-2009
33	RETAINER SEALING RING	16-2376
34	PIN RETAINER SEALING RING	16-2286
35	RING SUPPORT	16-2435
36	RING SEALING	16-2285
37	BUFFER PISTON	16-2287
I (38-39)	MAIN SPRING UNIT	16-2422
38	MAIN SPRING	16-0672
39	GUIDE TUBE MAIN SPRING	16-1987
J (40-53)	BACK BLOCK UNIT	16-2389
40	BACK BLOCK	16-1115
41	BACK BLOCK INC 42,43,44.	16-2431
42	CUP BACK BLOCK	16-2438
43	BUSH BACK BLOCK	16-2417
44	WASHER LOCKING	16-2442

45	TRIGGER	16-2040
46	SPRING TRIGGER	16-2031
47	PIN AXIS TRIGGER	16-0530
48	SCREW ADJUSTING TRIGGER	16-2025
49	SCREW STOP TRIGGER	16-2026
50	PIN LOCKING TRIGGER ADJ SCREW	16-2012
51	SEAR	16-2029
52	PIN AXIS SEAR	16-0589
53	SPRING SEAR	16-2317
54	STOCK INC RECOIL PAD	16-2389
55	BOLT STOCK	16-1115
56	WASHER PLAIN STOCK BOLT	16-2430
57	SCREW FIXING STOCK FRONT	16-1008
58	WASHER LOCKING	16-1010
59	RECOIL PAD	16-2230

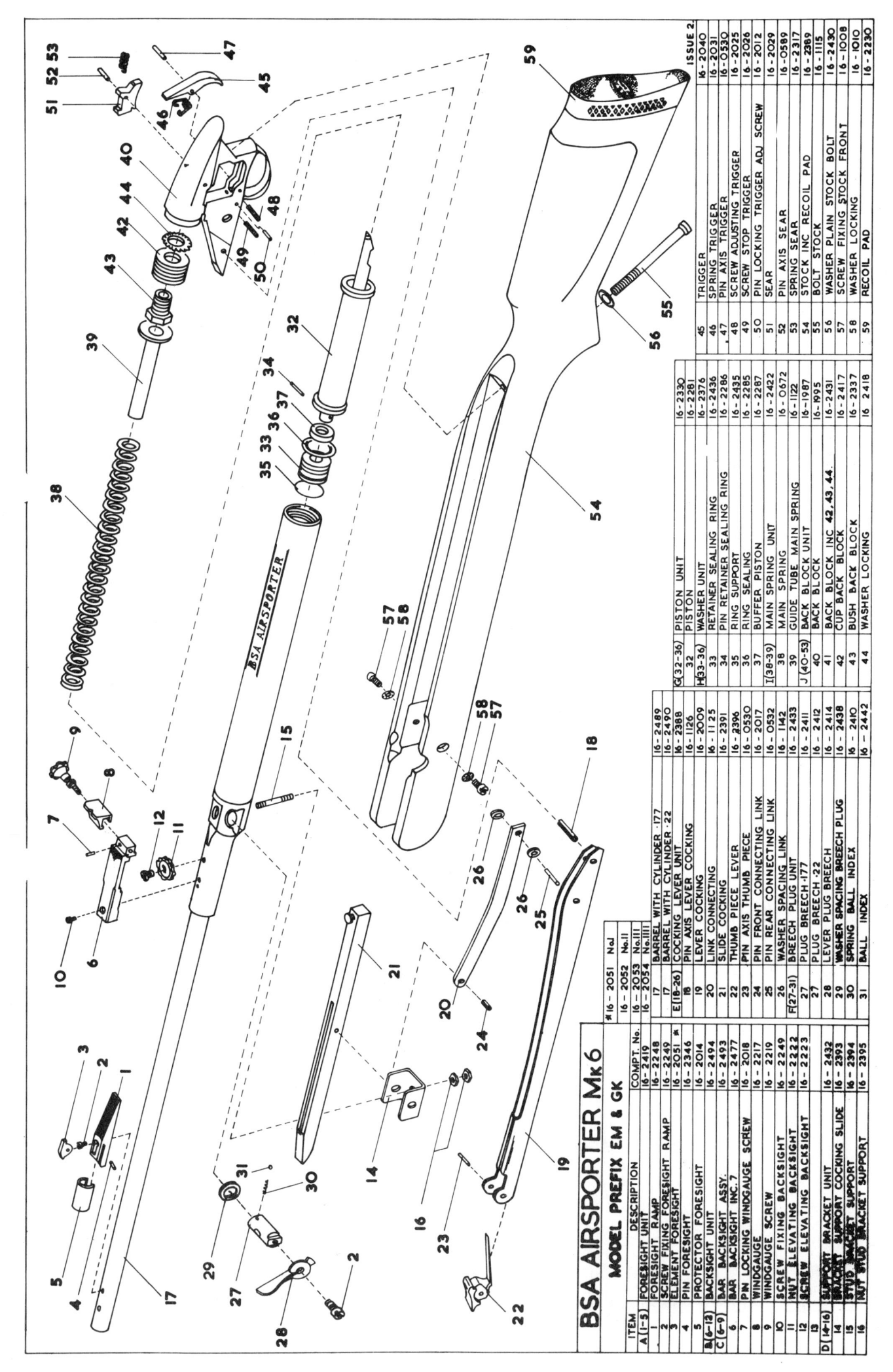

BSA AIRSPORTER Mk6
MODEL PREFIX EM & GK

ITEM	DESCRIPTION	COMPT. No.
A(1-5)	FORESIGHT UNIT	16-2419
1	FORESIGHT RAMP	16-2248
2	SCREW FIXING FORESIGHT RAMP	16-2249
3	ELEMENT FORESIGHT	16-2051 *
4	PIN FORESIGHT	16-2346
5	PROTECTOR FORESIGHT	16-2014
B(6-12)	BACKSIGHT UNIT	16-2494
C(6-9)	BAR BACKSIGHT ASSY.	16-2493
6	BAR BACKSIGHT INC.7	16-2477
7	PIN LOCKING WINDGAUGE SCREW	16-2018
8	WINDGAUGE	16-2217
9	WINDGAUGE SCREW	16-2249
10	SCREW FIXING BACKSIGHT	16-2222
11	NUT ELEVATING BACKSIGHT	16-2223
12	SCREW ELEVATING BACKSIGHT	
D(14-16)	SUPPORT BRACKET UNIT	16-2432
14	BRACKET SUPPORT COCKING SLIDE	16-2393
15	STUD BRACKET SUPPORT	16-2394
16	NUT STUD BRACKET SUPPORT	16-2395

*16-2051	No.I	
16-2052	No.II	
16-2053	No.III	
16-2054	No.IIII	
E(18-26)	COCKING LEVER UNIT	16-2388
17	BARREL WITH CYLINDER .177	16-2489
17	BARREL WITH CYLINDER .22	16-2490
18	PIN AXIS LEVER COCKING	16-1126
19	LEVER COCKING	16-2009
20	LINK CONNECTING	16-1125
21	SLIDE COCKING	16-2391
22	THUMB PIECE LEVER	16-2396
23	PIN AXIS THUMB PIECE	16-0530
24	PIN FRONT CONNECTING LINK	16-2017
25	PIN REAR CONNECTING LINK	16-0532
26	WASHER SPACING LINK	16-1142
F(27-31)	BREECH PLUG UNIT	16-2433
27	PLUG BREECH .177	16-2411
28	PLUG BREECH .22	16-2412
28	LEVER PLUG BREECH	16-2414
29	WASHER SPACING BREECH PLUG	16-2438
30	SPRING BALL INDEX	16-2410
31	BALL INDEX	16-2442

G(32-36)	PISTON UNIT	16-2330
32	PISTON	16-2281
H(33-36)	WASHER UNIT	16-2376
33	RETAINER SEALING RING	16-2436
34	PIN RETAINER SEALING RING	16-2286
35	RING SUPPORT	16-2435
36	RING SEALING	16-2285
37	BUFFER PISTON	16-2287
I(38-39)	MAIN SPRING UNIT	16-2422
38	MAIN SPRING	16-0672
39	GUIDE TUBE MAIN SPRING	16-1987
J(40-53)	BACK BLOCK UNIT	16-2317
40	BACK BLOCK	16-1115
41	BACK BLOCK INC. 42,43,44	16-2414
42	CUP BACK BLOCK	16-2431
43	BUSH BACK BLOCK	16-2337
44	WASHER LOCKING	16-2418

45	TRIGGER	16-2040
46	SPRING TRIGGER	16-2031
47	PIN AXIS TRIGGER	16-0530
48	SCREW ADJUSTING TRIGGER	16-2025
49	SCREW STOP TRIGGER	16-2026
50	PIN LOCKING TRIGGER ADJ SCREW	16-2012
51	SEAR	16-2029
52	PIN AXIS SEAR	16-0589
53	SPRING SEAR	16-2317
54	STOCK INC RECOIL PAD	16-2369
55	BOLT STOCK	16-N95
56	WASHER PLAIN STOCK BOLT	16-2430
57	SCREW FIXING STOCK FRONT	16-1008
58	WASHER LOCKING	16-1010
59	RECOIL PAD	16-2230

ISSUE 2

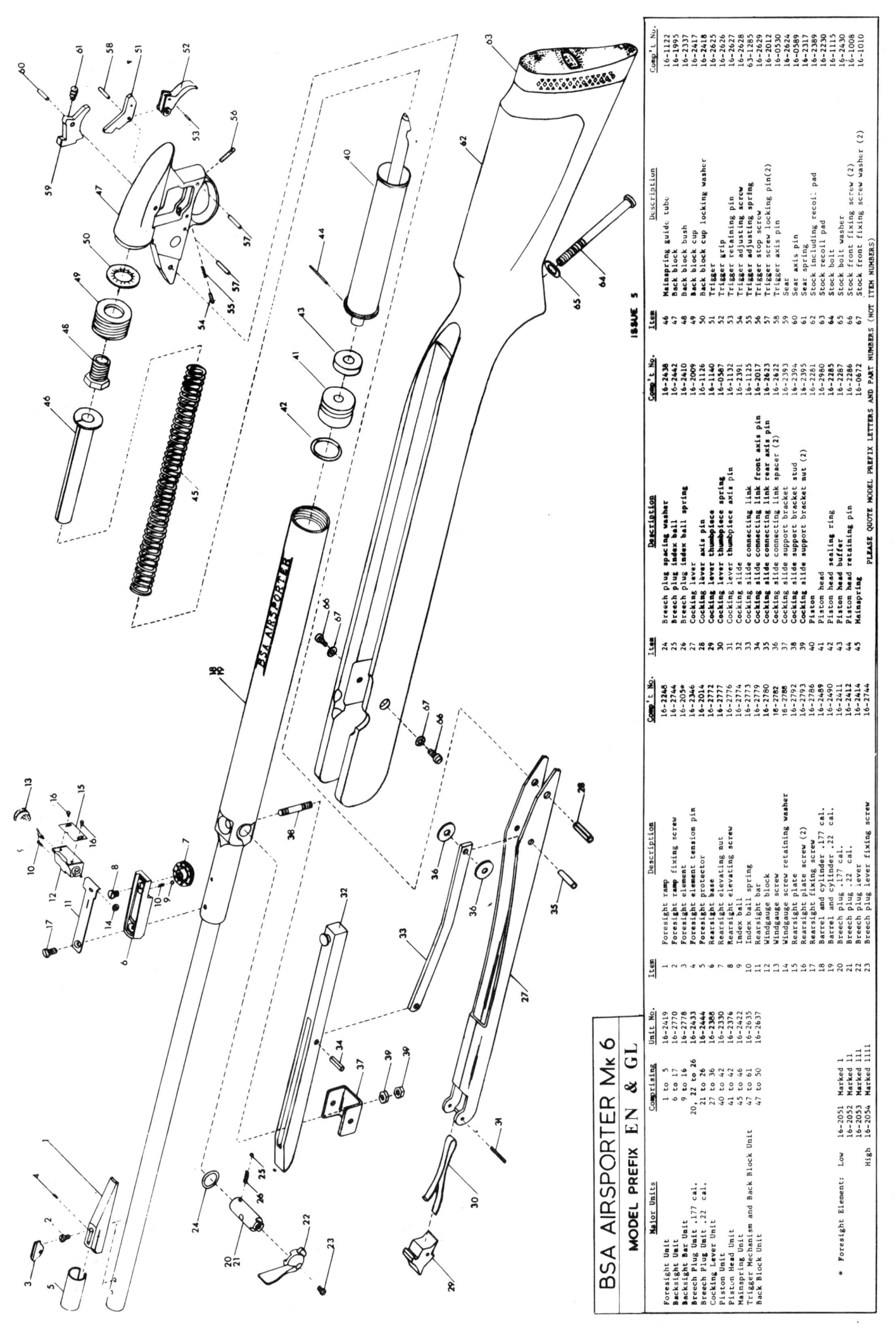

BSA AIRSPORTER Mk 6
MODEL PREFIX E N & GL

Major Units	Comprising	Unit No.
Foresight Unit	1 to 5	16-2419
Backsight Unit	6 to 17	16-2770
Backsight Bar Unit	9 to 16	16-2778
Breech Plug Unit .177 cal.	20, 22 to 26	16-2433
Breech Plug Unit .22 cal.	21 to 26	16-2444
Cocking Lever Unit	27 to 36	16-2388
Piston Unit	40 to 42	16-2330
Piston Head Unit	41 to 42	16-2376
Mainspring	45 to 46	16-2422
Trigger Mechanism and Back Block Unit	47 to 61	16-2635
Back Block Unit	47 to 50	16-2637

* Foresight Element:	Low	16-2051	Marked 1
		16-2052	Marked 11
		16-2053	Marked 111
	High	16-2054	Marked 1111

Item	Comp't No.	Description
1	16-2248	Foresight ramp
2	16-2744	Foresight ramp fixing screw
3	16-205*	Foresight element
4	16-2346	Foresight element tension pin
5	16-2014	Foresight protector
6	16-1126	Foresight base
7	16-2772	Rearsight elevating nut
8	16-2777	Rearsight elevating screw
9	16-2776	Index ball
10	16-2774	Index ball spring
11	16-2773	Rearsight bar
12	16-2779	Windgauge block
13	16-2780	Windgauge screw
14	16-2782	Windgauge screw retaining washer
15	16-2788	Rearsight plate
16	16-2792	Rearsight plate screw (2)
17	16-2793	Rearsight fixing screw
18	16-2786	Barrel and cylinder .177 cal.
19	16-2489	Barrel and cylinder .22 cal.
20	16-2490	Breech plug .177 cal.
21	16-2411	Breech plug .22 cal.
22	16-2412	Breech plug lever
23	16-0672	Breech plug lever fixing screw
24	16-2438	Breech plug spacing washer
25	16-2442	Breech plug index ball
26	16-2410	Breech plug index ball spring
27	16-2009	Cocking lever
28	16-1126	Cocking lever axis pin
29	16-1140	Cocking lever thumbpiece
30	16-0587	Cocking lever thumbpiece spring
31	16-1132	Cocking lever thumbpiece axis pin
32	16-2391	Cocking slide
33	16-1125	Cocking slide connecting link
34	16-2017	Cocking slide connecting link front axis pin
35	16-2623	Cocking slide connecting link rear axis pin
36	16-2622	Cocking slide connecting link spacer (2)
37	16-2624	Cocking slide support bracket
38	16-2394	Cocking slide support bracket stud
39	16-2395	Cocking slide support bracket nut (2)
40	16-2281	Piston
41	16-2960	Piston head
42	16-2285	Piston head buffer
43	16-2287	Piston head retaining pin
44	16-2286	Mainspring
45	16-0672	

Item	Comp't No.	Description
46	16-1122	Mainspring guide tube
47	16-1995	Back block
48	16-2337	Back block bush
49	16-2417	Back block cup
50	16-2418	Back block cup locking washer
51	16-2625	Trigger grip
52	16-2626	Trigger
53	16-2627	Trigger retaining pin
54	16-2628	Trigger adjusting screw
55	16-1285	Trigger adjusting spring
56	16-2629	Trigger stop screw
57	16-2012	Trigger screw locking pin (2)
58	16-0530	Trigger axis pin
59	16-2624	Sear
60	16-0589	Sear axis pin
61	16-2389	Sear spring
62	16-2230	Stock including recoil pad
63	16-1115	Stock recoil pad
64	16-2430	Stock bolt washer
65	16-1008	Stock bolt
66	16-1010	Stock front fixing screw (2)
67		Stock front fixing screw washer (2)

ISSUE 5

PLEASE QUOTE MODEL PREFIX LETTERS AND PART NUMBERS (NOT ITEM NUMBERS)

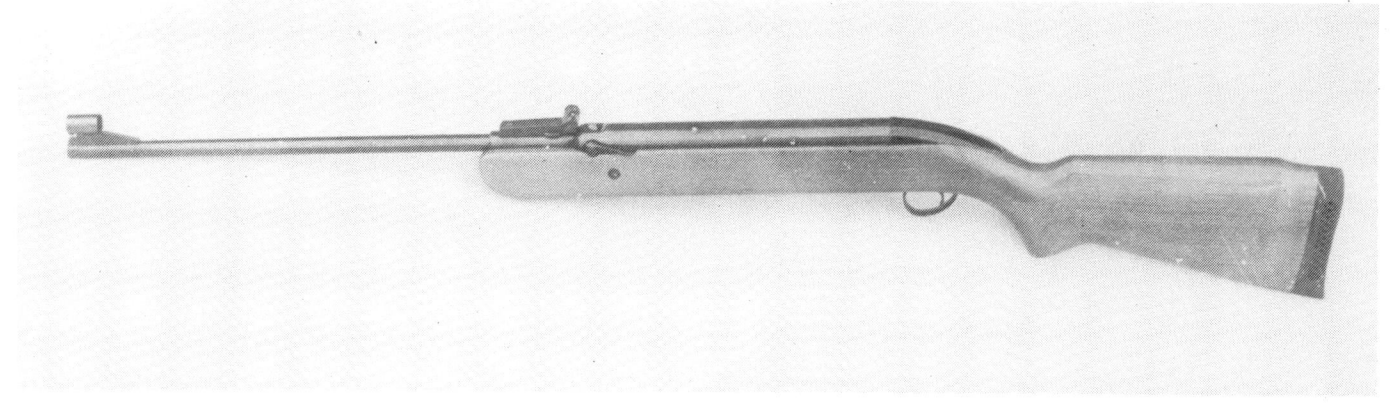

B.S.A. Airsporter Mk. VI

MODEL Airsporter Mk. VI.

MAKER B.S.A. Guns Ltd, Armoury Road, Birmingham B11 2PX.

DATE Mk. VI Airsporter dating by prefix letters. Appeared in 1974.
ISSUE NUMBER TWO   "EM" for .177 and "GK" for .22
ISSUE NUMBER FIVE   "EN" for .177 and "GL" for .22 (April 1976)
Mk. VII, Issue No.9 March 1983. "ER"/.177 and "GN"/.22

VALUATION £40—£80. ($60—$120).

DETAILS 44 inches in length. Serial number stamped on the underside of the barrel breech and can only be seen when underlever has been pulled back into cocked position. Same stampings as previous model Airsporters. The Mk. VI differs from the Mk. V in some internal features, i.e. improved foresight and rearsight, die-cast tap lever, simplified piston, and modified trigger mechanism. Trigger adjustment by way of small Allen key set in front of trigger guard.

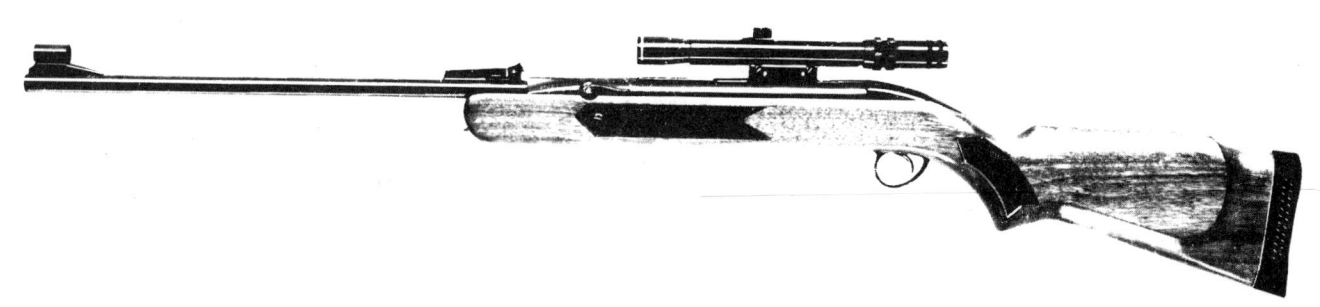

The B.S.A. Airsporter S

MODEL PREFIX EP & GM

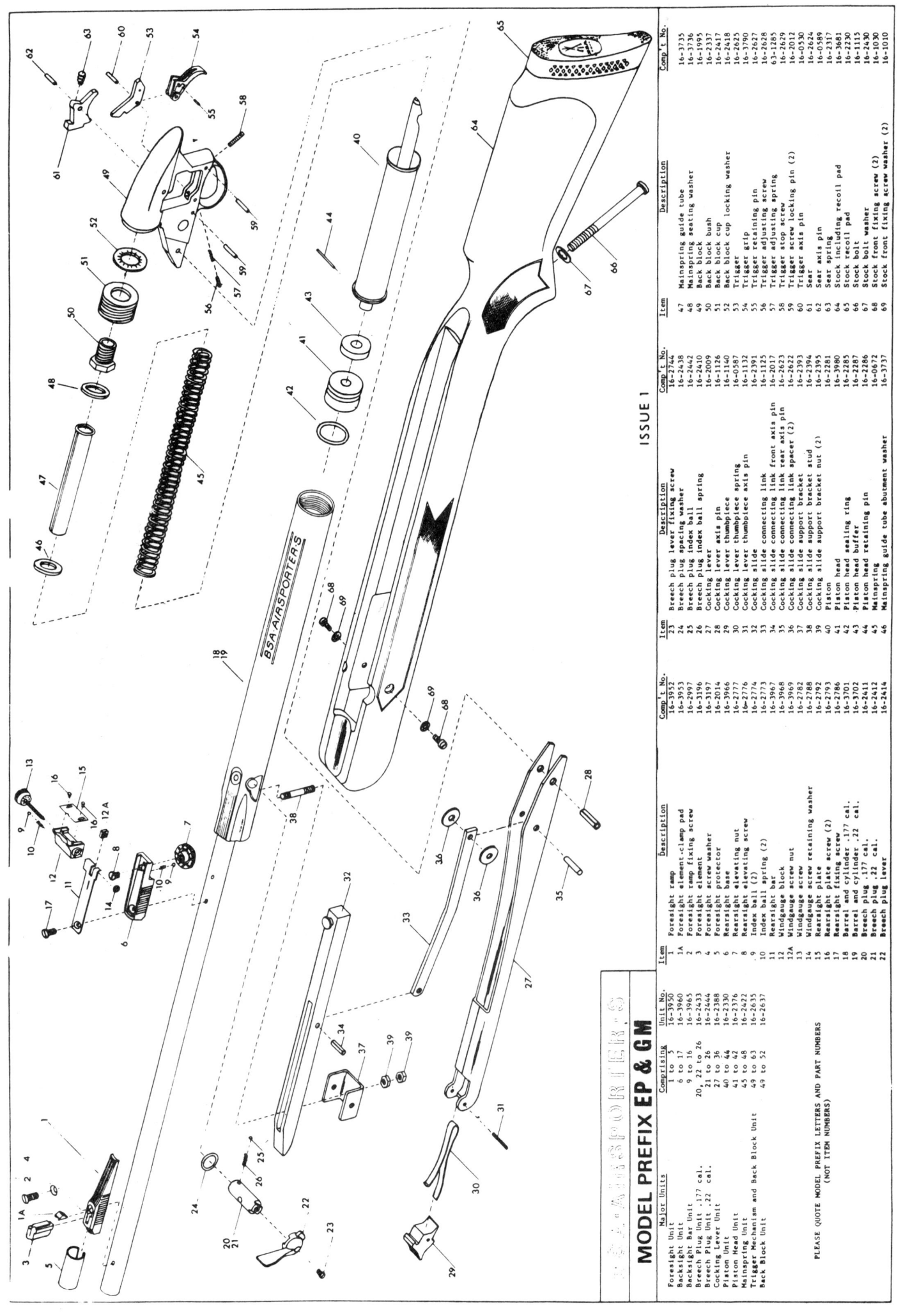

Major Units	Comprising	Unit No.
Foresight Unit	1 to 5	16-3950
Backsight Unit	6 to 17	16-3960
Backsight Bar Unit	9 to 16	16-3965
Breech Plug Unit .177 cal.	20, 22 to 26	16-2433
Breech Plug Unit .22 cal.	21 to 26	16-2444
Cocking Lever Unit	27 to 36	16-2388
Piston Unit	40 to 44	16-2330
Piston Head Unit	41 to 42	16-2376
Mainspring Unit	45 to 48	16-2422
Trigger Mechanism and Back Block Unit	49 to 63	16-2635
Back Block Unit	49 to 52	16-2637

PLEASE QUOTE MODEL PREFIX LETTERS AND PART NUMBERS
(NOT ITEM NUMBERS)

Item	Comp't No.	Description
1	16-3952	Foresight ramp
1A	16-3953	Foresight element-clamp pad
2	16-3965	Foresight ramp fixing screw
3	16-3196	Foresight screw washer
4	16-3197	Foresight element
5	16-2014	Foresight protector
6	16-3966	Rearsight base
7	16-2777	Rearsight elevating nut
8	16-2776	Rearsight elevating screw
9	16-2774	Index ball (2)
10	16-1125	Index ball spring (2)
11	16-3967	Rearsight bar
12	16-3968	Windgauge block
12A	16-3969	Windgauge screw nut
13	16-2782	Windgauge screw
14	16-2788	Windgauge screw retaining washer
15	16-2792	Rearsight plate
16	16-2395	Rearsight plate fixing screw (2)
17	16-2281	Rearsight fixing screw
18	16-2786	Barrel and cylinder .177 cal.
19	16-3701	Barrel and cylinder .22 cal.
20	16-3702	Breech plug .177 cal.
21	16-2411	Breech plug .22 cal.
22	16-2414	Breech plug lever

Item	Comp't No.	Description
23	16-2744	Breech plug lever fixing screw
24	16-2438	Breech plug spacing washer
25	16-2442	Breech plug index ball
26	16-2410	Breech plug index ball spring
27	16-2009	Cocking lever
28	16-1126	Cocking lever axis pin
29	16-1140	Cocking lever thumbpiece
30	16-0587	Cocking lever thumbpiece spring
31	16-1132	Cocking lever thumbpiece axis pin
32	16-2391	Cocking slide
33	16-1125	Cocking slide connecting link
34	16-2017	Cocking slide connecting link front axis pin
35	16-2623	Cocking slide connecting link rear axis pin
36	16-2622	Cocking slide connecting link spacer (2)
37	16-2393	Cocking slide support bracket
38	16-2394	Cocking slide support bracket stud
39	16-2395	Cocking slide support bracket nut (2)
40	16-2281	Piston
41	16-2786	Piston head
42	16-2285	Piston head sealing ring
43	16-2287	Piston head buffer
44	16-2286	Piston head retaining pin
45	16-0672	Mainspring
46	16-3737	Mainspring guide tube abutment washer

Item	Comp't No.	Description
47	16-3735	Mainspring guide tube
48	16-3736	Mainspring seating washer
49	16-1995	Back block
50	16-2337	Back block bush
51	16-2417	Back block cup
52	16-2418	Back block cup locking washer
53	16-2625	Trigger
54	16-3790	Trigger grip
55	16-2627	Trigger retaining pin
56	16-2628	Trigger adjusting spring
57	63-1285	Trigger adjusting screw
58	16-2629	Trigger stop screw
59	16-2012	Trigger screw locking pin (2)
60	16-0530	Trigger axis pin
61	16-2624	Sear
62	16-0389	Sear axis pin
63	16-2317	Sear spring
64	16-3881	Stock including recoil pad
65	16-2230	Stock recoil pad
66	16-1115	Stock bolt
67	16-2430	Stock bolt washer
68	16-1090	Stock front fixing screw (2)
69	16-1010	Stock front fixing washer (2)

ISSUE 1

The Centenary Airsporter S. (Acknowledgements to B.S.A.)

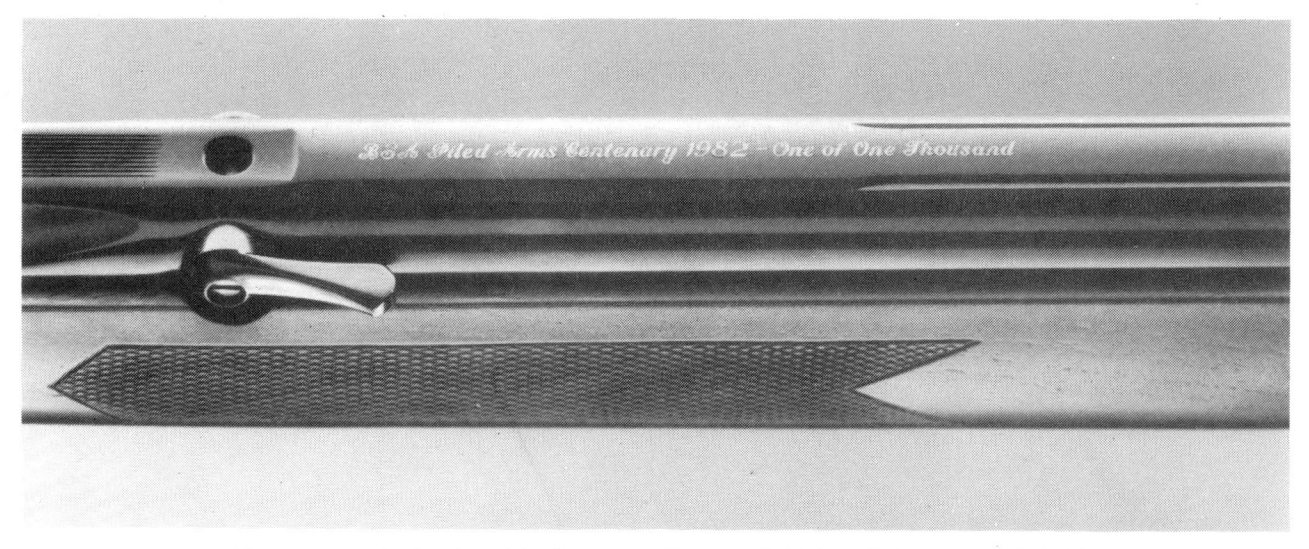

The engraved air chamber of the Centenary Airsporter S. (Acknowledgements to B.S.A.)

MODEL Airsporter S.

MAKER B.S.A. Guns Ltd., Birmingham B11 2PX, England.

DATE Introduced 1979 (May). Prefix letters EP for .177 and GM for .22. Issue No.2 March 1983, "ES"/.177 and "GP"/.22.

VALUATION Airsporter S, £60—£120. ($90—$180). Centenary Model £235n, although can be seen offered for as low as £200n, none as yet have appeared in auction. ($353n—$300n).

DETAILS A deluxe version of the Airsporter with a slight increase in power. Fitted with all metal sights with a foresight element that can be removed and inverted for either blade or bead, height can also be adjusted by slackening the adjuster screw. Increased accuracy as barrel has 12 groove rifling. Air chamber is of slightly larger diameter to the standard Airsporter. The most distinctive characteristic are the flutes cut on either side of the action between the loading tap and the rearsight. The stock is walnut and oil finished with pressed chequering. Advertised muzzle velocities for .22 being 600 f.p.s. and for .177, 825 f.p.s. It is recommended that the air chamber is not lubricated as it already contains Molyslip grease. The barrel is slightly wider, hence heavier than that fitted to the standard model. It is a screw fit into the air chamber. Overall length 44⅝ inches with a 19½ inch barrel. Advertised weight 8 lbs. A review appears in "Airgun World" December 1979. Each rifle is accuracy tested at 25 yards and for muzzle velocity before leaving the factory. The export muzzle velocity was the same for .177 but in .22 it was given as 635 f.p.s. Telescopic sight ramps measure 11.5 mm across. During the Game Fair of 1982 held at Tatton Park, Knutsford, Cheshire, B.S.A. launched a centenary air rifle based on the Airsporter S and the serial numbers ran from C0001 to C1000. The original specification is as follows:

BSA PILED ARMS CENTENARY RIFLE

Although the Company was established in 1861, it was not until 1882 that the now famous "Piled Arms" trademark was introduced. This was a representation of three Martini Henry .577 single shot rifles stacked or "piled" in military fashion. This particular rifle was in volume production by the Company at that time.

In 1982, to celebrate the Centenary of the Piled Arms trademark, B.S.A. are producing 1,000 special air rifles. These rifles will be modelled on the Airsporter S, but with a new three-quarter length Stutzen stock. The stock has a contrasting "Schnabel" fore-end tip and will be supplied with a pistol grip cap illustrating the trademark. Also incorporated is a new cocking lever which is completely concealed in the fore-end.

Each rifle will be engraved with the legend:

"BSA Piled Arms Centenary 1982 —
One of One Thousand"

and will be accompanied by a Certificate carrying the rifle number. Each Certificate will be individually signed and sealed with the original hand operated Company seal.

Included in the package will be:

1	Mk. X 4 x 40 Telescope
1 Pair	TM9 Telescope Mounts
1	'Scope Stop
1 Pair	"QD" Sling Swivels
1	Sling in Basketweave Leather*
1	BSA Deluxe Gun Cover with thick pile lining*
1	Embroidered B.S.A. Badge
1	Shooting Kit comprising: Target Holder, Targets, Pellets, Gun Oil

* These items will also be specially marked with the commemorative message.

The rifle will be available in either .177 or .22 calibre, but the total quantity to be produced will be strictly limited to 1,000.

As the number of rifles available is limited they will quickly become collectors items. The first rifles will be ready for despatch during July/August 1982.

The rifle is available only as a complete Kit, including the items shown and is priced at a suggested U.K. retail price of £235, including VAT.

(Reproduced by the kind permission of B.S.A. Ltd., Birmingham).

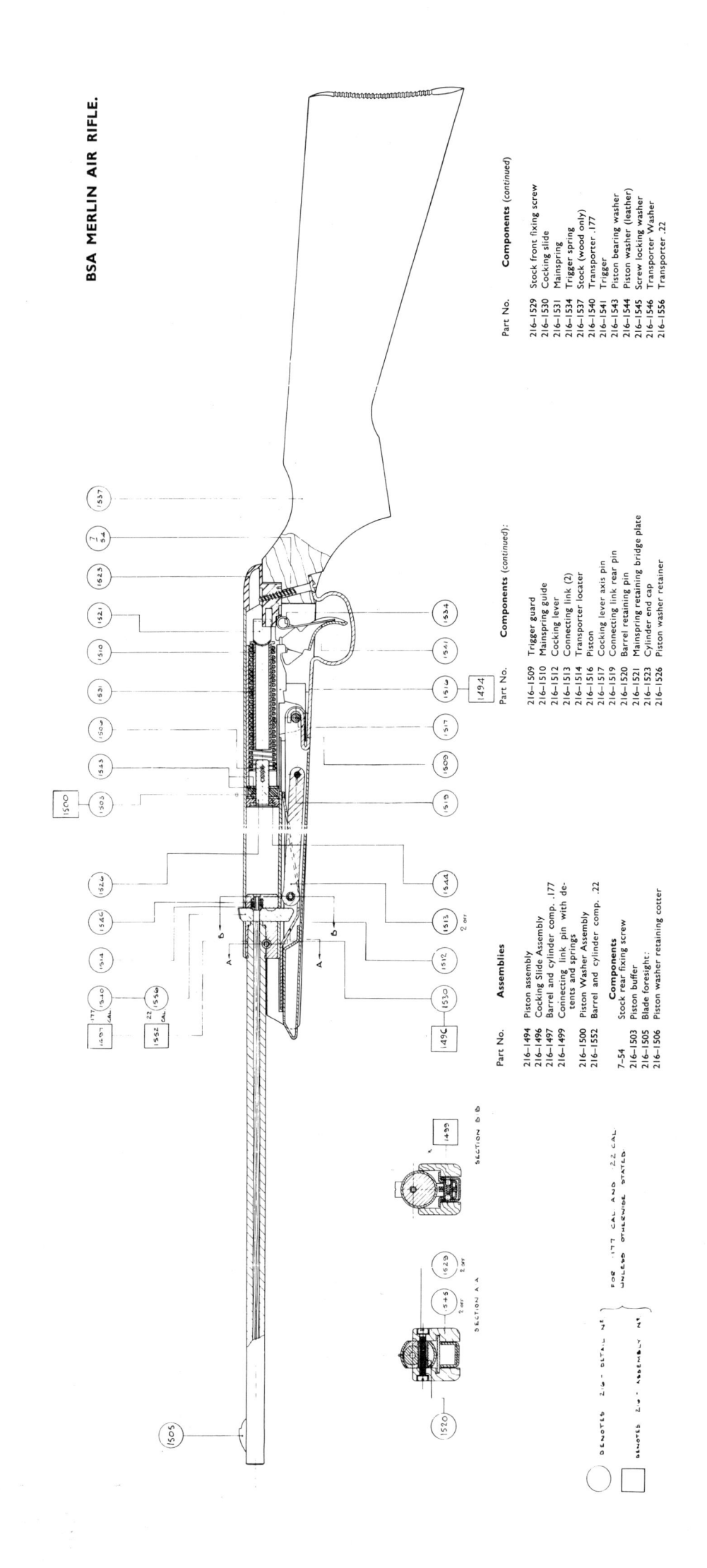

BSA MERLIN AIR RIFLE.

Part No.	Assemblies
216-1494	Piston assembly
216-1496	Cocking Slide Assembly
216-1497	Barrel and cylinder comp. .177
216-1499	Connecting link pin with detents and springs
216-1500	Piston Washer Assembly
216-1552	Barrel and cylinder comp. .22

	Components
7-54	Stock rear fixing screw
216-1503	Piston buffer
216-1505	Blade foresight
216-1506	Piston washer retaining cotter

Part No.	Components (continued):
216-1509	Trigger guard
216-1510	Mainspring guide
216-1512	Cocking lever
216-1513	Connecting link (2)
216-1514	Transporter locater
216-1516	Piston
216-1517	Cocking lever axis pin
216-1519	Connecting link rear pin
216-1520	Barrel retaining pin
216-1521	Mainspring retaining bridge plate
216-1523	Cylinder end cap
216-1526	Piston washer retainer

Part No.	Components (continued)
216-1529	Stock front fixing screw
216-1530	Cocking slide
216-1531	Mainspring
216-1534	Trigger spring
216-1537	Stock (wood only)
216-1540	Transporter .177
216-1541	Trigger
216-1543	Piston bearing washer
216-1544	Piston washer (leather)
216-1545	Screw locking washer
216-1546	Transporter Washer
216-1556	Transporter .22

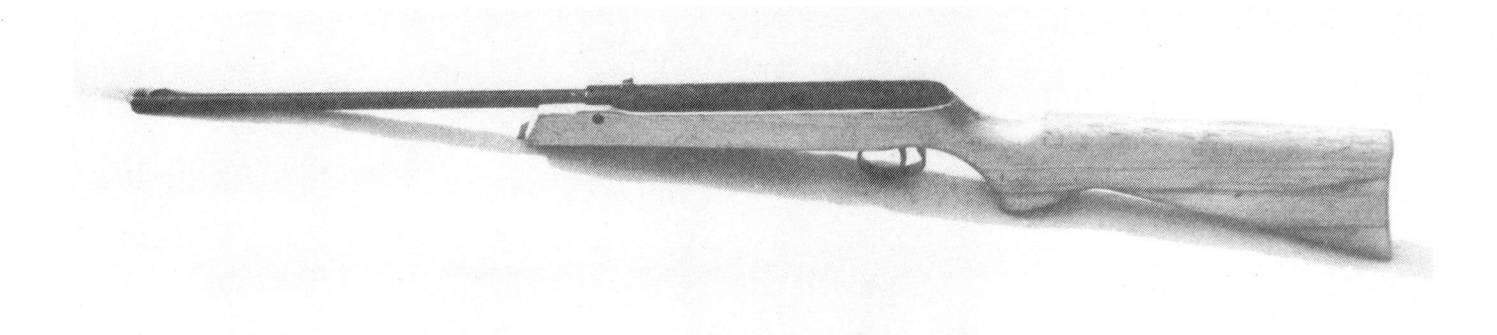

B.S.A. Merlin

MODEL Merlin.

MAKER B.S.A., Shirley, Solihull, Warwickshire. Address at time of manufacture.

DATE By prefix letter as follows:
October 1962 to December 1964   "K" for .177
  "L" for .22
December 1964 to December 1968   "KA" for .177
  "LA" for .22

VALUATION £40—£80. ($60—$120), should be worth more but they can still be purchased for less than their rarity warrants.

DETAILS 36 inches long. Stamped with B.S.A. in arrow on top of air chamber along with the name "MERLIN". Stamped on top of barrel "B.S.A. GUNS LTD, ENGLAND. .177 CAL" plus the three rifle trademark. Serial number of above K04678 stamped on L.H.S. of barrel breech near stock. Above has plastic pop-up pellet breech. This was changed to alloy in December 1964 and a separate rearsight was fitted instead of the sight being part of the loading port. Black lacquer finish with "Merlin" and B.S.A. painted in with gold paint. Breech popped up as the underlever was pulled down, pellet inserted and then manually pushed down. Dainty design and becoming quite rare. The trigger mechanism is not the same between the two models, i.e. K/L and the later KA/LA. On the earlier models the trigger guard had a curled extension that clipped on to the cocking lever pivot pin whilst the later type had two prongs that protruded up into the stock and rested on a lip of wood.

B.S.A. Merlin Mk. II

MODEL Merlin. MK. II.

MAKER B.S.A., Birmingham, England.

DATE Second series of Merlin air rifles. Dating by prefix letters as follows:
"KA" for .177
"LA" for .22 above for 1964 to 1968.

VALUATION £40—£80.
  ($60—$120).

DETAILS 36 inches in length. One piece stock with slightly wider fore-end. Metal work is lacquered black with gold lettering on the top of the air chamber. Stamped on top of air chamber between the two telescopic sight grooves appears "BSA MERLIN". The loading tap is alloy with a separate rearsight just in front. Adjustable for windage only. Serial number stamped on L.H.S. of barrel just under the rearsight. Stamped along the upper edge of the barrel is "B.S.A. GUNS LTD. ENGLAND .22 CAL" also the triple rifle trademark. Serial number of above LA3840. See "Airgun World" February 1979. Advertised weight 3½ lbs.

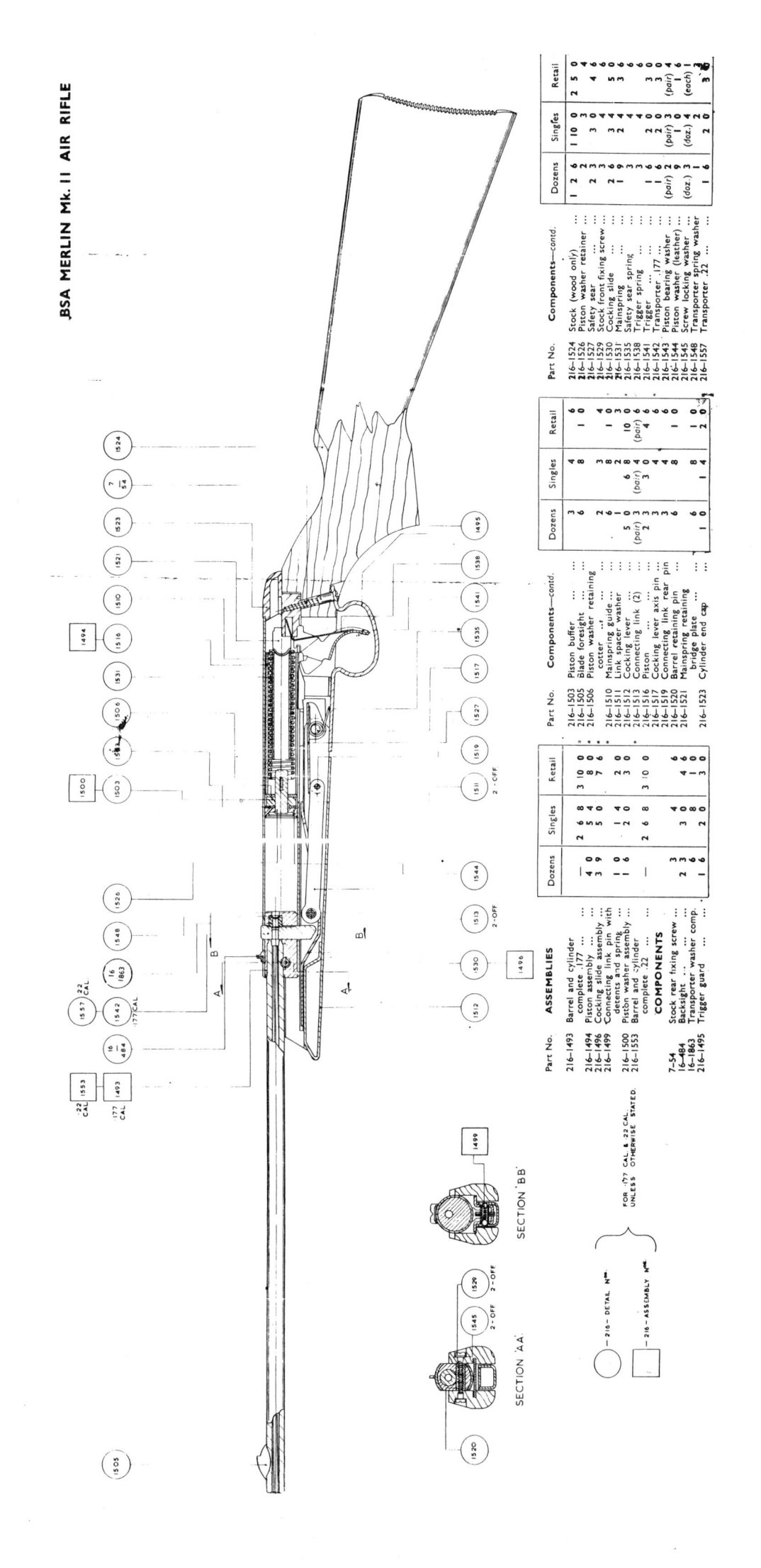

BSA MERLIN Mk. II AIR RIFLE

ASSEMBLIES

Part No.		Dozens	Singles	Retail
216-1493	Barrel and cylinder complete .177		2 6 8	3 10 0
216-1494	Piston assembly	4 0	5 4	8 0
216-1496	Cocking slide assembly	3 9	5 0	7 6
216-1499	Connecting link pin with detents and spring	1 1	1 4	2 0
216-1500	Piston washer assembly	1 6	1 6	2 3
216-1553	Barrel and cylinder complete .22		2 6 8	3 10 0

COMPONENTS

7-54	Stock rear fixing screw	2 3	3 0 8	4 6
16-484	Backsight		3 0	4 0
16-1863	Transporter washer comp.		8	1 0
216-1495	Trigger guard	1 6	2 0	3 0

Part No.	Components—contd.	Dozens	Singles	Retail
216-1503	Piston buffer		4	6
216-1505	Blade foresight	3 6	8	1 0
216-1506	Piston washer retaining cotter	2 6	3	4 0
216-1510	Mainspring guide	5 0	6 8	10 0
216-1511	Link spacer washer	(pair) 2 3	(pair) 3	(pair) 4
216-1512	Cocking lever	2 3	3 4	4 6
216-1513	Connecting link (2)	2 3	3 0	4 6
216-1516	Piston	6 0	8 4	10
216-1517	Cocking lever axis pin		4	6
216-1519	Connecting link rear pin		4	6
216-1520	Barrel retaining pin		8	1 0
216-1521	Mainspring retaining bridge plate	1 0	1 4	2 0
216-1523	Cylinder end cap			

Part No.	Components—contd.	Dozens	Singles	Retail
216-1524	Stock (wood only)	1 2 6	1 10 0	2 5 0
216-1526	Piston washer retainer	2 6	3 0 4	4 6
216-1527	Safety sear	2 3	3 3	6 0
216-1529	Stock front fixing screw		3 4	5 0
216-1530	Cocking slide	2 6	3 4	6 3
216-1531	Mainspring	1	2 9	3 6
216-1535	Safety sear spring		3 4	6
216-1538	Trigger spring		4	6
216-1541	Trigger	1 6	2 0	3 0
216-1542	Transporter .177	(pair) 6	(pair) 1 0	(pair) 3
216-1543	Piston bearing washer	2 3	3 0	4 0
216-1544	Piston washer (leather)	(doz.) 3	(doz.) 1	(each) 6
216-1545	Screw locking washer	1 6	2 0	3 0
216-1548	Transporter spring washer			
216-1557	Transporter .22			

61

MERCURY MODEL PREFIX W & Z

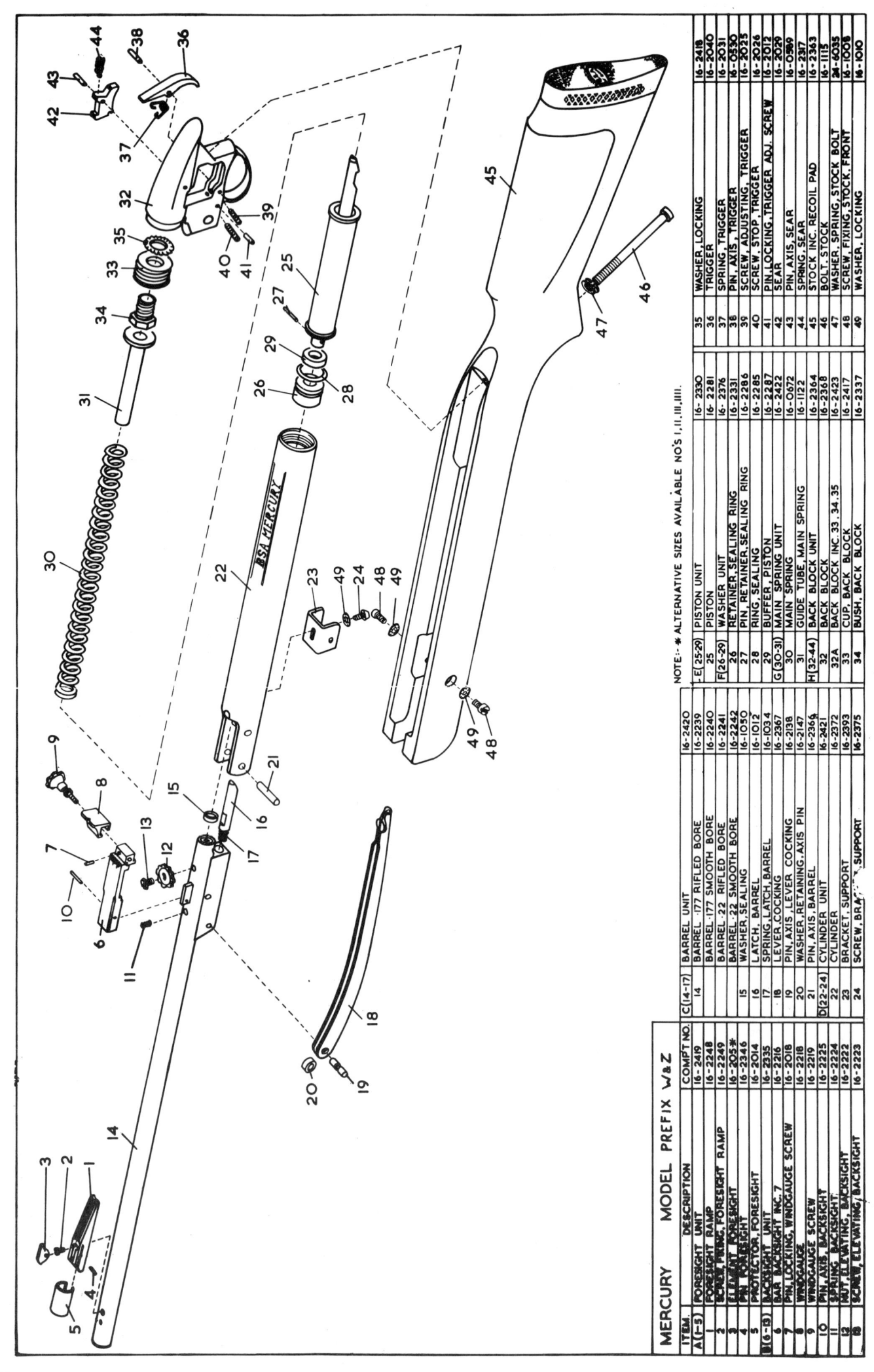

ITEM	DESCRIPTION	COMPT NO.
A(1-5)	FORESIGHT UNIT	16-2419
1	FORESIGHT RAMP	16-2248
2	SCREW, FIXING, FORESIGHT RAMP	16-2249
3	ELEMENT, FORESIGHT	16-205*
4	PIN, FORESIGHT	16-2346
5	PROTECTOR, FORESIGHT	16-2014
B(6-13)	BACKSIGHT UNIT	16-2335
6	BACKSIGHT INC. 7	16-2216
7	PIN, LOCKING, WINDGAUGE SCREW	16-2018
8	WINDGAUGE	16-2218
9	WINDGAUGE SCREW	16-2219
10	PIN, AXIS, BACKSIGHT	16-2225
11	SPRING, BACKSIGHT	16-2224
12	NUT, ELEVATING, BACKSIGHT	16-2222
13	SCREW, ELEVATING, BACKSIGHT	16-2223
C(14-17)	BARREL UNIT	16-2420
14	BARREL .177 RIFLED BORE	16-2239
	BARREL .177 SMOOTH BORE	16-2240
	BARREL .22 RIFLED BORE	16-2241
	BARREL .22 SMOOTH BORE	16-2242
15	WASHER, SEALING	16-1050
16	LATCH, BARREL	16-1012
17	SPRING, LATCH, BARREL	16-1034
18	LEVER, COCKING	16-2367
19	WASHER, RETAINING, AXIS PIN	16-2138
20	PIN, AXIS, LEVER COCKING	16-2147
21	PIN, AXIS, BARREL	16-2366
D(22-24)	CYLINDER UNIT	16-2421
22	CYLINDER	16-2372
23	BRACKET, SUPPORT	16-2393
24	SCREW, BRACKET, SUPPORT	16-2375

E(25-29)	PISTON UNIT	16-2330
25	PISTON	16-2281
F(26-29)	WASHER UNIT	16-2376
26	RETAINER, SEALING RING	16-2331
27	PIN, RETAINER, SEALING RING	16-2286
28	RING, SEALING	16-2285
29	BUFFER, PISTON	16-2287
G(30-31)	MAIN SPRING UNIT	16-2422
30	MAIN SPRING	16-0672
31	GUIDE TUBE, MAIN SPRING	16-1122
H(32-44)	BACK BLOCK UNIT	16-2364
32	BACK BLOCK	16-2368
32A	BACK BLOCK INC. 33, 34, 35	16-2423
33	CUP, BACK BLOCK	16-2417
34	BUSH, BACK BLOCK	16-2337
35	WASHER, LOCKING	16-2418
36	TRIGGER	16-2040
37	SPRING, TRIGGER	16-2031
38	PIN, AXIS, TRIGGER	16-0330
39	SCREW, ADJUSTING, TRIGGER	16-2025
40	SCREW, STOP, TRIGGER	16-2026
41	PIN, LOCKING, TRIGGER ADJ. SCREW	16-2012
42	SEAR	16-2029
43	PIN, AXIS, SEAR	16-0569
44	SPRING, SEAR	16-2317
45	STOCK INC. RECOIL PAD	16-2363
46	BOLT, STOCK	16-1115
47	WASHER, SPRING, STOCK BOLT	24-2035
48	SCREW, FIXING, STOCK, FRONT	16-1005
49	WASHER, LOCKING	16-1010

NOTE:- * ALTERNATIVE SIZES AVAILABLE NO'S I, II, III, IIII.

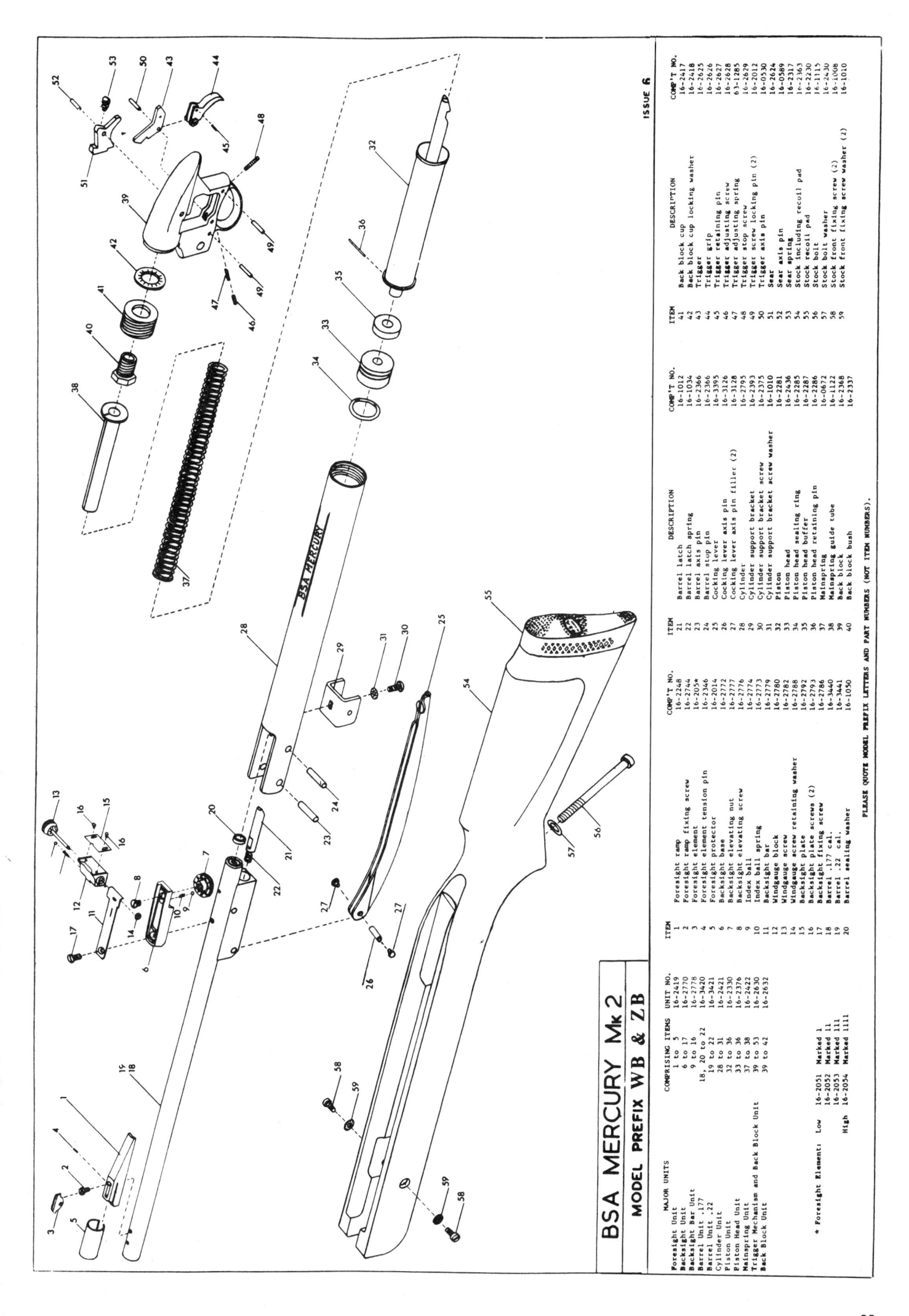

BSA MERCURY Mk2
MODEL PREFIX WB & ZB

ISSUE 6

MAJOR UNITS	COMPRISING ITEMS	UNIT NO.
Foresight Unit	1 to 5	16-2419
Backsight Unit	6 to 17	16-2770
Backsight Bar Unit	9 to 16	16-2778
Barrel Unit .177	18, 20 to 22	16-3420
Barrel Unit .22	19 to 22	16-3421
Cylinder Unit	28 to 31	16-2421
Piston Unit	32 to 36	16-2330
Piston Head Unit	33 to 36	16-2376
Mainspring Unit	37 to 38	16-2422
Trigger Mechanism and Back Block Unit	39 to 53	16-2630
Back Block Unit	39 to 42	16-2632

* Foresight Element:		
Low	16-2051	Marked 1
	16-2052	Marked 11
	16-2053	Marked 111
High	16-2054	Marked 1111

ITEM	DESCRIPTION	COMP'T NO.
1	Foresight ramp	16-2248
2	Foresight ramp fixing screw	16-2744
3	Foresight element tension pin	16-205*
4	Foresight protector	16-2366
5	Foresight base	16-2014
6	Backsight	16-2772
7	Backsight elevating nut	16-2777
8	Backsight elevating screw	16-2776
9	Index ball	16-2773
10	Index ball spring	16-2774
11	Backsight bar	16-2779
12	Windgauge block	16-2780
13	Windgauge screw	16-2782
14	Windgauge screw retaining ring	16-2288
15	Backsight plate	16-2287
16	Backsight plate screws (2)	16-2286
17	Backsight fixing screw	16-2786
18	Barrel .177 cal.	16-3440
19	Barrel .22 cal.	16-3441
20	Barrel sealing washer	16-1050

ITEM	DESCRIPTION	COMP'T NO.
21	Barrel latch	16-2268
22	Barrel latch spring	16-2744
23	Barrel axis pin	16-205*
24	Barrel stop pin	16-2366
25	Cocking lever	16-3395
26	Cocking lever axis pin	16-3126
27	Cocking lever axis pin filler (2)	16-3128
28	Cylinder	16-2795
29	Cylinder support bracket	16-2993
30	Cylinder support bracket screw	16-2375
31	Cylinder support bracket screw washer	16-1010
32	Piston	16-2281
33	Piston head	16-2436
34	Piston head sealing ring	16-2285
35	Piston head buffer	16-2287
36	Piston head retaining pin	16-2793
37	Mainspring	16-2786
38	Mainspring guide tube	16-3440
39	Back block	16-3441
40	Back block bush	16-2337

ITEM	DESCRIPTION	COMP'T NO.
41	Back block cup	16-1012
42	Back block cup locking washer	16-1034
43	Trigger grip	16-2366
44	Trigger	16-2366
45	Trigger retaining pin	16-3395
46	Trigger adjusting screw	16-3126
47	Trigger adjusting spring	63-1285
48	Trigger stop screw	16-2629
49	Trigger screw locking pin (2)	16-2012
50	Trigger axis pin	16-0530
51	Sear	16-2624
52	Sear axis pin	16-0589
53	Sear spring	16-2317
54	Stock including recoil pad	1--2363
55	Stock recoil pad	16-2230
56	Stock bolt	16-1113
57	Stock bolt washer	16-2430
58	Stock front fixing screw (2)	16-1008
59	Stock front fixing screw washer (2)	16-1010

PLEASE QUOTE MODEL PREFIX LETTERS AND PART NUMBERS (NOT ITEM NUMBERS).

63

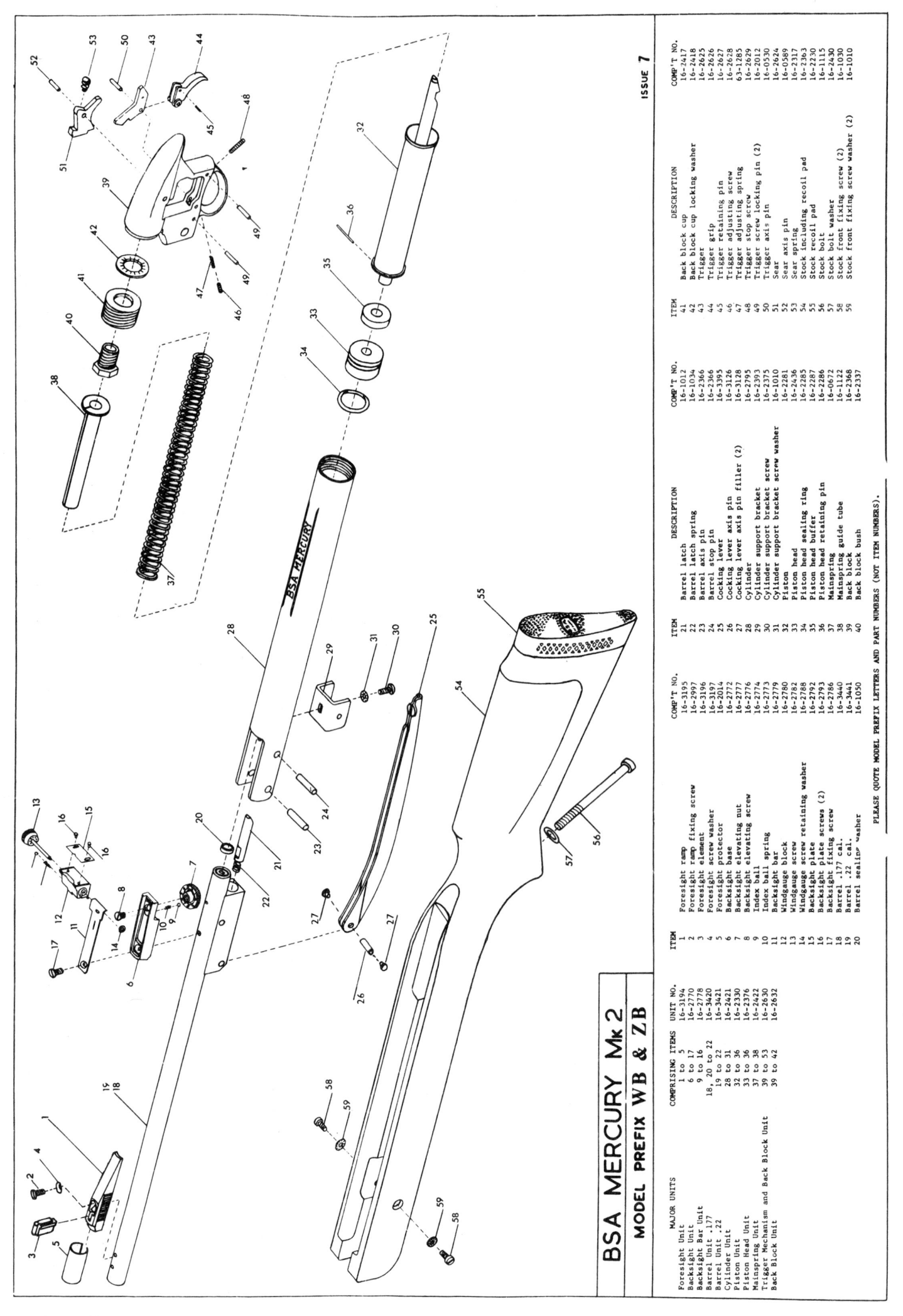

BSA MERCURY Mk 2
MODEL PREFIX WB & ZB

ISSUE 7

MAJOR UNITS	COMPRISING ITEMS	UNIT NO.
Foresight Unit	1 to 5	16-3194
Backsight Unit	6 to 17	16-2770
Backsight Bar Unit	9 to 16	16-2778
Barrel Unit .177	18, 20 to 22	16-3420
Barrel Unit .22	19 to 22	16-3421
Cylinder Unit	28 to 31	16-2421
Piston Unit	32 to 36	16-2330
Piston Head Unit	33 to 36	16-2376
Mainspring Unit	37 to 38	16-2422
Trigger Mechanism and Back Block Unit	39 to 53	16-2630
Back Block Unit	39 to 42	16-2632

ITEM	COMP'T NO.	DESCRIPTION
1	16-3195	Foresight ramp
2	16-2997	Foresight ramp fixing screw
3	16-3196	Foresight element
4	16-3197	Foresight screw washer
5	16-2014	Foresight protector
6	16-2772	Backsight base
7	16-2777	Backsight elevating nut
8	16-2776	Backsight elevating screw
9	16-2774	Index ball
10	16-2773	Index ball spring
11	16-2779	Backsight bar
12	16-2780	Windgauge block
13	16-2782	Windgauge screw
14	16-2788	Windgauge screw retaining ring
15	16-2792	Backsight plate
16	16-2787	Backsight plate screws (2)
17	16-2793	Backsight fixing screw
18	16-2786	Barrel .177 cal.
19	16-3440	Barrel .22 cal.
20	16-3441	Barrel sealing washer
21	16-1050	Barrel latch
22	16-1012	Barrel latch spring
23	16-1034	Barrel axis pin
24	16-2366	Barrel stop pin
25	16-2366	Cocking lever
26	16-3395	Cocking lever axis pin
27	16-3126	Cocking lever axis pin filler (2)
28	16-3128	Cylinder
29	16-2795	Cylinder support bracket
30	16-2393	Cylinder support bracket screw
31	16-2375	Cylinder support bracket screw washer
32	16-1010	Piston
33	16-2281	Piston head
34	16-2436	Piston head sealing ring
35	16-2285	Piston head buffer
36	16-2287	Piston head retaining pin
37	16-2286	Mainspring
38	16-0672	Mainspring guide tube
39	16-1122	Back block
40	16-2368	Back block bush
41	16-2417	Back block cup
42	16-2418	Back block cup locking washer
43	16-2625	Trigger
44	16-2626	Trigger grip
45	16-2627	Trigger retaining pin
46	16-2628	Trigger adjusting screw
47	63-1285	Trigger adjusting spring
48	16-2629	Trigger stop screw
49	16-2012	Trigger screw locking pin (2)
50	16-0530	Trigger axis pin
51	16-2624	Sear
52	16-0589	Sear axis pin
53	16-2317	Sear spring
54	16-2363	Stock including recoil pad
55	16-2230	Stock recoil pad
56	16-1115	Stock bolt
57	16-2430	Stock bolt washer
58	16-1030	Stock front fixing screw (2)
59	16-1010	Stock front fixing screw washer (2)

PLEASE QUOTE MODEL PREFIX LETTERS AND PART NUMBERS (NOT ITEM NUMBERS).

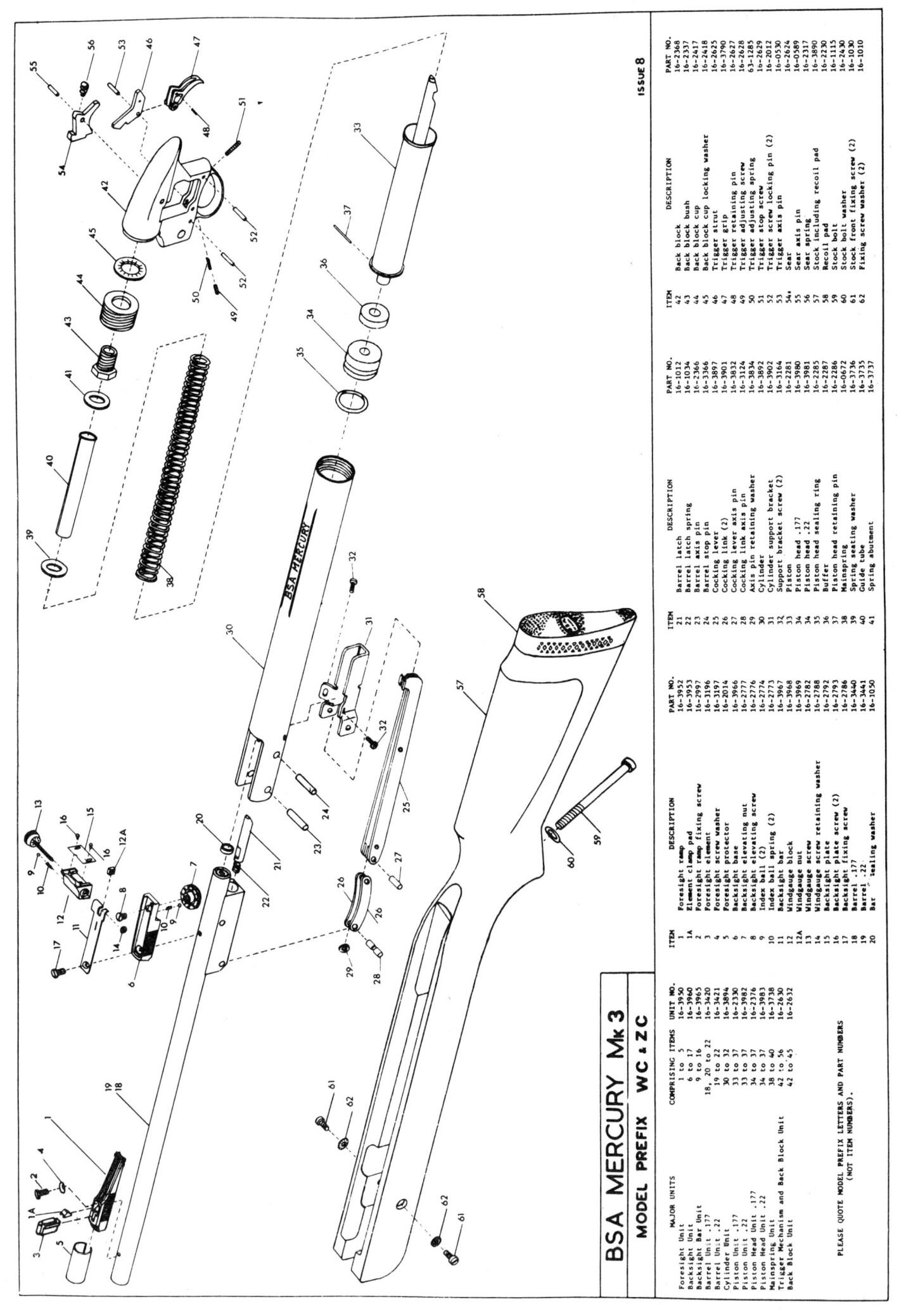

BSA MERCURY Mk 3
MODEL PREFIX WC & ZC
Issue 8

MAJOR UNITS	UNIT NO.	COMPRISING ITEMS
Foresight Unit	16-3950	1 to 5
Backsight Unit	16-3960	6 to 17
Backsight Bar Unit	16-3965	9 to 16
Barrel Unit .177	16-3420	18, 20 to 22
Barrel Unit .22	16-3421	19 to 22
Cylinder Unit	16-3894	30 to 32
Piston Unit .177	16-2330	33 to 37
Piston Unit .22	16-3982	33 to 37
Piston Head .177	16-3983	34 to 37
Piston Head .22	16-2012	34 to 37
Mainspring Unit	16-3738	38 to 40
Trigger Mechanism and Back Block Unit	16-2630	42 to 56
Back Block Unit	16-2632	42 to 45

PLEASE QUOTE MODEL PREFIX LETTERS AND PART NUMBERS
(NOT ITEM NUMBERS).

ITEM	PART NO.	DESCRIPTION
1	16-3952	Foresight ramp
1A	16-3953	Element clamp pad
2	16-2997	Foresight ramp fixing screw
3	16-3366	Foresight screw washer
4	16-3197	Foresight element
5	16-2014	Foresight protector
6	16-3966	Backsight base
7	16-2777	Backsight elevating nut
8	16-3124	Backsight elevating screw
9	16-2776	Axis pin retaining washer
10	16-2774	Cylinder
11	16-3892	Index ball spring (2)
12	16-2773	Backsight bar
12A	16-3967	Windgauge nut
13	16-3968	Windgauge block
14	16-3969	Windgauge screw
15	16-3981	Windgauge screw retaining washer
16	16-2788	Backsight plate
17	16-2285	Backsight plate screw (2)
18	16-2792	Barrel .177
19	16-2793	Barrel .22
20	16-2786	Barrel sealing washer

ITEM	PART NO.	DESCRIPTION
21	16-1012	Barrel latch
22	16-1034	Barrel latch spring
23	16-3366	Barrel axis pin
24	16-3897	Barrel stop pin
25	16-3901	Cocking lever
26	16-3832	Cocking link (2)
27	16-3124	Cocking lever axis pin
28	16-3834	Cocking link axis pin
29	16-2776	Axis pin retaining washer
30	16-2774	Cylinder
31	16-3892	Cylinder support bracket
32	16-3164	Support bracket screw (2)
33	16-2281	Piston
34	16-3980	Piston head .177
35	16-2317	Piston head .22
36	16-3890	Piston head sealing ring
37	16-2287	Piston head retaining pin
38	16-2286	Mainspring
39	16-0672	Spring seating washer
40	16-3736	Guide tube
41	16-3737	Spring abutment

ITEM	PART NO.	DESCRIPTION
42	16-2368	Back block
43	16-2337	Back block bush
44	16-2417	Back block cup
45	16-2418	Back block cup locking washer
46	16-2625	Trigger strut
47	16-3790	Trigger grip
48	16-2627	Trigger retaining pin
49	16-2628	Trigger adjusting screw
50	63-1285	Trigger adjusting spring
51	1o-2629	Trigger stop screw
52	16-0530	Trigger screw locking pin (2)
53	16-2624	Trigger axis pin
54	16-0589	Sear
55	16-3890	Sear axis pin
56	16-2230	Sear spring
57	16-1115	Stock including recoil pad
58	16-2430	Recoil pad
59	16-1030	Stock bolt
60	16-1010	Stock bolt washer
61	16-3736	Stock front fixing screw (2)
62	16-3735	Fixing screw washer (2)

65

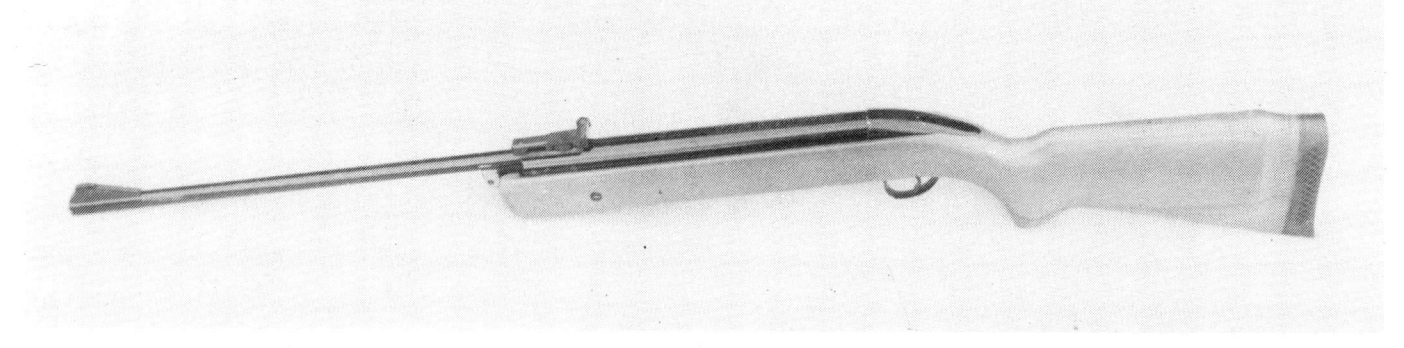

B.S.A. Mercury Mk. I

MODEL Mercury.

MAKER B.S.A. Guns Ltd., Birmingham, England.

DATE Appeared in 1971 as the Mk. I, W for .177 and Z for .22. By August 1976 the Mk. II had appeared WB for .177 and ZB for .22. By September 1979 the Mk. III had appeared WC for .177 and ZC for .22. The Mk. IV was also given the "WC" and "ZC" prefix letters.

VALUATION £40–£80.
($60–$120).

DETAILS The breakaction version of the Airsporter. Have found the above to be slightly more powerful than the Airsporter. Presents excellent value for the price. For a review of the Mercury see "Guns Review" June 1972. 43½ inches long with an 18½ inch barrel. Ramp foresight and plastic rearsight. Metal surfaces are blacked. Top of air chamber stamped "B.S.A. MERCURY" and the lettering is filled with gold coloured paint. Smooth stock with thick rubber butt plate. Serial number is stamped on the underside of the barrel near the cocking arm pivot. Trigger adjustment by way of small grub screw set in front of the trigger. Advertised weight 7¼ lbs. For stripping the Mercury see "Airgun World" December 1978. In the review of airguns featured in "Guns Review" April 1976 it mentions the Mercury Mk. II. For airgun test of the Mercury see "Airgun World" May 1978. In the latter half of 1975 B.S.A.'s brought out a target model of the Mercury. This being in .177 only, tunnel foresight with interchangeable elements, and fully adjustable rear aperture sight. This target model was not stocked by retailers but was obtainable from B.S.A. by special order. See "Guns Review" October 1975. During the middle of 1979 "Manchester Airguns" started to produce the above with .25 inch and 200 inch rifled barrels. Barrel length remained the same. Advertised in 1972 as being available in either .22 or .177 rifled or smoothbore.

On the Mk. II Mercury, prefix letters W, Z and WB, ZB, part number 29 can work loose and allow the action to slip about no matter how hard the fore-end screws are tightened. To correct this annoying fault remove action from stock and then knock out pin 26 complete with end caps, lever out the cocking lever part number 25. If you wish change the existing screw with an Allen key head for a normal screw type head and tighten down finger tight. Replace action into set and with the rear action bolt (56) tightened adjust the position of part number 29 so the two fore-end screws can be screwed home, now insert a screwdriver into the underside of the stock and tighten down part 29 and make sure that it has a locking washer fitted, now remove action and replace the cocking lever and re-assemble.

At a later date the air chamber was blued instead of the earlier "blacked" finish. It would appear that the foresight has a reversable element so that a choice of either blade or bead can be made.

A prototype of the Target Model Mercury was displayed at the Air Rifle Club's Association Annual National Championship Finals at Smethwick, on Sunday, 3 June 1973.

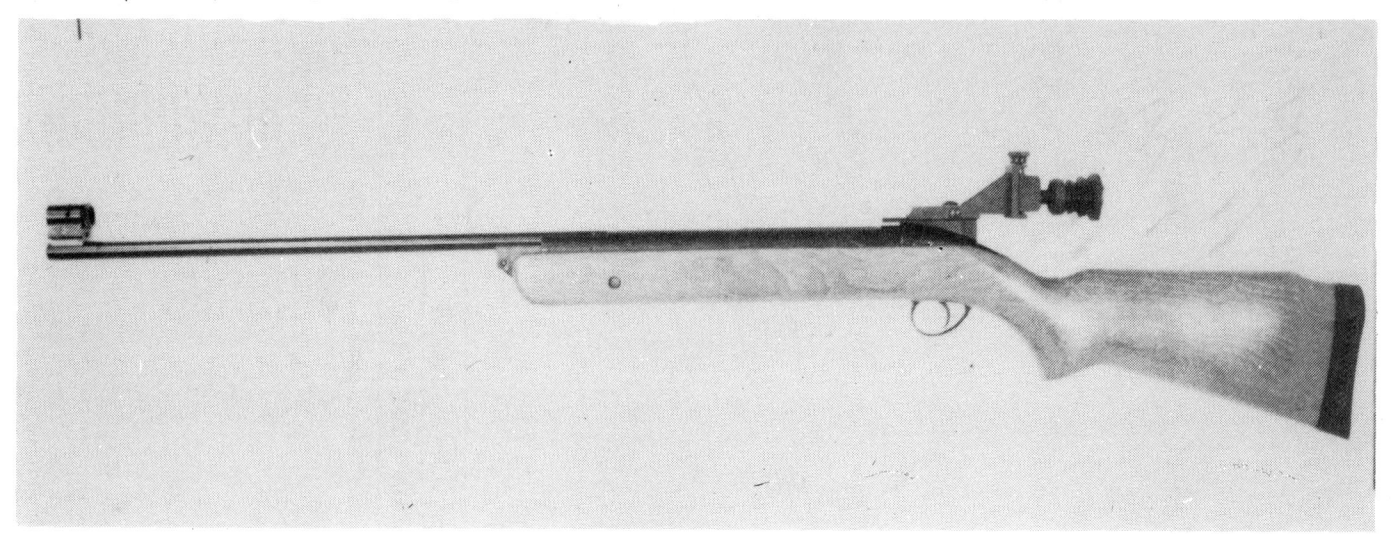

The B.S.A. Mercury Target Model.

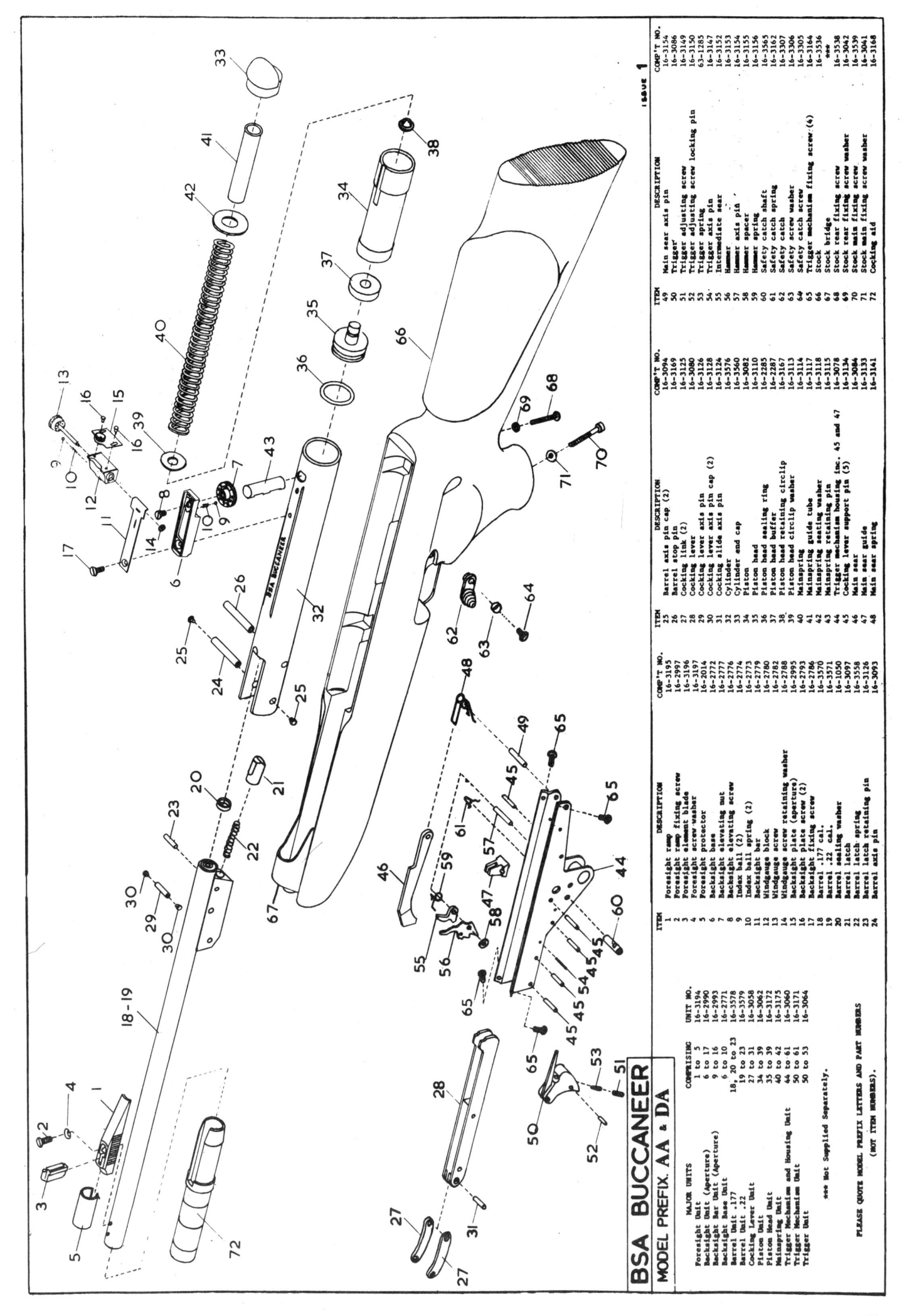

BSA BUCCANEER
MODEL PREFIX. AA & DA

Issue 1

MAJOR UNITS	UNIT NO.	COMPRISING
Foresight Unit	16-3194	1 to 5
Backsight Unit (Aperture)	16-2997	6 to 17
Barrel Unit (Aperture)	16-2990	9 to 16
Backsight Base Unit	16-2993	6 to 10
Barrel Unit .177	16-2771	18, 20 to 23
Barrel Unit .22	16-3578	19 to 23
Cocking Lever Unit	16-3579	27 to 31
Piston Unit	16-3062	34 to 39
Piston Head Unit	16-3175	35 to 39
Mainspring Unit	16-3060	40 to 42
Trigger Mechanism and Housing Unit	16-3171	44 to 61
Trigger Mechanism Unit	16-3064	50 to 61
Trigger Unit		50 to 53

*** Not Supplied Separately.

PLEASE QUOTE MODEL PREFIX LETTERS AND PART NUMBERS
(NOT ITEM NUMBERS).

ITEM	DESCRIPTION	COMP'T NO.
1	Foresight ramp	16-3195
2	Foresight ramp fixing screw	16-2997
3	Foresight element blade	16-3196
4	Foresight screw washer	16-3197
5	Foresight protector	16-2014
6	Backsight base	16-2772
7	Backsight elevating nut	16-2777
8	Backsight elevating screw	16-2776
9	Index ball (2)	16-2776
10	Index ball spring (2)	16-2773
11	Backsight bar	16-2779
12	Windgauge block	16-2780
13	Windgauge screw	16-2782
14	Windgauge screw retaining washer	16-2788
15	Backsight plate (aperture)	16-2995
16	Backsight plate screw (2)	16-2793
17	Backsight fixing screw	16-2786
18	Barrel .177 cal.	16-3570
19	Barrel .22 cal.	16-3571
20	Barrel sealing washer	16-1050
21	Barrel latch	16-3097
22	Barrel latch spring	16-3558
23	Barrel latch retaining pin	16-3126
24	Barrel axis pin	16-3093

ITEM	DESCRIPTION	COMP'T NO.
25	Barrel axis pin cap (2)	16-3094
26	Barrel stop pin	16-3169
27	Cocking link (2)	16-3080
28	Cocking lever	16-3125
29	Cocking lever axis pin	16-3126
30	Cocking lever axis pin cap (2)	16-3128
31	Cocking slide axis pin	16-3124
32	Cylinder	16-3576
33	Cylinder end cap	16-3560
34	Piston	16-3082
35	Piston head	16-3110
36	Piston head sealing ring	16-2285
37	Piston head buffer	16-2287
38	Piston head retaining circlip	16-3167
39	Piston head circlip washer	16-3113
40	Mainspring	16-3114
41	Mainspring guide tube	16-3117
42	Mainspring seating washer	16-3118
43	Mainspring retaining pin	16-3115
44	Trigger mechanism housing inc. 45 and 47	16-3078
45	Cocking lever support pin (3)	16-3134
46	Main sear	16-3084
47	Main sear guide	16-3133
48	Main sear spring	16-3141

ITEM	DESCRIPTION	COMP'T NO.
49	Main sear axis pin	16-3154
50	Trigger	16-3086
51	Trigger adjusting screw	16-3149
52	Trigger adjusting screw locking pin	16-3150
53	Trigger spring	63-1285
54	Trigger axis pin	16-3147
55	Intermediate sear	16-3152
56	Hammer	16-3153
57	Hammer axis pin	16-3154
58	Hammer spacer	16-3155
59	Hammer spring	16-3156
60	Safety catch shaft	16-3565
61	Safety catch spring	16-3162
62	Safety catch	16-3307
63	Safety catch screw	16-3306
64	Safety catch screw washer	16-3305
65	Trigger mechanism fixing screw (4)	16-3164
66	Stock	16-3336
67	Stock bridge	—
68	Stock rear fixing screw	16-3538
69	Stock rear fixing screw washer	16-3042
70	Stock main fixing screw	16-3134
71	Stock main fixing screw washer	16-3041
72	Cocking aid	16-3168

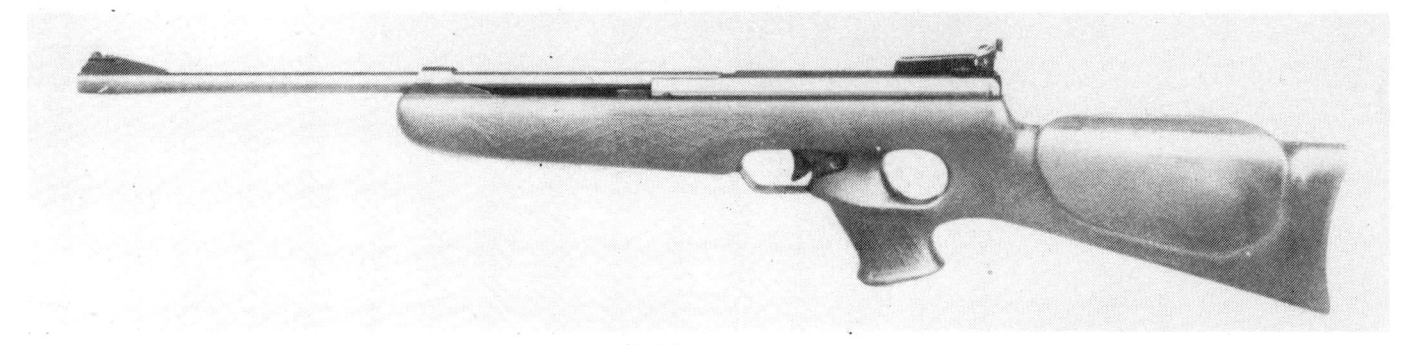

B.S.A. Buccaneer

MODEL Buccanneer.

MAKER B.S.A., Armoury Road, Birmingham B11 2PX.

DATE Introduced late 1977, and phased out of production during 1981, although old stock will have been advertised after this date. In years to come this model will be collectable — remember the Merlin.

VALUATION £40—£80. ($60—$120).

DETAILS Based on the Scorpion air pistol in that it has the same air chamber and trigger action. Measures 35 inches long with an 18½ inch rifled barrel. Brown one piece plastic moulded stock that makes left-handed use almost impossible. Air chamber grooved for telescopic sight and fitted with peep-sight at rear. Barrel blued as is the air chamber. Barrel stamped "B.S.A. GUNS LTD. ENGLAND .22 CAL." the triple rifle trademark appears between "ENGLAND" and the calibre. Serial number is stamped on the underside of the barrel breech. Unusual style of stock being a thumb-hole design. Advertised weight 6 lbs. There is also a specially designed telescopic sight for the above being the B.S.A. Mk. IX, 5x15. Advertised weight 6 lb. A review appears in "Airgun World" August 1981.

B.S.F. "Junior"

MODEL "Junior".

MAKER Bayer Sportswaffen Fabrik, West Germany. Imported by Norman May & Co., Bridlington, Humberside, England.

DATE Early 1950s to 1970s. Available in small numbers only.

VALUATION £30—£60, ($45—$90).

DETAILS Small sized air rifle for the lower end of the airgun market. 38 inches long with a 16¼ inch rifled barrel. Manufactured in .177 only. Foresight dovetail mounted with the largest hood I've ever seen. Rearsight fully adjustable. Side of barrel breech stamped "JUNIOR" with serial number on the underside. Double linked cocking lever. Air chamber has two circular rings cut around chamber and the B.S.F. trademark at the other end. "MADE IN GERMANY WEST" is stamped on the side of the air chamber. Trigger adjustment is at the rear of the air chamber. Wooden stock has butt plate and is stamped "SILE". Advertised weight 4 lbs 6 ozs.

B.S.F. air rifles were sold in America under the "BAVARIA" trade name and using a different trademark.

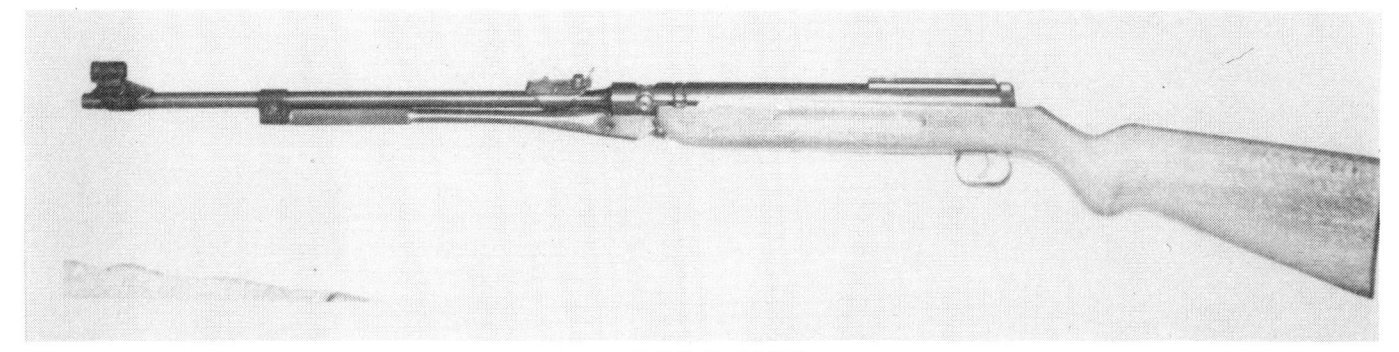

B.S.F. Model S54

MODEL S 54.

MAKER Bayer Sportswaffen — Fabrik, G.m.b.H., Erlangen, West Germany. Maker's name given as Hans Schutt in the 1970 catalogue of D. R. Hughes.

DATE Current model. Seen advertised as early as 1958.

VALUATION £120n—£130n, although have seen them priced at £140n and as low as £90n. Now quite rare £100—£200 ($150—$300).

DETAILS What an air rifle! As soon as you pick one up you know that this is different. 45½ inches long. Rather plain stock for the price. The metal work has a para-military look about it. The foresight, rearsight and catch for the underlever appear to be made from castings and then pinned on to the barrel. The rearsight is the largest I've ever seen fitted as standard on to an air rifle. The underlever and cocking arms are from heavy metal pressings. Underlever catch is the very distinctive tubular fastening. Stamped on top of air chamber is the circular B.S.F. trademark with an arrow through the "S" on the L.H.S. of the tap lever is stamped the model "S54 KAL 5.5" "MADE IN GERMANY" appears on the L.H.S. of the chamber with "WEST" printed after as though it's an after-thought. Serial number of above A5160, but has 5579 stamped on the underside of the barrel. Advertised weight 7 lb 6 ozs.

To remove the mainspring first undo the two stock screws and lift the action away from the stock. The chamber end plug should now be unscrewed. Now, believe it or not, unscrew the forward screw in the scope ramp and then gently tap the ramp towards the rear, you will notice that the trigger assembly will also travel rearwards and then stop as will the ramp. Now lift the ramp out and away from the chamber and then pull the trigger assembly out. The mainspring is held in place by the spring guide and stock bolt that is screwed into it. Taking up the spring tension the stock bolt plug should be unscrewed, it does NOT have a reserve thread. Assemble in reserve order.

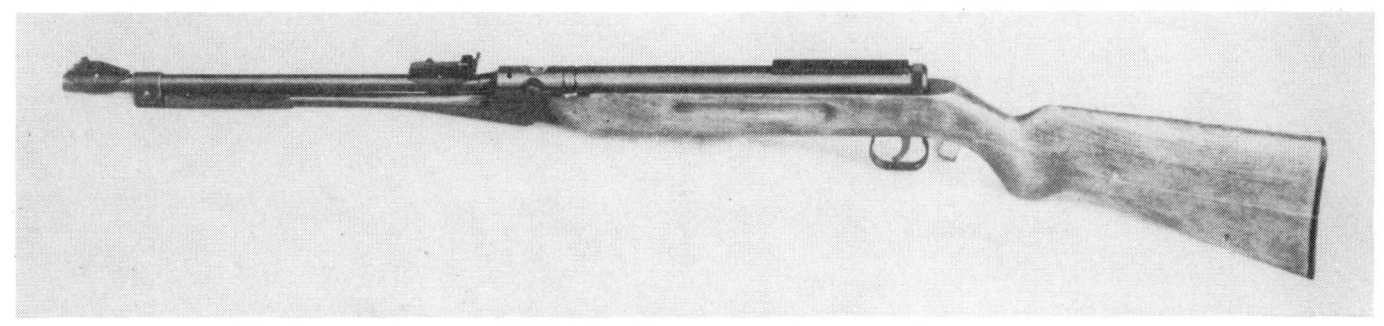

B.S.F. Model S54 with shortened barrel

B.S.F. Model 30

MODEL Bavaria Model 30.

MAKER Bayer Sportswaffen Fabrik (B.S.F.) G.m.b.H., Erlangen, West Germany. The name Bavaria was used for the American Market.

DATE Introduced very late 1950s or very early 1960s. Assume model was phased out in the middle 1960s.

VALUATION £30—£60. ($45—$90).

DETAILS A very small well made air rifle. 34 inches long with a 14½ inch rifled barrel available in .177 only. Blade foresight set in dovetail and rearsight adjustable for elevation only. Side of barrel breech stamped "BAVARIA 30" and serial number on the underside. Top of air chamber stamped with Bavaria trademark and "MADE IN GERMANY WEST" stamped on the side. Stock has no butt plate. "SILE" stamped on stock. Advertised accuracy ⅜ inch group at 25 feet. Trigger adjustment is at rear of air chamber. Advertised weight 3½ lbs. Advertised velocity 425 f.p.s.

"Sile" stamped on the stock indicates that the stock was made in Italy by Sile Spar, who made stocks for many airgun manufacturers including B.S.A. As with the B.S.F. airguns the A prefix indicates a .177 calibre, whereas .22 airguns had no prefix letter.

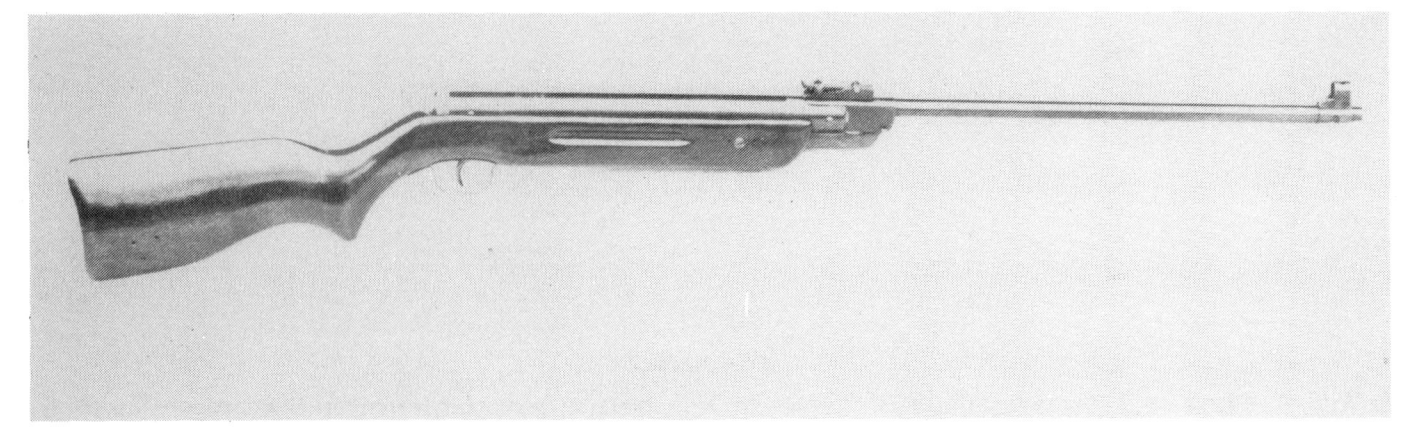

Chinese Air Rifle

MODEL "Hunter" or "Pioneer", Model 61, or under the "Arrows" trade name.

MAKER Manufactured in Shanghai, China.

DATE Introduced into Britain during the early 1970s and still a current model, although rarely advertised.

VALUATION £20—£30. ($30—$45).

DETAILS The small model to the .22 version. All metal with a stock which is rather short in length. .177 rifled barrel with pillar foresight and rearsight adjustable for elevation only. Top of air chamber bears the "ARROW" trademark along with Chinese writing and "MADE IN CHINA". Well varnished stock fitted with sling swivels. Stock length rather short. A very well made air rifle for the price. Trigger appears to be non-adjustable. 42¼ inches long with a 18¾ inch barrel. Advertised weight 7 lb. The Arrow used to be imported by Sussex Armoury. The air chamber is not fitted with a scope ramp. A review of the above appears in "Guns Review" April 1974.

Chinese school children being taught the art of shooting. Now we know why Chinese Air Rifles have such short stocks! (Courtesy of "American Rifleman" 1973).

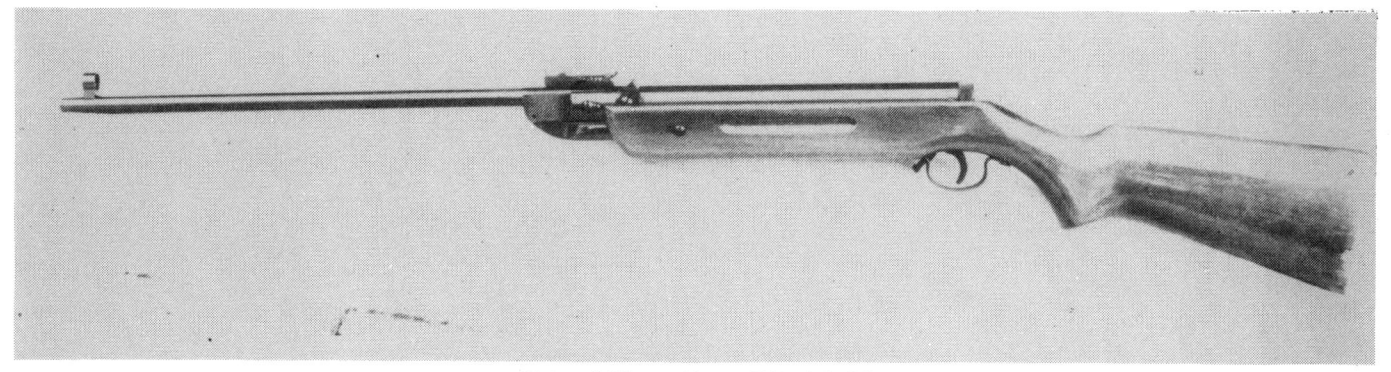

Chinese "Super-Hunter" Model 45-2

MODEL   Super Hunter or 45-2. Also called the Model 55, see "Guns review" April 1974.

MAKER   "Industry" Brand, Shanghia, China.

DATE   Appeared in Britain 1973 and still available in small numbers.

VALUATION   £20—£40. ($30—$60).

DETAILS   The deluxe version of the Hunter. 42¼ inches long with a 18¾ inch .177 rifled barrel. Dovetail mounted foresight with hood. Very solid ramp type rearsight calibrated from 10 to 35 yards. Barrel lock lever on side of breech that is pushed forward to release the barrel. Air chamber stamped with "I" in a diamond shape which is the trademark for "Industry" brand, also Chinese writing and "MODEL" 45-2". Many parts interchange with the Hunter or Arrow air rifle. Trigger adjustment by way of screw through trigger guard. Nice full length stock unlike the tiny stock fitted to the Arrow. What appears to be a date stamp is on the butt. The swivel sling attachments are fixed to the stock. Available in either .22 or 177 rifled. Advertised weight 6 lb 4 oz. The model 55 referred to the calibre of .22 (5.5 mm). When removing the stock note that the R.H. fore-end stock screw is under the swivel sling bracket and this has to be removed first of all.

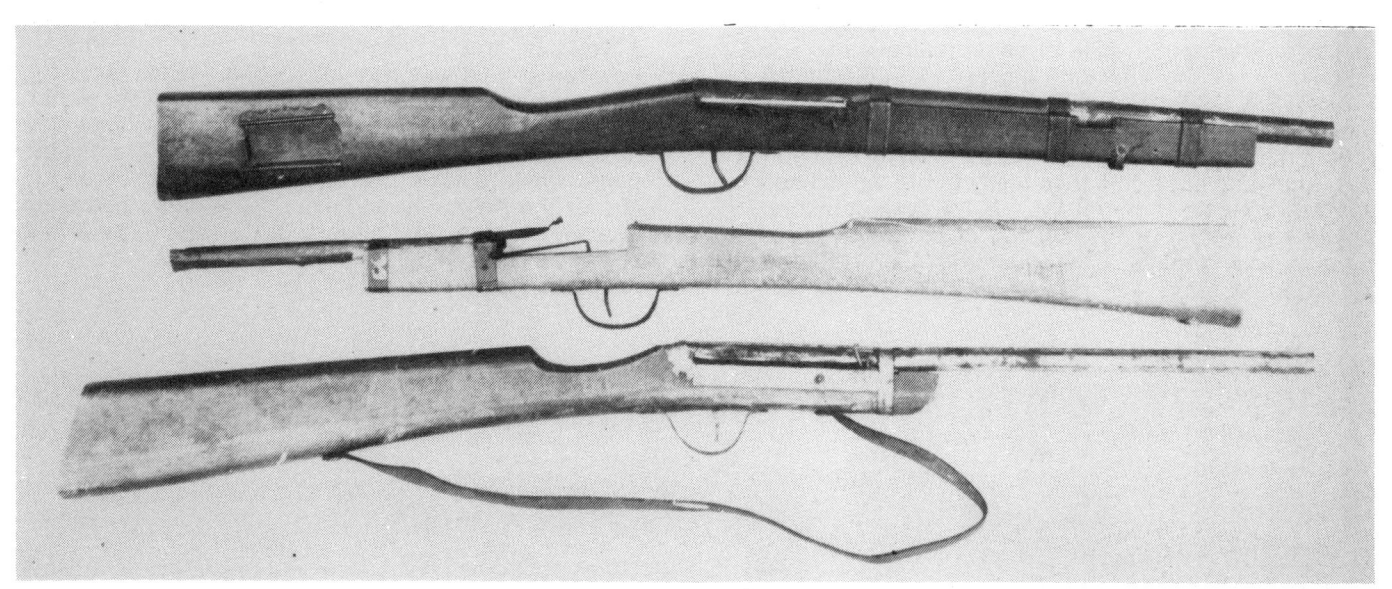

Three Clay-Ball Air Rifles. Bottom one is a double barrel Ball Gum.

MODEL   A clay ball air rifle.

MAKER   Could be of German origin. Advertised in German "Alfa" Catalogue.

DATE   From around 1908 to middle 1930s. Towards the 1930s these changed from clay ball to tethered cork guns.

VALUATION   £20—£40. ($30—$60).

DETAILS   Small light weight tinplate air rifle of child's proportions. 25¾ inches long with a 5⅝ inch tinplate rolled barrel. The barrel rotates within the barrel band and has a 1.5 cm hole through which clay balls are introduced into the barrel, before firing the barrel is rotated so that the hole is covered by the stock, thus effecting an air seal. There was a small handle soldered on the side of the barrel but this has since come off. Barrel bore is 1.5 cm and smoothbore! The other two bands hold the air chamber in place as well as an extension that is nailed into the stock. All metal parts are very thin and can easily be distorted with finger pressure. The action is cocked by pulling back the pull-bolt until it connects with the simple twin bent wire sear and single bent wire trigger. Now for the crunch, the main spring is that powerful that many a father would have spent a happy Christmas pulling his guts out on this small air rifle as it is well beyond the capabilities of a minor to accomplish. The mainspring cannot be replaced as to remove all the nails and tinplate ironwear would destroy the airgun. The stock has a very neat patchbox for storing clay balls with a sliding lid. Even tinplate sling swivels are fitted. The above was also sold for firing darts. From the catalogue they appear to have been sold by the dozen, twelve in old language. The above style of clay ball and cork gun were made in the following lengths, 38, 48, 53, 58, 65, 70, 78, and 80 cms long. They were nearly all sold complete with either a canvas or oil cloth sling and a tethered cork. Some even had nickel plated barrels. The above description applies to the top example illustrated.

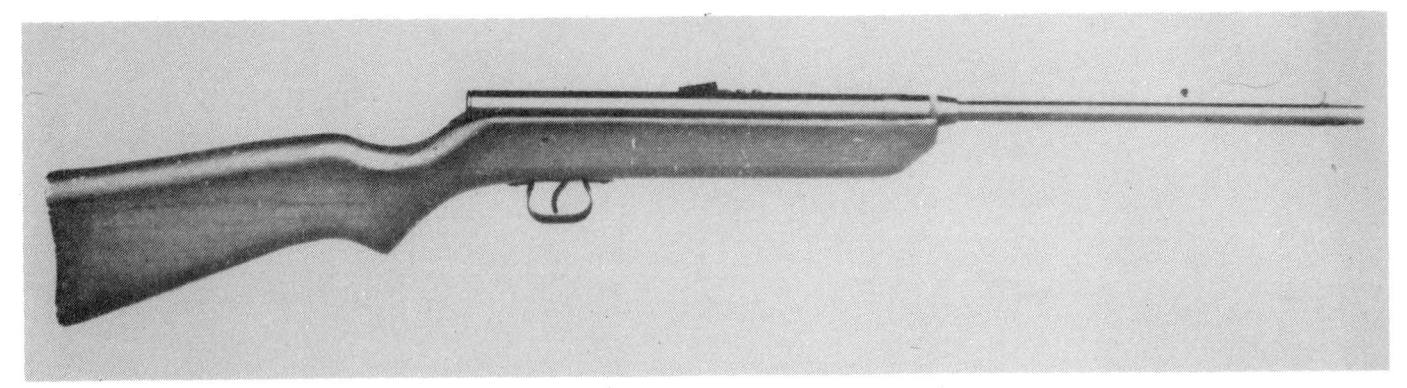

Crosman Model V-350 Pump Action BB Repeater

MODEL V-350.

MAKER Crosman Arms (Canada) Ltd., Dunnville, Ontario. Towards end of 1960s address had become Crosman Arms Co. Inc., Fairport, N.Y. Made in U.S.A.

DATE Introduced 1961 and ceased production 1970. Total production amounted to 263,546.

VALUATION £30—£60 ($45—$90).

DETAILS Measures 35 inches long. Serial number not visible. Rather tall foresight, rearsight has slider adjustment for elevation and pivot arrangement for windage. Stamped on side of barrel is above maker's address and on the other side appears; "V — 350 SLIDE — ACTION, B-B AIR RIFLE PAT. PENDING". To operate you fill magazine with BBs and holding air rifle upright push in barrel then pull forward until you hear engaging click, it is then ready to fire. Advertised as 22 shot repeater. Barrel 16 inches and smoothbore. Advertised weight 3½ lbs. On top of air chamber are three holes. Purpose as follows from barrel to rear of chamber; Hole one: for loading BBs these are dropped in one by one. Hole two appears to be inspection hole to ascertain if magazine contains any BBs, this appears just in front of rearsight. Last hole is for lubrication of spring and when cocked, the piston. To empty magazine it helps to cock the action and pull forward the barrel, until the barrel almost clicks into firing position, it is then possible to see the lip on the end of the magazine, then turn air rifle upside down and shake BBs into your hand as it is held over the loading hole. The above was the first BB airgun manufactured by Crosman. In 1969 the above was restyled to form the Model 3500, improvements being Monte Carlo stock, hooded foresight, redesigned rearsight, and alterations to trigger and feed mechanisms. Was still being advertised in 1974 and an optional scope and mount was then available. Advertised muzzle velocity 350 f.p.s. Could this be how the air rifle was named? "V-350". When removing the stock care should be taken not to loose the spring loaded ball bearing which rests against the underside of the action. There is no need to remove the trigger guard when removing action from stock. Towards the end of the 1960s the address on the barrel had been changed to that in Fairport, N.Y., also there might appear a date stamp on the top of the barrel, for example "KB.3.69".

Crosman M-1 Carbine

MODEL M-1 Carbine.

MAKER Crosman Arms Co. Inc., Fairport, N.Y., U.S.A. Imported by the Sussex Armoury, 34 North Street, Hailsham, Sussex BN27 1BR.

DATE Appeared in the early 1970s.

VALUATION £30—£60 ($45—$90).

DETAILS Similar action as the Crosman V-350. Could be a follow on design. 35½ inches long. Push-in barrel action to cock and load, then pull barrel out to be ready to fire. Very neat looking "fun" gun. Stamped on R.H.S. of barrel the above maker's name and on the L.H.S. "M-1 CARBINE B-B AIR RIFLE". To load BBs pull back the breech sliding lever and pour BBs into the first hole on top of barrel through the upper plastic casing. On the above 22 BBs could be inserted. The second hole appears to be an oiling hole, but unfortunately is about the same size as a BB pellet so if one falls down by mistake it will block the oil-way and should be removed. The magazine can be removed by pushing up, then forwards, this holds spare BBs and has a sliding lid. Rearsight is adjustable for windage and elevation. Serial number stamped on R.H.S. of rearsight housing. Advertised capacity of carrying magazine 270. Strong plastic one piece full length stock with separate upper barrel protector. Advertised weight 5 lbs.

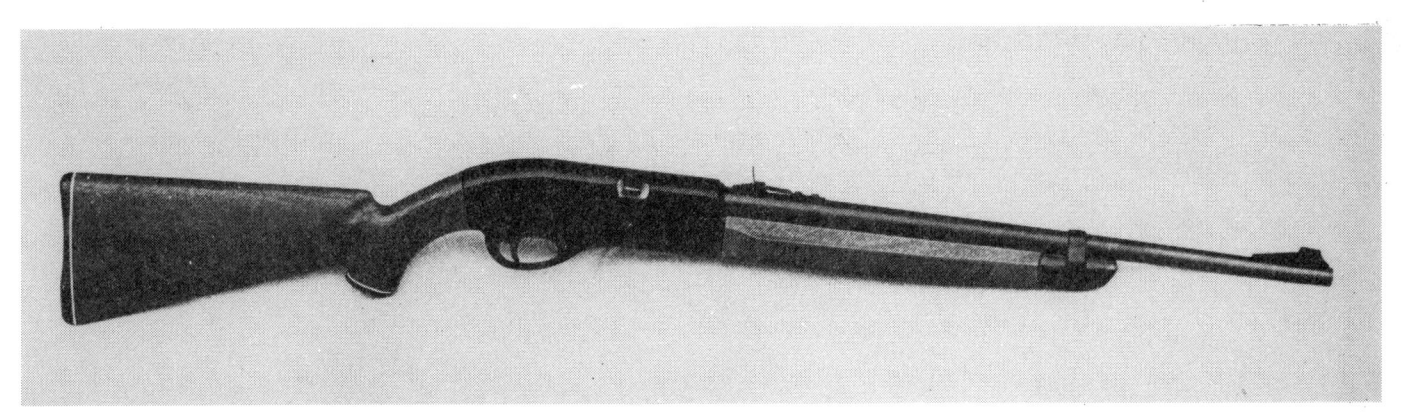

Crosman 766

MODEL 766.

MAKER Crosman Arms, 980 Turk Hill Road, Fairport, New York, U.S.A. and imported by Sussex Armoury, Sturton Place, Station Road, Hailsham, Sussex.

DATE Current model.

VALUATION £25—£50 ($38—$75).

DETAILS 38¾ inches long. Extensive use of plastics for stocks, and action parts. Black action, barrel, butt plate and pistol grip plate, with wood coloured stock and fore-end. Serial number of above 278036422, must be the longest that I have ever seen on an airgun. This is stamped on the R.H.S. of the action. For ease of use do not oil the BB repeater action as this tends to slow or impede the flow of BBs through the action. The loading of pellets can be a bit awkward at times. Advertised weight 4 lb 10 oz. For further details see "AIRGUN WORLD" January 1978. Advertised velocities for ten pumps BB/Pellets, 710/665. The butt reservoir holds 100 BBs and the magazine in the action holds 15 BBs. Advertised as having a limit of ten pumps only. The barrel is a rifled steel tube measuring 523 mm long, almost 21 inches in length. For a review of above see "Guns Review" October 1976.

An article on the Crosman 766 appears in "Shooting Magazine" February 1977 and deals with the practice for clay pigeon shooting using the Crosman air rifle with all sights removed. A similar application to the Daisy "Quick Kill" method of shooting, again using the BB type airgun. An American instruction leaflet for the Crosman 766 indicates that the BBs can be fed straight from the butt reservoir into the BB feed tube, this being the "visual magazine". To operate pull BB follower stem back and locate stem into the holding slot provided. Gripping rifle at the small of the butt, as you would to fire, point muzzle of air rifle straight down and twist hand in semi circular movement. Fifteen BBs will automatically feed from the reservoir into the visual magazine. Release follower from holding slot and gun is ready to fire, when pumped etc. The hand twisting motion appears to be the same as doing the "twist" with the gun held in a downward position. A choice of music may help in the above operation. To unload BBs from the rifle make sure the action is on SAFE, grip gun at small of stock, as above, hold rifle in upward position, and pull back the BB follower until it is located into the holding slot, then "let's twist again" with the gun, BBs should now roll back into the reservoir, continue twisting until all the BBs have left the visual magazine. The follower is now released to prevent BBs rolling back into the visual magazine. An article dealing with the stripping of the action appears in "Airgun World" July 1981. Advertised weight 5 lbs. The following muzzle velocities were also advertised:

Pellet	3 Pumps	6 Pumps	10 Pumps
BB	450	587	710 f.p.s.
.177	428	567	637 f.p.s.

During the late 1970s a streamline design appeared with no lettering at all on the sides of the action. Only the barrel bore the maker's name and address with the calibre. This style also had a simplified all plastic rearsight. A more direct way of loading the BBs into the spring tube magazine is to pull back the plunger, turn air rifle over and hold slightly pointing downward and then pat the stock butt plate as though you are winding a baby, or by thrashing it if BBs are stubborn!

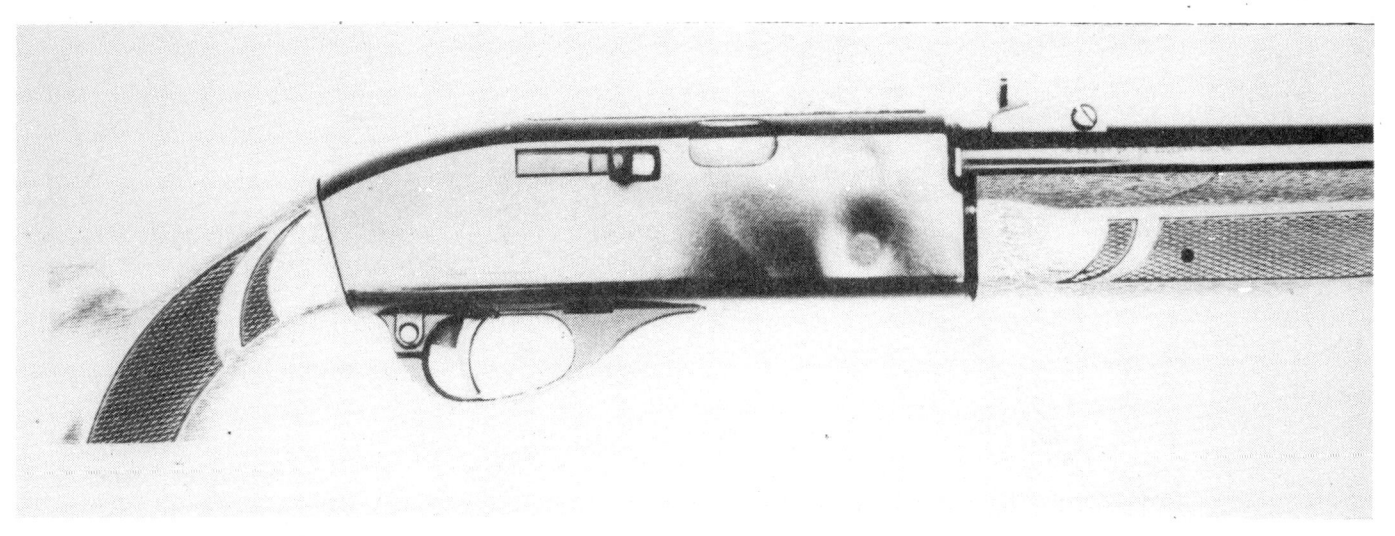

Crosman 766, later style with plain action and improver rearsight.

Fig. 1 Before July 1975 Series

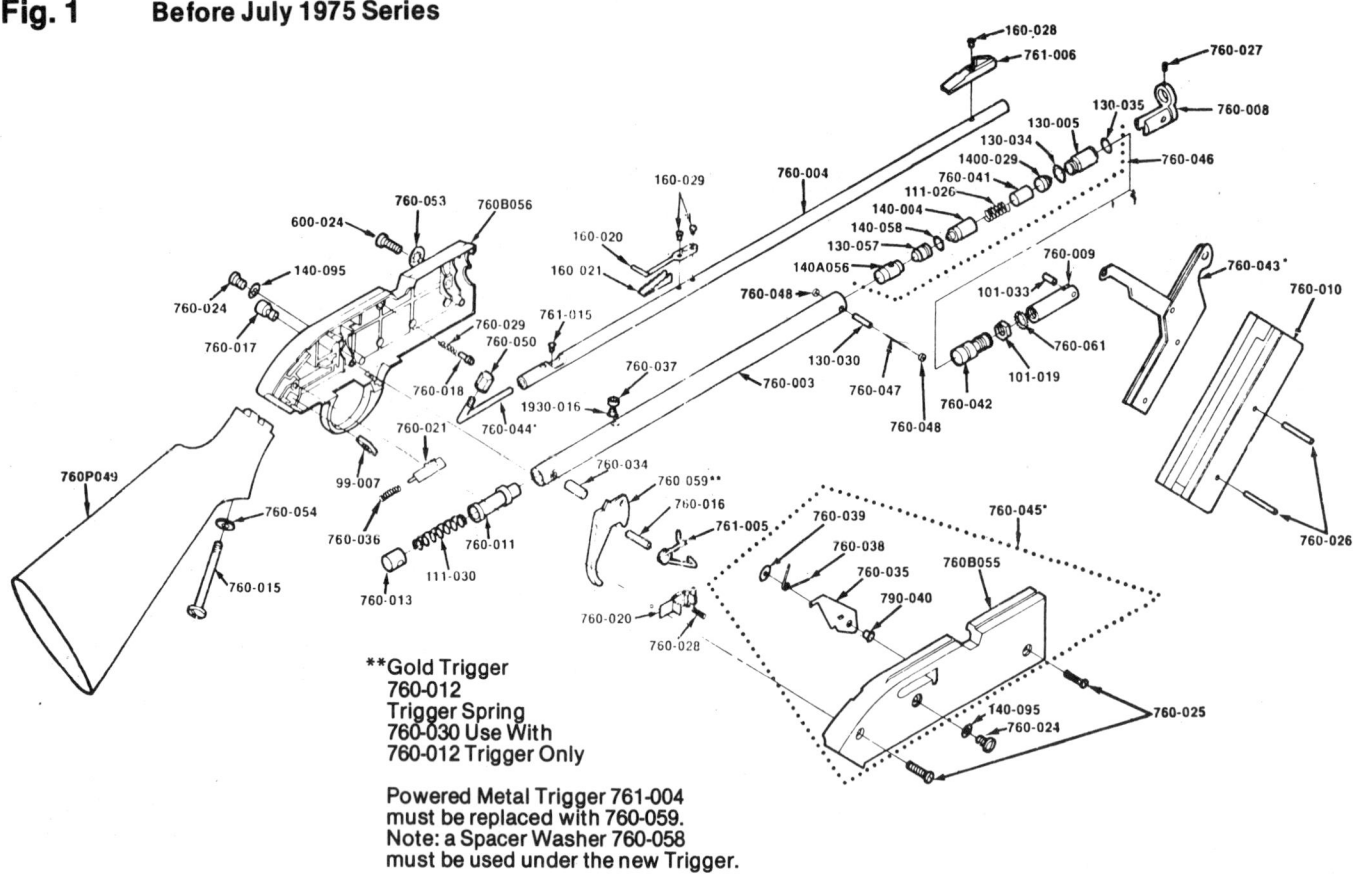

Gold Trigger 760-012 Trigger Spring 760-030 Use With 760-012 Trigger Only

Powered Metal Trigger 761-004 must be replaced with 760-059. Note: a Spacer Washer 760-058 must be used under the new Trigger.

* Factory Assembly Only

Fig. 2 After July 1975 Series

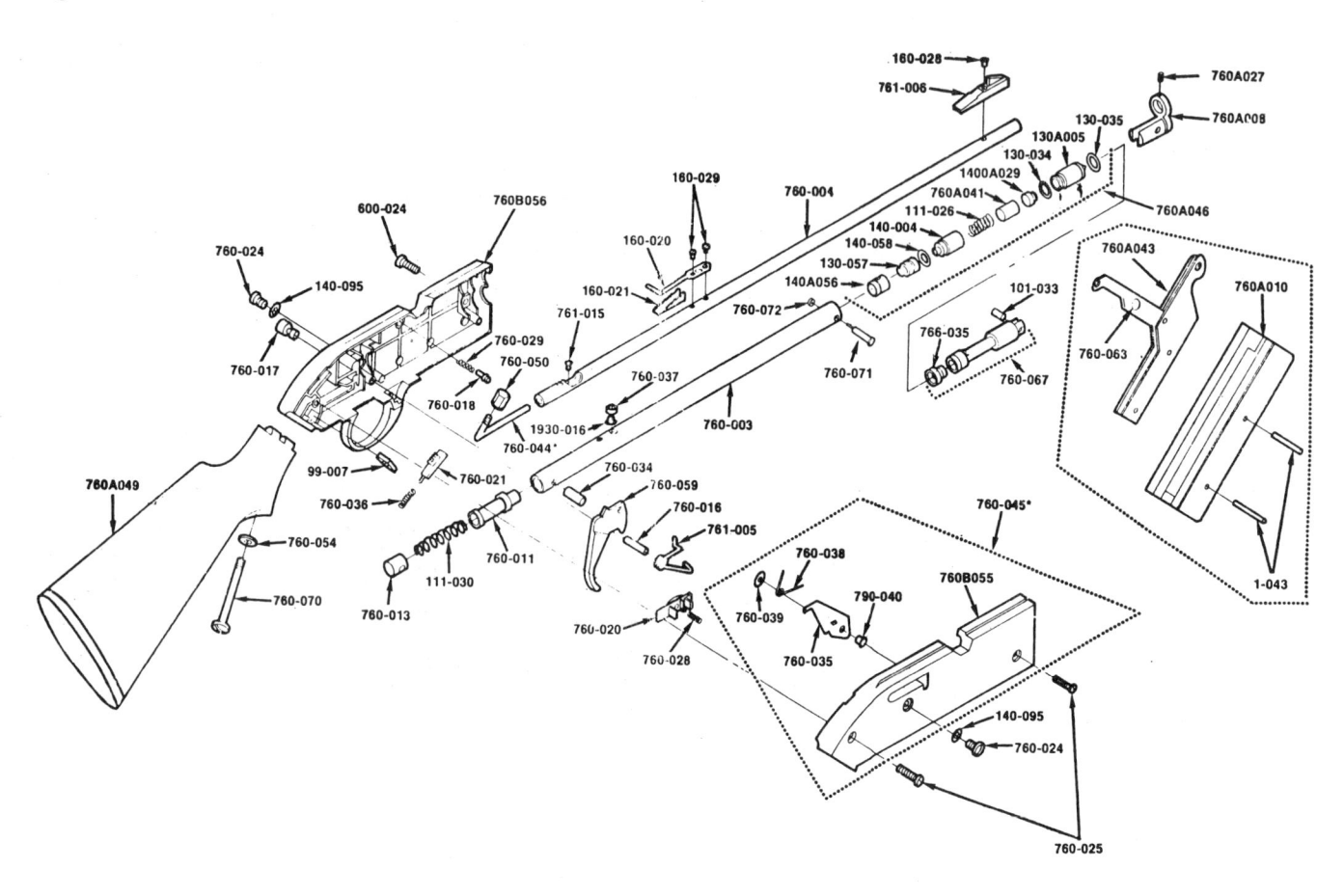

* Factory Assembly Only

Model 760 Assemblies and Parts List

PART NO.	QTY.	DESCRIPTION	FIG.NO.	PRICE
1-043	2	Forearm Pins	1	.10
99-007	1	Nut	1 & 2	.10
101-019	1	Lock Nut	1 & 2	.10
101-033	1	Plunger Guide Pin	1 & 2	.15
111-026	1	Check Valve Spring	1 & 2	.30
111-030	1	Sear Spring	1 & 2	.10
130-005	1	Check Valve Body	1	1.65
130A005	1	Check Valve Body	2	1.65
130-030	1	Pivot Pin		.10
130-034	1	O Ring	1 & 2	.10
130-035	1	O Ring	1 & 2	.10
130-057	1	Valve Cap	1 & 2	1.15
130-059	1	Piston Assembly (Use 760-042)	1 & 2	N/A
140-004	1	Exhaust Valve Body	1 & 2	1.20
140A056	1	Exhaust Valve Ring	1 & 2	.50
140-058	1	O Ring	1 & 2	.10
140-095	2	Lock Washer	1 & 2	.10
160-020	1	Rear Sight	1 & 2	.20
160-021	1	Elevator	1 & 2	.10
160-028	1	Front Sight Screw	1 & 2	.10
160-029	2	Rear Sight Screw	1 & 2	.10
600-024	1	Screw	1 & 2	.10
760-003	1	Pump Tube	1 & 2	3.45
760-004	1	Barrel	1 & 2	7.00
760-008	1	Front Barrel Guide	1 & 2	1.00
760A008	1	Front Barrel Guide	2	1.15
760-009	1	Pump Guide		.85
760-010	1	Wood Forearm	1	1.55
760A010	1	Plastic Forearm		1.55
760-011	1	Sear Block	2	.55
760-012	1	Gold Trigger (See Exploded View)	1 & 2	.60
760-013	1	Sear Block Stop	1 & 2	.30
760-015	1	Stock Screw (Use w/760P049)	1 & 2	.30
760-016	1	Trigger Pivot Pin	1 & 2	.10
760-017	1	Safety	1 & 2	.20
760-018	1	B.B. Detent	1 & 2	.10
760-020	1	B.B. Port Cover	1 & 2	.30
760-021	1	B.B. Retainer	1 & 2	.20
760-024	2	Clamping Screw	1 & 2	.10
760-025	2	Receiver Screw	1 & 2	.10
760-026	2	Forearm Pin	1	.10
760-027	1	Barrel Set Screw #8		.10
760A027	1	Barrel Set Screw #10	2	.10
760-028	1	Cover Spring	1 & 2	.10
760-029	1	Detent Spring	1 & 2	.10

PART NO.	QTY.	DESCRIPTION	FIG.NO.	PRICE
760-030	1	Trigger Spring	1	.40
760-034	1	Cross Pin	1 & 2	.45
760-035	1	Bolt Latch	1 & 2	.20
760-036	1	B.B. Retainer Spring	1 & 2	.10
760-037	1	Breech Gasket	1 & 2	.10
760-038	1	Bolt Latch Spring	1 & 2	.10
760-039	1	Spring Nut	1 & 2	.10
760-040	1	Pivot Pin	1	.30
760-041	1	Valve Spacer		.30
760A041	1	Valve Spacer	2	1.65
760-042	1	Piston Assembly	1	2.25
760A043	1	Lever and Link Assembly	2	2.40
760-043	1	Lever and Link Assembly	1 & 2	2.10
760-044	1	Breech Bolt Assembly	1 & 2	6.60
760-045	1	R.H. Receiver Assembly	1 & 2	6.00
760-046	1	Exhaust Valve Assembly	1	6.00
760A046	1	Exhaust Valve Assembly	2	.10
760-047	1	Pin	1	.10
760-048	2	Cap	1	7.00
760A049	1	Stock	1 & 2	N/A
760P049	1	Stock (Use 760A049 and 760-070)		.20
760-050	1	Bolt Knob	1 & 2	.10
760-053	1	Lock Washer	1 & 2	.10
760-054	1	Lock Washer	1 & 2	5.95
760B055	1	R.H. Receiver	1 & 2	4.50
760B056	1	L.H. Receiver	1 & 2	.10
760-058	1	Spacer Washer	1	1.05
760-059	1	Trigger	1	.10
760-061	1	Lock Washer		.10
760-063	1	Detent Plug	2	.10
760-067	1	Piston and Cup Assembly	2	2.90
760-070	1	Stock Screw (Use w/760A049)	2	.30
760-071	1	Pivot Pin	2	.45
760-072	1	Pivot Pin Retainer	2	.10
761-004	1	Trigger (Use 760-058 & 760-059)		N/A
761-005	1	Trigger Spring	1 & 2	.40
761-006	1	Front Sight	1 & 2	.20
761-015	1	Barrel Screw	1 & 2	.10
766-035	1	Pump Cup	2	.45
1400-029	2	Check Valve	1	.40
1400A029	1	Check Valve	2	.40
1930-016	1	Breech Gasket Sleeve	1 & 2	.10
3376-003	1	L.H. Receiver — Western Auto Model Only		4.50
3376-035	1	Western Auto Model Stock		7.50
		Exploded View and Parts List (E.V.P.)		1.50

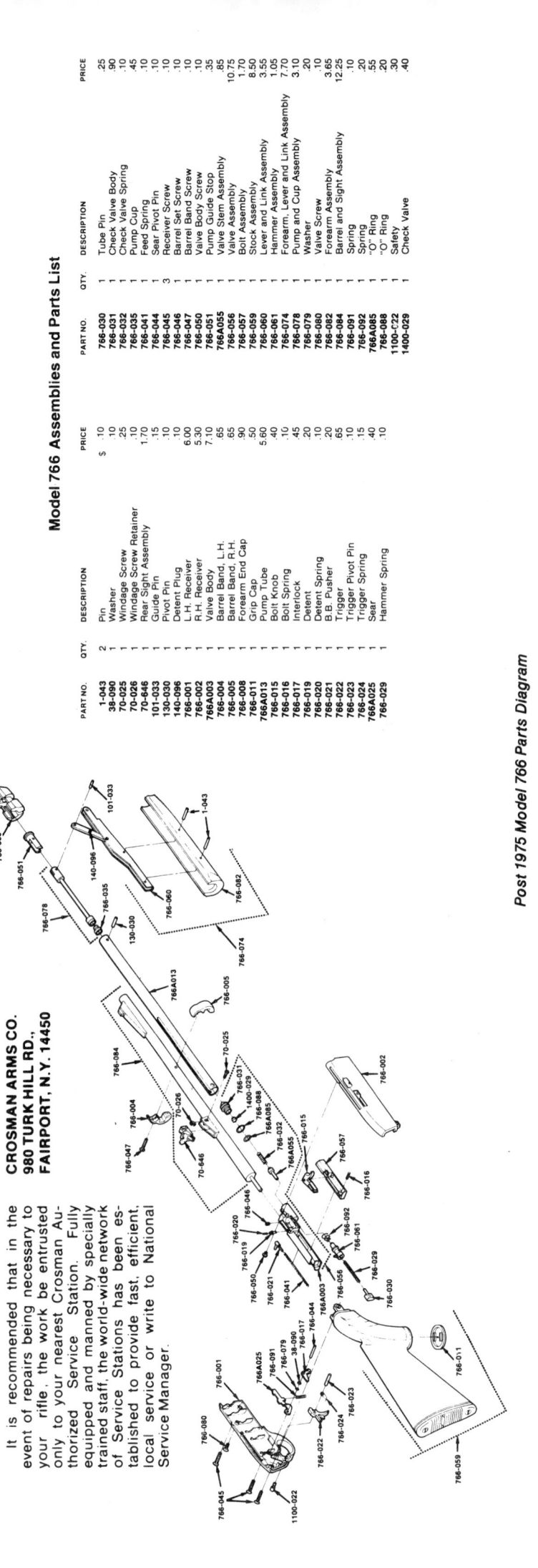

REPAIR SERVICE

It is recommended that in the event of repairs being necessary to your rifle, the work be entrusted only to your nearest Crosman Authorized Service Station. Fully equipped and manned by specially trained staff, the world-wide network of Service Stations has been established to provide fast, efficient, local service or write to National Service Manager.

CROSMAN ARMS CO.
980 TURK HILL RD.,
FAIRPORT, N.Y. 14450

Post 1975 Model 766 Parts Diagram

Model 766 Assemblies and Parts List

PART NO.	QTY.	DESCRIPTION	PRICE
1-043	2	Pin	$ .10
38-090	1	Washer	.10
70-025	1	Windage Screw	.25
70-026	1	Windage Screw Retainer	.10
70-646	1	Rear Sight Assembly	1.70
101-033	1	Guide Pin	.15
130-030	1	Pivot Pin	.10
140-096	1	Detent Plug	.10
766-001	1	L.H. Receiver	6.00
766-002	1	R.H. Receiver	5.30
766A003	1	Valve Body	7.10
766-004	1	Barrel Band, L.H.	.65
766-005	1	Barrel Band, R.H.	.65
766-008	1	Forearm End Cap	.90
766-011	1	Grip Cap	.50
766A013	1	Pump Tube	5.60
766-015	1	Bolt Knob	.40
766-016	1	Bolt Spring	.10
766-017	1	Interlock	.45
766-019	1	Detent	.20
766-020	1	Detent Spring	.10
766-021	1	B.B. Pusher	.20
766-022	1	Trigger	.65
766-023	1	Trigger Pivot Pin	.10
766-024	1	Trigger Spring	.15
766A025	1	Sear	.40
766-029	1	Hammer Spring	.10
766-030	1	Tube Pin	.25
766-031	1	Check Valve Body	.90
766-032	1	Check Valve Spring	.10
766-035	1	Pump Cup	.45
766-041	1	Feed Spring	.10
766-044	1	Sear Pivot Pin	.10
766-045	3	Receiver Screw	.10
766-046	1	Barrel Band Screw	.10
766-047	1	Valve Body Screw	.10
766-051	1	Pump Guide Stop	.35
766A055	1	Valve Stem Assembly	.85
766-056	1	Valve Assembly	10.75
766-057	1	Bolt Assembly	1.70
766-059	1	Stock Assembly	8.50
766-060	1	Lever and Link Assembly	3.55
766-061	1	Hammer Assembly	1.05
766-074	1	Forearm, Lever and Link Assembly	7.70
766-078	1	Pump and Cup Assembly	3.10
766-079	1	Washer	.20
766-080	1	Valve Screw	.10
766-082	1	Forearm Assembly	3.65
766-084	1	Barrel and Sight Assembly	12.25
766-091	1	Spring	.10
766-092	1	Spring	.20
766A085	1	"O" Ring	.55
766-088	1	"O" Ring	.20
1100-022	1	Safety	.30
1400-029	1	Check Valve	.40

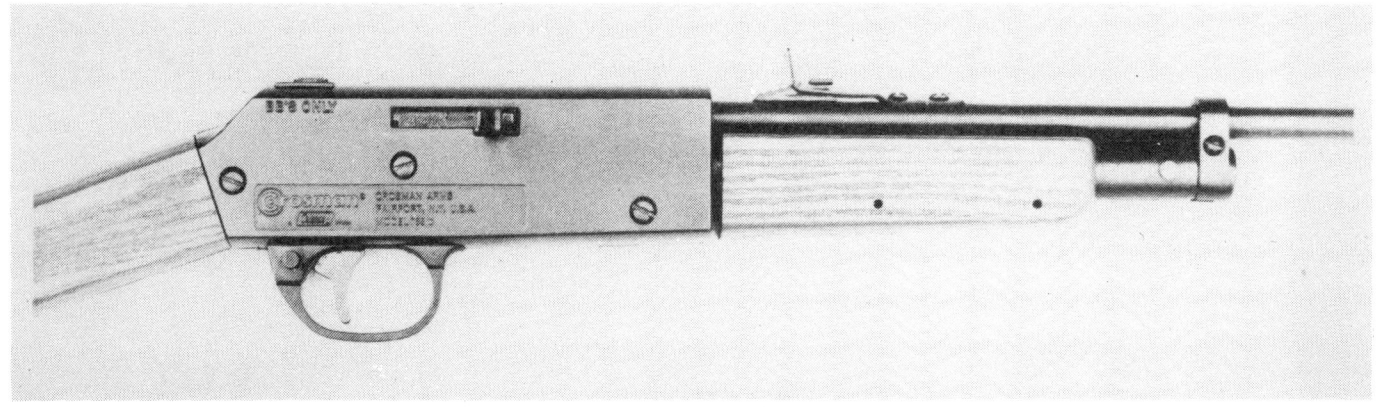

Crosman Model 788

MODEL 788. The BB Scout.

MAKER Crosman Arms Corporation, Fairport, New York 14450, U.S.A.

DATE Introduced 1978.

VALUATION £10—£25. ($15—$37.5).

DETAILS The junior model to the 766. A very nice little air rifle for the youngster. 30½ inches long with a 13¼ inch barrel. Fires BBs only and works on the same action as the larger Model 766. Solidly made with die cast action, steel barrel and plastic wood simulated stock. BBs are loaded through a slot in the top of the action with a sliding cover plate. A gap running along the top allows contents of magazine to be seen. Action is gravity fed and BBs are push fed into the barrel every time the bolt is drawn back and then pushed forward. Fixed foresight and fully adjustable rearsight. Advertised velocities for BBs only:

    3 pumps   330 f.p.s.
    6 pumps   437 f.p.s.
    10 pumps 470 f.p.s.

Magazine holds about 20 BBs. Advertised weight 2 lbs 3 oz. Barrel is smoothbore and action is not fitted with telescopic sight ramp. The 788 is not available in this country. Trigger guard is fitted with a manual push in/out safety button. The action is regulated to accept ten pumps and any more will only overstrain the action and cause a second shot without any further pumping and this *will* damage the airgun. When working the bolt the airgun must be held in a downward position. There is also the danger that over zealous pumping can over-heat the action and even burn valve faces.

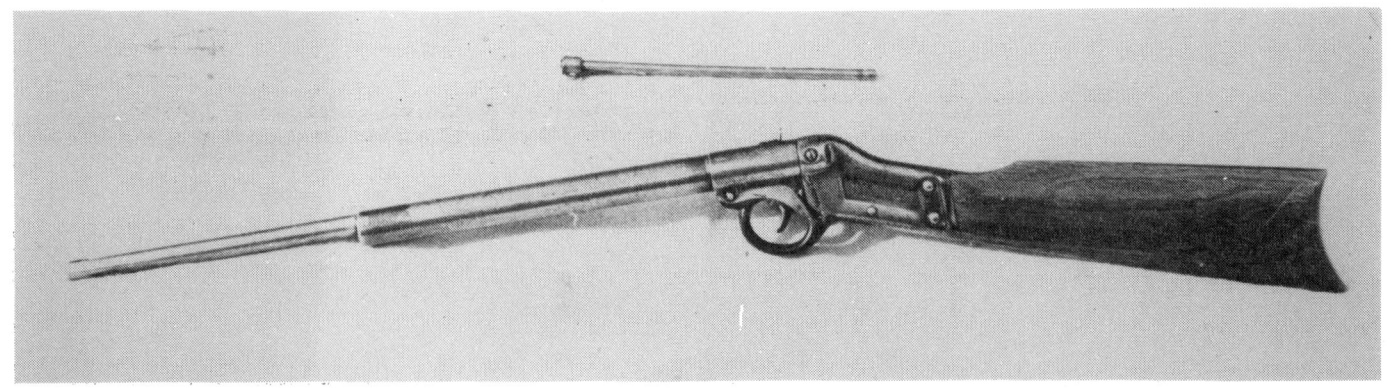

"1901" Patent Daisy

MODEL   Daisy Twentieth Century Single Shot.

MAKER   Daisy, Plymouth, Michigan, U.S.A.

DATE   From 1901 to 1908.

VALUATION £15—£40. ($23—$60).

DETAILS   Tin plate with wooden butt. Rear non-adjustable peepsight. Removable brass barrel to load. On side of trigger plate next to butt is printed "DAISY" and on other side "PATENTED AUG.13.1889—JUL.14.1891. JAN.21.1892—MAR.26.1901. JUL.30.1901 — OCT.1.1901. THE DAISY MFG. CO. PLYMOUTH, MICH. U.S.A. 30 inches long. Was also available in repeater form. Some were stamped with an oval trademark on the butt and had a well shaped stock whilst later models were not stamped and had a plainer parallel side stock.

To give you some idea of how thin the metal is on the above some have been seen where the chamber has a "ring" bulge where the leather washer has struck the end of the air chamber and pushed outwards and thus formed a faint ring around the outside. This should not affect performance.

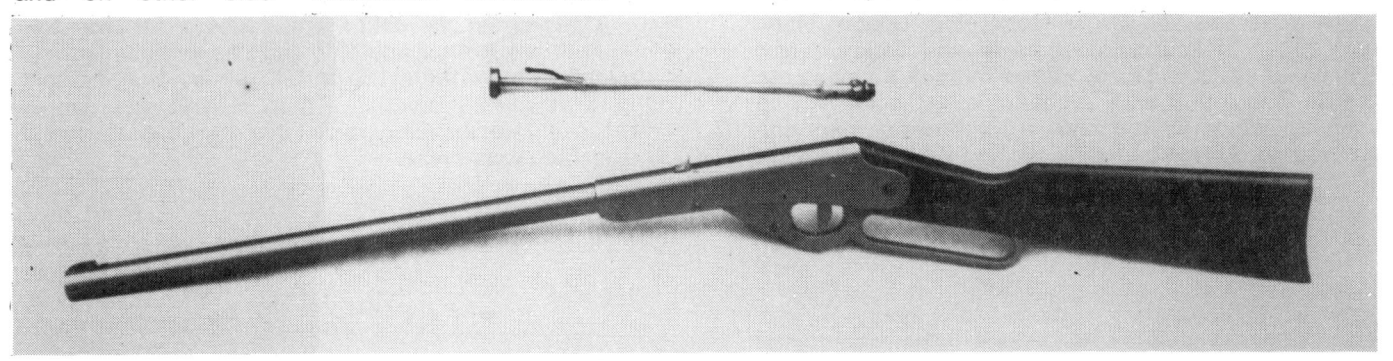

Daisy Model B-1000 shot repeater

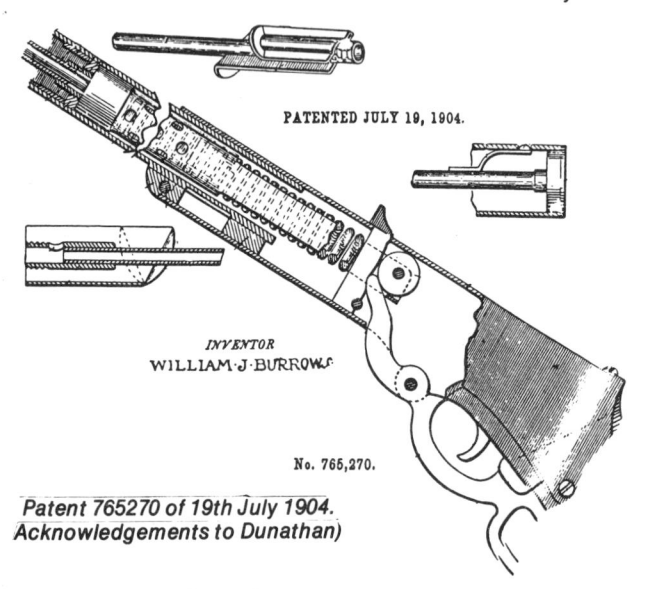

Patent 765270 of 19th July 1904. (Acknowledgements to Dunathan)

MODEL   B 1000 Shot Repeater.

MAKER   Daisy Manufacturing Company, Plymouth, Michigan, U.S.A.

DATE   1905 to 1915.

VALUATION £20—£40. ($30—$60).

DETAILS   Tinplate underlever cocking 1000 shot BB repeater. 35½ inches long (90 cms). Fixed foresight and rearsight, although the rearsight looks as though it could be dovetail mounted. The barrel unscrews for lubricating the air chamber, but to load just rotate the knurled front of barrel, this opens a small hole just behind the foresight, now pour in 1000 BBs and turn barrel to close up the hole. Top of air chamber stamped "1000 SHOT DAISY MODEL B — DAISY MFG, CO., PLYMOUTH, MICH., U.S.A., PAT. OCT.1.1901—JULY.19.1904". The first patent was by F. F. Bennett whose original patent granted in March, 26th, 1901 was for the Daisy Twentieth Century Model and applied to the difficulty in soldering the cast iron trigger housing to the sheet metal action, this very soon changed to tinplate and one would assume that this later patent in October of the same year applied to this change. The second patent, number 765270 invented by William J. Burrows appears to cover two aspects of the Model B, first the barrel tube with a multishot capability and the second being a protruding tongue on the cocking lever that engaged with a rotating bearing on the end of the piston rod for pulling back the piston when the cocking lever is pulled down. The cocking lever and rearsight are cast iron. The Model B was sold nickel plated although for a short time a black nickel finish was supplied by a part-time worker at Daisy. The black nickel was applied to the original plating and produced a very high lustre finish, but was easily scratched. To find one of these in excellent condition is indeed a rarity. The Model B had a walnut stock with a metal butt plate. The two side screws that fix the action to the stock are off centre to each other so that they can both enjoy the full thickness of the thin stock for strength. This design forethought may be common to most Daisy air rifles with wooden stocks.

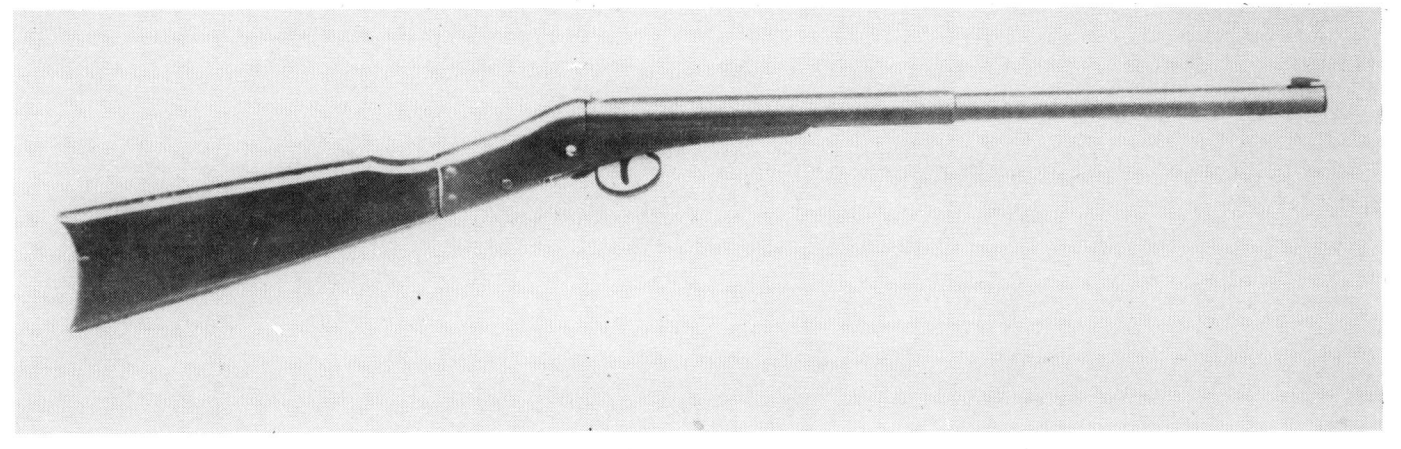

Daisy Model C, 1912 to 1914

Daisy Model C action with barrel removed. Note how trigger action forms cocking lever

MODEL C.

MAKER Daisy Manufacturing Company, Plymouth, Michigan, U.S.A., until 30th April 1958 when the firm moved to Rogers, Arkansas, U.S.A.

DATE From 1912 and manufactured for a short period only, up until 1914.

VALUATION Although rare they still only fetch between £20 and £40 only. ($30—$60).

DETAILS Described by Dunathan as being "very scarce". A single shot break action air rifle, although a 350 shot repeater was also available. Most unusual design in that the trigger guard and block act as the cocking lever, the mainspring rests against the trigger block and when the action is broken the trigger housing forces the mainspring forward until the trigger sear engages with the piston rod, on the return stroke the piston with the mainspring under tension is then drawn back to the rear of the air chamber with the action cocked all the time. The action can be released from the cocked state at either end of the air chamber. A very novel way of cocking an airgun. The above example was too pitted to read any lettering on the air chamber. Appears to have been sold nickel plated with either walnut or oak stocks. Being a single shot the barrel is a bayonet fit and needs to be removed for loading the BB, or has been suggested that you "spit" the BB down the barrel. The bayonet fitting also acted as the foresight and the rearsight was a non-adjustable peephole. Top of action marked "DAISY SINGLE SHOT MODEL C" and "DAISY" with bulls-eyes were featured on the side of the action. Other variations may have "DAISY SINGLE — MODEL C. DAISY MFG. CO., PLYMOUTH, MICH., U.S.A. U.S. PAT., SEPT.1-08-NOV.3-08, FRANCE FEB.8-08, GREAT BRITAIN FEB.8-08, GERMANY FEB.14-08, OTHERS PENDING". The patent for 3rd November 1908, number 903.092 was by Edward C. Hough, an employee of the Daisy Company and this was for the barrel with the bayonet fitting and the spring loaded rotating foresight that engaged with the bayonet lugs in the outer air chamber casing.

The British patent of the 8th February 1908 is number 2882 and refers to the action of cocking in which the piston is drawn back after the mainspring has been compressed. So when the airgun is broken for cocking first the mainspring is compressed against the piston and then both piston and mainspring are drawn back down the air chamber into the ready to fire position. The patent is featured in "Guns Review" January 1979. The actual action differs to the patent in that the trigger and sear is attached to the trigger guard/cocking arm. One small point to mention is that this patent does not apply to the Daisy Model 20 as referred to in the patent comment.

903,092.

Patented Nov. 3, 1908.

Inventor
Edward C. Hough.

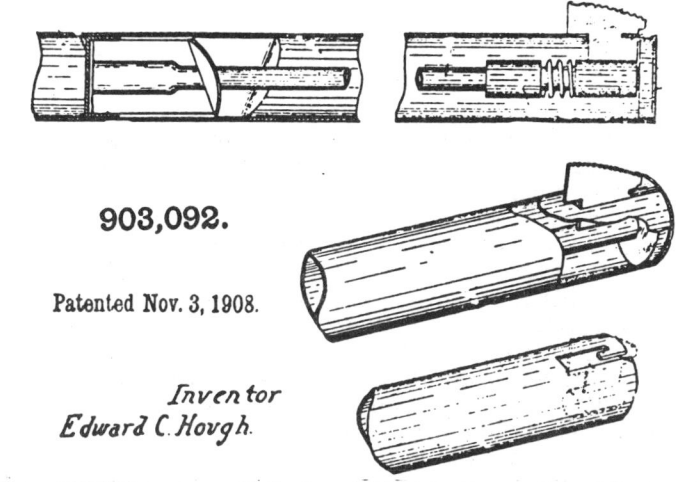

Patent 903092 dealing with the foresight bayonet mounting of the barrel. (Acknowledgements to Dunathan).

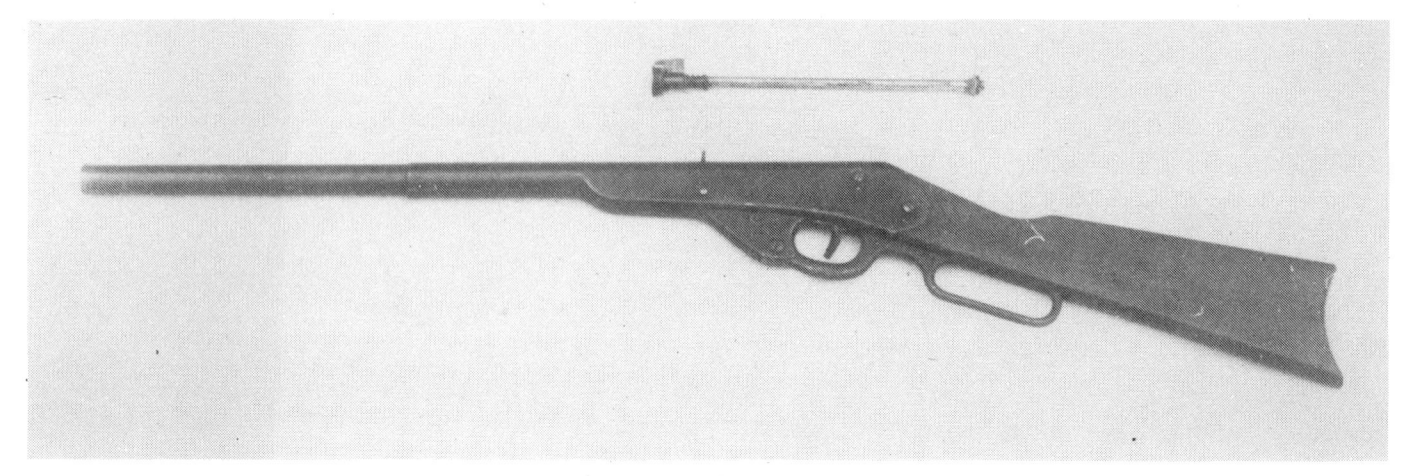

Daisy Model H tinplate underlever

MODEL Model H.

MAKER Daisy Manufacturing Company, Plymouth, Michigan, U.S.A.

DATE 1914 to 1920.

VALUATION £20–£40. ($30–$60).

DETAILS The collecting of tinplates is very neglected in Britain, but the subject does offer the chance of collecting rare items at ridiculously low prices. Until of course everybody wakes up and realises that tinplates offer good prospects in collecting. The Model H is a tinplate single shot underlever cocking air rifle loaded by removing barrel from barrel housing. 30¾ inches long with an 8¼ inch removable smoothbore barrel. Non adjustable sights. Top of air chamber stamped "DAISY SINGLE SHOT MODEL H DAISY MFG CO PLYMOUTH, MICH. US PAT. JULY 30-01, NOV.03-08 OTHERS PENDING". Flat sided stock with crescent shaped butt. Distinctive style underlever.

The above was named after the designer Edward C. Hough. It was the first all tinplate one piece frame and barrel design that Daisy's produced. During the 1930s the one piece frame became standard as by then Daisy had perfected the difficult task of butt and spot welding the underside of the frame and barrel in order to make the air chamber air-tight. The patent 3rd November 1908 was number 903,092, designed by E. C. Hough and was for the method of holding the barrel in place by having the spring tensioned foresight on the barrel clip into a bayonet slot on top of the outer barrel casing. So with the barrel in place the clip acted as the foresight. See Dunathan's "The American BB Gun" for further details. The Model H was first produced as a nickel plated model in 1913, but from 1914 to 1920 they were blued with walnut stocks. Underlever is cast iron with distinctive small loop. Sides of frame stamped "DAISY" between two bullseyes. Listed in Dunathan's as being "scarce". An easy method of firing the above was by pushing the pellets down the barrel with a thin rod. Thus leaving the barrel in place. The above was very accurate, far better than some modern rifled air rifles tested.

Daisy Model 21

MODEL 104, 21 and 410.

MAKER Daisy Manufacturing Co., Rogers, Arkansas, U.S.A.

DATE The Model 104 from 1940 to 1941 and the Model 21 and 410 from around 1965 to early 1970s.

VALUATION £50–£100. ($75–$150).

DETAILS A great fun-gun. The Author will always be amazed at the value and collectability of tinplate airguns. When introduced in 1940 the Model 104 was a 96 shot repeater, 48 from each barrel, tinplate construction with two loading tubes and two triggers. The shot tubes might interchange with the Model 25 trombone action air rifle. The metal work was blued and stamped with scroll edging and hunting scenes, almost identical to the later models, but with a change in finish. It was fitted with walnut stock and fore-end. This first model is quite rare bearing in mind that it was only manufactured for one year. There may have been an earlier issue of these in the middle 1930s, about 5,000 were produced and there is one recorded purchase during this time. The capacity of the loading tube also appears to vary from 50 down to 46.

The Model 21 is identical except for three major differences, gun-metal blue paint finish, plastic stock

Daisy Model 21 with action open and one loading tube removed

and fore-end, and is missing game bird scenes from the front of each side plate of the action as this part is masked by the fore-end. During 1968 25 were produced with chequered and carved walnut stocks as saleman's samples, these are very rare! 37 inches long (94 cms) with oil holes to each barrel, white bead foresight and fixed blade rearsight. Each loading tube is unscrewed and loaded then replaced and screwed down, top lever is pushed aside and stock drops down, further pressure will cock both barrels and activate the safety, this has to be pushed forward in order to fire the airgun. The front trigger fires and R.H. barrel and rear trigger fires the L.H. one.

At the time of writing it is not clear what the Model 410 is.

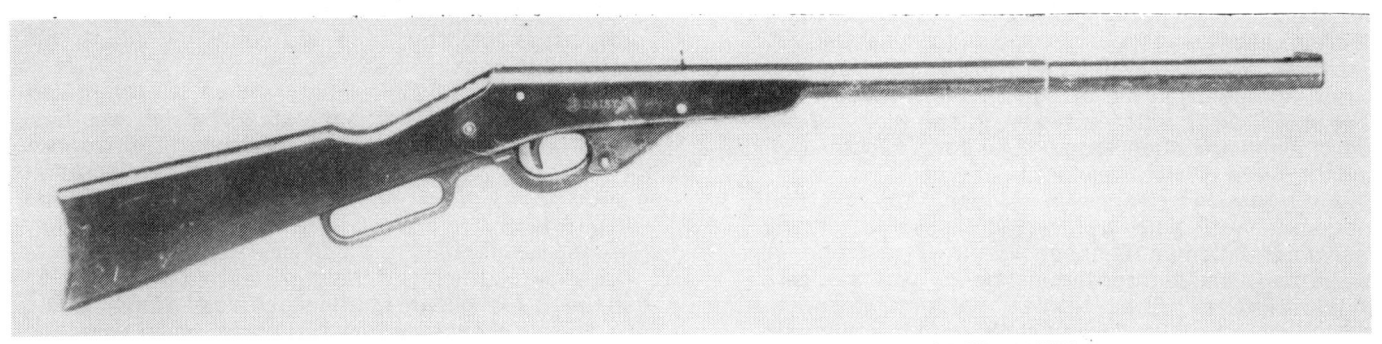

The Daisy No. 12, Model 24, introduced in 1924, 5 years before the Model 29

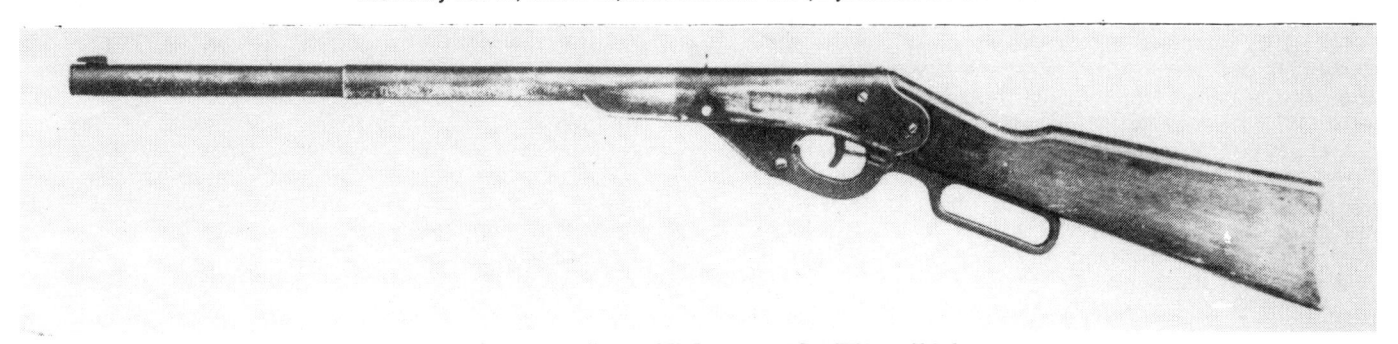

Daisy No. 12, Model 29 single shot tinplate air rifle

MODEL Number 12, Model 29.

MAKER Daisy, Plymouth, Michigan, U.S.A.

DATE The Number 12 was manufactured from 1918 to 1937 whilst the Model 29 from 1929 to 1937, so it could be that the above hybrid was manufactured from 1929 to 1937.

VALUATION £10—£25. ($15—$38).

DETAILS Single shot tinplate with removable barrel for loading. 30½ inches long with an 8 inch smoothbore barrel. Side of action stamped "DAISY" between two bulls-eyes and on top of receiver "DAISY No. 12 MODEL 29, SINGLE SHOT" and alongside "DAISY MFG. Co., PLYMOUTH, MICH., U.S.A., U.S.

PATS. NOV.3,1908—AUG.17,1915". The first patent was for the barrel and the method of fixing it into the outer casing by way of the foresight that slotted into a bayonet lug. This patent was number 903,092 and invented by Edward C. Hough, the son of Lewis Charles Hough one of the founders of the Daisy airgun industry. This model was the follow-on from the Model H. Simple non-adjustable sights and fitted with a cast iron cocking lever. The Number 12 was available nickel plated from 1918 to 1919 and blued from 1920 to 1933. Both finishes were then available from 1934 to 1937. Production ceased upon the introduction of the Model 101. Although the Number 12 was a single shot the Model 29 was advertised as a 350 shot BB repeater. The above had a very strong mainspring and needed more than a child's effort to cock. For sometime the Model H was advertised as the Model 12. During 1924 the Number 12 was stamped Model 24, this would appear to be an earlier variation and puts its introduction as 1924 and changing of Model number as being 1929, hence "Model 29". The lettering on top of the air chamber is identical on both the Model 24 and 29 air rifles.

Daisy Model 25. (Acknowledgements to the "American Rifleman")

MODEL   25 and 325.

MAKER   Daisy Manufacturing Company, Rogers, Arkansas, U.S.A.

DATE   1914 to late 1970s.

VALUATION   £20—£40. ($30—$60).

DETAILS   One of Daisy's most popular designs, over a 65 year period over 20 million have been produced. The Model 25 began life about 1912 when the designer, Charles Lefever a member of a family of St. Louis shotgun designers wrote to Edward Hough of Daisy, upon inspection the design was bought and Charles Lefever was induced to go and work at Daisy's. Unsure at first, he stayed for 44 years and was granted about 60 patents in the design of Daisy airguns. His first patent dealt with the Model 25 and included the elbow pump operation, ease of take down construction and the screw elevated rearsight.

Should you wish to dismantle a Model 25 the following procedure will help as it first appeared in the "American Rifleman" October 1980; it will help to refer to the parts diagram for the numbered parts and care should be taken not to force any parts of the action, but to rather manipulate and jiggle until it either falls apart or goes back together.

First make sure the airgun is unfired and empty, remove barrel (1) by unscrewing, remove stock (27) and tang screw (24), pull stock down and back to remove. Now take out the screw (25) and pull receiver (23) from the barrel (11). Now take note of trigger and spring position, 28 and 29, before removing the trigger screw (26), this allows the trigger to come out. Next take out the slide bar screw (13) and then pull the pivot forearm (14) and slide bar (15) downwards and at the same time unlatching the slide bar from its seat in the outer barrel. Now push out the spring anchor (12) from the barrel slide the lever and plunger out at the rear of the outer barrel. Now pull the plunger case (8) to the rear through the outer tube (9) until the lever pin (18) is visible in the lever assembly (16), remove the pin and withdraw the lever assembly. Now take the plunger and compress the mainspring (10) until you can pull out the piston head pin with pliers, slowly release the mainspring and this will push the piston head off. This piston arrangement is very similar to that on the Haenel and Anschutz bolt action repeaters.

The Model 25 is a 50 shot force fed repeater with a long 14 inch as opposed to a short 14 inch elbow cocking action that deals well with the 4 inch piston travel. The first model which appeared in 1914 was blued with a case hardened cocking lever. The stock and cocking handle were walnut, cocking handle has five grooves. Adjustable foresight and step elevating rearsight. The slide rod was held in place with claw mounts that extended up and over the side of the outer barrel housing. The trigger guard is from sheet metal with a reinforced square shaped rear. Very early models had large headed take down screws that might be mistaken for not being original. Commonly sold with a blued finish, rarely nickel plated and very scarce with a black nickel finish. This first model was made from 1914 to 1924.

From 1925 to 1933 it was produced with a blued finish only, had a fixed foresight and sometime during this period the cocking slide handle went from 5 to 6 grooves. For the 1936 model stamped engraving was used on the receiver and the slide housing was now blued instead of being case hardened. The wooden bits became "gum"? and/or birch instead of walnut. Period of production of this variation was from around 1936 to 1953 with a break from 1941 to 1946 when they won the War for us! From 1951 onwards a serial number was added to the top of the outer barrel casing. In 1954 the first use of plastic for the stock was introduced and the finish became the now customary blued paint and the engraving was replaced by stamping a design with a loss of design detail. The foresight became a ramp type and the rearsight changed to a twin leaf "V" and peepsight. By 1956 the stamped engraving was dropped and replaced by stencilled designs that changed annually. Up to 1957 the Model 25 was manufactured at Plymouth and after at Rogers, address on air rifle may give indication of the change and date.

Due to its long period of production various special models have appeared including one with a telescopic sight Model number 40 in 1952 as well as a shooting kit that comprised of targets, a cork-ball target, extra barrel and other accessories which again appeared in 1952. During 1958, the year of transfer from Plymouth to Rogers, a model with a bronze finish and blonde coloured stock was issued. Average length of the Model 25 and 38 inches and weight 3¼ lbs. When production ceased in the very late 1970s or 1980 the last one was presented to the NRA Museum in America. The engraving was golded in until it became stencilled. The advertised rate of fire from the shoulder was 30 rounds per minute.

The Model 325 issued during 1952 and mentioned earlier was a two-way target outfit based on the Model

82

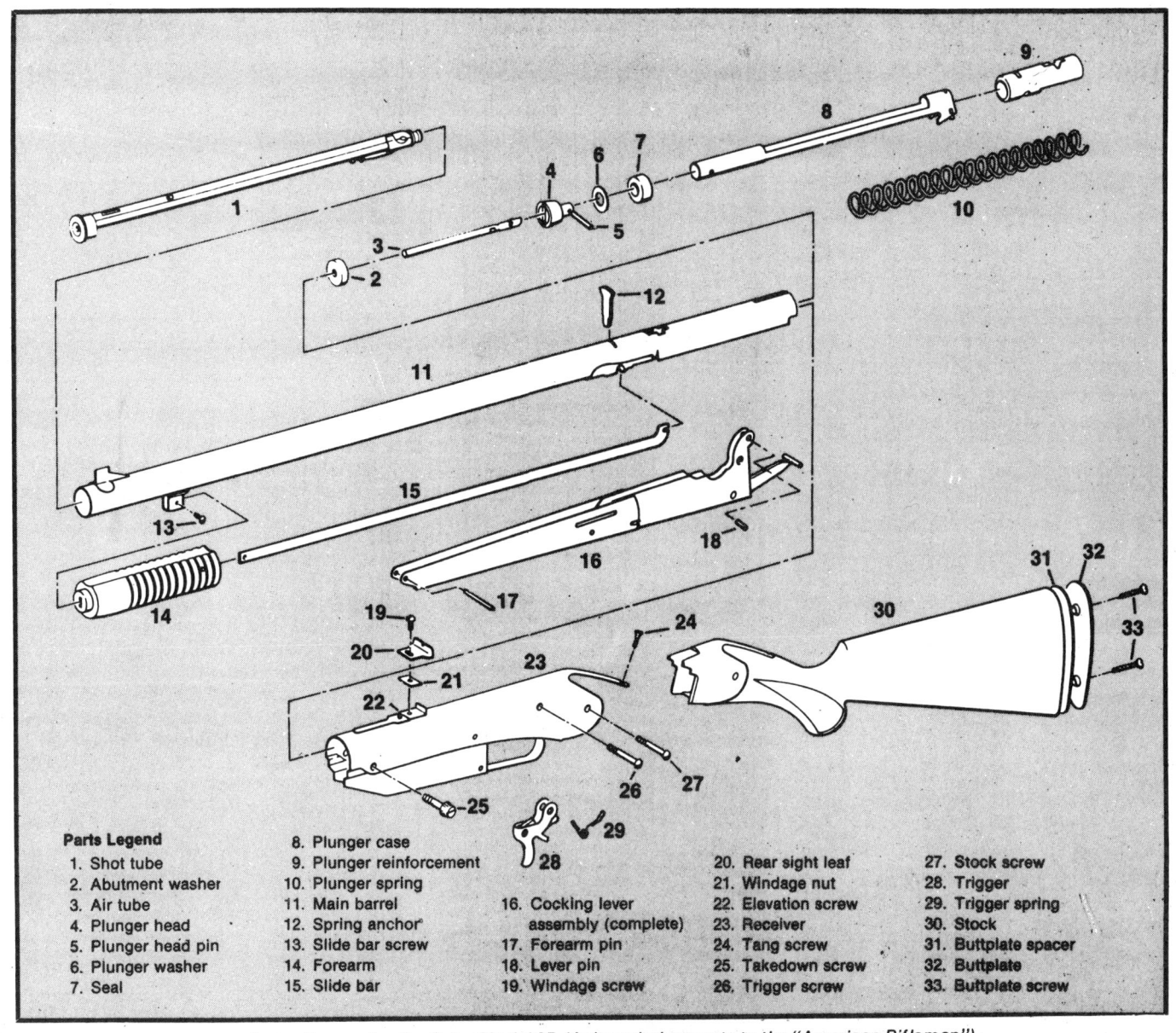

Parts Legend
1. Shot tube
2. Abutment washer
3. Air tube
4. Plunger head
5. Plunger head pin
6. Plunger washer
7. Seal
8. Plunger case
9. Plunger reinforcement
10. Plunger spring
11. Main barrel
12. Spring anchor
13. Slide bar screw
14. Forearm
15. Slide bar
16. Cocking lever assembly (complete)
17. Forearm pin
18. Lever pin
19. Windage screw
20. Rear sight leaf
21. Windage nut
22. Elevation screw
23. Receiver
24. Tang screw
25. Takedown screw
26. Trigger screw
27. Stock screw
28. Trigger
29. Trigger spring
30. Stock
31. Buttplate spacer
32. Buttplate
33. Buttplate screw

Parts diagram for the Daisy Model 25. (Acknowledgements to the "American Rifleman")

25. It was issued with two barrels, one for normal BB shooting and the other with a widened mouthpiece for accepting jumbo cork BBs and targets. It is doubtful if the air rifle repeated with these jumbo cork BBs and in fact they had to be pressed into the mouth of the barrel each time the action was cocked. The air rifle was mounted with a long 2x power telescopic sight. For BB shooting the kit contained a supply of BBs and a target holder with spare cards, all this was sold in a "sturdy corrugated carton". In post-war adverts the Model 25 was described as the "King of all BB Guns". In 1958 it was advertised as having a bright metal trigger and as having a full figured plastic stock to resemble walnut. Now comes the offer of a lifetime — it was sold with a new Daisy screwdriver formed from the words DAISY and the "I" being extended to form the screwdriver, this being for the large receiver screw for removing the barrel assembly. It was sold complete with a gun carrying case and supply of BBs. I'm surprised that America doesn't sink when one thinks of the countless millions of BBs lying about on its surface.

In 1958 it was sold as the "Air Rifleman Set" that comprised of the Model 25 air rifle, a wall or table thick wire gun rack with wooden base, a Daisy gun cleaning kit in a metal case, a "Special Screwdriver" and a metal BB storage box. Sounds like a clear-out jumble box from Daisy. During the 1960s the action was pre-tapped for mounting the Daisy "Eagle-Eye" 2x power 11 inch Model 303 telescopic sight complete with FOUR lenses. This was also available for models 102, 94, 90 and 25. Muzzle velocity of the Model 25 is about 320 to 340 f.p.s.

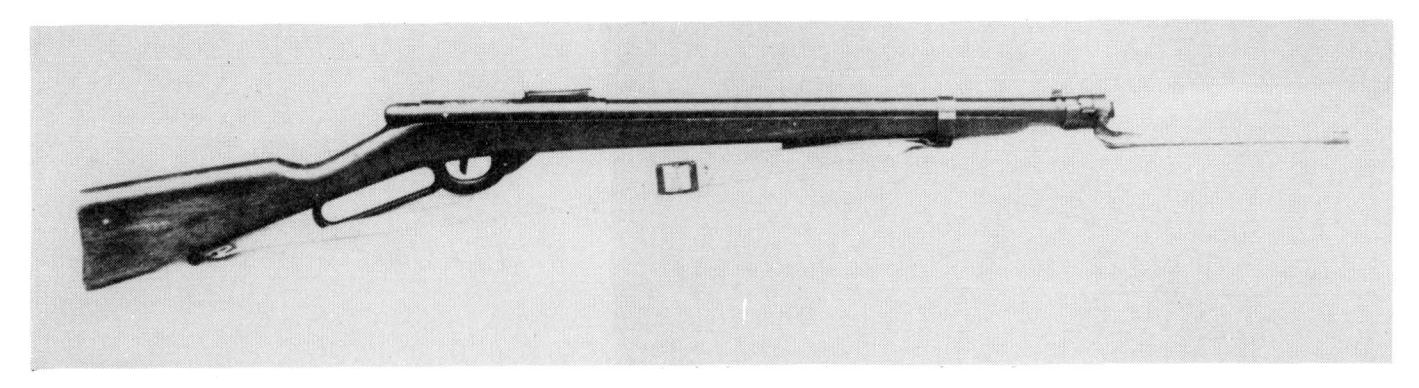

Daisy Model 40 Military Model

MODEL 40.

MAKER Daisy Manufacturing Company, Plymouth, Michigan, U.S.A.

DATE 1916, appears to have been manufactured in decreasing quantities up to 1932. A very scarce tinplate air rifle.

VALUATION £50—£150. ($75—$225).

DETAILS Nearly all military style air rifles are generally very scarce and command high prices. This one is no exception. The Model 40 appeared just after the outbreak of First World War and was sold complete with socket bayonet and canvas sling. 36½ inches long with a 9½ inch bayonet with a black rubber safety insert in the end. The workmanship and fit of the bayonet is extraordinary. Bayonet has a locking ring that would do justice to its military counterpart. Screw-out barrel with a force fed tubular magazine running under the barrel. Advertised as a 50 shot repeater. Dovetail mounted foresight on a spot welded raised platform and ramp rearsight with slide operated elevation. Top of air chamber stamped "DAISY No.40 DAISY MFG. CO., PLYMOUTH, MICH., U.S.A., PAT. OCT.20-14, AUG.17-15". The rear extension to the air chamber is described as a dummy bolt but without a bolt handle. Action fitted with full length walnut finished stock. All metal parts were blued. An article on the above appears in "Antique Arms & Militaria" August 1979. Advertised weight 3¼ lbs without bayonet. For further details see "The American BB Gun" by Dunathan.

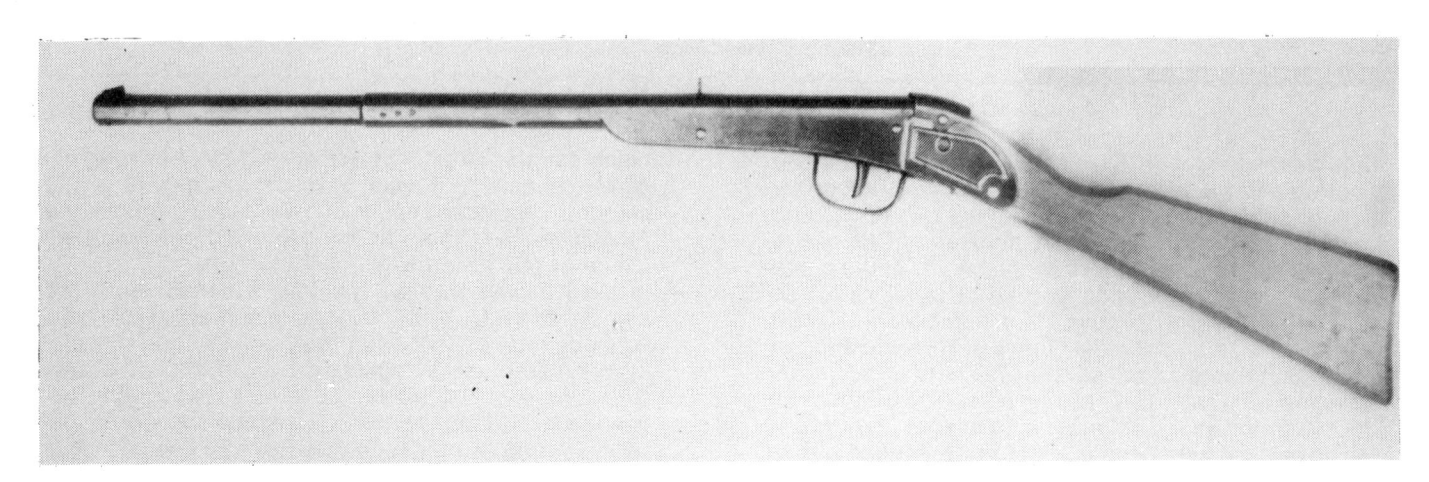

Daisy single shot Model 38, No. 100

MODEL Single shot Model 38, Number 100.

MAKER Daisy Manufacturing Co. Ltd., Plymouth, Michigan, U.S.A.

DATE Two phases of production, 1938 to 1941 and 1946 to 1949. Rated by Dunathan as being common.

VALUATION £5—£30. ($8—$45).

DETAILS Unusual tinplate in two respects, non-removable barrel and has a single thick cocking wire. Blued tinplate construction with single non-adjustable sights. 31 inches long. Top of air chamber stamped "DAISY, No.100-MODEL 38, SINGLE SHOT, DAISY MFG. CO., PLYMOUTH, MICH., U.S.A., U.S. PAT. 1150248". Action is stop-welded and micro-welded together. A sealed for life air rifle. When the action is broken for cocking there is one stout wire cocking link, unlike the earlier twin wires. Light coloured wooden flat sided stock. The Model 38 was fitted with the Hough pattern frame and barrel, see Daisy Model H for similarity of design.

As the above has a non-removable barrel the steel BBs must be rolled or spat down the barrel, they are held in place by a slight taper within the barrel. On no account should lead pellets be pushed down the barrel as it has barely enough power to vomit the BB!

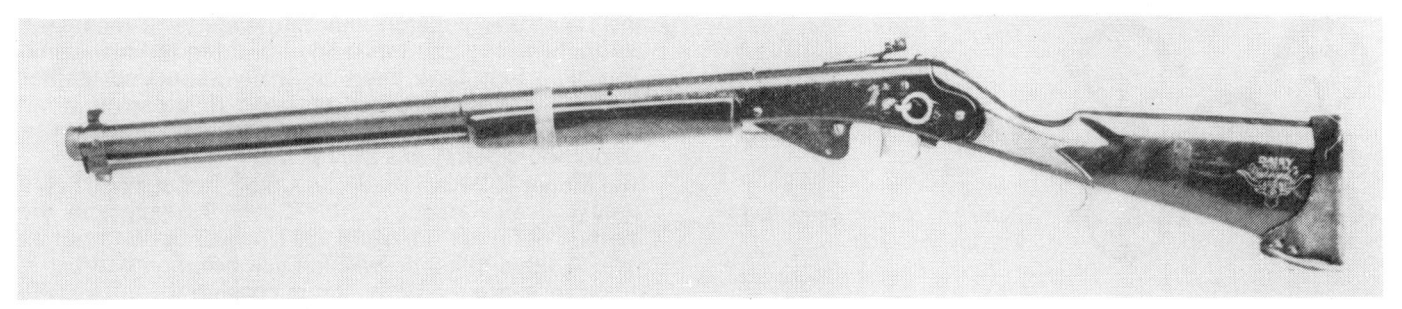

Daisy Model 94 "Red Ryder" carbine

MODEL Model 94 "Red Ryder" Carbine.

MAKER Daisy Manufacturing Co. Ltd., Plymouth, Michigan, U.S.A.

DATE 1958—1962.

VALUATION £30—£60. ($45—$90).

DETAILS The above is the successor to the Number 111 Model 40 Red Ryder Carbine that was manufactured from 1940 to 1958 when the Company moved to Rogers. It would appear from the address of manufacture that this is a transitional model in that it has the characteristics of both models, so would date the above as 1958. 34½ inches long. Barrel tube can be unscrewed from body but this is unnecessary, to load, just rotate end of barrel until the loading tube has been opened by the metal flap spot welded to the lower part of the barrel. The BBs can now be poured into the magazine. Would assume the above to hold 1,000, but at later dates the overall length of the airgun was reduced from 34½ inches to 32 inches and magazine capacity also reduced. All metal parts are covered with blue paint except for the barrel ring which has "DAISY" and Indian style designs pressed on it and the aluminium underlever, saddle ring and dummy trigger. Underside of fore-end has "IT'S A DAISY" cast around the hole for fixing screw. The sides of the trigger action have a gold paint spray-on scene of a cowboy lassoing a steer. Top of air chamber has small hole for oiling and stamped near it appears "MODEL No 94 RED RYDER CARBINE LICENCED BY STEPHEN SLESINGER N.Y. PATS 2,724,897 2,226,620 DAISY MFG. CO., PLYMOUTH, MICHIGAN, U.S.A. REGISTER No C133476". Rearsight is fully adjustable and has flip-up arrangement for either "V" or peepsight. The stock and fore-end are plastic and pressed into the side of the butt is "DAISY MODEL 94 RED RYDER CARBINE" with a horned steer's head underneath. Base of butt has a real leather sew-on butt boot. Daisy certainly put a lot into a tinplate air rifle. The saddle ring may have had a leather thong originally.

Copper coated BBs were also available in packs called the, you guessed it, "RED RYDER". The above was also sold as "THE RED RYDER COWBOY OUTFIT" it contained the air rifle plus one pint capacity canteen for water, or whisky, leather belt and leather canteen carrier, this was advertised in the late 1950s. In the early 1960s it was advertised as the "WESTERN CARBINE". Advertised in 1974 as the Model 7938 Red Ryder Commemorative. Identical to illustration but with different motif branded on wooden stock. It also had a wooden fore-end. Repeating action with an advertised capacity of 700 BBs. Some confusion may be caused by the fact that the Model 7938 is in fact stamped "No.1938".

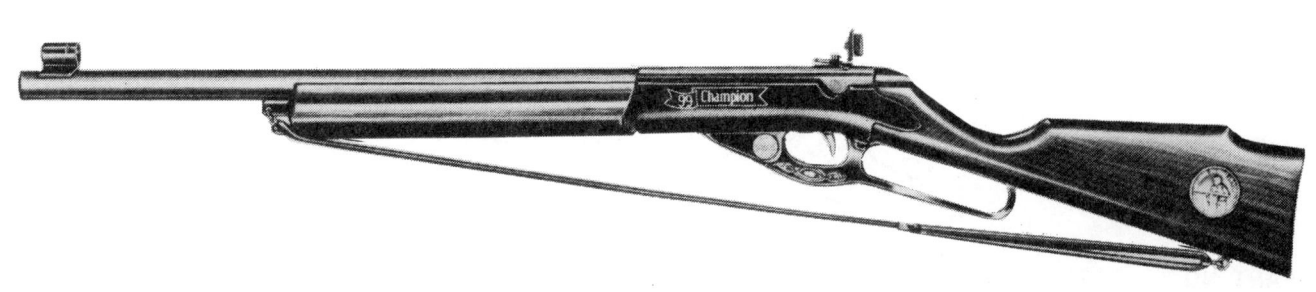

Daisy Model 99 "Champion"

MODEL 99 and 499B

MAKER Daisy, Rogers, Arkansas, U.S.A.

DATE Introduced 1959 and still manufactured to date.

VALUATION £30—£60. ($45—$90).

DETAILS The Model 99 must surely represent the top range of BB guns available with double pull trigger, peepsight with interchangeable foresight elements, canvas sling, and wooden fore-end and butt. Why don't schools over here take shooting as seriously as the Americans, Russians and Chinese?

The Model 99 is sold with four foresight elements as shown, samples of Daisy BBs and oil, a Daisy BB gun instruction manual, the operation manual for the Model 99, a Daisy Air Rifle Instruction booklet, another little booklet called "The Daisy Book", and finally instructions on how to fit the Daisy precision sight mount No. 2169, this is a graduated fully adjustable rear peepsight. This sight can also be fitted to Models 299 and 1498.

The Model 99 has the blued enamelled paint finish with "MODEL 99 B-B GUN DAISY, ROGERS, ARKANSAS, U.S.A." stamped on the top of the barrel, whilst on the underside, "PAT. 2,758,586 & 3,030,708 LOT NO. C311439". The wooden stock has a medallion with "OFFICIAL SHOOTING EDUCATION B-B GUN BY DAISY". The force-fed magazine tube may be difficult to re-insert into the outer barrel tube, to ease it in pull down on the cocking lever part of its travel downwards and even fully cock the action but do not release the action until the magazine tube has been fully screwed down. The foresight elements are held in place by spring tension.

Foresight elements supplied with the Model 99

During its first year of manufacture the Model 99 was fitted with an 850 gravity fed magazine, but in 1960 the force fed magazine tube was introduced. This first model should be quite rare. This type of BB gun was intended for the American NRA 15 foot target shooting and was introduced in response to a demand from the Camp Perry match shooting experts. It measures 36½ inches long and has a 50 shot force fed magazine. The sling may have been originally simulated leather grained and by 1974 was changed to a canvas army style webbing. Advertised muzzle velocity with a smoothbore barrel was 230 f.p.s.

The Model 499B is a single suck/blow target air rifle very similar in appearance to the Model 99 except in the method of firing. The 499B is a single shot BB target air rifle. A BB is rolled down the wide bell mouthed barrel and it rolls into the barrel, upon cocking the action, the BB is sucked into the barrel and it can actually be heard as it is being sucked into and down the barrel. Action has safety slide on the R.H.S.. Top of barrel stamped "DAISY MODEL 499B, ROGERS, AR. U.S.A.. B-B CAL (4.5mm) STEEL AIR GUN SHOT". Example seen was fitted with a pistol grip stock as opposed to the straight hand stock as seen on the Model 99 in the illustration.

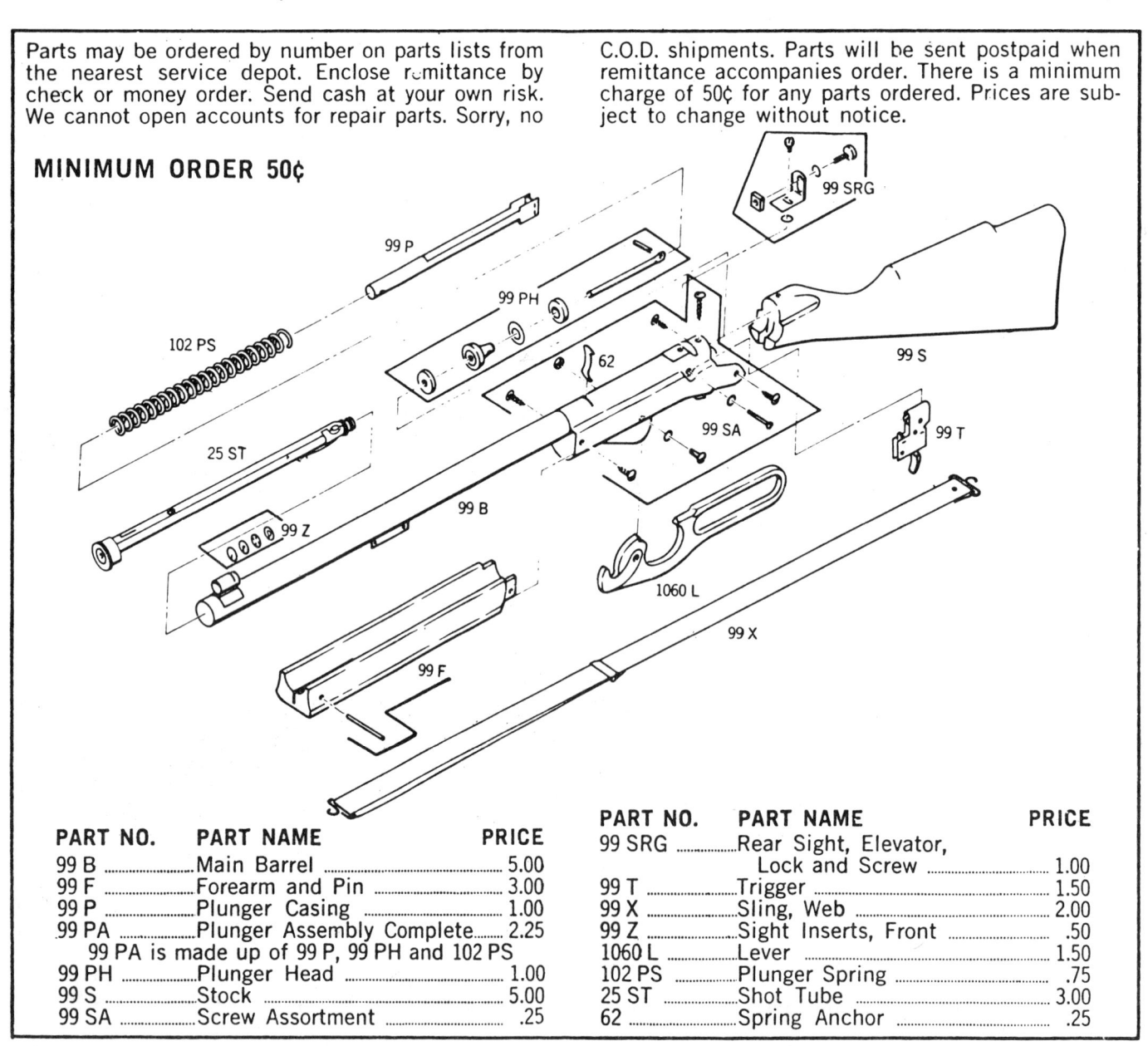

Parts may be ordered by number on parts lists from the nearest service depot. Enclose remittance by check or money order. Send cash at your own risk. We cannot open accounts for repair parts. Sorry, no C.O.D. shipments. Parts will be sent postpaid when remittance accompanies order. There is a minimum charge of 50¢ for any parts ordered. Prices are subject to change without notice.

MINIMUM ORDER 50¢

PART NO.	PART NAME	PRICE
99 B	Main Barrel	5.00
99 F	Forearm and Pin	3.00
99 P	Plunger Casing	1.00
99 PA	Plunger Assembly Complete	2.25
	99 PA is made up of 99 P, 99 PH and 102 PS	
99 PH	Plunger Head	1.00
99 S	Stock	5.00
99 SA	Screw Assortment	.25

PART NO.	PART NAME	PRICE
99 SRG	Rear Sight, Elevator, Lock and Screw	1.00
99 T	Trigger	1.50
99 X	Sling, Web	2.00
99 Z	Sight Inserts, Front	.50
1060 L	Lever	1.50
102 PS	Plunger Spring	.75
25 ST	Shot Tube	3.00
62	Spring Anchor	.25

Looks, feels, performs like famed Western carbine. Spring-forced feed. Loads 45 B·B's through side port. Ramp front, adjustable buckhorn rear sights. Two-way cocking lever; hammer safety, slim-line barrel. 38" long. Model 1894.

"Spitting Image" 1894 Winchester style BB repeater

MODEL "Spitting Image" Model 1894 B-B Air Rifle.

MAKER Daisy Manufacturing Co., Rogers, Arkansas, 72756, U.S.A.

DATE From 1961 to date.

VALUATION £50n, £20—£50, £13a.
($75n, $30—$75, $20a).

DETAILS One hell-of-a fun-gun. Looks and operates exactly like the Winchester underlever rifle that it represents. The cocking lever half cocks the action on the downward stoke and completes the cocking action on the upward stroke. BBs are fed into the magazine by way of the spring loaded side gate and then by holding the air rifle stock upper-most and pulling forward the spring plunger on the underside of the barrel up to 40 BBs are introduced into the force-fed magazine tube. Before the action can be fired the hammer must be pulled back into the cocked position. This was the first totally new design to come out of Daisy's since the Lefever Targeteer air pistol in 1936 and along with the other "Spitting Image" models they have broke all the previous records of Daisy airguns sold. To date there have been three special editions, the Buffalo Bill, the Cody Scout, and the Sears Replica Centennial Models. The above are so life-like that they have been used in parades, films and many other purposes when the real thing was either too expensive to throw about or for security reasons could not be used. After the introduction of the 1894 Model in 1961 the "Cody Model" came out during 1969 and had a bright anodised frame with "LAND OF BUFFALO BILL, CODY, WYOMING" stencilled on the side. Besides the usual saddle ring there was a medallion set into the stock. This model

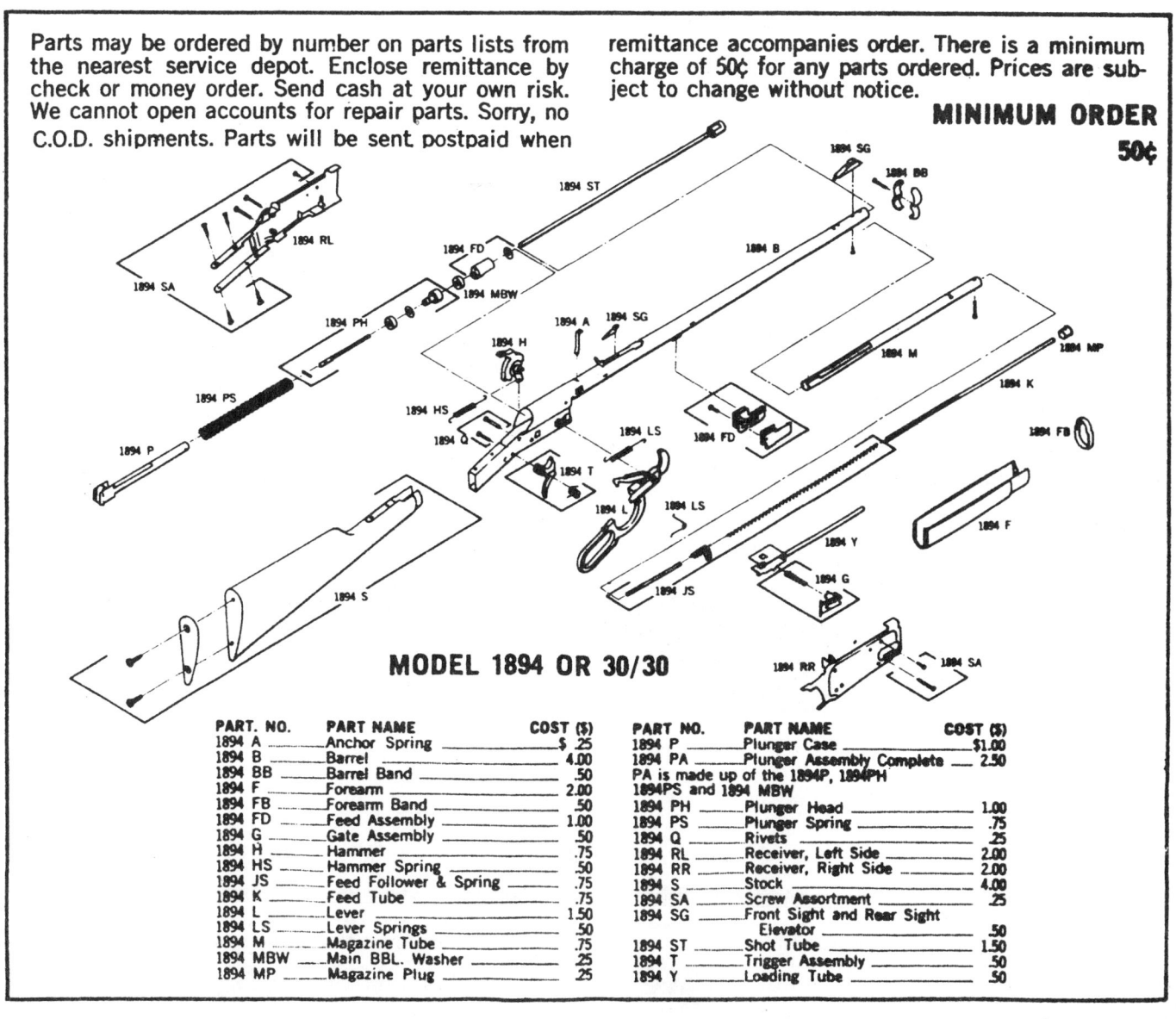

Parts may be ordered by number on parts lists from the nearest service depot. Enclose remittance by check or money order. Send cash at your own risk. We cannot open accounts for repair parts. Sorry, no C.O.D. shipments. Parts will be sent postpaid when remittance accompanies order. There is a minimum charge of 50¢ for any parts ordered. Prices are subject to change without notice.

MINIMUM ORDER 50¢

MODEL 1894 OR 30/30

PART. NO.	PART NAME	COST ($)
1894 A	Anchor Spring	$ .25
1894 B	Barrel	4.00
1894 BB	Barrel Band	.50
1894 F	Forearm	2.00
1894 FB	Forearm Band	.50
1894 FD	Feed Assembly	1.00
1894 G	Gate Assembly	.50
1894 H	Hammer	.75
1894 HS	Hammer Spring	.50
1894 JS	Feed Follower & Spring	.75
1894 K	Feed Tube	.75
1894 L	Lever	1.50
1894 LS	Lever Springs	.50
1894 M	Magazine Tube	.75
1894 MBW	Main BBL. Washer	.25
1894 MP	Magazine Plug	.25

PART NO.	PART NAME	COST ($)
1894 P	Plunger Case	$1.00
1894 PA	Plunger Assembly Complete	2.50
PA is made up of the 1894P, 1894PH 1894PS and 1894 MBW		
1894 PH	Plunger Head	1.00
1894 PS	Plunger Spring	.75
1894 Q	Rivets	.25
1894 RL	Receiver, Left Side	2.00
1894 RR	Receiver, Right Side	2.00
1894 S	Stock	4.00
1894 SA	Screw Assortment	.25
1894 SG	Front Sight and Rear Sight Elevator	.50
1894 ST	Shot Tube	1.50
1894 T	Trigger Assembly	.50
1894 Y	Loading Tube	.50

was manufactured for sale only from the Buffalo Bill Museum as is quite rare. At the same time for general sale a "Buffalo Bill Model" was introduced with his signature stencilled across the frame. The other model was the Sears Centennial Model that copies the Winchester Golden Spike rifle; this had an octagonal barrel, a brass coloured frame and a fore-end cap and butt plate. Only 50,000 were made in 1970 and must be pretty rare. One other variation appeared during 1971 and this was the Model 5894 Carbine NRA COMMEMORATIVE MODEL. A limited edition with an antique bronze finish to the frame and inscribed "1871 — NRA CENTENNIAL — 1971" and having an NRA medallion set in the stock. This must be the rarest of the 1984 variants. It was supplied in a combination display and carrying carton.

The Buffalo Bill Model was also sold as the Daisy Model 3030 Buffalo Bill Scout. In 1973 a 5694 Texas Commemorative BB Carbine was issued to honour the Texas Lawmen. This had a case hardened plated receiver with a metallic replica of a Rangers badge and on the other side "1823 — TEXAS RANGERS — 1973" there was also a medallion set into the stock. It was specially packed with a 48 page booklet on the history of the Rangers. The 1894 measures about 39 inches long, had a smoothbore barrel and had a muzzle velocity of around 300 f.p.s. It had a 40 BB shot spring fed magazine tube.

One such Model 3030 Buffalo Bill Scout seen was obviously intended for export as it was stamped with the F-in pentagon. Most parts were silver anodised except for the barrel and magazine tube. The barrel was stamped "MODEL No. 1894 — DAISY MFG. CO. — PRESTON — ONTARIO — CANADA — REG. NO.", the sling leather thong hung from the rear barrel band and not from the action as on the standard 1894 model.

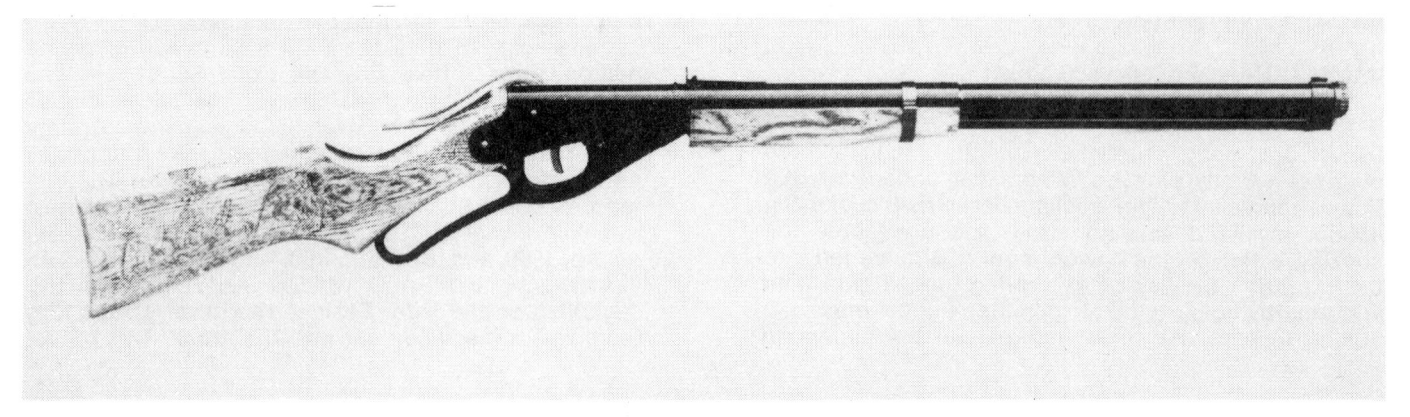

Daisy Red Ryder BB repeater No. 1938 (7838)

MODEL No. 1938 Red Ryder Carbine BB Gun. Also listed in America as the Model 7938 Red Ryder Commemorative Model.

MAKER Daisy, Rogers, Arkansas, U.S.A.

DATE 1974 to 1980s.

VALUATION £10—£30. ($15—$45).

DETAILS One of the breed of perfect "fun-guns". A magazine BB repeater that holds 700 on one loading. The first model appeared in 1940 and this was a 1,000 shot repeater. 35¾ inches long. Deep blue enamelled metal work with cast alloy cocking lever/trigger guard. Fixed blade foresight and rearsight adjustable for elevation only. Top of air chamber stamped, "NO. 1938 RED RYDER CARBINE BB GUN, DAISY ARKANSAS, ROGERS, U.S.A., PAT. NO. 2,758,586, REG. NO. K848587". Air chamber also has two holes in top, one for oiling and other for inspection of magazine to see if any BBs are remaining. To load, front of barrel is rotated through 90° in any direction and BBs are poured into receiver under barrel. After this the airgun becomes quite heavy. Fitted with wooden fore-end and stock. Stock is stamped with Red Ryder cowboy playing with his lariat and forming the name of the Model. L.H.S. of action has a saddle ring with a leather thong attached. Advertised weight 1.1 kg. The barrel is smoothbore and advertised muzzle velocity is 280 f.p.s. By 1981 they were advertised with a manual safety catch. The magazine feed is magnetically aided.

By the middle 1980s the Red Ryder Special had become one of Daisy's most popular selling airguns and was even featured in the movie "A Christmas Story". By 1984 a sundial and compass was added to the wooden stock.

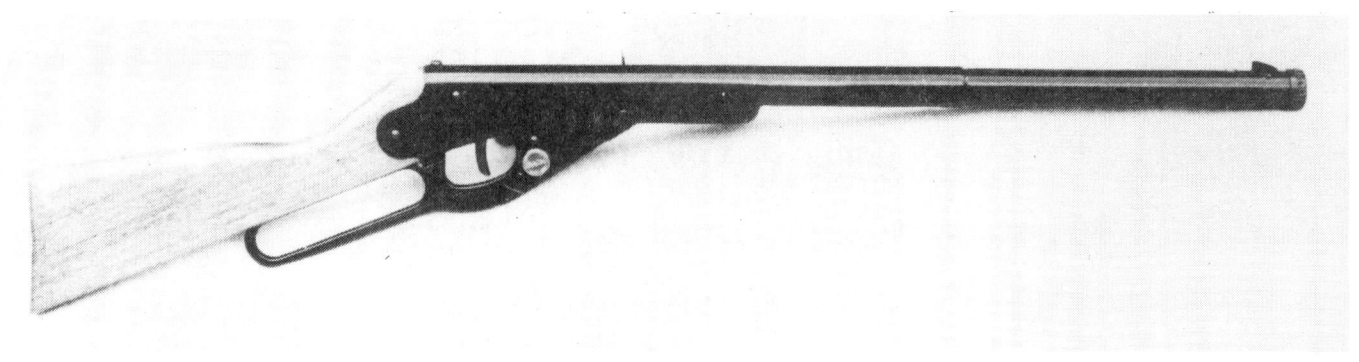

Daisy Model 102 BB repeater

MODEL 102 "BB" Repeater. (Also called the CUB).

MAKER Daisy, Rogers, Arkansas, U.S.A.

DATE The first model 102 appeared in 1933 and has remained virtually unaltered until present day. Later it was called the Model 36. The above variation is a current model and appeared in the early 1950s.

VALUATION £10—£30. ($15—$45).

DETAILS Current model. Metal parts painted a deep pale blue. Fixed sights. "BB" repeater. Front muzzle cap is rotated to reveal a loading hole just behind the foresight. The above holds 350 "BBs". Top of air chamber stamped "DAISY MODEL 102 B-B GUN, ROGERS, ARKANSAS, U.S.A." and on the underside of the barrel stamped "PAT. 2,758,586 LOT NO. A703567". The underlever is cast alloy with the name "DAISY" on each side and a "DAISY" stick-on label. Where the lever clips up into the action is a polythene insert. All screws have "Phillip" heads. Non-adjustable sights. Plain parallel sided stock with a warning label stuck to butt warning of the dangers of firing anything else but "BB" pellets. Later advertised as a 1,000 shot repeater. During the late 1950s to early 1960s it was advertised with a chequered simulated walnut stock. Overall length 30 inches. Advertised muzzle velocity 260 f.p.s. Imported by Milbro, Millard Bros. Ltd. Address see under Milbro. In the middle 1960s they were advertised as being pre-tapped for fitting the Daisy "Eagle-Eye" telescopic sight.

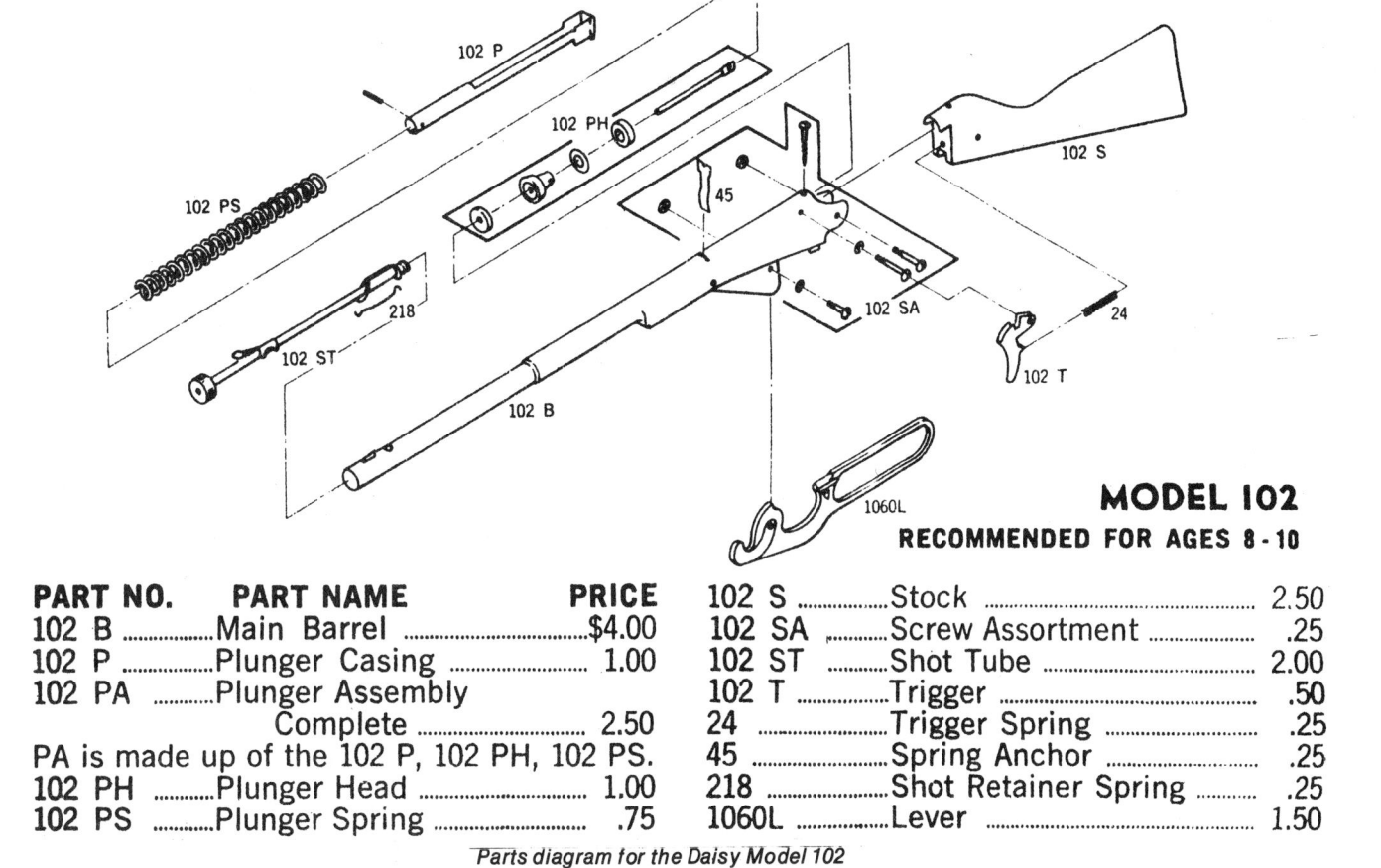

MODEL 102
RECOMMENDED FOR AGES 8-10

PART NO.	PART NAME	PRICE
102 B	Main Barrel	$4.00
102 P	Plunger Casing	1.00
102 PA	Plunger Assembly Complete	2.50
PA is made up of the 102 P, 102 PH, 102 PS.		
102 PH	Plunger Head	1.00
102 PS	Plunger Spring	.75
102 S	Stock	2.50
102 SA	Screw Assortment	.25
102 ST	Shot Tube	2.00
102 T	Trigger	.50
24	Trigger Spring	.25
45	Spring Anchor	.25
218	Shot Retainer Spring	.25
1060L	Lever	1.50

Parts diagram for the Daisy Model 102

The Daisy 1000-shot Model 155

MODEL 155.

MAKER Daisy Manufacturing Co., Plymouth, Michigan, U.S.A.

DATE Two periods of manufacture, first from 1931 to 1941 in quite small numbers and from 1946 to 1949. A relatively rare model and have yet to see an advert for the above.

VALUATION £15–£30. ($23–$45).

DETAILS A 1,000 shot repeater and manufactured as Daisy's lowest priced air rifle with this repeating capacity. 34½ inches long (88 cms), sheet metal construction with underlever cocking. Pre-war models had a cast iron lever whilst post-war were fitted with an aluminium one. The steel BBs were loaded via a hole in the top of the barrel just in front, or behind the foresight. The front outer barrel sleeve is rotated to reveal the loading hole. On the post-war model the following is stamped on the air chamber "MODEL No. 155 — DAISY MANUFACTURING CO., — PLYMOUTH, MICH., U.S.A. — PATENT NOS. 1062855, 880555". The first Patent deals with the cocking lever mechanism whilst the second I'm not sure about. The example seen was post-war with a blued finish to the action and an either very deep blue finish, or black painted cocking lever. Straight-sided stock in either birch or "gum"? The Model 155 is based on the previous Model H.

It is little wonder that the original boxes do not survive as printed on the back is a variety of circular bulls-eye targets with the instructions "Use these targets. Learn to shoot straight. Stuff box with *folded* newspapers, set against a safe back-stop indoors or out. Have fun and shoot safe, Buddy!!!" Hence very few survive. The front of the box was priced £3 5s. 0d. which in present day coinage is £3.25.

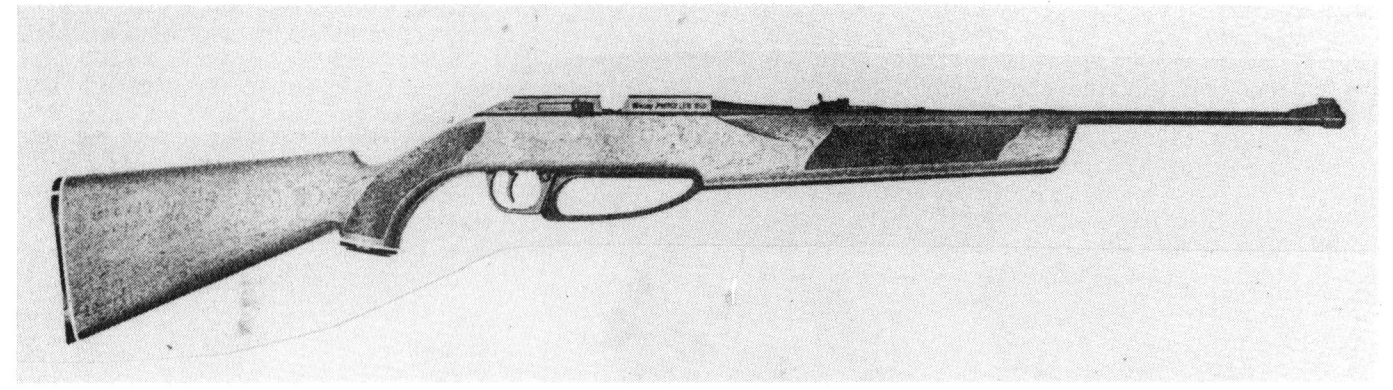

Daisy Model 850

MODEL 850.

MAKER Daisy Manufacturing Co., Rogers, Arkansas, 72756, U.S.A.

DATE Introduced in America during 1982.

VALUATION £20—£40. ($30—$60).

DETAILS Similar to the Model 922 Powerline series, the major difference being that the Model 850 is a single pump pneumatic. It is an adult sized air rifle for recoiles shooting with .177 pellets or BB's. The BB's are stored in a 100 shot magazine. The single stroke pneumatic mechanism is similar to that fitted to the Model 717 airpistol. Advertised weight 4 lbs. 5 ozs. Stock is a one piece woodgrained moulded plastic with chequering on grip and fore-ends. Rearsight is fully adjustable and action is fitted with standard scope rails. Average muzzle velocity with pellets was around 450 f.p.s.

With the single pump action it is possible to rapid fire BB's and upwards of 10 shots per minute are possible. The sequence for loading is printed on the pumping lever and is as follows:

1) Put on safe. 2) Open bolt. 3) Pump. 4) Load. 5) Close bolt. 6) Aim. 7) Take off safe. 8. Fire!!!!

Advertised length 38⅜ inches, barrel length 21¼ inches with 12 grooves and one turn in 16 inches with a right hand twist. Although fitted with plastic stock a model 851 was offered with a woodstock. A review of the above appears in "American Rifleman" April, 1982 and "Guns Magazine" April, 1982. Advertised muzzle velocities are 510 f.p.s. with BB's and 480 f.p.s. with lead pellets. During 1982 the Model 850 retailed for around $60 and the woodstock 951 for $80.

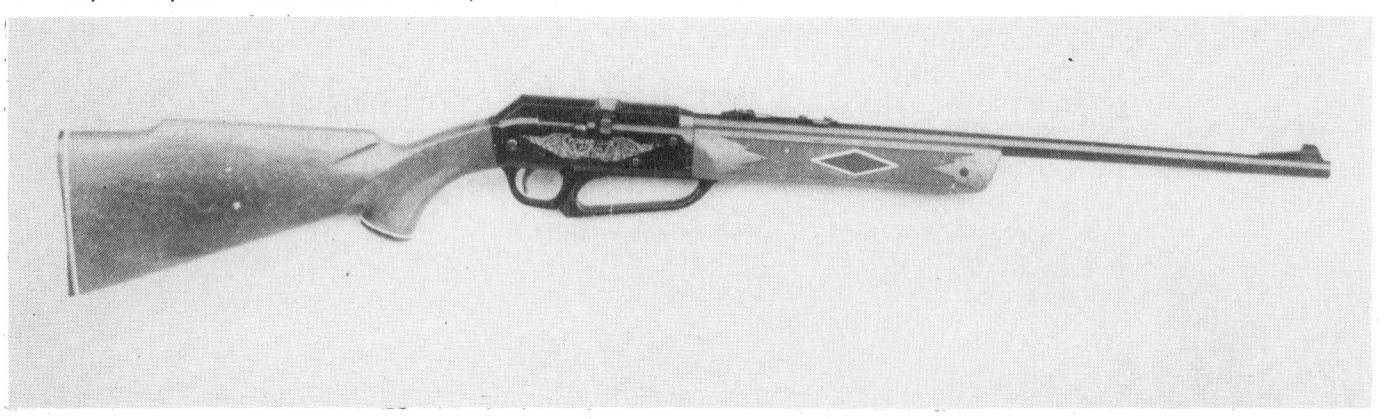

Daisy "Powerline" Model 922

MODEL "Powerline" Model 922.

MAKER Daisy Manufacturing Co., Rogers, Ark. 72756, U.S.A. Address for Canada: Victor Recreation Products, Cambridge, Ontario N1R5T1, Canada.
Imported by Millard Bros., P.O. Box 24, Motherwell, Lanarkshire ML1 4UP, Scotland.

DATE Introduced 1978 and still a current model, although the Model 880 and 881 were available in the U.S.A. 1974.

VALUATION £15—£35, £25a. ($23—$53, $38a).

DETAILS Neat handy little pump-up air rifle. Plastic stock and fore-end. Metal parts covered with deep blue coloured paint. 37½ inches long. Each side of body stamped with "POWERLINE" surrounded by a floral design. Fitted with non-automatic safety. Side of barrel stamped "POWERLINE MODEL 922 22 CAL. (55 mm) PELLET ROGERS, ARKANSAS, U.S.A." and under the barrel towards the foresight "LOT NO J801705 PAT. No. 3,855,990 & 3,810,455. The action can either be fitted with a sledge for single firing of pellets, or a longer plastic slide can be inserted across the breech that holds five pellets. The sledge can only be moved when the bolt has been drawn back. The advertised muzzle energy is as follows:

```
            2 pumps — 2.6 ft lbs   285 f.p.s.
            4 pumps — 5.2 ft lbs   405 f.p.s.
            6 pumps — 7.2 ft lbs   475 f.p.s.
            8 pumps — 8.6 ft lbs   520 f.p.s.
           10 pumps — 9.8 ft lbs   555 f.p.s.
```

The airgun can only be pumped when the bolt has been drawn back. The rearsight is fully adjustable for windage and elevation. Advertised weight 4¼ lbs. The earlier Model 880 is in .177. With continuous use the stock is liable to work loose as this takes some of the strain of pumping. Brass liner barrel is ten groove rifled with one complete turn in 16 inches.

Although the Model 922 was introduced into Britain during 1979 it was available in the U.S.A. much earlier. A 1976 American advertised praised the fact that with ten pumps the Model 822, as it was known in the States, could punch a .22 pellet through a 22 gauge aluminium plate at 15 feet. The pumping of ten pumps gave it an advertised muzzle velocity of 600 f.p.s.

"Junior" Diana

MODEL "Junior" Diana. Also seen as "No.I".

MAKER "Diana" Mayer & Grammelspacher, Germany.

DATE From the early 1920s to 1945. Post-war production began November 1952.

VALUATION £5—£20, £3a—£7a.
($8—$30, $4a—$11).

DETAILS Nickel plated. 30½ inches long. Barrel needs to be removed for loading pellet. 8½ inch barrel. "Tinplate" construction. Diana trademark stamped on top of trigger block, "DIANA" stamped either side at rear of trigger. On underside of metalwork at rear of trigger is stamped "MADE IN GERMANY". Sights non-adjustable.

Diana Model I

MODEL MOD I.

MAKER "Diana", Mayer & Grammelspacher, Germany.

DATE Early 1920s to 1945, production recommenced November 1952.

VALUATION £5—£20, although have seen them for as high as £25 in antique shops.
£3a—£7a. ($8—$30, $4a—$11a).

DETAILS See "Junior" Diana, almost identical except for minor differences in "tinplate" pressings. The break action lock is circular and underside of air chamber does not have a seam. Removable barrel for loading pellet. On top of trigger block is stamped Diana trademark with "DIANA MOD I MADE IN GERMANY". Almost 31 inches long. Has traces of nickel plating. A variation of the above called the "Milbro Scout" has two spring loaded ball bearings as latches to keep action in place. It would appear that the above design was used by retailers with their own name or trademark stamped on them. Have seen the above called the "Hector", and "Hot-Shot". The average rate of production of the Model I was around 60,000 per year.

German Diana Model 15

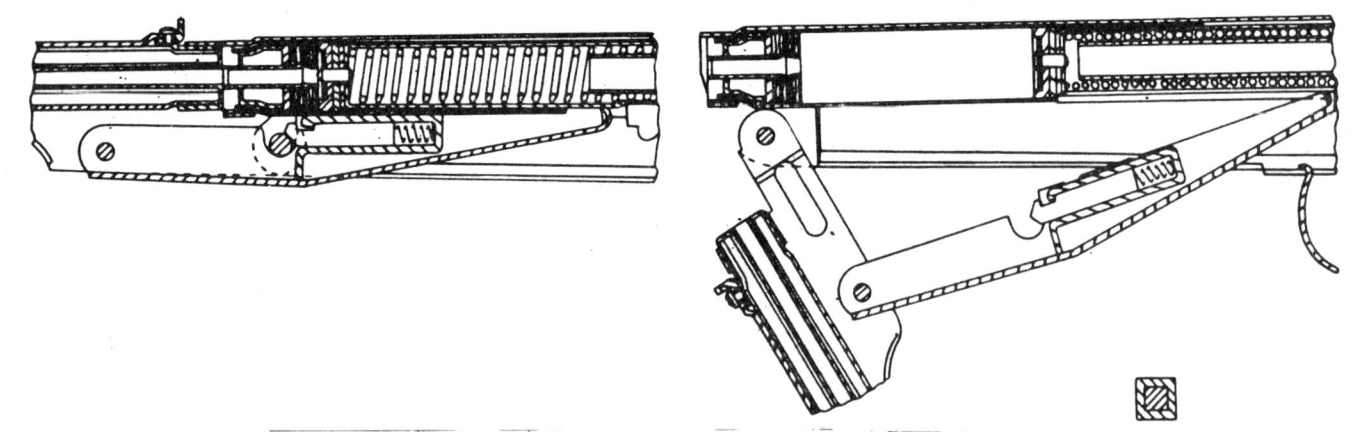

Patent 359870, 1930, dealing with barrel detent being contained in the cocking lever

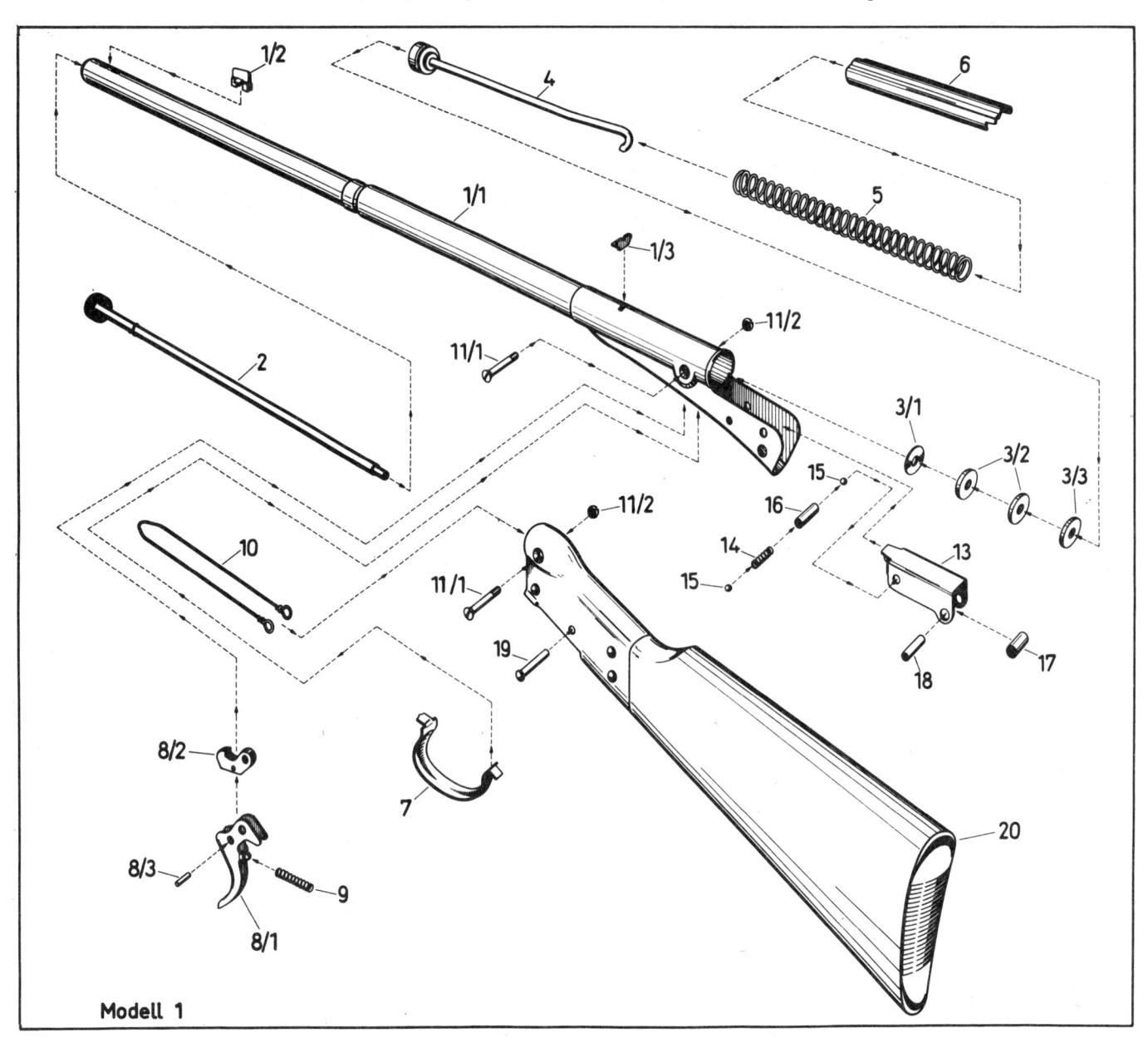

Modell 1

MODEL 15.

MAKER Edwin Mayer and Rudolf Mayer trading as Mayer & Grammelspacher, Dianawerk, Rastatt, Baden, Germany.

DATE 1930 to 1945.

VALUATION £15—£30. £23—£45).

DETAILS A tinplate, or sheet metal, construction air rifle that has been copied worldwide and even converted to an airpistol. See the Voere airpistol in "Airpistols" Third Edition. 32⅝ inches (83 cms) long, although usually advertised as being 34 inches, and having a 12 inch (30.5 cms) .177 smoothbore barrel, the foresight is screw mounted and non-adjustable whilst the rearsight is adjustable for elevation only, but is not worth altering when you consider the accuracy achieved.

The air chamber is stamped with the Diana trademark, i.e. the Huntress, but some will have "DIANA" going over the chamber at an angle with a curved line underneath, not the usual trademark associated with Diana. It is also marked "MOD. 15" and "MADE IN GERMANY". Usually stamped on the butt is a date stamp, i.e. 7,36 stands for July 1936.

For further details see entries under Diana 15 and 16 pre- and post-war and under "Original" 15 and 16. The Model 16 is the stocked version of the above. Although the barrel latch on the Model 15 clips on to the barrel pivot pin there may be some first models about that do not have this arrangement, what they will have are clips on either side of the cocking link that clip up into the underside of the air chamber, similar to the action of the Haenel Model 15.

During the early 1930s they were advertised as having a "Splendid nickel finish" and weighing 2 lbs. It would appear from adverts that the Model 16 came after the Model 15.

The barrel latch was patented during 1930 by Edwin and Rudolf Mayer trading as the famous Mayer & Grammelspacher. Patent number 350870 and dealt with doing away with having to machine a barrel latch and detent into the action, but rather having a spring loaded plunger set into the cocking link that acted on the barrel pivot pin, which is already there anyway. An efficient system for small low powered air rifles.

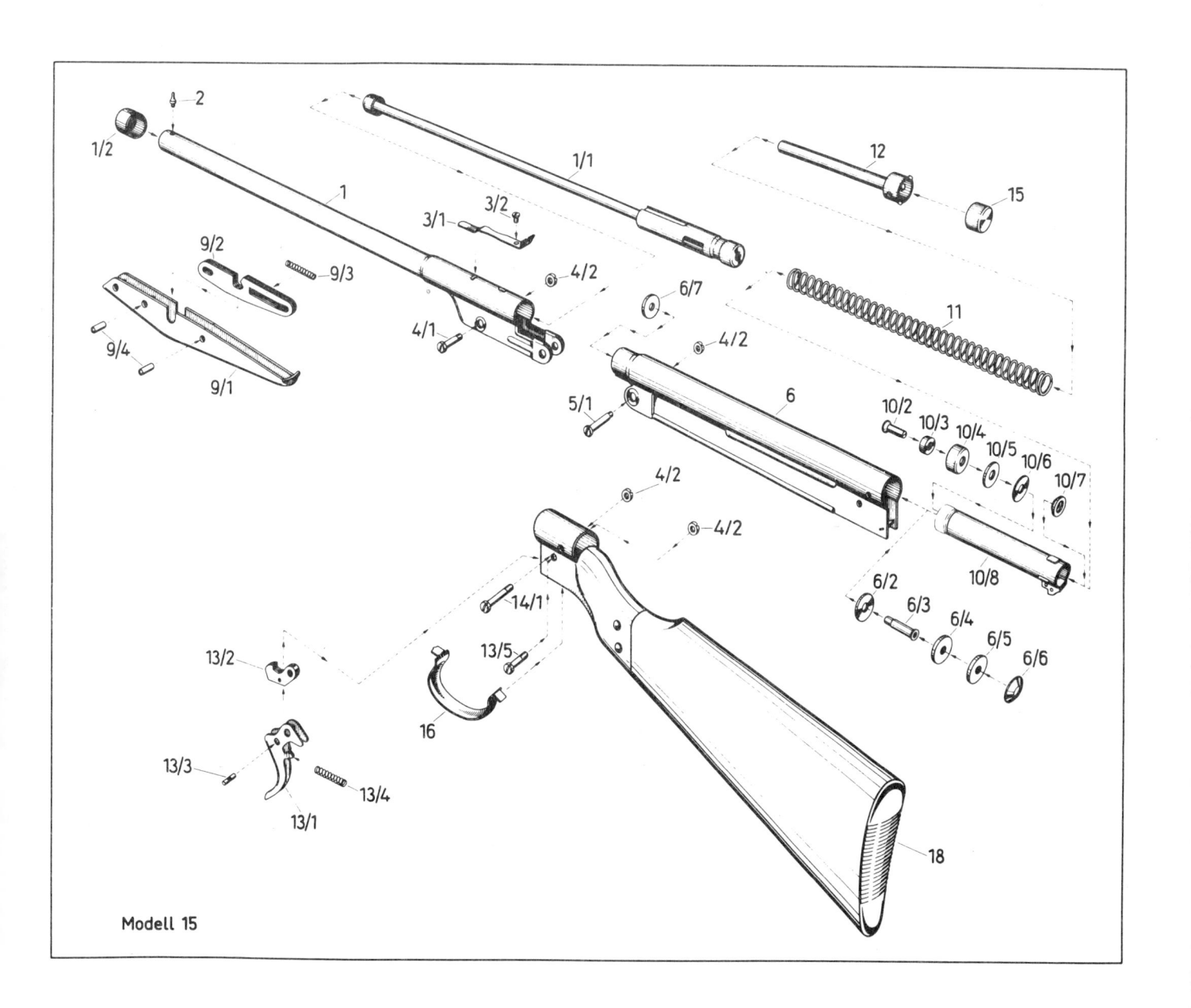

Modell 15

Diana pre-war Model 16. Rope repair to stock is not "original"

MODEL 16.

MAKER "Diana", Mayer & Grammelspacher, Rastatt, West Germany.

DATE 1933 to about 1945, and re-appeared in September 1950 as the "Original" Model 16.

VALUATION £5—£20, £3a—£5a. ($8—$30, $4a—$9a).

DETAILS The stock version of the Model 15. 32½ inches long with a 12 inch .177 smoothbore barrel. Tinplate construction with a blued finish. Screw-in piller foresight and a simple rearsight adjustable for elevation only. Top of air chamber stamped "DIANA" with cursive line underneath. Unusual trademark as the Huntress is missing also has "MOD. 16 MADE IN GERMANY". Butt of stock is stamped with date, i.e., "2.38". When it first appeared in 1933 it may have been called the Model 15, but as the stocked model. This model was not as popular as the Model 15. Mayer & Grammelspacher produced around 25,000 Model 16s each year.

Diana Model 20

MODEL Model 20.

MAKER "Diana", Mayer & Grammelspacher, West Germany.

DATE Middle 1920s to 1945.

VALUATION £20—£40. ($30—$60).

DETAILS "Tinplate" construction. Above has been nickel plated. 34 inches long. Solid metal smoothbore barrel, set in a tinplate wrap-around cover. Breakaction. Stamped on top of trigger block is Diana trademark and the name "DIANA". Stamped in the stock is "MADE IN GERMANY". Sometimes a date stamp appears on the upper part of the stock butt. These were also available nickel plated, same markings on air chamber etc., Date stamp can also appear on underside of stock near trigger action. Nickel plated example seen had date stamp "5,31".

Modell 16

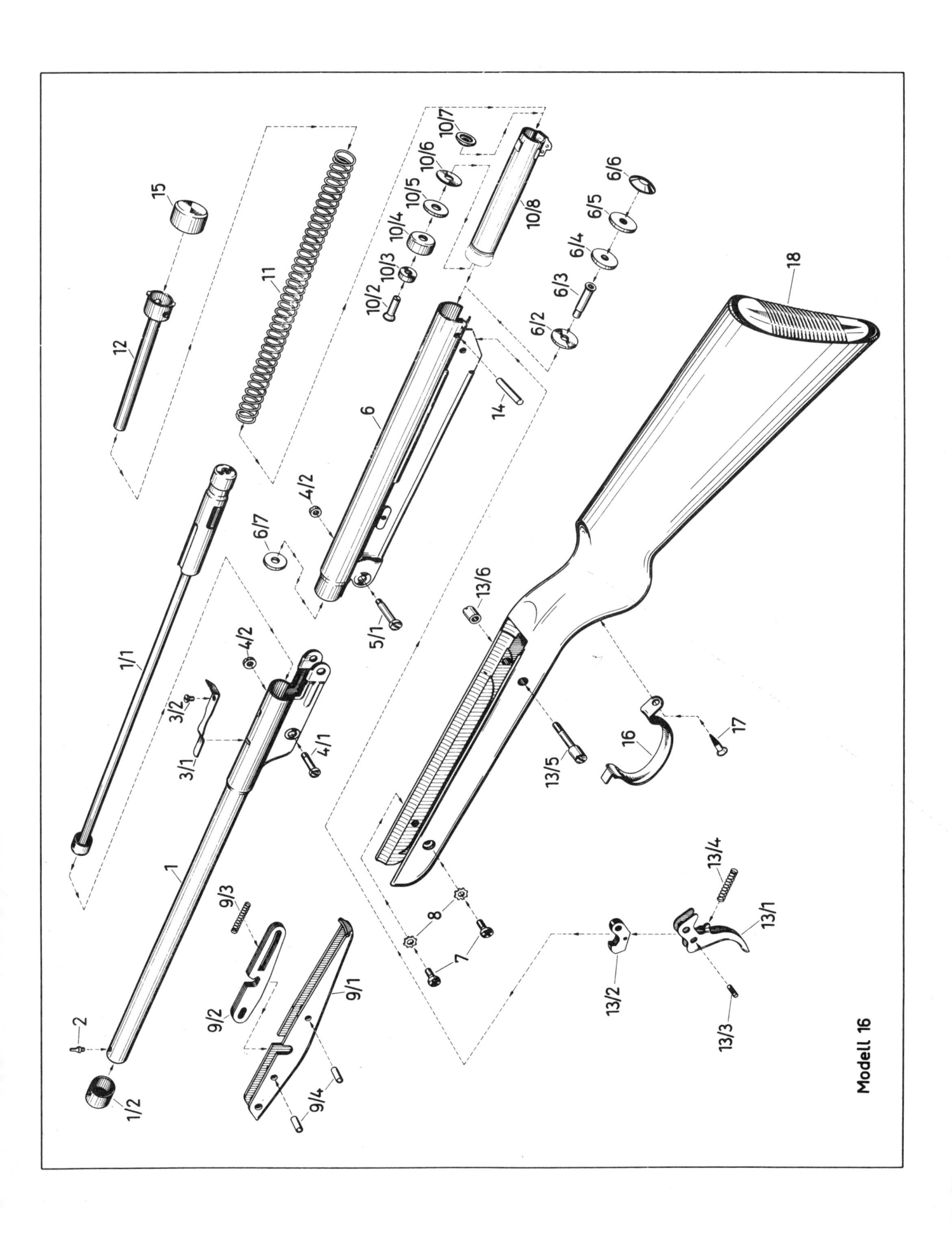

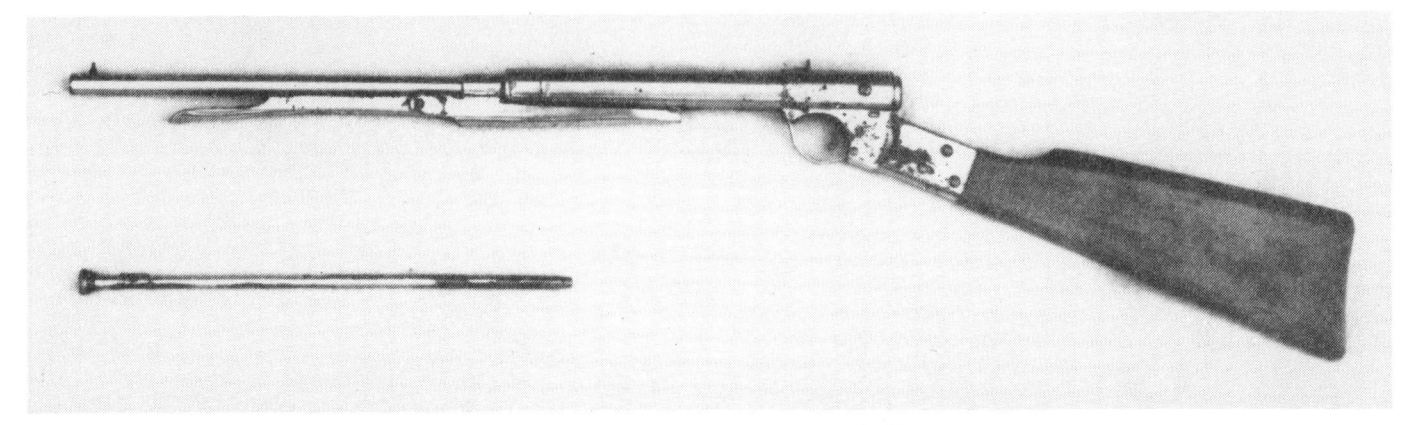

German Diana Model 20 underlever air rifle

MODEL Underlever cocking Model 20.

MAKER Mayer & Grammelspacher, Rastatt, Germany.

DATE Around 1910, rather a short period of manufacture for a Diana air rifle.

VALUATION £30—£60. ($45—$90).

DETAILS A rare Diana tinplate air rifle. Appears to fall into the same trap as the B.S.A. Merlin and Bucanneer. Too much air rifle for too little power. Underlever cocking with a removable barrel for loading. Nickel plated all over. Removable barrel is in .177 and smoothbore, measures 12¼ inches long and is very strong, being a brass liner in a solid steel shell. Air rifle measures 20 inches long, could this be how the Model 20 was so named? Both sides of the trigger block are stamped "DIANA LUFT GEWEHR" which roughly translates to "Diana Air Rifle" and on top of the trigger block is the Diana Huntress trademark with "SCHUTZMARKE". Advertised weight was 1.200 kg and was sold in .177 only, nickel plated and with a "Matted walnut stock".

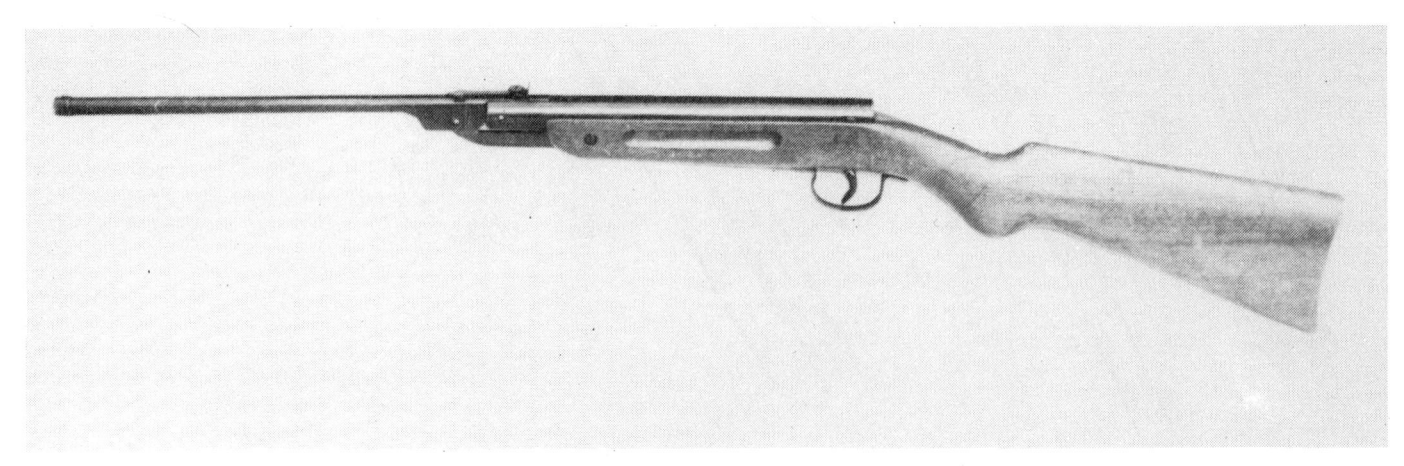

Diana Model 22

MODEL 22.

MAKER Dianawerk, Mayer & Grammelspacher, Rastatt, Bavaria, Germany.

DATE Late 1920s to 1945. Identical to the post-war Diana Model 22 that appeared in the very late 1940s from Scotland under the Diana trademark of Millard Brothers (Milbro).

VALUATION £20—£40. ($30—$60).

DETAILS 36 inches long with a 14¼ inch .177 smoothbore barrel. Screw mounted foresight and dovetail mounted rearsight. Top of air chamber stamped with Diana Huntress trademark and "DIANA—MOD. 22—MADE IN GERMANY". Butt has date stamp. This design appeared after the war under the British Diana trade name. In the 1930s they were obtainable either rifled or smoothbore and blued or nickel plated. Advertised weight 3¼ lbs. Average production of the Model 20 was about 25,000 per year.

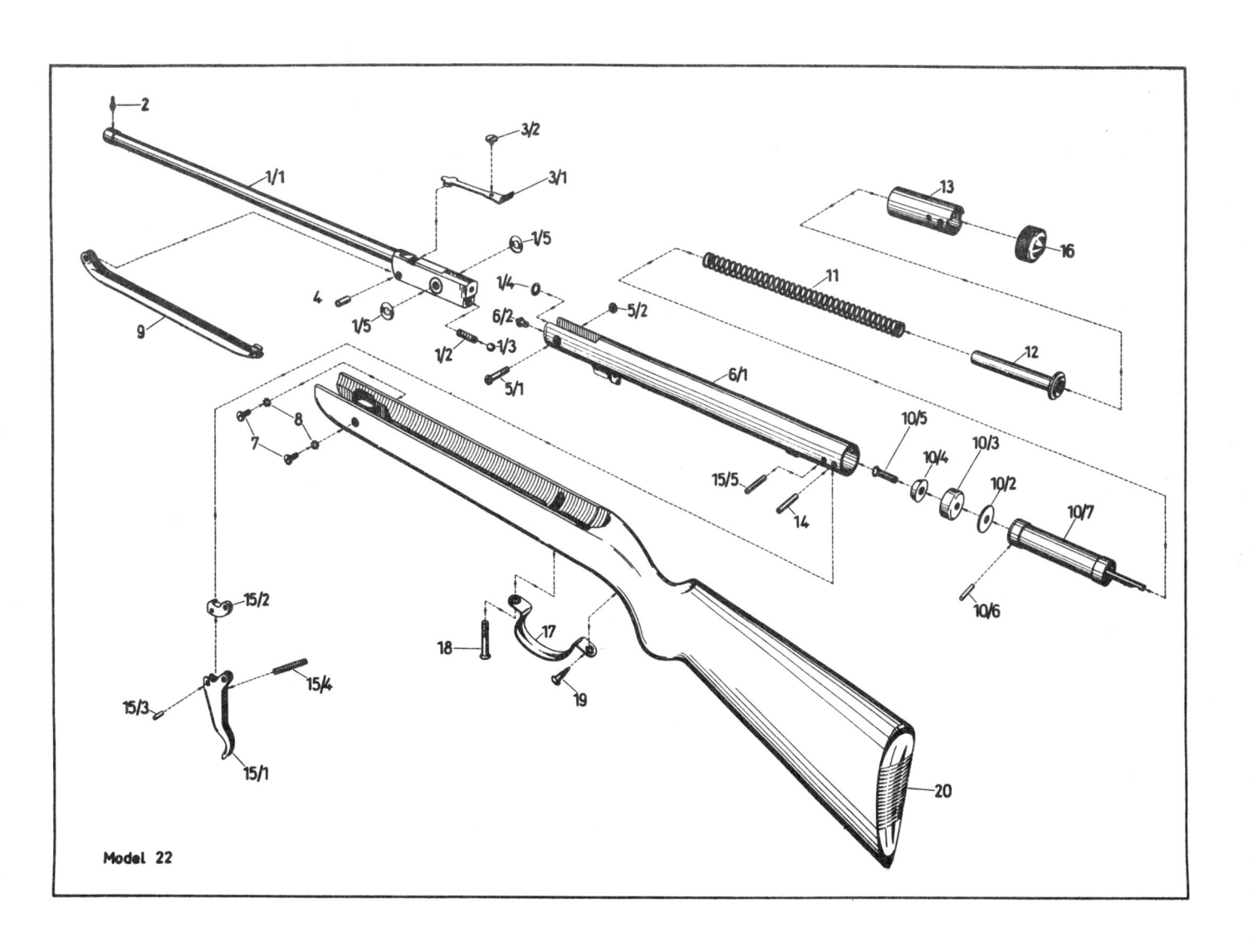

Model 22

Item No.		Code No.	Price Index
1/1—1/3, 1/5, 2)	Barrel complete rifled	301232	G 4
	Barrel complete smooth	301239	G 4
1/2	Locking spring	300146	A 2
1/3	Locking ball	300147	A 1
1/4	Breech washer	300194	A 1
1/5	Hinge ring	300192	A 1
2	Foresight	300148	A 2
3/1—3/2	Rearsight complete	300149	B 3
3/1	Rearsight blade	300150	B 1
3/2	Rearsight screw	300153	A 3
4	Lever pin	300155	A 2
5/1	Barrel axis screw	300193	A 3
5/2	Nut for axis screw	300083	A 1
6/1—6/2	Compression tube	300157	G 3
6/2	Locking cone	300165	A 6
7	Side stock screw	300131	A 2
8	Toothed spring washer	300130	A 1
9	Cocking lever	300154	D 3
10/2—10/7	Piston complete	300166	F 3
10/2—10/5	Piston washer complete	301236	C 1
10/2	Rear fibre washer	300173	A 1
10/3	Leather washer	300175	B 3
10/4	Front fibre washer	300176	A 2
10/5	Piston screw	300177	A 2
10/6	Piston set pin	300178	A 1
11	Main spring	300179	B 3
12	Main spring guide	300180	A 8
13	Trigger housing	300184	B 2
14	End piece pin	300185	A 2
15/1—15/3	Trigger with sear and pin	300186	C 2
15/4	Trigger spring	300199	A 1
15/5	Trigger pin	300190	A 2
16	End piece	300195	A 7
17	Trigger guard	300198	A 7
18	Front guard screw	300200	A 2
19	Rear guard screw	300199	A 1
20	Stock	300196	H 1

Please state Code Number

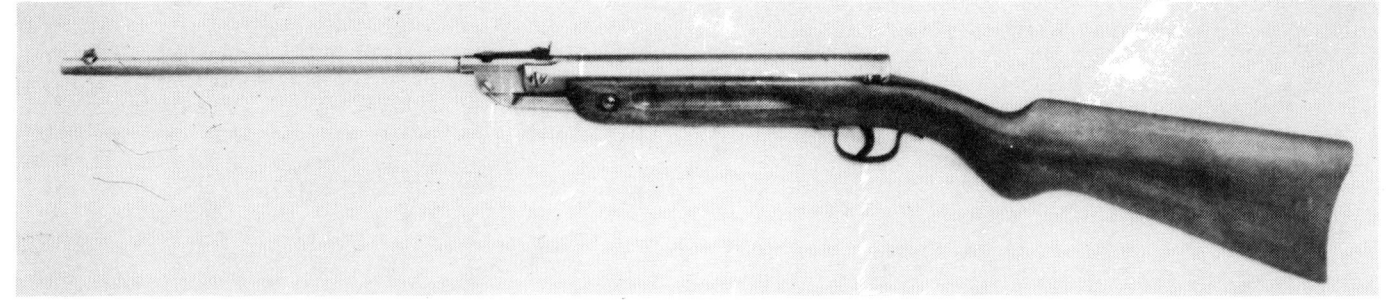

Early German Diana Model 25

MODEL   Appears to be early Model 25.

MAKER   Mayer & Grammelspacher, Rastatt, West Germany.

DATE   The late 1920s to 1945.

VALUATION   £20—£40. ($30—$60).

DETAILS   38½ inches long with a 15½ inch smoothbore barrel. Serial number is stamped on the underside of the breech and is obscured by the cocking lever. Serial number of above is 331. Rear of air chamber is stamped with the "Huntress" trademark and the word "DIANA". Top of barrel stamped "DIANA — LUFT — GEWEHR" whilst on the underside appears "MADE IN GERMANY". Seen advertised in a 1926/7 catalogue as the "new model Diana No. 25". It would appear from catalogue illustrations that a new Model 25 was introduced around 1933. It had an increased length of 40 inches and was available with rifled or smoothbore barrels. Advertised weight 5 lbs. Supplied in .177 only. The serial number appears to be a date stamp with a comma between the month and year, hence one example seen had a number "11,27" stamped on the underside of the barrel breech, this would stand for "November, 1927".

The "Improved" Model 25

MODEL   25.

MAKER   "Diana", Mayer & Grammelspacher, Rastatt, Bavaria, Germany.

DATE   Around 1934/5 to 1945. Although it was reproduced after the war by the Original firm and by Diana of Great Britain. It re-appeared after the war in December 1951.

VALUATION   £20—£50. ($30—$75).

DETAILS   This was the improved model of the first version that appeared in the late 1920s. Visual improvements are a lengthening of the fore-end of the stock towards the barrel pivot screw, no decrease in barrel width just in front of the rearsight, and an outer screw-on cap to the air chamber. A date stamp was stamped on the butt, in this case "10,35". The action lettering was changed to just "DIANA MOD. 25, MADE IN GERMANY" with the Huntress trademark. Available in either .22 or .177 smoothbore or rifled. The sights were the same as fitted to the first model. 38 inches long (96 cms) with a 15¾ inch (40 cms) barrel. Advertised weight around 4¾ lbs. During the late 1930s and early 1940s on average 25,000 were produced each year.

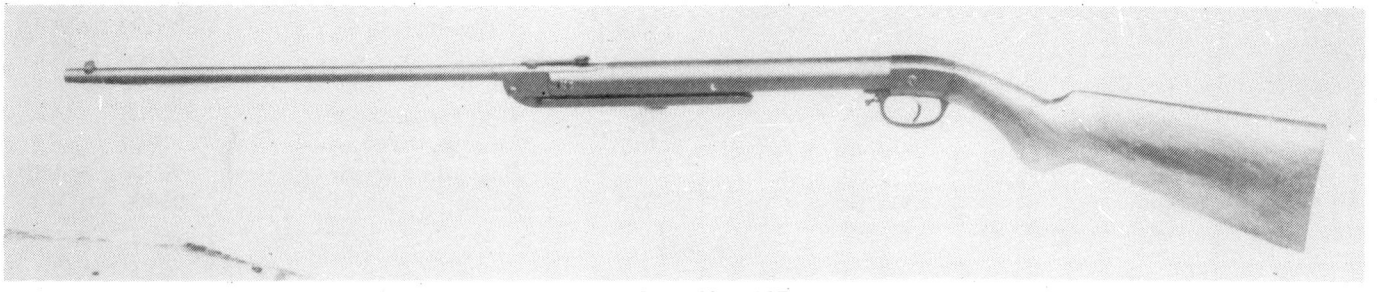

Pre-war Diana Model 27

MODEL   27 pre-war.

MAKER   German "Diana" by Mayer & Grammelspacher, Rastatt, Germany.

DATE   Around 1910—1930s.

VALUATION   £30—£60. ($45—$90).

DETAILS   42¼ inches (107 cms) long with 18¾ inch (48 cms) smoothbore barrel. Serial number stamped on the underside of the barrel breech and is concealed by the cocking lever when barrel is closed. Serial number of above 428. Stamped on top of barrel "DIANA — LUFT— GEWEHR" and on top of the air chamber near trigger block appears the "Huntress" trademark with small arrow and "DIANA". Trigger adjustment is by screw through the trigger guard. Stock has metal butt plate. If above is the early Model 27 then its advertised length is 109 cms, also appeared as the Model 2700. Around 1930 was advertised alongside the more modern Model 127 with a full length stock. Have seen one of the above with date stamp "10,25" bearing a Midland Gun Company brass medallion tacked on to the stock. Could have been retailed by the said Company. Some models may have "MANUFACTURED IN GERMANY" stamped on the underside of the barrel.

The serial number quoted above, 428 may be a date stamp, i.e. April, 1928. Was also sold in .177 rifled calibre. Towards the late 1930s the Diana Huntress trademark appeared on the above along with "DIANA MOD. 27, MADE IN GERMANY". Towards the end of production the date stamp appears to have been stopped and a serial number used in its place as three have been seen bearing numbers 986, 62895, and 70211. The highest date stamp seen is 5,31 (May, 1931).

German Diana Model 27

MODEL 27.

MAKER "Diana" Mayer & Grammelspacher, Rastatt, Germany.

DATE Pre-1945 as Diana trade name used, after Second World War Mayer & Grammelspacher used the "Original" trademark. The above model appeared as an improvement on earlier models sometime in the middle 1930s. The German "Original" Model 27 re-appeared in December 1951.

VALUATION £30—£60.
($45—$90).

DETAILS 41¼ inches long with 17¼ rifled barrel. Serial number not visible. Stamped on rear of air chamber near trigger appears the Diana Huntress trademark holding aloft the air rifle and discarding her bow and arrow. Underneath appears "DIANA MOD. 27 MADE IN GERMANY". Double pull trigger with two adjuster screws set in the trigger. Metal butt plate on early models. The trigger can be dry fired if the action is only allowed to partly cock. On some examples a date stamp appears on the base of the butt. Towards the end of the 1930s the average yearly production rate was 15,000.

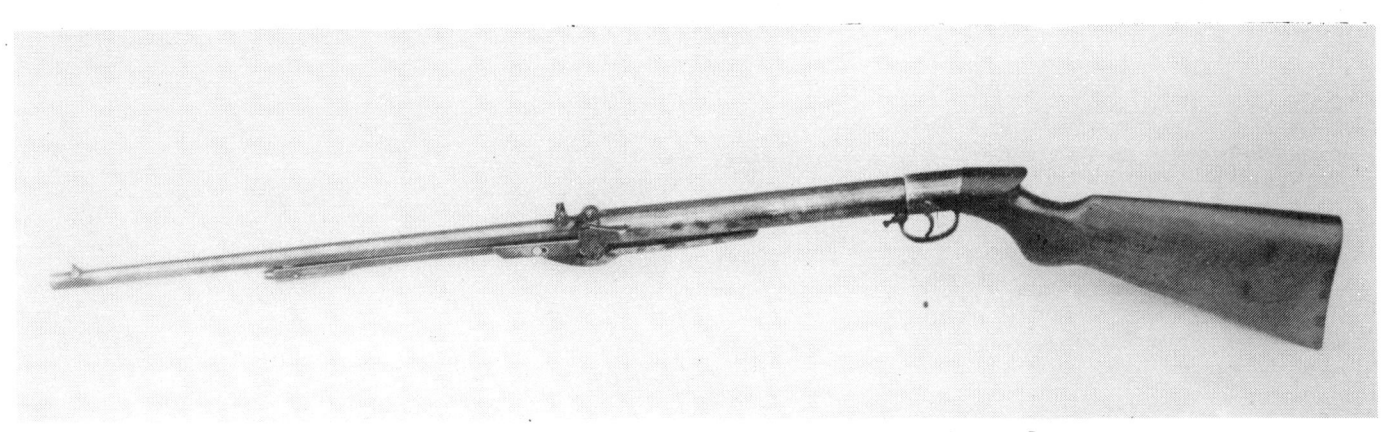

Diana Model 48. Early Model. Note distinguishing shape of cocking lever

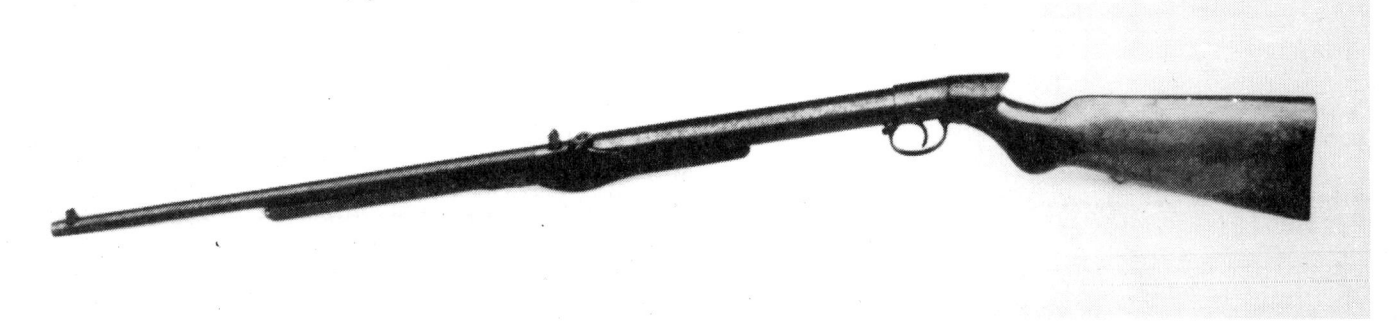

Diana Model 48, later model

99

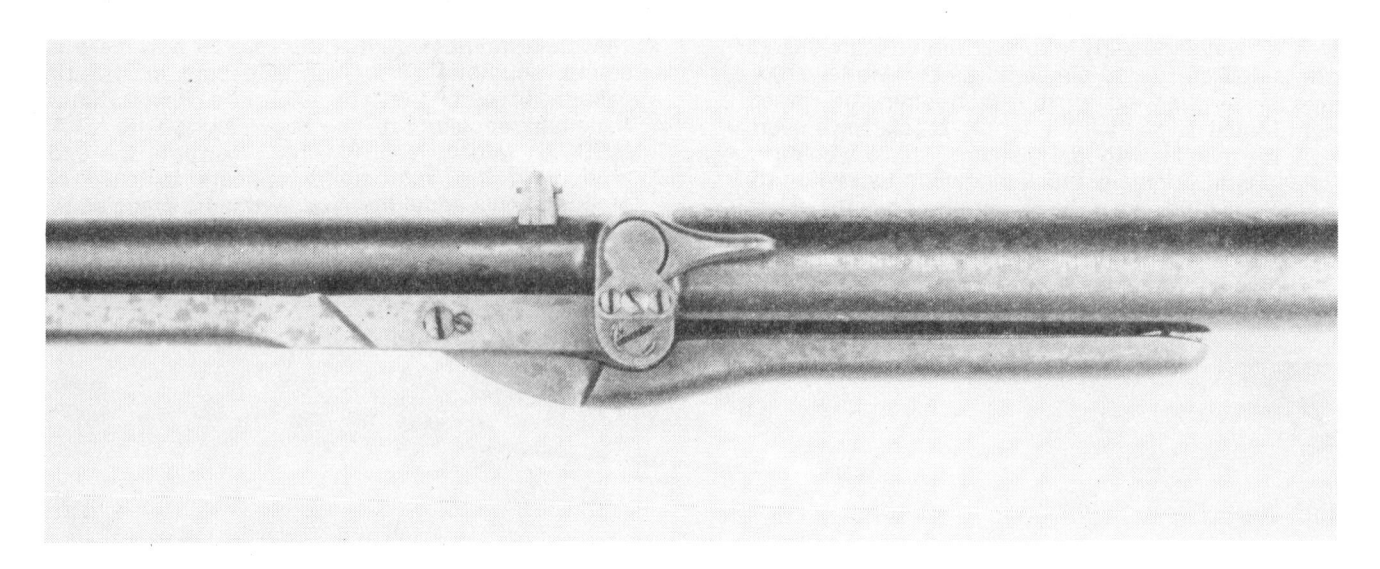

Diana Model 48. Note locking screw between the two tap-plate screws

MODEL 48.

MAKER Mayer & Grammelspacher, Rastatt, Germany.

DATE The predecessor to the Model 50. Seen advertised as early as 1923, but the above has a later style underlever with a smooth profile similar to the pre-war B.S.A. underlevers, whilst the early Diana Model 48s had a narrow waist shaped underlever. The above could well be just before Second World War or just after. Would date the above from around the middle 1930s to the early 1940s.

VALUATION £100—£150. ($150—$225). Becoming quite a rare air rifle and rarely seen these days.

DETAILS Very similar to the pre-war B.S.A. underlever. 46 inches long with a 19½ inch .22 rifled barrel. Underlever cocking action. Barrel appears to be braized into the action just in front of the rearsight. High blade foresight similar to that fitted to the Haenel airpistols. Serial number and/or date stamp not visible. Top of air chamber stamped with Huntress trademark and "DIANA — MOD 48". There was also a Model 48E. Fitted with metal butt plate. Pistol grip stock with pressed chequering. Advertised weight 7½ lbs. Sold in either .177 or .22 calibre with rifled barrels. Interesting tap plate has two outer screws for holding plate to action and inner locking screw. Have seen many pre-war B.S.A. underlevers with loose tap plates. May have "MADE IN GERMANY" stamped on the underside of the barrel, and a number may appear on the stock. Should the tap be loose then unscrew the keeper screw and remove, then loosen the main screw and the plate under this can be rotated around the tap square end so that you have four positions in which to take up any slack in the main screw position when tightened down. Quite a rare air rifle as only about 3,000 were produced each year. The top of the barrel may be stamped "DIANA—LUFT—GEWEHR", but on many this is very faint and might be overlooked.

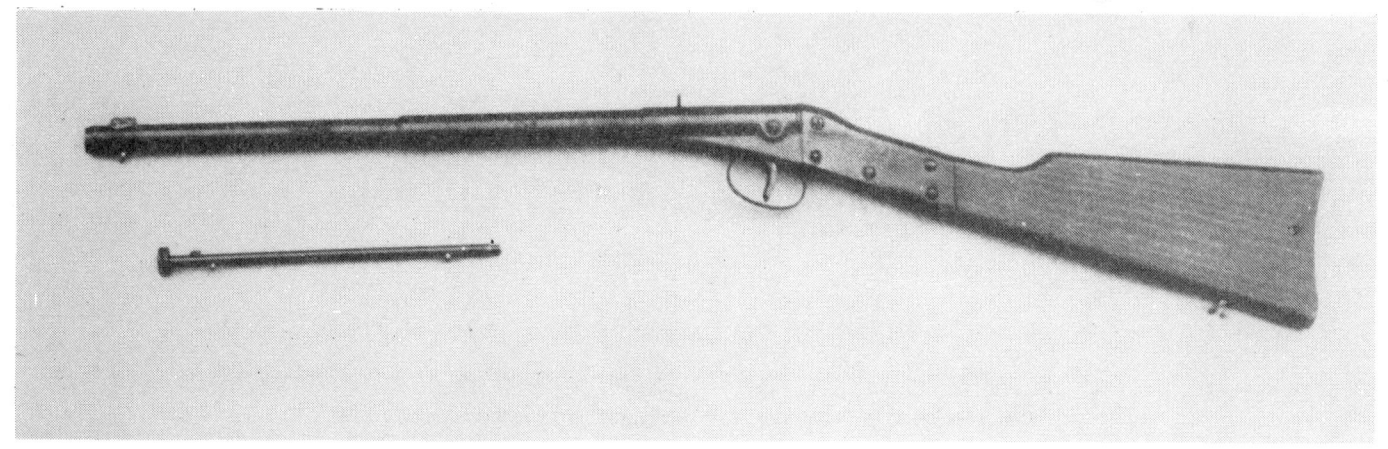

Diana Model 1

MODEL Model 1.

MAKER "Diana", Millard Bros., Motherwell, Lanarkshire, Scotland.

DATE Post-war, so assume around 1949 onwards, seen advertised until 1959. Price then 27/9.

VALUATION £5—£20, £3a—£7a). ($8—$30, $4a—$11a).

DETAILS Almost identical to the pre-war German Model 1. Main differences being a single crimp in the barrel half way along and two small ball bearings spring loaded for the action catch. Stamped on either side of the rear section appears "DIANA — MADE IN GT. BRITAIN" whilst on the top of the air chamber is stamped "DIANA — MOD I — MADE IN GREAT BRITAIN", with the "Huntress" trademark holding aloft her Diana air rifle and throwing away her now obsolete bow and arrow. Removable smoothbore barrel for loading. Early models may have a date stamp on the underside of the stock where it joins the action. Have seen one stamped "12 49".

Diana Model 1 parts diagram

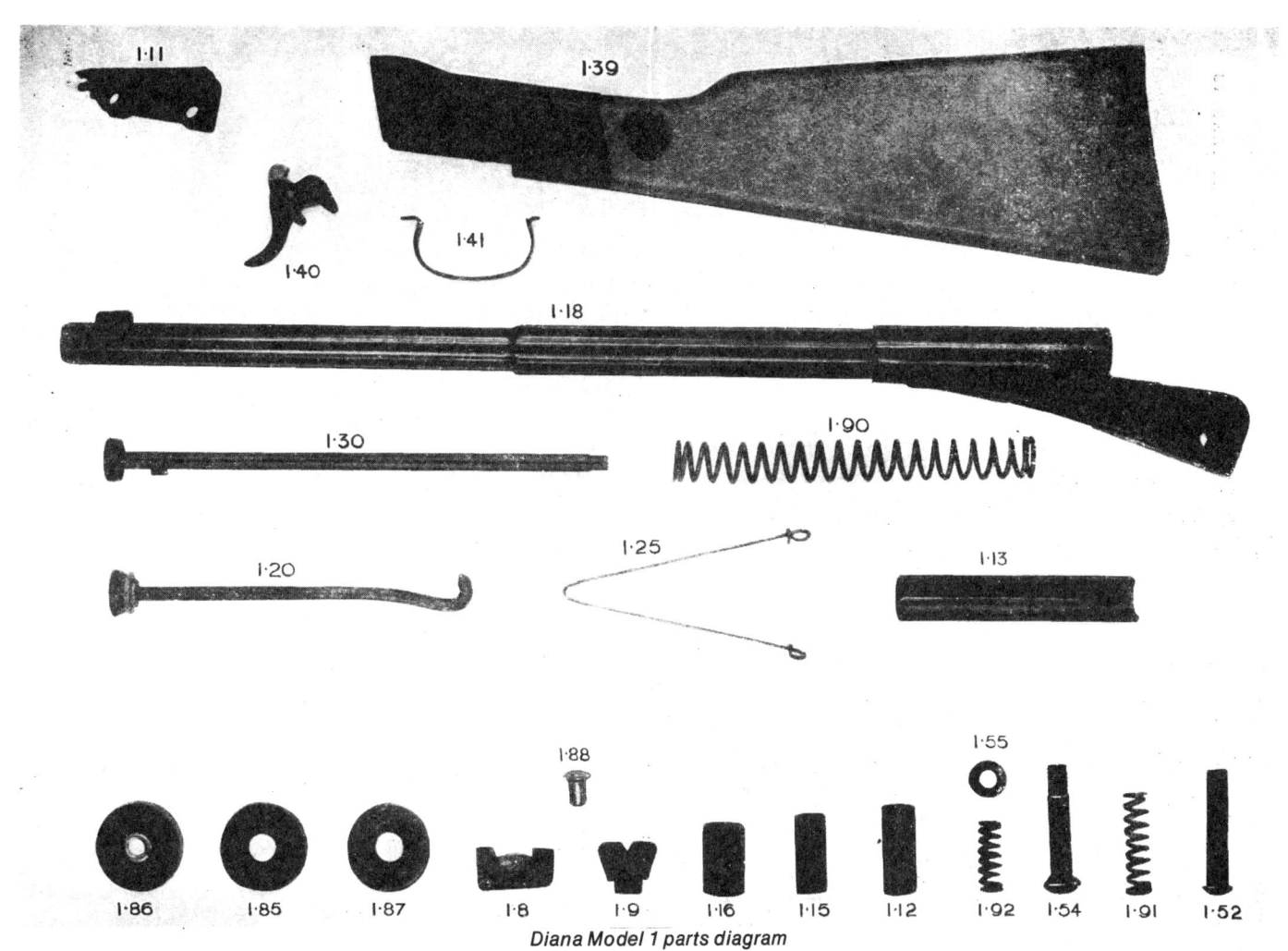

SPARE PARTS LIST — MODEL No. 1

Detail	Price		Description	Location, etc.
1-8	6d.	Each	Front Sight	
1-9	4d.	"	Rear Sight	
1-11	1/3	"	Trigger Housing	Assembled to breech end of 1-18 barrel. Location for trigger assembly.
1-12	4d.	"	Spacing Tube	Spacer used in 1-11 housing.
1-13	9d.	"	Plunger Sleeve	Guide for 1-20 plunger assembly.
1-15	4d.	"	Ball Spring Tube	Take two 7/32 in. steel balls and provide locking action with dimple on housing on 1-39 butt assembly.
1-16	4d.	"	Spacing Tube	Spacer holding 1-15 in 1-11 housing.
1-18	10/6	"	Barrel Assembly	Complete with sealing washers.
1-20	4/-	"	Plunger Assembly	Fitted with main spring 1-90 and 1-25 "V" wire provides cocking and firing action.
1-25	9d.	"	"V" Wire	See 1-20.
1-30	3/-	"	Pellet Tube Assembly	Detachable loading medium for slug or dart. Fitted to 1-18.
1-39	9/-	"	Butt Assembly	
1-40	1/9	"	Trigger Complete	See 1-11.
1-41	7d.	"	Trigger Guard	
1-52	3d.	"	Rivet	Hinge pin locating through 1-11, 1-18 and 1-39.
1-54	5d.	"	Screw	Attaches "V" wire to 1-39.
1-55	4d.	"	Nut	Used with 1-54.
1-85	1/-	"	Packing Washer	Used as seal at clenched section on 1-18.
1-86	1/-	"	Eyeletted Washer	Used as seal at clenched section on 1-18.
1-87	1/-	"	Packing Washer	Used as seal at clenched section on 1-18.
1-88	2d.	"	Eyelet	With 1-85 makes up 1-86.
1-90	1/6	"	Main Spring	
1-91	7d	"	Trigger Spring	Trigger Spring.
1-92	7d.	"	Ball Catch Spring	Used with 1-15.

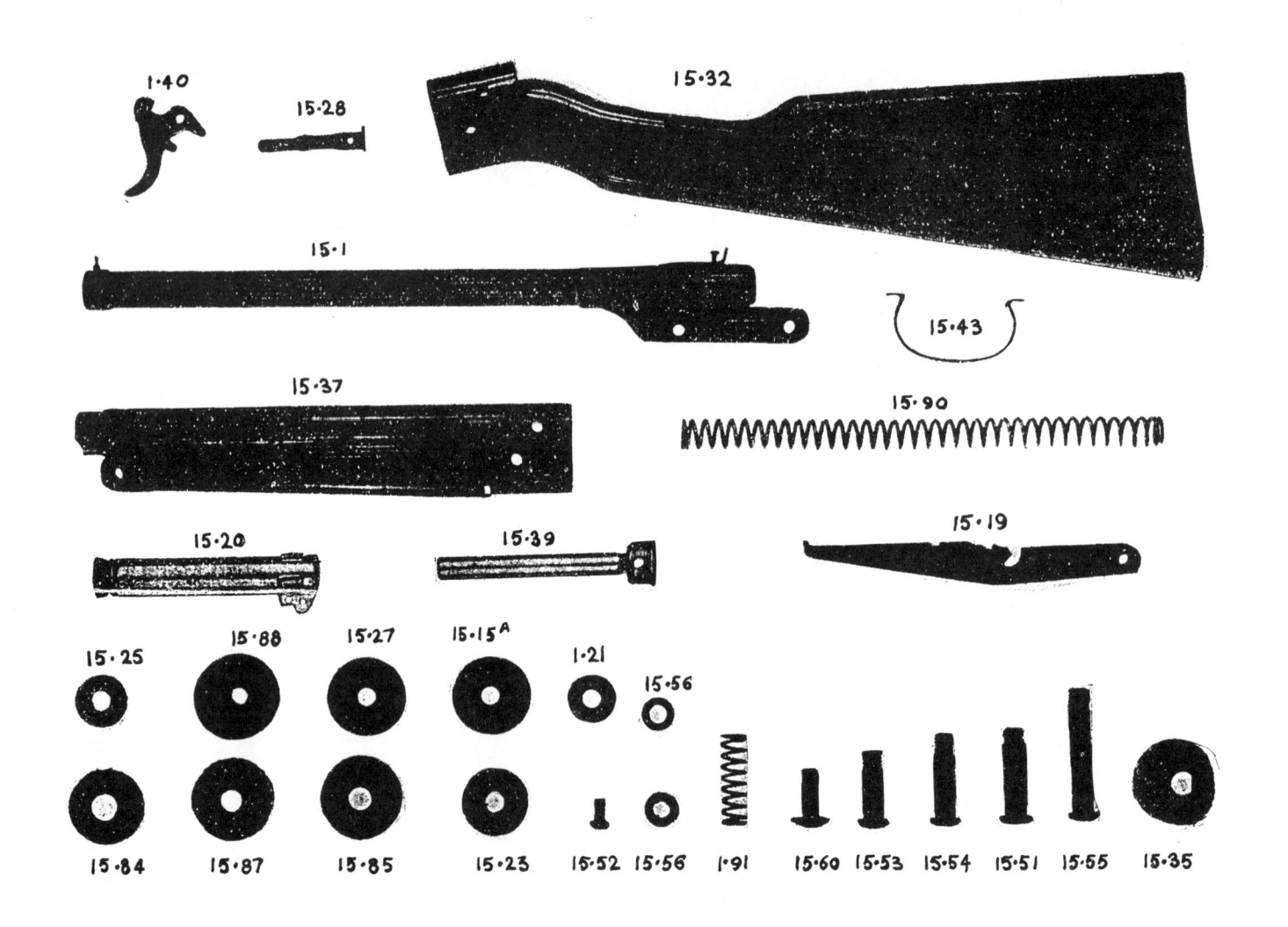

SPARE PARTS LIST — MODEL No. 15

Detail	Price		Description	Location, etc.
1-21	3d.	Each	Piston Washer	See 15-20.
1-40	1/9	"	Trigger Assembly	
1-91	7d.	"	Trigger Spring	
* 15-1	15/-	"	Barrel Assembly	Complete with front sight and rear sight.
* 15-19	4/6	"	Cocking Lever Complete	
15-15A	3d.	"	Cylinder Washer	Used in cylinder end 15-37.
* 15-20	5/-	"	Piston Assembly	1-21, 15-23, 15-24, 15-25, 15-27 and 15-88 washers comprise piston head riveted with 15-60.
15-23	3d.	"	Piston Washer	See 15-20.
15-24	3d.	"	Piston Washer	See 15-20.
15-25	3d.	"	3 BA. Steel Washer	See 15-20.
15-27	4d.	"	Fibre Washer	See 15-20.
15-28	1/3	"	Rear Sight Assembly	Complete with screw 15-52.
* 15-32	10/-	"	Butt Assembly	
15-35	7d.	"	Cylinder End Cap	Sealing cap in 15-37.
* 15-37	7/6	"	Cylinder	The shell into which is fitted 15-20, 15-39 and 1-40.
* 15-39	1/9	"	Spring Guide Assembly	Guide for main spring 15-90.
15-43	7d.	"	Trigger Guard	
15-50	6d	"	Front Sight	Not illustrated.
15-51	5d	"	Hinge Screw	Attaches barrel to cylinder.
15-51M	4d.	"	Nut	Illustrated as 15-56. See 15-51.
15-52	4d.	"	Rear Sight Screw	See 15-28.
15-53	5d.	"	Cocking Lever Screw	Attaches cocking lever to cylinder.
15-54	5d.	"	Trigger Screw	Hinge screw for trigger through 15-37.
15-55	6d.	"	L.S.B. Screw	Hinges cylinder to L.S.B. housing on 15-32.
15-56	4d.	"	Nut	Used with 15-53, 15-54 and 15-55.
15-60	3d.	"	Piston Rivet	See 15-20.
15-85	4d.	"	Leather Washer	As 15-84.
15-86	4d.	"	Leather Washer	Packing washer for cylinder end 15-37.
15-87	4d.	"	Breech Washer	Sealing medium between barrel 15-1 and cylinder 15-37.
15-88	9d.	"	Cup Washer	See 15-20.
15-90	1/9	"	Main Spring	

Prices are for supply of parts only — fitting is charged extra.
Items marked * are subject to purchase tax, in addition to retail prices shown, in United Kingdom.
These prices apply in United Kingdom only.
If inexpensive Spares have to be specially ordered from the works, Dealers may require a minimum charge of 2/6d. to cover the cost of postage and handling, despite any lower price quoted in our Spares List.

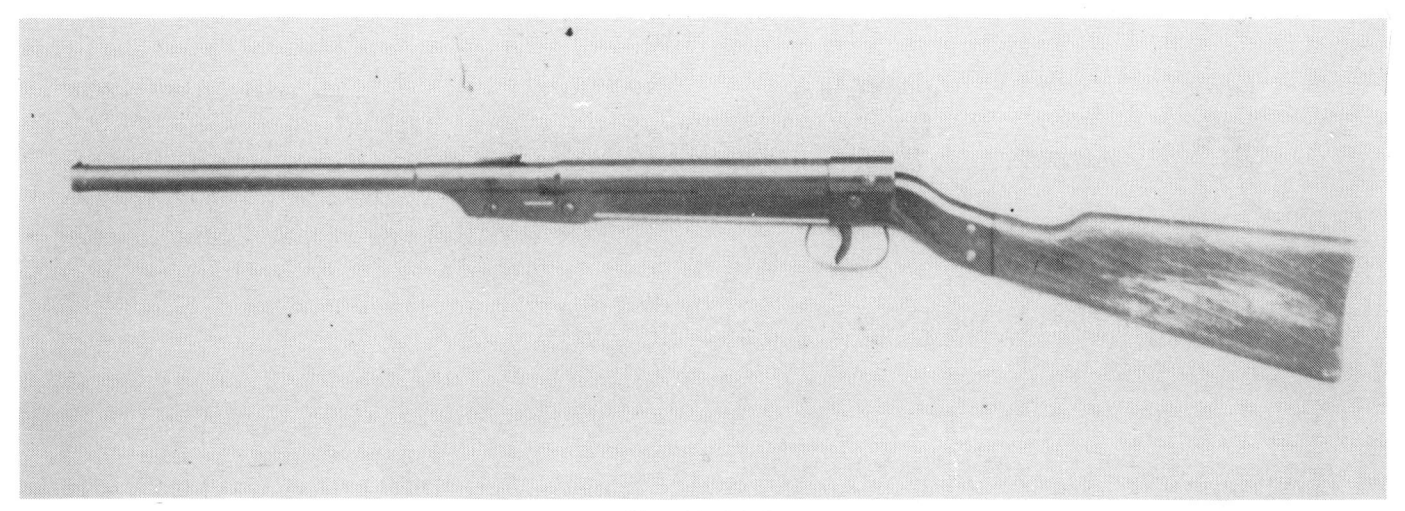

Diana Model 15

MODEL Model 15.

MAKER "Diana", Millard Bros. Ltd., Motherwell, Lanarkshire, Scotland.

DATE Advertised around 1930 in German catalogue, but the above was made in England so made sometime after Second World War. Listed in Smith's book so would assume manufacture in the 1950—1960 region. Later became the Diana Model G74 with extended stock, see G.R. April 1976. Production ceased in 1980.

VALUATION £10—£30.
($15—$45).

DETAILS "Tinplate" construction. Very similar to a "Slavia" air rifle. 32 inches long. Barrel brass liner and smoothbore. Held together by nuts and bolts except for the two rivets holding stock to action. Stamped on top of air chamber is "DIANA MOD. 15 MADE IN GREAT BRITAIN" along with the Diana trademark. "DIANA MADE IN GT. BRITAIN" is also stamped either side of the rear on trigger block. Have seen some with a rifled brass barrel liner. To remove or replace the barrel liner first remove the foresight by unscrewing take off end barrel cap, then push liner back towards the rearsight when barrel has been broken for cocking the action. The front barrel plug has a threaded hole for the foresight and when barrel liner has been replaced this must be lined up with the hole in the outer barrel casing for the foresight to be replaced.

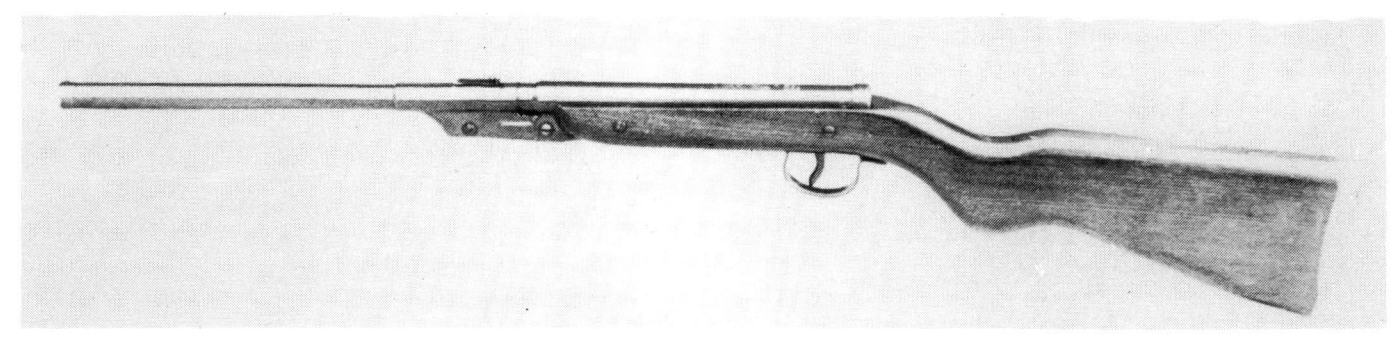

Diana Model 16 (The Plainsman)

MODEL 16. The Plainsman Model.

MODEL "Diana", Millard Brothers Ltd., Motherwell, Lanarkshire. Scotland.

DATE From the late 1940s to 1974.

VALUATION £10—£30.
($15—$45).

DETAILS The fully stock version of the Model 15, see Diana Model 15 and "Original" Models for comparison. Nicely blued finish with stock which has date stamp on the butt. Top of air chamber is stamped with the Diana Huntress trademark followed by "DIANA, MOD. 16, MADE IN GT. BRITAIN" this dates the air rifle as from the 1960s because at a later date the inscription was changed to "BRITISH MADE", one would assume that Britain was no longer considered GREAT! Advertised weight 2 lbs 11 oz. 32½ inches long with a 12 inch smoothbore barrel. Screw-in pillar foresight and simple rearsight adjustable for elevation only. Was only sold in .177. During the middle 1970s Winchester of America sold the above as the Model 416 and Hy-score as the Model 805, "THREE GUNS IN ONE" because you could use it for pellets, darts and BBs. Even Daisy had a go at selling the above as their Model 160. The follow-on from the above appears to be the Model Series 70, Model 74. During the 1960s some were fitted with a small telescopic sight ramp that was spot welded on to the air chamber, two spot welds were used and the lettering was stamped in front of the ramp and "Golded-in".

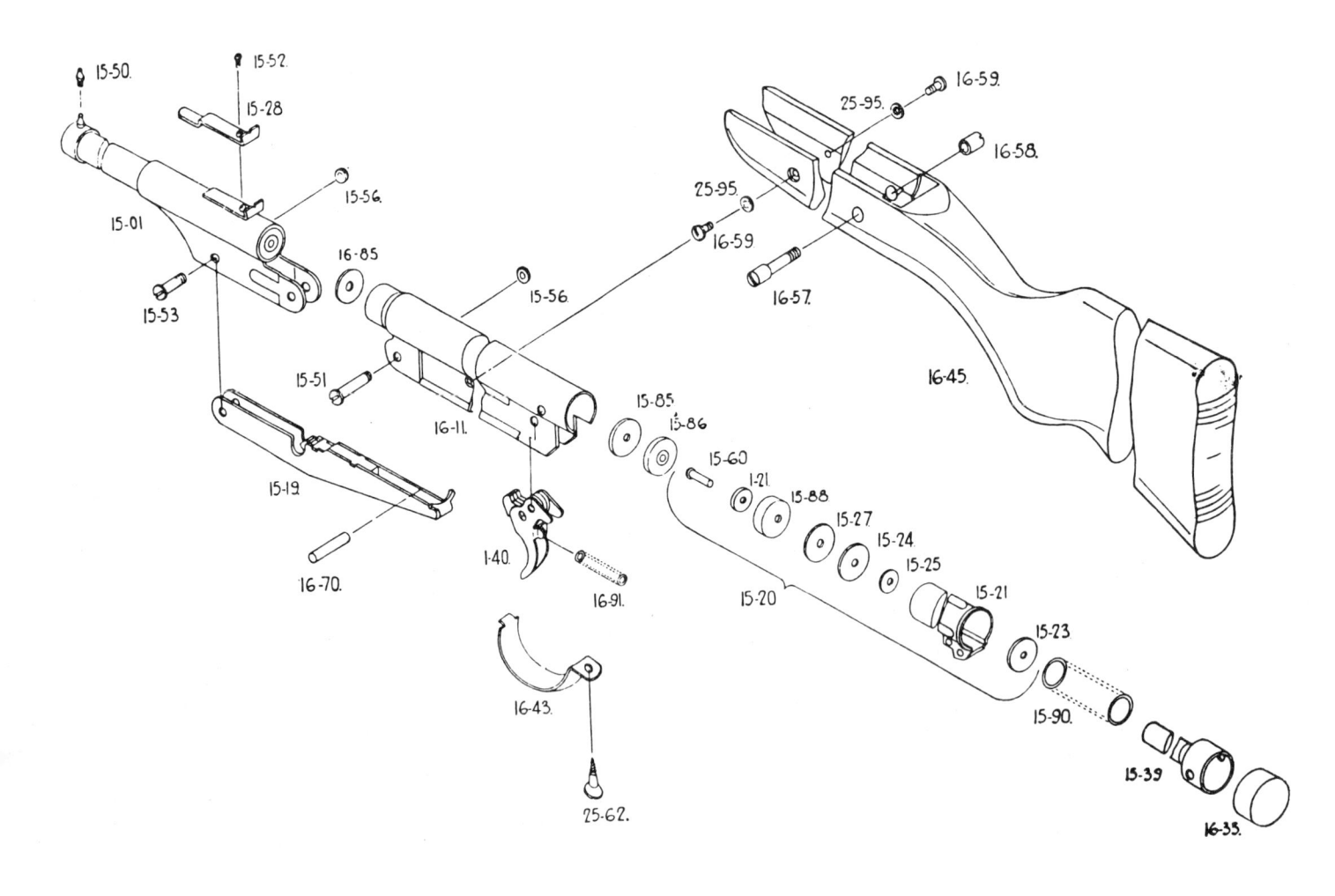

SPARE PARTS LIST
MODEL No G16

Stock No.	Description	Designation	Beschreibung	Beskrivning
01-21	Piston Washer	Cuvette du cuir de piston	Kolbenscheibe	Pistongbricka
01-40	Trigger Assembly	Détente	Abzug	Avtryckare, komplett
15-01	Barrel Assembly	Canon lisse	Lauf, glatt	Pipa, komplett
15-19	Cocking Lever	Levier d'armement	Spannhebel	Spännarm
15-20	Piston Assembly	Piston complet	Kolben komplett	Pistong, komplett
15-23	Piston Washer	Rondelle du piston	Kolbenscheibe	Pistongbricka
15-24	Piston Washer	Rondelle dur piston	Kolbenscheibe	Pistongbricka
15-25	3 B.A. Steel Washer	Rondelle d'acier	Staalscheibe	Stålbricka
15-27	Fibre Washer	Plaque ébonite du cuir de piston	Kolbenfiberscheibe	Fiberbricka
15-28	Rear Sight	Hausse	Visier	Sikte
15-39	Spring Guide Assembly	Guide du ressort de piston	Federführung	Fjäderstyrstång
15-50	Front Sight	Guidon	Korn	Korn
15-51	Hinge Screw	Vis du charniere	Scharnierschraube	Scharnierskruv
15-52	Rear Sight Screw	Vis de la hausse	Visierschraube	Siktskruv
15-53	Cocking Lever Screw	Vis du levier d'armement	Hebelschraube	Spännarmsskruv
15-56	Nut	Ecrou	Mutter	Mutter
15-60	Piston Rivet	Rivet du piston	Kolbenniete	Nit till pistong
15 85	Leather Washer	Rondelle du cylindre	Zylinderscheibe	Läderpackning
15-86	Leather Washer	Rondelle du cylindre	Zylinderscheibe	Läderpackning
15-88	Cup Washer	Cuir du piston	Ledermanschette	Skålformad läderpackning
15-90	Main Spring	Ressort Principal	Kolbenfeder	Pistongfjäder
16-11	Cylinder	Cylindre	Zylinder	Cylinder
16-35	Cylinder End Cap	Cuvette du cylindre	Abschlussdeckel	Ändhylsa till cylinder
16-43	Trigger Guard	Sougarde	Abzugbügel	Varbygel
16-45	Butt	Crosse	Schaft	Stock
16-57	Trigger Screw	Vis du détente	Abzugschraube	Avtryckarskruv
16-58	Trigger Screw Nut	Ecrou de la vis de détente	Abzugschraube & Mutter	Mutter till avtryckarskruv
16-59	Cylinder Screw	Vis du cylindre	Zylinderschraube	Cylinderskruv
16-70	Locking Pin	Goupille du cylindre	Zylinderstift	Låsbult
16-85	Breech Washer	Rondelle de culasse	Laufdichtung	Pippackning
16-91	Trigger Spring	Ressort de détente	Abzugfeder	Avtryckarfjäder
25-62	Rear Guard Screw	Vis de la Sougarde (arrière)	Hintere Abzugbügelschraube	Bakre skruv till varbygel
25-95	Washer	Rondelle	Dichtung	Packning

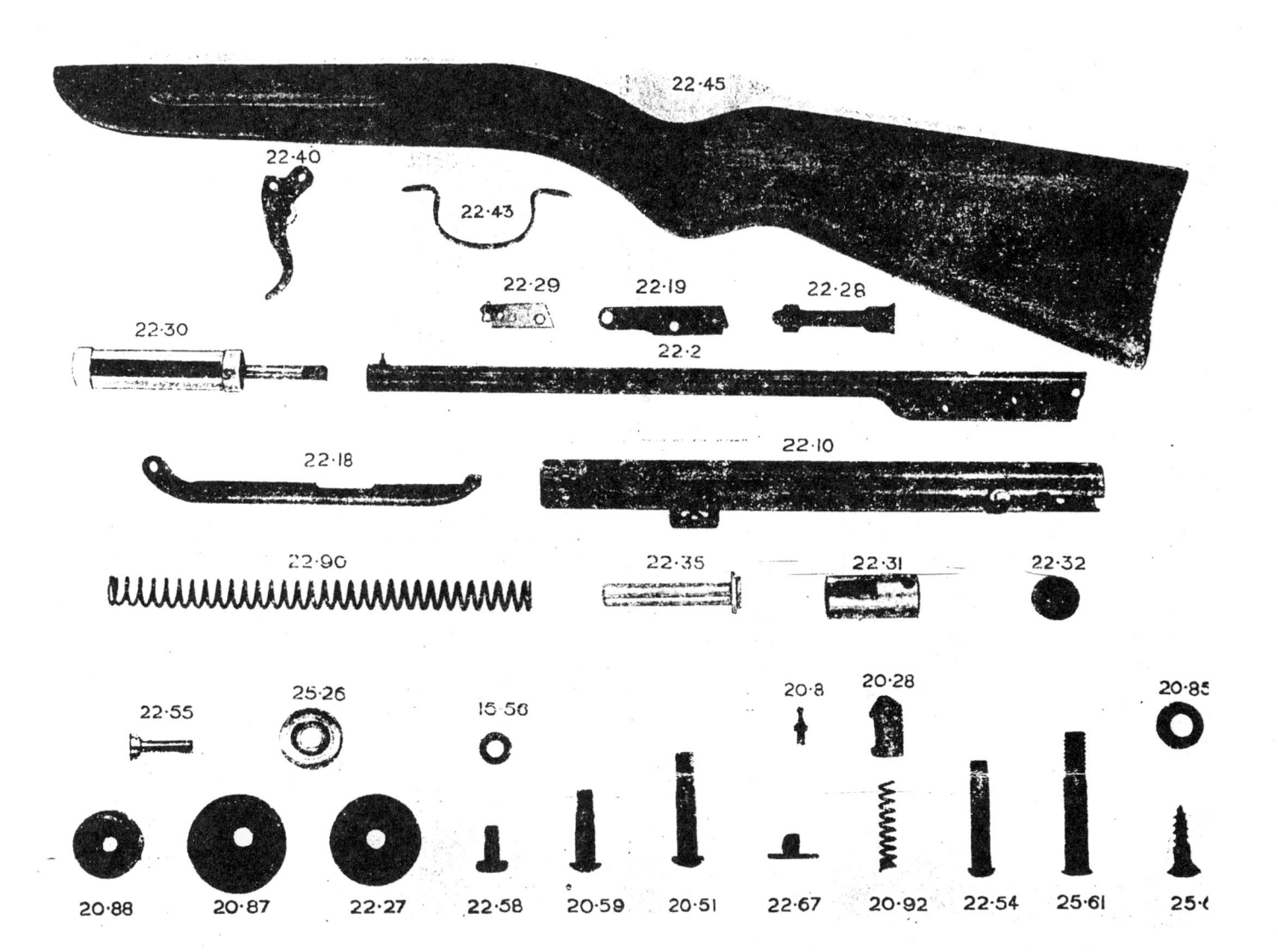

SPARE PARTS LIST — MODEL No. 22

Detail	Price	Each	Description	Location, etc.
15-56	4d.	Each	Nut	Used with 20-51 and 20-59 (2 off)
20-8	6d.	”	Front Sight	
20-28	2/-	”	Catch Pin	Locking Pin inserted to cylinder 22-10.
20-51	7d.	”	Hinge Screw	Hinges barrel 22.8 to cylinder 11-10.
20-59	6d.	”	Cocking Lever Screw	
20-85	4d.	”	Breech Washer	Leather sealing washer on 22-10.
20-87	1/-	”	Piston Cup Washer	Used on 22-30 in conjunction with 20-88, 22-27, 22-55, and 25-26 constitutes piston head.
20-88	6d.	”	Piston Leather Washer	Used as on 20-87.
20-92	6d.	”	Catch Pin Spring	Is spring loading medium for 20-28 used on 22-10.
* 22-8s	17/6	”	Barrel Assembly	Smooth. Complete with front sight. Illustrated as 22-2.
* 22-8r	20/-	”	Barrel Assembly	Rifled.
* 22-10	30/-	”	Cylinder Assembly	The tube into which is fitted 22-30 piston with washers, 22-81 trigger housing, 22-35 spring guide assembly and 22-40 trigger assembly.
* 22-18	4/6	”	Cocking Lever Case	
22-19	1/-	”	Catch Block Case	Assembly fitted to 22-8 barrel, providing locking action with 20-28 in cyl.
32-27	4d.	”	Fibre Washer	Used as on 20-87.
22-28	2/-	”	Rear Sight	Complete with adjustable screw fitted.
22-29	3/6	”	Catch Block	Part of 22-19 Assembly.
* 22-30	8/6	”	Piston Rod Assembly	To complete requires washers 20-87, 20-88, and 22-27, 22-55 screw and 25-26 washer.
22-31	2/3	”	Trigger Housing	Internal housing in 22-10 for 22-40 trigger assembly.
22-32	1/-	”	Cylinder End Cap	Sealing cap on butt end of 22-10 cylinder.
* 22-35	1/9	”	Spring Guide Tube	Guide for main spring 22-90, housed in 22-10.
22-40	2/-	”	Trigger Assembly	
22-43	1/-	”	Trigger Guard	
* 22-45	22/6	”	Butt	Stained and Polished.
22-53	4d.	”	Grub Screw	Stop for 20-28 lock pin (not illustrated).
22-54	6d.	”	Trigger Screw	Hinge screw attaching trigger to 22-21 (this has been replaced by Pin 22-93).
22-55	5d.	”	Piston Screw	Used with piston washers (see 22-30) to complete assy.
22-58	4d.	”	Screw	2 off required to screw butt to bridge on 22-10.
22-67	8d.	”	Rear Sight Screw	
22-90	2/-	”	Main Spring	
25-26	6d.	”	Piston Washer	As on 20-87.
25-61	9d.	”	Guard Front Screw	Fixed 22-43 to welded nut on 22-10.
25-62	3d.	”	Guard Rear Screw	Fixes 22-43 to butt 22-45.
25-91	9d.	”	Trigger Spring	(not illustrated).

Prices are for supply of parts only — fitting is charged extra.
Items marked * are subject to purchase tax, in addition to retail prices shown, in United Kingdom.
These prices apply in United Kingdom only.
If inexpensive Spares have to be specially ordered form the works, Dealers may require a minimum charge of 2/6d. to cover the cost of postage and handling, despite any lower prices quoted in our Spares List.

Diana Model 22

MODEL Model 22.

MAKER Diana, Millard Bros. Ltd., Motherwell, Lanarkshire, Scotland.

DATE Post-war, but almost identical to Model 22 that was made by Diana in Germany. Advertised as early as 1930. Would assume manufacture of above to be around 1946—1970s.

VALUATION £15—£40. ($23—$60).

DETAILS Tinplate construction, but similar in looks to the "Original" Model 23. .177 smoothbore brass barrel liner. 36 inches long. Double pull trigger but does not appear to adjust. Stamped on top of air chamber Huntress trademark plus "DIANA MOD. 22 MADE IN GT. BRITAIN". At a later date ".177 CAL." was added to the above lettering. What appears to be a date stamp is marked on the base of the butt. Advertised weight 3½ lb. Sold in the U.S.A. as the Model 202-R. the "R" stood for "Rifled". Earlier models were stamped "BRITISH MADE" instead of "Made in Gt. Britain". Most parts will interchange with the Milbro G23 and the Webley "Junior" air rifles.

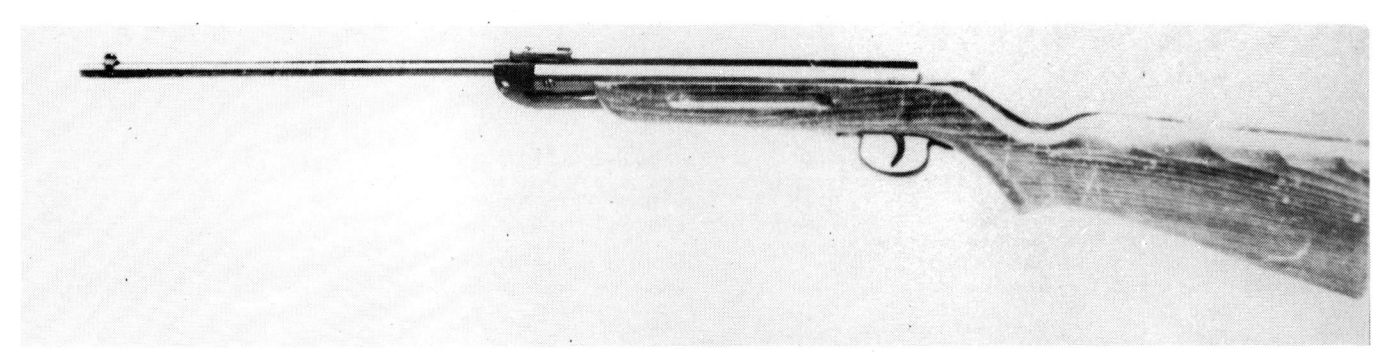

Diana Model 23

MODEL 23.

MAKER Millard Bros. Ltd., Carfin, Motherwell, Scotland and 467 Caledonian Road, London N.7. Address at time of manufacture.

DATE Late 1940s to around 1960.

VALUATION £15—£40. ($23—$60).

DETAILS The solid barrel version of the Model 22. Falke and other manufacturers did the same sort of thing. 37 inches long (94 cms) with a 15⅛ inch rifled barrel (38.5 cms). Side of barrel breech bears the serial number and code letter. Top of air chamber stamped with the Diana Huntress trademark and "MOD 23 — MADE IN GT. BRITAIN". Butt bears what appears to be a date stamp. The Model 23 is quite rare when compared with the Model 22 and 25, and now that Diana have ceased producing airguns now might be a good time to collect Diana products. During the early 1960s this model became the G23 with very little change.

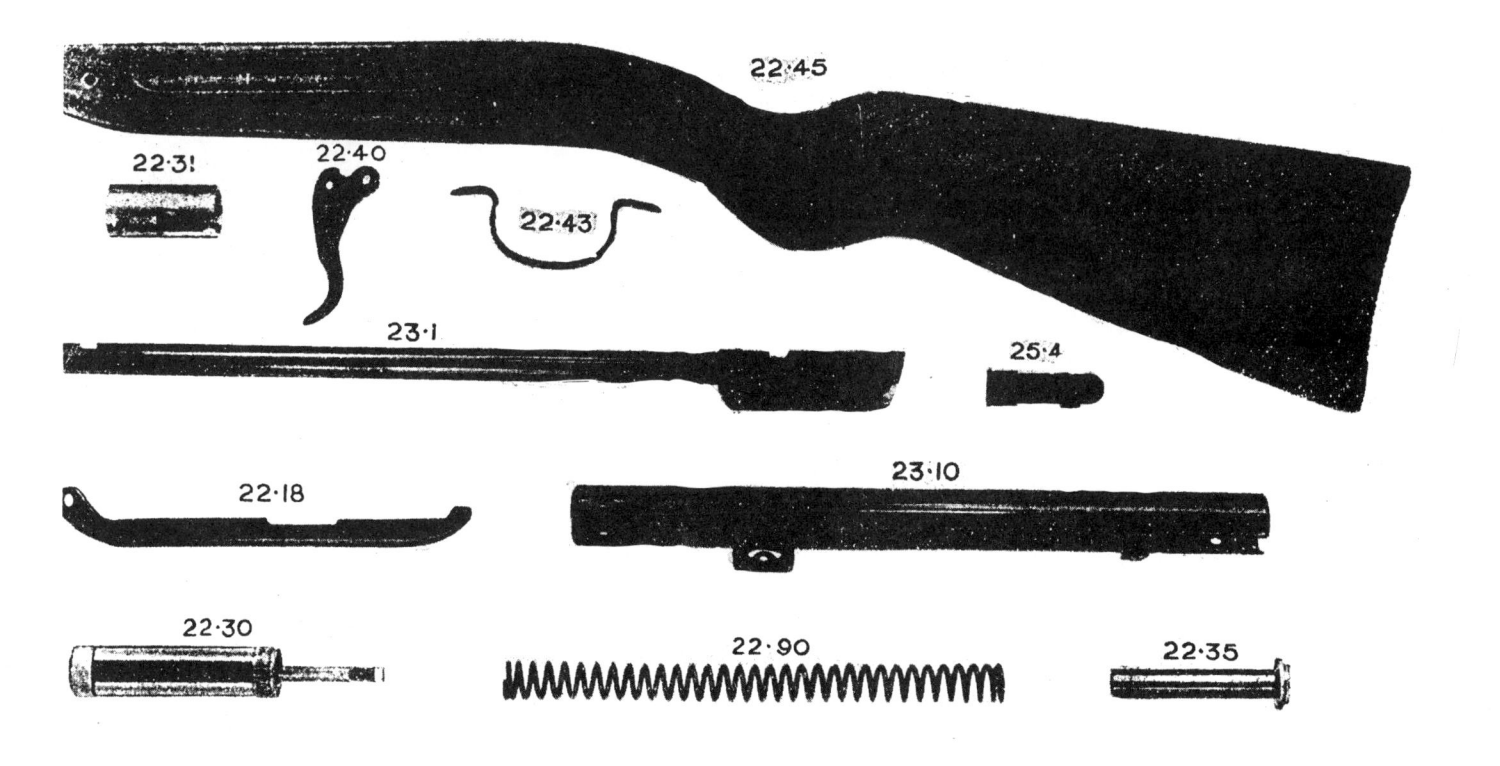

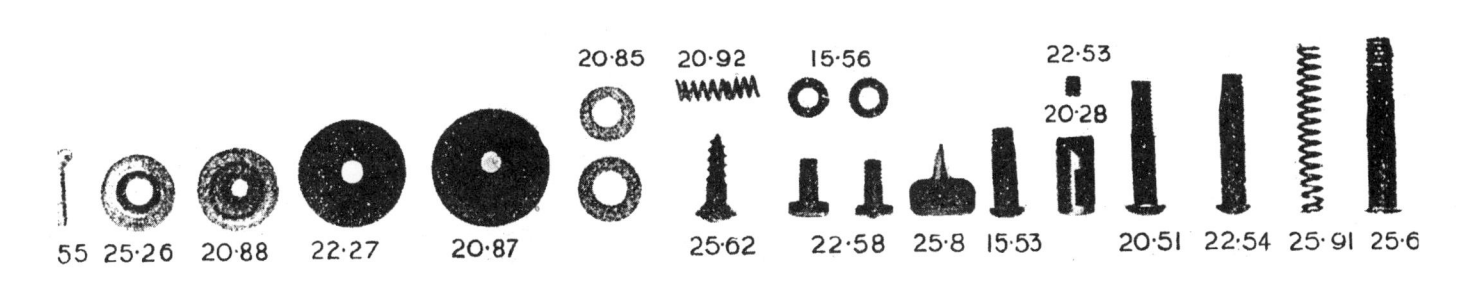

SPARE PARTS LIST — MODEL No. 23

Detail	Price		Description	Location, etc.
15-53	5d.	Each	Cocking Lever Screw	
15-56	4d.	”	Nut for C. Lever Screw	
20-28	2/-	”	Catch Pin	Locking Pin inserted to Cylinder No. 23-10.
20-51	7d.	”	Hinge Screw	Hinges Barrel 23-1 to Cylinder 23-10.
20-85	4d.	”	Breech Washer	Leather Sealing Washer on 23-10.
20-87	1/-	”	Piston Cup Washer	Used on 23-30. In conjunction with 20-88, 22-27, 22-55, and 25-26 constitutes Piston Head.
20-88	6d.	”	Piston Leather Washer	Used as on 20-87.
20-92	6d.	”	Catch Pin Spring	Is spring loading medium for 20-88 used on 23-10.
* 22-18	4/6	”	Cocking Lever	
22-27	4d.	”	Fibre Washer	Used as on 20-87.
* 22-30	8/6	”	Piston Rod Assembly	To complete requires Washers 20-87, 20-88 and 22-55 screw, and 25-26 Washer.
22-31	2/3	”	Trigger Housing	Internal Housing in 23-10 for 22-40 Trigger.
* 22-35	1/9	”	Spring Guide Tube	Guide for main spring 22-90, housed in 22-10.
22-40	2/-	”	Trigger Assembly	
22-43	1/-	”	Trigger Guard	
* 22-45	22/6	”	Butt	Stained and Polished.
22-53	4d.	”	Grub Screw	Stop for 20-28 Lock Pin.
22-54	6d.	”	Trigger Screw	Hinge Screw attaching Trigger to 22-31.
22-55	5d.	”	Piston Screw	Used with Piston Washers to complete assembly. See 22-30.
22-58	4d.	”	Screw	2 off required to screw butt to bridge on 23-10.
22-90	2/-	”	Main Spring	
* 23-1s	33/-	”	Barrel Assembly Smooth	Fitted with 25-28 and 20-92.
* 23-1r	35/6	”	Barrel Assembly Rifled	Fitted with 25-28 and 20-92.
* 23-10	30/-	”	Cylinder	
25-4	4/-	”	Rear Sight Assy. Complete	
25-8	4/6	”	Front Sight	
25-26	6d.	”	Washer	Used as on 20-87.
25-29	2/-	”	Catch Pin	Fitted to Breech End of 23-1.
25-61	9d.	”	Guard Front Screw	Fixes 22-43 to welded nuts on 23-10.
25-62	3d.	”	Guard Rear Screw	Fixes 22-43 to Butt 22-45.
25-91	9d.	”	Trigger Spring	

Prices are for supply of parts only — fitting is charged extra.
Items marked * are subject to purchase tax, in addition to retail prices shown, in United Kingdom.
These prices apply in United Kingdom only.
If inexpensive Spares have to be specially ordered from the works, Dealers may require a minimum charge of 2/6d. to cover the cost of postage and handling, despite any lower prices quoted in our Spares List.

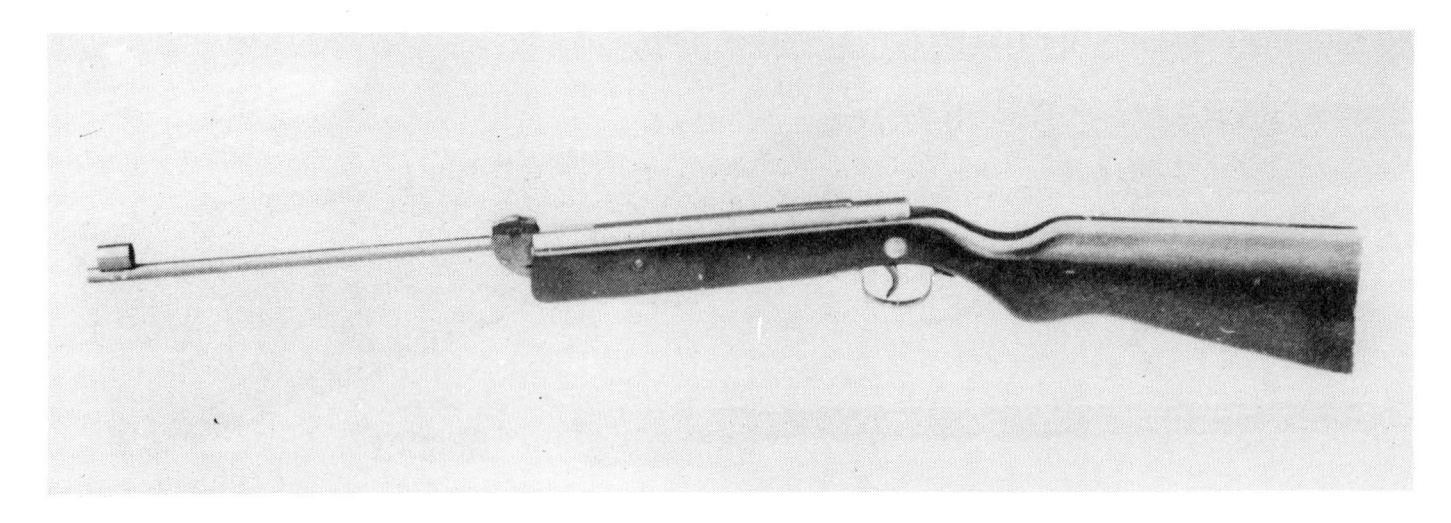

Milbro G23

MODEL G23. (The Bushman).

MAKER Milbro, Milbro Sports Department, P.O. Box 24, Motherwell, Lanarkshire ML1 4UP, Scotland.

DATE Would assume early 1970s.

VALUATION £20–£40. ($30–$60).

DETAILS Well made air rifle for the youngster. Semi-tinplate construction. 37 inches long with a 15 inch .177 rifled barrel. Pillar foresight with a very long tunnel hood. Serial number not visible. Side of air chamber stamped "MILBRO G23" followed by "MADE IN GT. BRITAIN". Small ramp for telescopic sight spot welded to top of air chamber. Non-adjustable trigger, but trigger guard has small hole for screwdriver, suggests that guard was also intended for more advanced model. One piece stock with "6 71 8" stamped on the butt. Could be date stamp. Unusual in that the above is called Milbro instead of the more usual name Diana. During 1969 the Model G23 was advertised with a slender stock, similar to the pre-war Diana air rifles, a sliding ratchet rearsight and a long hooded foresight. Advertised weight 3½ lbs. This earlier style has been dated into 1971.

Diana Model 25

MODEL 25.

MAKER British "Diana" by Millard Bros., Lanarkshire, Scotland.

DATE Post-war. Appeared in early 1950s. New models were introduced in 1966 with safety catches and other up to date improvements.

VALUATION £20–£40. ($30–$60).

DETAILS Almost identical to the German "Original" Model 25. 38¼ inches long with a 15¾ inch heavy rifled barrel. Serial number stamped on L.H.S. of barrel breech. Ramp rearsight set in dovetail for windage adjustment. Stamped on top of air chamber at the back appears the Diana Huntress trademark with "DIANA — MOD 25 — MADE IN GT. BRITAIN". A small removable plate for telescopic sight is fitted by two screws and ".177 CAL" is stamped next to it. Available in either .22 or .177 rifled. Full length beechwood stock. Advertised weight 5 lbs. A date stamp may appear on some models stamped on the upper half of the stock butt. Was also sold smoothbore.

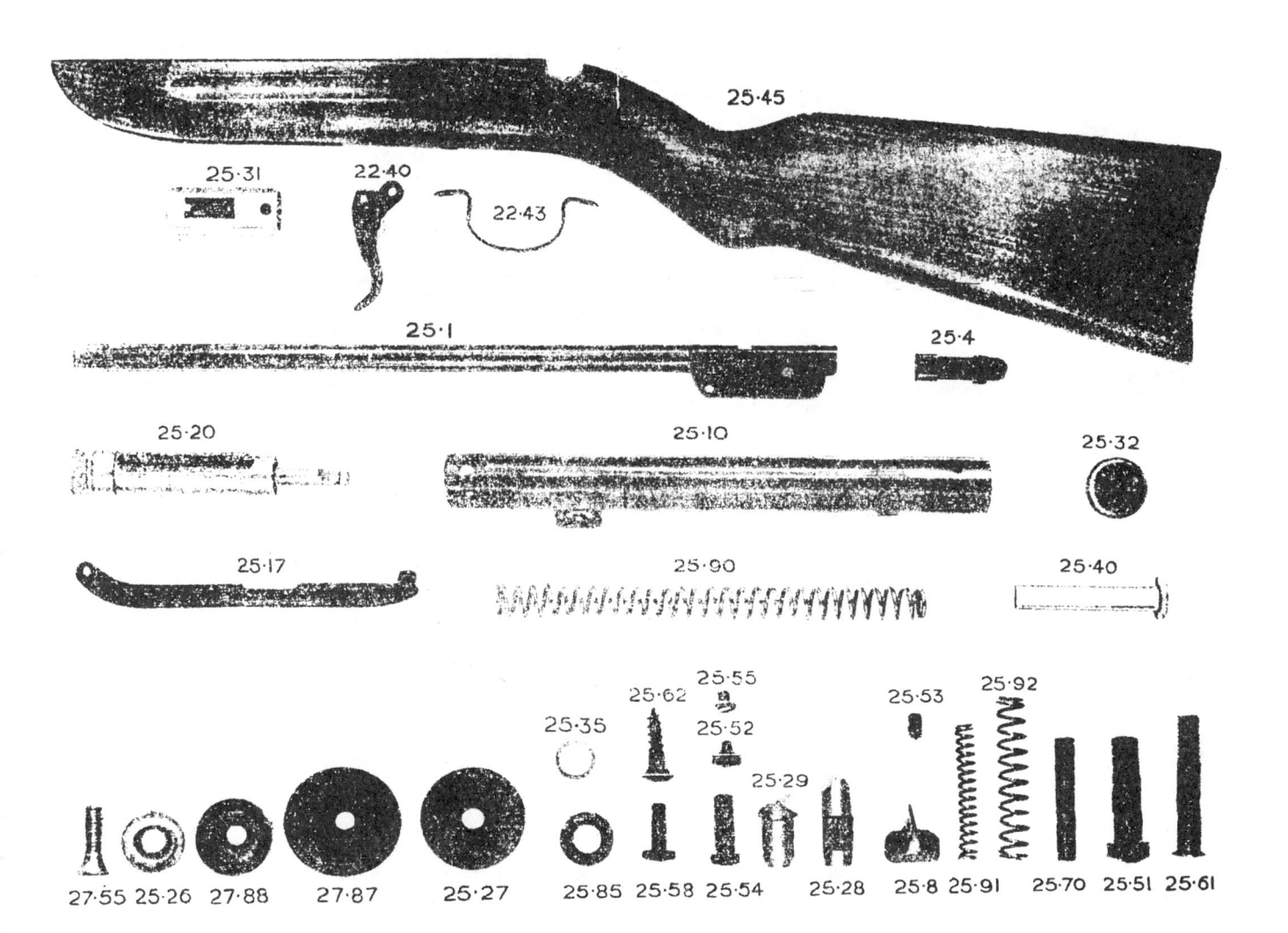

SPARE PARTS LIST — MODEL No. 25

Detail	Price		Description	Location, etc.
* 25-1S	45/-	Each	Barrel Assembly	Less front sight 25-8 and rear sight 25-4.
* 25-1R	48/-	"	Barrel Assembly	
25-4	4/-	"	Rear Sight	
25-6	2/-	"	Rear Sight Elevating Blade	
25-7	9d.	"	Rear Sight Slide	
25-8	4/6	"	Front Sight	
* 25-10	33/-	"	Cylinder	
25-17	5/-	"	Cocking Lever Assembly	
* 25-20	12/6	"	Piston Assembly	25-25, 25-26, 25-27, 27-87, and 27-88 washers complete piston head with screw 27-55.
25-26	6d.	"	Piston Washer	See 25-20.
25-27	4d.	"	Piston Washer	See 25-20.
25-28	2/-	"	Lock Pin	Fitted to breech end of 25-1.
25-29	2/-	"	Catch Pin	Fitted to fork end of cylinder to provide locking action with 25-28.
25-31	2/6	"	Trigger Housing	Internal housing in 25-10 for 22-40.
22-32	2/6	"	Cylinder End Cap	Sealing cap on butt end of 25-10 cylinder.
25-35	3d.	"	Shim Washer	Used as required with 25-51 hinge screw.
* 25-40	1/9	"	Spring Guide Assembly	Guide for main spring 25-90 housed in 25-10.
* 25-45	32/6	"	Butt	Stained and polished.
25-51	1/3	"	Hinge Screw	Hinges 25-1 barrel to cylinder 25-10.
25-52	6d.	"	Safety Screw	Locks 25-51.
25-53	4d.	"	Lock Pin Screw	Stop for 25-28 lock pin.
25-54	6d.	"	Fulcrum Screw	Cocking Lever Screw.
25-55	6d.	"	Safety Screw	Locks 25-54.
25-58	6d.	"	Front Stock Screw	Locates through butt to bridge on 25-10 (2 off).
25-61	9d.	"	Guard Front Screw	Fixes 22-43 to welded nut on 25-10.
25-62	3d.	"	Guard Rear Screw	Fixes 22-43 to butt 25-45.
25-70	6d.	"	Trigger Hinge Pin	
25-71	2d.	"	Rear Sight Pin	
25-85	6d.	"	Breech Washer No. 1 Bore	Sealing washer in breech end of barrel.
25-86	6d.	"	Breech Washer No. 2 Bore	Sealing washer in breech end of barrel.
25-90	3/-	"	Main Spring	
25-91	9d.	"	Trigger Spring	
25-92	9d.	"	Lock Pin Spring	
25-93	3d.	"	Rear Sight V-Spring	
25-94	2d.	"	Rear Sight Coil Spring	
* 22-40	2/-	"	Trigger Assembly	
22-43	1/-	"	Trigger Guard	
27-55	6d.	"	Piston Screw	See 25.20.
27-87	1/6	"	Piston Cup Washer	See 25.20.
27-85	1/-	"	Piston Washer	See 25.20.

Prices are for supply of parts only — fitting is charged extra.
Items marked * are subject to purchase tax, in addition to retail prices shown, in United Kingdom.
These prices apply in United Kingdom only.
If inexpensive Spares have to be specially ordered from the works, Dealers may require a minimum charge of 2/6d. to cover the cost of postage and handling, despite any lower prices quoted in our Spares List.

Diana 'Comet' rifle kit based on the Diana Model 25 air rifle

MODEL Comet Air Rifle Kit.

MAKER Millard Bros., Diana Works, Carfin, Motherwell, Scotland. Address at time of manufacture.

DATE Short period of manufacture, from early 1960s to the middle of 1963 when the G25 appeared.

VALUATION The complete kit is quite rare.
£50—£80. ($75—$120).

DETAILS The Comet outfit is based around the Model 25 air rifle. See previous page for details of the Model 25 British Diana. To find any old air rifle in its original box is quite a rarity as unlike air pistols which can easily be placed in a drawer, with air rifles the cardboard box is the first thing to go. The kit comes complete with targets and target holder with wooden back block for firing darts. A packet of darts and pellets are also included. A plastic 2x magnification telescopic sight complete with black plastic eyepiece caps. Advertised in 1962 as the "new Diana Comet Outfit" and priced at £10 19s. 6d. for .177 and £11 2s. 6d. for .22. The air rifle in the above kit bears no serial number but does have a date stamped on the base of the butt "4 60". Usually a letter follows the year but is obscured. Further to the above a serial number does appear stamped on the L.H.S. of the barrel breech and can only be read when the action has been cocked. Number of above 59228C.

Diana Model G25

MODEL G25.

MAKER Millard Bros. Ltd., Carfin, Motherwell, Scotland, and 467 Caledonian Road, London N.7. Address at time of manufacture.

DATE 1963 to 1966. Quite a rare variation.

VALUATION £20—£40. ($30—$60).

DETAILS Although quite a rare variation this appears not to increase the value of airgun in question. Purely from the collecting point of view it represents another stage in the Model 25 and Model 27 pedigree story. Almost identical to the Model 25 but has been updated with the minimum expense. Improvements include a hooded dovetail mounted foresight as fitted to the Diana Model 4 airpistol. A scope ramp was spot welded on in true Webley fashion, but this model had two pairs of telescope mount stops and was striated for extra grip. The cocking lever bolt and locking screw was replaced by a simple pin. A telescopic sight, the "famous" G29, was available for the above as well as the Models G23 and G27. The G25 was sold in either .22 or .177. A date stamp is on the upper part of the butt and on the one examined it was "12-66-1 DA". 38 inches long with a 15¾ inch rifled barrel. Advertised weight 5 lbs. Side of air chamber near the scope ramp stamped, "DIANA G25 CAL .177 MADE IN GT. BRITAIN". Date stamp on the butt.

The spares diagram gives some idea of the interchange ability that exists from model to model, as with nearly all Diana products, the part numbers are in two sections, the first being the model number which will nearly always be the lowest number from which the part has been taken from or is used upon. So the Model G25 has parts prefixed 25, but towards the bottom of the parts list uses parts from Model 27 and 36, even Model 100! By the way, has anybody seen a Model 100?

MODEL No. G25

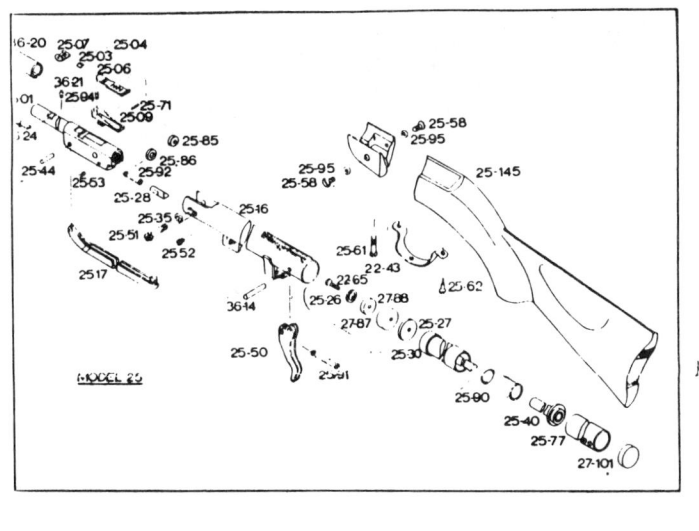

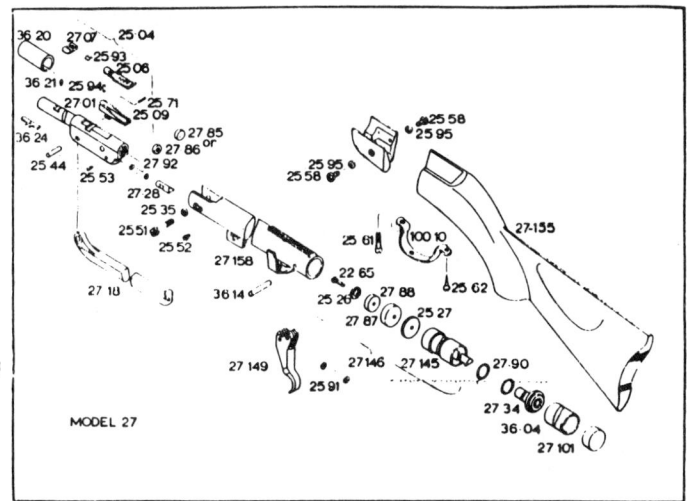

MODEL No. G27

SPARE PARTS LIST - MODELS G25 and G27

Stock No.	Description	Designation	Beschreibung	Beskrivning
22-43	Trigger Guard	Sougarde	Abzugbügel	Varbygel
22-65	Piston Screw	Vis du piston	Kolbenschraube	Fästskruv till pistongpackning
25-01/1	Barrel Assembly (.177 Rifled)	Canon rayé	Lauf gezogen	Pipa, komplett, räfflad
25-01/3	Barrel Assembly (.177 Smooth)	Canon lisse	Lauf glatt	Pipa, komplett, slätborrad
25-02/1	Barrel Assembly (.22 Rifled)	Canon rayé	Lauf gezogen	Pipa, komplett, räfflad
25-02/3	Barrel Assembly (.22 Smooth)	Canon lisse	Lauf glatt	Pipa, komplett, släborrad
25-04	Rear Sight	Hausse	Visier	Sikte
25-06	Blade	Partie supérieure de la hausse	Visier-platte	Siktram
25-07	Slide	Glissière de hausse	Visier-versteller	Löpare
25-09	Base	Socle de la hausse	Visier sockel	Siktfot
25-16	Cylinder	Cylindre	Zylinder	Cylinder
25-17	Cocking Lever	Levier d'armement	Spannhebel	Spännarm
25-..	Piston Assembly	Piston complet	Kolben komplett	Pistong, komplett (kanna)
25-..	Piston Washer	Rondelle du piston	Kolbenscheibe	Bricka till pistong (kanna)
25-27	Fibre Washer	Plaque ébonite du cuir de piston	Kolbenfiberscheibe	Fiberpackning
25-28	Lock Pin	Verrou de fermeture au cylindre	Verschlusskegel	Låsstift
25-35	Shim Washer	Pastilles de serrage	Ausgleichscheibe	Mellanläggsbricka
25-40	Spring Guide Assembly	Guide du ressort de piston	Federführung	Styrhylsa till pistongfjäder
25-44	Pin	Goupille pour la hausse	Stift zu visier	Stift till sikte
25-50	Trigger Assembly	Détente assemblé	Abzug	Avtryckare, komplett
25-51	Hinge Screw	Vis du charnière	Scharnierschraube	Scharnierskruv
25-52	Safety Screw	Contre-vis de vis de charnière	Sicherungsschraube	Fästskruv till 25-51
25-53	Lock Pin Screw	Vis de verrou de fermeture au canon	Verschlussschraube	Stoppskruv till låsstift 25-28
25-58	Front Stock Screw	Vis de fixation du cylindre	Schaftbefestigungsschraube	Främre fästskruv till stocken
25-61	Guard Front Screw	Vis de la sougarde (avant)	Vordere Abzugbügelschraube	Främre skruv till varbygel
25-62	Guard Rear Screw	Vis de la sougarde (arrière)	Hintere Abzugbügelschraube	Bakre skruv till varbygel
25-71	Pin	Goupille pour la hausse	Stift zu visier	Stifte till sikte
25-77	Trigger Housing	Logement de détente	Schlossstück	Avtryckarhylsa
25-85	Breech Washer No. 1 Bore	Rondelle de culasse	Laufdichtung	Pippackning för kaliber 4.5 mm.
25-86	Breech Washer No. 2 Bore	Rondelle de culasse	Laufdichtung	Pippackning för kaliber 5.5 mm.
25-90	Main Spring	Ressort principal	Kolbenfeder	Pistongfjäder
25-91	Trigger Spring	Ressort de détente	Abzugfeder	Avtryckarfjäder
25-92	Lock Pin Spring	Ressort du verrou de fermeture au canon	Verschlussfeder	Fjäder till låsstift
25-93	Leaf Spring	Ressort pour la hausse	Blattfeder zu Visier	Bladfjäder till sikte
25-94	Spring for Rear Sight	Ressort de la hausse	Visierfeder	Siktfjäder
25-95	Washer	Rondelle	Dichtung	Packning
25-145	Butt	Crosse nue	Schaft	Stock
27-01/1	Barrel Assembly (.177 Rifled)	Canon rayé	Lauf gezogen	Pipa, komplett, räfflad
27-01/3	Barrel Assembly (.177 Smooth)	Canon lisse	Lauf glatt	Pipa, komplett, slätborrad
27-02/1	Barrel Assembly (.22 Rifled)	Canon ou rayé	Lauf gezogen	Pipa, komplett, räfflad
27-18	Cocking Lever	Levier d'armement	Spannhebel	Spännarm
27-28	Lock Pin	Verrou de fermeture au cylindre	Verschlusskegel	Låsstift
27-34	Spring Guide Assembly	Guide du ressort de piston	Federführung	Styrhylsa till pistongfjäder
27-85	Breech Washer	Rondelle de culasse	Laufdichtung	Pippackning för kaliber 4.5 mm.
27-86	Breech Washer	Rondelle de culasse	Laufdichtung	Pippackning för kaliber 5,5 mm.
27-87	Piston Cup Washer	Cuir du piston	Ledermanschette	Skålformad läderpackning
27-88	Piston Block Washer	Rondelle du piston	Ledermanschette	Pistongläderpackning
27-90	Main Spring	Ressort principal	Kolbenfeder	Pistongfjäder
27-92	Lock Pin Spring	Ressort de verrou de fermeture au canon	Verschlussfeder	Fjäder till låsstift 27-28
27-101	Cylinder End Cap	Cuvette du cylindre	Abschlussdeckel	Ändhylsa till cylinder
27-146	Piston Assembly	Piston complet	Kolben komplett	Pistong, komplett (kanna)
27-149	Trigger Assembly	Détente assemblé	Abzug	Avtryckare, komplett
27-155	Butt	Crosse nue	Schaft	Stock
27-158	Cylinder Assembly	Cylindre	Zylinder	Cylinder
36-04	Trigger Housing	Logement de détente	Schlossstück	Avtryckarhylsa
36-14	Hinge Pin	Goupille	Abzugstift	Avtryckarstift
36-20	Shield	Protection	Visierschutz	Kornskydd
36-21	Front Sight	Guidon	Korn	Korn
36-24	Base	Plaque de Base	Visiersockel	Kornfot
100-10	Trigger Guard	Sougarde	Abzugbügel	Varbygel

Diana Model 27, later to become the G27

First Model Diana 27 post-war, but of pre-war design. Double pull trigger and was not fitted with telescopic sight ramp

MODEL   Diana Model 27.

MAKER   Millard Bros., Lanarkshire, Scotland.

DATE   Featured in Smith's so would assume around the 1950s. Although German Diana Model 27 was advertised as far back as the 1930s. Seen advertised as far back as the 1930s. Seen advertised until 1963.

VALUATION £30—£60.
($45—$90).

DETAILS   41½ inches long. All metal, but has alloy trigger. Ramp adjustable rearsight. Has small telescopic sight ramp screwed on top of air chamber, this is often missing and leaves two small holes that will not affect performance. Next to ramp is stamped the calibre and at the rear of chamber is stamped the trademark, "Diana, Mod. 27, Made in Gt. Britain". The serial number of above is 275573 and is found on the side of barrel breech, so cannot be seen when barrel is closed. Double pull trigger, but does not appear to be adjustable.

Some of the above have what appears to be a date stamp on the top of the butt. Have seen with "3 60" with a serial number 270664 C in .177 calibre. Advertised weight 5 lb 13 oz. Lettering on top of air chamber was "golded" in including the calibre. Available in either .177 or .22 rifled or smoothbore.

First models produced just after Second World War were fitted with the pre-war double pull trigger that can be dry fired. This has a steel trigger with two small adjuster screws that can only be reached when the trigger guard has been removed. Apparently this trigger system was also used on the first Model Webley Mk. IIIs.

The air chamber of the first models were stamped "BRITISH MADE". Without any mechanical change this became the Model G27, and later still the safety catch was added, see next air rifle. These first G27s were not stamped with the Diana Huntress trademark, but were marked "DIANA G27 CAL. .22, MADE IN GREAT BRITAIN" along the side of the air chamber. They were drilled for the very small telescopic scope ramp.

The Milbro G27

MODEL G27.

MAKER Millard Bros. Ltd., P.O. Box 24, Motherwell, Lanarkshire, Scotland ML1 4UP.

DATE Seen advertised 1963 and was discontinued towards the end of 1967 with the introduction of the G34 and G36. The G27 continued on into the early 1970s as the Milbro G27.

VALUATION £20—£40. ($30—$60).

DETAILS Must be the last of the long line of the Model 27 air rifles. 41½ inches long with a 17¼ inch rifled barrel. Pillar foresight with long hood, ramp rearsight could be drifted for windage adjustment. Solid metal construction with locking screws on the barrel and cocking lever pivot screws. Double pull trigger. Telescopic ramp spot welded on as on the Webley Mk. III. Scope ramp has arrestor projections. L.H.S. of air chamber stamped "DIANA G27 CAL .22 MADE IN GT. BRITAIN". Advertised weight 5 lbs 10 ozs. On one example date stamped "1 71 8" the air chamber was marked "MILBRO G27" and the barrel and cocking lever pivots were pins and not screws as for the Diana G27. Such is the rate of progress. The Milbro model also had a safety catch on the side of the trigger block. One model of the Diana G27 seen had no safety catch, dated 1967, it could be that the Diana G27 was earlier and had no safety catch whilst the later Milbro G27 had one fitted. The Diana G27 was available in .177 rifled or smoothbore, and .22 rifled only.

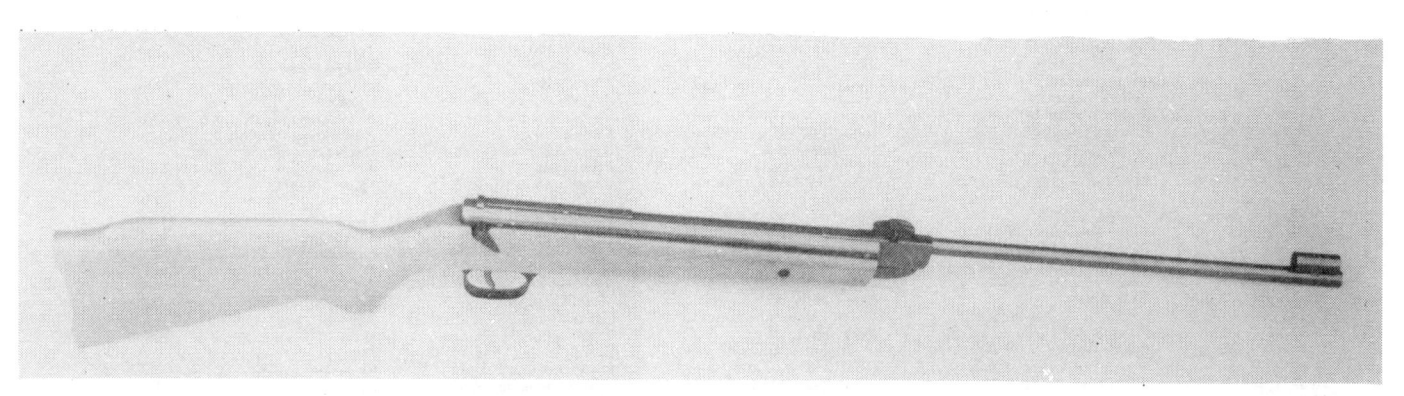

British Diana Model G36

MODEL Diana G36.

MAKER Millard Bros. Ltd., Lanarkshire, Scotland.

DATE First advertised around late half of 1966. Does not appear in the airgun guide in "Guns Review" April 1976. Could have ceased production when the "Series 70" appeared.

VALUATION Did cost £13 17s. 6d. in 1966.
£20—£40. ($30—$60).

DETAILS Does not appear to have a serial number. 41½ inches long with a 17¼ inch rifled barrel. Double pull trigger with adjustment through the trigger guard. Safety catch on the R.H.S. of the air chamber. Long tunnel foresight and plastic rearsight as still fitted to the G4 airpistol. Has a fitted telescopic sight ramp with arrestor. Stamped on side of air chamber "DIANA G36 CAL .22 MADE IN GT. BRITAIN". Has a machined cocking lever. Advertised in 1966 as "the only British made air rifle with a safety catch". Advertised muzzle velocities up to 700 feet per second (must be for .177) and to "find the bull as far as 60 yards away". Had a pillar foresight. Models were coded "G36/1" for .177 and "G36/2" for .22. On upper part of butt has what appears to be a date stamp "3 68 10".

MODEL No. G34

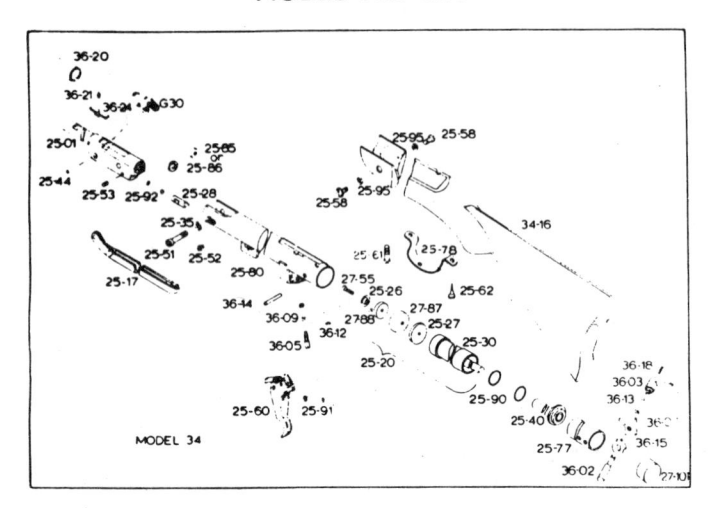

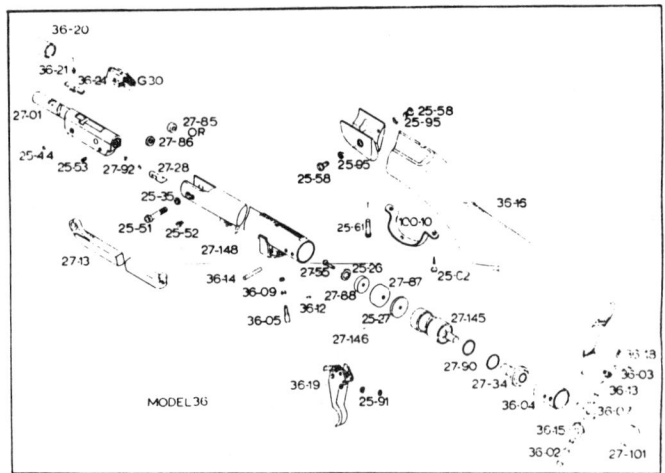

MODEL No. G36

SPARE PARTS LIST – MODELS G34 and G36

Stock No.	Price	Description	Designation	Beschreibung	Beskrivning
25-01.3	60 - Each	Barrel Assembly (·177" Smooth)	Canon lisse 4,5 mm.	Lauf glatt 4,5 mm.	Pipa, komplett, slätborrad (Kal. 4,5 mm.)
25-01.1	60 - „	Barrel Assembly (·177" Rifled)	Canon rayé 4,5 mm.	Lauf gezogen 4,5 mm.	Pipa, komplett, refflad (Kal. 4,5 mm.)
25-02.1	60 - „	Barrel Assembly (·22" Rifled)	Canon rayé 5,5 mm.	Lauf gezogen 5,5 mm.	Pipa, komplett, refflad (Kal. 5,5 mm.)
25-02.3	60 - „	Barrel Assembly (·22" Smooth)	Canon lisse 5,5 mm.	Lauf glatt 5,5 mm.	Pipa, komplett, slätborrad (Kal. 5,5 p
25-17	6 8 „	Cocking Lever	Levier d'armement	Spannhebel	Spännarm
25-20	16 3 „	Piston Assembly	Piston complet	Kolben komplett	Kanna komplett
25-26	9d. „	Piston Washer	Rondelle du piston	Kolbenscheibe	Metallbrickatill akanna
25-27	6d. „	Fibre Washer	Plaque ébonite du cuir de piston	Kolbenfibrescheibe	Fiberpackning
25-28	2 3 „	Lock Pin	Verrou de fermeture au cylinder	Verschlusskegel	Pipspärr
25-35	6d. „	Shim Washer	Pastilles de serrage	Ausgleichscheibe	Låsbricka
25-40	2 7 „	Spring Guide Assembly	Guide du ressort de piston	Federführung	Styrhylsa till slagfjäder
25-44	9d. „	Pivot Pin	Goupille	Abzugstift	Avtryckarstift
25-51	1 6 „	Hinge Screw	Vis du charnière	Scharnierschraube	Scharnierskruv
25-52	9d. „	Safety Screw	Contre-vis de vis de charnière	Sicherungsschraube	Stoppskruv till scharnierskruv
25-53	9d. „	Lock Pin Screw	Vis de verrou de fermeture au canon	Verschlussschraube	Stoppskruv till pipspärr
25-58	9d. „	Stockholder Screw	Vis de fixation du cylindre	Schaftbefestigungsschraube	Främre kolvskruv
25-60	2 7 „	Trigger Assembly	Détente assemblée	Abzug	Avtryckare, komplett
25-61	9d. „	Guard Screw	Vis de sous-garde	Vordere Abzugbügelschraube	Korsskruv
25-62	6d. „	Guard Rear Screw	Vis de la sougarde (arrière)	Hintere Abzugbügelschraube	Träskruv till varbygel
25-77	3 - „	Trigger Housing	Logement de détente	Schlossstück	Avtryckarhus
25-78	1 3 „	Trigger Guard	Sougarde	Abzugbügel	Varbygel
25-80	43 6 „	Cylinder Assembly	Cylindre	Zylinder	Cylinder
25-85	9d. „	Breech Washer No. 1 Bore	Rondelle de culasse 4,5 mm.	Laufdichtung 4,5 mm.	Pippackning för (Kal. 4,5 mm.)
25-86	9d. „	Breech Washer No. 2 Bore	Rondelle de culasse 5,5 mm.	Laufdichtung 5,5 mm.	Pippackning för (Kal. 5,5 mm.)
25-90	3 6 „	Main Spring	Ressort principal	Kolbenfeder	Slagfjäder
25-91	1 - „	Trigger Spring	Ressort de détente	Abzugfeder	Avtryckarfjäder
25-92	1 - „	Lock Pin Spring	Ressort du verrou de fermeture au canon	Verschlussfeder	Fjäder till pipsparr
25-95	6d. „	Washer	Rondelle	Dichtung	Låsbricka
27-01.3	78 6 „	Barrel Assembly (·177" Smooth)	Canon lisse 4,5 mm.	Lauf glatt 4,5 mm.	Pipa, komplett (Kal. 4,5 mm. slätborrad)
27-01.1	78 6 „	Barrel Assembly (·177" Rifled)	Canon rayé 4,5 mm.	Lauf gezogen 4,5 mm.	Pipa, komplett (Kal. 4,5 mm. refflad)
27-02.1	78 6 „	Barrel Assembly (·22" Rifled)	Canon ou rayé 5,5 mm.	Lauf gezogen 5,5 mm.	Pipa, komplett (Kal. 5,5 mm. refllad)
27-18	25 3 „	Cocking Lever	Levier d'armement	Spannhebel	Spännarm
27-28	3 6 „	Lock Pin	Verrou de fermeture au cylindre	Verschlusskegel	Pipspärr
27-34	3 6 „	Spring Guide Assembly	Guide du ressort de piston	Federführung	Styrhylsa till slagfjäder
27-55	9d. „	Piston Screw	Vis du piston	Kolbenschraube	Skruv till kannpackning
27-85	9d. „	Breech Washer No. 1 Bore	Rondelle de culasse (4,5 mm.)	Laufdichtung (4,5 mm.)	Pippackning för Kal. 4,5 mm.
27-86	9d. „	Breech Washer No. 2 Bore	Rondelle de culasse (5,5 mm.)	Laufdichtung (5,5 mm.)	Pippackning för Kal. 5,5 mm.
27-87	1 9 „	Piston Cup Washer	Cuir du piston	Ledermanschette	Kannpackning
27-88	1 3 „	Piston Block Washer	Rondelle du piston	Ledermanschette	Inläggspackning
27-90	4 6 „	Main Spring	Ressort principal	Kolbenfeder	Slagfjäder
27 92	1 - „	Lock Pin Spring	Ressort du verrou de fermeture au canon	Verschlussfeder	Fjäder till pipspärr
27-101	3 - „	End Cap	Capuchon	Abschlussdeckel	Ändhylsa till cylinder
27-146	14 - „	Piston Assembly	Piston complet	Kolben komplett	Kanna, komplett
27-148	48 - „	Cylinder	Cylindre	Zylinder	Cylinder
G30	7 6 „	Rear Sight	Hausse	Visier	Sikte
34-16	42 8 „	Butt	Crosse	Schaft	Kolv
36-02	1 - „	Safety Catch Spindle	Axe du levier	Hebelspindel	Säkringsaxel
36-03	9d. „	Safety Catch Lever	Levier	Hebel	Säkringsarm
36-04	1 9 „	Trigger Housing	Logement de detente	Schlossstück	Avtryckarhus
36-05	6d. „	Trigger Adjusting Screw	Vis	Schraube	Stallskruv
36-07	6d. „	Ratchet Plate	Plaque d'engrenage	Sperrplatte	Säkringsbleck
36-09	6d. „	Trigger Adjusting Spring	Ressort d'ajustement	Anpassungsfeder	Fjäder till ställskruv
36-12	6d. „	Circlip	Clip	Verzierungsring	Låsbricka
36-13	6d. „	Safety Catch Spring	Ressort de sureté	Sicherungsfeder	Säkringsfjäder
36-14	6d. „	Trigger Hinge Pin	Goupille	Abzugstift	Avtryckarstift
36-15	6d. „	Safety Catch Cam	Plaque à came	Nockenplatte	Säkringsbricka
36-16	45 6 „	Butt	Crosse	Schaft	Kolv
36-18	6d. „	Safety Catch Lever Screw	Ecrou du lévier	Hebelschraube	Stoppskruv
36-19	7 9 „	Trigger Assembly	Détente assemblée	Abzug	Avtryckare, komplett
36-20	6d. „	Front Sight Shield	Protection	Visierschutz	Kornskydd
36-21	6d. „	Front Sight	Guidon	Korn	Korn
36-24	1 6 „	Front Sight Platform	Plaque de base	Visiersockel	Kornfot
100 10	3 6 „	Trigger Guard	Sougarde	Abzugbügel	Varbygel

G46 Targetmaster

MODEL G44 and G46 "Targetmaster".

MAKER Millard Brothers Ltd., Motherwell, Lanarkshire, Scotland. Address at time of manufacture as the firm ceased trading during 1982.

DATE 1967—1970 or thereabouts.

VALUATION Have only seen one, and that was rough! That sold for £20 ($30). In excellent condition these should fetch around £60. ($90).

DETAILS Must be the only air rifle produced by British Diana without a middle rearsight, and in true British style this target air rifle was also available in .22! These are quite rare, but are still not worth a great deal. Advertised length of 42 inches (107 cms) and having a weight of 6 lb 3 oz (2.8 kilograms). All metal construction with a solid cocking lever. Peepsight ramp was spot welded on and had little side projections to prevent sight creepage. Side of action was stamped "DIANA G46 CAL .22 MADE IN GT. BRITAIN". The stock has a date stamp just in front of the trigger guard and in the above example is was "1 68 3" which tallies with the production dates. The stock also had a hard black rubber butt plate that was not only screwed on but glued as well! It advertised accuracy and power range was given as 60 yards (56 metres). The standard peepsight fitted was the Milbro G31. The trigger mechanism had a side safety catch and trigger adjustment screw just in front of the trigger. The Model 44 was based on the barrel and cylinder components of the Model 25 whilst the G46 had the barrel and chamber of the Model 27. The G44 was available in .177 and .22 both rifled and smoothbore whilst the G46 in .177 rifled and smoothbore and only rifled in .22. On both models the trigger mechanism originated from the Model G36 and many parts would interchange.

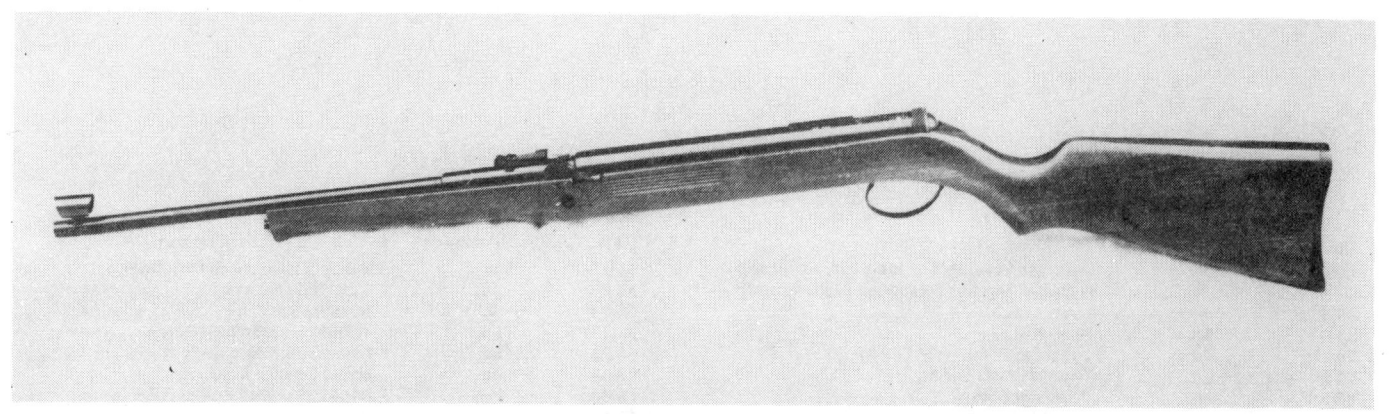

British Diana Model G55

MODEL 55 also called the Model G55.

MAKER Diana, Millard Bros. Ltd., Motherwell, Lanarkshire, Scotland.

DATE Seen advertised 1963 and not mentioned by Wesley or Smith, so would assume manufacture to be between late 1950s to early 1960s.

VALUATION A rare model, £50—£150. ($75—$225). Have yet to find one in auction.

DETAILS Similar in design to the "Original" Model 50. 42 inches long with 17¼ inch barrel. Hooded pillar foresight and ramp adjustable rearsight in groove for windage adjustment. Automatic opening tap when underlever is pulled down. Have seen an "Original" Model 50 with automatic tap. Very distinctive tap design. Top of air chamber stamped with Huntress trademark discarding her bow and arrow, has ".22 CAL" near the scope ramp that is held in position by two small grub screws. When ramp is removed has "DRILLED FOR SCOPE" stamped on the chamber. At the rear of the chamber appears "DIANA MOD 55 — MADE IN GT. BRITAIN". Smooth stock with course ribs on fore-end and hard black rubber butt plate. Stamped on underside of stock near the cocking lever groove "8 62H". Could be a date stamp. Fitted with a heavy alloy trigger that appears to have no adjustment. Advertised weight 7 lb 2 oz. Available in either .177 or .22. Serial number usually appears stamped on the underside of the barrel just in front of the button for the cocking lever.

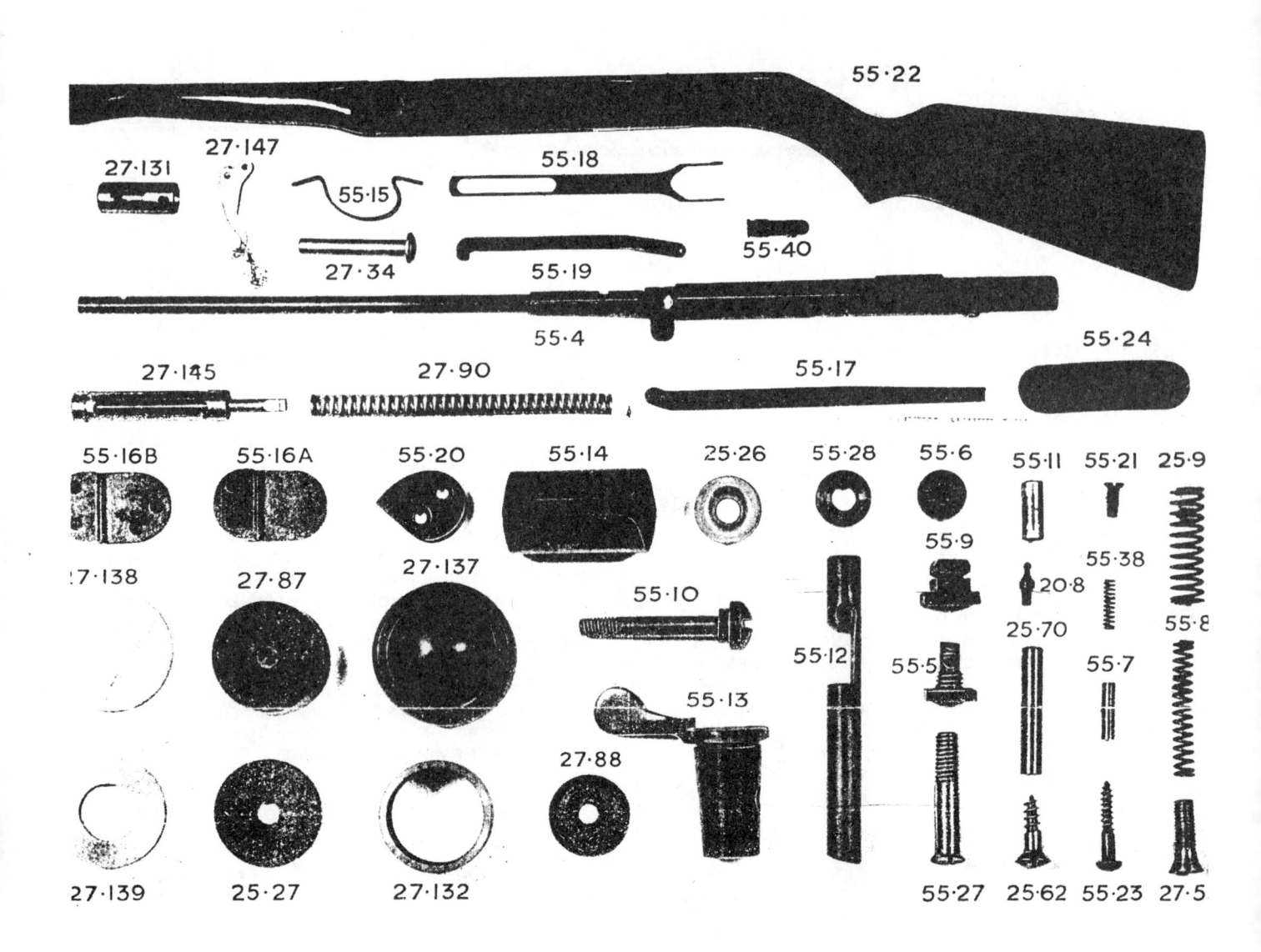

SPARE PARTS LIST — MODEL G55

Detail No.	Price each	Description
* 55-4	150/-	Cylinder Assembly — includes Barrel and Cylinder (but not Telescope Sight Mount).
55-5	4/6	Lever Catch.
55-6	6d.	Pivot Nut.
55-7	6d.	Lever Pin (Pivots 55-19 to 55-17).
55-8	6d.	Thumb Catch Spring.
55-9	5/-	Fore Sight Block.
20-8	6d.	Fore Sight Bead.
55-10	1/3	Pivot Screw.
55-11	6d.	Thumb Catch Pin.
55-12	2/-	Thumb Catch.
55-13	15/-	Pellet Chamber. State whether No. 1 bore .177 (4.5 m/m.) or No. 2 bore .22 (5.5 m/m). Rifle should be returned to Works to have this part fitted. — See special instructions.
55-14	1/-	Fore Sight Shield.
55-15	3/-	Trigger Guard.
55-16A	6/9	Retaining Block. Plain.
55-16B	6/9	Retaining Block. Dimpled.
* 55-17	12/6	Cocking Arm.
55-18	7/6	Pellet Chamber Slide.
* 55-19	9/-	Cocking Lever.
55-20	1/-	Cam Stop.
55-21	6d.	Cam and Retaining Block Screw.
* 55-22	55/-	Stock (Stained and Polished).
55-23	3d.	Butt Plate Screw.
J 55-24	3/6	Butt Plate.
55-27	9d.	Trigger Guard Front Screw.
55-28	6d.	Lever Catch Nut. Secures 55-5 to 55-22.
55-38	6d.	Pellet Chamber Spring.
55-39	2d.	Pellet Chamber Ball (not illustrated).
55-40	4/-	Rear Sight.
25-26	6d.	Piston Steel Washer.
25-27	4d.	Piston Fibre Washer.
22-62	3d.	Trigger Guard Rear Screw.
25-70	6d.	Trigger Hinge Pin.
25-91	9d.	Trigger Spring.
* 27-34	2/6	Spring Guide Assembly.
27-55	6d.	Piston Screw.
27-87	1/6	Piston Cup Washer.
27-88	1/-	Piston Block Washer.
27-90	4/-	Main Spring.
27-131	2/9	Trigger Housing.
27-132	3/6	Spacing Sleeve.
27-137	2/6	Cylinder End Cap.
27-138	9d.	Cylinder End Cap Washer.
27-139	9d.	Cylinder End Washer.
* 27-145	10/6	Piston Assembly.
* 27-147	11/6	Trigger Assembly.

GF28   40/- each   Diana Telescope Sight.

If inexpensive parts have to be specially ordered from Works, dealers may require to make a minimum charge of 2/6 to cover cost of postages and handling.

**Prices are for supply of parts only. Fitting is charged extra.
Items marked * are subject to purchase tax, in addition to retail prices shown.
These prices apply in United Kingdom only.**

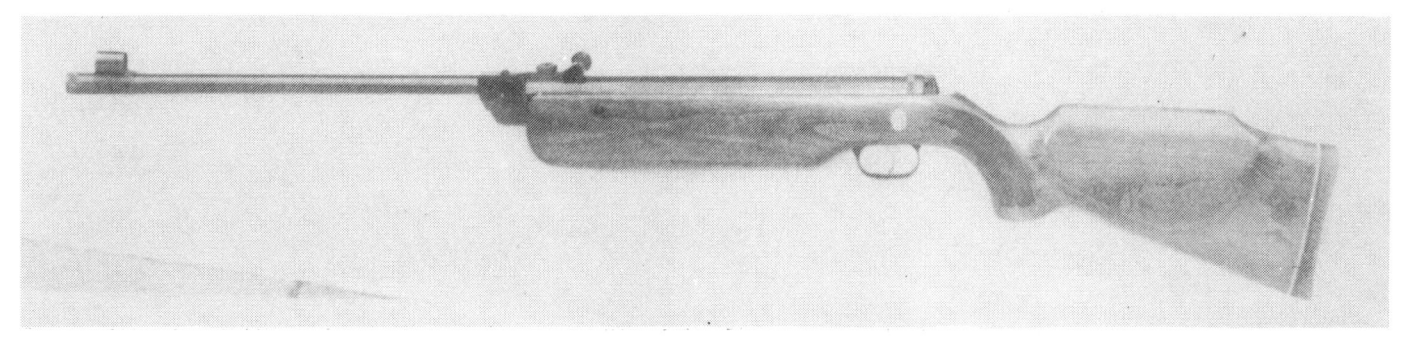

Diana Series 70 Model 71

MODEL Series 70 Model 71.

MAKER Millard Bros. Ltd., Motherwell, Lanarkshire, Scotland.

DATE From 1971 to early 1980s when Millard Bros. ceased trading.

VALUATION £40—£60. ($60—$90).

DETAILS Not the usual Diana air rifle. Have never seen this version of the Model 79/80 advertised and can only assume that it was for special order or export only. 42¾ inches long (1.85 m) with a 17⅝ inch (45 cm) rifled barrel. Barrel fitted with outer sleeve, plastic foresight with spring metal hood, fully adjustable rearsight. Top of air chamber stamped "SERIES 70, MODEL 71, MADE IN GT.BRITAIN". Stock has what is assumed to be a date stamp on the underside of the fore-end (9 76 6). The safety catch is at the rear of the chamber cap and NOT on the side as is usually the fashion. When action is cocked the safety can be pushed in and the action then released. Beautiful stock with relum like fore-end. Pressed chequering and white band to butt recoil pad. All in all a very nice quality Diana air rifle, a pity we did not see more of it when it was available.

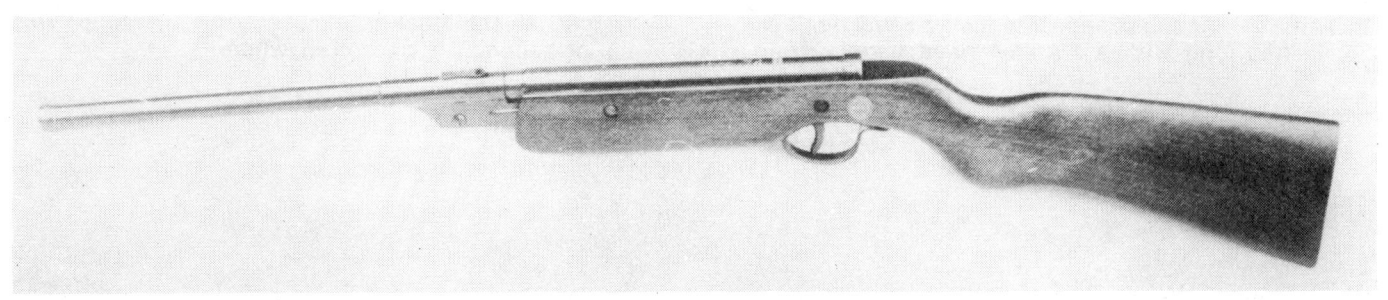

Diana Series 70 Model 74

MODEL Model 74, Series 70. Also known as the Model G74.

MAKER Milbro Sports Ltd., P.O. Box 24, Motherwell, Lanarkshire, Scotland ML1 4UP. Address at time of manufacture.

DATE From early 1970s to late 1970s. About 1980 it was renamed the Model 75 and produced with a rifle barrel.

VALUATION £5—£20. ($8—$30).

DETAILS Almost identical to "Original" Model 16, but with updated stock. 32½ inches long with a 12 inch .177 smoothbore brass liner barrel. Pillar foresight and rearsight adjustable for elevation only. Patent barrel latch forming part of the cocking link. For details of the Patent see "Guns Review" April 1980. Top of air chamber stamped "SERIES 70 MODEL 74 MADE IN GT. BRITAIN". Base of stock stamped "7 77 2". Could be a date stamp. Advertised weight 3 lbs. When it first appeared it may have just been called the "SERIES 70" and not the Model 74.

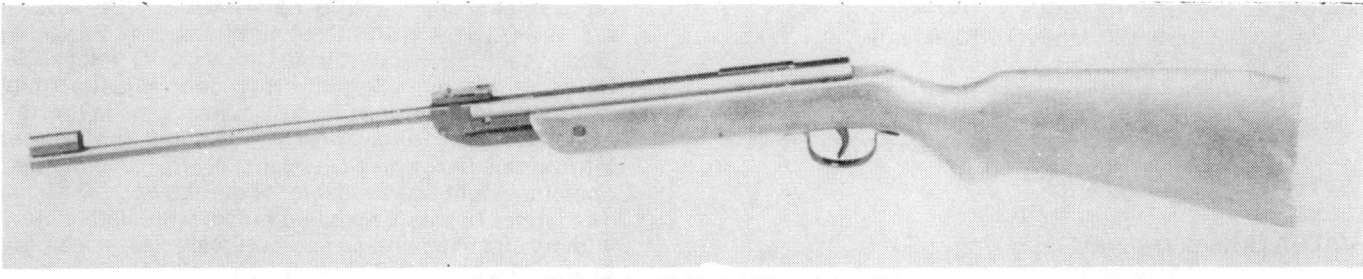

British Diana Sries 70 Model 76, early model

MODEL Series 70, Model 76.

MAKER Millard Bros., P.O. Box 24, Motherwell, Lanarkshire ML1 4UP.

DATE The New Diana Series 70 was introduced during 1972.

VALUATION £20—£40. ($30—$60).

DETAILS Semi-tinplate lightweight construction. 37 inches with a 15¾ inch rifled barrel. Barrel has pillar foresight with tunnel protector. Rear plastic sight as fitted to most of the smaller Diana airguns, this has a patent number 13057-61 cast on the side of the dovetail. Top of air chamber has a telescopic sight ramp spot welded on and stamped on the side "SERIES 70, MODEL 76, MADE IN GT. BRITAIN". Stock has slightly swollen fore-end with a brass medallion bearing the "DIANA" name with laurel leaves set in the L.H.S. Stamped on the butt are the numbers "9 46", so much for the date stamp idea! Advertised weight 4 lb 5 oz. Stock is of stained beech. Advertised muzzle velocities .177-400 f.p.s. and .22-300 f.p.s. Newly designed stock with sloping fore-end was introduced in 1980.

The Diana Sries 70 Model 77 air rifle

MODEL Model 77.

MAKER Millard Bros. Ltd., Motherwell, Lanarkshire, Scotland.

DATE Advertised in 1972 as the "new Diana Series 70" and are still produced. See "Airgun World" September 1978 and "Guns Review" April 1976.

VALUATION £20—£40. ($30—$60).

DETAILS Does not appear to have a serial number. 38½ inches long with a 15¾ inch rifled barrel. White plastic disc set in stock bearing the "Huntress" trademark with the words "DIANA SERIES 70". Between the telescopic sight grooves is stamped "SERIES 70 MODEL 77 MADE IN ENGLAND". Has a safety catch on the R.H.S. of the air chamber. Tunnel foresight and fully adjustable rearsight. Advertised weight 6 lb. Double pull trigger which appears adjustable. Rearsight looks very similar to one fitted to A.S.I. "Paratrooper". Later models appear to be fitted with recoil pad.

Have a care when removing the stock as there is a small coil spring that goes between the trigger adjuster screw and the trigger mechanism just in front of the trigger. As the stock is removed from the action this spring becomes free to fall anywhere.

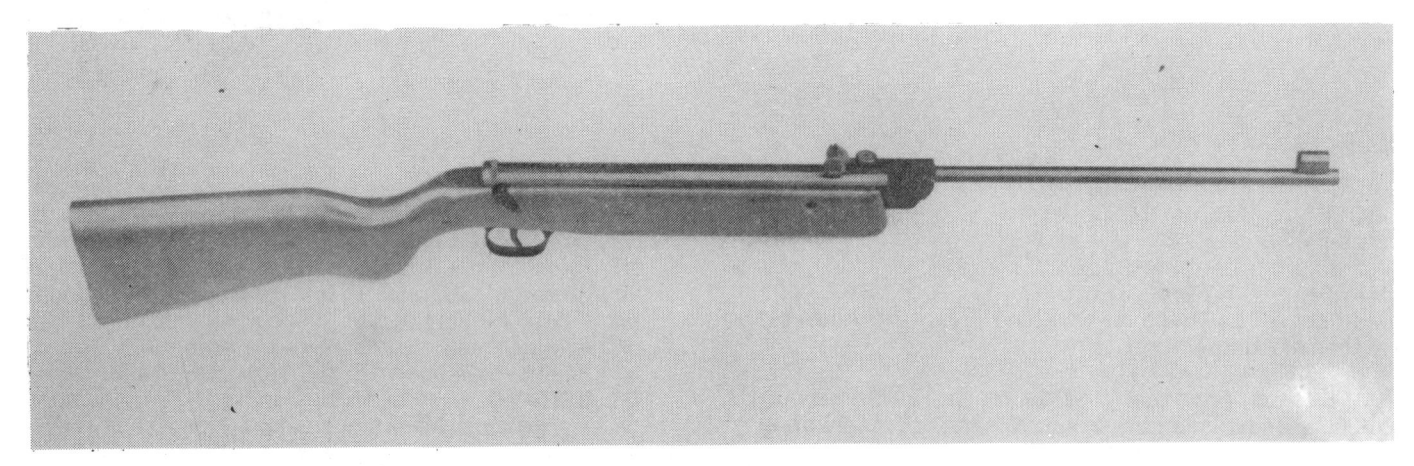

British Diana Series 70 Model 78

MODEL Series 70, Model 79 (De luxe)
Series 70, Model 78 (Standard).

MAKER Diana, Millard Bros., Motherwell, Lanarkshire, Scotland.

DATE Introduced 1972.

VALUATION £30—£60.
($45—$90).

DETAILS 42 inches long with 17¼ inch rifled barrel. Fully adjustable rearsight. Serial number not visible. Air chamber grooved for telescopic sight. Between the grooves appears "SERIES 70 — MODEL 79 MADE IN GT. BRITAIN". On R.H.S. of air chamber is the safety catch, back for safety on and forward for release for firing. Single pull trigger with trigger adjustment by way of hole in trigger guard. "Diana" medallion set in stock above trigger on L.H.S. Chequering pressed into stock. Advertised weight 6¾ lb. A simplified aperature sight was available for the above.

The Model 78 was a standard model with simple stock without the cheek piece and butt plate. Have seen one Model 78 with "4 36" stamped on the base of the butt, so much for thinking the above was a date stamp! Unless someone at the factory made a mistake. The above models were guaranteed for two years. Price in 1972 was £17.25 for Model 79 and £15.00 for Model 78. Advertised muzzle velocities .177-625 f.p.s. and 22-500 f.p.s.

MODEL 79
SERIES 70

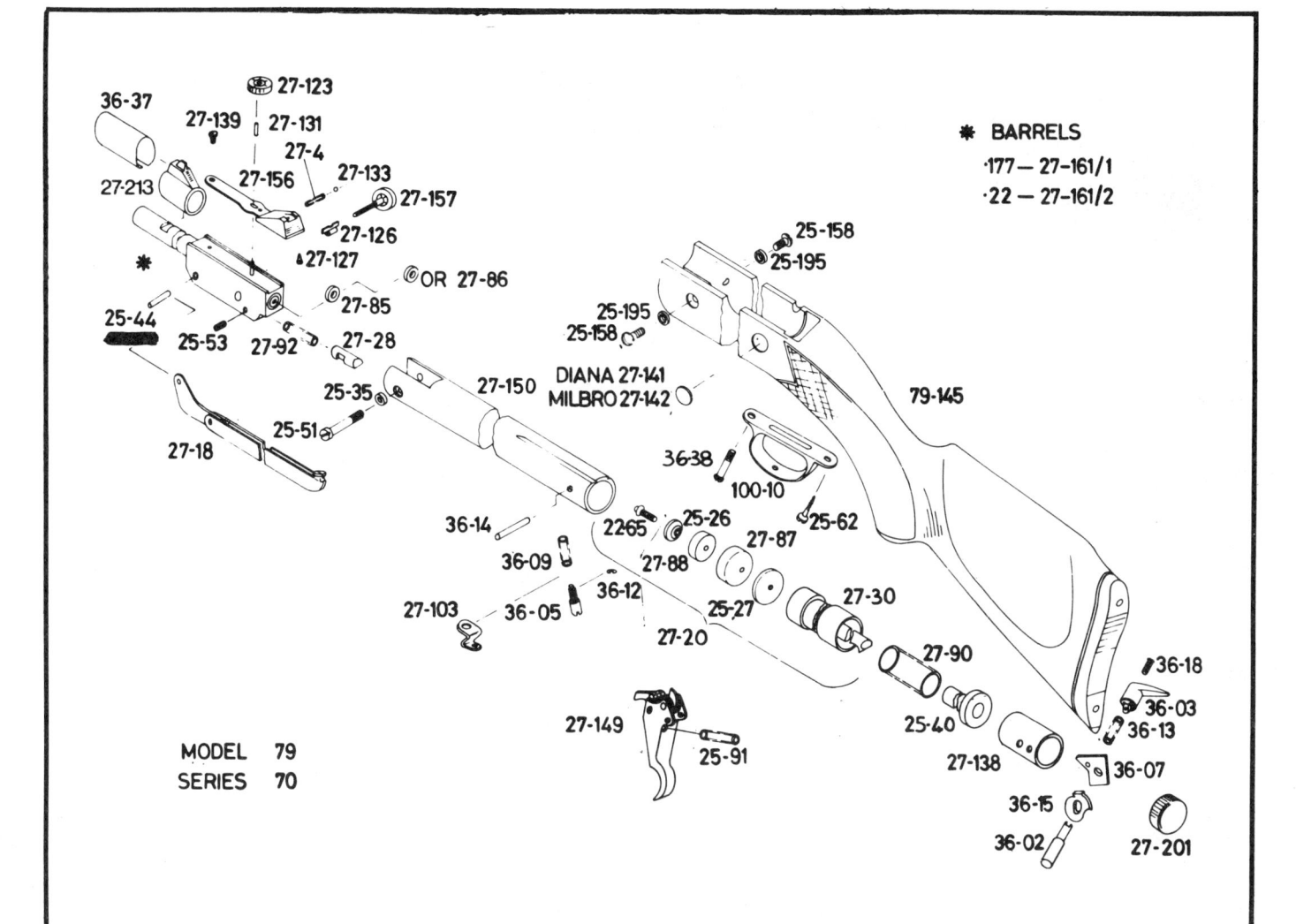

✱ BARRELS
·177 — 27-161/1
·22 — 27-161/2

SPARE PARTS LIST

PART NO.	DESCRIPTION	PART NO.	DESCRIPTION
22–65	Screw	27–133	Ball
25–26	Washer	27–138	Housing
25–27	Washer	27–139	Screw
25–35	Shim Washer	27–141	Diana Motif
25–40	Guide Tube	27–142	Milbro Motif
25–44	Pin	27–149	Trigger
25–51	Pivot Screw	27–150	Cylinder
25–53	Grub Screw	27–156	Sight
25–62	Screw	27–157	Spindle
25–91	Spring	27–161/1	·177 Barrel
25–158	Screw	27–162/2	·22 Barrel
25–195	Washer	27–213	Front Sight
27–4	Spring	28–8	Washer
27–18	Cocking Lever	36–2	Spindle
27–20	Piston Complete	36–3	Lever
27–28	Lock Pin	36–5	Screw
27–30	Piston	36–7	Plate
27–85	·177 Washer	36–9	Spring
27–86	·22 Washer	36–12	Circlip
27–87	Cup Washer	36–13	Spring
27–88	Washer	36–14	Pivot Pin
27–90	Main Spring	36–15	Cam
27–92	Spring	36–18	Screw
27–103	Bracket	36–37	Shield
27–123	Wheel	36–38	Screw
27–126	Blade	79–145	Butt
27–127	Screw	100–10	Trigger Guard
27–131	Stud		

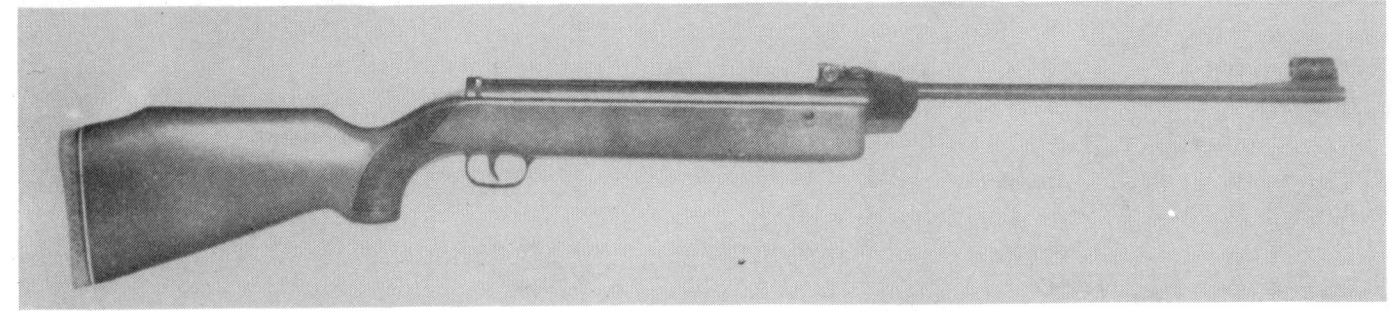

Diana G80

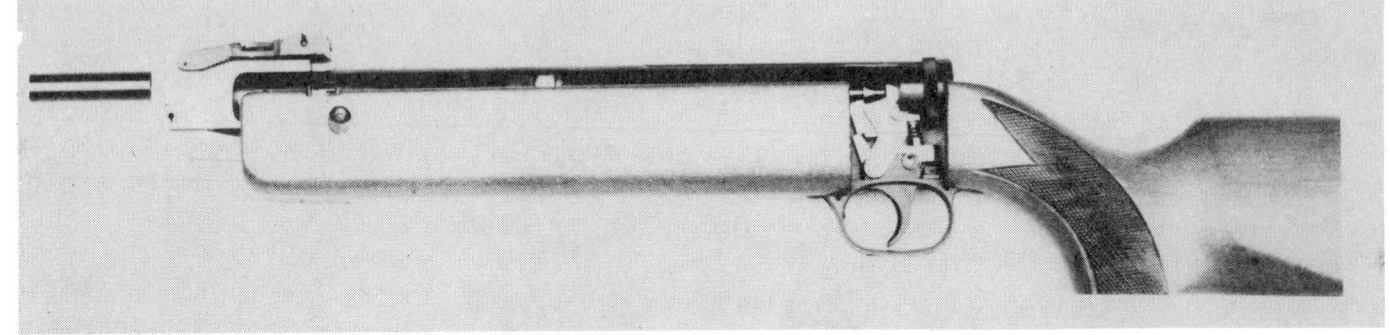

Diana G80 cut-away demonstration model

MODEL G80.

MAKER Milbro Sports Ltd., Motherwell, Lanarkshire, Scotland.

DATE Introduced early 1977 until 1982.

VALUATION £30–£50. ($45–$75).

DETAILS A well made air rifle giving good value for the price. 42 inches long with a 17¼ inch rifled barrel. Tunnel foresight with interchangeable sights. All metal rearsight fully adjustable. Cocking action appears to suffer from the "Weihrauch" click. Top of air chamber stamped "DIANA G80 MADE IN GT. BRITAIN". Telescopic sight grooves are 13 mm wide. Full length wooden stock with pressed chequering and rubber butt plate. Stamped on underside near trigger guard "4 77 4" could be a date stamp. Serial number not visible. Stock forescrews have Allen key heads. Trigger adjustment by way of small holes through the plastic trigger guard. Advertised weight 6 lbs 12 oz. See "Airgun World" September 1977 for gun test. The above is the de luxe version of the Model G79. The airgun is supplied with three foresight elements: post, aperture, and bead. The trigger is double pull, first adjustment is by way of screw in the trigger itself and the final pull is adjusted by the screw behind the trigger. Unusual nowadays in that the piston has a leather washer. Advertised muzzle velocities .177-625 f.p.s. and .22-500 f.p.s. In 1980 a newly designed stock with sloping fore-end was introduced. A micrometer peepsight (G31) is available for the above.

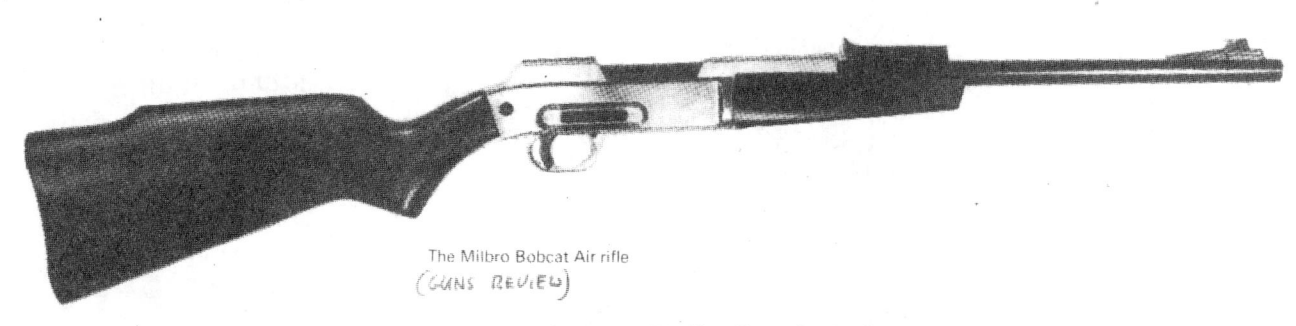

The Milbro Bobcat Air rifle. (Guns Review)

MODEL Diana G85, commonly referred to as the Bobcat.

MAKER Millard Brothers, PO Box 24, Motherwell, Lanarkshire, Scotland.

DATE From around 1978 to 1982.

VALUATION £20–£40. ($30–$60).

DETAILS The most updated version of the Model 16. Uprated sights with wooden stock and fore-end, sheet metal barrel and chamber with alloy die cast receiver and trigger guard. Automatic safety on the R.H.S. that operates when the action was being cocked. Example seen had lacquer finish barrel with a blued chamber, black stock and fore-end with silver/blue receiver. Overall a very stunning looking little air rifle. The rearsight was adjustable for elevation only. The above was sold with a booklet of instructions including the advice "Never shoot where you cannot see up to 360 yards"!! It was sold in .177 only and smoothbore at that. When new the Bobcat sold for around £17.00. Details of stripping etc can be gained from "Guns Review", November, 1978.

Overall length was 34 inches (86.4 cm), and weight given as 3.75 lb. It was also sold with a "Special Cloth Badge", what a collectors' item. The piston was fitted with an "O" ring seal and not the usual riveted leather washer. A review appeared in "Airgun World", October, 1978.

Although this was a junior air rifle it is seldom seen these days, and would be well worth collecting.

Em-Ge Model 2

MODEL 2.

MAKER Em-Ge, Moritz & Gerstenberger, Waffenfabrik, Zella, Mehlis, Thuringia, Germany.

DATE Assume the above to be pre-1939.

VALUATION £20 – £40. ($30 – $60).

DETAILS 38¾ inches long with a 15¾ inch. 177 smoothbore barrel. Stamped on side of barrel breech "KAL 4.5 m/m". Cocking arm is pivoted just under the barrel pivot. Top of air chamber stamped " EM — GE<ZELLA — MEHLIS (THUR.)" and at the rear of the air chamber "MOD. 2 EM-GE D.R.G.M." D.R.G.M. stands for Deutsches Reichs Gebrauchsmuster, German Empire Utility Design. The stock bears the circular "EM-GE" medallion that also appears on the pre-war Zenit air pistol, see Smith's "Airguns of the World" page 151. Trigger adjustment is by way of a screw through the front of the trigger guard. On the top part of the ribbed butt may appear a date stamp.

Falke Model 10 (W. H. B. Smith)

Falke Model 20 (W. H. B. Smith)

Falke Model 30 (W. H. B. Smith)

Falke Model 40 (W. H. B. Smith)

Falke Model 50 (W. H. B. Smith)

Falke Model 60 (W. H. B. Smith)

Falke Model 70 (W. H. B. Smith)

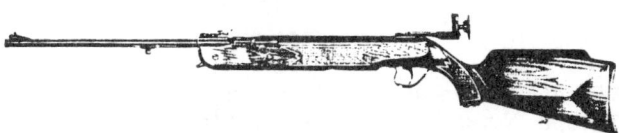

Falke Model 90 (W. H. B. Smith)

MODEL Falke Model 40.

MAKER Albert Fohrenbach, G.m.b.H., Bennigsen, Hannover, Germany.

DATE Early 1950s to early 1960s.

VALUATION Falke Model 40 £30—£60. ($45—$90).

DETAILS Very similar to the tinplate Haenel air rifles and those of Diana. The Model 40 is of sheet metal construction. 35¼ inches long with a 14⅛ inch .177 smoothbore barrel. For its size would imagine that it was sold in .177 only. Simple screw-in pillar foresight and dovetail mounted rearsight. Top of trigger block housing tube stamped "FALKE-MOD.40". It might also have been stamped with the falcon head crest trademark: but on the example seen this was not present. Single pull trigger and lacks adjustment. Simple stock that may have been stamped with a date stamp, but example seen was heavily varnished.
The range of Falke air rifles ran from the cheap tinplate up to a heavyweight underlever, briefly they are as follows:

MODEL 10 Lightweight tinplate small air rifle of a somewhat very distinctive shape. Has been likened to pre-war Haenel design. Short stock up to trigger only.

MODEL 20 Same as the Model 10 but fitted with a separate fore-end.

MODEL 30 Would appear very similar to Diana Model 16. Fitted with stock up to the breech.

MODEL 40 Similar to Diana Model 22.

MODEL 50 Same as Model 40 but fitted with a solid metal barrel.

MODEL 60 The first of the stronger air rifles. Adjustable trigger by way of screw through trigger guard. Ramp type rearsight with slider.

MODEL 70 The largest break barrel action they made. Fitted with barrel latch. Improved trigger mechanism and adjustment. Stock is chequered on on pistol grip. Looks very much like Haenel Model 2 D.R.P. 37 inches long and weighing 6 lbs 9 ozs. Sold in either .22 or .177 smoothbore or rifled.

MODEL 80 Underlever cocking air rifle with tap loading for the pellet. Chequered stock on grip and fore-end with falcon emblem. Same cocking action as the B.S.A. Airsporter. 44 inches long with a weight of 8 lbs. 13 ozs. Sold in .22 and .177 rifled. Would appear to have a self opening loading tap. On a Falke Model 80 air rifle, serial number 129, the following has been noted. The number, if it is a serial number also appears on the tap handle, rear of air chamber stamped "FALKE MODELL 80" with a falcom emblem, this emblem also appears on the stock. Top of barrel stamped "KAL. 4.5 m/m gez", this denoting that the barrel is rifled, underside of barrel stamped "MADE IN GERMANY". The action is held in the stock by SIX screws, the largest number of fixing screws the Author has ever encountered.

MODEL 90 Same as the Model 80, but fitted with sling swivels, de luxe stock with high combe, and made from walnut as opposed to elm on the Model 80. The Model 90 was also fitted with an aperture peepsight. Weight of the Model 90 was 9 lbs 7 ozs.

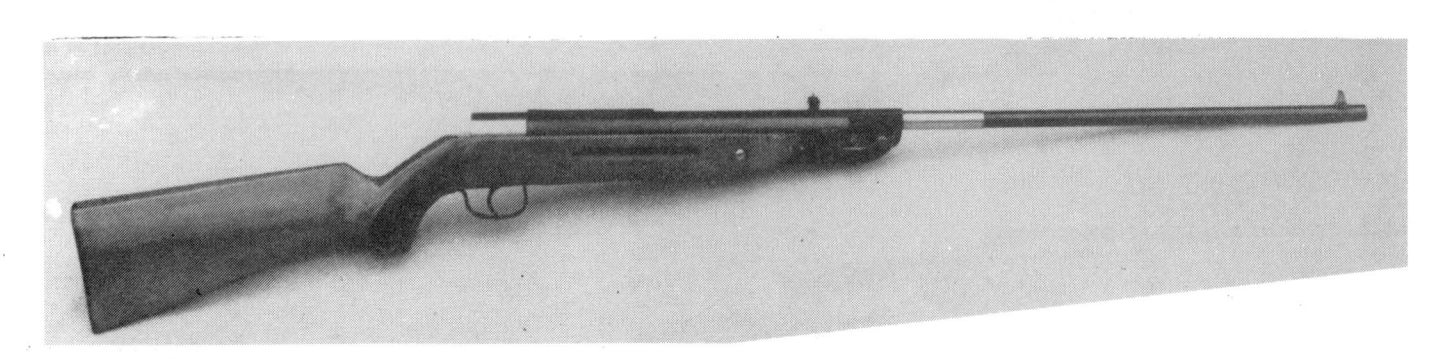

Falke Model 70

MODEL 70.

MAKER Trade name "Falke" used by Albert Fohrenbach, G.m.b.H., Benigsen, Hannover, Germany, although very similar to Haenel air rifles and would not be surprised if Haenel supplied some of the components, if not the complete air rifles!

DATE Late 1940s to very early 1950s.

VALUATION £40—£80. ($60—$120).

DETAILS Falke air rifles appeared just after Second World War, but were not to last long. They were never widely advertised in this country and must have been sold in relatively small numbers compared to other makes of airguns, even if they were very well made and renowned for power. 42¾ inches long with a 19 inch barrel, available in .22 or .177 rifled or smoothbore. Dovetail mounted pillar foresight and turret blade rearsight adjustable for elevation only. Top of barrel stamped "KAL 5.5 m/m gez" the gez stands for Gezogen-rifled, as opposed to "glat." meaning Glatter smoothbore. On the underside of the barrel is stamped "MADE IN GERMANY" and is identical to that on Haenel airguns. On the R.H.S. of the barrel breech is a barrel latch that is pushed towards the air chamber in order to release the barrel, similar action to the Haenel air rifles. Plain air chamber with separate trigger block with the Eagle trademark and "FALKE MODEL 70" stamped underneath. Stock fitted with metal butt plate and hand chequered. Trigger adjustment through hole in trigger guard. Jointed cocking link. Advertised weight 6 lbs 9 ozs.

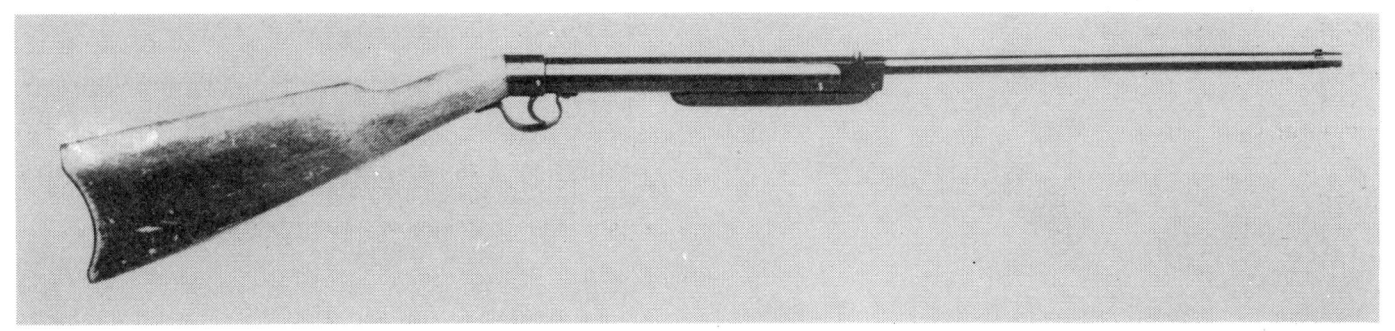

The "Favorit 1" by F. Langenham

MODEL "Favorit I".

MAKER Friedrich Langenham, Zella-Mehlis (Thuringen), Germany.

DATE About 1930 to 1939, although the above style appeared in the early 1920s with an octagonal to round barrel.

VALUATION £20–£40. ($30–$60).

DETAILS Looks very much like the Haenel Model 45. Small sized air rifle measuring 35¾ inches long with a 15¾ inch smoothbore barrel, although rifled barrels were available in the one calibre, .177. Simple non-adjustable sights set in dovetails. Stamped on the underside of the barrel breech is the last three digits of the serial number and F.L.Z. in the sectors of a circle. The serial number, 16603 in this case, is stamped near the trigger block on the air chamber. All metal parts are blued including the butt plate. Stamped into the wood under the butt plate is a capital H. Barrel catch is a spring tensioned ball bearing. Similar to the "Original" of Mayer & Grammelspacher. Although the above bears the trademark of F. Langenham it still looks very similar to the "Tell" air rifles made by Oscar Will who sold out to Wilheyn Foss who later became Mayer & Grammelspacher. Advertised weight 1.650 kilograms.

The Flecha Model 14 (foresight is not original)

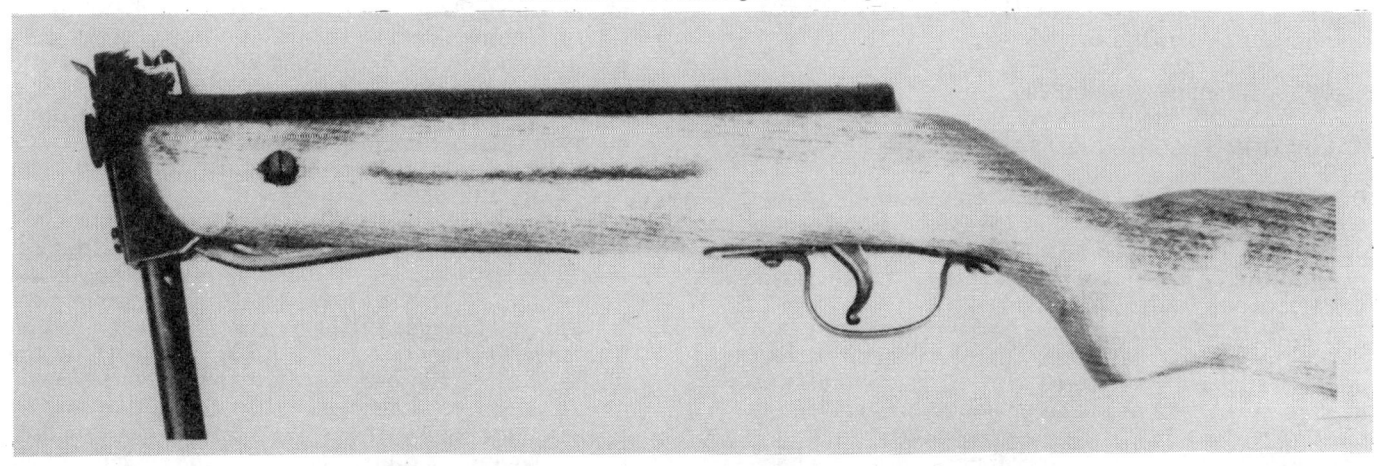

Action of Flecha Model 14. Note trigger adjustment slide linked to trigger guard.

MODEL 14.

MAKER "Flecha" who could either be the manufacturer or retailer.

DATE From the look of the thing would suggest 1950/1960s.

VALUATION £20–£40. ($30–$60).

DETAILS Break action air rifle, 40½ inches long with a 17⅜ inch .22 rifled barrel. Foresight is not original and rearsight is adjustable for elevation only. Serial number not visible. Top of air chamber stamped "FLECHA" with an arrow running through it and "MOD — 14" underneath. All in all a very basic air rifle. The only thing of note is the trigger adjustment. This is a flat piece of metal held against the stock by the trigger guard. The forward guard screw is loosened and the piece of metal is pressed against the trigger and pushed to any position of adjustment required. It is then locked into place by tightening the forward guard screw. From the look of the air rifle I think it has European origins.

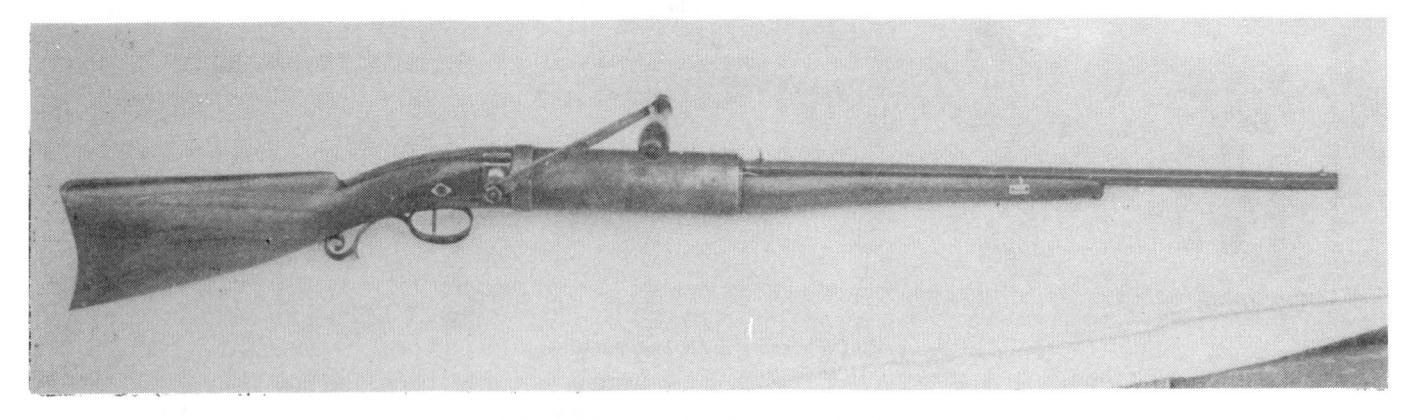

R.H.S. with crank in position to cock action

Crank wind Gallery air rifle

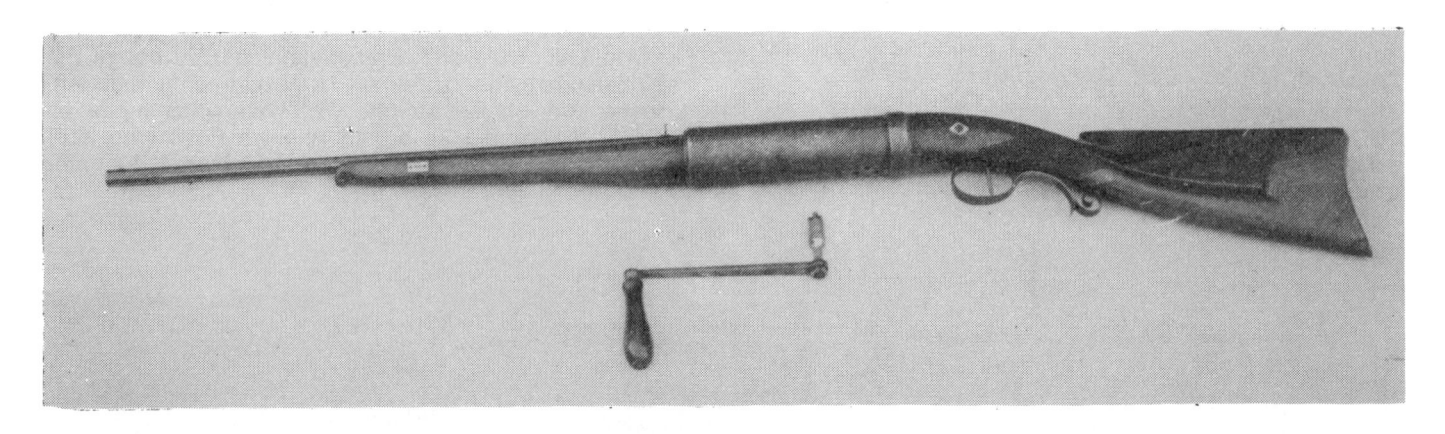

L.H.S. with crank removed

MODEL Crank wind Gallery Air Rifle.

MAKER The initials "F.M." or "T.M." (probably "F.M.") appear stamped on the barrel with a small crown over the initials. There also appears an elongated hexagonal stamp with something deeply pressed in the centre but is undecipherable. No other mark or serial number appears on the air rifle.

DATE Early to late 1800s.

VALUATION £300—£600. ($450—$900).

DETAILS Muzzle loading crank wound gallery smoothbore .25 target air rifle. Measures 46 inches in length with a 22 inch barrel including thread for screwing into the air chamber. The air rifle splits into three parts: fore-end, barrel, and action with butt.

The fore-end measures 13 inches and is fixed on to the barrel by one flat cross pin. Horn insert at rear appears to have held some sort of catch that was located in the face of the air chamber, but this is now missing.

The barrel is .25 and smoothbore with a brass restriction at the air chamber. Octagonal and parallel sided with front and rearsights set in dovetails that bear simple marks as having been zeroed in at sometime in its life. The slot for the fore-end pin has also been dovetailed into the barrel.

The air chamber measures $8\frac{1}{4}$ inches in length and almost $2\frac{1}{4}$ inches in diameter. Appears to be fitted with a convalute spring and chamber has four air holes drilled in the underside to allow free flow of air as the massive piston trundles down the air chamber on its journey to deliver power to the cowering pellet lurking in the barrel. Rear of action has an upper and lower back strap that holds action to butt. Action appears to have a set trigger with adjustment by way of small screw at rear of trigger. Trigger guard has well proportioned scroll work and screws into the lower back strap at front and into butt at rear. Roach bellied stock with well figured wood. Metal butt plate. The crank is inserted into the right-hand side just behind the air chamber and rotated twice and a bit in order to cock the action. The set trigger needs very little pressure to fire.

The crank handle has been well made. Straight shaft with six toothed cog for cocking the action. Length of shaft handle $7\frac{3}{8}$ inches. All metal parts are smooth and in the "white". Traces of original blueing or plating are lacking. The European style crank wound gallery airgun was advertised as late as the 1930s. The fact that the above is a muzzle load means that somewhere, lying about, is the separate ram rod as the airgun has no provision for holding the ram rod. For further details of crank wound airguns see "Airguns and other Pneumatic Arms" by Arne Hoff, Chapter three titled "Strike-Pump Guns". In the book "Airguns" by Eldon G. Wolff the above pattern gallery gun is termed the "Primary New York City" type. When barrel has been removed it can be seen that the end of the piston is covered with leather, a flat section and not cupped as found in modern airguns.

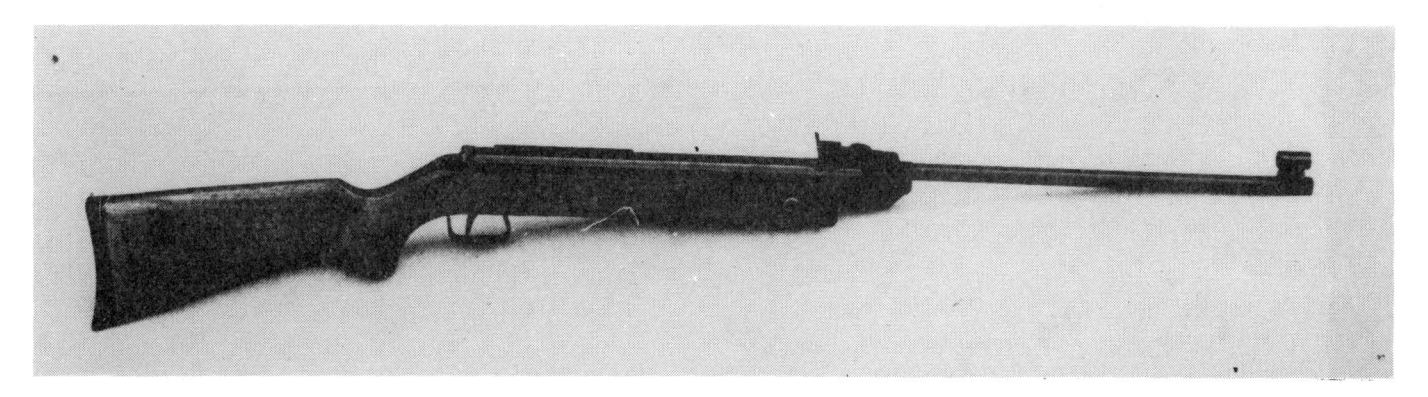

Geco Model 55R

MODEL 55R.

MAKER "Original", Mayer & Grammelspacher, Rastatt, West Germany. The Geco trade name was for the American Market. "GECO" was the trade name of the distributors G. Genschow of Hamburg, Germany. They also supplied airguns to America after the Second World War.

VALUATION £30–£60. ($45–$90).

DETAILS 42¼ inches with a 17¾ inch rifled barrel. Hooded foresight clamped on groove. L.H.S. of barrel breech stamped with the calibre and an "F" in pentagon denoting lower muzzle energy required in Europe. Ball-bearing barrel lock. Action cannot be released when cocked and must be fired. Rich deep blueing to all metal parts. Top of air chamber stamped with "GECO" and "MOD 55R". Towards the rear end on the L.H.S. appears "MADE IN GERMANY" and "03 73" similar to the supposed date stamps on "Original" airguns. The last figure three could be either an eight or nine. Fitted with telescopic sight ramp with a serrated surface. All in all looks very much like the "Original" type airgun. Double pull trigger with two adjusting screws. Very similar to the "Condor" that appeared in this country in the early 1979s. For further details of the "Condor" see "Airgun World" June 1979. "Geco" was also the trade name of Gustav Genschow & Co., Berlin and were in business from 1919 to 1944 when for some reason the firm stopped production, maybe it was a bit short of the "Eastern Promise"!

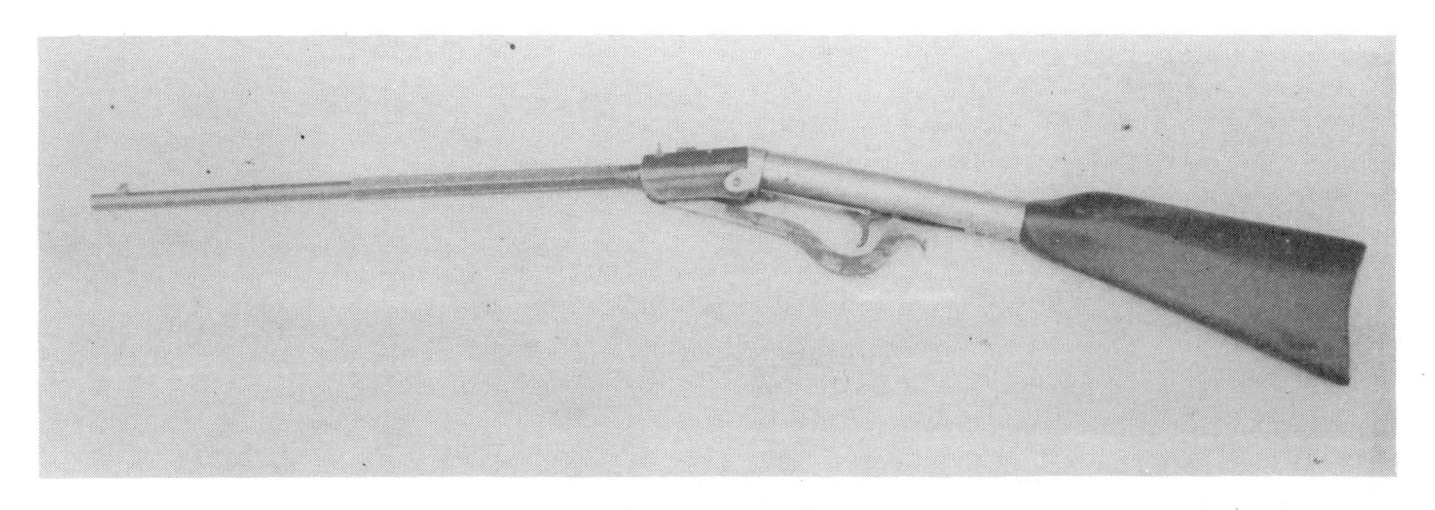

Gem style air rifle

MODEL Gem style air rifle.

MAKER Not known, but has all the characteristics of manufacture by Langenham of Zeller Street, Blasii, Thuringia, Germany.

DATE Would assume from late 1890s to around 1920.

VALUATION £30–£60. ($45–$90).

DETAILS Typical "Gem" style but with simple external spring trigger action. Same pattern of nickel plating, i.e. the air chamber, trigger guard, trigger and spring, and the butt plate, also the barrel latch. Usual sloppy action that appears to be the ear-mark of the Gem pedigree. 33½ inches long with a 17⅜ inch barrel, smoothbore. Serial number is stamped in the usual place on the barrel breech face and on the opposing transfer port face. Number of above, 2540. The stock plugs straight into the rear of the air chamber. Very similar design to air rifle featured on page 123. The above could be a larger version made at the same time. Note similar trigger action. Rear and foresights are set in dovetails across barrel and have no elevation adjustment. Gem style barrels appear to screw into the supporting breech and have seen replacement barrels made from other air rifles including the Webley Mk. II service barrel in place of the original barrel. Another hybrid that has crept out of the "Woods".

Have only seen three of the above with serial numbers 492, 2540 and 8417. Care should be taken when firing the above as if gripping the air chamber at the rear of the chamber the mainspring can nip the hand as it compresses.

Gem style air rifle, left-hand side

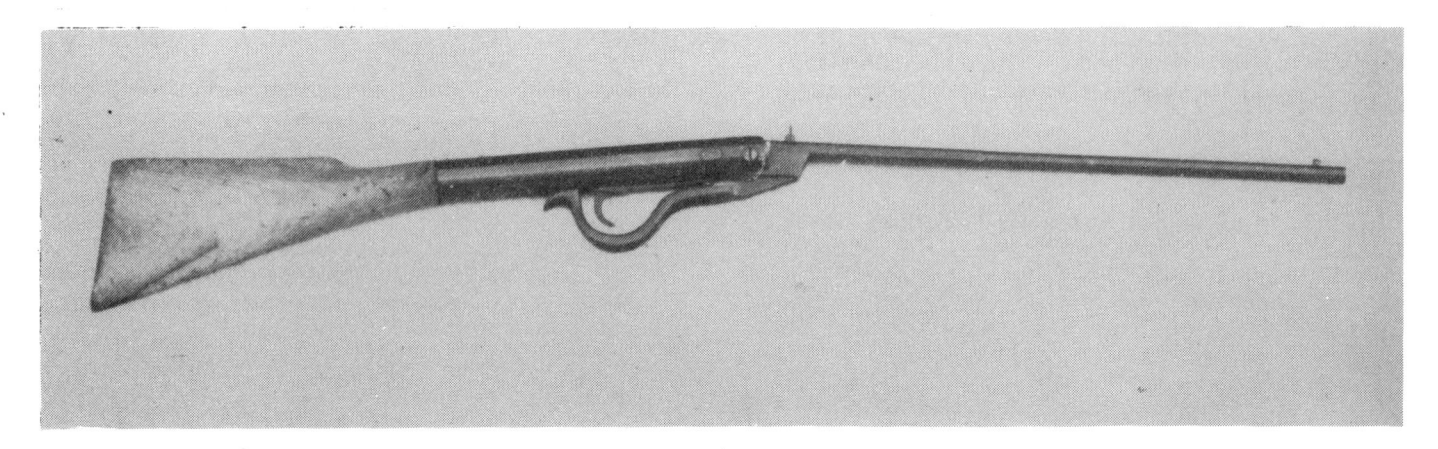

Gem style air rifle, right-hand side

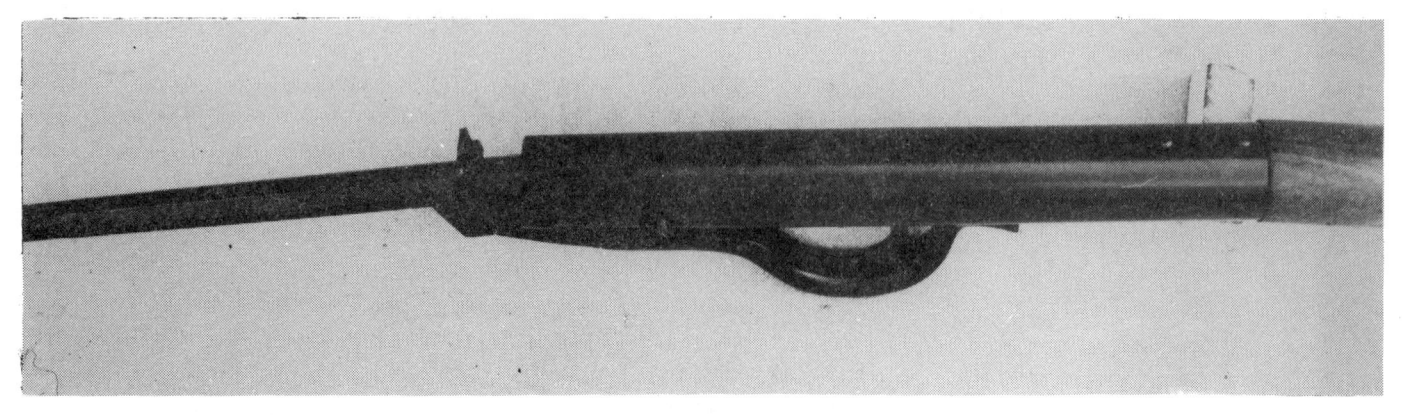

Gem style air rifle action

MODEL Millita style Gem air rifle.

MAKER F. Langenham of Zeller Street, Blasii, Thuringia, Germany.

DATE Would assume from around 1910 to 1930s but only in small numbers.

VALUATION For anything unusual in this line of Gem style air rifles one would expect from around £20 to £60. ($30—$90).

DETAILS Gem style air rifle with Millita style barrel release button. Serial number 2 stamped on almost all parts. 17¼ inch smoothbore barrel. Measures 30 inches in length. Barrel braized on to barrel support block. Air chamber is pegged on to the stock. Stock bears the retailer's name "H.H.B. — S.U.G.G. — ANGEL ST. — SHEFFIELD". So must have been a production air rifle, but with such a low serial number would seem improbable. The button barrel release is identical to that fitted to the early Millita air rifles imported by Martin Pulvermann. So manufacture of the above must have been after 1901. For details of this patent see "Guns Review" March 1978. This barrel latch style was later changed by another patent in 1905, see "Guns Review" June 1978. Rear and foresights look too wide for the slender barrel and both overhang each side of the barrel.

Have only seen two of the above with serial numbers 2 and 41, see "Airgun World" April 1981.

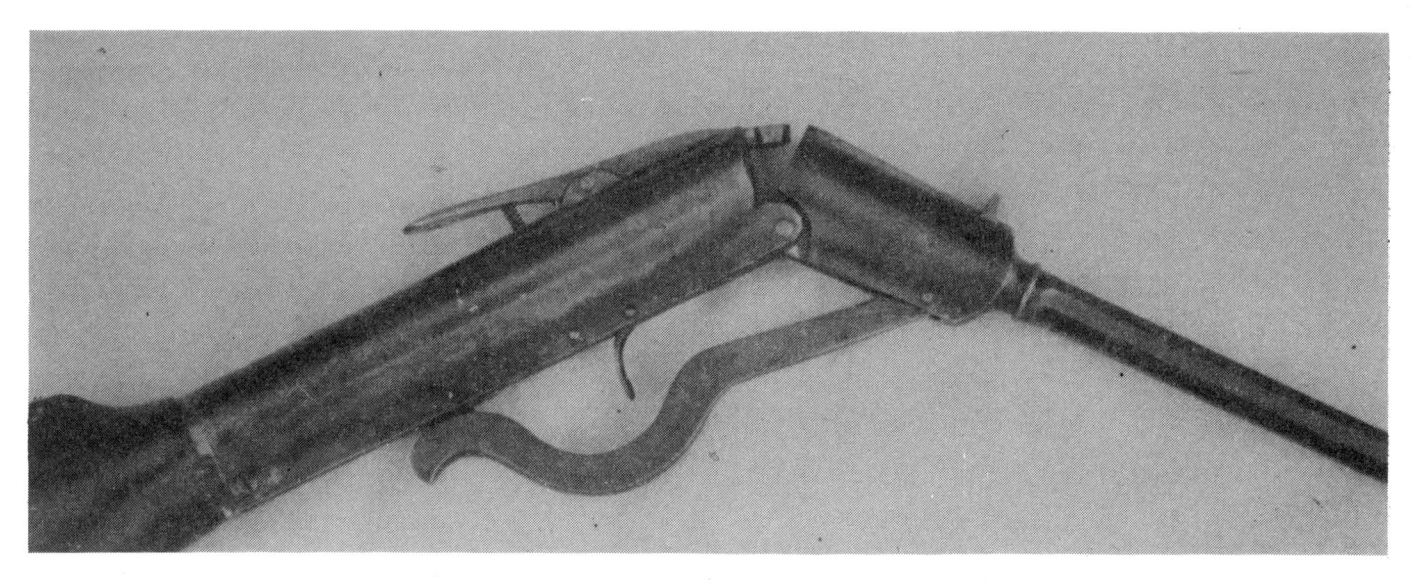

Side view: Gem air rifle with patent "long lever bolt"

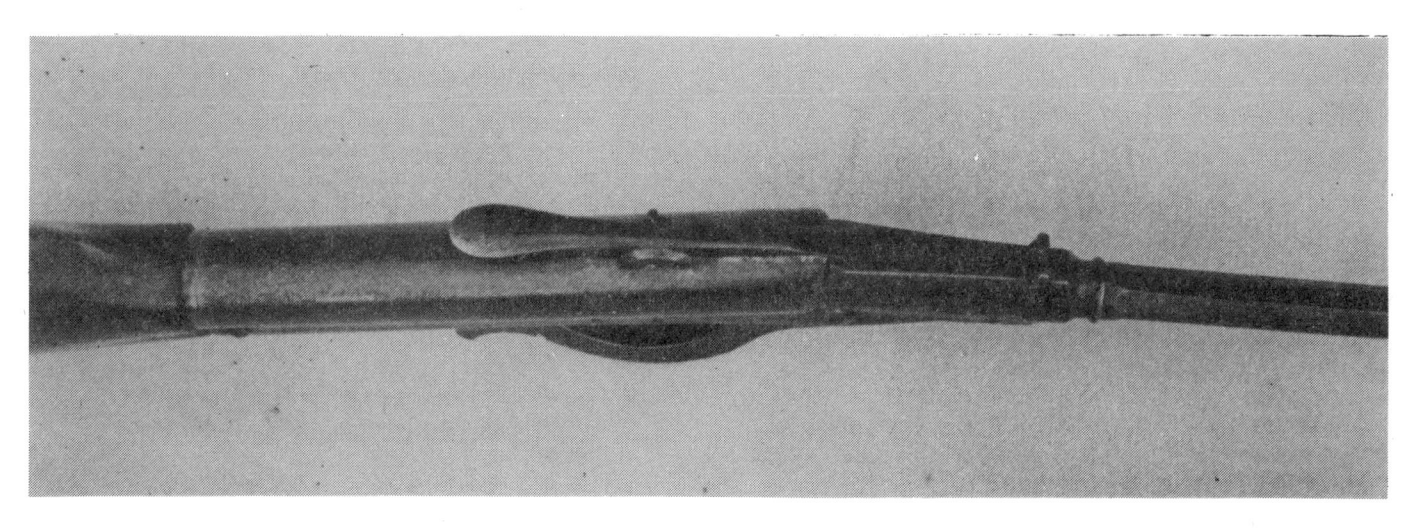

Top view

MODEL Gem air rifle with "long lever bolt".

MAKER Friedrich Langenham of Zeller Street, Blasii, Thuringia, Germany.

DATE Patent for the above barrel latch was made out in 1894 and have seen adverts for the above style Gem air rifle as late as 1911.

VALUATION £30–£60. ($45–$90).

DETAILS Not the usual style of barrel latch for a Gem air rifle. For further details of the patent for the above see "Guns Review" December 1977. The air rifle follows the patent exactly. Measures 87 cm or 37¼ inches in length with an 18⅜ inch smoothbore barrel. The unusual barrel latch was patented by Friedrich Langenham through the agents Martin Pulvermann who imported Gem and Millita air rifles and a G. F. Redfern. Octagonal to round barrel. Breech of barrel stamped "5223 -2-" as is the face of the air chamber. Serial number also appears on the cocking lever which acts as a trigger guard. Top flat of barrel stamped "GEM", the crossed rifle trademark with the letters "LZ" and further along towards the rearsight "MANUFACTURED IN GERMANY". Behind the rearsight is stamped "D.R.G.M.". Metal butt plate with "256" stamped on the underside and in the bare wood, could be that the butt came from another Gem air rifle. The Langenham trademark at a later date took on the shape of a circle with three sectors with the letters "F.L.Z." appearing in each sector.

Only three have been seen with the above style barrel and they had the following serial numbers: 30882, 2-43751, and 2-5223.

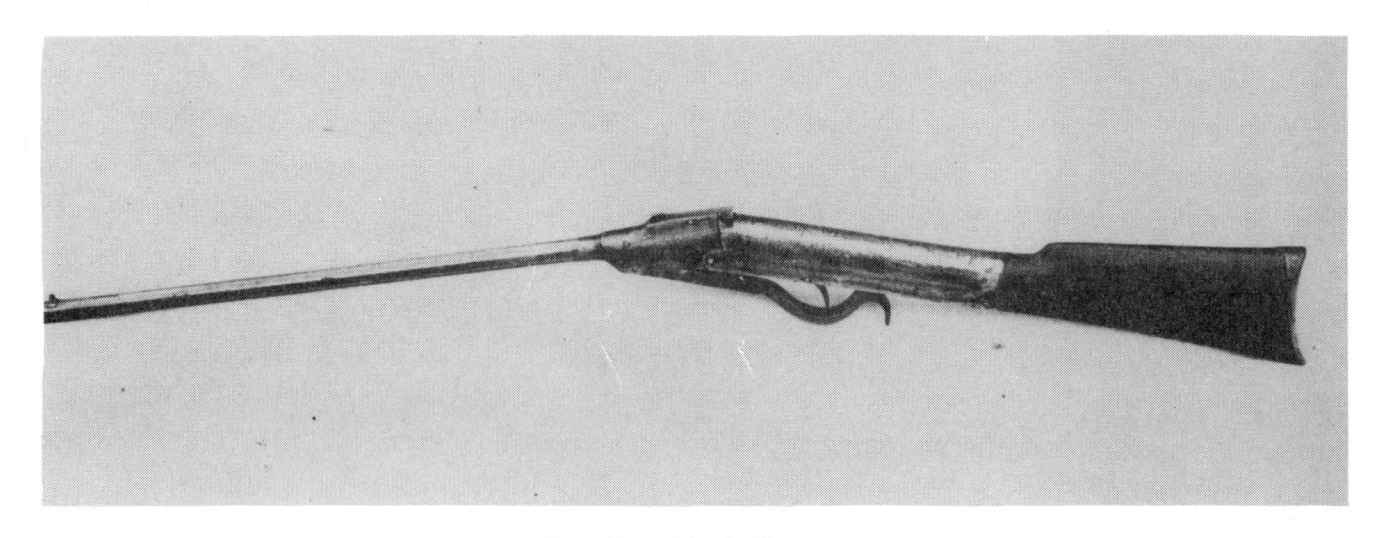

Heavy Gem style air rifle

MODEL Gem style air rifle.

MAKER Have seen this type stamped "MADE IN BELGIUM" on one of the barrel flats.

DATE From around 1885 to early 1900s.

VALUATION £30—£60, £26a. ($45—$90, $39a).

DETAILS A heavy model with an anti-clockwise rifled barrel. This is the second rifled gem I've seen and even more unusual in that the rifling is anti-clockwise, normally rifling is clockwise. 41½ inches long with a 23¼ inch rifled barrel. Octagonal barrel full length with simple sights. Barrel screws into the breech. Rearsight forms part of the "T" bar latch. Stamped on top of latch "12 91". Serial number not visible. Does have "58" stamped under the heavy cast butt plate. Simple wooden stock bears the trader's stamp "HOOTON JONES, CODALE ST. LIVERPOOL". Could be that the above was made by some other firm than the manufacturer of "Gem" air rifles. The above could be a "Laballe" air rifle advertised to give 50 per cent more penetration than the "Gem". Seen advertised 1892. Weighs between 7 to 8 lbs. Have seen shotguns bearing the name Hooton Jones. An earlier example, serial number 37, had "DEPOSE 18,5,88" engraved on the "T" bar barrel latch. Of the three seen the following pattern emerges:

Date	Serial Number
18,5,88	37
12,90	38
12,91	58

Can't possibly believe that only one was made between 1888 and 1890 and 20 between 1890 and 1891.

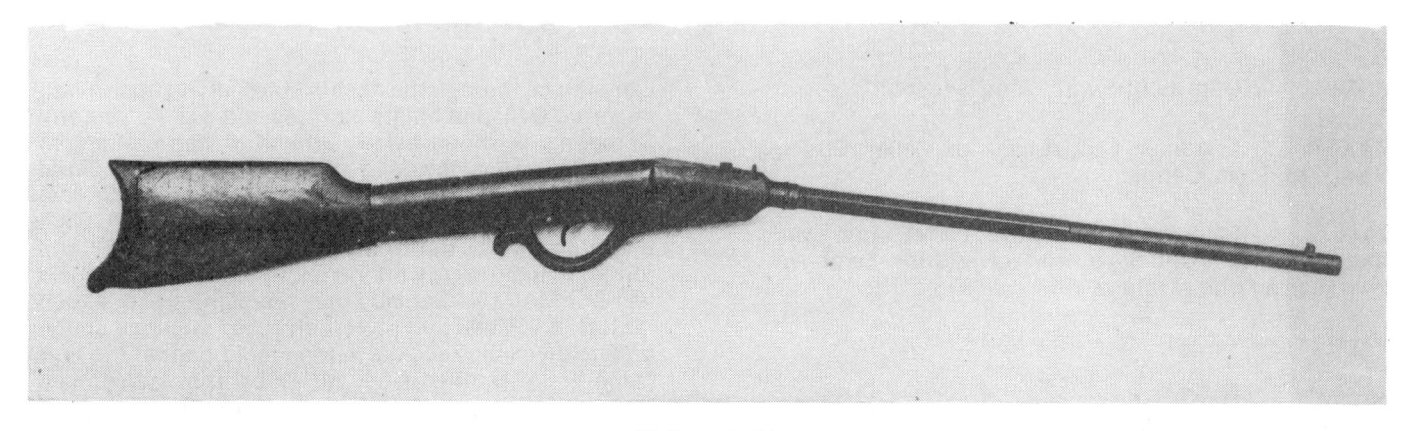

.25 Gem air rifle

MODEL Gem .25 smoothbore model.

MAKER F. Langenham, Blasii Street, Thuringia, Germany.

DATE First advertised in 1882 and up till the late 1930s.

VALUATION For .25 Gems £30—£70, £14a—£55a. ($45—$105, $21a—$78).

DETAILS 39½ inches long with 21½ inch smoothbore .25 barrel. Very heavy with an equally heavy stock butt plate. Cocking lever and air chamber bear traces of nickel plating. Serial number 11981 stamped on barrel breech and air port faces with the last three digits on the cocking lever. Barrel octagonal to round with "GEM, MANUFACTURED IN GERMANY" stamped on the upper flat. Rearsight just in front of the barrel latch and adjustable for windage only. Advertised in 1911 as the "HEAVY MODEL" and weighed 3,400 kilograms. Most Gem style air rifles suffer from various degrees of sloppy breeches, i.e. barrel wobbles from side to side. For this style of .25 Gem air rifle I've seen the following: 3. 11981. 81888. and 87878.

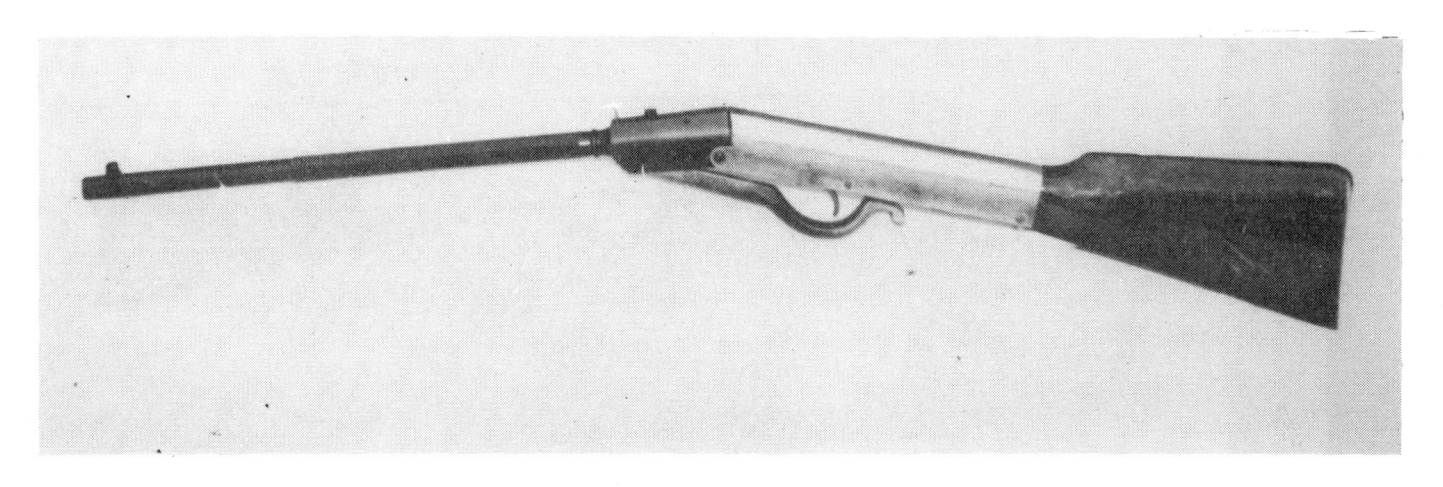

.25 Gem air rifle (light pattern)

MODEL Gem .25 smoothbore. Appears to be a lighter model to the "Heavy" model described elsewhere.

DATE From around the 1890s to the late 1920s.

VALUATION £30—£70, £14a—£55a. ($45—$105, $21a—$78a).

DETAILS 38½ inches long with a 20½ inch .25 smoothbore barrel. Serial number 5 stamped on all major parts. Air chamber, cocking lever, trigger and thin butt plate bear traces of nickel plating. Barrel stamping as above. The "Harpoon" trademark looks like a flintlock pistol firing from left to right. A barbed arrow protrudes from the barrel. Rearsight is separate from the barrel latch, denoting a later style of manufacture.

"Heavy" style .177 Gem

MODEL "Heavy" style Gem air rifle.

MAKER Assume either Fritz or Friedrich Langenham of Zeller Street, Blasii, Thuringia, Germany, or by Flurscheim & Bergman, "Eisenwerke", Gaggenau, Baden, Germany.
Imported by Adolphe Arbenz, 107/108 Great Charles Street, Warwick, Birmingham.

DATE Assume from early 1900s to late 1920s.

VALUATION £30—£60. ($45—$90).

DETAILS Heavy model. .177 smoothbore 19⅝ inch barrel. Simple blade foresight with rearsight part of the barrel latch. Octagonal to round barrel with a trademark of two gat-like pistols crossed with "G" underneath. The gat air pistols look very much the "Dolla" so could be that they were manufactured by either of the above. Also marked on top of barrel flat "PATENT GEM No. 2224". Barrel latch has doll's head extension. Serial number stamped on face of barrel breech and the last two digits appear on transfer port face and on the inside surface of the cocking lever. Number of above example 415. Traces of nickel plating appear on air chamber, cocking lever, and butt plate. Nice wide butt with a heavy cast butt plate. Often on the underside of butt plates for Gem air rifles appears pencilled writing that appears to be the serial number for matching to the gun. On others have seen the serial number stamped. Overall length 37¼ inches. The "Heavy" model was advertised in either .177 or .25 calibre. The "G" under the trademark could stand for "GEM", or for Gaggenau if manufactured by Flurscheim & Bergmann. An air pistol manufactured by Flurscheim & Bergmann is featured in "Guns Review" May 1975 and bears a similar trademark to the above. It seems very likely that the above was manufactured by Flurscheim & Bergmann. An identical model in .25 had a harpoon-like trademark stamped on the barrel with "GEM". The following serial numbers have been seen for the above style heavy Gem 5, 415, 551 and 3360.

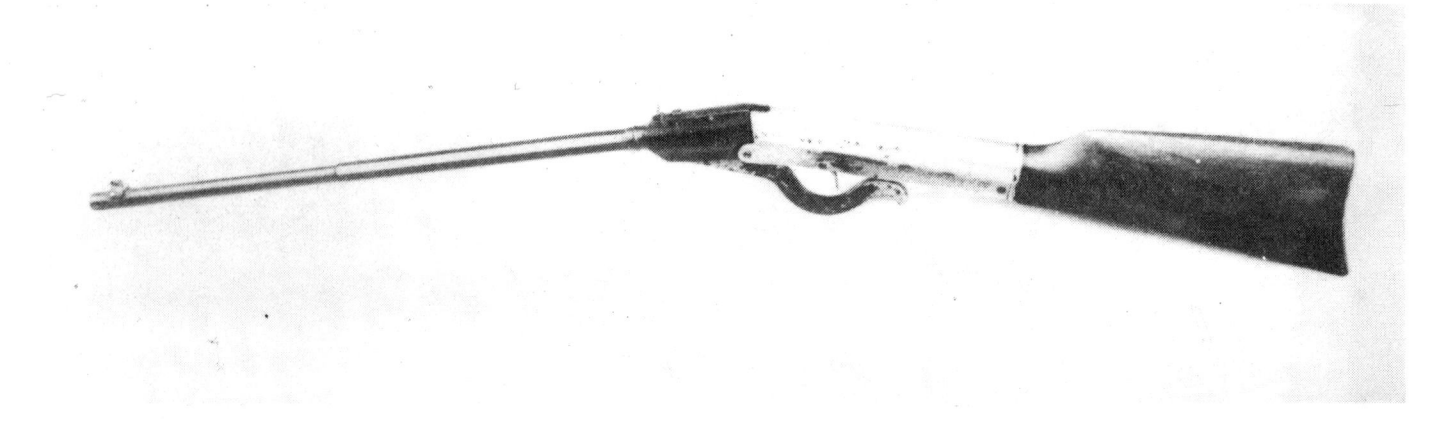

"Gem" air rifle. 2-45484

MODEL "Gem".

MAKER Has a crossed rifled trademark with the initials "LZ" this could be Friedrich Langenham of Zeller Street, Blasii, Thuringia, Germany. He patented various improvements for Gem style air rifles, see "Guns Review" December 1977 and onwards.

DATE Assume 1890 to 1930s.

VALUATION £30—£50.
($45—$75).

DETAILS Serial number 49437. 34¾ inches long with octagonal to round barrel. Smoothbore. Last three digits stamped on underlever. Air cylinder, cocking lever, trigger and butt plate bear traces of nickel plating. Top flat of barrel stamped "GEM" in cursive writing, followed by a crossed rifle trademark with initials "LZ" could stand for "Langenham". The final stamping is "MANUFACTURED IN GERMANY". Rearsight is separate from the barrel latch. Barrel measures 18½ inches long. Have seen a light model Millita with side button barrel release bearing the above "LZ" trademark, so would assume that the above Gem and Millita air rifles came from the same source. The action pins appear to be tapered so with airgun held trigger pointing up and barrel pointing away from you, you remove pins from right to left and replace left to right. On Gem, serial number M54956, the barrel was stamped "MADE IN GERMANY SPECIALLY FOR THE INTRODUCER A. ARBENZ, BIRMINGHAM" and "THE ORIGINAL GEM QUALITY" with an open cross with "B" in the centre. Adolf Arbenz had a shop in Great Charles Street, Birmingham during the late 1800s. The "B" could stand for Baden. As a coincidence Theodore Bergmann manufactured and patented Gem airguns about this time and his address was Eisenwerke, Gaggenau, Baden, Germany. This message about the introducer has also been seen etched on top of the air chamber in much larger letters. This style of Gem represents the commonest variety to be found hence the list of recorded serial numbers is quite long, so here goes: 3401, 9225, 14178-2, 20986, 29568, 38277-2, 42894-2, 45482-2, 47239, 49437, 54068-2 first appearance of "MADE ABROAD" stamped on the action, this is also seen on other German airguns. 71618, 81267, 84752 retailed by R. Jones, Manchester Street, Liverpool, stock number 1539, 84967, 85957, 92120, 98056 this had an etched air chamber with "THE ORIGINAL GEM 'B' QUALITY 'B' MANUFACT. IN GERMANY SPECIALLY FOR THE INTRODUCER 'B' A. ARBENZ BIRMINGHAM". This etching also appears on M94349, B55509, B68255, M54956 barrel was stamped "THE GERMAN GEM QUALITY FOR THE INTRODUCER A. ARBENZ BIRMINGHAM", M94349 see 98056, and lastly S40819.

The life expectancy of the Gem was not thought of highly as demonstrated by Townshend in his excellent book "The Complete Airgunner" (1907) and he went on to state "Although it sold in thousands and tens of thousands it earned the reputation of quickly going wrong; in fact, these airguns frequently became unserviceable after a few days use. (A little savage compared to the survival rate of today). The chief cause of trouble was the over-loading of the propelling spring, and the severe strain on the piston-releasing mechanism working in conjunction with the trigger. No one, in fact, but a clever mechanic could keep one of these early type airguns in a constant state of efficient repair. The piston was always slipping from its supports at a critical moment in the loading operation, with the result that the connecting-link received a severe blow which put most of the parts out of gear." From the above comments, it is surprising how many Gems have survived.

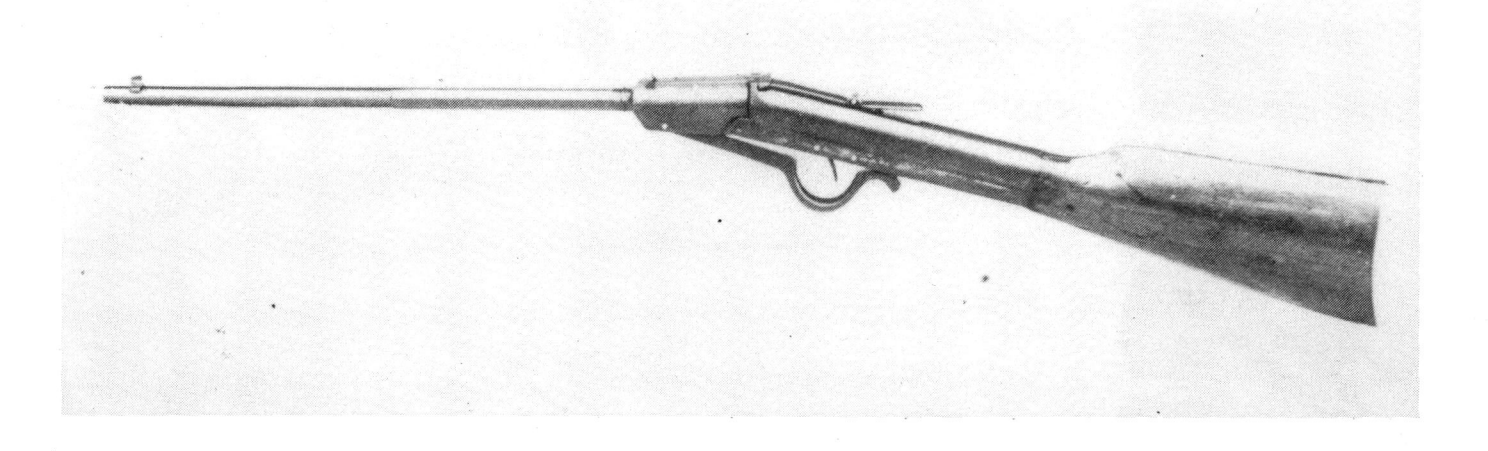

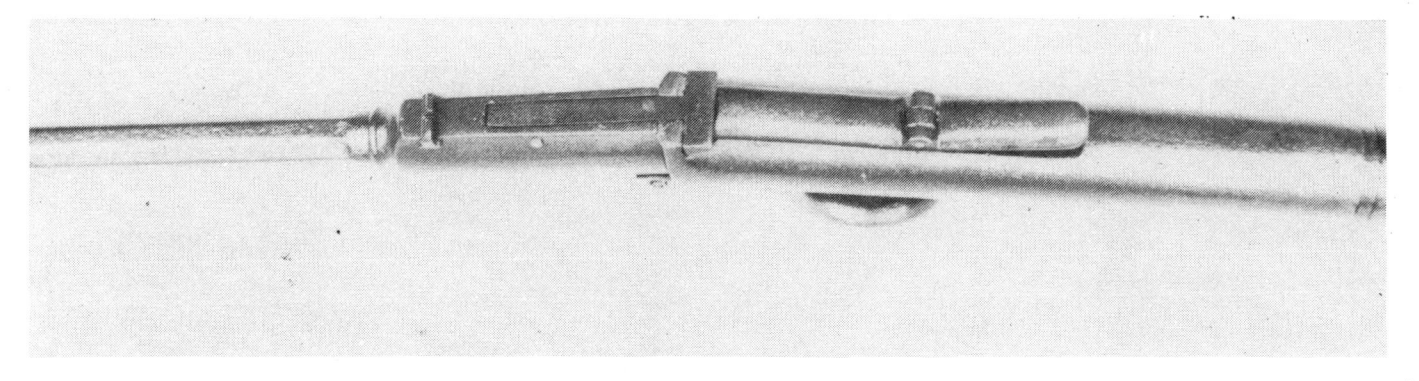

"T" bar barrel latch Gem

MODEL "Gem" type air rifle.

MAKER Could be Theodor Bergmann, "Eisenwerke", Gaggenau, Baden, Germany.

DATE From the very late 1800s to the 1930s.

VALUATION £30—£60. ($45—$90).

DETAILS Serial number of above 75446. 32½ inches long. "T" bar catch with extra lever to press down to release barrel. This similar to Lanes type barrel lock action, and to patent 6879 of 1893 (see "Guns Review" December 1977), airgun still has traces of nickel plating. Smoothbore, have not come across a rifled barrel "GEM" with original barrel. On upper flat of barrel is stamped "PATENT" and "GEM" with an odd looking trademark between them that looks like a gun firing an arrow and supported on a box. Serial number stamped on breech of barrel, as it is on all Gems that I have seen. Have seen one rifled Gem, this was in .177 and followed the same design as the "composite" style Gem featured elsewhere. The rifled barrel was completely circular and lacked the octagonal rear section. Theodor Bergmann patented three types of barrel latches as improvements for the Gem style air rifle. The above style is one of them.

Three only have been seen and had the following serial numbers: 75446, B52085, and S42879.

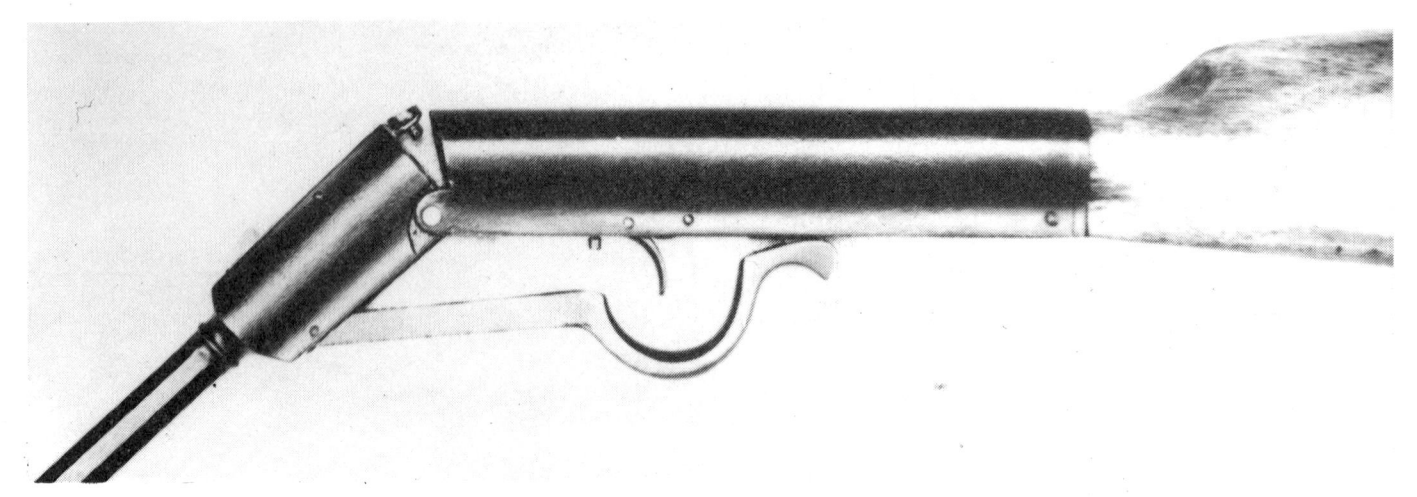

"Gem" type air rifle. Rearsight part of barrel latch

MODEL "Gem" type air rifle.

MAKER Theodor Bergmann, "Eisenwerke", Gaggenau, Baden, Germany. On air rifle stamped "GEM" with crossed air pistols trademark with "G" on barrel flat. Serial number 15647.

DATE 1882 to 1928.

VALUATION £30—£60. ($45—$90).

DETAILS Smoothbore. Top lever barrel catch that also incorporates the rearsight. Heavy barrel. 34 inches long. Distinguished from other Gems in that the rearsight is not separate, but forms part of the barrel latch. Serial number usually appears on the breech and air transfer port faces. 17¾ inch .177 smoothbore barrel. On air rifle seen had the serial number stamped on the side of the barrel, 15647, and had the last two digits stamped on all major parts including under the butt plate. The original finish for these Gems was all parts nickel plated except for the barrel which was blued. This style is very common for German pre-war air rifles. Examples seen:

11 — Harpoon trademark.
15647 — Crossed pistols trademark with "GEM No. 8322" on barrel.
26672 — No marks.
33145 — .25, crossed pistols trademark and stock stamped "No. 847, SOLD BY ROBERT JONES, MONARCH GUNWORKS, MANCHESTER STREET, LIVERPOOL".
M27746 — No marks.
W36288 — No marks.
X-3694 — Crossed pistols trademark and stamped "GEM PATENT No. 2003".
X11344 — No marks, but stamped "ROBERT JONES, MANCHESTER STREET, LIVERPOOL".

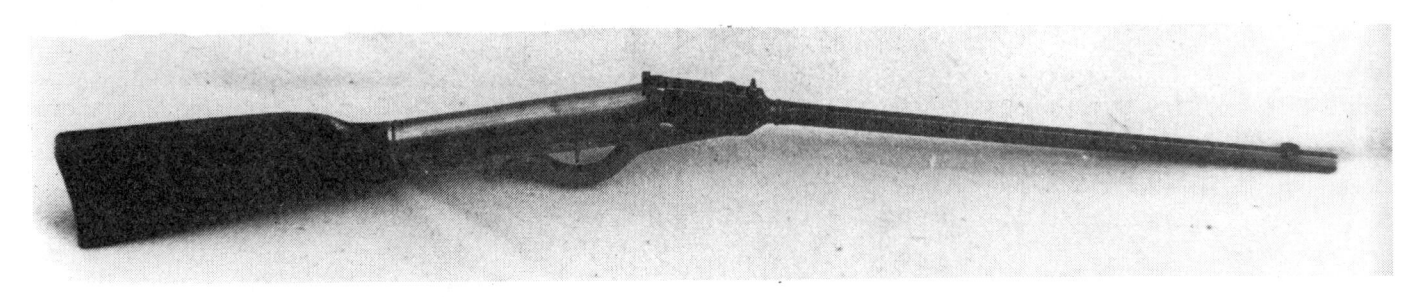

"T" bar Gem

MODEL "T" bar Gem. Listed in an "original" catalogue as the Model 3 and made in 1913.

MAKER "Dianawerk". Originally Mayer & Grammelspacher, Germany.

DATE Early 1900s to middle 1930s.

VALUATION £30—£60. ($45—$90).

DETAILS Octagonal barrel, smoothbore. Serial number of above 19931 stamped on barrel breech face and last two or three digits stamped on other metal parts. Has a "T" bar catch barrel latch, 34½ inches long. The above model is featured in a 1980 catalogue as having been made by Diana in 1913. Later models were fitted with the more usual octagonal to round section barrel. One example stripped by the author, Gem air rifle that is, had a piston with a flat profile leather washer. To remove the piston from a standard Gem follow the following procedure:

Loosen the lower air chamber screw, this is at the bottom end of the chamber near where the stock screws into the air chamber. The stock can now be unscrewed care being taken that a small wood screw is not protruding from the stock backing plate. If so then lever screw back into place so that is is flush with the stock backing plate. Continue to unscrew stock taking care towards the end that it does not fly out under spring tension. Now remove mainspring. In order to take out the piston the cocking slide must come out as well so either tap out the cocking lever pin or the barrel pivot pin, remember that these pins are tapered so remove from left to right as looking down on top of the air chamber with the barrel pointing away from you. With cocking arm now free pull piston out and pull trigger at same time so that the sear is down and allows free travel of piston. Assemble in reverse.
Have only seen two of the above and they had serial numbers 19931 and 60167.

The accuracy of the "T" Bar Gem air rifle was testified by Townshend who stated "I once saw seven consecutive shots placed in a bull one third of an inch in diameter at seven yards with an unrifled T-bar airgun (Gem), which had been in use over ten years, shooting the common flanged slugs, but it was only a fluke. They never did it before or after."

A combination "T" bar Gem air rifle, serial number 3043 has been seen. These combination airguns are very rare and working on the principle of an inner Morris tube that slid into the barrel for firing pellets, upon removal it allowed shotgun cartridges, or even bullets to be firing. The piston falling onto a firing pin placed in the transfer port for igniting the primer of the cartridge. Example seen with serial number 3043 had an octagonal barrel with "GEM" and "manufactured in Germany" stamped on the upper barrel flats, on the side appears "0,2grN.G.P. M/71 4,gr Bl"; on the underside of the barrel appears what I assume are the proof marks — three crowns, not all the same, with the letters "B,G,U" and a number "29,43", although there might be another prefix number, but not sure. The barrel was smoothbore with no sign of the Morris tube.

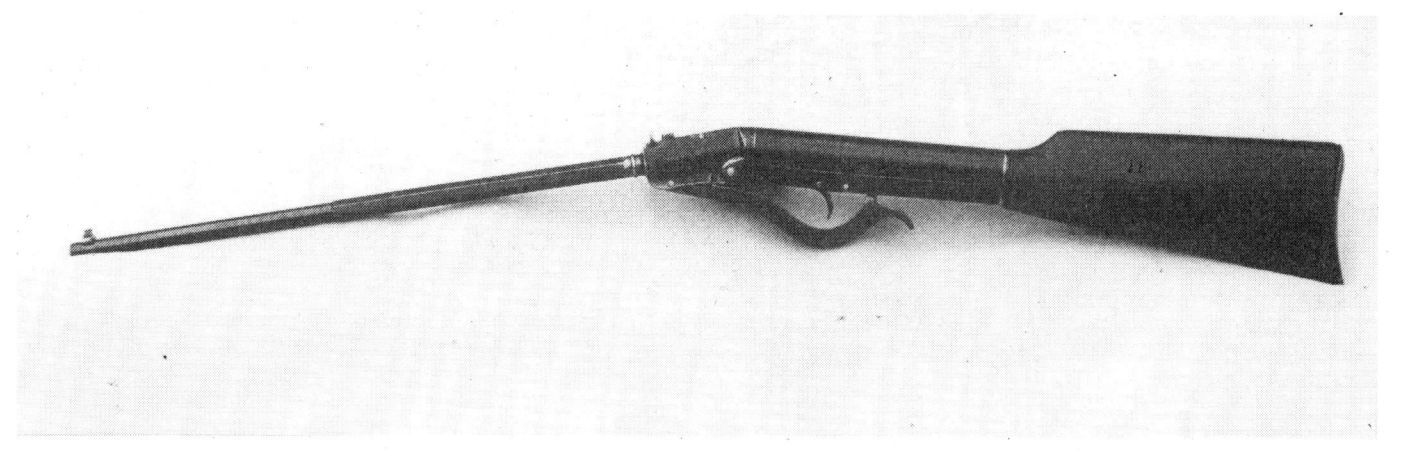

"Composite" type Gem

MODEL "Composite Gem".

MAKER Friedrich Langenham, Zeller Street, Thuringia, Germany.

DATE Late 1920s to 1939.

VALUATION £30—£60. ($45—$90).

DETAILS Almost 35 inches long. Octagonal to round smoothbore barrel. Unusual in the fact that it is a "composite" type Gem. Air chamber has removable trigger assembly and the transfer port end also appears to be detachable. Usually the air chamber is made from one piece of metal so would assume this model to be late on in the period of the "Gem" air rifle. Barrel unscrews from the breech block. Serial number of above 11806. Stamped on top of barrel "GEM" and on the underside "MADE ABROAD". Rearsight is separate from the top barrel latch. Above has been seen bearing the circular trademark of Friedrich Langenham, this being the letters FLZ set in a circle divided into three sectors. The only rifled Gem that I have seen is of the above pattern, barrel was circular from tip to breech and was in .177. It also had the F.L.Z. trademark as mentioned above. The earlier type trademark has been seen on Millita air rifles, so would assume the Friedrich Langenham manufactured the Gem and Millita air rifles. The above style surely represents the last of the Gem line. Improvements have been made in order to keep up with the general trend of more efficient and stylish air rifles, but a Gem is always a Gem no matter how you try to disguise the fact. The "Composite" model was fitted with a leather washer and the sear acted on a separate ring around the piston. The trigger block is held on by two screws that appear not to be interchangeable. To remove the stock first remove the rear trigger block screw then unscrew stock, you can then change mainspring if required. The last three digits of the serial number are stamped on all major parts. To remove the cocking link/trigger guard first knock out forward pivot pin then position cocking link in line with the two semi-circular cut-outs in the piston guide then rotate link through 90° and then withdraw the cocking arm. The "composite" Gem was blued, whereas most other models had nickel plated air chambers, butt plates, etc. The following "Composite" Gems have been seen:
2417 — Marked "GEM" on barrel.
5894 — No marks.
11806 — FLZ trademark and "Gem".
20618 — FLZ trademark.
20682 — FLZ trademark.
22673 — FLZ trademark.

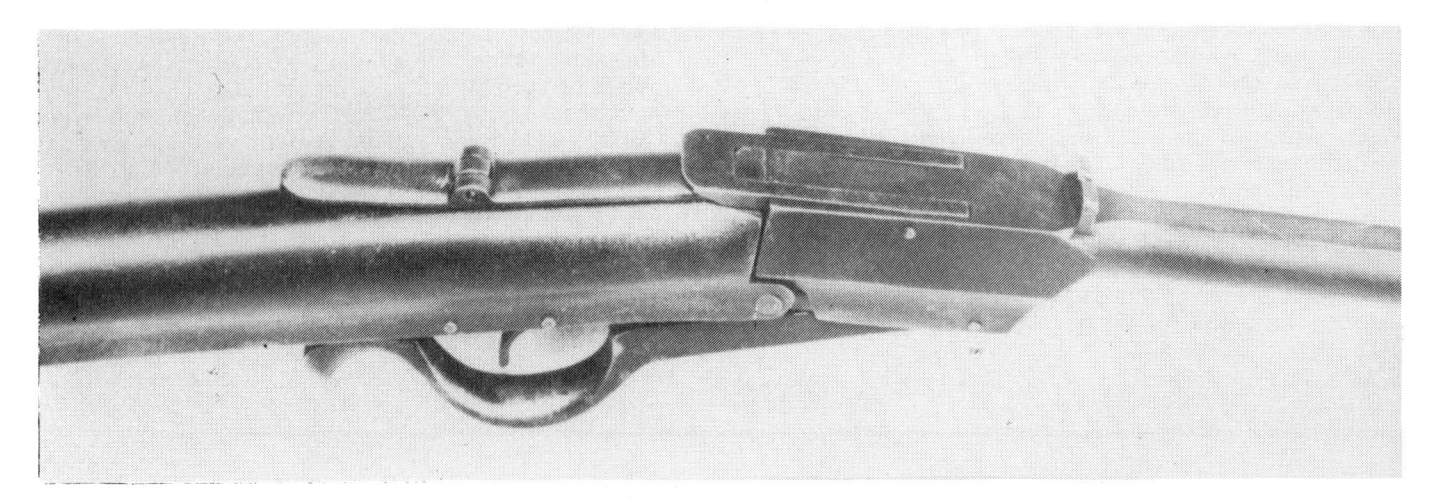

Lane's type barrel lock "Gem"

MODEL Lane's type barrel locking action. Placed under "Gem".

MAKER Either manufactured or adapted from existing Gem air rifles by Lane Brothers, 45a New Church Street, Bermondsey, London S.E. Address at time of manufacture.

DATE High serial number 59485, so would assume 1920 to 1930. Actual dates of production could be from early 1900s to late 1920s.

VALUATION £30–£60. ($45–$90).

DETAILS Unusual double barrel lock, but does not have the patent Lane's ball-bearing trigger action. Heavy construction with a .177 smoothbore barrel. Stock is originally black painted. Barrel has a flat filed rib running the whole length. Very well made, but the power is low. All parts are numbered with the last three digits of the serial number and the air cylinder, and other parts bear traces of nickeling. 35 inches long. The above model was adapted by Lane Brothers for firing their Patent Shot Cartridge. This was a .177 calibre tube filled with either No. 9 or No. 7 shot for airgun use. They were sold in boxes of 100 or 50 and were "invaluable to naturalists, collectors of specimen birds, etc., SPLENDID EFFECTS! So much for the "Good Old Days", eat your heart out R.S.P.C.A.

Two models were available of the above Gem; "Improved" and "Jewel". The Improved Model was adapted for firing the shot cartridge and was obviously intended for field use. No parts were nickel plated so as not to scare our feathered friends. This model cost 17/- whilst the nickel plated "Jewel" cost 16/-. Both were available in .177 only. At the same time as the above was being sold the Lane's Catalogue offered the following combination of "Gem" air rifles.

No. 0, 4½ mm. Light pattern fixed sights press down catch	12/6
No. 1, 4½ mm. Heavy pattern, fixed sights, T catch	13/6
Ditto, extra strong	15/6
No. 2, 5¼ mm. Heavy pattern, fixed sights, T catch	13/6
Ditto, extra strong	15/6
No. 3, 6½ mm. Heavy pattern, fixed sights, press down catch	22/6
Ditto, extra strong	25/-

"The extra strong are fitted by us (Lane Brothers), and thoroughly tested before leaving the Works".

The following have been seen:
23785 — Stock stamped "ROBERTS GUNMAKERS, STEELHOUSE LANE, BIRMINGHAM".
51950 — No marks.
59485 — No marks.
87208 — Action stamped "JEWEL GEM" and stock "HOOTON JONES, CODALE STREET, LIVERPOOL".
93113 — No marks.

The Greener air rifle

Greener air rifle, breech closed

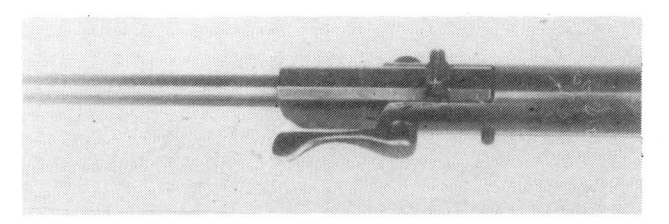

Greener air rifle, breech unlocked

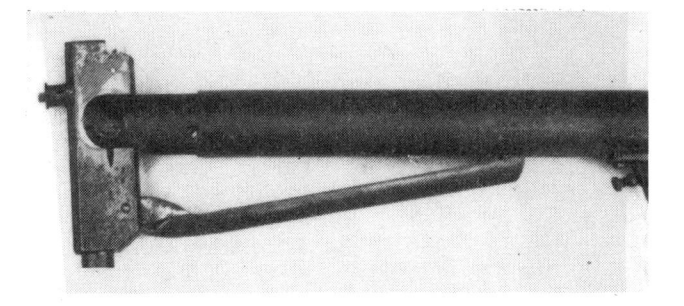

Greener, number 578, note complete lack of side lever, and the lever stop screw is flush with chamber surface

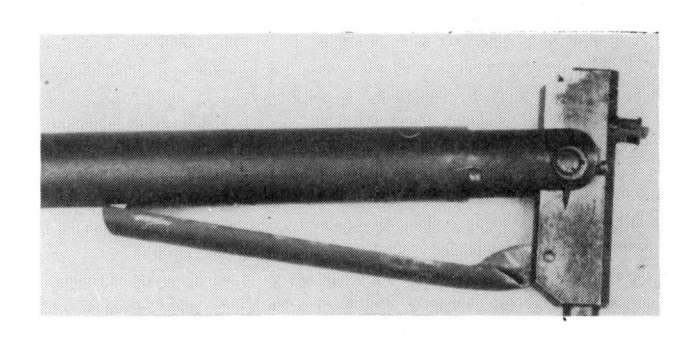

R.H.S. of Greener 578, note forward facing cam locking screw through the barrel support arm

MODEL "The Greener Air Rifle".

MAKER W. W. Greener, Birmingham.

DATE Around 1933 to 1940. Some could even have been made as late as the 1960s. See text.

VALUATION A rare item. £300—£500. ($450—$750).

DETAILS Serial number 337 stamped with ".177 BORE" on the R.H.S. of the barrel breech. On each side of the barrel pivot appears the word "OIL". Engraved on top of air chamber appears "W. W. GREENER, MAKER, BIRMINGHAM". 43 inches long with 19½ inch rifle barrel. Advertised weight of 7½ lbs. Could be bought in .22 or .177. Rearsight adjusted for elevation by large centre screw whilst for windage there are two set screws on either side of the sight and adjustment of these moved the blade from side to side. Lever on L.H.S. is turned up towards end of barrel and barrel moves forward away from the tap port about $\frac{1}{16}$ of an inch, then barrel can be broken for insertion of pellet. A cam makes this possible and prevents air leakage. Noticed that pellets were a tight fit on the above example, almost needed a pellet push to insert them into the barrel. Illustrations in catalogues differ from the above in that the trigger block appears to hang down from the air chamber whilst on the above the trigger arrangement is similar to pre-war B.S.A.'s with trigger adjustment by way of a screw through the trigger guard. Also advertised with a projection on the face of the tap port that forced the pellet forward into the barrel when the lever was operated seating the pellet firmly and at a set distance into the barrel. On Greener air rifle number 234 the top of the air chamber is stamped "THE GREENER AIR RIFLE — W. W. GREENER LTD., LONDON & BIRMINGHAM — PATENT APPLIED FOR". Also had last two digits of serial number stamped on the cocking lever.

Patent 411520 deals with the cam operated breech seal and seating of the pellet. Patent dated 1932/33. See "Guns Review" May 1980. The Author when talking to an ex-employee of Greeners was told that the air rifle was still being produced well into the middle 1960s, but that only about three to four per week were being produced.

There would appear to be Greeners about without the cam lever but still fitted with a rotatable cam main barrel bearing pin. This can be set in different positions in order to take up any wear in the action. One such example had a serial number 578. Had the Greener ramp foresight and blade rearsight with the little lateral adjusting screws. Top of air chamber engraved "W. W GREENER, MAKER, BIRMINGHAM". 43½ inches long with a 19¾ inch .177 barrel that could have been rifled, but is more rippled due to age! Side of the breech is stamped "578, .177 BORE" and "78" is stamped under the air chamber. Underside of butt plate is stamped "741" whilst stock is 262. Now comes the oddity, the cam lever is non-existent. Two collar nuts hold the main pin in place and the barrel latches on to the cross-pin that does not stick out from the side as that fitted to the cam model. The oil wedge-shaped channels are on each side of the min pin but the major difference is the little screw on the R.H.S. of the action. This is not original but the hole is threaded and extends into the cam mechanism so that when a grub screw is inserted it is tightened down into the cam after the hole has been alined by rotating the cam bearing with the barrel in cocked position so that no undue tension is on the bearing and it is free to rotate. Is the above a cheaper version of the Greener or is it someone's cock-up? All the parts are equally weathered and only the small side screw had been added. Serial numbers seen range from 234 up to 832.

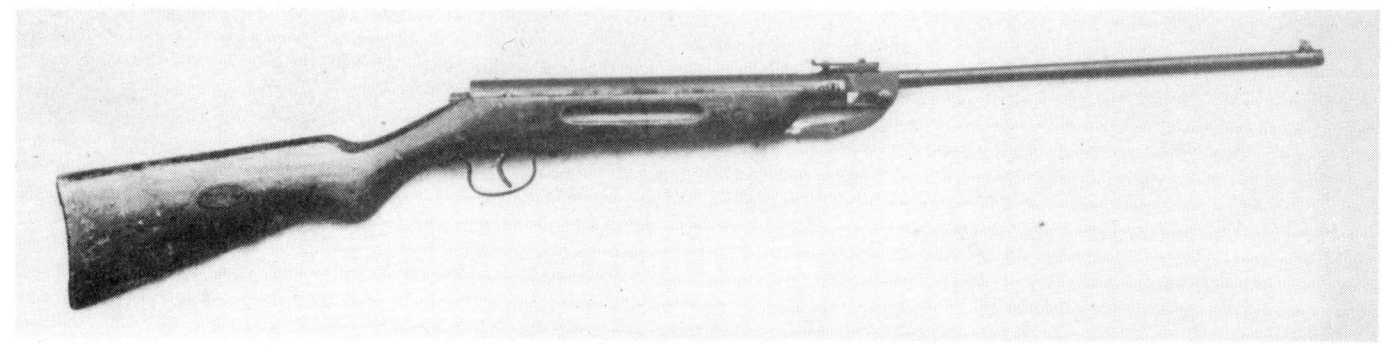

Model I D.R.P.

MODEL   I D.R.P.

MAKER   C. G. Haenel, Suhl, Thuringer, Wald, Germany.

DATE   Pre-war origins, but the above model post-war. Available from around 1925 to the 1960s. Pre-war version seen advertised as early as 1927.

VALUATION   £20—£50.
($30—$75).

DETAILS   38¼ inches long with a 15¾ inch rifled barrel. Top of barrel stamped "CAL. 4.5 m/m" whilst the underside is stamped "MADE IN GERMANY". Foresight adjustable for windage and the rearsight for elevation. Rearsight being a ramp with sliding adjuster. Barrel lock the usual Haenel type that is pushed towards the air chamber to release the barrel. Serial number not visible. Top of air chamber stamped "HAENEL MOD.I D.R.P." with "HAENEL" in the arrow trademark at the rear near the turn-over safety catch. Advertised in 1939 as having the following improvements upon the pre-war model; linked cocking action, safety catch, barrel lock, and the tangent rearsight. Weight 4 lb 10 ozs. Price advertised in 1939 was 35/- same as in 1935! The trade badge on the stock appears to be original as it also appeared in adverts around 1939. Advertised in 1927 as the "Thistle" Air Gun in the catalogue by G. C. Bell & Sons of Glasgow. It apeared without the medallion on the butt, no safety catch, and rearsight was long leaf spring with knurled adjuster screw. Available in rifled and smoothbore models at 26/6 and 25/- respectively. Pre-war models may not be fitted with the stock medallion and rearsight fitted is similar to that on the Model 45. Advertised as the "Boy's Model" and sold in .22 or .177, smoothbore or rifled. Appears to have been blued only, but I dare say nickel specimens will turn up. Barrel had 12 groove rifling. Listed in a 1939 Stoeger Catalogue as their Model 3100. Advertised weight 4lbs. 10ozs.

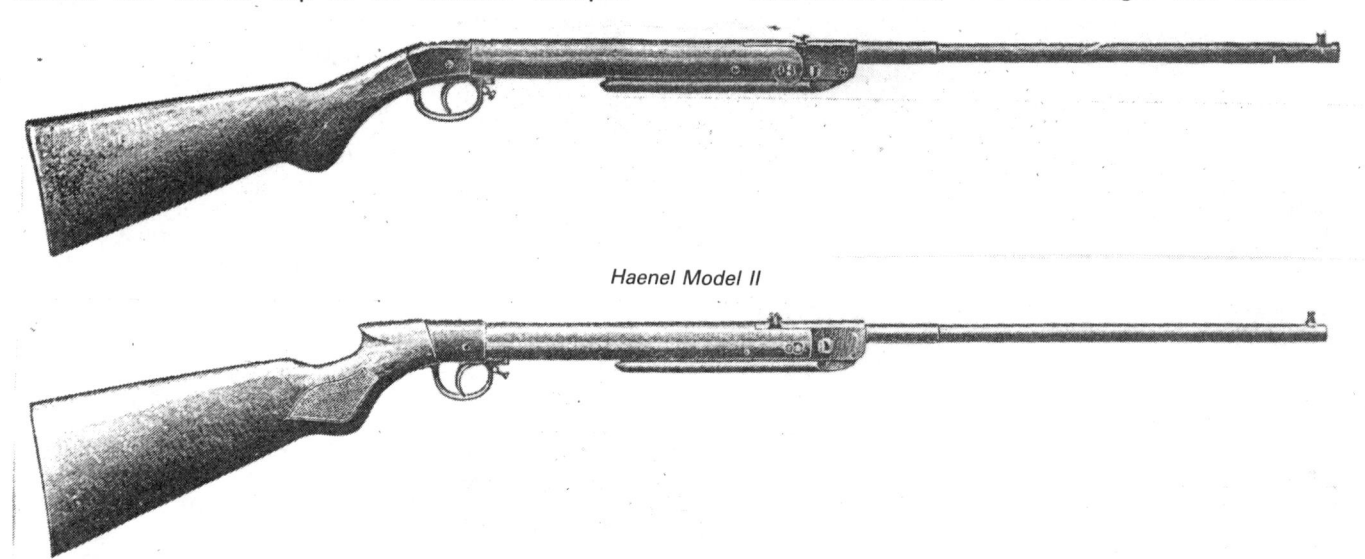

Haenel Model II

Haenel Model II-E

MODEL   Model II D.R.P. D.R.P. stands for Deutsches Reichs Patent", German Republic Patent.

MAKER   C. G. Haenel, Suhl, Germany.

DATE   Pre Second World War. From 1925 onwards although this may not be the initial date of manufacture.

VALUATION   £40—£80.
($60—$120).

DETAILS   43 inches long, barrel catch that pushes in towards the air cylinder. Stamped on top of air chamber "HAENEL MOD.II D.R.P." Circular "H" trademark is stamped on top of trigger block. On top of barrel is stamped the calibre and on the underside is "MADE IN GERMANY". Serial number stamped on underside of barrel near cocking lever pivot and is 928. The trademark can also be the word Haenel forming part of an arrow. On the underside of the barrel can also appear a serial number made up from the day, month, and year of manufacture, i.e. 1 5 38 could mean that it was made on the 1st May 1938. The 19¼ inch barrel is rifled, but smoothbore barrels were available. Trigger adjustment by way of screw through front of trigger guard. A variation of the above has slab sided trigger block and drooping sides to the barrel support arms very similar to Millita air rifles. Advertised as having a polished walnut stock and sold in .22 or .177, rifled or smoothbore.

The Webley Mark III mainspring should fit the above as a replacement if you cannot find original mainsprings. The models II and II-E differed in minor details and these can best be seen by comparing the two catalogue illustrations shown. Advertised weight 6lbs. 10ozs.

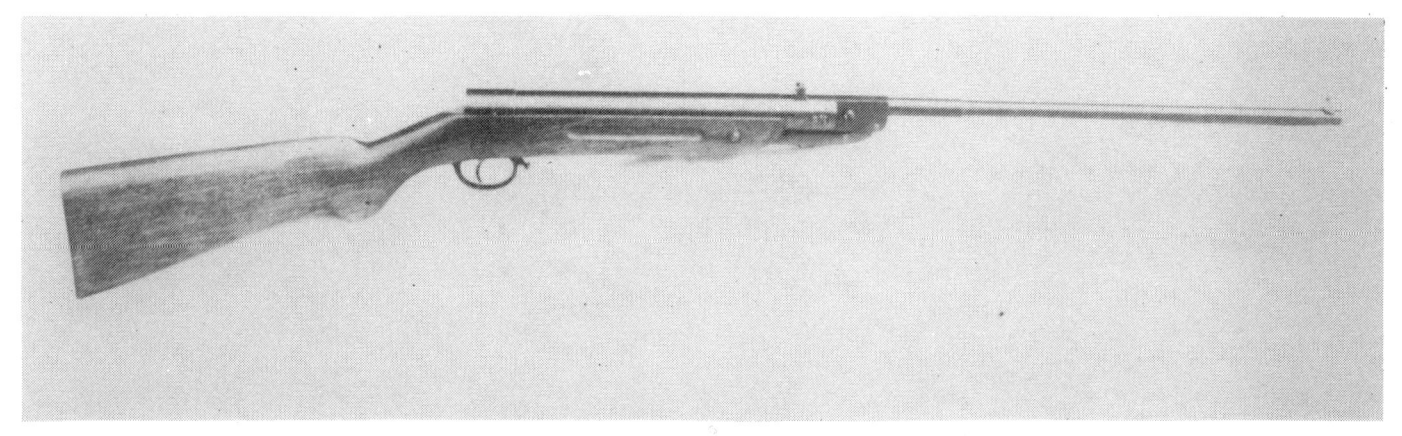

Haenel Model III D.R.P.

Later style Haenel Model III D.R.Pa. (1930—1939). Note downward extensions to barrel pivot support arms

MODEL   III D.R.P.

MAKER   C. G. Haenel, Suhl, Germany.

DATE   From around the late 1920s to 1939, although may still be available after the Second World War.

VALUATION   £40—£90. ($60—$135).

DETAILS   43 inches long with a 19 inch rifled barrel. Pillar foresight set in a dovetail groove. Top of barrel stamped "CAL. 4.5 m/m (.177)" and on the underside appears the serial number and "MADE IN GERMANY". Serial number of above 33090. Fitted with the push-in barrel lock. Very well made rearsight calibrated for 15 m. Top of air chamber stamped "HAENEL MOD III D.R.P." and the circular "H" trademark appears on the trigger block. Fully stocked with a metal butt plate. Trigger adjustment by way of screw through the trigger guard. On other models the arrow Haenel trademark is stamped. The number stamped on the underside of the barrel appears to form a date stamp. Example "1.10.31 E" would assume manufacture to have been on the first of October 1931 and destined for export, maybe to Britain. Sold in both .22 and .177, either rifled or smoothbore. Advertised weight of 6 lb 10 oz and barrel having 8 grooves.

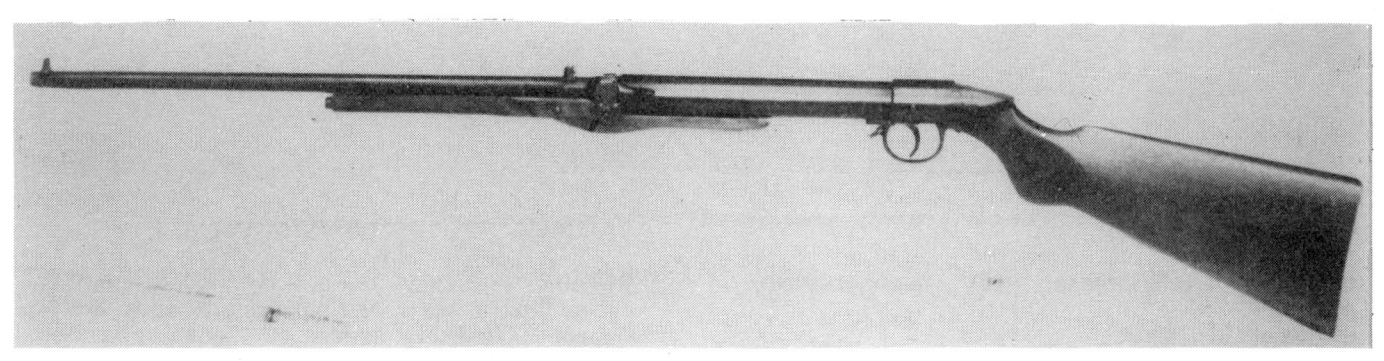

Haenel Model IVE air rifle

MODEL   IVE.

MAKER   C. G. Haenel, Suhl, Germany.

DATE   Assume 1930s to 1950s. Mentioned in Smith's book as the "Haenel New Model IV" whilst in Wesley's he mentions the IVE as being the more powerful .22 calibre, also lists the Model IVE as pre-war.

VALUATION   £50—£150. ($75—$225).

DETAILS   Very similar to the pre-war B.S.A. underlever. Measures 43 inches long. Top of air chamber stamped "HAENEL MOD IVE" and the circular "H" trademark appears on the top of the trigger block. Serial number 40879 appears on the underside of the barrel and on the underlever. .177 calibre. Stock is hand chequered with metal butt plate. Photographed in Smith's book as a repeater with drum magazine. Earlier models had the flat-sided trigger block. Available in either .22 or .177 rifled. At a guess I would assume that air rifles with a date stamp were pre-war and those with a serial number were post-war. Have seen three Haenel Model IVE's.
Pre-war — 1, 10, 31E arrow trademark.
Post-war — 40474 ad 40879 circular Haenel trademark.

137

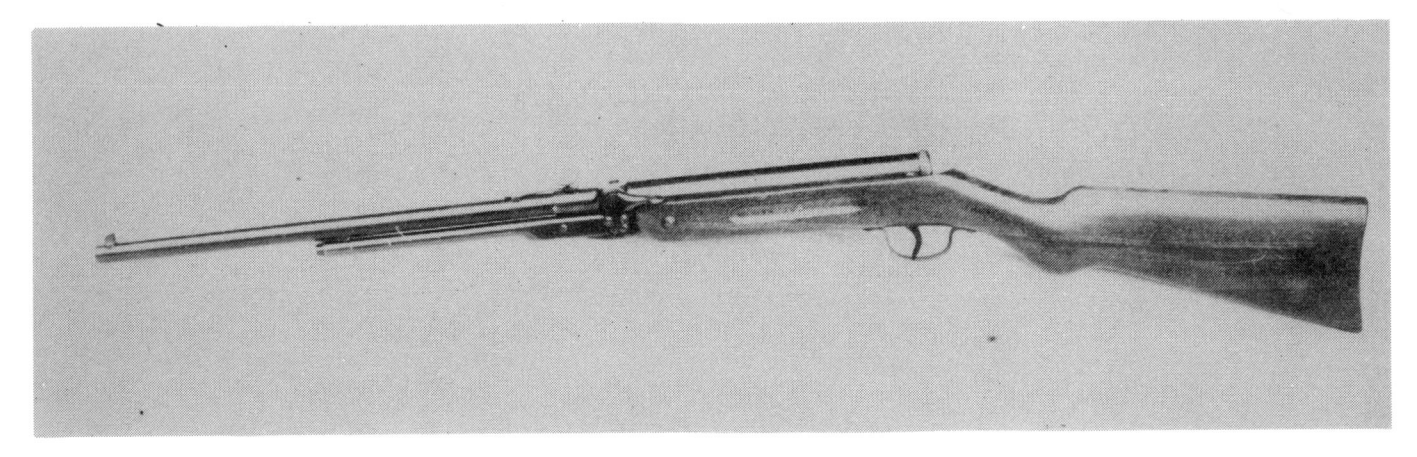

Haenel Model V Junior

MODEL "V" Junior.

MAKER C. G. Haenel, Suhler Jagdwaffen Gmbh, 60 Suhl, Strasse der Freundsschaft 10, Postfach 161, East Germany.

DATE Around 1933 to the outbreak of the Second World War, 1939, may have been offered for sale after the War for a short period only.

VALUATION £50—£100. ($75—$150).

DETAILS The above was also available with a drum repeating mechanism. 38½ inches long. A small well made and compact underlever air rifle. Blade foresight set in dovetail, rearsight also mounted in dovetail. Stamped on top of barrel "CAL. 4.5 m/m (.177)" and on the underside stamped "MADE IN GERMANY". Underlever and cocking lever are semi-tinplate construction, although very well made. Near the underlever pivot pin appears the figure "9". Top of air chamber stamped "HAENEL MOD V JUNIOR D.R.G.M.", and the end of the air chamber is marked with the Haenel trademark in an arrow. One piece stock with a Haenel medallion set on the R.H.S. Base of butt is stamped with the date "1,8,38". Later models were fitted with a safety catch. Advertised weight 5 lbs 2 ozs. Listed by Smith as being post-war, it would appear that these were fitted with safety latches. The above uses the same stock as the Haenel Model 1 Junior air rifle. Was also available with drum repeater mechanism. Available in .177 only.

One type of finish seen on a later style with safety latch was a navy grey enamel paint overall. This could be a war-time utility finish.

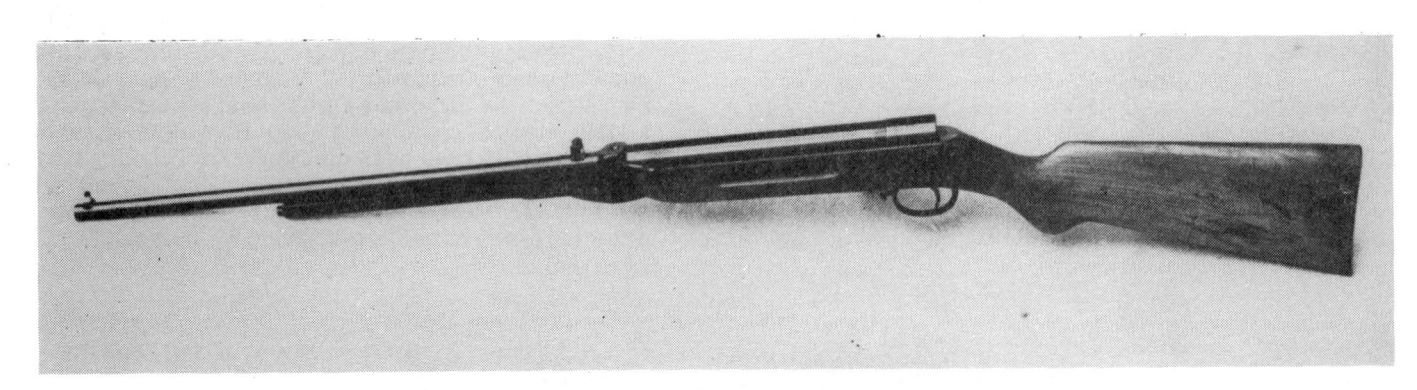

Haenel "Model V"

MODEL Model V.

MAKER C. G. Haenel, Suhl, Thuringer Wald, Germany.

DATE Listed at back of Wesley's book "Airguns and Air Pistols" as a pre-war model, whilst in Smith's "Airguns of the World" it is listed as a Post-war II production model, this could be a pre-war model that was improved for post-war production. Pre-war production from middle 1920s to 1939.

VALUATION £50—£100. ($75—$150).

DETAILS Similar to pre-war underlever B.S.A. except that it has a one piece stock up to the tap. Underlever cocking action. 43 inches long. Serial number I 7.38 stamped on underside of barrel. "HAENEL MODELL V" stamped on top of chamber, "HAENEL" in arrow trademark appears on top of trigger block. Calibre of above .177. Stock had a retailers mark "F. W. VANDREY & Co, HAMBURG". Advertised weight of 6 lbs 10 oz.

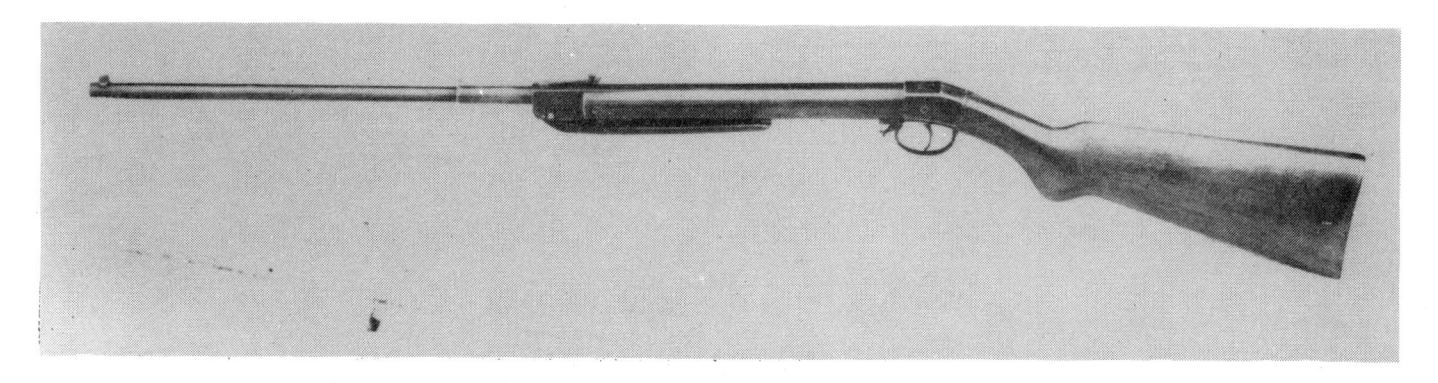

Haenel Model VIII

MODEL Model VIII.

MAKER C. G. Haenel, Suhl, Germany.

DATE Approx. 1925 to 1939.

VALUATION £40–£60. ($60–$90).

DETAILS Serial number of above 1229, unusual in being smoothbore. Over short range have found smoothbores to be just as accurate as rifled barrels. 43 inches long. Stamped on top of air chamber "HAENEL MOD VIII", and on top of barrel "CAL.4.5 m/m (.177)" and on underside of barrel "MADE IN GERMANY" followed by serial number. Number stamped on underside of barrel could also be a date stamp, i.e. 1,3,36 could stand for manufactured 1 March 1936. Usually rifled models have an asterisk stamped after the calibre number. Sold in rifled or smoothbore .177 or .22 with a blued finish. Advertised weight 6lbs. 4ozs.

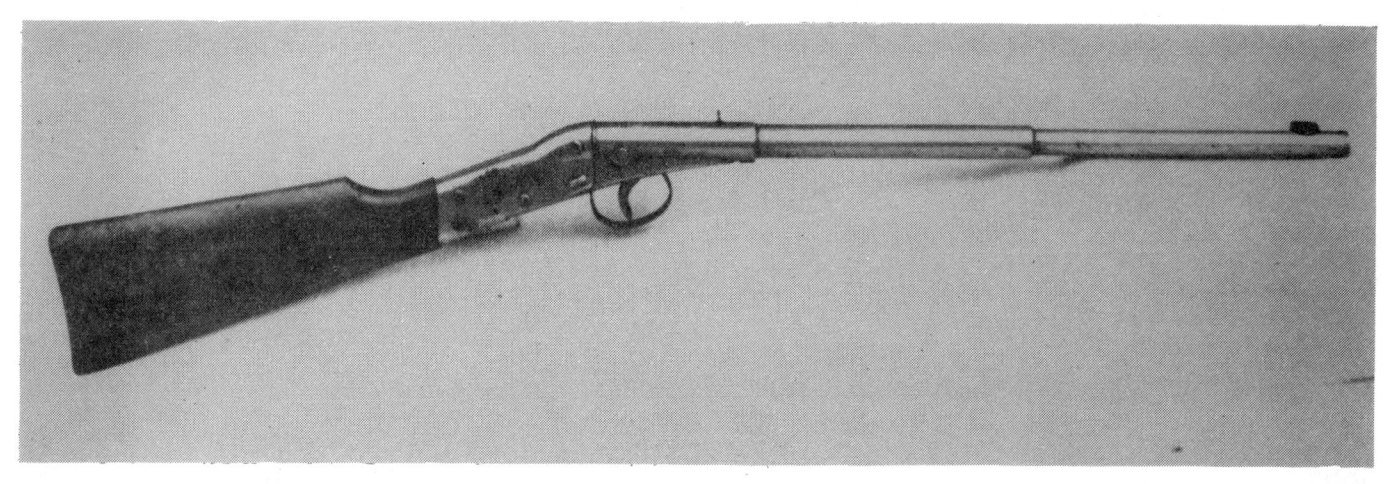

Haenel Model X or 10

MODEL X or 10.

MAKER Either by Haenel or under licence by Diana (Germany).

DATE 1930s just prior to Second World War and may even have appeared just after the War.

VALUATION £5–£20. ($8–$30).

DETAILS Nickel plated tinplate construction. Removable smoothbore barrel. 31 inches long with 8⅞ inch barrel. Simple non-adjustable sights. Top of air chamber stamped "X" and "HAENEL" and a date stamp appears on the underside of the stock. The above stamped "1 2 38". Another variation had machined rippling over part of the air chamber. Stamped "MADE IN GERMANY" on the metal part near the stock. They were also sold with the normal blued finish. Advertised weight 1lb. 5ozs.

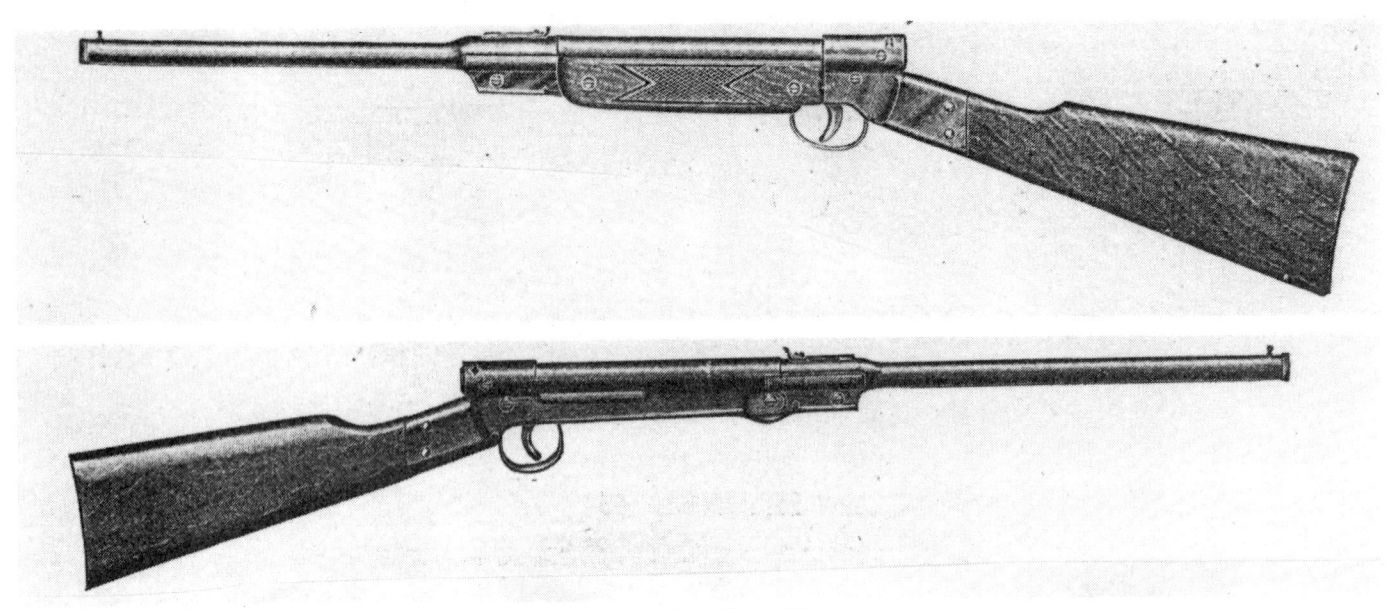

Haenel Model XV or 15

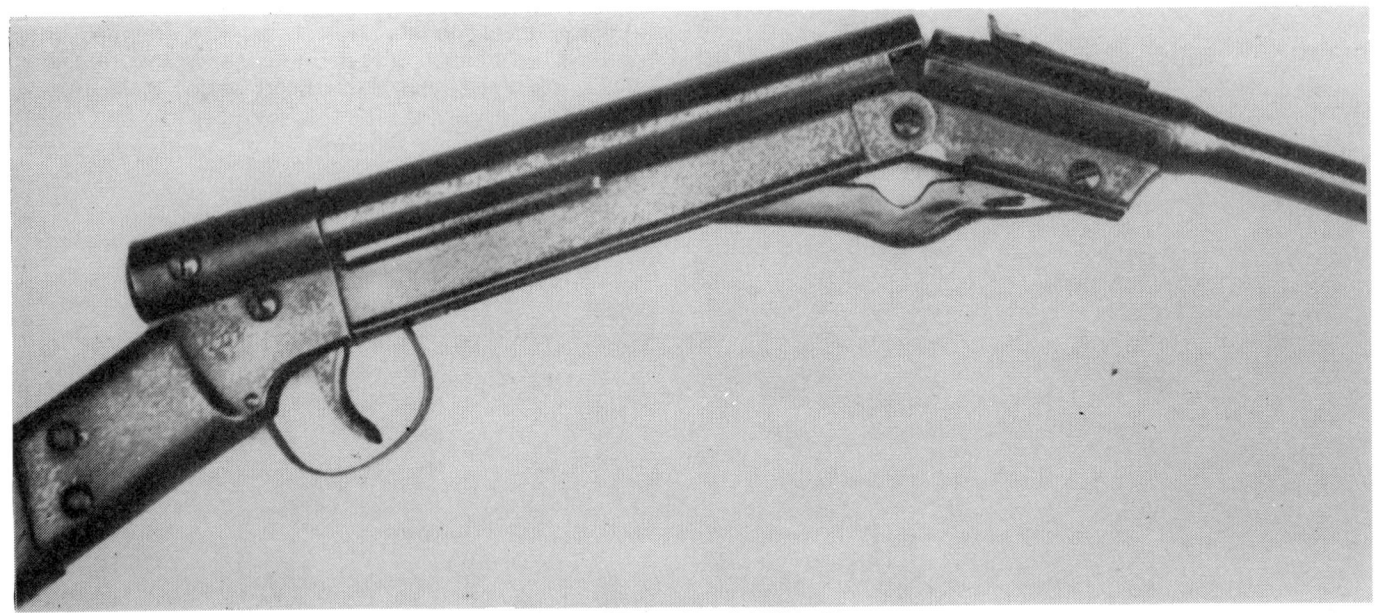

Action of Haenel Model XV or 15

MODEL XV or 15.

MAKER Would assume Haenel, Suhler, Kagdwaffen Gmbh, 60 Suhl, Strass der Freundsschaft 10, Postfach 161, East Germany, but may have been under licence by another manufacturer.

DATE Early to late 1930s and may even have appeared for a very short time after Second World War.

VALUATION £10—£30. ($15—$45).

DETAILS Tinplate construction with short flat sided stock. Very similar to the Diana Model 15 except for the major difference in the fixing of the barrel. 33½ inches long with a 14¼ inch .177 smoothbore barrel. The inner brass barrel liner easily unscrews without the removal of the foresight. Pillar foresight and simple rearsight spot welded into place and adjustable for elevation only. Air chamber has an extended lip that overlaps the barrel, very similar to the Markham Model 17. The cocking lever also acts as the barrel latch, but instead of clipping on to the barrel pivot pin as with the Diana tinplate air rifles, the cocking lever has been expanded at the barrel end and this acts as a holding clip when the barrel is returned to the firing position. Wear can easily be taken up by widening the gap in the cocking lever or squeezing the underside of the barrel support mounting. Top of trigger housing stamped "XV D.R.P.a." followed by "HAENEL" in arrow trademark. Underside of action stamped "MADE IN GERMANY" whilst the stock bears the date stamp "1 1 39E" the E stands for "EXPORT". Also sold nickel plated.
Advertised weight 2lbs. 9ozs.

A much more rare variation was the Model VA which differed from the above in that it was fitted with chequered wooden fore-end. Advertised weight being 3lbs.

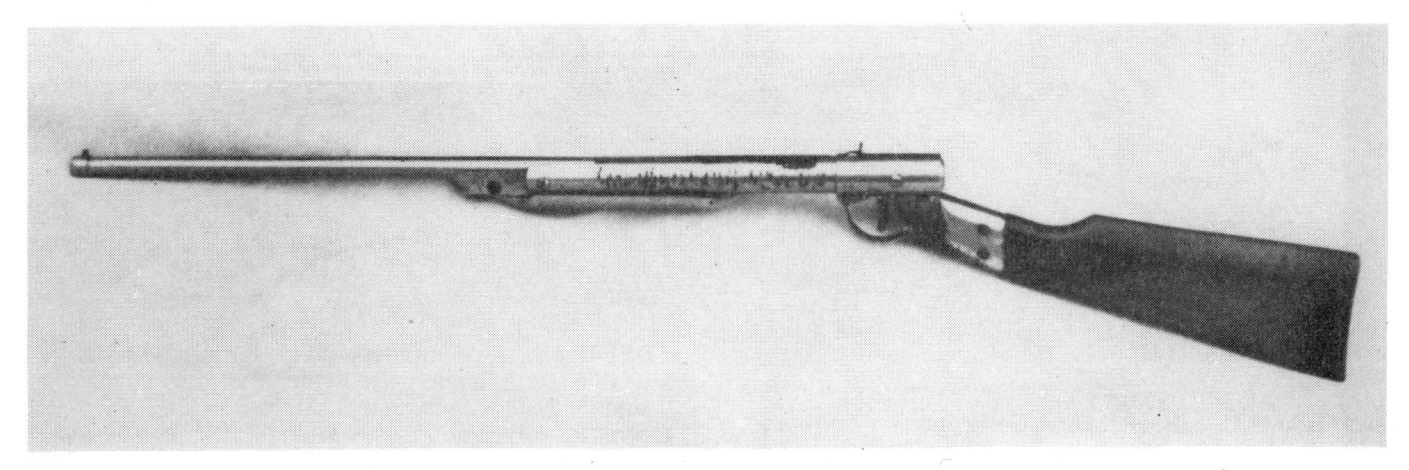

The Haenel Model XX (20)

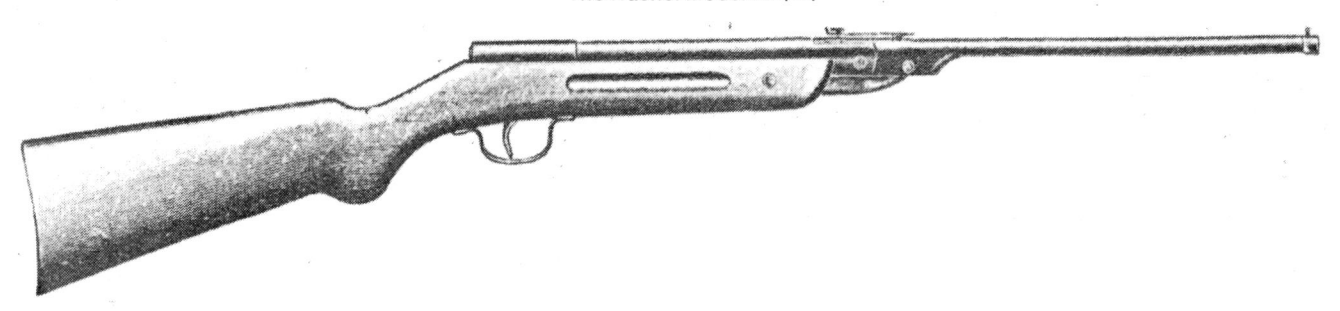

Haenel Mark XXX (30)

Haenel Mark XXXX (40)

MODEL "XX" or 20.

MAKER Haenel, Suhler Jagdwaffen Gmbh, 60 Suhl, Strasse der Freundsschaft 10, Postafch 161, East Germany. Beyond the "Wall".

DATE Middle 1920s to 1930s, but some may have appeared just after the War. These could have been unsold pre-war stock.

VALUATION £20—£40. ($30—$60).

DETAILS Similar to the Diana pre-war Model 20, but is not identical. 34¼ inches long with a 14¼ inch .177 smoothbore barrel. Appears to have been sold in .177 smoothbore only. All parts nickel plated except for the fore and rear sights. Tinplate construction with a heavier than usual gauge metal. Pillar foresight and spring type rearsight. Underside of barrel stamped "MADE IN GERMANY". Cocking lever has chequering pressed into the metal. Top of trigger block stamped "XX" and has the Haenel trademark in the arrow. "MADE IN GERMANY" also stamped on the underside of the action where it joins the stock. Stock bears the date stamp. Advertised weight 3 lb 2 oz. Early examples will have the circular trademark instead of the arrow. Sold .177 smoothbore only and either had a nickel or blued finish. By the late 1930s the rearsight was mounted on the barrel and not on the air chamber.

The Model XXX (30) was the Model 20 but fitted with an extended stock up to the barrel Joint. It was available in .177 rifled or smoothbore and weighed 3lbs. 2ozs.

The Model XXXX (40) was the above but fitted with a solid barrel in either rifled or smooth bores .177. Advertised weight 3lbs. 12ozs.

Haenel "Model 45"

MODEL   Model 45.

MAKER   C. G. Haenel, Suhl, Germany.

DATE   Early 1930s to 1939.

VALUATION   £20−£50. ($30−$75).

DETAILS   Almost identical to "PRECISION" Junior air rifle. Note Roach-bellied stock that now appears on some clay pigeon shotguns. 35 inches long. All metal construction as opposed to tinplate. Stamped on top of air chamber "HAENEL MOD 45", and has "HAENEL" trademark above trigger block. On the underside of barrel is stamped "MADE IN GERMANY" and the serial number, in this case 11235. Top of barrel has "CAL.4.5 m/m (.177)". Advertised weight 3lb. 10ozs. Available in either rifled or smoothbore .177 only.

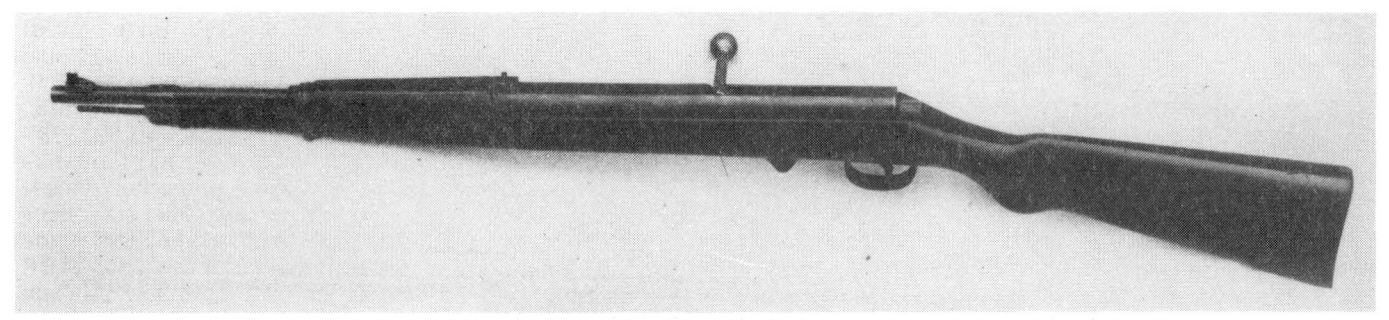

Haenel "Sport Modell 33 Junior"

Haenel "Sport Modell 33 Junior"

MODEL   Sport Modell 33 Junior.

MAKER   C. G. Haenel, Suhl, Thuringer Wald, Germany.

DATE   Introduced in 1933 as the Schmeisser bolt action repeater and then sold under the Haenel name, see Smith's page 83. Smith also mentions that the above model was back in production, see page 142. So production resumed about 1957. Above seen advertised in 1939.

VALUATION   £45−£100, £40a. ($68−$150).

DETAILS   38½ inches long, fully stock in the military fashion. Foresight adjustable for windage, has dummy cleaning rod under barrel. Top of barrel stamped "MADE IN GERMANY". Fitted with swivel sling fore and aft. Has six shot force fed magazine clip although the twelve shot was also available. Rearsight on the above is not original. Stamped on top of air chamber "HAENEL SPORT MODELL 33 JUNIOR — SCHMEISSER'S PATENT", with the Haenel in arrow trademark at the rear near the swivel safety catch. Butt has plain metal butt plate. Serial number not visible. Rifled barrel for shot only. Advertised weight 5½ lbs. Originally the rearsight was adjustable for elevation only. The diameter of shot to be used was 4.45 which was equivalent to .174. In 1939 this was available from Kynoch who sold the shot in small tubes containing about 200. Of all the repeating airguns tested the above action has been, until now, proved absolutely flawless in operation. A cheap supply of shot may be obtained by buying "BB" size shotgun pellets. A bag of these should last a lifetime.

Details of the "Schmeisser's Patent" can be had from "Guns Review" June 1980. The patents dealt with the magazine clip used. The early magazine clips could have been of tinplate design. The other patent applies to the cocking action that was also used on the later Anschutz and Haenel bolt action air rifles. The serial number appears to be stamped on the underside of the action near the trigger assembly, on the R.H.S. A "Senior Modell 33" was advertised, this being larger than the Junior Model and has a military sling, tangent military rearsight and a metal butt plate. The barrel is rifled.

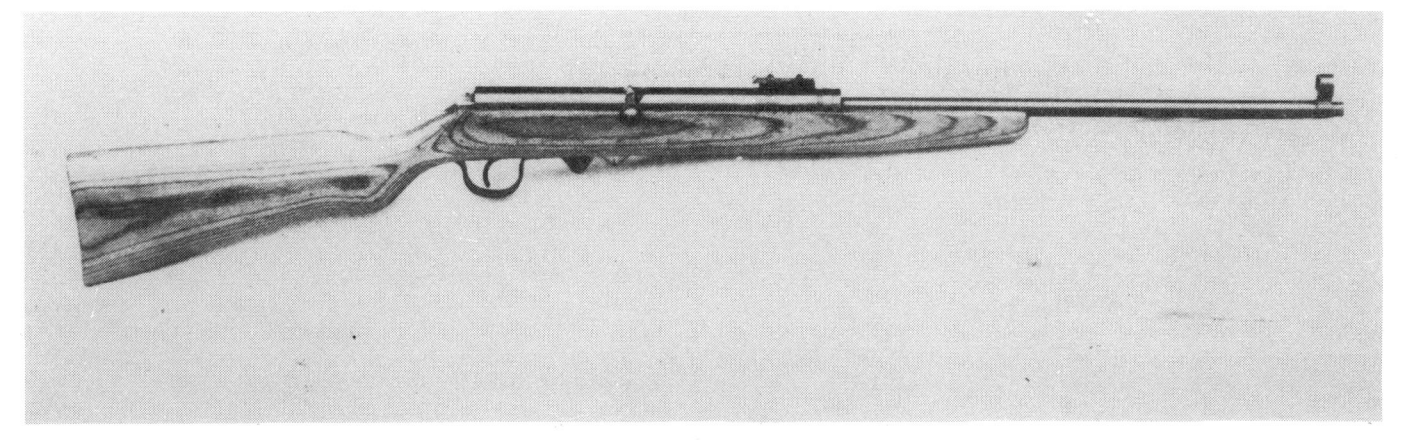

Haenel Model 49a

MODEL 49a.

MAKER Haenel, Suhler Kagdwaffen Gmbh, 60 Suhl, Strasse der Freundsschaft 10, Postfach 161, East Germany.

DATE From early 1950s to either very late 1950s or even to early 1960s.

VALUATION £50−£100. ($75−$150).

DETAILS Bolt action repeater very similar to the other Haenel repeaters and to the Anschutz Model 275. Could be the forerunner to the Target Model 311 bolt action single shot tap loaded air rifle. 41½ inches long. Blade foresight with hood, ramp rearsight adjustable for elevation only. Top of air chamber marked "SPORT MODELL 49a" followed by "S" in a triangle with 32/1108/1007 underneath. Rear of action bears the Haenel name in an arrow with the Suhl trademark of standing man hammering the hell out of an anvil. Usual wing mauser like safety at the back of the action. Antibear trap device on trigger. Date stamp on butt plate, "5,59", on example examined with "ML001338" stamped on side of stock. A real novelty air rifle to use and have always found this type of action almost foolproof. 4.45 mm calibre which means that steel BB's are NOT to be used, either use the specially made copper coated lead round shot or purchase a bag of BB lead shot for loading shotgun cartridges, and this will last a lifetime. Although supplied with a six shot magazine an eight and twelve shot were also available.

The Haenel Model 302

MODEL 302.

MAKER C. G. Haenel, Suhl, Thuringer, Wald, Germany.

DATE The above is the model that preceded the Haenel Model 303. Seen advertised in 1969, also 1970. Sometime between 1970 and 1978 the Mode 303 appeared.

VALUATION £30−£60. ($45−$90).

DETAILS Heavy well made air rifle. 17¾ inch rifled barrel, 44 inches long. Stock has metal butt plate. Ramp rearsight for elevation and foresight for windage. Serial number of above 437590 and appears stamped on the L.H.S. of the barrel breech. Top of barrel marked "KAL 5.6 mm". Three circular rings are set around the air chamber near the transfer port end, similar to the B.S.F. range of airguns. On top of air chamber is stamped "MODELL 302" followed by a man standing at an anvil with "SUHL" underneath. At the rear, near the trigger safety is "HAENEL" in an arrow going from left to right. Safety operates when airgun is cocked but can be pushed in to release action without having to fire when it is cocked. Above is made in Eastern Germany. Beechwood stock and advertised weight 7 lb.

The Haenel Model 303

MODEL 303.

MAKER C. G. Haenel, Suhl, Thuringer, Wald, Germany. Imported by Parker Hale.

DATE Superseded the Model 302. Appeared sometime between 1970 and 1978.

VALUATION £30–£60.
($45–$90).

DETAILS 43¾ inches in length with a 19¼ inch barrel. Top of barrel stamped with the calibre. On the L.H.S. of the barrel breech appears the serial number. Number of above 499625. Top of air chamber has "MODELL 303" with a "Sulh" trademark of man and anvil. At rear near the safety catch appears "HAENEL" set in an arrow with "MADE IN GDR" underneath. The safety catch operates as the gun is cocked but can be pushed in against a spring to release the action when it is required to uncock instead of firing the action. One piece heavy stock has metal butt plate. Advertised weight 6 lbs 10 ozs. Trigger adjustment by way of screw in trigger guard.

A gun test of the Haenel Model 303 appears in "Sporting Air Rifle" November 1984. By the mid 1980's the stock design had been changed to one with a more fuller fore-end and semi check piece to stock.

Haenel 310-8 Model air rifle

MODEL 310-8.

MAKER Haenel, Suhler Kagdwaffen Gmbh, 60 Suhl Strasse der Freundsschaft 10, Postfach 161, East Germany.

DATE Middle 1970s to 1980s.

VALUATION £50–£100.
($75–$150).

DETAILS Appears never to have been advertised in Britain. Seems to be an improved model of the 49a. Main differences being cheaper grade wood stock and pressed metal cover for the lower cocking lever pivot so as to hide the pivot pin. More streamlined rearsight although still the tangent ramp with slider that will also interchange with the Model 303 air rifle. Safety catch is no longer the famous Mauser winged type, but is now the pull-out/push-in pattern as on the other Haenel air rifle, and is manual in operation.

41¾ inches long (1.60 m), top of barrel stamped "KAL.4.4mm" so still have to use the 4.4 mm ball and NOT steel BB's. Six and twelve shot alloy magazine clip fits into the slot on the underside of the stock. Top of chamber stamped "MODELL 310" followed by the Suhl trademark of a man and anvil. Towards the rear is the arrow Haenel trademark and "MADE IN GDR". Does GDR stand for God-dam Russia?

The serial number is stamped on the R.H.S. on the stock in very small figures. By the mid 1980's the stock had changed to one with a deep fore-end and pronounced pistol grip. There was also a change in the design of the backsight.

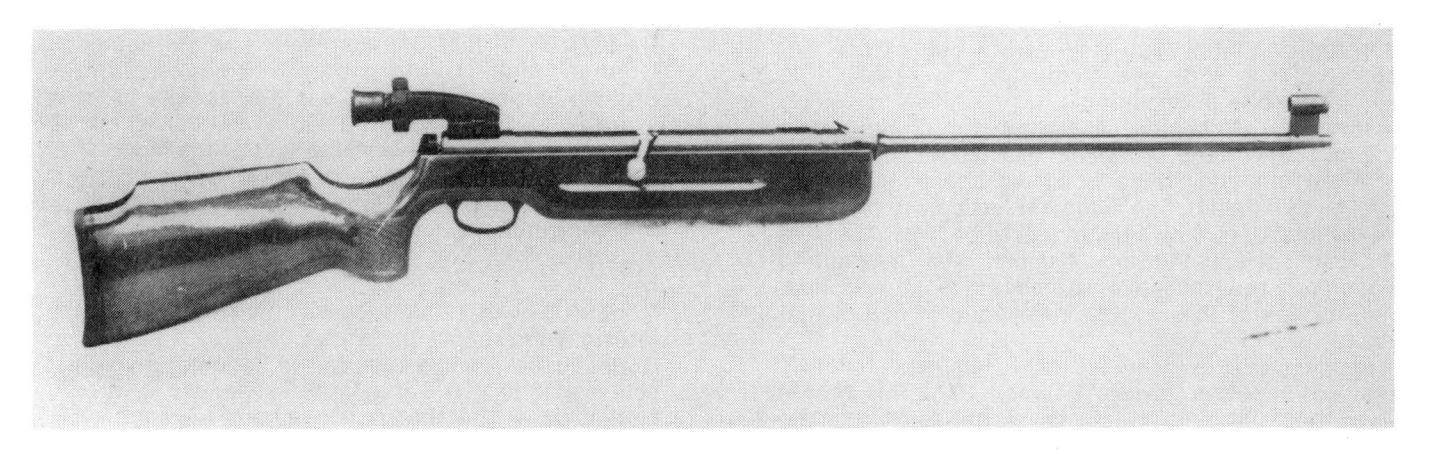

The Haenel Model 311 bolt action target air rifle

MODEL 311.

MAKER Haenel, VEB Ernst-Thalmann-Werk, Suhl, Thuringen, East Germany.

DATE 1970 to early 1980s, but was never widely advertised and sold in relatively small numbers.

VALUATION £50 — £150.
($75 — $225).

DETAILS Bolt action single shot target air rifle based on the action of the Scheisser Patent action air rifles. Tap loading. 44 inches long with a 16¾ inch .177 rifled barrel. Rather high foresight pegged on to the barrel with interchangeable sight elements. Top of barrel stamped with calibre and serial number near tap orifice. Top of air chamber stamped "MODELL 311, the Suhl trademark of man standing at anvil, "HAENEL" in arrow and "MADE IN GDR". Peepsight is screw mounted on to a block which is then mounted on to the action. It would appear that the peepsight can be unscrewed from the mounting block and the block be re-sighted on to a dovetail just behind the loading tap and a rearsight then screwed to the mounting block and the air rifle then used with open sights, although have never seen the secondary rearsight advertised. Very nice stock with generous proportions and is hand chequered. Safety catch at rear of chamber under the peepsight and must be pushed in each time the action is cocked before airgun can be fired. Trigger adjustment by way of two screws, one in the trigger whilst the other is tucked away inside the action behind the trigger. When the Model 311 first appeared in 1970 it was modestly priced at £32, but as the decade progressed this crept up to almost £90. The air rifle was sold with a neat cardboard box, the peepsight, screwdriver, spare foresight elements, piston washer, and mainspring, which only measured 6⅜ inches in length. The box was stamped with the serial number of the air rifle in question. Advertised weight 7 lb 14 oz and muzzle velocity about 600 f.p.s., bearing in mind that this is a target air rifle and not a sporting miracle maker. They were imported into Britain by Parker Hale Ltd., Birmingham, England. Details of stripping the action can be found in "Guns Review" July 1970 and April 1977. The peepsight has a six hole rotating disc of varying apertures. One thing you have to admire about these Russian imports is that once they are being imported they never alter the design. Since the introduction of the 311 it has remained unaltered since 1970. Try that in the car industry!

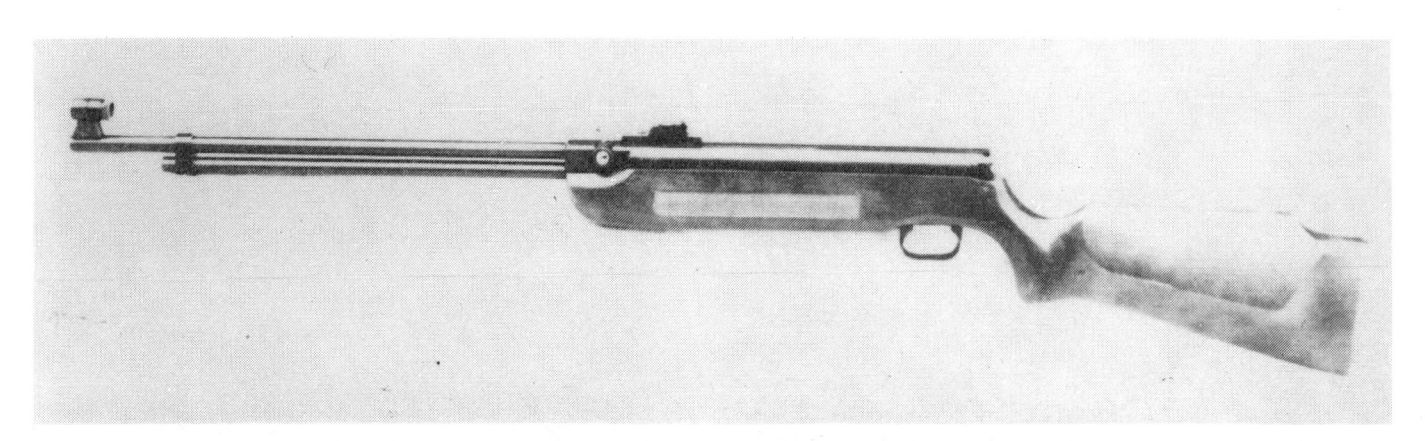

the Hammerli Model 4 HS 03 with solid round bar barrel weight

MODEL Hammerli Model 4 HS 03.

MAKER Hammerli Gmbh, D-7897 Tiengen/ Hochrhein, BR Deutschland, Germany, Postfach 1147.

DATE Very short period of production in this form with the under barrel weight. From around 1973 to 1975.

VALUATION £50 — £100.
($75 — $150).

DETAILS Typical Hammerli design with side lever cocking and the little turn tap loading key. Unusual feature is the solid steel bar that acts as a barrel weight, this adds considerably to the overall weight of the air rifle. 43¼ inches long with an 18 inch .177 rifled barrel. Side of barrel breech is stamped "Cal. 4.5/.177 — 'F' in pentagon — MADE IN GERMANY". The L.H.S. of the air chamber is stamped "MOD.4 HS 03". The top of the breech housing has "HAMMERLI" with a target logo over the "i". The serial number appears at the far end of the chamber on the L.H.S. The tunnel foresight is

145

dovetail mounted and has screw-out centre for changing the foresight elements. The rearsight is somewhat odd in design and has an off-set elevation screw. Top of chamber is grooved for 12 mm scope mounts. The stock is walnut stained beech with a grooved fore-end. There does not appear to be any trigger adjustment. The side lever has an anti-bear trap devise that only allows the trigger to be fired when it is at rest against the air chamber. The mainspring uncompressed is just over 13 inches in length and must rate as one of the longest mainspring in use at that time.

A similar model to the above is the Hammerli Model 10, featured in "Guns Review" February 1972. This did not have the solid steel weight below the barrel, but the barrel weight was an outer tube over the barrel. It also had no rearsight and was assumed to have been supplied with a peepsight. Muzzle velocity for the Model 10 ranged from 630 to 650 f.p.s.

Hyscore, of America, sold the Model 4 as their Model 894, with barrel weight and in either .177 or .22. They advertised a muzzle velocity of 775 f.p.s. for the .177. Advertised weight 8½ lbs. 1974 adverts mention the above.

By 1974, in Britain the Hammerli was distributed by Norman May, Union House, Princess Terrace, Bridlington and they advertised the Model 4 as being available in .177 only, and the equivalent air rifle in .22 and without the under-barrel weight as the Model 2. By 1975 a more angular style of stock appeared and by 1977 the Hammerli range had been expanded into the following models:

Model 400 — Standard model of the range with tunnel foresight and simple blade rearsight.
Model 401 — Same as 400 but fitted with fully adjustable rearsight.
Model 402 — This time both front and rearsights were not fitted, but a telescopic sight was fitted and supplied in their place.
Model 403 — The target model that superseded the Model 4. Fitted with outer barrel sleeve weight, aperture rearsight, and adjustable butt plate to stock.
Model 420 — A very stylish military side lever air rifle.
All of the above models were sold in both .177 and .22.
Details of how to strip the Model 4 and others appears in "Airgun World" April 1980.

Home-made .25 underlever

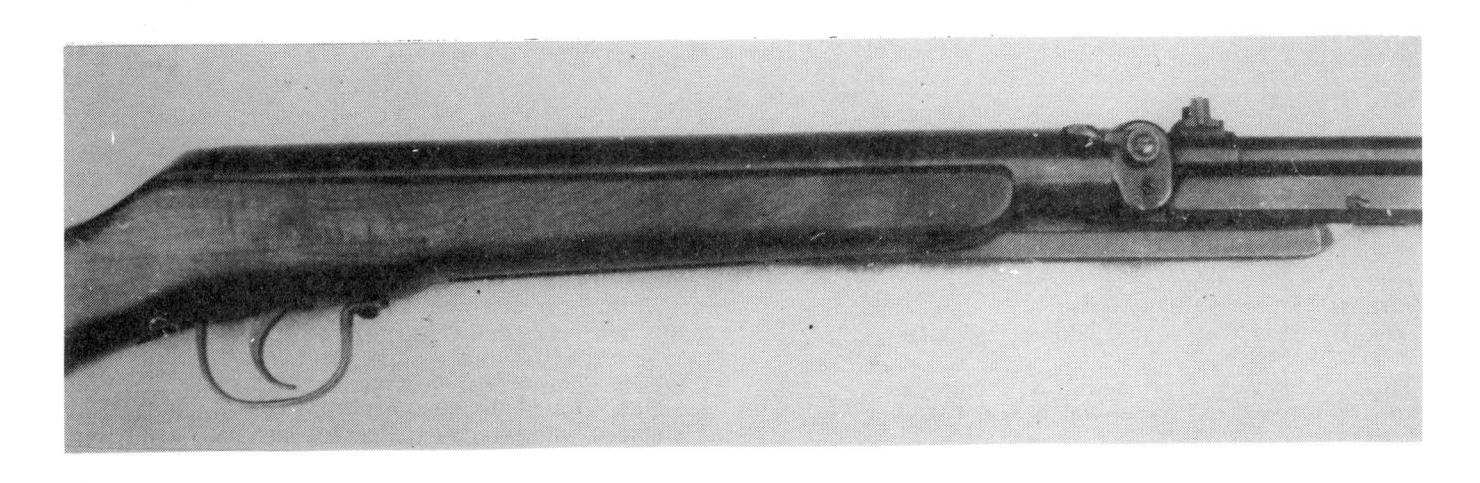

Close-up view R.H.S.

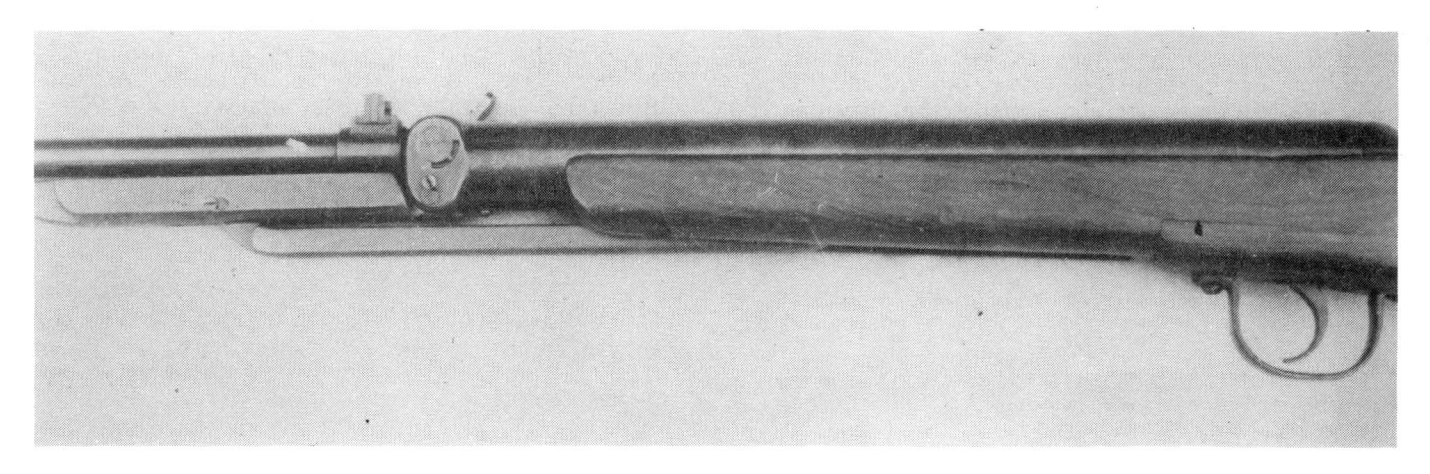

L.H.S. of home-made air rifle

MODEL   Home-made air rifle.

MAKER   Not known.

DATE   Not known, but would assume post-war as the trigger assembly looks very much like Webley Mk. III.

VALUATION   These home-made airguns either fetch high prices or next to nothing, this model changed hands during the early 1980s for around £80 ($120).

DETAILS   A home-made air rifle in .25. The barrel is from the Webley Service Mk. II, so is the rearsight, whilst the trigger block and assembly looks very much as though it has Webley Mk. III origins. Everything else looks as though it has been made from virgin steel. No markings appear whatsoever on either the metalwork or stock. Notice the unusual join in the stock between the hard and soft wood used. If any reader can supply any information on the above the Author would fully acknowledge any help given.

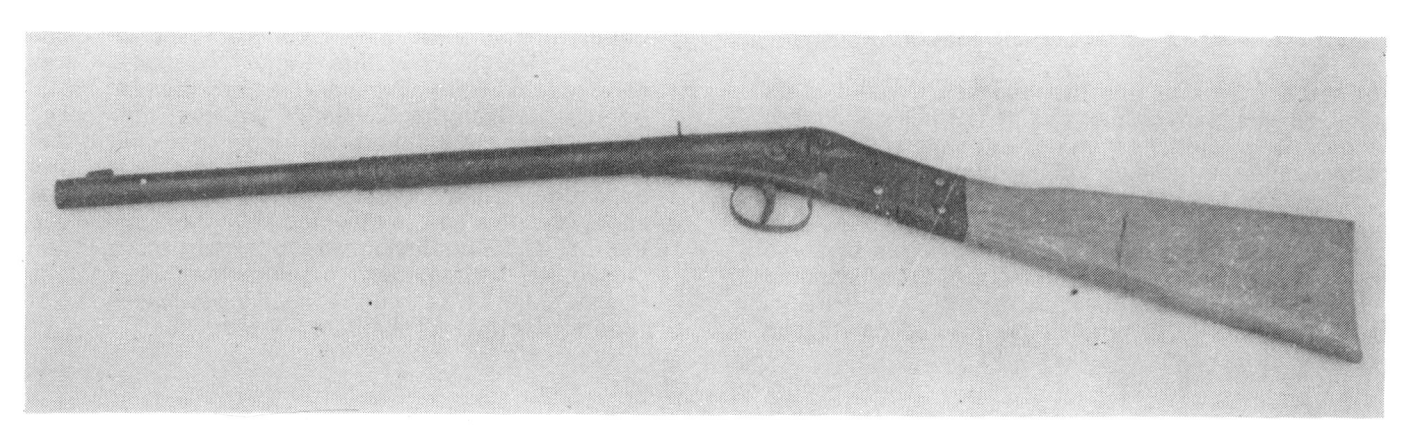

"Hot Shot" tinplate air rifle

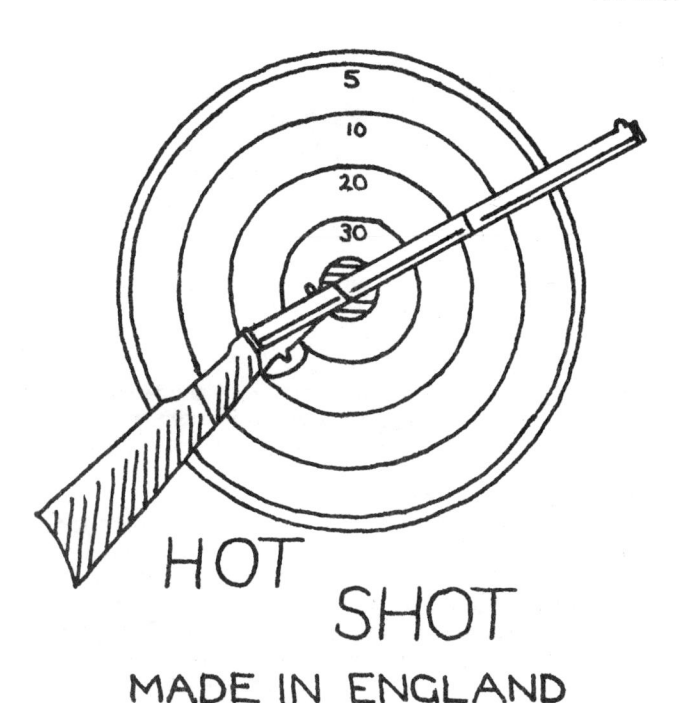

"Hot Shot" trademark. 3x magnification

MODEL   Hot Shot.

MAKER   Not known, but was claimed to be British when advertised.

DATE   Pre-1939.

VALUATION   £5—£30. Would assume the above to be a rare example of a tinplate air rifle.

DETAILS   Could well have been made by Diana of Germany or Britain if post-war. Removable barrel for loading. 30¾ inches in length. Simple non-adjustable sights. Top of air chamber behind the rearsight is stamped with a target trademark with an air rifle and "HOT SHOT" underneath with "MADE IN ENGLAND". Appears to be identical to the Diana Model 1 and the Hector tinplates.

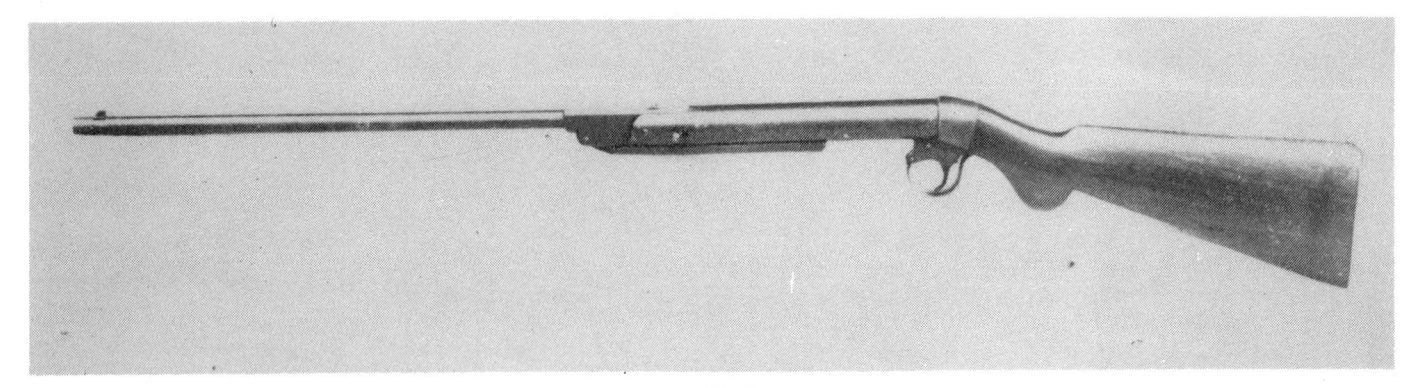

Lane's Musketeer

MODEL   Musketeer.

MAKER   Confusion, Lane Brothers advertised the Musketeer as being "entirely British made" yet do not appear to claim any manufacturing rights. The trigger design was patented by the Greener family of shotgun fame so they may have made the above, on the other hand a Midland Gun Catalogue claimed that they made it, or parts of it. I dare say that a lot of "jobbing" went on in the Birmingham gun trade in that quite a few specialist workshops had a hand in manufacturing components before it ended up at Lane's.

DATE   From around 1903 to 1910 although unsold stock may have been advertised after this date.

VALUATION   £100–£200. ($150–$300).

DETAILS   An air rifle that was years ahead of its time, as was many British air rifles of this period, but appeared to suffer from a lethargic advertising campaign and foreign competition. Have times changed? All steel airgun with quarter stock. 40¾ inches long with a 20 inch barrel. Simple front and rearsights set in dovetail mountings. Last two digits of serial number are stamped all over the place. Barrel stamped "MUSKETEER" and "LANE BROS., LONDON BRITISH MADE". Barrel latch is a simple pivoted bar that is pulled back to release the barrel. Trigger mechanism hangs down below the rear of the air chamber and is stamped with Greener's patent number "PATENT No.9644" and the serial number. Plain stock with metal butt plate. Lane's address at time of manufacture, 45a New Church Street, Bermondsey, London S.E. Price in 1907 was 35/- equivalent to £1.75 in modern foreign British money. Lane's also offered to rifle any smoothbore airgun. The above example is smoothbore .177. The first appearance of the Musketeer was in a patent, 15773, of 1901 by Charles, John, and Ernest Lane and covered the cocking and trigger mechanism for a barrel pivoted air rifle with a wedge on the trigger engaging directly into a split in the underside on the piston. This type of Musketeer has not appeared yet in collector's circles, but one may appear yet. The original patent does show the barrel latch used as above. Details of the above patent can be found in "Guns Review" March 1978. The trigger mechanism was patented by Harry Greener in 1903, number 9644. Address as being of St. Mary's Square, Birmingham. This patent was an improved trigger mechanism that used a tumbler between the trigger and piston. The upper porting of the tumbler had two pointed horns that engaged with a hole in the underside of the piston and the rear end. The design was followed exactly in the Musketeer without any modification. See "Guns Review" May 1978 for further details. Have seen two of the above with serial numbers 570 and 2768.

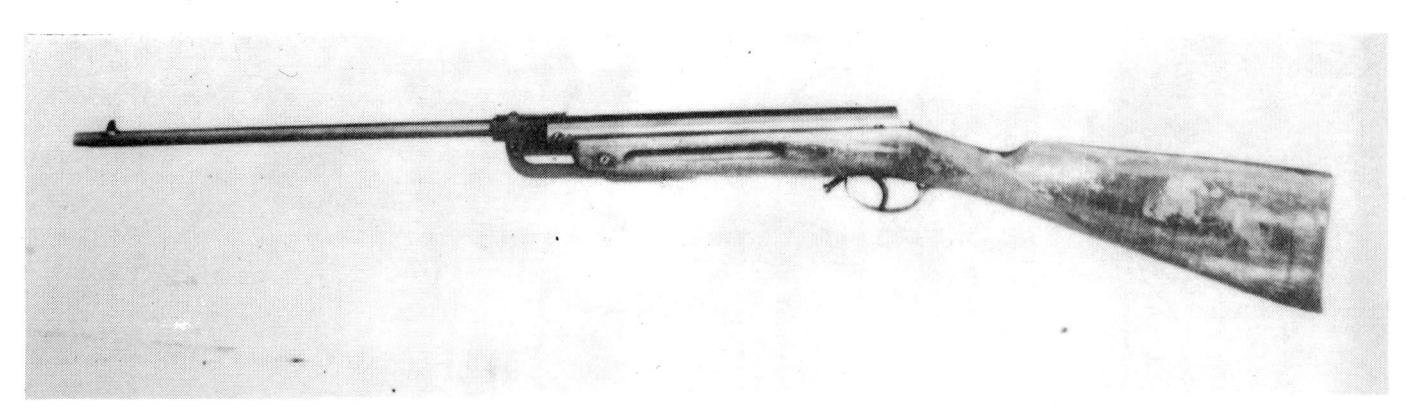

A Lepco air rifle

MODEL   "Lepco" air rifle.

MAKER   "Lepco", of Belgium. Could have the same origins as the Browning as one advert refers to the above as being made by "F. N. Lepco", the initials standing for "Fabrique Nationale" of Belgium.

DATE   Middle to late 1930s.

VALUATION   £30–£60. ($45–$90).

DETAILS   Quite rare to find a Belgium airgun. A well made air rifle with a few distinctive features, i.e. a kinked cocking lever, tangent rearsight that is screw mounted on to the dovetail mounted block, rounded surface to rear of trigger block and finally the novel method of stock to action fitting which we'll deal with later.
40 inches long (1.100 m), with a 16½ inch (42 cm) barrel in .177 and rifled. Underside of breech stamped with serial number (1985), as is the chamber, trigger block and other parts. It would appear to be a sign of European airguns that they are smothered with serial numbers. Side of breech is stamped "MADE IN BELGIUM". Simple blade foresight dovetail mounted as is the rearsight, but the rearsight is screw mounted to the dovetail block that fits into the groove across the barrel. The cocking lever pivot screw and barrel pivot screws

both have locking screws. The air chamber is nicely blued with "LEPCO" in a diamond logo on top of the air chamber. The stock is hand chequered and is of the straight hand variety often seen on shotguns. Heavy metal trigger guard with adjustment screw through the front.

Stock removal can be quite a puzzle for the first time, but here goes; remove trigger adjuster screw then by undoing the two trigger guard screws remove the guard. Under this there is the main action screw, remove this and then undo the cross bolt through the fore-end and pull it out. Now you may wonder why the action is still attached to the stock, but don't worry for you now have to undo the cocking lever screws and drop the cocking arm and swing it sideways so as to reveal a small screw on the underside of the air chamber at the front of the stock, insert a screwdriver and remove. Action can now be removed by drawing the cocking arm through the slot towards the rear of the stock. Remember to insert cocking arm in action and thread through same slot in stock when refitting action to stock.

As a coincidence the Lepco airguns were sold by L. LePersonne & Co. Ltd., 7 Old Bailey, London E.C.4 which easily sounds like Lepco when shortened. They also sold F. N. Lepco "All-Metal Shotgun Cartridges", Lepco Automatic Bird Scarer and Crop Protector, as well as .22 Lepco Rim Fire Cartridges.

The Lucznik Model 141

MODEL 141.

MAKER Lucznik, Poland.

DATE Would assume 1970s.

VALUATION £30–£60. ($45–$90).

DETAILS Small sized air rifle for the junior end of the market. Not generally available in Britain. 36½ inches long with a 14½ inch .177 rifled barrel. Dovetail mounted foresight and rearsight. Rearsight adjustable by a rider that rests in serrations actually cut into the top of the barrel. Serial number, C00230, on side of barrel breech and on air chamber. Top of air chamber milled for telescopic sight. Rear of chamber stamped "LUCZNIK 141, KAL. 4.5 mm, MADE IN POLAND". Single pull trigger that lacks adjustment.

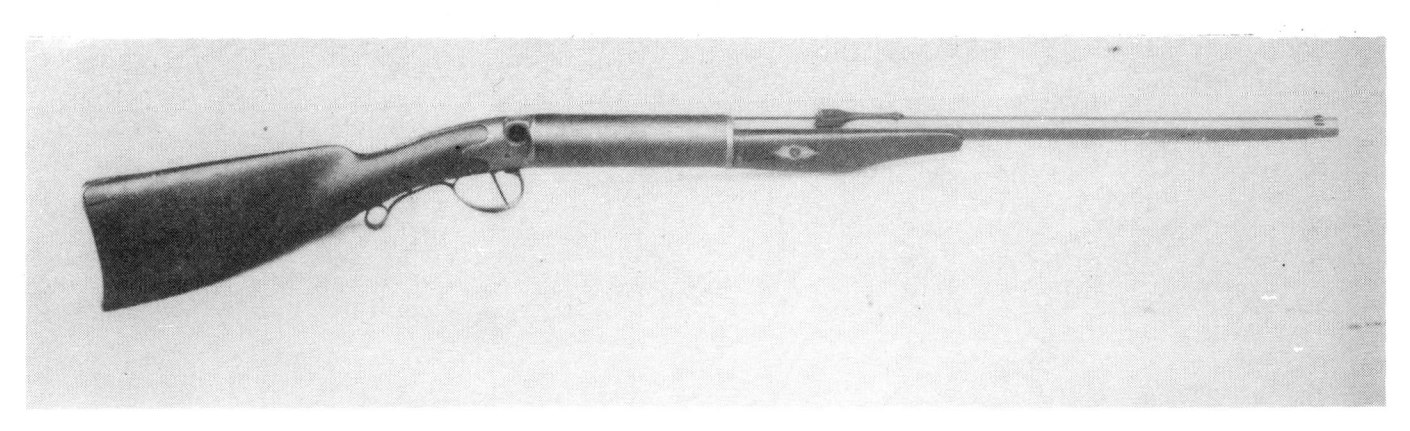

David Lurch Gallery air rifle

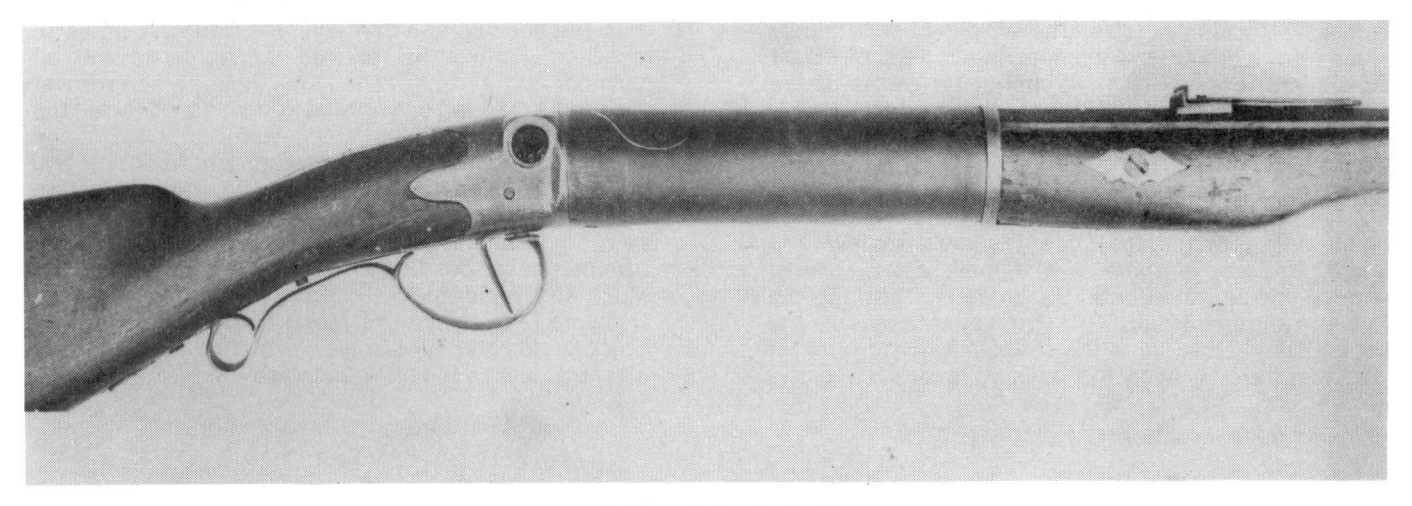

Action of a Lurch air rifle

MODEL Primary New York City Type Gallery Air Rifle.

MAKER David Lurch, 157 Grand Street, New York, U.S.A.

DATE David Lurch is listed as a gunsmith from around 1863 to 1890 or thereabouts. The address varied from 142 Grand Street to 157 and the move took place during 1866, so the above gallery gun was made sometime between 1866 and 1890.

VALUATION £300—£600. ($450—$900).

DETAILS Crank would gallery air rifle. 43 inches long with a 21 inch smoothbore barrel of bore larger than .25, appears to be $\frac{5}{16}$ inch. Octagonal barrel full length. Foresight set in dovetail and rearsight unusual in that it is a reverse dovetail setting, the sight blade is over the dovetail mounting and the spring of the sight faces forward. Stamped on top of barrel flat "DAVID LURCH, 157 GRAND ST., N.Y.". To load the barrel is turned 90° clockwise, same action as the A. F. Wirsing gallery air pistol, see "Airpistols" Second Edition by D. E. Hiller. Wooden forepiece held in place by one stock screw. Iron air chamber with double convolute mainspring. Top of air chamber bear traces of scroll pattern engraving. Transfer port has thin metal blade set across the opening to act as a pellet trap so as to prevent pellets entering the air chamber when the action is cocked. Trigger action housing and guard are brass. Hole for crank is iron lined. Trigger adjustment is by way of small screw behind trigger, in the above this is missing. To remove action from air chamber first unscrew the small grub screw on the underside of the air chamber near the trigger guard. The action can then be unscrewed from the air chamber. The only number visible is a figure "3" stamped on the butt plate.

The Primary New York Type is known also in Europe, but for two differences, the barrel tips down for loading and the crank hole usually has a pivoted cover plate. The stock has a cheek piece and a brass butt plate. The trigger mechanism is identical to that used in a crossbow of German origin. Besides being a gallery airgun manufacturer, he also manufactured guns, mechanical targets, springs, darts and other "sporting goods". For further details see "Airguns" by Eldon G. Wolff.

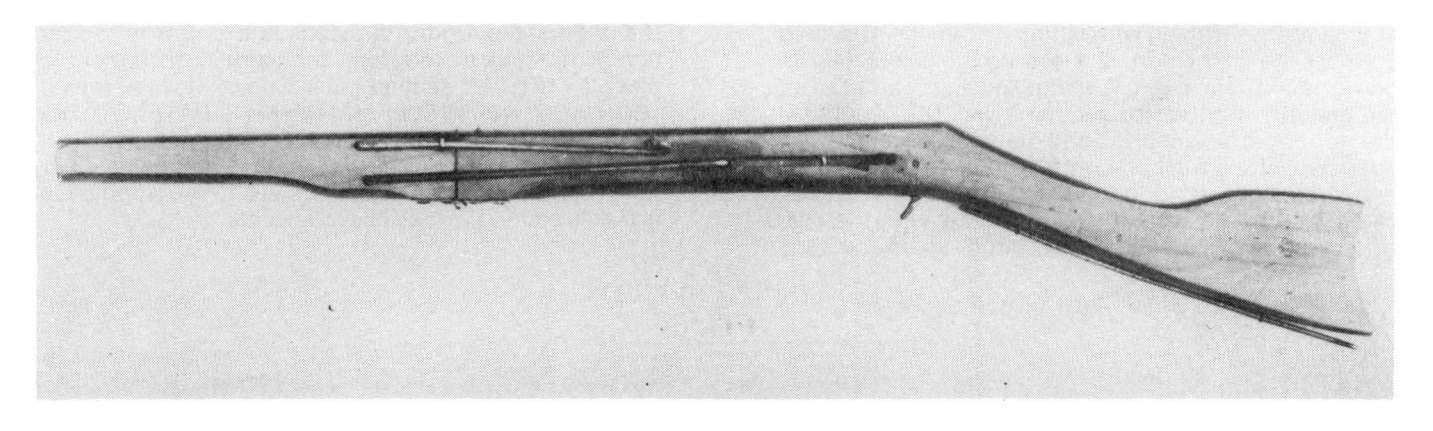

Markham "Chicago" air rifle

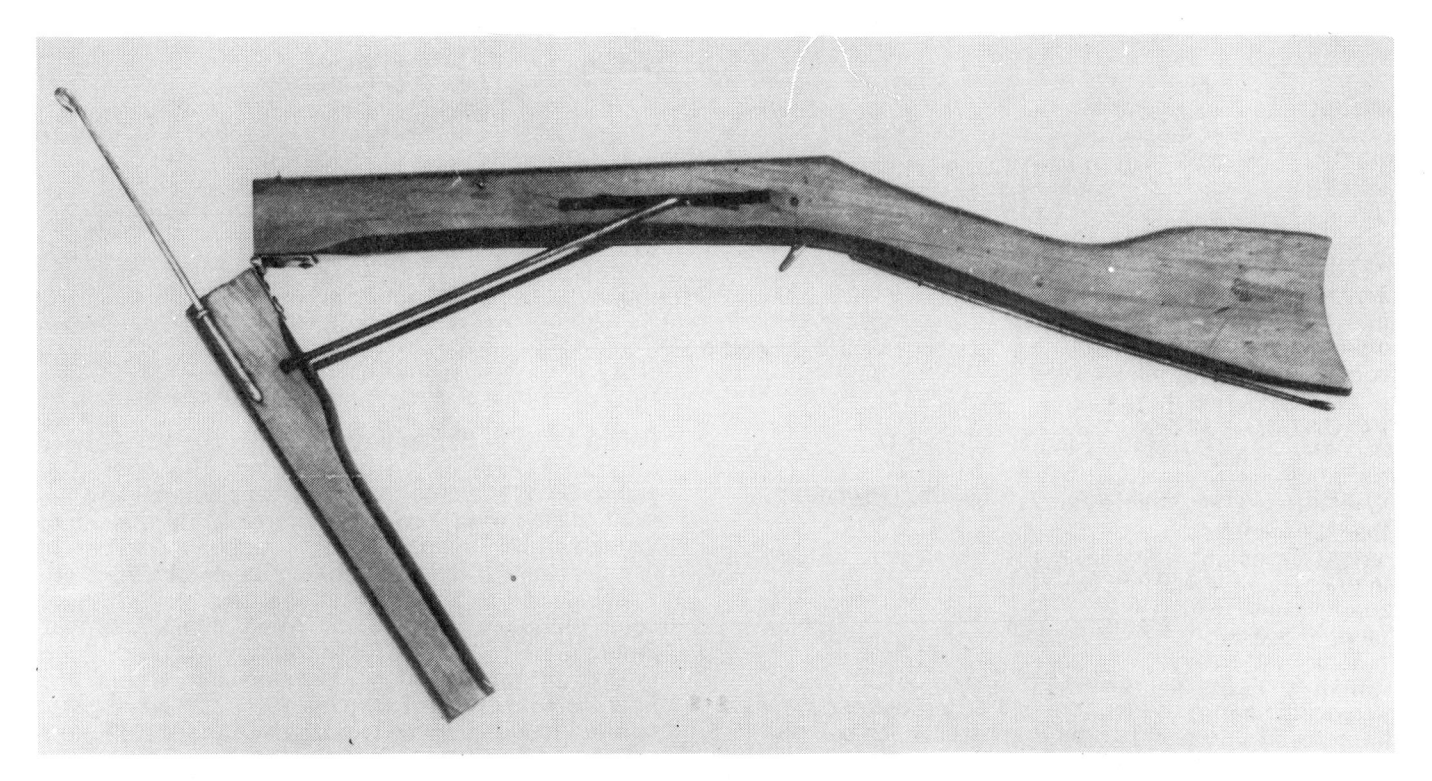

Markham "Chicago" in cocked position

"The American Rifleman" November 1966

Mr. Harold W. Glassen, Vice President of the National Rifle Association, is pictured with a plaque presented to the NRA museum by the Daisy Mfg. Co. The plaque contains the all-wood "Chicago" BB Gun, and a rare model of the first Daisy all-metal BB Gun.

MODEL Chicago.

MAKER The Markham Air Rifle Co., Plymouth, Michigan, U.S.A.

DATE From 1888 to around 1890.

VALUATION £100—£200. ($150—$300).

DETAILS Most unusual and must be quite rare. Almost all wooden with a few minor metal parts. 32 inches long with a 9¾ inch smoothbore brass barrel. A case of using more furniture polish than oil in keeping it clean. The barrel is set in a groove and held in position by a strip of wood glued on top. Small brass foresight stuck in front. A piece of wire is passed through the wood above the barrel and bent back towards the air chamber to form the barrel lock. This clips over a "U" shaped pin. Any looseness can easily be taken up. The wire barrel locking arm is tethered by a smaller gauge wire. The barrel pivot is a hinge, what else using wood, the hinge is held by four screws on either side. Stock and air chamber are set in once piece of wood. The air chamber is brass which is open ended, ¾ of an inch. The seal arrangement is on the barrel side.

The barrel has a small wire spring just inside, this is to hold the pellet or dart in place until the build-up in power is sufficient to get things moving. The head of the piston is slotted for a screwdriver. This would aid the refitting of mainspring and the above example was not fitted with a washer, only a solid brass piston. Thin brass rearsight set in groove across the air chamber. One piece trigger that engages directly with the sear that runs from the solid brass piston, as on the early Diana tinplates. Under the stock is a long wire rod for removing stuck pellets form the barrel. This is held in place by two "U" shaped pins. Side of stock stamped "CHICAGO AIR RIFLE, MARKHAM'S PATENT". The above was the third model produced by Markham. It was advertised as being able to kill small game at 50 feet "Death to sparrows and rats etc.". The wood used is maple stained to look like rosewood.

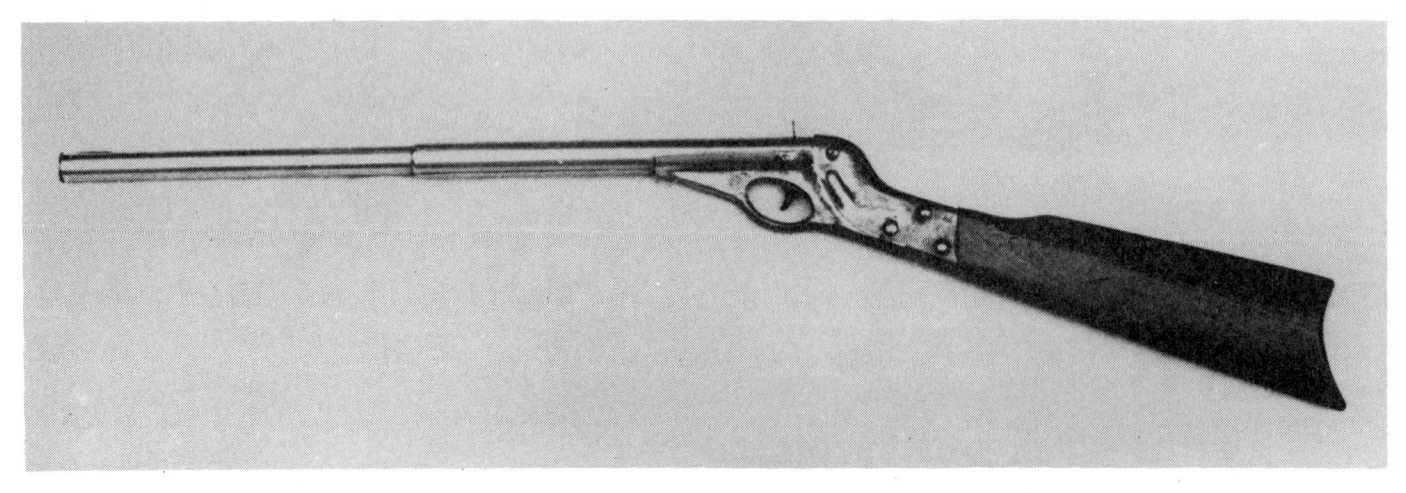

King No. D

MODEL "New Model King Air Rifle No. D".

MAKER The Markham Air Rifle Co., Plymouth, Michigan, U.S.A.

DATE 1908 to around 1910.

VALUATION £10—£30. ($15—$45).

DETAILS Nickel plated tinplate construction. Removable barrel to load, the end of the barrel could be pressed into a potato as a substitute for pellets. Single shot. 30½ inches long with a 9½ inch smoothbore barrel. Non-adjustable sights. Blade foresight and peephole rearsight. Top of air chamber stamped:
KING No.D THE MARKHAM AIR RIFLE
CO, PLYMOUTH, MICH., U.S.A.
PATENTED
SEPT.27,1892.
JAN.28,1896.
APR.,7,1896.
APR.,1,1902.
OCT.,27,1903.
JAN.,29,1907.

Patent for 27th September 1892, number 483159, was for cocking the action by breaking. The April 1902 patent 696461 related to the removable barrel and the front sight fitting into a locking slot. The patent of January 1896, number 553716 appears to be an improvement to the two cocking wires. The 7th April 1896 referred to a repeater model that may not have been produced, this patent being number 557849. Patent number 742734 of 27th October 1903 appears to refer to an improved trigger and sear arrangement. The final patent of 29th January 1907, number 842324 referred to an improved locking device for holding the barrel into the mouth of the air chamber. As can be seen some of the listed patents were in fact not used. For further details see Dunathan's "The American BB Gun".

An assumed earlier Model D has the following stamped on the air chamber: "KING MODEL D, THE MARKHAM AIR RIFLE CO., PLYMOUTH, MICH., U.S.A. PAT. NOS., 483159, 553716, 557849, 655170, 696461, 742734, 842324. These have been explained previously.

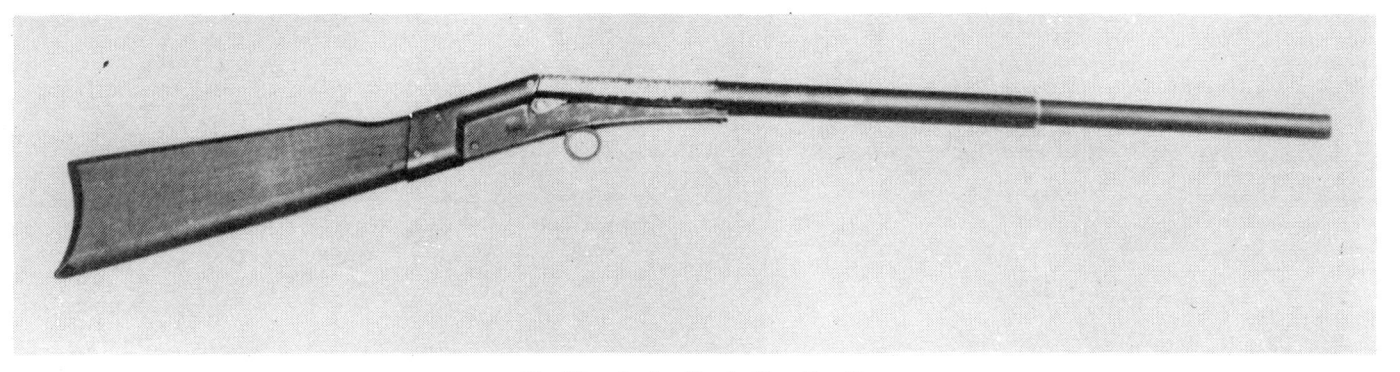

The King Junior Single Shot No. 10

(Acknowledgement to "The American BB Gun")

*Sell 20 packets of garden seeds and you were given an air rifle.
The Markham Number 10 was such one of these premium give-away airguns.*

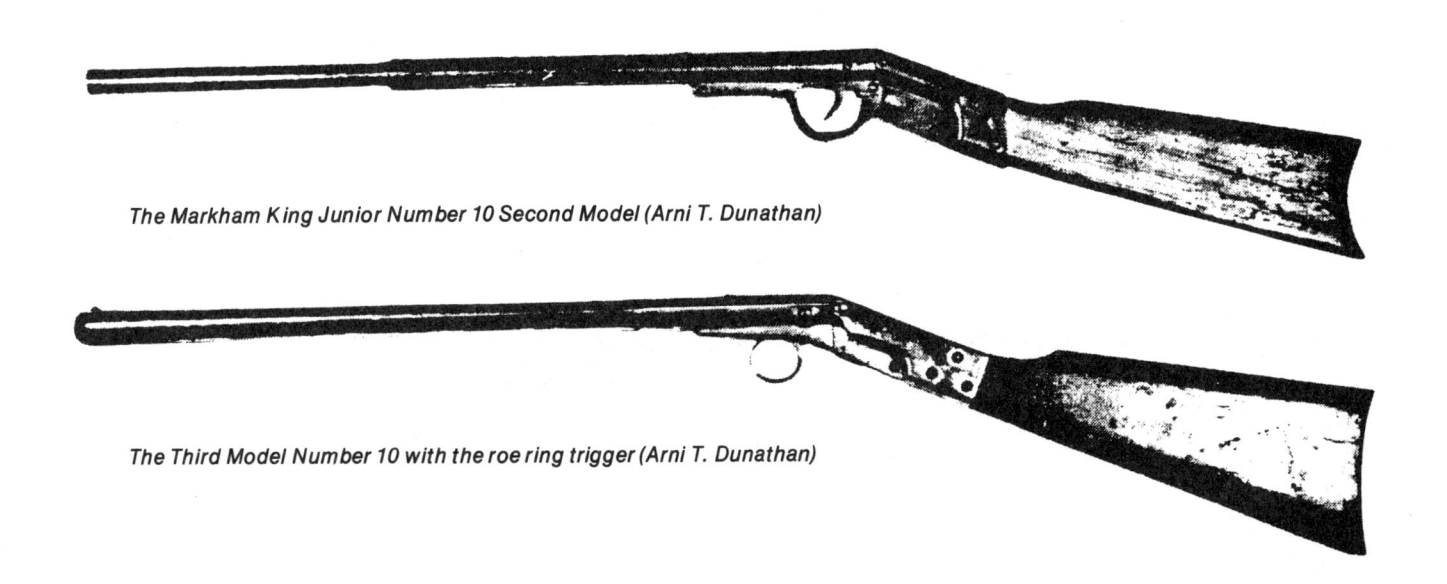

The Markham King Junior Number 10 Second Model (Arni T. Dunathan)

The Third Model Number 10 with the roe ring trigger (Arni T. Dunathan)

MODEL King Junior Single Shot Number 10.

MAKER The Markham Air Rifle Co., Plymouth, Michigan, U.S.A.

DATE 1910 to 1940. About three to four variations.

VALUATION £20—£40. ($30—$60).

DETAILS The above is a perfect example of the "Premium" airgun that was common in the States during the 1910s and 20s. They were small and cheap to make and were offered as an incentive to promote sales of other products. Sell so many packets of "garden seeds" and you receive two dollars plus the above air rifle free. 27½ inches long (70 cm), with a non-removable smoothbore .177 barrel. You either pushed or spat the BB's down the barrel. Fixed sights and no trigger guard. Unusual ring trigger. The mainspring was quite powerful for the size of the airgun. Lettering stamped on top of air chamber just behind the rearsight. Arni T. Dunathan in his book "The American BB Gun" lists three models of the Number 10, but the above does not quite fit in. The three listed are:

Model 1. Nickel plated frame and barrel, cast-iron trigger guard that extended into the grip and acted as the fulcrum for cocking. Barrel was one piece and had no step in it between barrel and air chamber. Dates about 1910 to 1915.

Model 2. From about 1915 to 1925. Same as above but barrel and air chamber was made in two pieces.

Model 3. The common one. Made from 1926 to 1940. Still had the two piece barrel and chamber but the action dropped the trigger guard and replaced it with a ring trigger.

Now for the confusion, Dunathan shows the late model as having a one piece barrel and chamber, but the above definitely has a two piece construction. It also appears very much shorter than that featured in the book, also the stock is of smaller proportion. Could the above be a Junior Junior? The above was also blued and not nickel plated.

153

King No. 17

MODEL Number 17.

MAKER The Markham Air Rifle Co., Plymouth, Michigan, U.S.A.

DATE Introduced 1917 and seen advertised as late as the middle 1930s in this country.

VALUATION £20—£40. ($30—$60).

DETAILS Tinplate construction and similar in design to the "Chicago". 31 inches long with a 12 inch smoothbore barrel. Simple non-adjustable sights. Breech washer in the air chamber side. Two wire rods form the cocking lever and they latch over the barrel pivot rivet to hold barrel in place for firing. Top of air chamber stamped "KING BREECH LOADER SHOT OR DARTS No. 17 THE MARKHAM AIR RIFLE CO. PLYMOUTH. MICH. U.S.A. PAT PEND'G TRADE MARK REG. U.S. PATENT OFFICE". Available with blued finish only and in .177. In 1928 it cost 7/-. The above was unique in that it started the trend in break barrel action air rifles, this was patented by an employee of Markham, E. S. Roe. For further details see Donathan "The American BB Gun". At a later date the lettering on top of the air chamber was changed to "KING BREECH LOADER SHOT OR DARTS No. 17 THE MARKHAM AIR RIFLE CO. PLYMOUTH. MICH. U.S.A. PAT. JUNE.13,1922, TRADE MARK REG. U.S. PATENT OFFICE. There appears to be a small pellet holder underneath the air chamber. If air rifle is turned upside down, where the barrel pivot pin is, towards the air chamber end is a flat piece of metal, if this is lifted slightly and pulled towards the barrel pivot pin a small drawer is revealed into which a store of pellets can be placed.

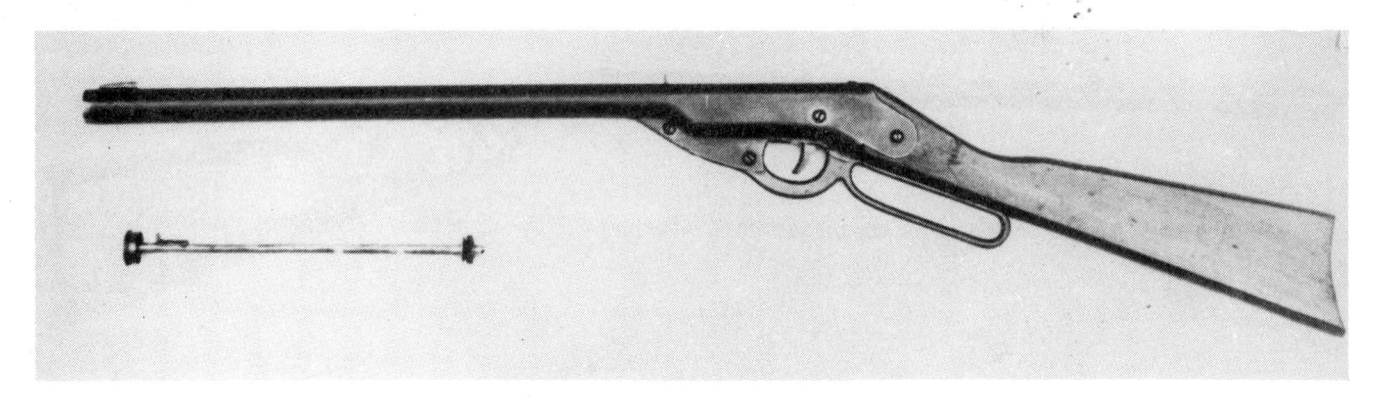

"King" Air Rifle Model 21. Identical to King Model 22 which was a 500 shot repeater

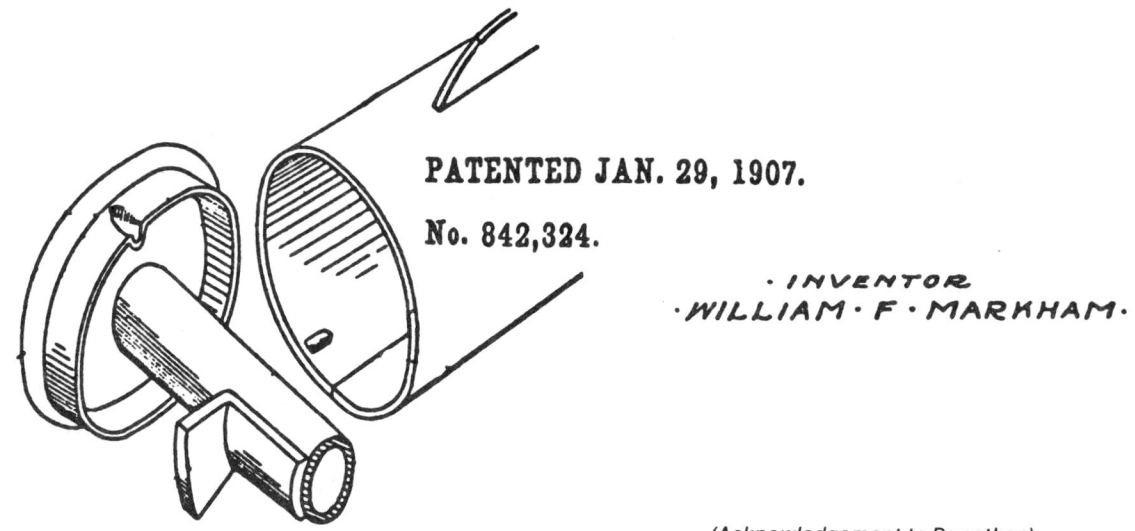

PATENTED JAN. 29, 1907.
No. 842,324.

·INVENTOR·
·WILLIAM·F·MARKHAM·

(Acknowledgement to Dunathan)

Patented May 27, 1913.

1,062,855.

(Acknowledgement to Dunathan)
The two patents associated with the King No. 21

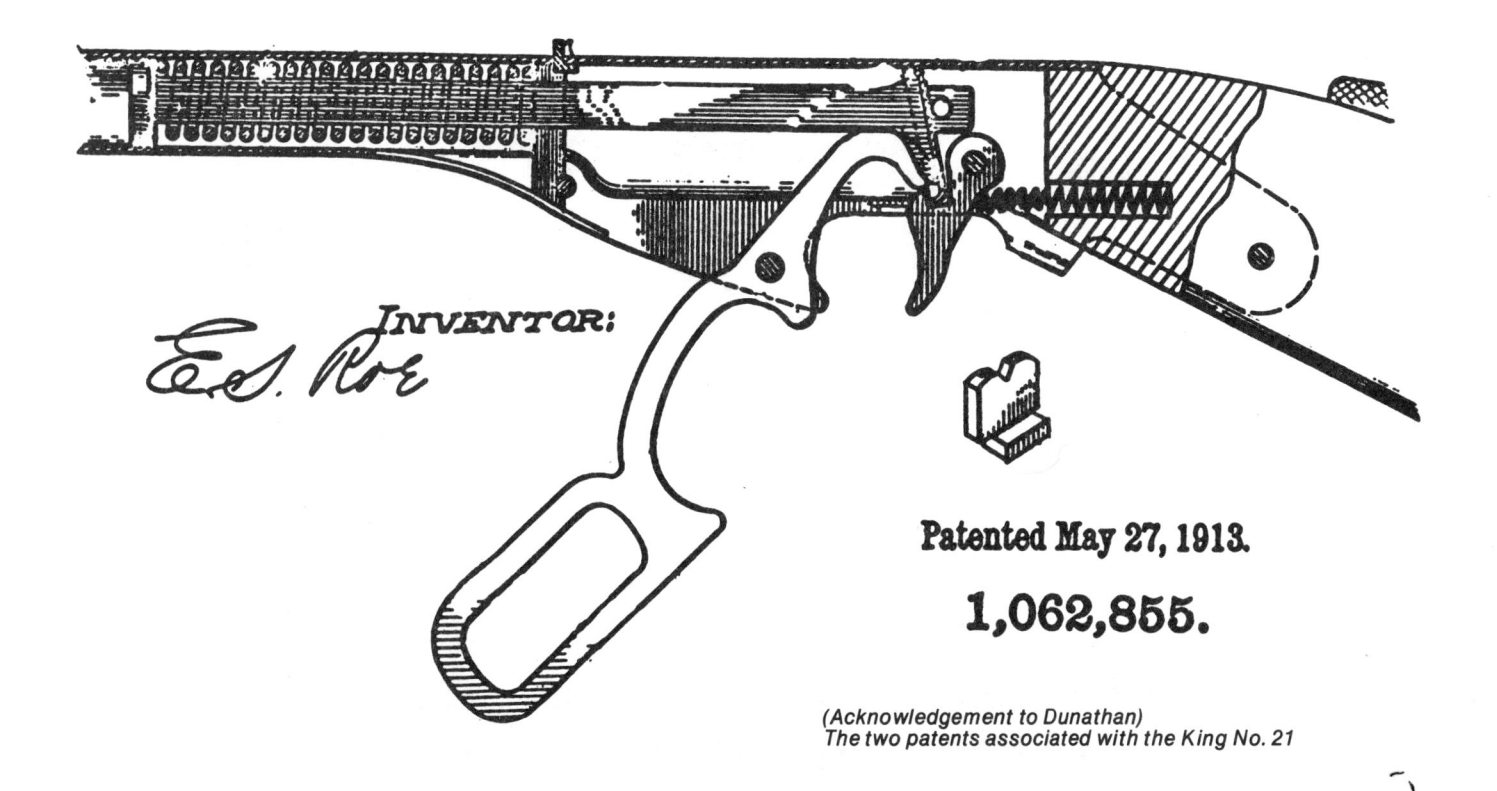

MODEL No. 21 "King" Single Shot.
No. 22 "King" 500 Shot.
No. 2233 "King" 500 Shot.

MAKER Markham Air Rifle Company, Plymouth, Michigan. the Markham Company was later taken over by Daisy.

DATE From around 1916 to 1934.

VALUATION £20—£40. ($30—$60).

DETAILS Tinplate construction with wooden butt. Underlever action with removable barrel for loading. When pellets ran out, the end of the barrel could be pressed into a potato and used as a "spud" gun. 30½ inches long with 8⅞ inch barrel. Roach bellied stock. Stamped on L.H.S. of action frame "KING SINGLE SHOT No. 21". The "K" appears in a circular bulls eye trademark. Underneath is stamped "PAT.JAN.29,1907 — May 27 1913" and near the stock appears "MFD. BY THE MARKHAM ??????, PLYMOUTH, M????", the stampings are faint in this region. Rearsight is simple leaf with no adjustment. Metal work shows signs of having been nickel plated in the past. Although the above was nickel plated there was also a blued model advertised. Was also available in a 500 shot repeater model. Another model seen had a straight hand stock thinner than the above and had the following stamped on top of the action "KING SINGLE SHOT No. 21" followed by "THE MARKHAM AIR RIFLE CO., PLYMOUTH, MICH., U.S.A. PAT JAN.29,1907 — MAY,27,1913, TRADE MARK REG. U.S. PATENT OFFICE". It can be assumed that this is an earlier model of the Number 21. The first of these patents is for number 842324 by William F. Markham and was for the bayonet fitting of the barrel into the outer barrel sleeve, before this a screw thread was used. The second patent was number 1062855 and was patented by E. S. Roe and dealt with the lever cocking action along with a method of placing the mainspring on to the plunger.

First models of the Number 21 were stamped "MODEL No. 21, KING MANUFACTURING Co., PLYMOUTH, MICH., U.S.A. SINGLE SHOT, PATENT NUMBERS 1062855—880555". This patent applies to the action of the underlever cocking lever. The removable barrel was not a bayonet fit, but a screw-in type.

The Model 22 was identical to the 21 except that it was a 500 shot repeater. The power of these tinplate underlevers can be quite surprising. The loading orifice is just under the foresight and to open turn the front milled rim of the barrel anti-clockwise as you face it. After pouring in the BB's rotate the front barrel face clockwise to close the hole.

By the middle 1930s the 500 shot had become the Model 2233 with the loading hole now on the R.H.S. of the foresight and having a three nut/bolt action with a more rounded and extended portion to the front of the trigger housing, also the forward nut/bolt had been replaced by a rivet. The barrel is a bayonet fit and may be eased out when the barrel has been rotated to open the loading orifice position.

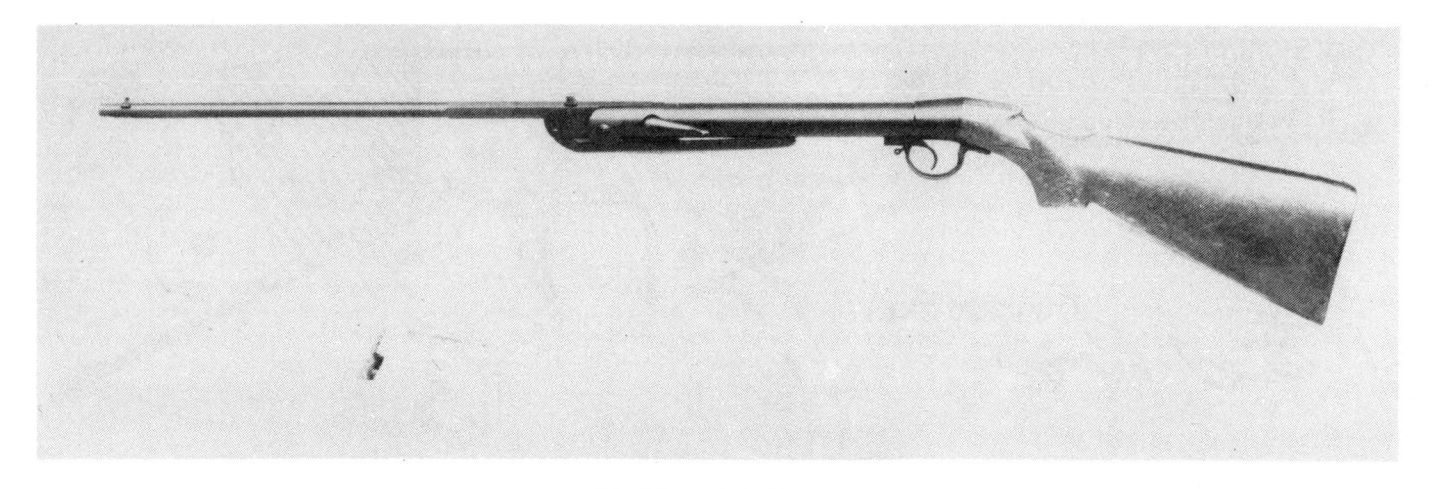

The "Marco" air rifle

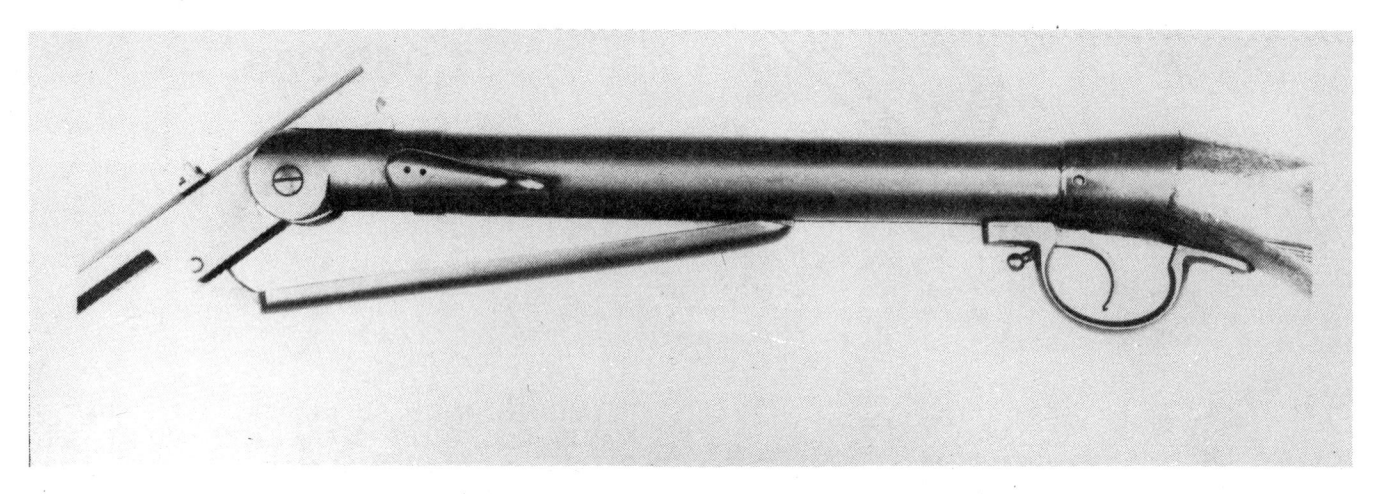

Close-up of action. Compare action with that of Roland Model 1927 for similarities in design

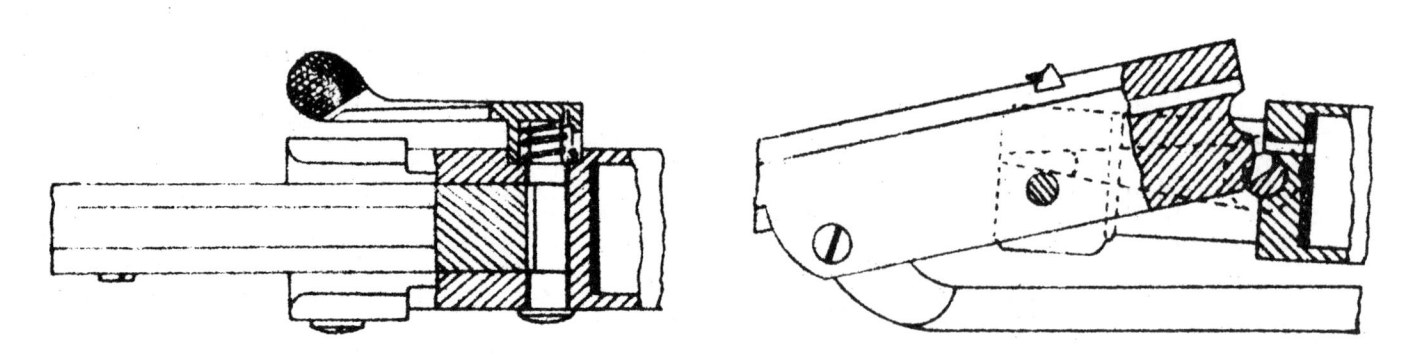

Details for patent 20246 (1903/4). By G. L. Jeffries. (Acknowledgement to Guns Review)

MODEL "Marco", but is very similar to the Roland 1927. Could be "Tell" air rifle sold to retailer "Marco" and has placed his trade name on the airgun. As did Lincoln Jeffries with Millita air rifles. Also seen with "SPORT 2" stamped on the barrel flat.

MAKER Oscar Will/Wilheyn Foss, Venuswaffenwerk, Zella-Mehlis (Thuringia), Germany.

DATE The above style of Tell air rifle with the side lever barrel catch appeared around 1920 and was still available right up to the outbreak of the Second World War, this being around 1939/40.

VALUATION £40–£80. ($60–$120).

DETAILS A very solid and well made air rifle. $42\frac{1}{8}$ inches long with an $18\frac{7}{8}$ inch .177 rifled barrel. The sights are identical to those fitted to the Roland Model 1927, i.e. foresight has a German silver tipped bead. Rearsight is also identical to those fitted to the Haenel Model 45 air rifle. Both sights are dovetail mounted. Octagonal to round barrel with "MARCO" stamped on the top. Underside stamped with serial number, so is underside of air chamber and in various other places. The barrel support mounts are very similar to those of the "Original V" of F. Langenham pedigree. Side lever barrel catch has the two small characteristic holes drilled in the side. Again these have been offered as Greener air rifles to less knowledgeable collectors, it pays to invest in a good book such as Hiller's! Many of the above were sold to retailers and offered to the public with many retailers' trademarks on them. The trigger block is identical to that on the Roland 1927. Trigger adjustment by way of screw with round head through trigger guard. Metal butt plate to stock. These "Club Airguns" were sold in the 1930s either blued or nickel plated, and sold in either .22 or .177 rifled or smoothbore. It was also advertised as the Tell Model 1704. During the early 1930s the Midland Gun Company was selling these as the "Perfecta" in .177 only. During this time it was identical to the Roland Model 1927. The barrel latch was patented by George Lincoln Jeffries of 1212 Steelhouse Lane, Birmingham during 1903 and 1904. This was patent number 20246 and the only difference from that latch fitted to the German Tell was the handle faced in the opposite direction. Was this a patent infringement or a business arrangement? See "Guns Review" May 1978 for further details of the above patent. During its passage through time it was also sold as the Tell Model 50. See "Airgun World" March 1980.

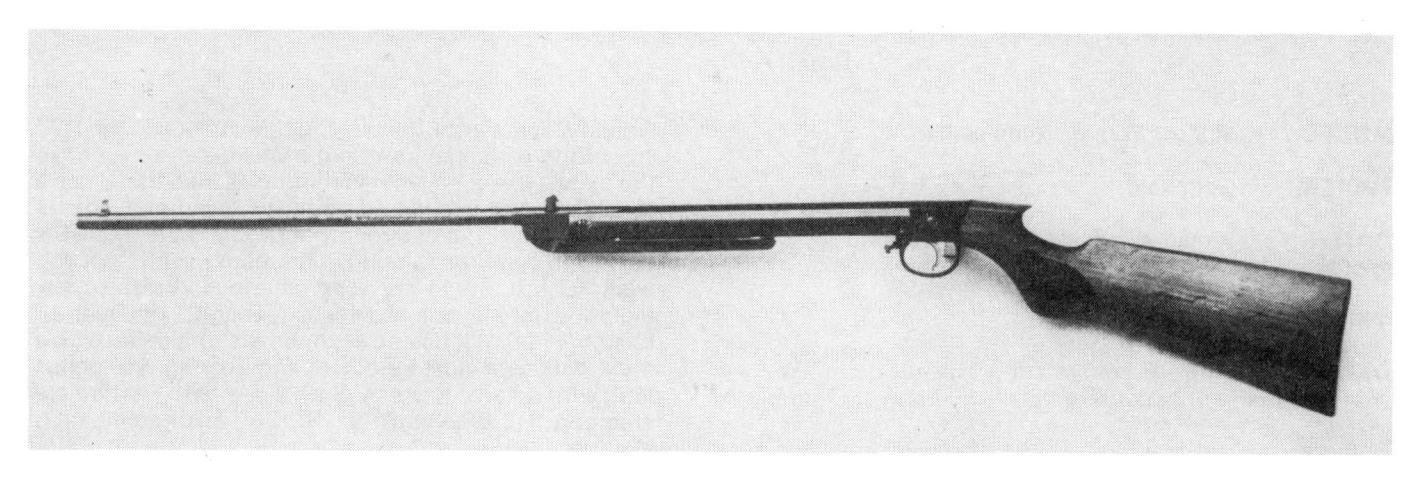

Midland Gun Co. "Demon"

MODEL "Demon".

MAKER Assumed Midland Gun Company, Bath Street, Birmingham.

DATE Production appears to be from 1919 to around 1935.

VALUATION £100–£200. ($150–300).

DETAILS Serial number of above 1028, break action, above has no engraving, or name, but the giveaway is the barrel braized on to the breech support block. B.S.A. type stock, but no measurement stamped on the underside. 42½ inches long, .22 rifled barrel. Have seen examples with heavy scroll engraving chiselled into the trigger block, also some have "MIDLAND GUN CO" stamped on to top of chamber. Very well made and have known them to give high muzzle velocities when tested. In 1925 they cost 30/- for .177 and 36/- for .22 model. See "Shooting Times and Country Magazine" 7th—13th April 1977 and "Guns Review" January 1976. Weight 6 lb.
Seen advertised as "MODEL DE LUXE AIR RIFLE" in a 1932—1933 copy of a Midland Gun Catalogue. Uses letter published in "The Shooting Times" 14th May 1932. Advertised as having a double spring and a solid plunger. Sold in .177 or .22 and could even be fitted to purchaser's measurements for small extra charge. A "CLUB" model was also offered fitted with a rear flip-up peepsight that looks like the one fitted to B.S.A. air rifles of the same period. Above air rifle was sold as MODEL DE LUXE or STANDARD. This difference could apply to the degree of engraving. They may have been manufactured by the Midland Gun Company.

The stock is held in place by a bolt that also has the trigger guard screw going through it. To remove stock:
(a) Remove trigger guard.
(b) Remove butt plate.
(c) Unscrew long stock nut, i.e. use screwdriver to ease nut off. After its removal it helps to grind the nut down to ⅝ inch size for future use with a socket spanner.
(d) The stock can now be removed.
To replace stock:
(a) Replace stock.
(b) Pack end on stock bolt with washers and replace the now ⅝ inch nut, do not tighten.
(c) Replace trigger guard with all screws fitted loosely.
(d) Tighten front trigger guard screws, then stock nut and finally the rear trigger guard screw.
(e) Replace butt plate.
The B.S.A. Airsporter Mk. I rearsight will fit the above as a replacement. A pre-war Diana Model 27 has been seen bearing a brass medallion stamped, "MIDLAND GUN Co., BATH ST., BIRMINGHAM" tacked on to the stock. Some of these may appear on the Demon air rifle, unless they were used only for stock retailed by the Midland Gun Co. The pre-war Diana air rifle date stamped "10,25". By serial number 1635 the top of the air chamber was stamped, "MIDLAND GUN Co., BIRMINGHAM, MADE IN ENGLAND".
The following have been seen:
 577 — .22 with engraved trigger block only.
1028 — .177 with no engraving.
1635 — "Midland Gun Co." circular stamp under butt plate, top of chamber stamped "Midland Gun Co., Birmingham, Made in England".
1979 — No engraving, but same chamber markings as 1635.

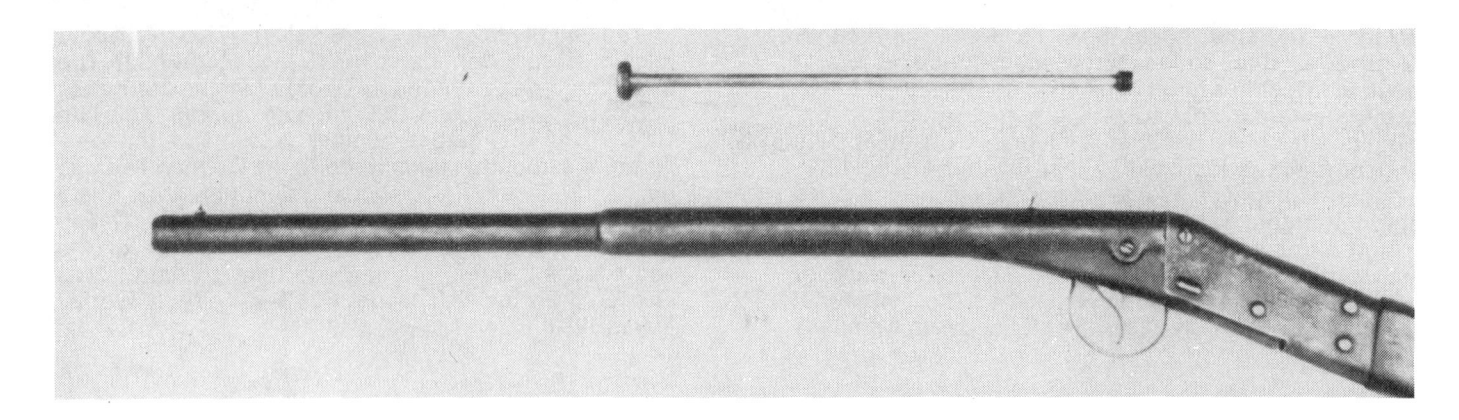

Milbro "Foreign" Number 1

MODEL Milbro "Foreign Number 1.

MAKER Germany.

DATE Would assume either late 1940s or early 1950s.

VALUATION £10−£20. ($15−$30).

DETAILS Tinplate construction but not quite like that usually associated with Mayer and Grammelspacher of Diana or "Original" fame. The .177 smoothbore barrel screws out of the outer tube, unlike the usual type of bayonet mounting. 9¾ inch barrel has a threaded portion soldered on to the lower end. This is obviously the type of airgun where you "spit" the BB's down the barrel as to remove the barrel each time you wish to fire would be very laborious. Brass screw mounted foresight and simple rearsight. Unusual air chamber in that it has no seam on the underside which must rank as a masterpiece of engineering. 31½ inches long with a flat side stock. Both sides of the action are stamped "MILBRO" with "FOREIGN" on one side only.

Milbro "Scout"

MODEL Milbro Scout.

MAKER Milbro, Motherwell, Lanarkshire. Scotland.

DATE Late 1940s to early 1950s.

VALUATION £10−£20. ($15−$30).

DETAILS Another "Diana" tinplate appears under another name! Identical to the post-war Diana Number 1. Tinplate construction with removable barrel for loading. Top of air chamber behind rearsight stamped with figure of boy scout holding his trusty staff and underneath "MILBRO SCOUT MADE IN ENGLAND". Either side of the stock part of the metal action stamped "MILBRO SCOUT MADE IN ENGLAND". Just on the underside of the stock is stamped "6 or 9" depending which way up you view the figure. 30½ inches long with an 8½ inch .177 smoothbore pull-out barrel. The above could also be used as a "spud-gun". The end of the barrel being pressed into one of Mother's potatoes and then barrel replaced in gun ready for firing.

Milbro "Foreign" air rifle

MODEL   Milbro air rifle.

MAKER   Not known, but air rifle is marked "FOREIGN" which usually means of German origins.

DATE   Would assume just after Second World War, i.e. middle to late 1940s. But actual design is pre-war, even as far back as the early 1930s.

VALUATION   £20—£40. ($30—$60).

DETAILS   Could be a stop-gap model until Milbro had time to produce their own airguns. As was the Milbro Cub air pistol, see "Airpistols" Second Edition. All in all a very pre-war looking air rifle. Solid construction with simple non-adjustable sights. 37½ inches long with a 16¼ rifled .177 barrel. Serial number stamped on underside of barrel support block and air chamber. Number of above 878. Top of air chamber stamped "MILBRO — FOREIGN". Simple stock with blued metal butt plate. The above looks very like the "Favorit" Model 3 which was advertised in the 1930s, it was also linked with the name "Precision" and have seen air rifles bearing this name that also appear to be linked with Tell air rifles. So take your pick! The above is definitely German. Serial number also appears on the trigger block. Another pointer to German origins is the fact that the stock is held in place by the customary nut screwed on to the long threaded shaft, as is seen on almost all of the Gem air rifles.

A larger model of the above has been seen, this was about the same size as the pre-war Diana Model 27, the first model with a stock that only went up to the trigger block. The example seen was without stock, but measured 30½ inches along the barrel/air chamber and had a 19 inch .177 rifled barrel. Barrel had a dovetail mounted foresight and simple ramp rearsight. Top of air chamber was stamped "MILBRO — FOREIGN". Its serial number, 792, was stamped all over the place, barrel, chamber, trigger guard, trigger block, etc. The trigger block was slab sided and curved downwards away from the chamber in true Diana style. It is safe to assume that these were brought back from Germany after the Second World War and sold in Britain.

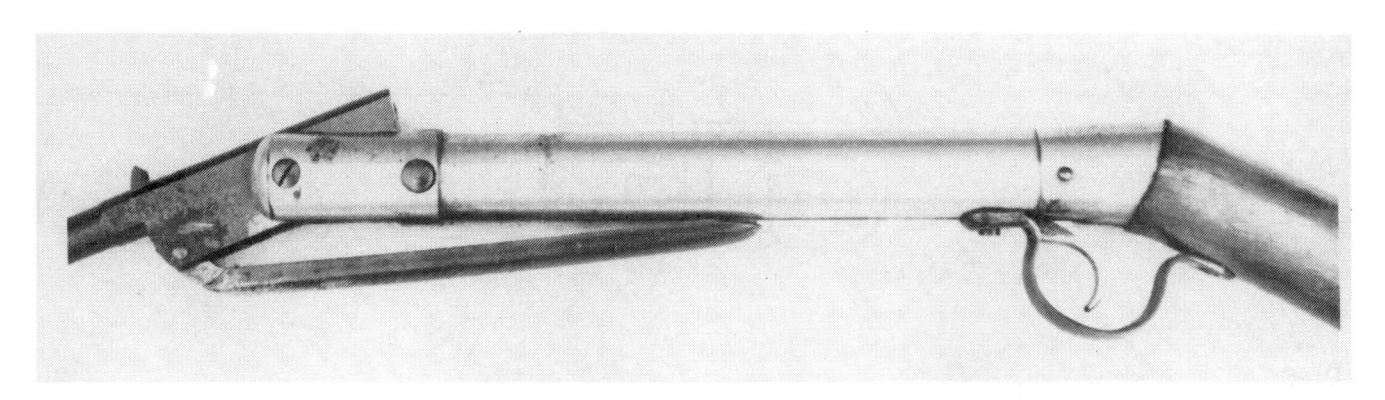

The lightweight Millita style air rifle retailed by "Lepco"

MODEL   Millita style air rifle.

MAKER   Theodore Bergmann, Gaggenau, Baden, Germany.

DATE   This style of side button barrel release from around 1930 to 1939. Note the following changes in design, round section barrel and rifled bore, chamber end plug incorporating the barrel support arms and side button machined in one piece and braized on to the chamber, pressed metal trigger guard, whereas earlier ones were cast. All these are pointers to the fact this is a late version of the middle and light pattern Millita air rifle.

VALUATION   £30—£60. ($45—$90).

DETAILS   Typical Germanic finish, the nickel plated chamber, trigger and guard, and cocking lever with the blued barrel. 39½ inches long with a 17¼ inch rifled .177 barrel. A serial number "8" appears on all major parts and "138" stamped inside the metal butt plate and written in pencil on the butt face, could be that the butt plates and stocks were matched up elsewhere. The above example had "LEPCO" in a diamond shaped logo with "MADE IN GERMANY" stamped on the stock. Lepco being the trade name for LePersonne & Co. Ltd., 7 Old Bailey, London E.C.4., a retailing firm that also placed their name on air rifles made in Belgium. Many of these are found with "B" cast into the butt plate and for this reason I have chosen Bergmann as the manufacturer.

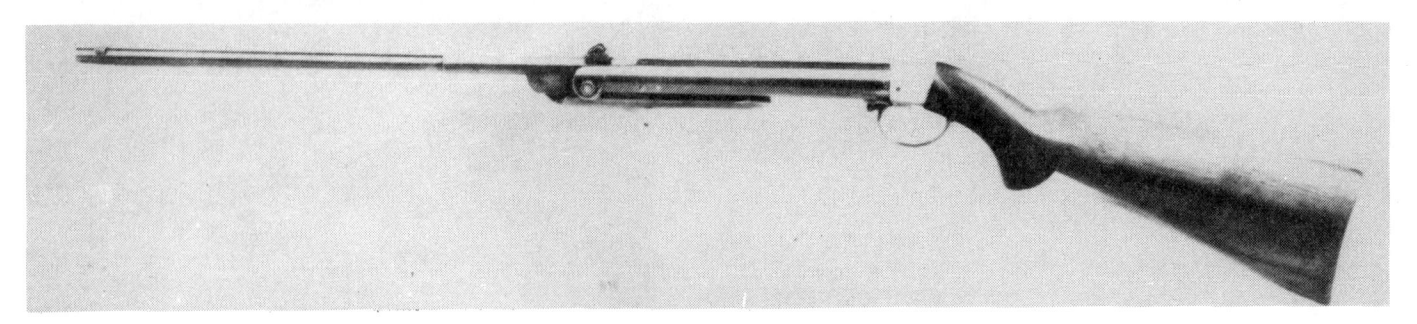

The "Millita" D-Model Club air rifle

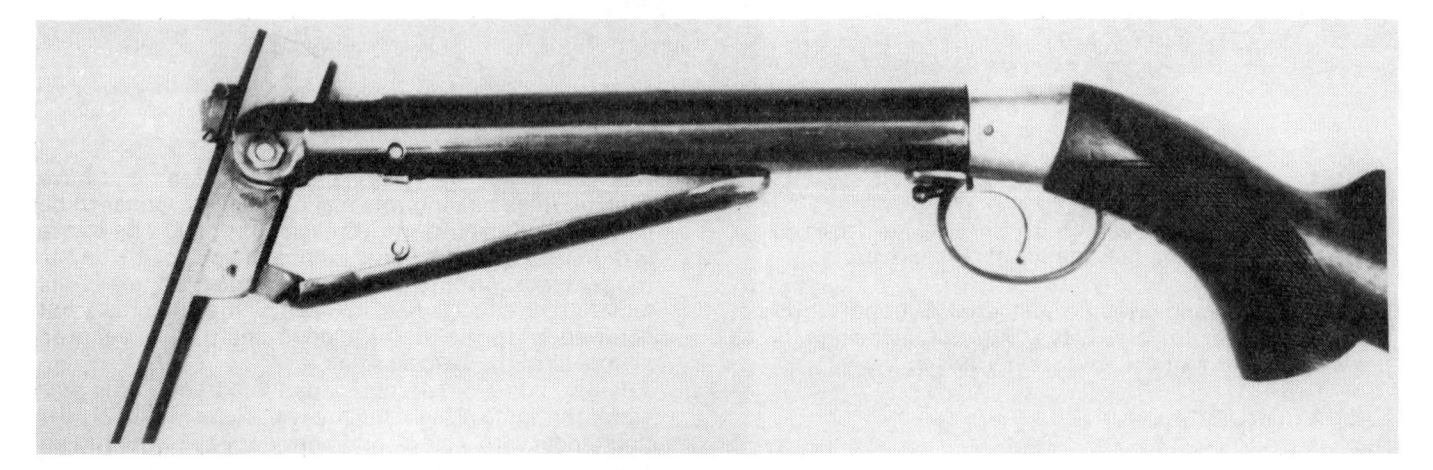

Close up of Model D action

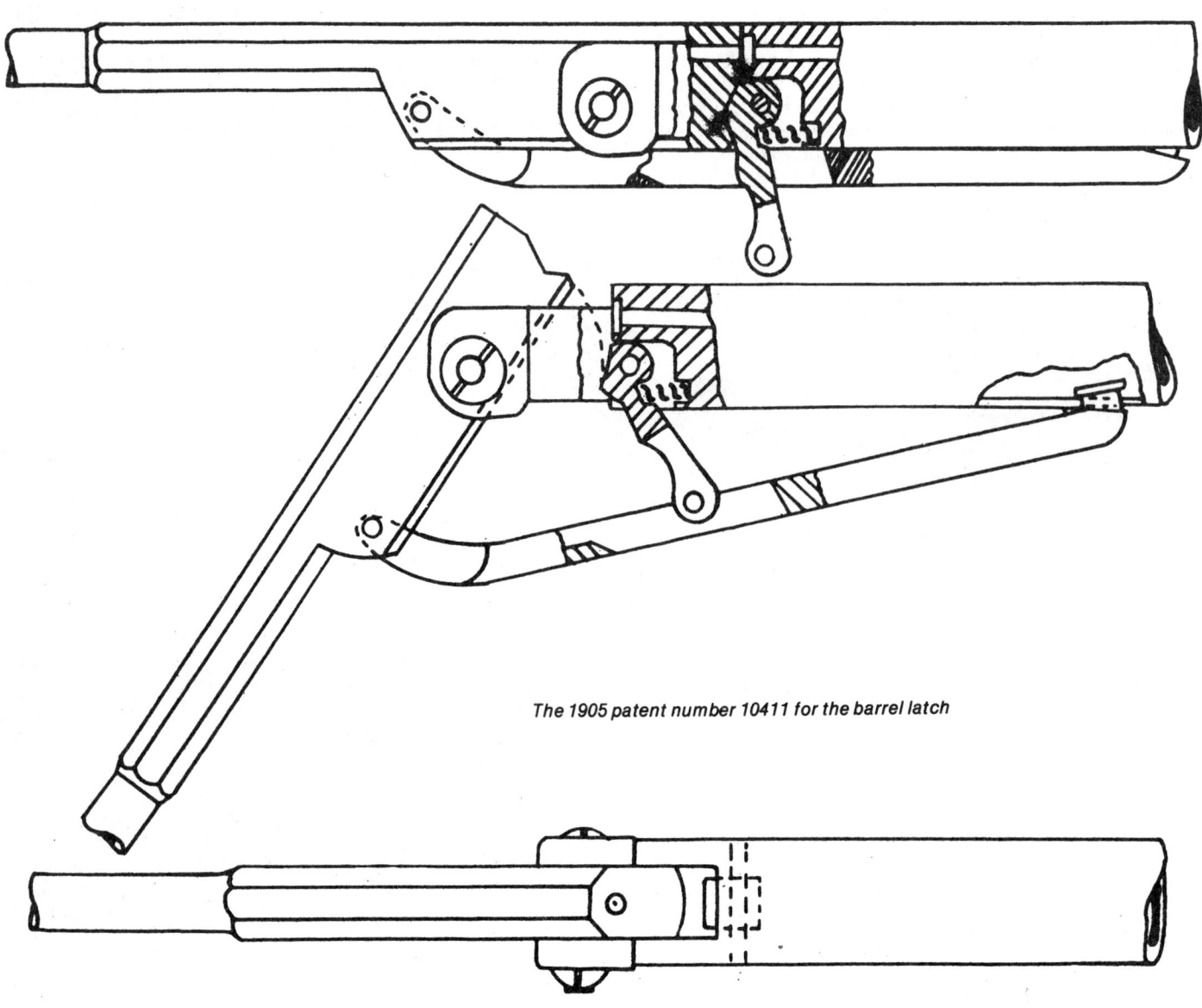

The 1905 patent number 10411 for the barrel latch

THE PATENT "MILLITA" AIR RIFLE (Underlever)
NEW MODEL

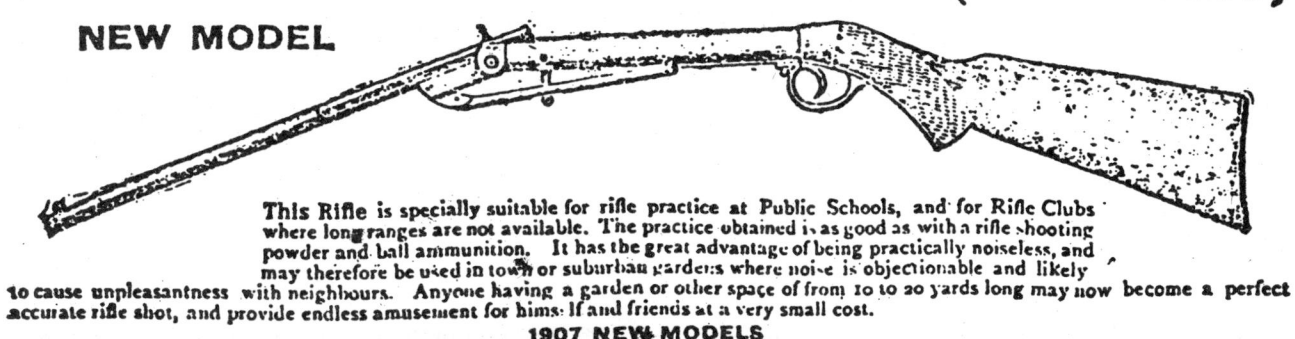

This Rifle is specially suitable for rifle practice at Public Schools, and for Rifle Clubs where long ranges are not available. The practice obtained is as good as with a rifle shooting powder and ball ammunition. It has the great advantage of being practically noiseless, and may therefore be used in town or suburban gardens where noise is objectionable and likely to cause unpleasantness with neighbours. Anyone having a garden or other space of from 10 to 20 yards long may now become a perfect accurate rifle shot, and provide endless amusement for himself and friends at a very small cost.

1907 NEW MODELS
D Model Millita Club Air Gun, rifled, specially sighted, pistol grip stock, heavy weight, 35/-. D Model Millita Club Air Gun, rifled, specially sighted, pistol grip stock, light weight, 25/-. Ordinary Model Millita, 16/-, 22/6 and 32/6.

MARTIN PULVERMANN & CO., 31 MINORIES, LONDON, E.C.

A November 1907 advert illustrating the D Model Millita Club air rifle

MODEL "Millita" D Model Club Air Rifle — Lightweight.

MAKER F. Langenham, Zella Street, Blasii, Thuringia, Germany. Imported into Britain by Martin Pulvermann, Lancaster Buildings, 26 Minories, London.

DATE 1906 to 1945.

VALUATION £40—£80. ($60—$120).

DETAILS The "Lightweight" model of the "Original V" air rifle as elsewhere. 39 inches (99 cms) long with a 17¾ inch (45 cms) .177 rifled barrel. Barrel is octagonal to round with dovetail mounted sights. Originally the finish was a blued barrel with nickel plated chamber, cocking lever and everything else. The foresight was advertised at one time as having a pearl tip, whilst the rearsight is not the usual one encountered, it usually being a screw adjustable blade rearsight. The one featured on air rifle serial number 34569-W has also been seen on large Gem air rifles. The bar is pivoted and just swings up and down at will, so if loose will also fall at will. The top barrel flat is stamped "MILLITA PATENT" and the serial number appears on the breech face. The serial number will also be stamped on the air chamber and the last three digits on other minor parts. Traces of nickel plating can be seen on all parts except for the barrel which was always blued. The stock on these air rifles is very well designed and feels good when held. Hand chequered stock, usually hardwood, and often has a pistol grip cap as well as the metal butt plate. Trigger adjustment is by way of screw through the front of the trigger guard. The size of the above corresponds to the Middle of the range of three lengths, but is often referred to as the Lightweight.

During 1906 the Millita was advertised in two sizes, heavyweight at 35/- and lightweight for 25/- and were available from the importers Martin Pulvermann & Co., whose address at that time was 31 Minories, London. By 1907 the above became the D Model Millita Club air rifle and the following were on offer; D Model Millita Club airgun, rifled and specially sighted, pistol grip stock, heavyweight, 35/-. D Model Millita Club airgun, rifled, specially sighted, pistol grip stock, lightweight 25/-. The above example is this lightweight Model D Club. Finally; Ordinary Model Millita, 16/-, 22/6, 32/6. These last three models could well be the first models with the side button barrel release as these appeared in three lengths and three weights. By 1911 the stock was advertised as being walnut, they were usually fitted with a screw adjustable rearsight with blade, but the above example must have been fitted to special order. The heavyweight D Model Club was 106 cms long weighed 3 kilograms. They were both available in .177 rifled only. The heavyweight became the "Original V".

The patent for the underlever barrel catch through the cocking link was number 10411 and was placed and accepted in 1905. It covered the design of the catch and the fact that it took up any wear by closing tighter on itself. It failed to mention that the slot in the cocking lever caused a point of weakness.

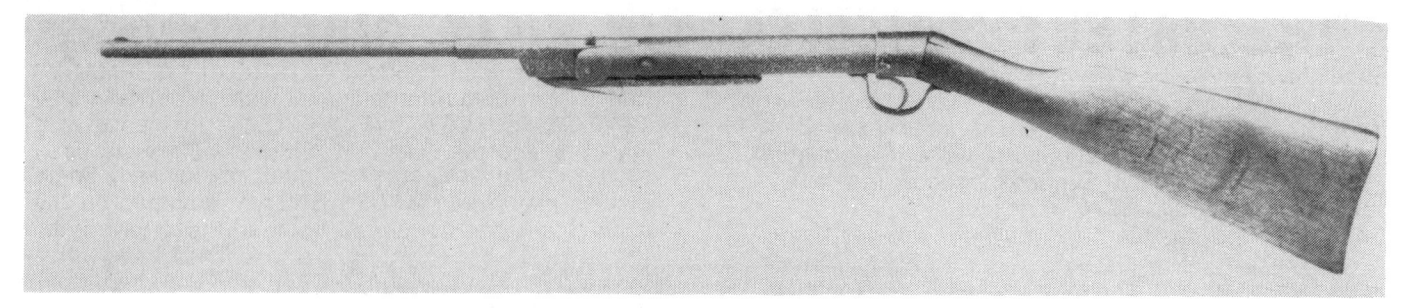

"Small" Model Millita air rifle

MODEL Three models of push button action Millita air rifles appear to have been manufactured. See other pages. Assume the above to be the smallest model, "unless you know differently".

MAKER Friedrich Langenham, Zelle Street, Blasii, Thuringia, Germany. Imported into Britain by Martin Pulvermann, 31 Minories, London. Address at time of import.

DATE With side button barrel release from around 1902 to 1912. Also sold under the "Pfeil" name in the 1930s with minor design alterations.

VALUATION £20—£40, £11a—£26a.
($30—$60, $17a—$39a).

DETAILS Example of the above in rather a dilapidated state, but gives some idea of the model involved. Measures three feet long with a 15¾ inch smoothbore barrel. Foresight appears to be a simple blade set into the barrel whilst the rearsight is missing but does have a dovetail fitting. Barrel octagonal to round with "MANUFACTURED IN GERMANY" stamped on one of the flats, other markings are not visible due to pitting of metal work. Serial number 580 stamped on breech of barrel, air chamber near trigger. The metal butt plate is missing but stamped into the wooden butt is the number "87", could be a date stamp, but stock made before the introduction of the above model. Length of air chamber from barrel pivot to trigger block 8⅛ inches. Trigger guard missing from the above. A common occurrence was for these Millita air rifles to be sold to a retailer and then be sold under a different name. Such an airgun bearing the "ARROW" trade name with an arrow running through the name has been seen, serial number 55. This model being unusual in that it was blued all over instead of the more standard finish of nickel plated air chamber etc. Barrel pivot pin is tapered and should only be removed from left to right as the airgun is pointed away from you. Pins replaced from right to left.

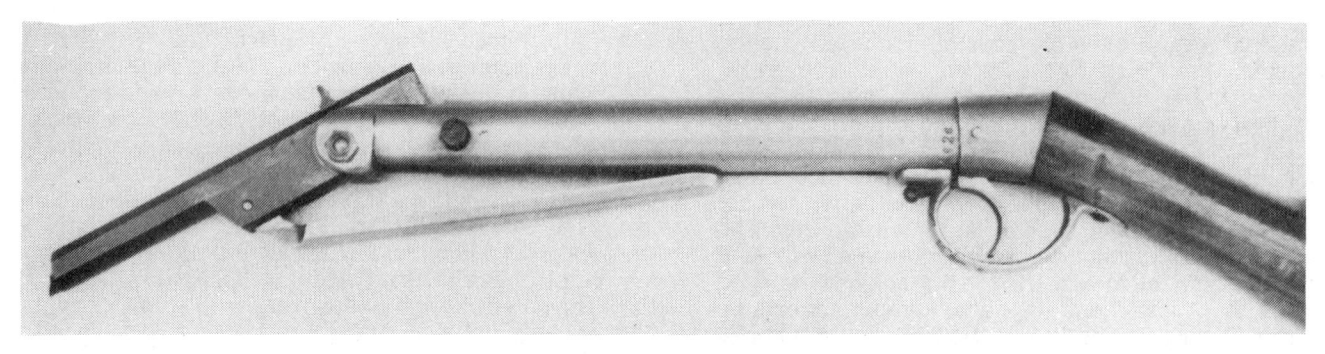

"Lightweight" Millita

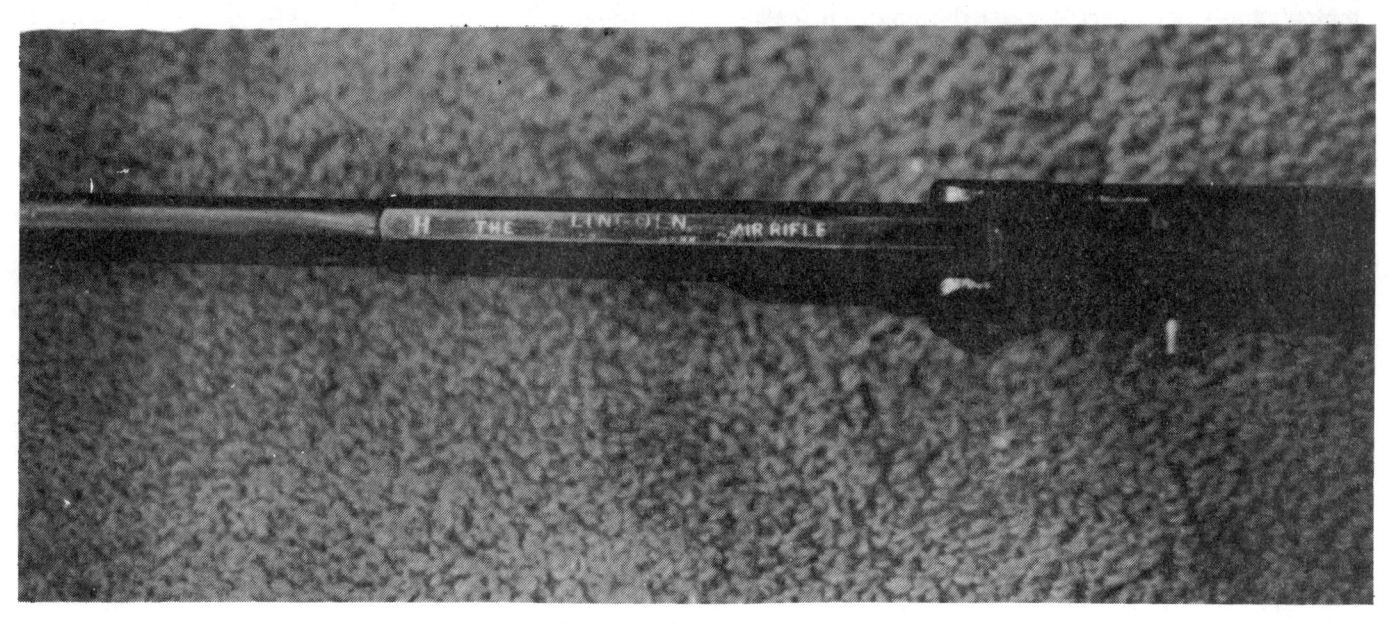

"H The Lincoln Air Rifle" German Millita. (This may also appear as the 'LJ Air Rifle')

MODEL Three models were manufactured, assume the above to be the middle of the range. These three only apply to the push button barrel action.

MAKER Friedrich Langenham, Zelle Street, Blasii, Thuringia, Germany. Imported into this country by Martin Pulvermann, 31 Minories, London. Previously of 26 Minories, London.

DATE With the side push-in button barrel release around 1902 to 1912. Later sold under various trade names up until 1939.

VALUATION £30–£60. ($45–$90).

DETAILS Serial number (64626) appears stamped on trigger block and on rear of air chamber, also stamped on breech of barrel. Last three digits appear on the inside surface of the cocking lever. 39½ inches with 17¾ inch smoothbore barrel. Trigger adjustment screw is through the front of the trigger guard. For details of the patent barrel catch see "Guns Review" March 1978. On top three flats of octagonal part of barrel is stamped "MANUFACTURED IN GERMANY" then the crossed rifle trademark with the letters "L — Z" finally "MILLITA REGISTERED". The above also manufactured the "Gem" air rifle as both have been seen bearing the crossed guns trademark. Some models may have "MADE ABROAD" stamped on the underside of the barrel flat. Some of these have been seen with "H THE LINCOLN AIR RIFLE" stamped on the barrel flat and bearing the standing man trademark on the butt with "REGISTERED LINCOLN JEFFERIES". These have been assumed to be Lincoln Jeffries when in actual fact they are not. It is safe to assume that they were imported and the actions were given the same lettering as their underlever air rifles which were made by B.S.A. By present day standards this would have been considered a little naughty.

Serial numbers seen for the middle size Millita air rifle range from 446 upto 64626. One of which, serial number 46577, bore a repair label dated 2—1—12.

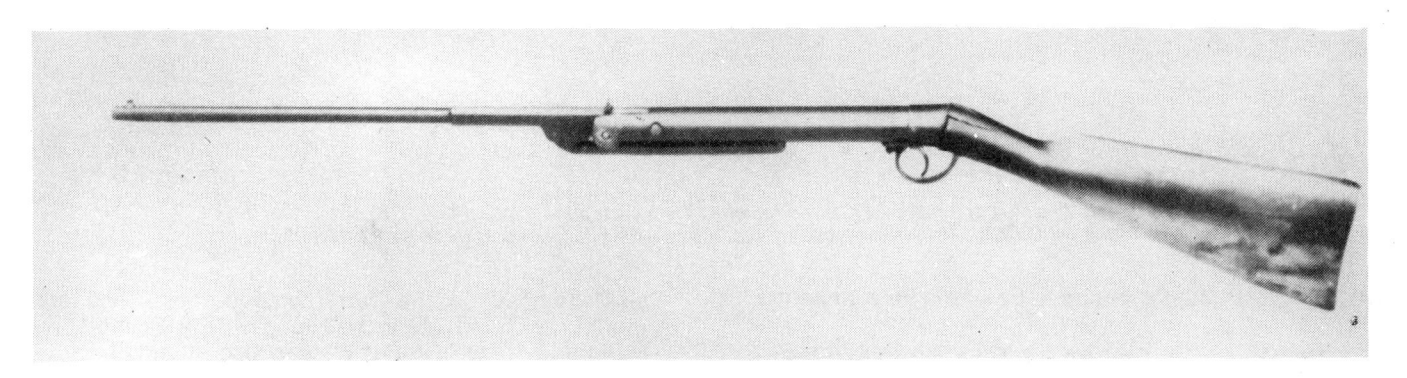

The "Heavyweight" Millita air rifle

MODEL Millita. (Heavyweight Model). See also "The Ansonia".

MAKER Friedrich Langenham, Zella Street, Blasii, Thuringia, Germany.

DATE The push button barrel catch was patented in 1901. A later improvement was patented in 1905, see "Guns Review" March 1978. Advertisements seen for the above barrel catch run from around 1906 to 1911. Sold under many traders names until 1939.

VALUATION Heavyweight Militia, £40–£80, ($60–$150). Ansonia side button air rifle £30–£150. ($75–$225).

DETAILS Serial number 2413 appears on the trigger block, air cylinder, face of barrel breech and the last three digits on the inside of the cocking lever. 42 inches long with 19 inch barrel. Octagonal to round barrel with the crossed rifle trademark, "MANUFACTURED IN GERMANY" and "MILLITA REGISTERED" stamped on the octagonal flats. All external surfaces except for barrel bear traces of nickel plating. The above were imported into this country by Martin Pulvermann, Lancaster Buildings, 26 Minories, London. Trigger guard has trigger adjustment screw through the front, screw has spherical head. Above model has been advertised as the "Bull's Eye" with a rifled barrel and available in .177 only.

E. Anson of 14 Steelhouse Lane, Birmingham, also retailed the above heavyweight Model Millita air rifle. One such specimen has been seen with serial number 17763 with "THE ANSONIA" RIFLED BARREL" stamped on the top barrel flat and "E. ANSON & CO., 14 STEELHOUSE LANE, BIRMN." stamped on the stock. It also had a white metal oval set in the comb of the stock. This being a very clear case of a British manufacturer importing German air rifles, and putting his own name on them and causing some confusion in later years, as with the break barrel Lincoln Jeffries air rifles! These might have been made to special order as contrary to the more usual Germanic finish of nickel plated action the "Ansonia" Millita air rifle was blued overall, we British being somewhat less flamboyant, and being more practical. They might have even been worked at the Anson factory before being released as the stock was fitted with an escutcheon and the barrel pivot cross bolt and nut were cross hatched chequered.

Serial numbers seen range from 2413 up to 24139 with 7595 being in .25 and 17763 being stamped "THE ANSONIA RIFLED BARREL" and the stock marked "E. ANSON & CO. 14 STEELHOUSE LANE, BIRM.", and air rifle 19890 was stamped "H THE LINCOLN AIR RIFLE" and its stock marked "LINCOLN JEFFRIES, 121 STEELHOUSE LANE, BIRMINGHAM".

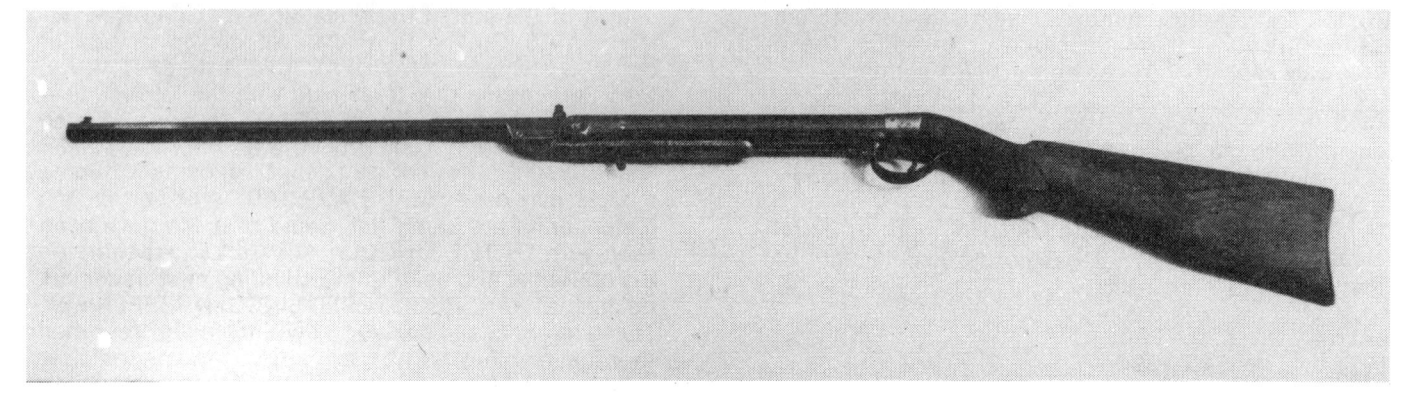

Millita "Original V" early model

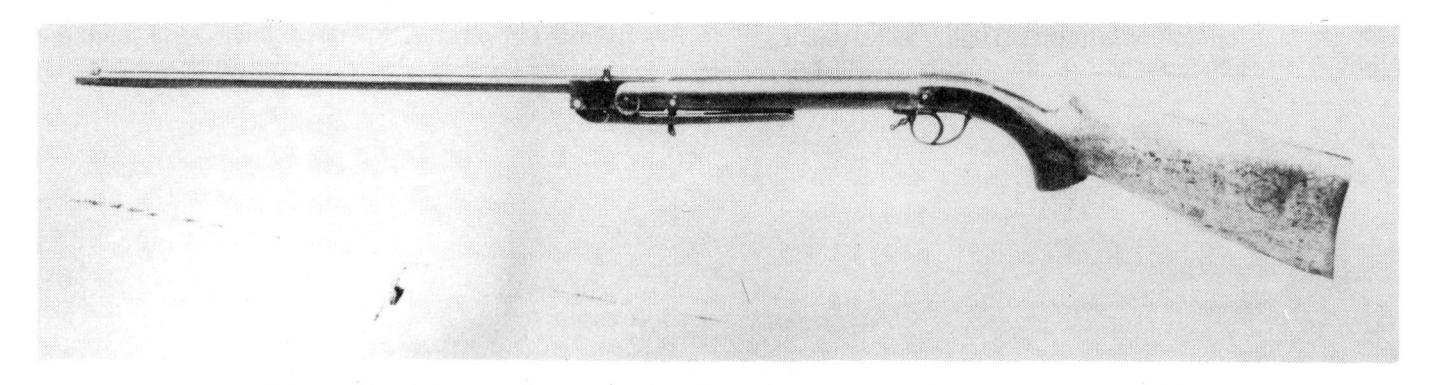

"Original V" by F. Langenham. Later model with rifled, and round section barrel. Note circular logo on stock with "Original V". The above was stamped with F.L.Z. circular trademark on air chamber

MODEL "Millita" imported by Martin Pulvermann.

MAKER F. Langenham of Zella Strasse, Blasii Thuringia, Germany.

DATE Middle 1920s to early 1940s.

VALUATION £40—£80.
($60—$120).

DETAILS Two versions were made, rifled or smoothbore. Most of the smoothbores had a side push in button barrel release, whilst rifled with the underlatch. First advertised around 1907 as the "D Model Club" but the above has "Original V" stamped on the top barrel flat. The "Original V" was advertised around the 1930s. Serial number of above 92492. Serial number also appears on the breech of barrel. 42 inches long.
Seen advertised in a 1927 catalogue by G. C. Bell & Sons of Glasgow as the "Clyde" Club Air Rifle. It would appear that they were imported into Britain and distributed to various retailers for sale under their own trade names. Have also seen the above stamped with Lincoln Jeffries name and erroneously advertised as such. In 1927 stated as having the "new pattern locking bolt". Advertised weight 6 lbs. Available in .177 rifled at 40/- and .25 smoothbore for 44/-. Was also advertised with an adjustable back sight similar to that fitted to the pre-war B.S.A. underlever. On air rifle number L34226 the air chamber was stamped with the circular trademark bearing the letters F.L.Z. and a smaller logo was stamped on the barrel breech face. This later model measured 45¾ inches long with a 22 inch .177 rifled barrel. "ORIGINAL V" was also stamped on the stock. During 1933 it was advertised in two lengths, 42½ inches (108 cm) and 46 inches (117 cm). The smaller model had a straight hand stock with no chequering, a shorter barrel and simple sights. It was made in .177 and .22 smoothbore. The larger version had a chequered pistol grip stock, elevation adjustable rearsight and white metal tipped foresight. Walnut stock with two metal caps, one for the butt and the other for the pistol grip. This was sold in .177 and .22 rifled.
A further variation of trademarks appears on serial number 121477, this had the circular logo on the stock with "ORIGINAL V" and on the barrel flat, "FREDR. JACOB BARTELS, WEISBADEN", this can safely be assumed to be the retailer, whilst on the air chamber "PRAZIONS LUFTGEWEHR — ORIGINAL V — CAL 4½ m/m — FR. LANGENHAM — ZELLA MEHLIS".
Another retailing name under which these were sold was "THE BISLEY AIR RIFLE". The example seen, serial number G23226, had the crossed air rifles trademark stamped on the uppermost barrel flat. It had a .177 rifled barrel and a chequered pistol grip stock with metal butt plate. One little extra was the stamping of "1" near the breech to indicate the calibre.
On air rifle 129535 the barrel was stamped "ORIGINAL V MODEL. 1929". It was the 46 inch version and was fitted with a much uprated trigger mechanism with machined trigger/sear unit and pinned machine trigger guard. In all a very well made air rifle, and is certainly more collectable than the smaller Model V.

A WONDERFUL AIR RIFLE.

.. The New "Millita" Air Rifle. ..

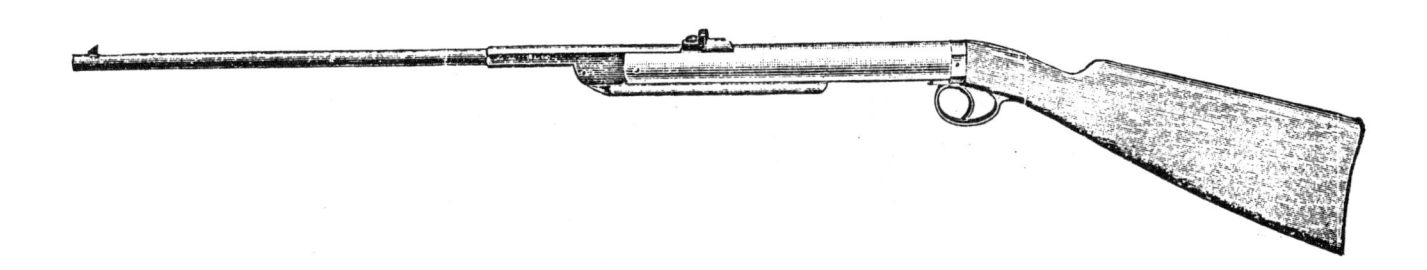

MODEL "New" Millita Air Rifle.

MAKER Friedrich Langenham, Zeller Street, Blasii, Thuringia, Germany.

DATE From around 1910 to the early 1930s.

VALUATION £50—£100. ($75—$150).

DETAILS The third style of barrel latch from the Langenham factory. First was the side push-in button followed by the underneath lever through the cocking link, finally came this combined sliding rearsight and latch. The sides of the sight are serrated for gripping. Only the foresight is adjustable and this for windage only. Calibre of above is .25 smoothbore. The above design left a very simple breech face with no further milling required other than just finishing off. Serial number (1055) stamped on all major parts. Top of barrel flats stamped "MANUFACTURED IN GERMANY" and "MILLITA REGISTERED" with the crossed rifles trademark and the letters "L + Z". Trigger adjustment by way of screw through front of trigger guard, these adjuster screws had a circular rounded solid head. Above fitted with a straight hand stock with metal butt plate, but pistol grip stocks were also fitted.

According to a 1911 German catalogue the following combinations of the above were sold, strangely enough they were all listed as being 4.5 calibre, but I'm pretty sure that this might be a mistake. It was also stated that they were blued all over, but ones seen have all been nickel plated except for the barrel which was blued.

Straight hand stock   **Pistol grip stock**
1. 2 kg. 2. 2.5 kg. 3. 3.0 kg. 4. 2.6 kg. 5. 3.1 kg.
96 cm. 104 cm. 110 cm. 105 cm. 109 cm.

4.5 mm cal. (All listed as 4.5 mm, but all seen have been either .177 or .25). During the middle 1920s the G. C. Bell Gun Company of Glasgow sold the above as the "Bell-Craig" with a rifled bore in two sizes, straight grip for 25/6 and the heavier model with a pistol grip for 30/6.

Although the above variation did not appear until about 1910 the rearsight barrel latch appeared in a patent dated 1895. This was for a repeating action but clearly shows the above style of rearsight. The patent was by Theodor Hornhauer of Schmeidegasse, Dresden, Germany. There could be some connection.

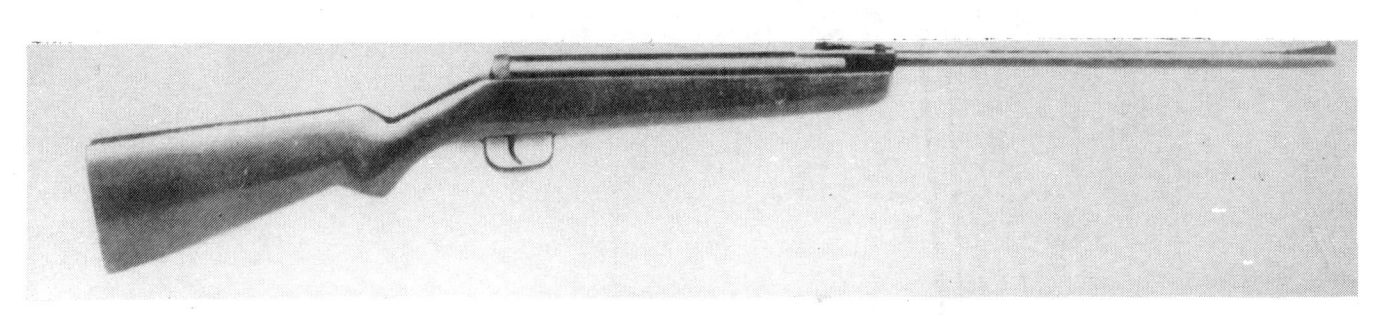

The NAC/Norica "Commando"

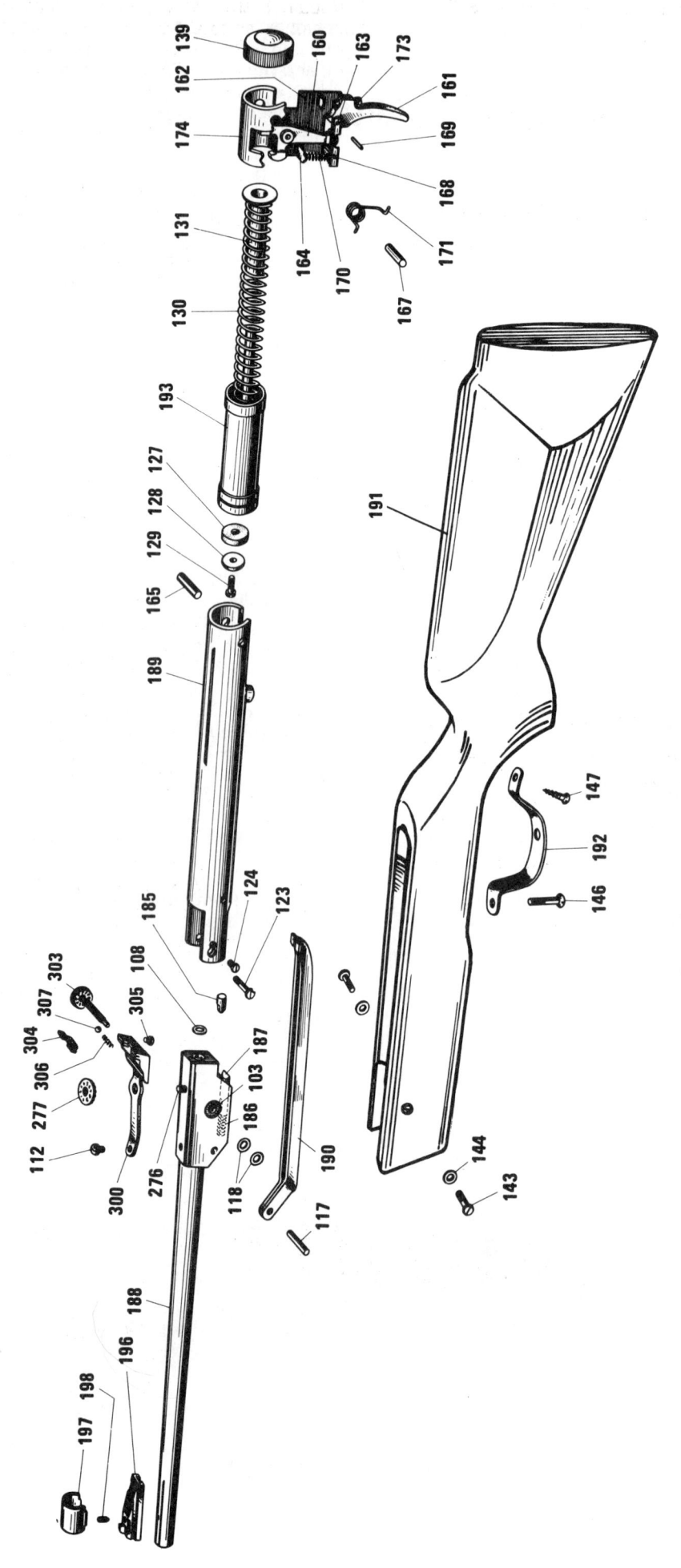

Parts diagram for the NAC/Norica Commando 61-C

MODEL Commando.

MAKER 'NAC" by Norberto Arizmendi S.A., Avda de Bilbao, 16 Eibar (Guipuzcoa), Spain. The Commando may also appear under the Norica trade name from the same firm.

DATE From early 1960s to date with changes to style and specification.

VALUATION £30–£60. ($45–$90).

DETAILS A full length and strongly made air rifle. Sold in either .177 or .22 calibre. 40½ inches long (103 cms), with a 17⅜ inch (45 cms) barrel. The blade foresight is dovetail mounted and usually has a hood protector. L.H.S. of breech black stamped "NAC" in a diamond with the calibre and serial numbers. The other side has "MADE IN SPAIN". Air chamber is grooved for telescopic sight. Two stage trigger with adjustment through hole in guard at rear. The Mk. II has a very nicely styled but plain stock. The rearsight is screw mounted on to a dovetail block. During the late 1960s it was described as the Commando Mk. II by A.S.I. Usually there was a gold and black transfer on the air chamber, as found on nearly all the A.S.I. range of air rifles. In 1972 it was advertised as the Commando Mk. III, and then by 1975 we were back to the Mk. II again! Advertised weight 6¼ lbs. At some stage in its life it may have been fitted with a two stage non-adjustable trigger. By 1976 the Commando had changed its style of stock from the rather nice plain shape to a futuristic thing with a swollen fore-end similar to the present day Relums. During the early 1980s it became the Commando 61-C. It is of interest the way foreign catalogues manage to construct the English part so here is an actual quote from the Norica catalogue about the Commando 61-C; "Compressed airgun type Commando for to shoot with a lead pellet or dart. With graduables sight and trigger. Smooth and very easily compression. We served this airgun with plain or rifled barrel and blued metal parts. Four characteristics of this gun; great solidity, easy handling, precision and very beautiful".

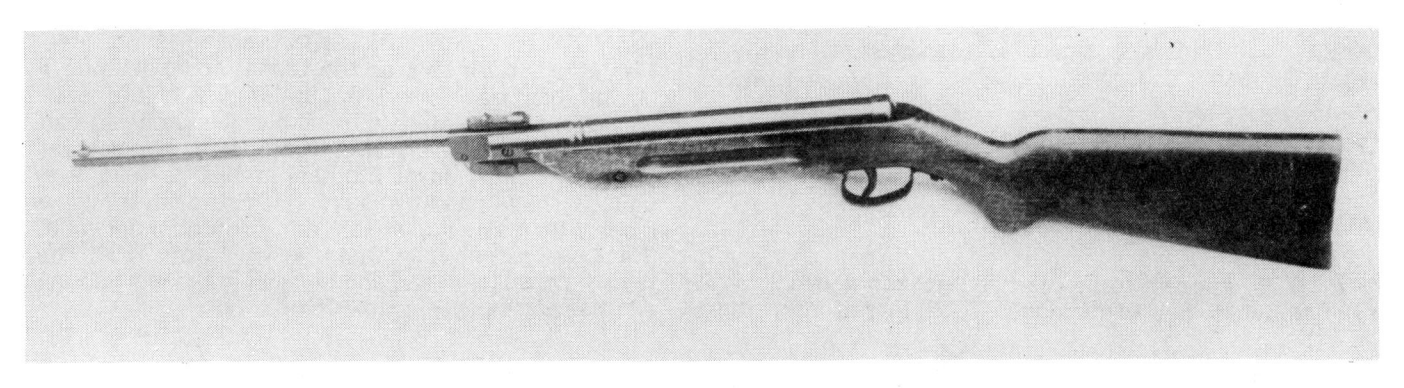

Ojmar Model 12

MODEL 12.

MAKER Ojmar.

DATE Would assume 1970s.

VALUATION £20–£40. ($30–$60).

DETAILS Small size air rifle. 35⅝ inches long with a 13⅞ inch .177 rifled barrel. Unusual pillar foresight and ramp rearsight. Underside of barrel breech stamped "O". Air chamber has two distinct grooves similar to the B.S.F. air rifles. Double link cocking lever. Top of air chamber has oil hole and further towards rear stamped "OJMAR MOD 12". Looks very much like European manufacture. A similar style was imported under the "Comet" trade name.

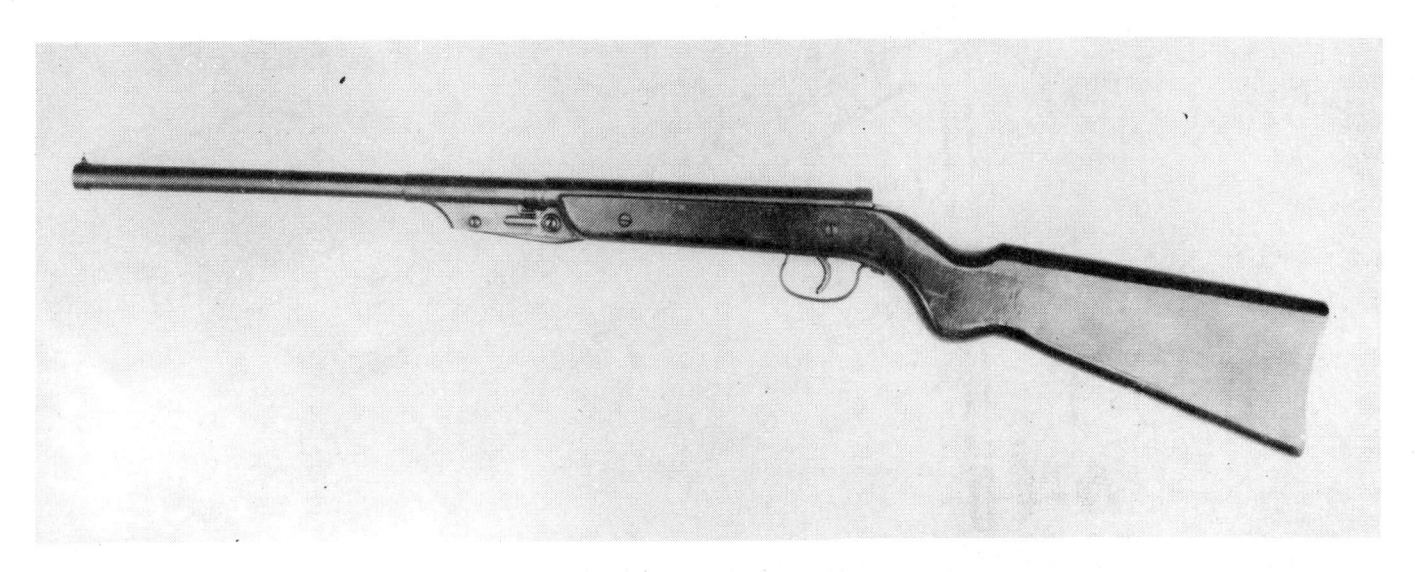

Original Model 16 air rifle

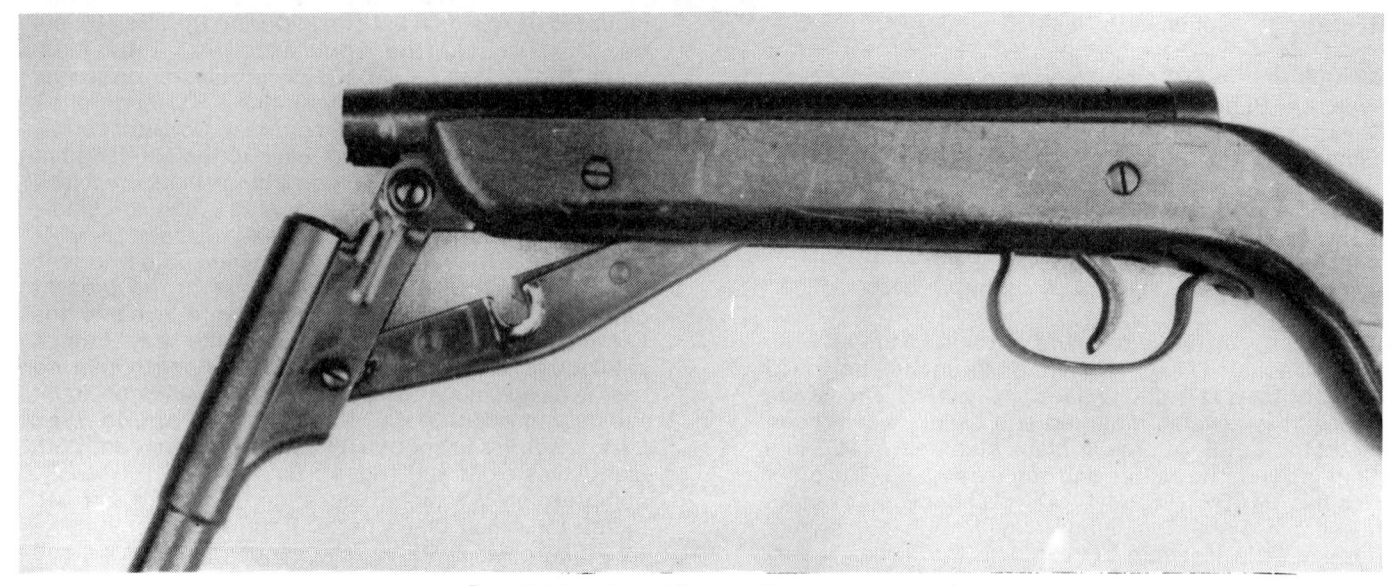

Barrel latch action of Original Model 16 air rifle

MODEL 16.

MAKER "Original", Mayer & Grammelspacher, Rastatt, Germany.

DATE Production resumed after the War in September 1950.

VALUATION £10—£30. ($15—$45).

DETAILS Appears to be the fully stocked version of the Model 15. See Diana Model 15. 32½ inches long with a 12 inch brass smoothbore .177 barrel. Tinplate construction. Top of air chamber stamped "ORIGINAL — MOD 16" with "FOREIGN" stamped on side. Mentioned in Smith's as the Diana Model 16. Above design has been used by British Diana and seen Slavia/Relem tinplates. Unusual barrel latch being part of the cocking lever. The barrel latch system was patented by the Mayer Brothers in 1930 to 1931. It is unusual that a patent was brought out to cover such a modest item as a tinplate air rifle. For further details of the above patent see "Guns Review" April 1980. The type of barrel latch can still be seen in today's tinplate air rifles and has been copied world-wide.

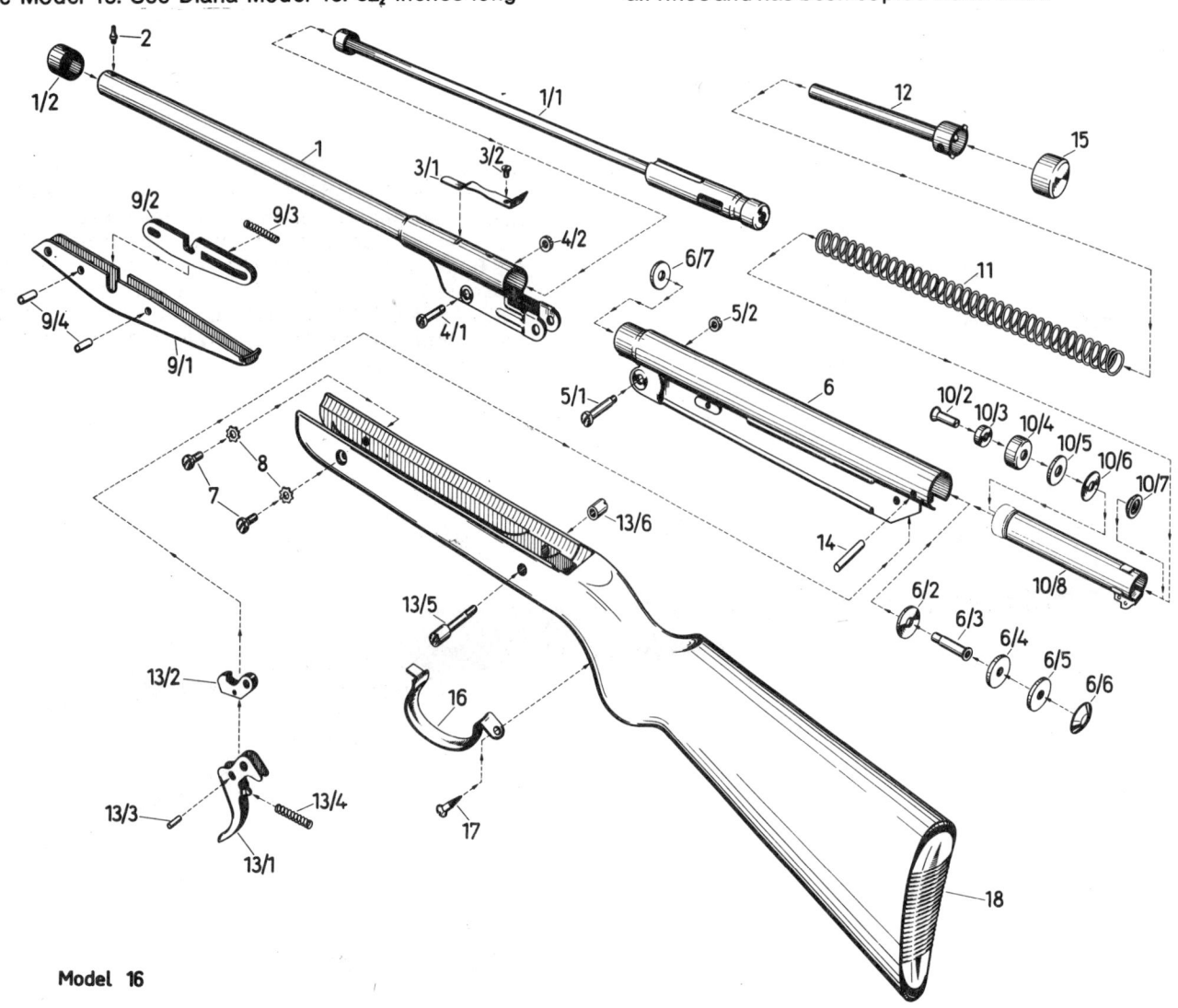

Model 16

168

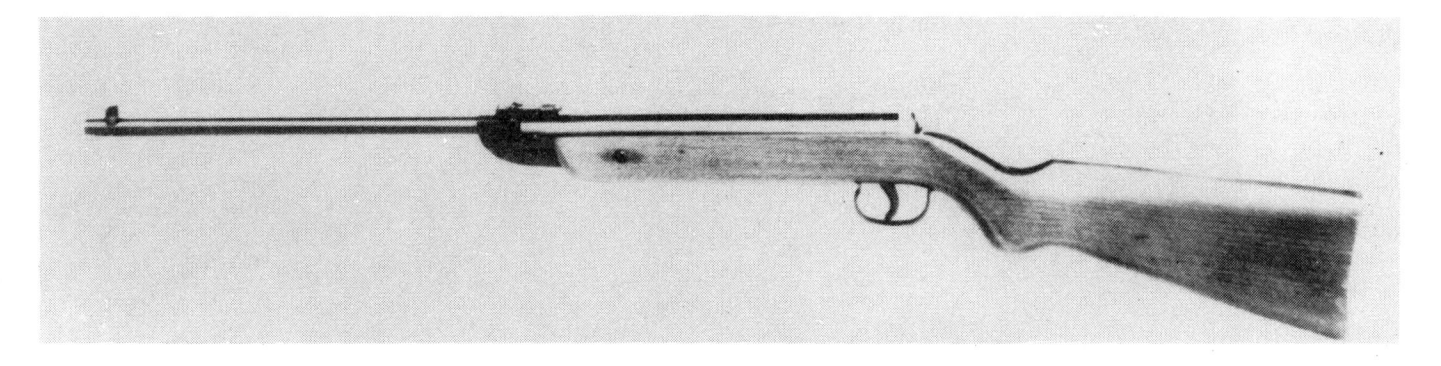

Original Model 23

MODEL Model 23.

MAKER "Original" Mayer and Grammelspacher, Rastatt, Germany.

DATE From August 1951.

VALUATION £10—£30. ($15—$45).

DETAILS 35½ inches long. Slightly smaller than the model 25. .177 rifled barrel. All metal and has ball bearing barrel release. Double pull trigger release, but does not appear to be adjustable. Ramp rearsight. Stamped on top and air cylinder "ORIGINAL MOD 23" and "MADE IN GERMANY" on the side. Serial number not visible, may be under the stock.

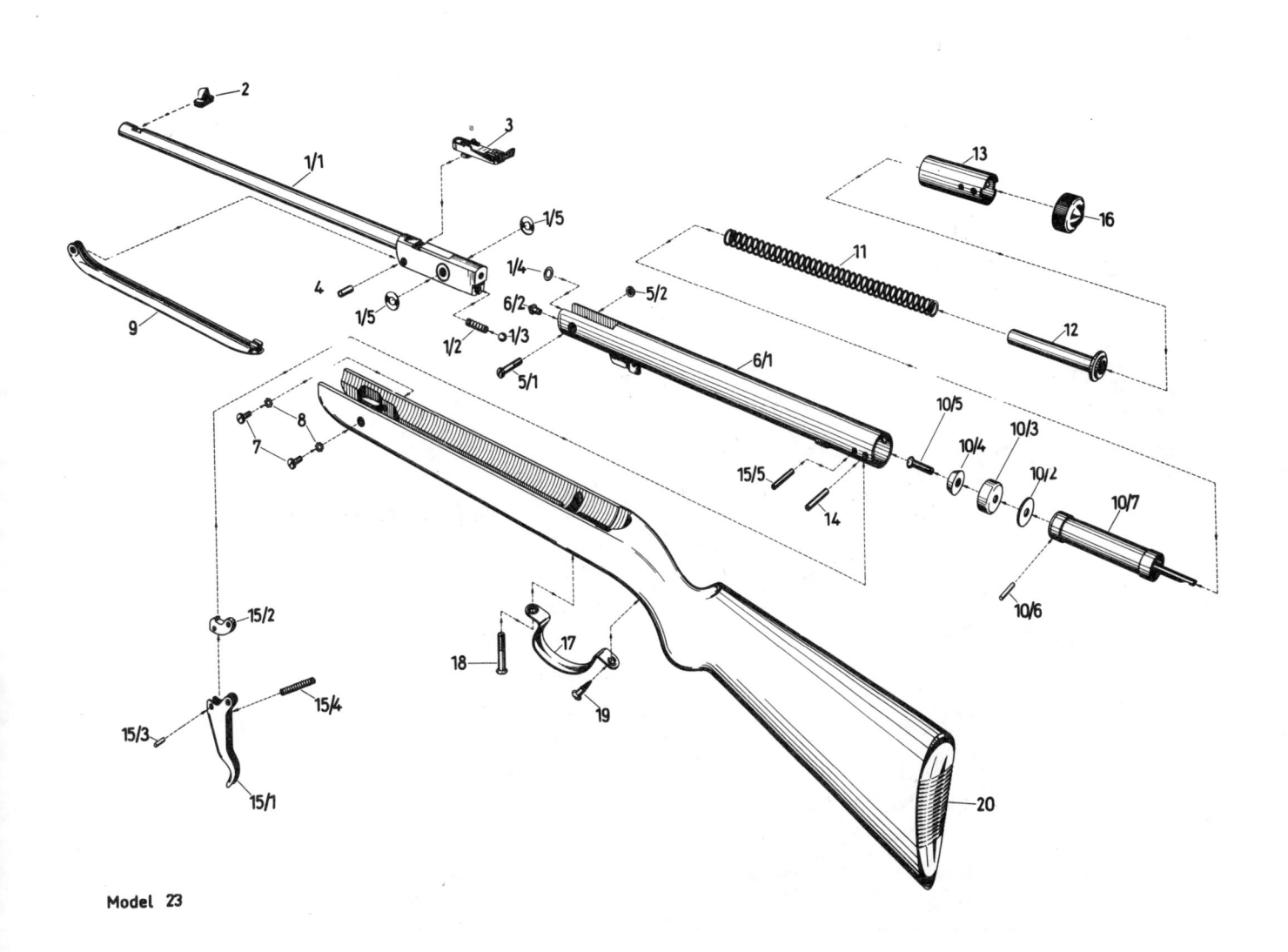

Model 23

169

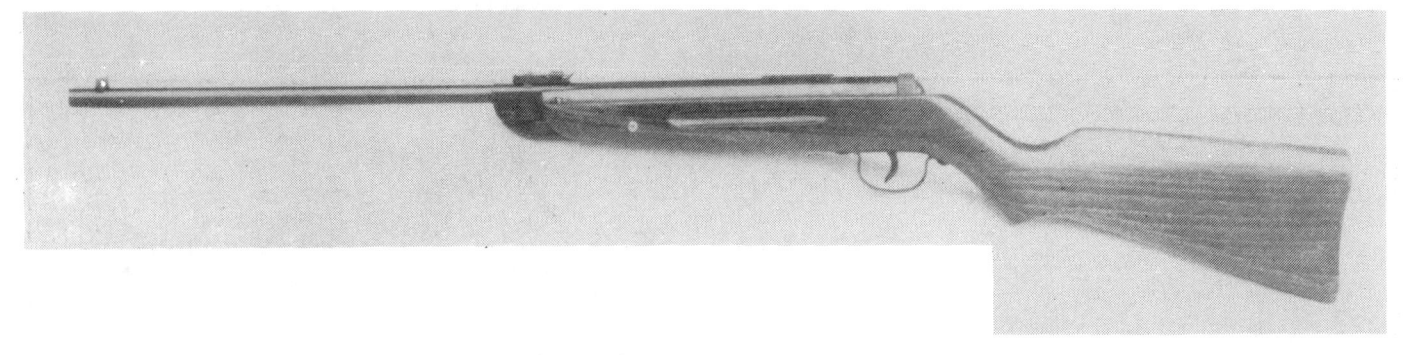

Original Model 25

MODEL 25.

MAKER Mayer & Grammelspacher, Rastatt, Germany.

DATE The "Original" trade name appeared in the early 1950s. Above style from the early 1950s to the early 1970s when an improved rearsight appeared, all plastic and fully adjustable. The Model 25 became available during December 1951.

VALUATION £20−£40. ($30−$60).

DETAILS Identical to the late pre-war Diana Model 25 and the post-war British Diana Model 25. A confusing picture, but such are the "Spoils of War"!

Very sturdy little air rifle that can still be seen giving mule-like service on many a fairground shooting gallery. 38 inches long with a 15⅞ inch rifled barrel in either .177 or .22 calibre. Blade foresight and ramp style rearsight adjustable for elevation only. Serial number not visible, but is stamped on other examples inspected. Top of air chamber stamped "ORIGINAL MOD 25" with "MADE IN GERMANY" on the side. Advertised weight 5 lb. Solid one piece stock without butt plate. Double pull trigger with no adjustment. Earlier models may have been stamped with "DIANA" and the Huntress trademark. They had a ball bearing barrel latch. Although the rearsight was unaltered the foresight was made from black plastic and mounted on parallel dovetails. Sold in America as the "Gecado" Model 25.

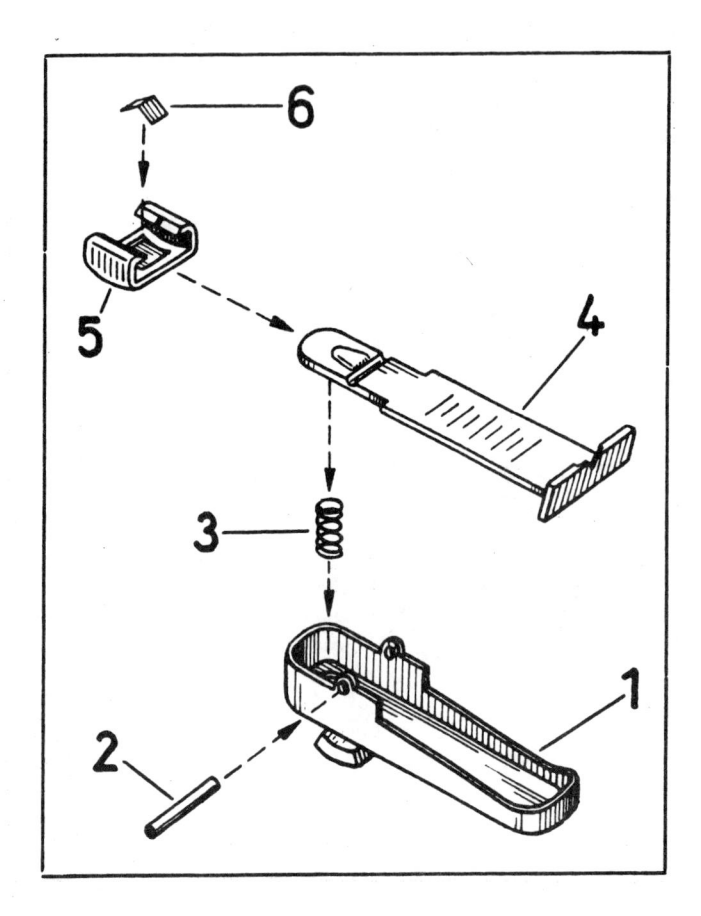

Spare Parts for Tangent Rearsight

No.	
1	Rearsight base with foot
2	Rearsight pin
3	Rearsight blade spring
4	Rearsight blade
5	Rearsight slide
6	Spring for rearsight slide

Tangent rearsight as fitted to early Diana and "Original" airguns

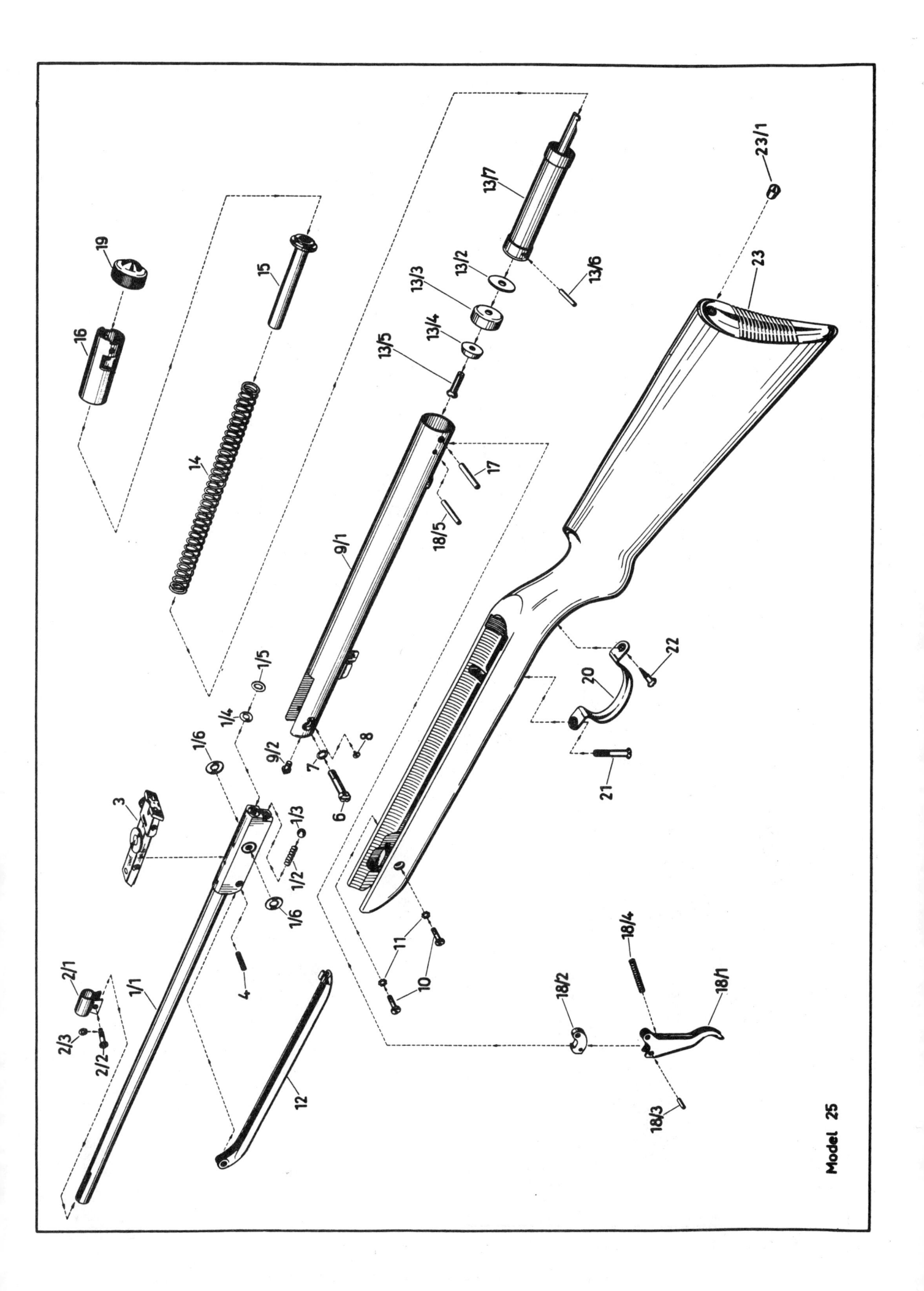

Model 25

Model 25 D

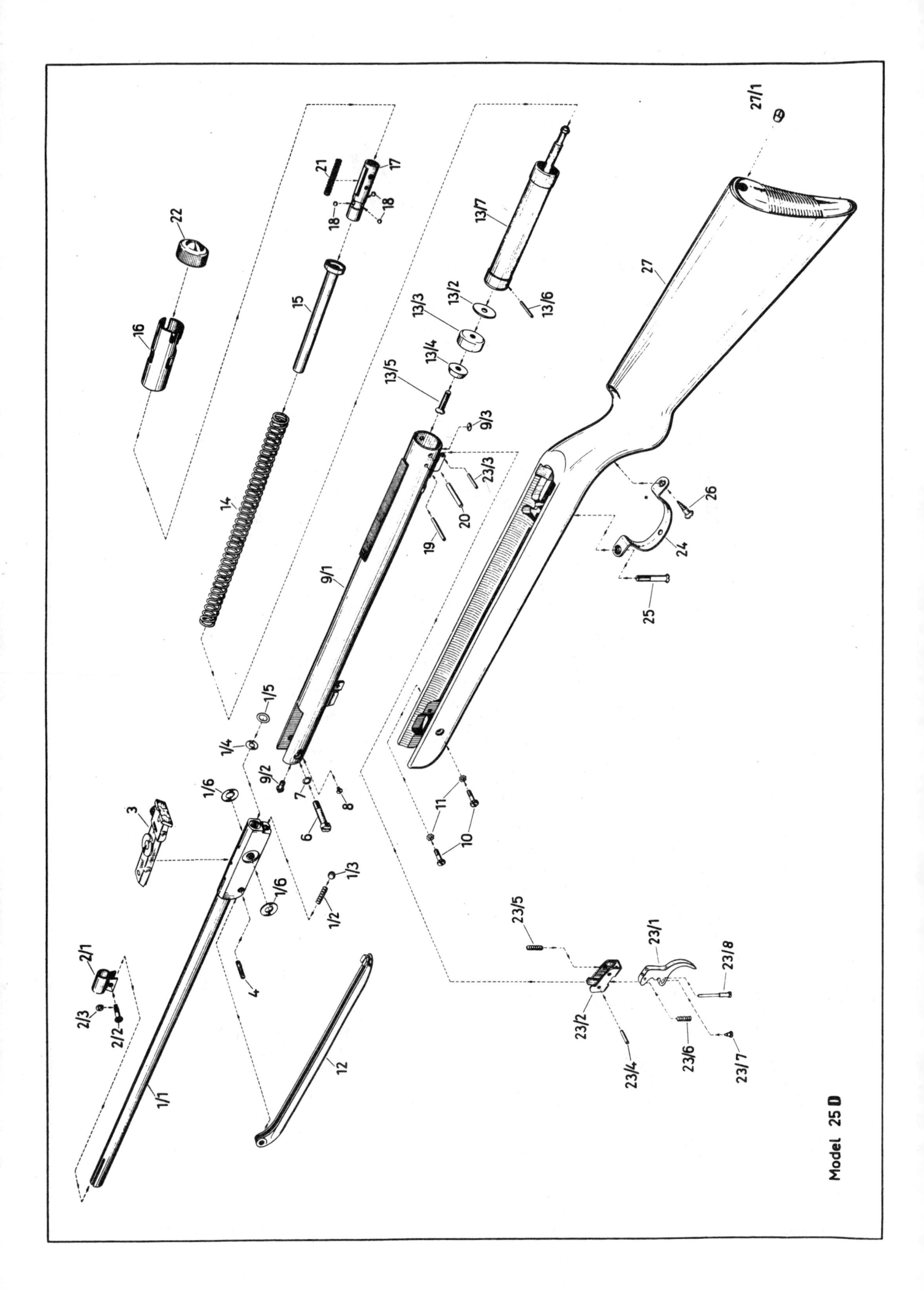

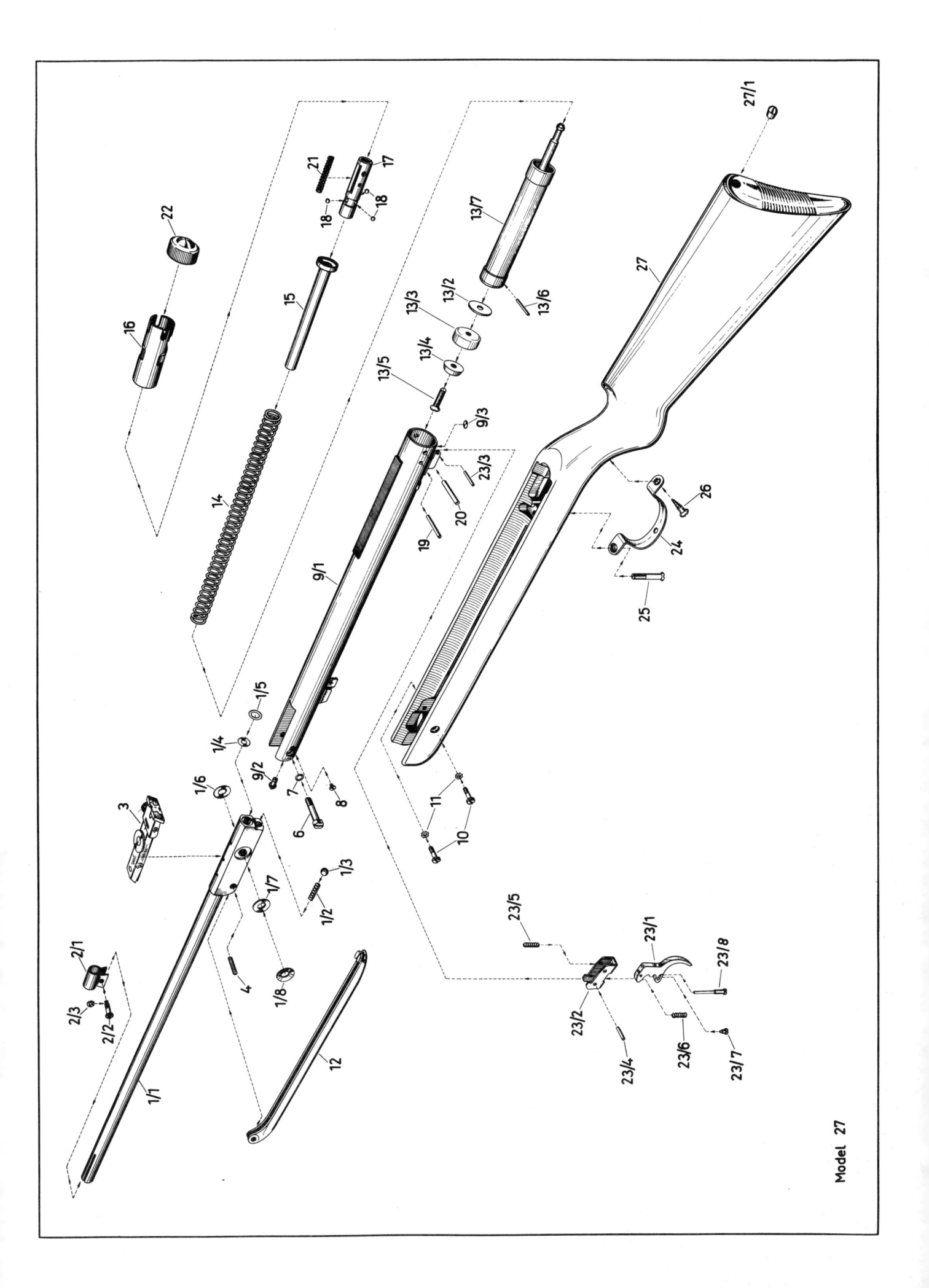

Model 27

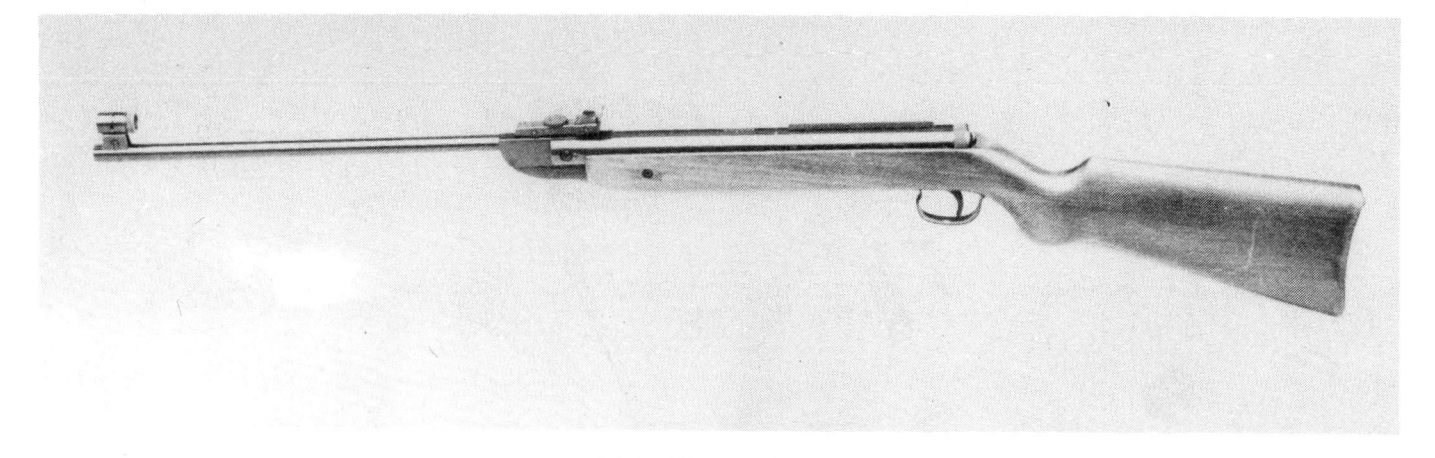

Original Model 27 De Luxe

MODEL   27D.

MAKER   "Original", Mayer & Grammelspacher, Dianawerk, 755 Rastatt, West Germany. Imported by Frank Dyke & Co.

DATE   Improved version of the Model 27 introduced 1976. The Standard Model 27 appeared during December 1951.

VALUATION   £30—£60. ($45—$90).

DETAILS   Improved model with the famous ball bearing trigger action, and all metal rearsight. 41¼ inches long with a 17¼ inch rifled barrel. Tunnel foresight with interchangeable sight elements. All metal fully adjustable rearsight with a revolving sight element to give four types of grooves. Side of barrel breech stamped with calibre and "F" in pentagon. Top of air chamber stamped "ORIGINAL MOD 27" and a date stamp appears towards the rear, "05 76". Serial number not visible. The butt has a small rubber end stop to prevent damage when airgun is propped up, a good idea. Top of air chamber is fitted with a serrated scope ramp which can also be used for fitting the peepsight. Advertised weight 5 lb 14 oz. A review of the Model 27 appears in "Airgun World" May 1981. Will also be found with the Diana trademark on top of the air chamber.

Metal Micrometer Rearsight for Mod. 25 — 25D — 27 — 35 — 50

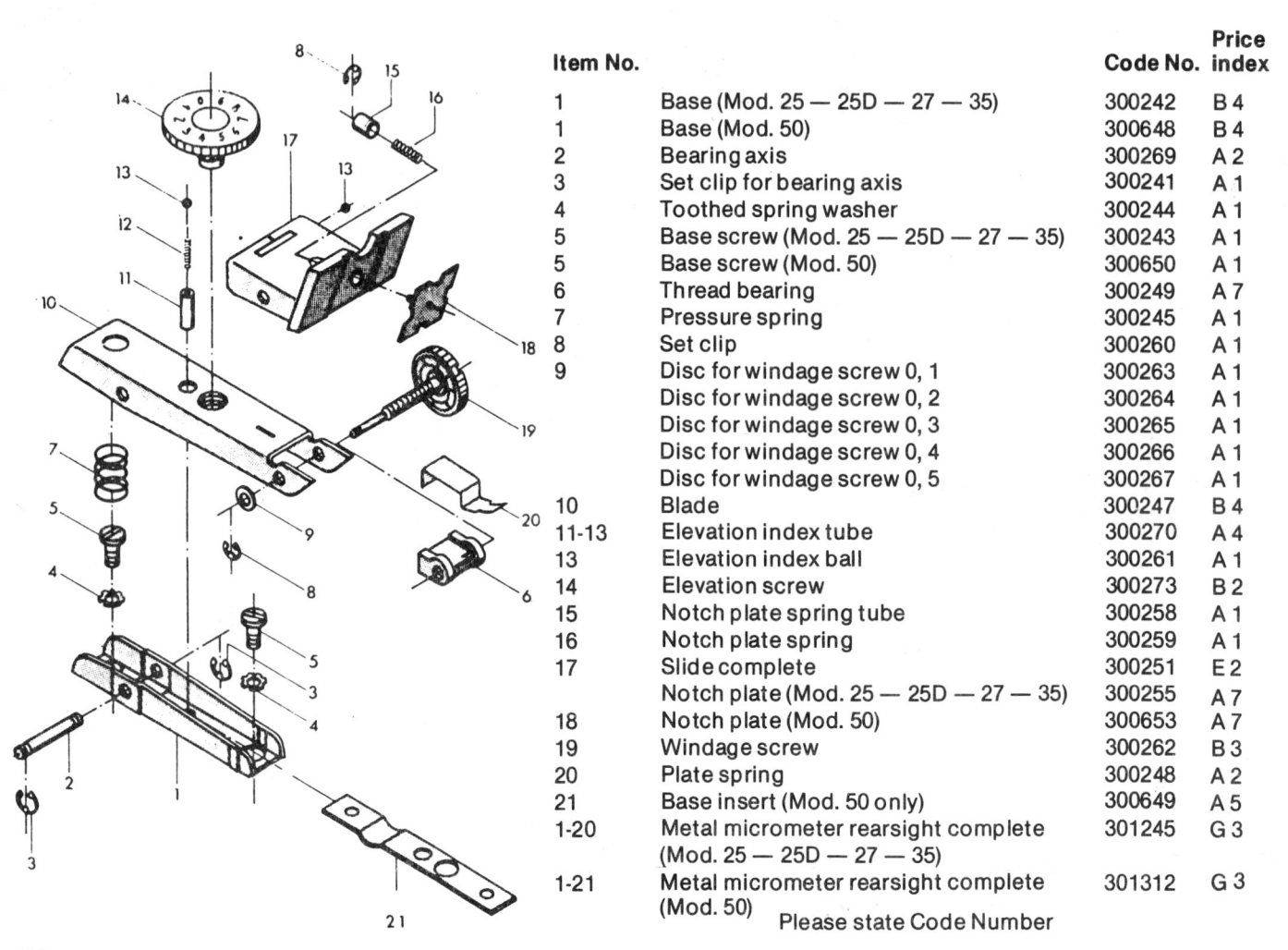

Item No.		Code No.	Price index
1	Base (Mod. 25 — 25D — 27 — 35)	300242	B 4
1	Base (Mod. 50)	300648	B 4
2	Bearing axis	300269	A 2
3	Set clip for bearing axis	300241	A 1
4	Toothed spring washer	300244	A 1
5	Base screw (Mod. 25 — 25D — 27 — 35)	300243	A 1
5	Base screw (Mod. 50)	300650	A 1
6	Thread bearing	300249	A 7
7	Pressure spring	300245	A 1
8	Set clip	300260	A 1
9	Disc for windage screw 0, 1	300263	A 1
	Disc for windage screw 0, 2	300264	A 1
	Disc for windage screw 0, 3	300265	A 1
	Disc for windage screw 0, 4	300266	A 1
	Disc for windage screw 0, 5	300267	A 1
10	Blade	300247	B 4
11-13	Elevation index tube	300270	A 4
13	Elevation index ball	300261	A 1
14	Elevation screw	300273	B 2
15	Notch plate spring tube	300258	A 1
16	Notch plate spring	300259	A 1
17	Slide complete	300251	E 2
	Notch plate (Mod. 25 — 25D — 27 — 35)	300255	A 7
18	Notch plate (Mod. 50)	300653	A 7
19	Windage screw	300262	B 3
20	Plate spring	300248	A 2
21	Base insert (Mod. 50 only)	300649	A 5
1-20	Metal micrometer rearsight complete (Mod. 25 — 25D — 27 — 35)	301245	G 3
1-21	Metal micrometer rearsight complete (Mod. 50)	301312	G 3

Please state Code Number

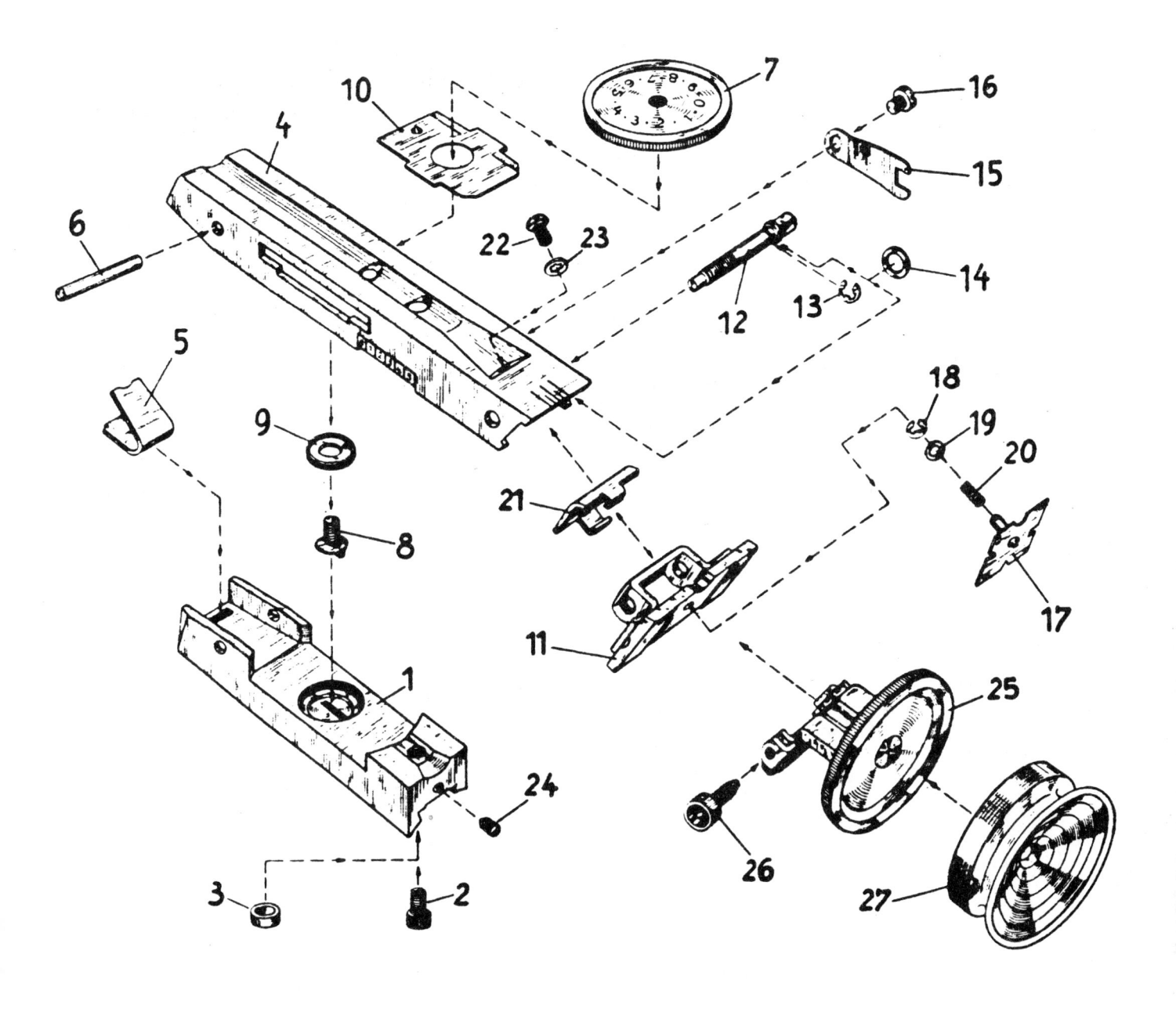

Micrometer rearsight for Models 35/b-M, 50/b-M

No.		No.	
	Micrometer rearsight without peepsight	14	Adjustment disc
1	Rearsight base	15	Windage index spring
2	Binding screw with plug	16	Set screw for No. 15
3	Rubber washer for No. 2	17	Notch plate with plug
4	Rearsight blade	18	Axle set washer for No. 17
5	Rearsight blade spring	19	Washer for No. 18
6	Rearsight pin	20	Notch plate spring
7	Elevating wheel	21	Windage brake
8	Elevating screw	22	Screw for No. 11
9	Thread for No. 8	23	Washer for No. 22
10	Elevating index spring	24	Guiding screw for No. 2
11	Rearsight plate complete with parts Nos. 17, 18, 19, 20	25—27	Peepsight complete with rubber cap
		25	Peepsight
12	Windage screw	26	Peepsight set screw
13	Axle set washer for No. 12	27	Peepsight rubber eye cup

ACCESSORIES

Screwdriver   Plastic envelope for screwdriver

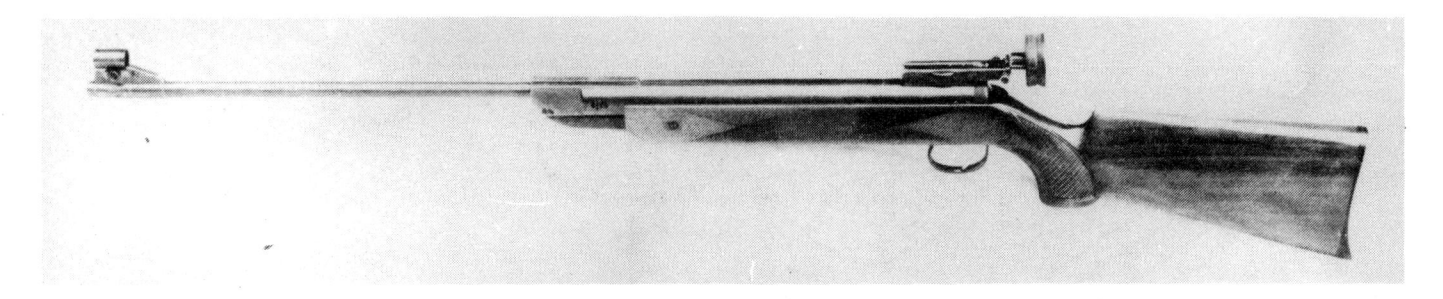

Original Model 35B

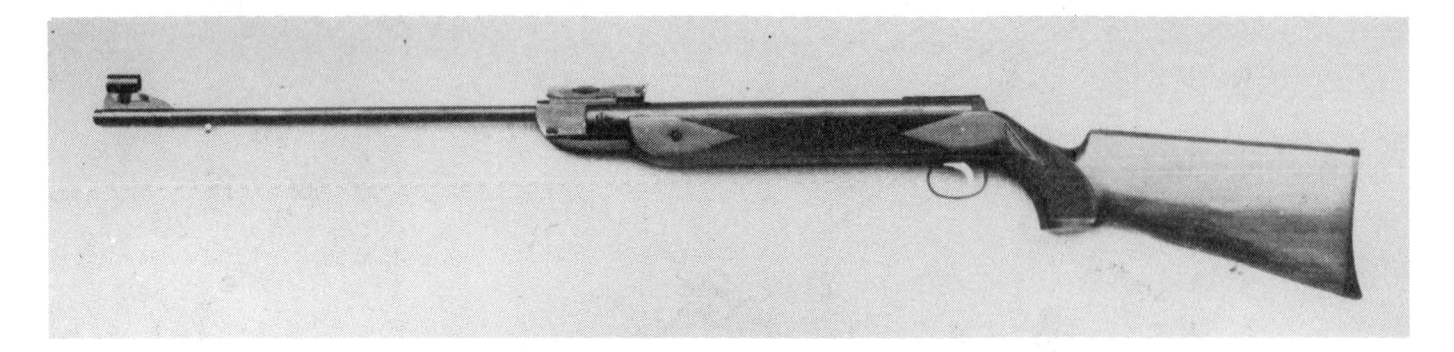

Original Model 35B

Original Model 35B rearsight

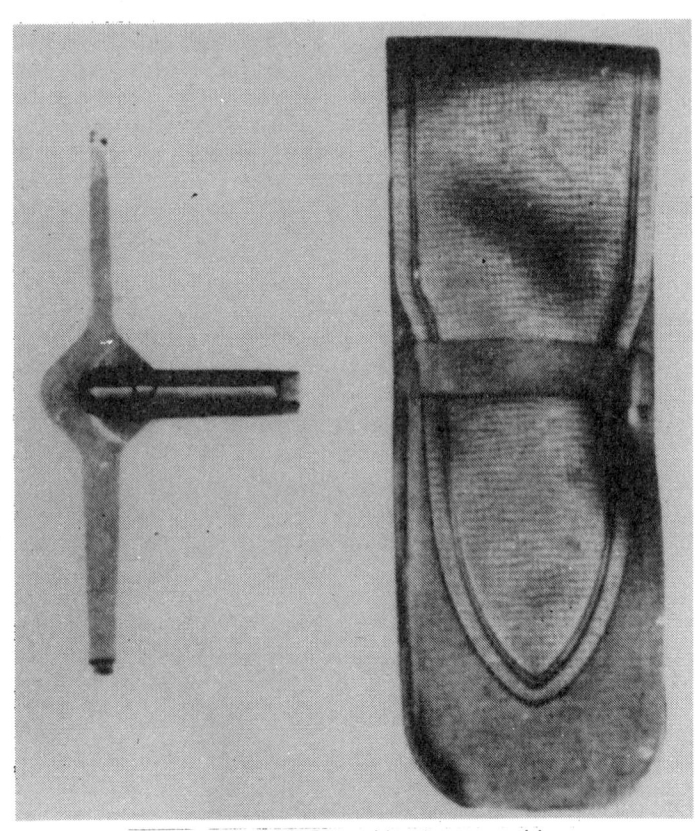

Original Model 35B combination screwdriver and socket spanner with plastic case

MODEL 35.

MAKER "Original", Mayer & Grammelspacher, Rastatt, Germany.

DATE The Model 35 started production during July 1953 and the above version lasted until the middle 1960s.

VALUATION £50—£150, £30a. ($75—$225, $45a).

DETAILS 44½ inches long with a 19½ inch rifled barrel. Foresight has four elements that can be rotated at will for choice of sighting blade, a sprung blade needs to be depressed before rotation can take place. Rearsight very well made, can be removed and placed on ramp at rear of air chamber for peepsight attachment. Rearsight is fitted with a locking screw for the blade sight and this must be loosened before adjustment can take place. The actual blade is spring held and can be rotated for a choice of four types of grooves. Top of air chamber stamped "ORIGINAL" and "MODEL 35" on the L.H.S. is "MADE IN GERMANY". Stock fore-end and pistol grip are very well chequered. Alloy trigger with two adjustment screws. The Model 35S is the current "Super" series, see "Airgun World" November 1978 for review. The first model 35 appears to have been introduced around the early 1930s. The 35 series has the same air chamber and trigger arrangement as the Model 50, i.e. the break action equivalent. Mentioned in D. R. Hughes Catalogue 1969, as having a muzzle velocity of 693 for .177. The Model

35B was supplied with the above arrangement of multi-sights but could be fitted to the Model 35 as an extra. Advertised weight 7½ to 7¾ lbs. This also applied to the Model 50, which according to a 1957 Thomas Bland Catalogue could be fitted with the above selection of sights and was called "MODEL 50B". The peepsight is a screw-on attachment. The four blades available at the front sight are, large bead, small bead, blade and barleycorn. See Wesley's Page 50. Sold in the U.S.A. under the "PEERLESS" trade name.

A small pivoted screwdriver and socket tool was sold with the Model 35B. The screwdriver was for removing the sights and the socket tool was for the windage screw. The special tool came complete with a plastic holdall.

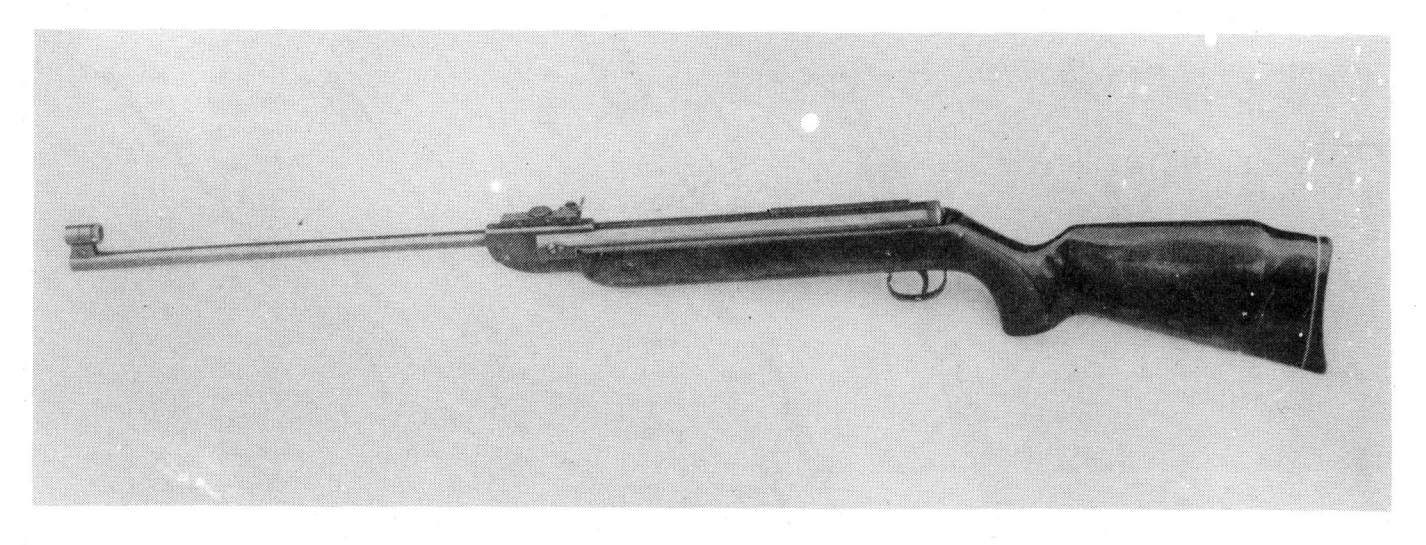

Original Model 35

MODEL 35.

MAKER Mayer & Grammelspacher, Rastatt, Germany.

DATE Above version introduced late 1960s and remained almost unaltered to around 1978. The basic model appeared in 1953.

VALUATION £50–£100. ($75–$150).

DETAILS 44 inches long with a 19 inch rifled barrel. Foresight altered to a tunnel with interchangeable blades. Rearsight all metal with rotating sight plate spring held with four widths of sight blades. Break action version of the Model 50. Serial number of above stamped on side of barrel near rearsight 107245. The above does not have the "F" in pentagon. Small "20" stamped on the underside of the barrel. Top of air chamber stamped "ORIGINAL" MOD 35 and on L.H.S. "MADE IN GERMANY" also the date stamped " 07 75". Calibre stamped on side of barrel breech "CAL. 5.5/.22". Full length stock with machine pressed chequering and ribbing on the inside of the pistol grip. Rubber butt plate with white liner, the butt plate may not be original as the fit is not too good. The above has had a very small hole drilled through the raised rear telescopic sight ramp for a back-stop peg. Advertised weight 7½ lbs. For a review of the Model 35S see "Airgun World" November 1978. The model prior to the above was fitted with the all plastic rearsight, the same sight as fitted to the Original air pistols.

Sold as the Model 809 Mk. V by the Hy-score Gun Company, 200 Tillary Street, Brooklyn, New York, U.S.A. during the middle to late 1970s.

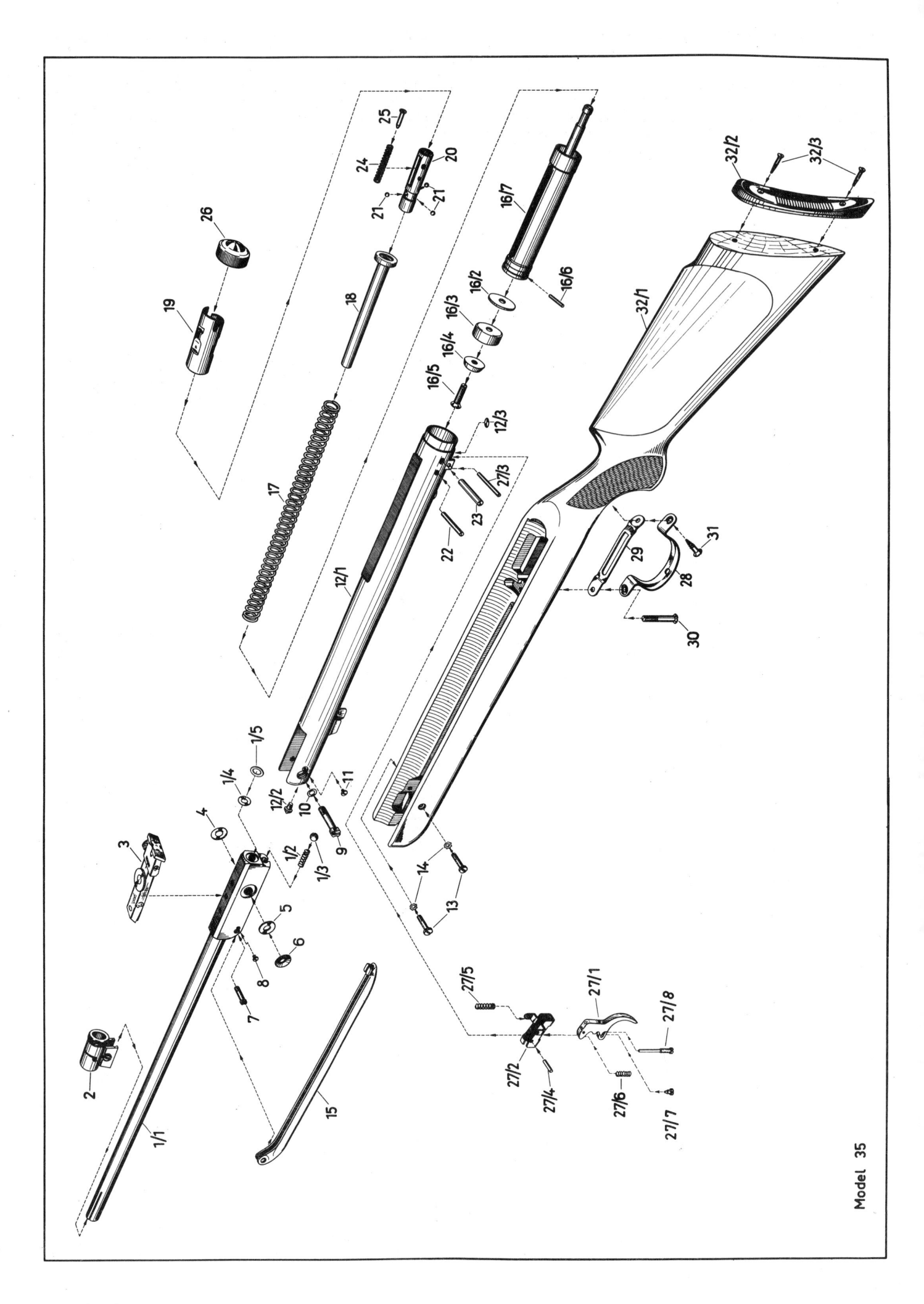

Model 35

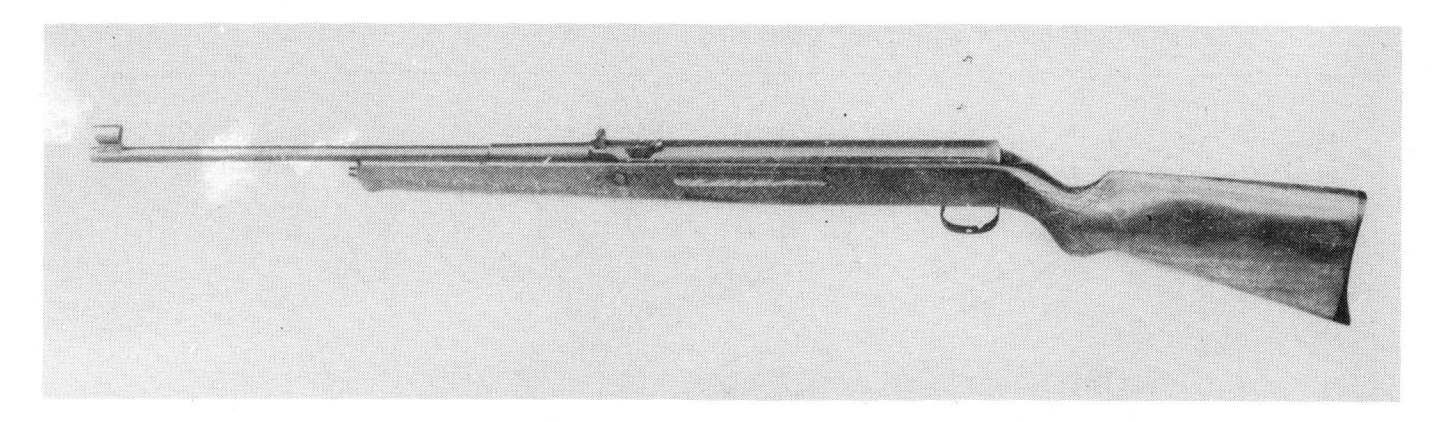

"Original" Model 50E (chequering is not original)

MODEL 50E. Would imagine the "E" stands for "EXPORT".

MAKER Mayer & Grammelspacher, Rastatt, Western Germany.

DATE This first model appeared in May 1952, the above first model may have lasted until the early 1960s.

VALUATION £50—£100.
($75—$150).

DETAILS Slender stock model with no chequering. Judging by the rather dated type of rearsight would assume manufacture to be of the earlier type. The "Export" model would be of higher muzzle energy than that allowed by the European countries. Does not have the "F" in pentagon stamped on it. 45 inches long. Tunnel foresight clamped on to grooves. Turret rearsight set in groove across barrel. Top of air chamber stamped "ORIGINAL MOD. 50E", and on L.H.S. of air chamber "MADE IN GERMANY". Alloy trigger with two adjuster screws. Smooth well finished stock with black vulcanite butt plate. Stock has slight lip at front to coincide with lip of cocking lever. Advertised weight 7¾ lbs. Appears that the above was also sold as MODEL 50B as having "FOUR IN ONE" revolving foresight and removable rearsight that also doubled as an aperature sight. This also applied to the Model 35 and 35B. By 1969 the butt plate was changed to one of rubber. By this date also the more common plastic rearsight was fitted, as appeared on Model 5 and 6 air pistols. Model 50 was an improved version of the earlier Diana Model 48. See Smith's "Airguns of the World" page 130. Mentioned in an undated article by Denis Commins in "Guns Review" that the first two digits of "Original" air rifle serial numbers are the year of manufacture. The Model 50E was sold in the U.S.A. under the "PEERLESS" trade name. On earlier models the word "FOREIGN" was used in place of "MADE IN GERMANY". Some of these early Model 50s had self-opening loading taps, similar operation to the Mk. I and Mk. II Airsporter.

Gecado (Original) Model 50E

MODEL 50E.

MAKER Dianawerk, (Original), Rastatt, Germany.

DATE From around 1952 to 1963 for the above model, or even later as this style was still being sold in America up until the very late 1960s.

VALUATION £50—£120.
($75—$180).

DETAILS One of the finest shapes given to an air rifle. All nicely wrapped up in a slender, sleek stock. 44¾ inches long with a 19¾ inch rifled barrel. Dovetail mounted foresight that looks very much a pre-war B.S.A. left over. This is mounted on a raised portion of the barrel. Ramp type rearsight. Top of air chamber stamped "GECADO MOD. 50E" and side marked "MADE IN WEST GERMANY". The air chamber is not grooved for either telescopic nor peepsight. Very nice smooth slender stock with sexual overtones. Aluminium trigger has adjuster screws mounted in it and are reached through the trigger guard. The trade name Gecado is the American equivalent to "Original". They were called "Peerless" air rifles in the middle 1950s. Apparently this was for airguns made for the Stoeger Arms Company of America. The "E" could stand for "Export". Advertised weight 8 lb 6 oz. This style also appeared in England with the same combination of sights under the "Original" trade name, although the foresight was shown hooded in adverts. The Model 50 was a follow-on from the pre-war Model 48 which looked very much like the B.S.A. pre-war Standard Model.

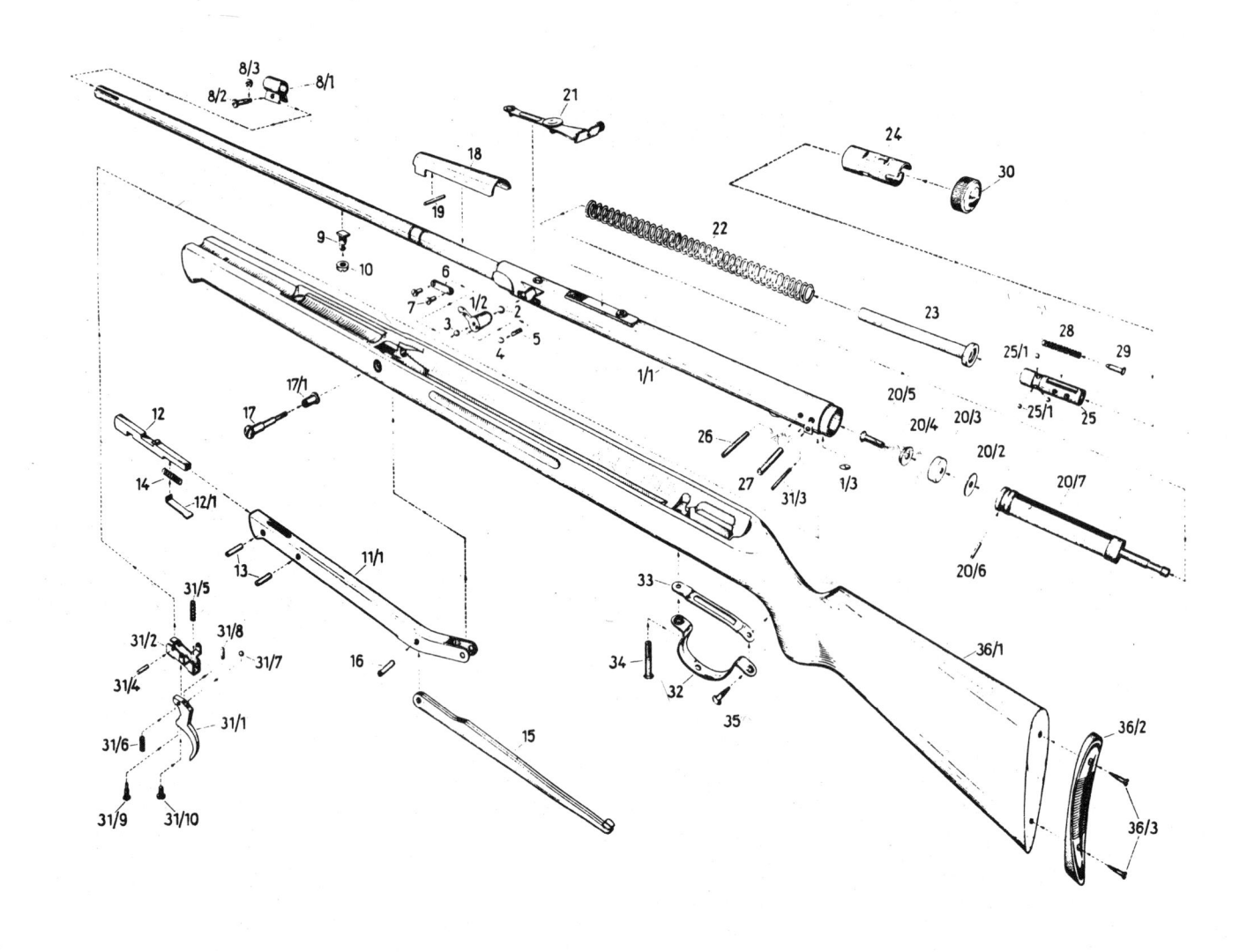

Spare Parts for Air Gun Model 50 (1962)

No.		No.	
1	Barrel rifled, calibre .177 or .22, with compression tube and loading chamber	20/5	Piston screw
		20/6	Piston set pin
1/1	Compression tube	20/7	Piston with rod
1/2	Loading chamber	21	Rearsight (as per list for micrometer rearsight — page 31; not for Model 50E)
1/3	Trigger stay		
2	Large ball bearing, if necessary with adjustment disc	22	Main spring
		23	Main spring guide
3	Small ball bearing	24	Trigger housing
4	Index ball	25	Main spring bearing
5	Index spring	25/1	Locking ball
6	Loading chamber plate	26	Trigger housing pin
7	Set screw for loading chamber plate	27	End piece pin
8	Foresight complete, parts 8/1-8/3	28	Locking spring
8/1	Foresight for Model 50E	29	Locking spring guide
8/2	Foresight screw	30	End piece
8/3	Foresight set clip	31	Trigger complete (parts 31/1 and 31/7 to 31/10)
9	Cocking lever catch		
10	Nut for cocking lever catch	31/1	Trigger
11	Front cocking lever complete (parts 11/1 to 14)	31/2	Trigger support
		31/3	Trigger support pin
11/1	Front cocking lever	31/4	Trigger pin
12	Lever locking bolt	31/5	Trigger support spring
12/1	Locking stay	31/6	Trigger spring
13	Locking bolt pin	31/7	Trigger ball
14	Locking spring	31/8	Trigger adjustment pin
15	Rear cocking lever	31/9	Trigger adjustment screw
16	Lever hinge pin	31/10	Set screw for adjustment screw
17	Lever hinge screw	32	Trigger guard
17/1	Nut for lever hinge screw	33	Trigger guard plate
18	Barrel cover	34	Front trigger guard screw
19	Spring pin for barrel cover	35	Rear trigger guard screw
20	Piston complete (parts 20/2 to 20/7)	36	Stock with butt plate (Bakelite) and screws (not for Model 50M)
20/1	Piston washer complete (parts 20/2 to 20/6)		
		36/1	Stock without butt plate
20/2	Rear fibre washer	36/2	Butt plate (Bakelite)
20/3	Leather washer	36/3	Butt plate screw
20/4	Front fibre washer		

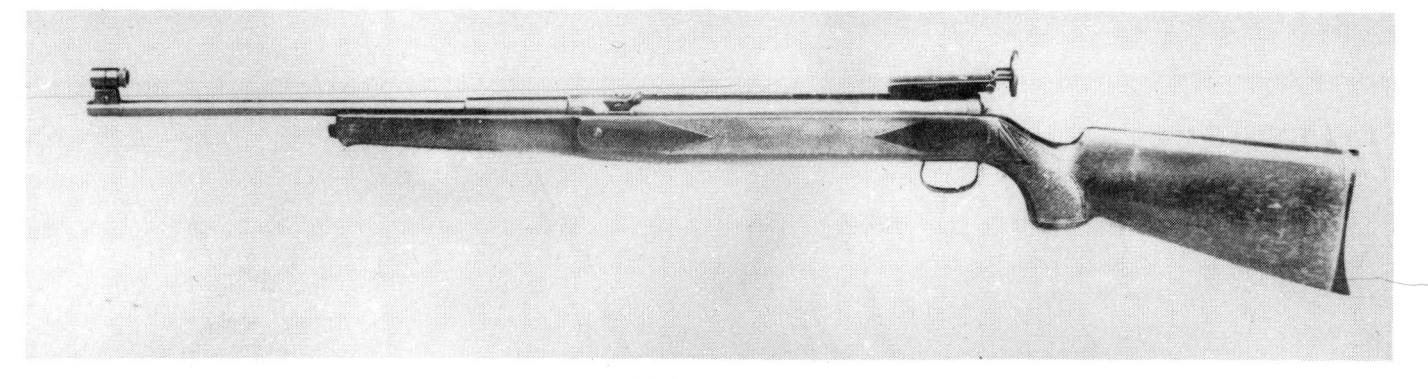

Original Model 50B

MODEL 50B.

MAKER "Diana" and/or "Original", Mayer & Grammelspacher, Rastatt, Germany. May appear with either of the two trade names mentioned above, or even "Gecado".

DATE Middle 1950s to very early 1960s. Around 1957 to 1962.

VALUATION £80−£150.
($120−$225).

DETAILS The 50B variation was described as the "Target Model" and was first available in .22. It was identical to the Model 50 except for the sights. The foresight was fitted with a notched cart-wheel arrangement with four sight blades, but at a later date this was dropped and a normal tunnel foresight fitted. The rearsight could be mounted on top of the air chamber and used as a normal open rearsight, or it could be removed and remounted on the back of the air chamber and fitted with a peepsight attachment. 44¼ inches long with a 19 inch rifled barrel. On the above example the foresight was dovetail mounted with interchangeable sight elements. Rearsight with peepsight attachment. Top of air chamber stamped "ORIGINAL MOD. 50" with "MADE IN GERMANY" on the side. The stock is one of the most profusely chequered production stocks I have ever seen. Aluminium trigger with adjuster screws actually set in the trigger. Advertised weight 8 lbs 6 ozs. By 1960 it was available in .177 as well, although the 50B was still advertised as being in .22 only. By 1961 the Model 50B was discontinued but the Model 35B was still being advertised.

Original Model 50

MODEL 50.

MAKER Dianawerk, Mayer & Grammelspacher, Rastatt/Baden, Germany.

DATE The above variation from about 1969 to 1976 when the square shaped stock appeared and the all metal rearsight was fitted.

VALUATION £60−£100.
($90−$150).

DETAILS Smooth, clean lines for an air rifle. Tunnel foresight with interchangeable sight elements. Underlever tap loading action. Serial number stamped on top of air chamber just in front of the loading tap. Serial number of above 70101932. Plastic rearsight and fitted with serrated ramp for either telescopic or aperature sights. Side of air chamber stamped with date stamp "09 70". Smooth stock with pressed chequering, raised combe and rubber recoil butt plate. Available in either .177 or .22. 45 inches long with 19¾ inch rifled barrel. Advertised weight 7¾ lbs and muzzle velocity for .177 690 f.p.s. The Micrometer Diopter peepsight No. 60 will also fit Models 35 and 65, whilst the plastic rearsight will fit all models of Original air rifles and air pistols manufactured during this period. It has been suggested that during this period of manufacture the first two digits of the serial number are in fact the year of manufacture. For a review see "Guns Review" January 1972. When first available it could also be purchased as the Model 50B with the aperture rearsight supplied with the air rifle. Advertised muzzle velocity for .22 is 490 f.p.s. To back up what has been said about the serial numbers, have seen air rifle number 70101883 with "09 70" stamped on air chamber.

The Model 50B, on the example seen, had two serrated ramps attached to the top of the air chamber, the front one was for the rearsight, whilst the rear was for the rearsight repositioned and the screw-on eye piece in place. The foresight was of the revolving type with four foresight blades each set at 90°.

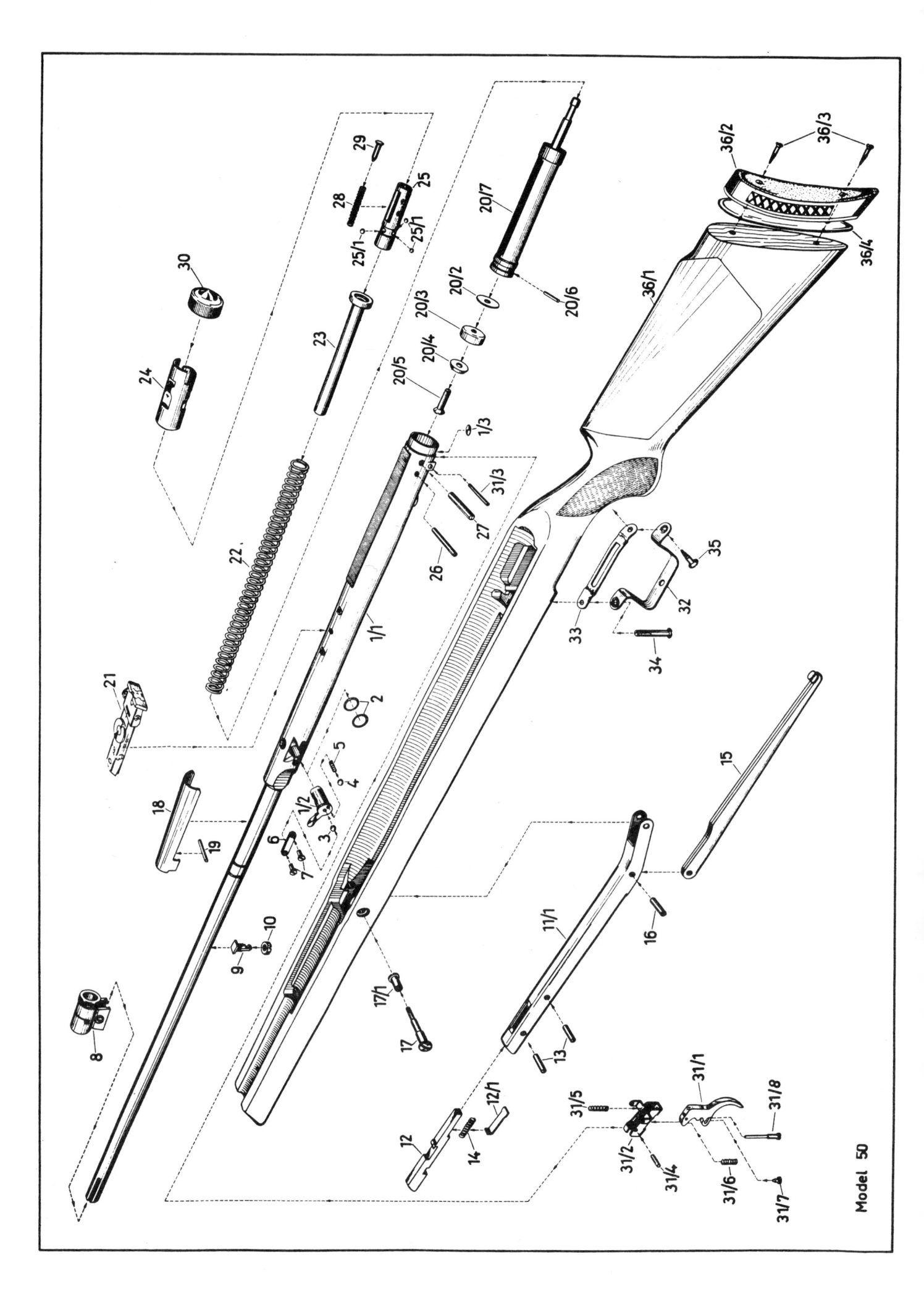

Model 50

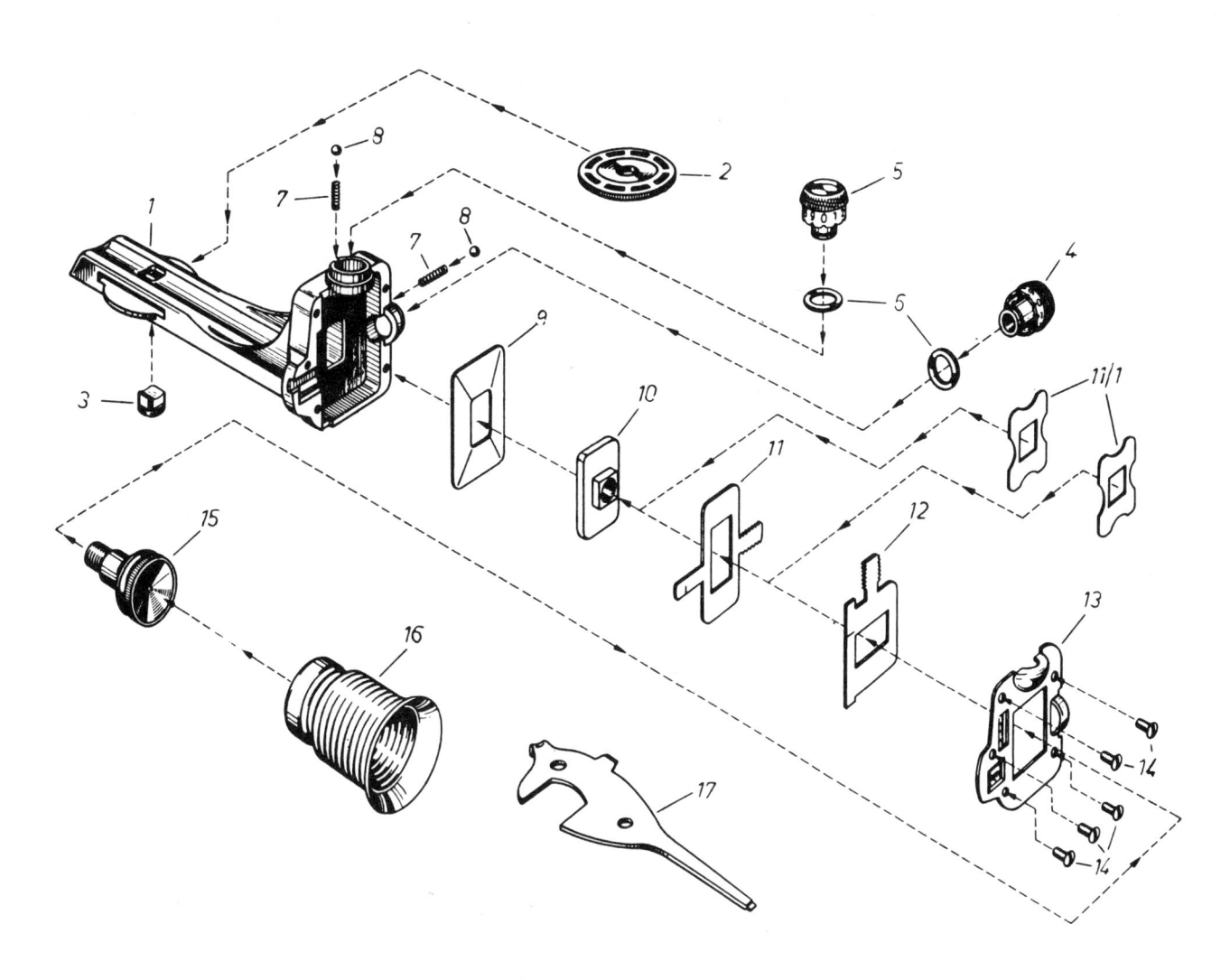

Peepsight for Model 35 — 50 — 60 — 66

Item No.		Code No.	Price index
1	Base	300792	G 3
2	Locking wheel	300793	C 1
3	Fastening screw	300794	C 4
4	Windage screw	300799	C 3
5	Elevation screw	300795	C 3
6	Adjustment disc 0, 05 mm	300803	A 1
	Adjustment disc 0, 1 mm	300804	A 1
	Adjustment disc 0, 2 mm	300805	A 1
	Adjustment disc 0, 3 mm	300806	A 1
	Adjustment disc 0, 5 mm	300807	A 1
7	Index spring	300816	A 1
8	Index ball	300261	A 1
9	Spring plate	300808	A 7
10	Slide piece	300810	C 3
11	Windage slide	300814	B 5
11/1	Insert piece 0, 1 mm	300811	A 3
	Insert piece 0, 2 mm	300812	A 3
	Insert piece 0, 4 mm	300813	A 3
12	Elevation slide	300815	B 5
13	Cover	300817	C 3
14	Cover screw	300818	A 1
15	Aperture sight	300819	E 1
16	Rubber cap	300820	C 1
17	Special screwdriver	300821	B 5

Please state Code Number

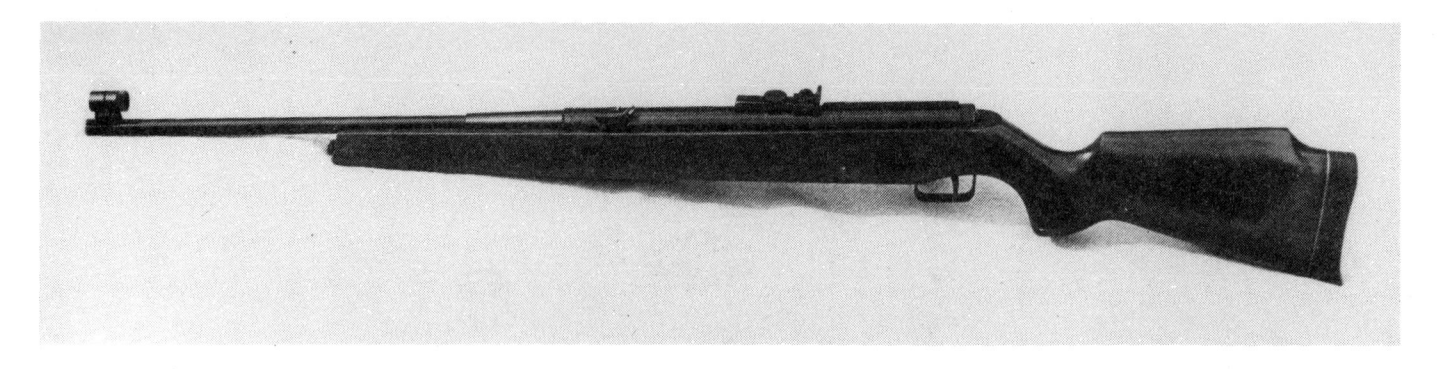

"Original" Model 50

MODEL Model 50. "Original".

MAKER Mayer & Grammelspacher, Rastatt, Germany.

DATE From around 1976 up to the introduction of the 501T during the late 1970s.

VALUATION £50—£100. ($75—$150).

DETAILS Above is the latest design change. 44½ inches long. One of the "quality" airguns. Underlever folds up into stock. Finish to stock and metal work excellent. Grooved for telescopic sight or peepsight. Advertised with an increase in muzzle velocity from serial number 173010. Serial number of above 149179. Serial number stamped on side of barrel, calibre and model stamped on top of air chamber. Tunnel foresight has interchangeable elements whilst the rearsight is fully adjustable. Advertised weight 7¾ lbs. See "Airgun World" February 1978 for preview of above.

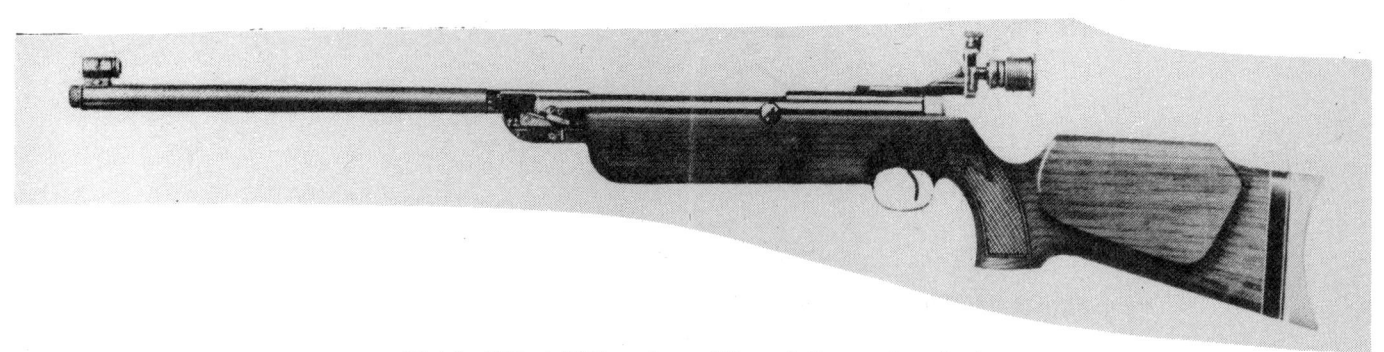

"Original" Model 65 (courtesy of Mayer & Grammelspacher)

MODEL 65. Sold in America by Hyscore as the Model 810 Olympic International rifle.

MAKER Mayer & Grammelspacher, Rastatt, Germany.

DATE 1965 to 1975.

VALUATION £100—£200. ($150—$300).

DETAILS The predecessor of the Model 66. Available in .177 only and worked on the principle of double reciprocating pistons that take off in opposite directions when the action is released. Hence no recoil. The barrel is supplied with a latch so that absolute rigidity is maintained. A barrel sleeve is supplied with each air rifle as is the peepsight. The double pull trigger is adjustable from 100 grams to 400 grams. Advertised length is 44 inches (120 cms) with a 19¼ inch (49 cms) barrel. The total weight was 11 lbs (5 Kgs) and average muzzle velocity given was 576 f.p.s. The stock was walnut with a cheek piece and chequered pistol grip. The barrel sleeve weighed 21 ozs. It can be assumed that when the Model 65 appeared it may not have been fitted with a barrel latch. Around 1970 the above was supplied with seven foresight elements, three baldes and four ring elements, the blade sights ranged from 1.8 mm to 3.4 mm and the rings from 2 mm to 5 mm. Due to the use of synthetic piston washers it is recommended that mineral oil is NEVER used to lubricate the insides.

Apparently the Model 66 stock will fit the above and vice versa.

Breakdown diagram of the Diana Air Rifle Model 65

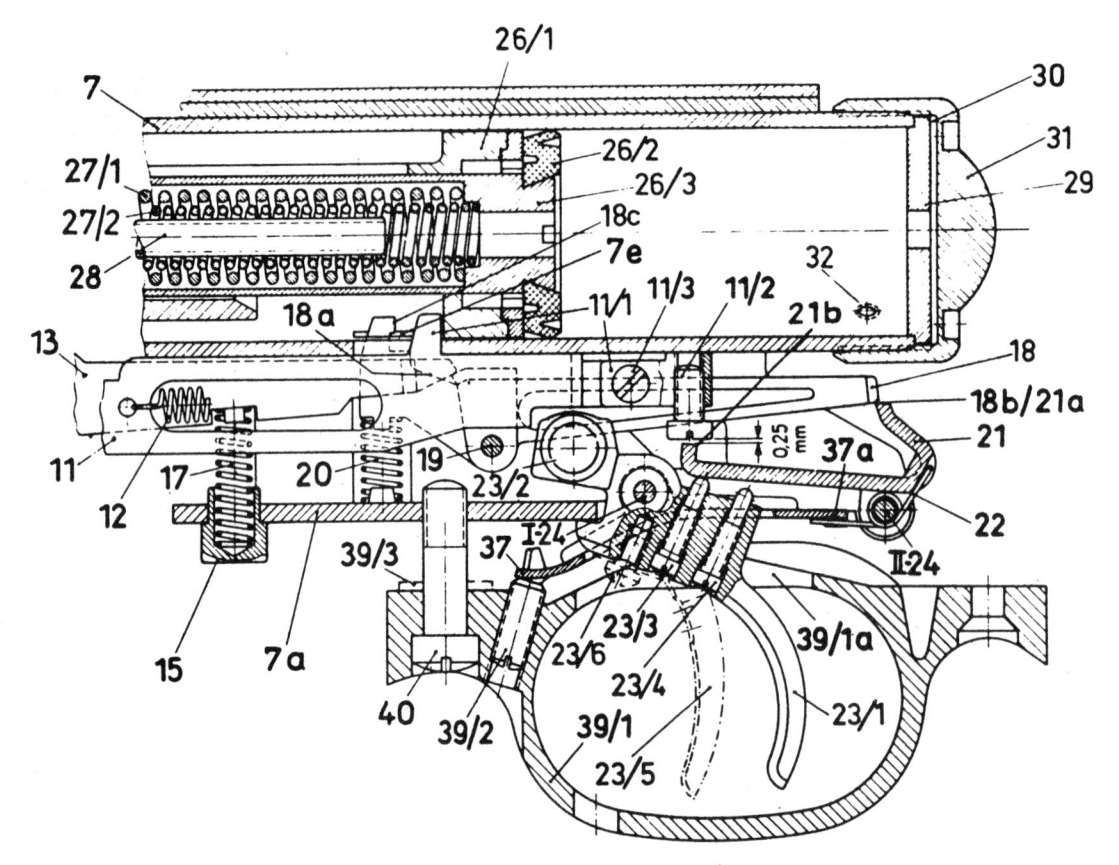

The "Original" 65 trigger mechanism

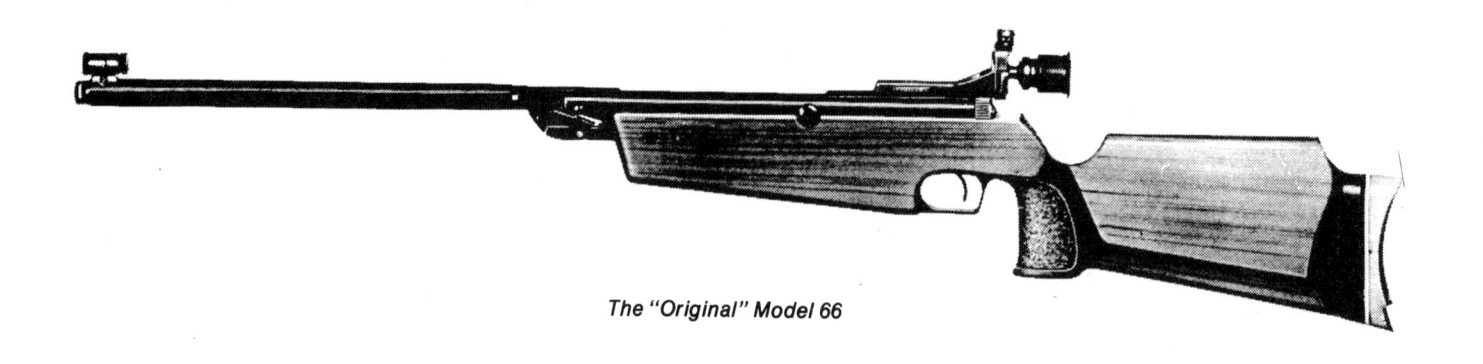

The "Original" Model 66

MODEL 66. Sold in America as the Hyscore Model 811 SM.

MAKER "Original" and/or "Diana", Mayer & Grammelspacher, Rastatt, West Germany.

DATE Introduced 1975.

VALUATION £100—£200, £125a. ($150—$300, $188a).

DETAILS The air rifle equivalent of the Model 10 air pistol. Works on the principle of two opposite pistons, one working and the other a counterweight, thus giving a recoiless action. Fitted with a barrel sleeve and locking lever at pivot. The match trigger adjustable from 0.2 to 0.8 lbs. A test target card was issued with each air rifle. Advertised length 43 inches (109 cm) and having a 19 inch (48 cm) barrel. Advertised weight 11 lbs. The barrel has twelve groove rifling. Two adjustments are available on the trigger mechanism, screw in front of trigger adjusts pull from 0.2 to 0.8 lbs, whilst screw in trigger itself is for adjusting the sear engagement. If fitted with the auxiliary trigger in front of the main trigger this increases the length of trigger pull. This auxiliary trigger is not normally fitted when sold and can be ordered as an accessory. The European walnut stock has an oil finish and a fully adjustable butt plate. Advertised velocity was 530 f.p.s., measured 5.5 feet from the muzzle. Stock measurements for length of pull being from 13¼ inches to 14¼ inches, drop at combe almost 2 inches and drop at heel 3 inches. The Model 66 is sold with tunnel foresight and aperture rearsight. Interchangeable foresights being 1.8 and 2.2 mm blade sights and 3.4, 3.8, and 4.0 mm ring sights. Others are available in blade from 1.8 to 2.2 mm and in ring form from 2.0 to 6.0 mm all in 2/10 graduations. A review appeared in "Airgun World" June 1978. The Model 66 was the continuation of the Model 65. The mainspring is composed of three springs, one outer and main with two smaller inner springs with a floating spring guide inside, also the rear piston counter weight has a guide tube, all in all a well cushioned power unit. It is recommended that the action is NOT oiled with mineral oil as there are plastic piston washers. The Model 66 is sold in either right or left hand stock.

Model 66

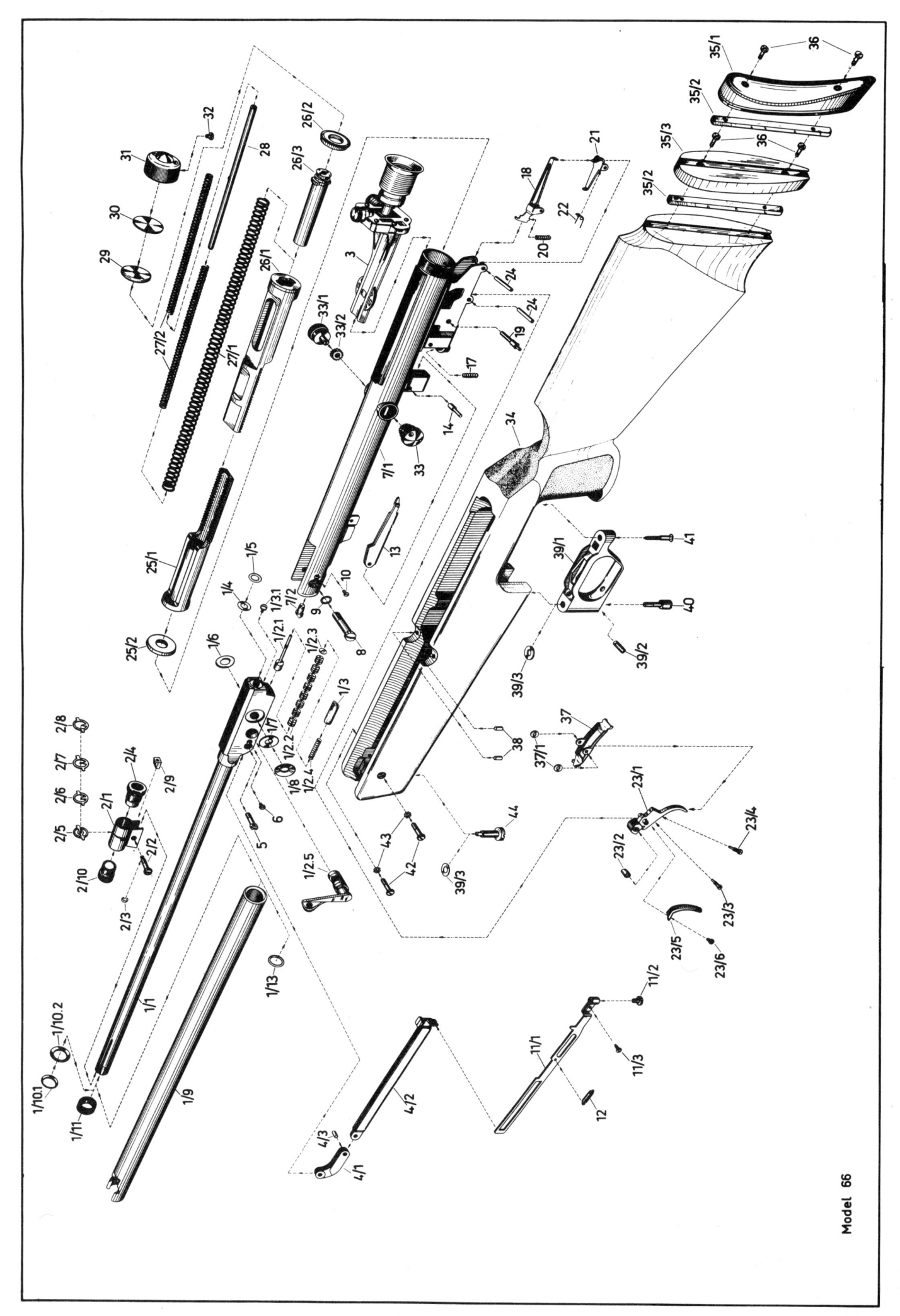

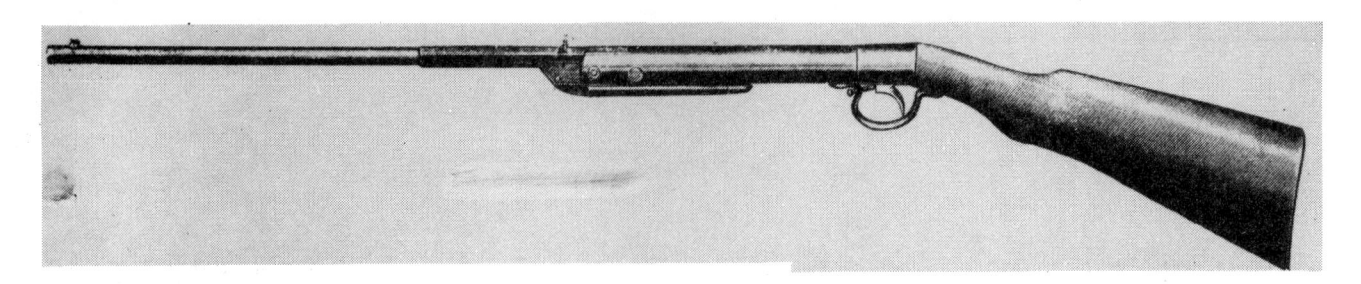

The Pfeil Standard 95 cm air rifle (working class)

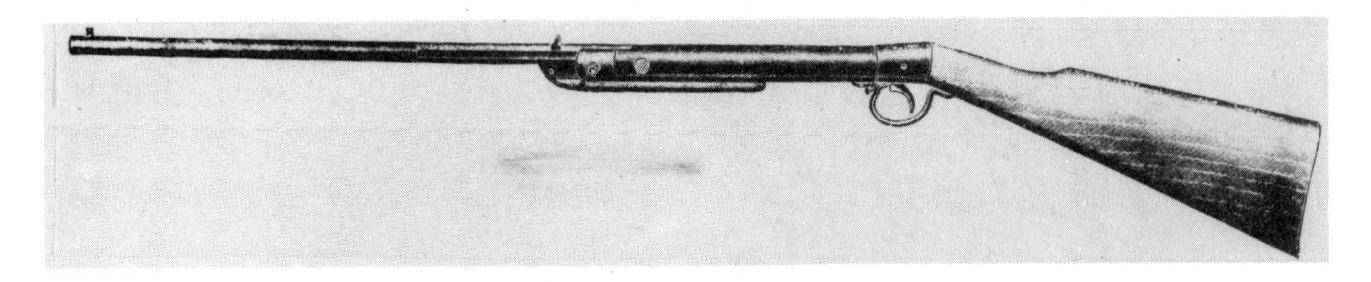

The Pfeil Standard 105 cm air rifle (middle class)

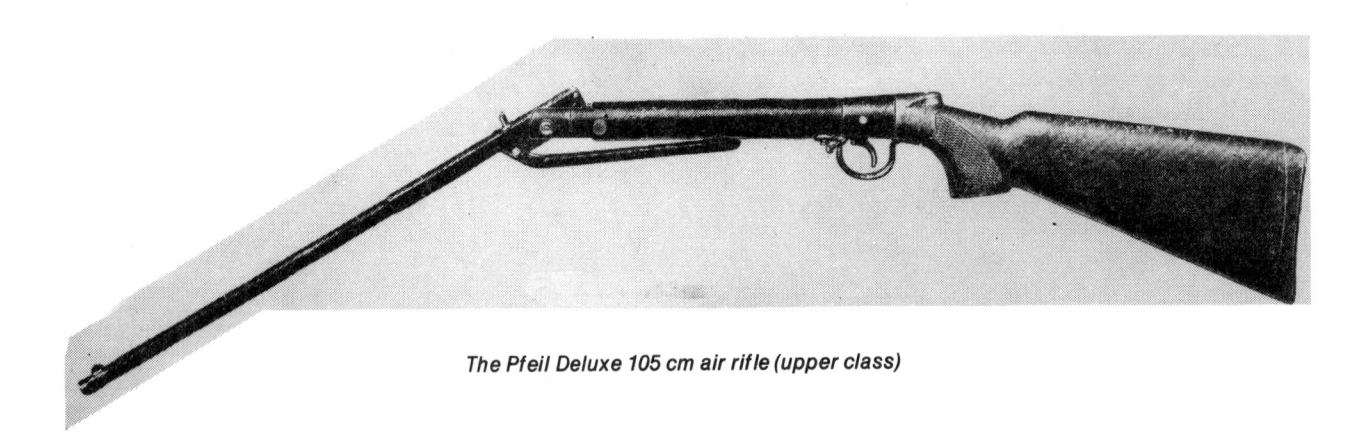

The Pfeil Deluxe 105 cm air rifle (upper class)

MODEL "Pfeil" air rifles.

MAKER It looks like a "Tell" air rifle from the Oscar Will stable, almost identical to the "Tell" air rifle mentioned on page 204. The only difference being that the above has a side button in the same fashion as the Millita air rifle. The "Pfeil" trade name apparently stands for "ARROW" and some air rifles may even have an arrow emblem marked on them. It has been suggested that because of this, and the fact that the Haenel trademark was an arrow, that they made the Pfeil air rifles, I doubt this. They were also advertised in a German catalogue bearing the retailers' name Robert Pfeiffer, Suhler Waffenhaus, Suhl, Thuringen, Germany and dated 1925. His surname being very similar to the Pfeil trade name, but until further information comes to light I'm putting my money on Oscar Will, Venuswaffenwerk, Zella Mehlis, Germany.

DATE The Pfeil trade name appeared in the 1910s and lasted up until the early 1940s.

VALUATION Generally speaking £40—£80. ($60—$120).

DETAILS Three models were advertised in the 1930s with a side button barrel release, although in 1913 two models were advertised, length 90 cms and 104 cms. They would appear to be at that date left overs, or bulk purchase, of the Millita air rifle of the same design. The three appear to differ in overall length and shape of stock. They are best described as follows:
Working Class Model. Blued with walnut stock having a slight pistol grip. 95 cm long and sold either .22 or .177 rifled and smoothbore. Weight 1.5 kilogram.
Middle Class Model. Blued with straight hand stock. Length 105 cms. Weight 2.5 kilograms. Available in either .22 or .177 smoothbore and rifled.
Upper Class Model. Length 105 cms. Blued with chequered stock having a pronounced pistol grip. Fitted with adjustable rearsight and pearl tipped foresight.
All the above were sold with a trigger adjustment screw through the trigger guard. The trigger guard often being a flat length of metal bent and curved to form the guard. Serial number is stamped on the face of the breech in true Millita or Gem fashion.

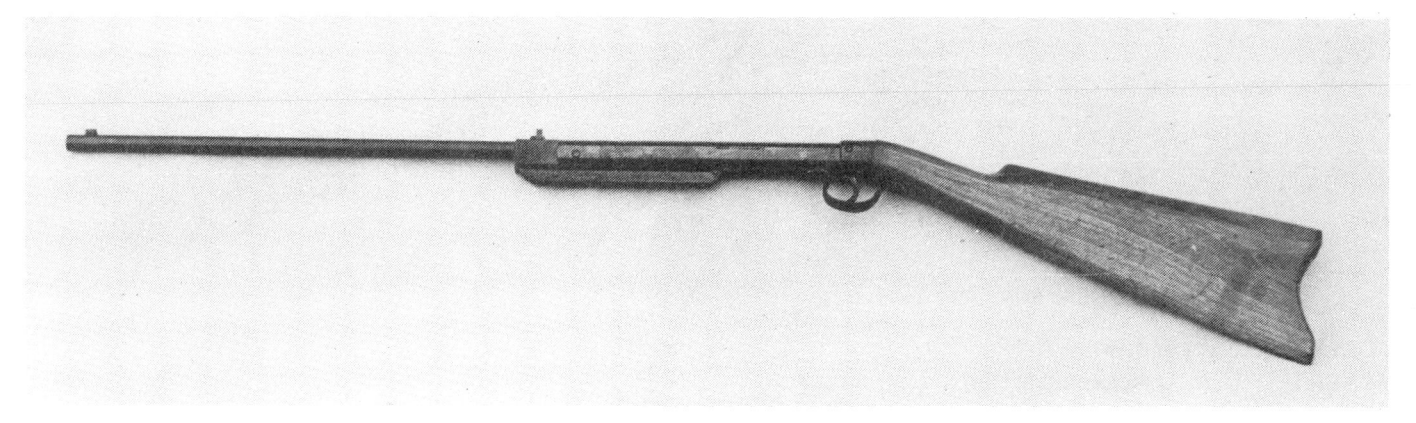

"Precision Junior"

MODEL "Precision Junior".

MAKER Appears to be linked with "Diana" of Germany. Mayer & Grammelspacher's Dianawerks.

DATE 1930s.

VALUATION £30—£60. ($45—$90).

DETAILS Serial number of above 10628. 36 inches long. All metal construction. Similar to Haenel Model 45. Rifled barrel. On top of air chamber "PRECISION JUNIOR" and serial number next to trigger block. "MADE IN GERMANY" on side of cylinder. Very well made with ball bearing barrel catch similar to some modern "Originals".

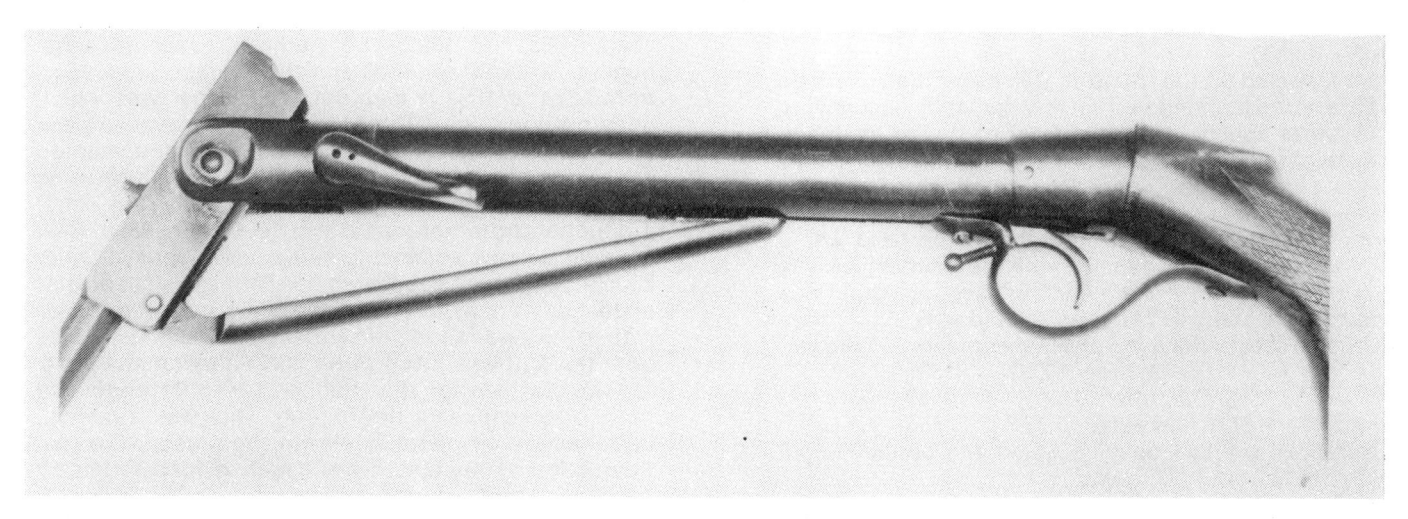

"Precision" side lever air rifle

MODEL "Precision" air rifle.

MAKER Oscar Will, who was later taken over by Wilheym Foss, Venuswaffenwerk, Zella-Mehlis, Thuringen, Germany. The above model is identical to the Roland Model 1927.

DATE This style with the rounded barrel support arms dates from 1927 to 1939.

VALUATION £40—£80. ($60—$120).

DETAILS Another trade name for the above air rifle appears. This one bears the "Precision" trade name and dates from the middle 1920s to 1939. 41¾ inches long with a 18¾ inch .177 rifled barrel. Dovetail mounted foresight with white metal tipped bead and dovetail mounted rearsight. Octagonal to round barrel with "PRECISION" stamped on the upper most flat. Serial number 19, appears on barrel and air chamber. Trigger adjustment is by screw through the trigger guard. Side lever barrel latch. Stock is hand chequered and is fitted with a metal butt plate. During the early 1930s the Midland Gun Company sold the above as the "Perfecta" in .177 only, for 50/- each, £2.50.

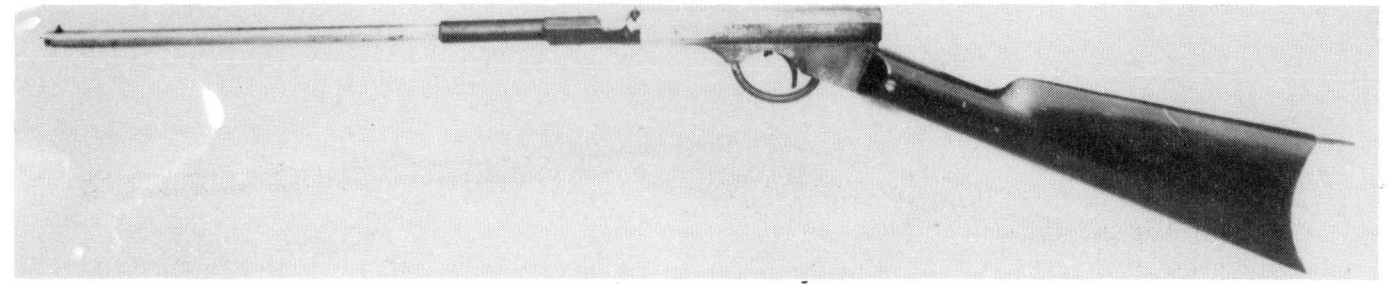

Quackenbush Number 1

MODEL Number 1.
MAKER H. M. Quackenbush, Herkimer, New York, U.S.A.
DATE From around 1876 to 1933 when H. M. Quackenbush died, but old stock was being sold after this date.
VALUATION £50—£150, £55a. ($75—$225, $83a).

DETAILS This air rifle was the one that put the American gallery gun out of business. Its simplicity of design and use of mass production meant that it was offered to the public at a fraction of the price asked for the gallery airguns by Lurch, Blackensdeorfer, etc. The Number 1 has only fifteen component parts as the typical New York style gallery airgun had over 27. 34¼ inches long with a 16¼ inch .21 calibre smoothbore barrel. The barrel is pushed in to cock the action and then partially drawn out to reveal the cut-away in the top of the barrel, a pellet or dart is inserted and the barrel is then drawn out fully. Air rifle is now ready to fire. Stamped on the side of the octagonal air chamber "H. M. QUACKENBUSH, HERKIMER, N.Y., PAT. JUNE,6,1876, — JULY,19,1881". The serial number is also stamped on the frame as well as on the underside of the barrel housing. Action is stripped by unscrewing the barrel housing from the front of the air chamber. Usually found nickel plated. Trigger adjustment screw is just in front of the trigger. Both sights were fixed. The steel piston was not fitted with a leather washer and as with the German Gem air rifle the piston head was a close fitting metal to metal fit with the air chamber. The mainspring was rectangular in section and was machined wound. In "Airguns" by Eldon G. Wolff there are three dated allocation of serial numbers as follows:

1st September 1909	31336
3rd October 1915	33539
6th May 1926	36553

The above publication also listed the production of Number 1s from 1893 to 1922.

Year	Production	Recorded serial number	Assumed serial numbers equated from addition & subtraction from point *
1884	1760		
GAP IN COMPANY RECORDS			
1893	286		21790
1894	348		22138
1895	357		22495
1896	269		22764
1897	473		23237
1898	442		23679
1899	551		24230
1900	1097		25327
1901	769		26096
1902	826		26922
1903	767		27689
1904	636		28325
1905	750		29075
1906	628		29703
1907	738		30441
1908	360		30801
1909	535	31336 ***	31336 ***
1910	440		31776
1911	320		32096
1912	457		32553
1913	352		32905
1914	233		33138
1915	357	33539 Only 44 out from the registered serial number	33539
1916	296		33791
1917	563		34354
1918	318		34672
1919	481		35153
1920	383		35536
1921	177		35713
1922	74		35787
GAP IN COMPANY RECORDS			
1926		**36553**	

The gap in company records from 1922 to the recorded serial number of 1926 represent four years and an average production rate of 191 per year is reached by dividing the difference between 36553 and 35787 by four. This appears to be about right when comparing it with other figures of previous years. It is assumed that even higher serial numbers will be seen as production is assumed to have finished in the early 1930s. The beginning of production paints a similar picture, assuming production to start in 1876, the earliest production figure is 1760 Number 1s for the year 1884, this averages out to 220 made per year which sounds about right. The Bermuda Triangle occurs between the years 1884 and 1893. The Author's assumed serial number is 21790 for 1893 and the average production from 1884 to 1893 comes out at 2225 per year which does not look right. The Author would appreciate any ideas on the above and knowledge of documented serial numbers. To confuse matters even further an article in "Airgun World" states that the total production from before 1883 to 1938 was 18560, then goes on to show a dismembered example serial number 25056! There would appear to be change in style on butt plate. Early examples were fitted with a heavy cast plate with an extended top horn for almost 1⅛ inches, whilst later the butt was fitted with a plain sheet metal plate. The mechanism for the Number 1 air rifle originated from Quackenbush's first airgun. This was a push-in barrel action air pistol similar to the present day gat. Production of this first model began in 1876. Referring back to the production number confusion in "Airguns & other Pneumatic arms" by Arne Hoff there is a reference to one example in the National Museum of History, Washington, U.S.A. with a serial number of 81475! One wonders if they were still being produced in heaven after 1933 when Henry Marcus Quackenbush passed on and according to Eldon G. Wolff production of airguns stopped at this date as well.

The first patent mentioned on the air chamber refers to U.S.A. patent number 178233 whose application date was 4th March 1876 and was made by A. C. Carey the agent and assigned to Pope, who obviously had connections with Quackenbush. This covered the push-in barrel action of the air pistol and was used in the design of the Number 1 air rifle. From an 1876 advert, see W. H. B. Smith's "Gas, spring, and Airguns of the World", the Number 1 was available either fully nickel plated or with a plated barrel and browned frame. Each was sold complete with 6 darts, 6 paper targets, 100 slugs and a dart claw and wrench. By 1908 it was advertised as being available fully nickel plated only. On the example seen the piston was very similar in shape to a hollow cup shaped airgun slug. The cap was fitted with a rubber stopper to act as a cushion, the mainspring was conical, the narrow end fitted into the base of the piston and then became wider to fill the compression chamber.

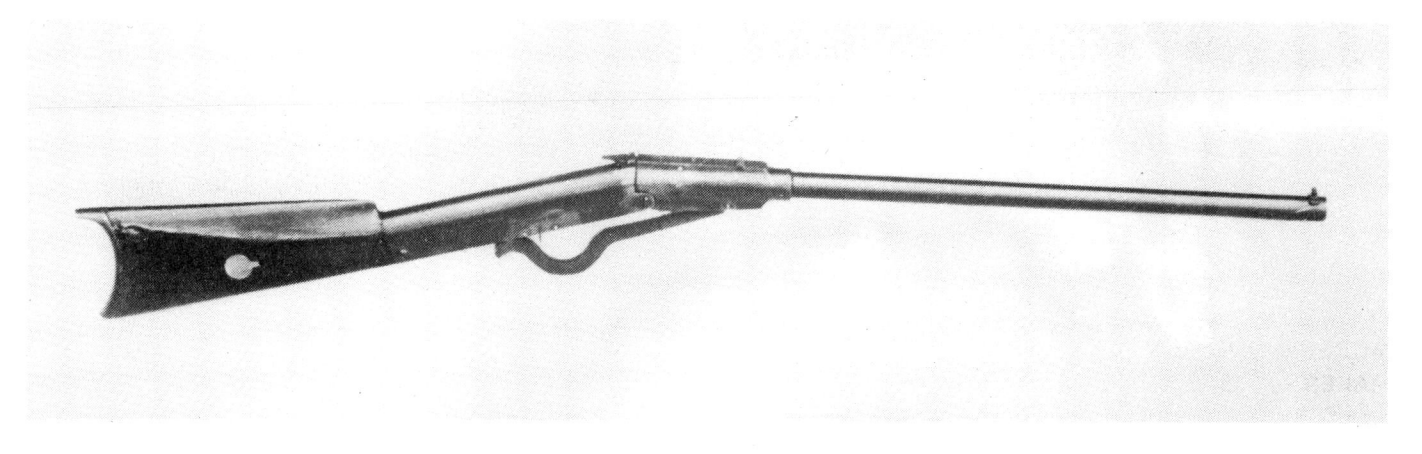

Quakenbush Model 5

MODEL 5.

MAKER Henry Marcus Quackenbush, 220 Prospect Street, Herkimer, New York, U.S.A. Address at time of manufacture.

DATE From around 1887 to 1911, or even as late as 1913. Although mention is made of the Model 5 as early as 1884.

VALUATION £100–£200. ($150–$300).

DETAILS Heavy construction, 39 inches long with a 21⅞ inch smoothbore barrel. Foresight set in dovetail with side screw for raising or lowering blade as required. Rearsight is simple blade in dovetail. Serial number stamped on underside of barrel, breech, and air chamber, these should all match. Number of above 1912. Top of air chamber stamped "H. M. QUACKENBUSH, HERKIMER, N.Y., U.S.A., PAT. SEP.20 & OCT.,4.1887". Stock similar to Gem air rifle, but has a patch box with spring held lid set in the R.H.S. Butt plate heavy with extended tips. The above style of airgun was patented by Haviland and Gunn and in 1883 Quackenbush purchased the patent from them and produced the No. 5. It appeared in two forms, the above with a smoothbore barrel of around .215 inch calibre and a combination air rifle that could be converted to rim fire cartridges. Only some 1500 to 2000 were manufactured. Total number produced as given by Eldon Wolff in "Airguns" a Milwaukee Public Museum publication is 1570 and dating by serial numbers as follows, further information can be obtained from the above publication. Earlier years are missing from factory records.

Year	Total Production
1885	136
1886	426
1887	553
1888	687
1889	844
1890	1020
1891	1187
1892	1334
1893	1478
1894	1659
1895	1764
1896	1822
1900	2289
1907	3107
1911	3185 (last entry)

Production may have continued until 1913, but in very small numbers. There is some confusion in the production dates for the Quackenbush Number 5 Model air rifle. One would assume that models made before 1887 would not have the 1887 patent dates stamped on the air chamber! Maybe the pre-1887 models were made by Haviland & Gunn before they sold the patent to Quackenbush. The above production figure does not take into account any production in the earlier years for which factory records are unavailable. So taking the last entry as fact it would appear that the total production figure could be as high as 3185 or even slightly higher. Spare parts were still being advertised in the late 1970s for all the Quakenbush air rifles and could be obtained from Numrich Arms Corporation, West Hurley, New York 12491, U.S.A. Telephone 914-679 2417.

Quackenbush started business in 1871 and as far as I know are still in business, but not producing airguns. Before 1871 H.M.Q. was an apprentice at the Remington Arms Company, Illion, New York. During 1943 they discontinued all manufacture of airguns because the entire plant was converted to the manufacture of machine bullets upon the Governments request when they entered the War, late! They still make .177 darts and this is the only product still manufactured connected with the airgun industry.

Since 1946 the firm has produced nut-crackers, nut-picks, nut-bowls, Lobster crackers and seafood forks. The firm seems to enjoy producing items that no one else would dream of. When production started in 1871 they made a dental tool and in 1878 the tool was modified to also act as a nut-pick. One can only assume that there were a lot of nuts about at that time. The nut-cracker started its life in 1880 and is still produced today with little change in the original design, mind you, how do you change the design of a nut-cracker? A bag of sweets sold with the above would have been called "Nutcracker Sweets". Nut-bowls were conceived in 1932 and the lobster crackers and seafood forks appeared in 1952.

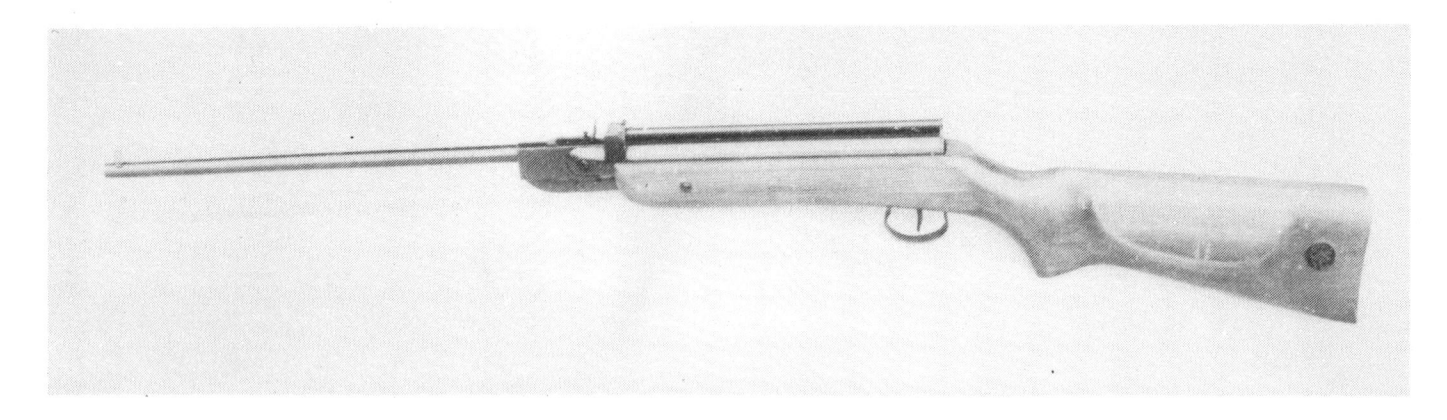

Relum "Repetier"

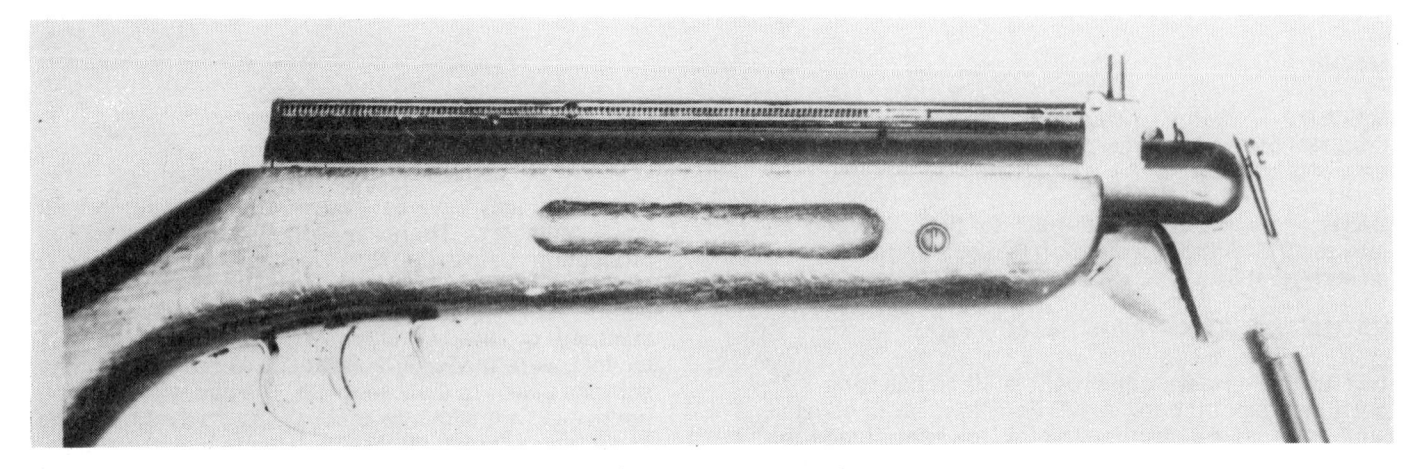

"Repetier" in cocked position

MODEL "Repetier".

MAKER Not known, suspect Relum import from Czechoslovakia.

DATE Seen advertised 1963.

VALUATION £40—£60. ($60—$90).

DETAILS Similar repeating action to the A.S.I. Magazine tube is non-removable and will hold 36 BBs. Above the loading gate is a bar, if pushed from right to left this cuts off the magazine and can be used for single shot pellet shooting, if the bar is pushed from left to right a red spot can be seen through a hole in the top, this opens the magazine for BB shooting. The movement of the bar is made easier by pulling back on the magazine bolt, this takes the pressure off the sliding bar. .177 rifled barrel. 38½ inches long. Serial number stamped on L.H.S. of air chamber near air port is 020163. On the L.H.S. of the stock is a brass medallion with a circular "REPETIER" and "CAL 4.5" around the outside and a bow and arrow with "JELLY" in the inside of the bow, the arrow points upward. When using BBs they tend to roll down the barrel if the airgun is held in a downward position. Seen advertised in a "Denhill" Catalogue, price then was 21/6. Advertised 32 shot magazine, but it will hold 36. It has been reported to the Author that the above was also available in .22 as one has been seen, serial number 539.

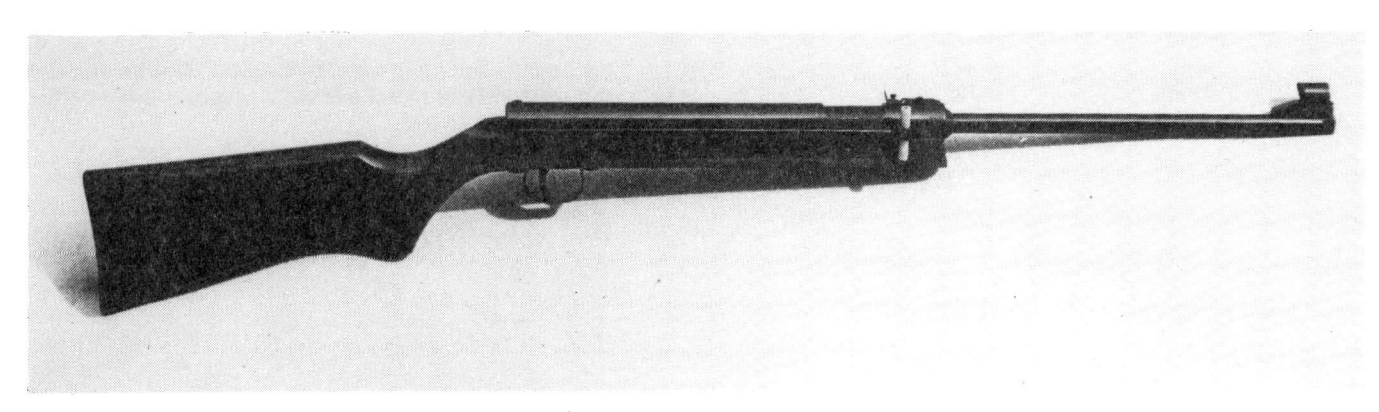

"Foreign" side lever air rifle

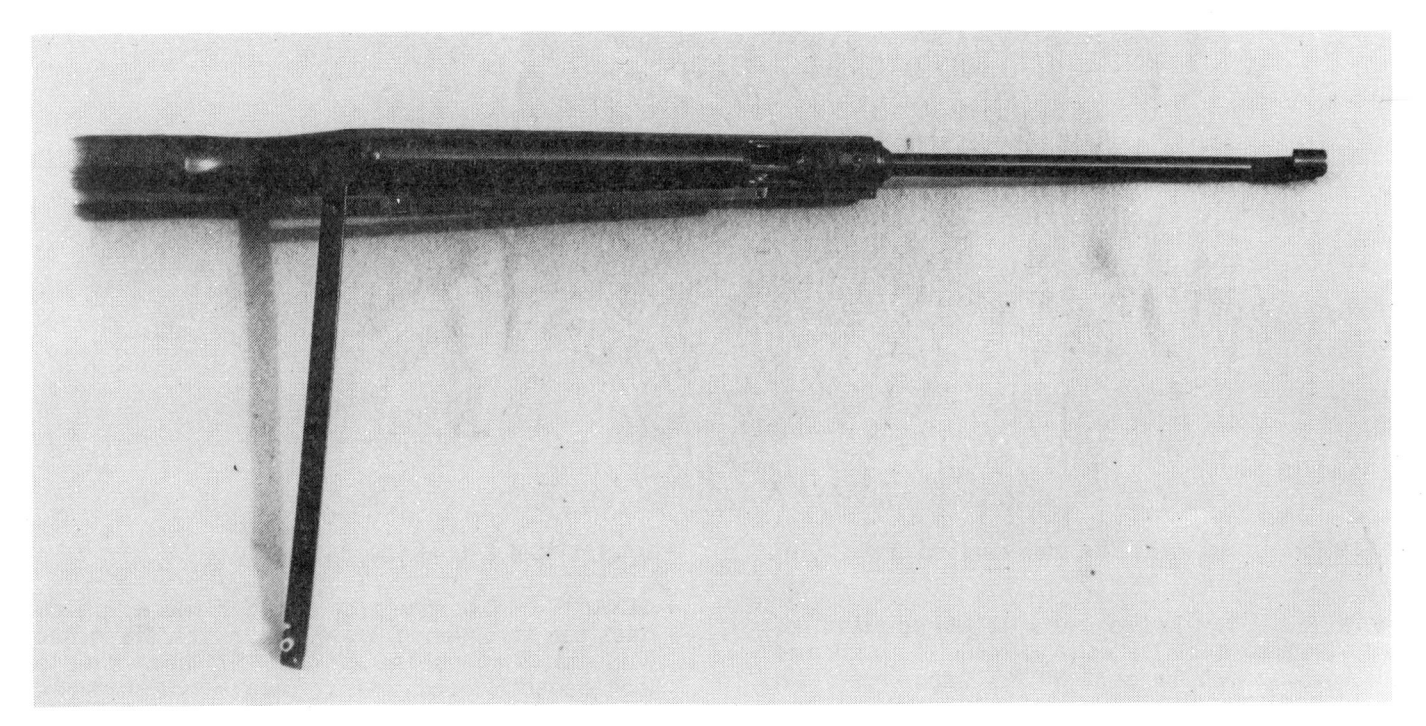

"Foreign" side lever in cocked position

MODEL Not known.

MAKER Not known. Placed under Relum — see below.

DATE Production not known as not available in this country, but would assume the late 1960s to middle 1970s.

VALUATION £30—£60. ($45—$90).

DETAILS Side lever action with no safety ratchet. Can be dangerous if sear fails and you have fingers in the breech loading pellet. I braced barrel against wall when I used the above and took the strain of the main spring on the cocking lever with one hand and loaded pellet with the other. 36½ inches long. Serial number of above 7612 stamped on side of barrel and also has "FOREIGN" stamped on barrel breech. Same type of stamp as that which appears on "RELUM" air rifles so would assume that it might originate from Czechoslovakia, or from one of the Eastern block buffer states.

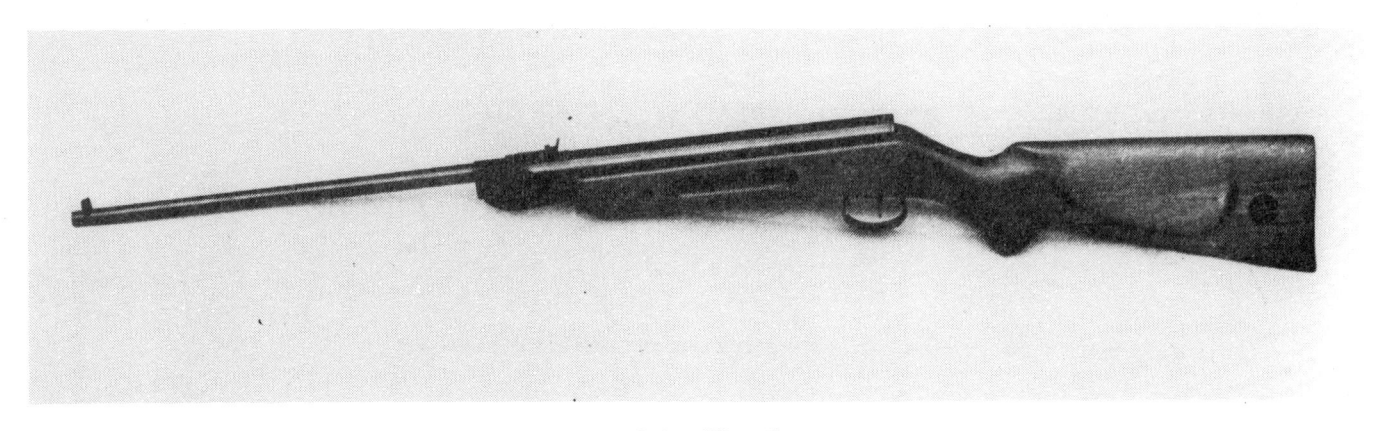

Relum "Sport"

MODEL "Relum Sport". Also known as the Model 822.

MAKER Not known, see next page.

DATE Current model.

VALUATION £20—£40. ($30—$60).

DETAILS Smaller of the two Relum break actions. 38½ inches long with a 15¼ inch rifled barrel. Stock has cheek piece, no butt plate, but has metal plate at base of pistol grip. Stamped on L.H.S. of barrel breech "RELUMSPORT & FOREIGN" also the serial number. An earlier variation may have a metal butt plate and pistol grip cap, barrel breech stamped "FOREIGN" and the metal stock medallion marked "SUPER CAL 4.5 JELLY" and bearing the drawn bow and arrow trademark. It would appear that all the Relum stocks will interchange whatever the model, so that you can fit the jumbo Tornado stock to the smallest Relum air rifle with somewhat out of proportion effects.

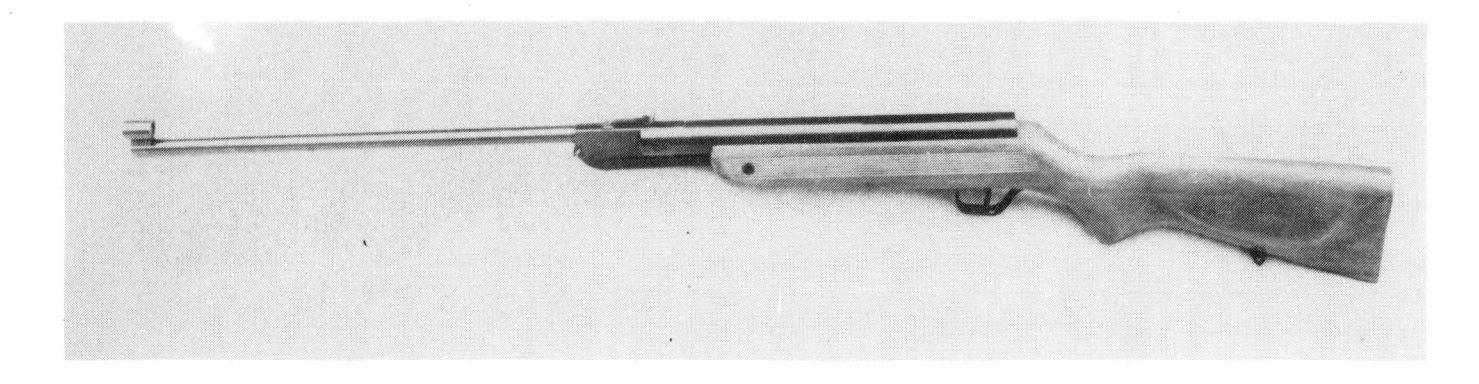

Relum Model LP25

MODEL Relum air rifle. Also stamped LP25.

MAKER Not known, but a RELUM advert in the mid 1960s printed a Galleon trademark on a black oval background with the word "ARTEX", and underneath "BUDAPEST". Address for Relum then was Relum Ltd., Ossulton House, London N.W.1., but may have moved since then.

DATE Discontinued 1978.

VALUATION £20—£40. ($30—$60).

DETAILS Two types of Relum break action air rifles can be obtained, these vary in size, 38½ inches long and 43 inches. The above is 43 inches with a 19 inch barrel. Hooded foresight and simple rearsight. Fitted with swivel sling rings. Only marks are "FOREIGN" and serial number stamped on L.H.S. of breech. Trigger adjustment by way of inner screw in trigger guard fore-screw. Metal butt plate. Grooved for telescopic sight. At a later date these appeared with "LP25" stamped on side of barrel breech.

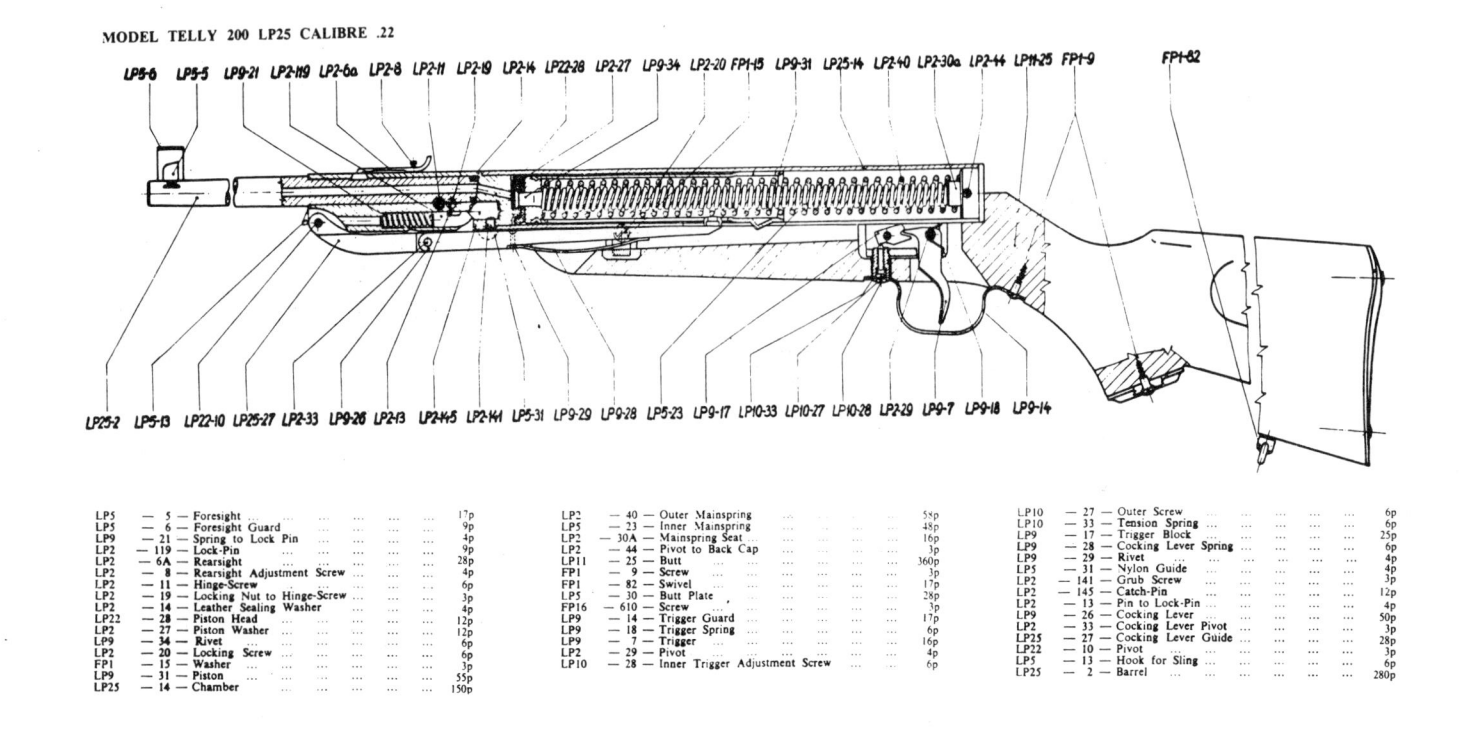

MODEL TELLY 200 LP25 CALIBRE .22

Part	Description	Price
LP5 — 5	Foresight	17p
LP5 — 6	Foresight Guard	9p
LP9 — 21	Spring to Lock Pin	4p
LP2 — 119	Lock-Pin	9p
LP2 — 6A	Rearsight	28p
LP2 — 8	Rearsight Adjustment Screw	4p
LP2 — 11	Hinge-Screw	6p
LP2 — 19	Locking Nut to Hinge-Screw	3p
LP2 — 14	Leather Sealing Washer	4p
LP22 — 28	Piston Head	12p
LP2 — 27	Piston Washer	12p
LP9 — 34	Rivet	6p
LP2 — 20	Locking Screw	6p
FP1 — 15	Washer	3p
LP9 — 31	Piston	55p
LP25 — 14	Chamber	150p
LP2 — 40	Outer Mainspring	58p
LP5 — 23	Inner Mainspring	48p
LP2 — 30A	Mainspring Seat	16p
LP2 — 44	Pivot to Back Cap	3p
LP11 — 25	Butt	360p
FP1 — 9	Screw	3p
FP1 — 82	Swivel	17p
LP5 — 30	Butt Plate	28p
FP16 — 610	Screw	3p
LP9 — 14	Trigger Guard	17p
LP9 — 18	Trigger Spring	6p
LP9 — 7	Trigger	16p
LP2 — 29	Pivot	4p
LP10 — 28	Inner Trigger Adjustment Screw	6p
LP10 — 27	Outer Screw	6p
LP10 — 33	Tension Spring	6p
LP9 — 17	Trigger Block	25p
LP9 — 28	Cocking Lever Spring	6p
LP9 — 29	Rivet	4p
LP5 — 31	Nylon Guide	4p
LP2 — 141	Grub Screw	3p
LP2 — 145	Catch-Pin	12p
LP2 — 13	Pin to Lock-Pin	4p
LP9 — 26	Cocking Lever	50p
LP2 — 33	Cocking Lever Pivot	3p
LP25 — 27	Cocking Lever Guide	28p
LP22 — 10	Pivot	3p
LP5 — 13	Hook for Sling	6p
LP25 — 2	Barrel	280p

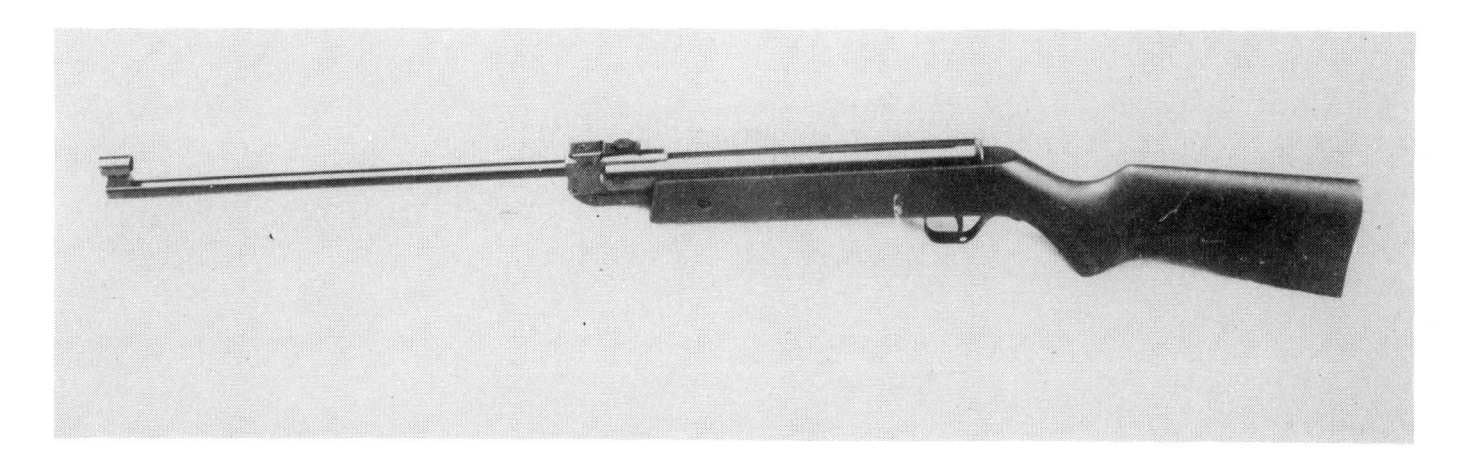

Relum "Taurus" (LG527)

MODEL LG527, also called the "Taurus".

MAKER Stamped "Made in Hungary" actual manufacturer not known. Current importer Relum Ltd., Carlton Park, Industrial Estate, Kelsole, Saxmundham, Suffolk.

DATE Appeared in the late 1970s, assume during 1978. Above model took the place of the large model Relum break action.

VALUATION £20—£40. ($30—$60).

DETAILS Updated version of the Relum break action. Improved sights, cocking lever, trigger action and stock. 40 inches long with an 18 inch rifled .22 barrel. Solid foresight mounted on a dovetail running in line with the barrel and screw held. Protected by push-on hood. All metal rearsight and fully adjustable for windage and elevation. Air chamber grooved for telescopic sight. Trigger adjustment by way of hole through the trigger guard and screw behind the trigger. Stock on the example examined was rather short in reach from the shoulder. Stamped on the side of the barrel breech is the serial number, "LG527" and "MADE IN HUNGARY", also stamped on the barrel the triangle in a circle that could be some sort of barrel inspection mark. The cocking lever is now one piece and certainly aids the ease of cocking. Grooves for telescopic sight are 13 mm apart.

The "Baby" Tornado

MODEL "Baby" Tornado.

MAKER Originated from Hungary.

DATE Would assume early 1960s as action is identical scale-down to the large .22 Tornado available at that time.

VALUATION £30—60. ($45—$90).

DETAILS I did not know that a .177 Relum Tornado was made until I saw the above. 37¾ inches long, 96 cms. It would appear that the large .22 Tornado had been scaled down in almost every aspect. The sights are of the same type as fitted to the Tornado. "FOREIGN" is stamped on the side of the tap breech. Serial number is not visible. Very slender air chamber, one inch in diameter. Plain stock with no chequering on butt plate. Have never seen the above advertised in Britain. The air chamber is obviously too small to accommodate a scope ramp. Tap lever rotates downward in the usual Relum fashion. Trigger adjustment is by way of secondary screw through the main action screw through the trigger guard.

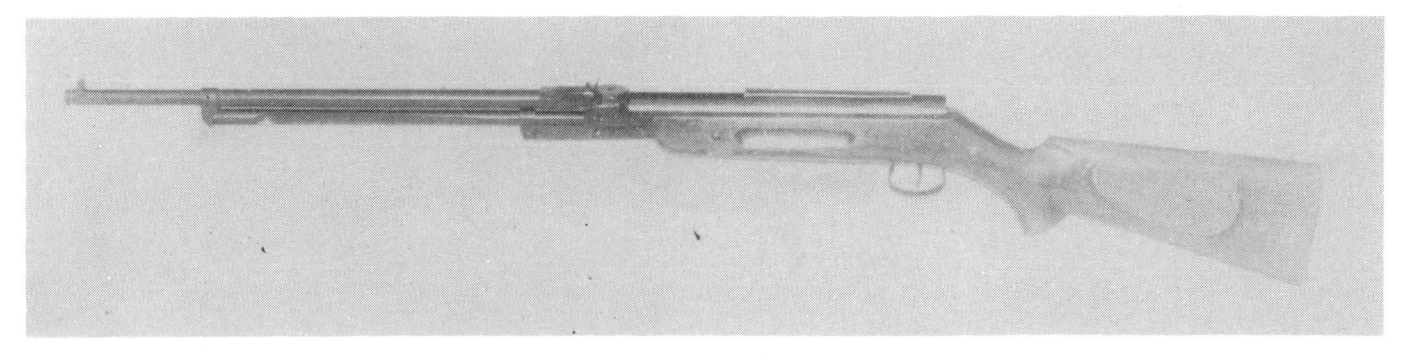

First model Relum Tornado, the LG322

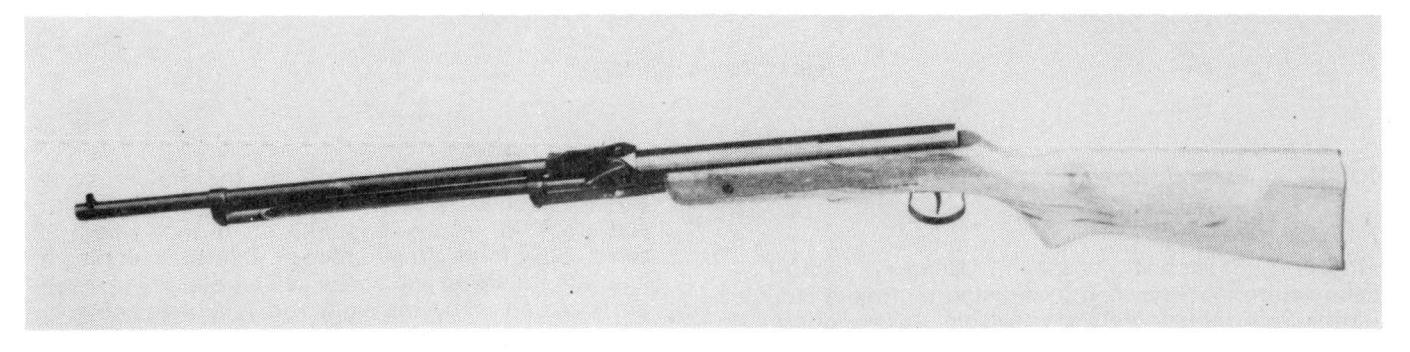

Early model Relum Tornado (LG322)

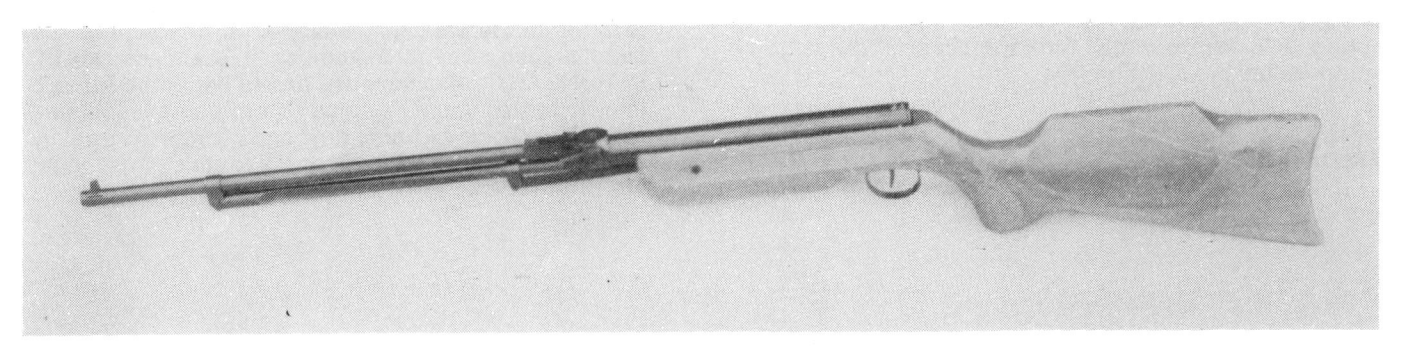

Relum Tornado

MODEL "Tornado".

MAKER Imported by Relum Ltd., Carlton Park Industrial Estate, Kelsole, Saxmundham, Suffolk.

DATE Advertised in 1963 with a more slender stock and metal butt plate. The above pattern of "Tornado" seen advertised late 1966. Remodelled in the very late 1970s and called the "Super Tornado". Super Tornado introduced 1978.

VALUATION £30—£60. ($45—$90).

DETAILS 45 inches in length with heavy well formed stock, 19 inch rifled barrel with foresight blade set in dovetail with spring held hood. Rearsight also set in groove with adjustment for windage and elevation. Tap has downward facing lever. Cocking lever has double link so final part is parallel to air chamber. Cocking lever has spring loaded plunger set in end for engaging socket on underside of barrel. L.H.S. of barrel near tap stamped "MADE IN HUNGARY" whilst on the other side appears the serial number. Number of above 67708. Stamped on the barrel appears a small triangle set in a circle. Top of air chamber has been dovetailed for telescopic sight and at rear is stamped "RELUM TORNADO". These letters have been "golded" in. Trigger adjustment is by way of small inner screw set in the main stock screw through the trigger guard. Butt has large proportions, deep fore-end has been grooved and grip hand chequered. Advertised weight 7 lb 5 oz. Advertised with the "ARTEX" trademark from Budapest and as having been made for Relum of London by "one of the Continent's leading arms factories". The Tornado is fitted with two main springs, one inside the other. Only available in .22. For a review of the Super model see "Airgun World" July 1979. All in all a hard working air rifle of robust design that could take much abuse. Fitted with leather washer, leather being a natural product made from animal skin.

First Model 322 appears to have been produced without serial numbers. These had the slender stock, but without the many parallel grooves down each side of the fore-end. Stock was fitted with metal butt plate and pistol grip cap. Telescopic groove was held in place by three screws. "MODEL 322" was stamped on the side of the air chamber. The world "FOREIGN" appeared on the side of the barrel breech. The B.S.A. Meteor mainspring should fit the above. Have seen other models stamped "LP 11". First models with the well proportioned stock were fitted with a screw-on folded metal scope ramp. Three screws held this in place. Artex was the State run, isn't everything over there, export agency and they sold the air rifles to Relum the import agency in England. Their Hungarian address was Via Hador 31, Budapest.

Hints on how to tune the Relum may be found in "Sporting Air Rifle" November 1984.

First models for the Relum air rifles were fitted with three mainsprings, one inner as per usual and two outer thin mainsprings that were would onto each other. The whole set looked like a mass of coiled wire.

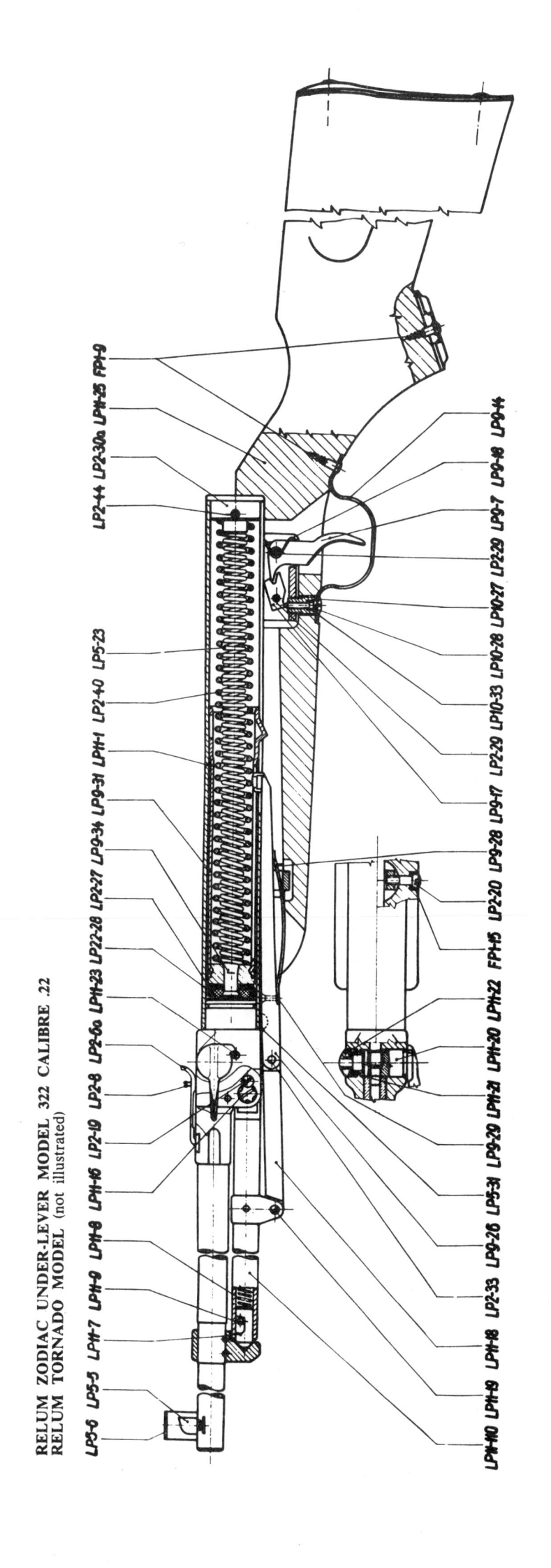

RELUM ZODIAC UNDER-LEVER MODEL 322 CALIBRE .22
RELUM TORNADO MODEL (not illustrated)

PARTS LIST – LG15V

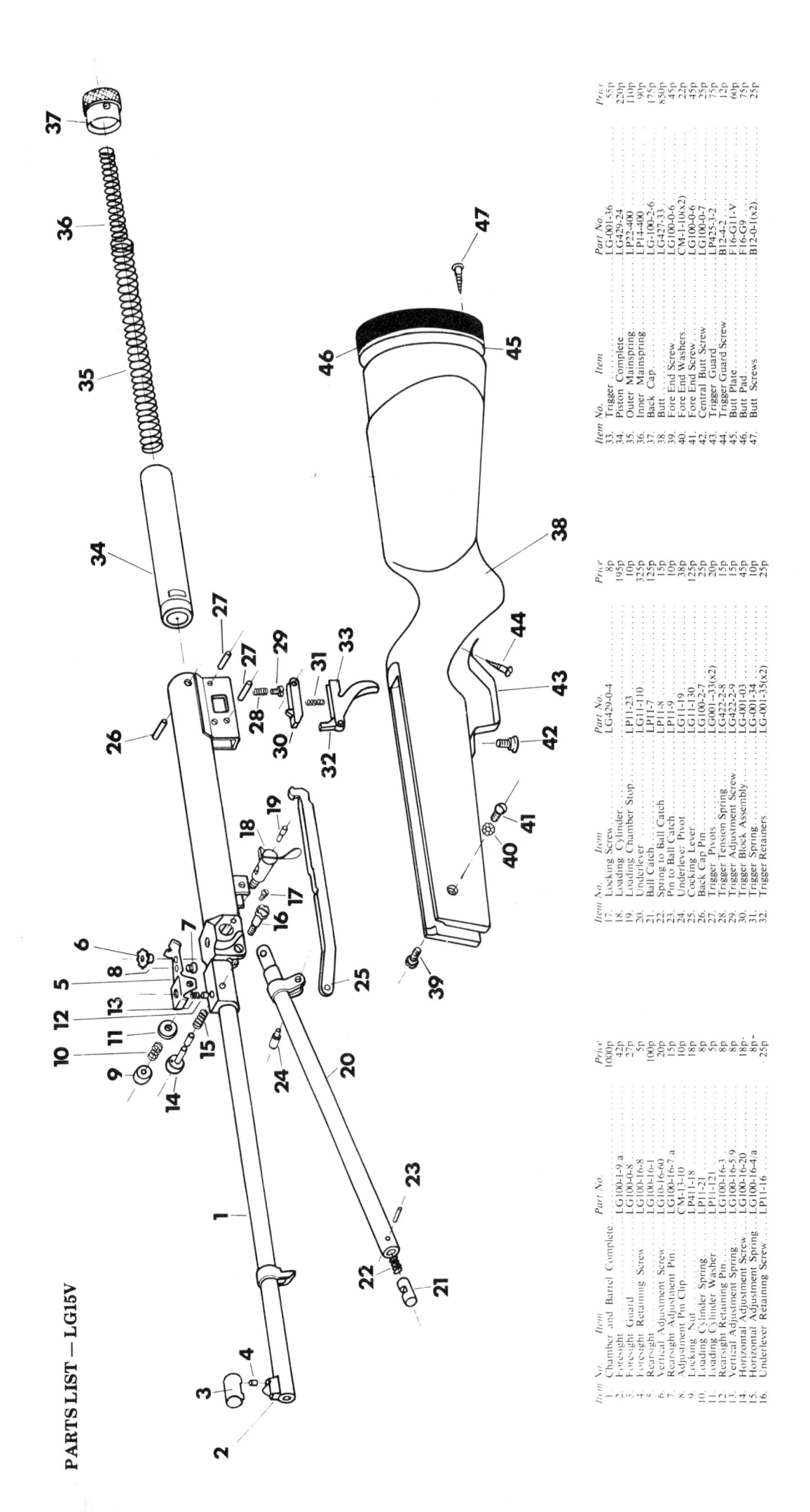

Item No.	Item	Part No.	Price
1.	Chamber and Barrel Complete	LG100-1-9a	1000p
2.	Foresight	LG100-0-8	42p
3.	Foresight Guard	LG100-16-8	27p
4.	Foresight Retaining Screw	LG100-16-1	5p
5.	Rearsight	LG10-16-60	100p
6.	Vertical Adjustment Screw	LG100-16-7a	20p
7.	Rearsight Adjustment Pin	CM-13-10	15p
8.	Adjustment Pin Clip	LP411-18	10p
9.	Locking Nut	LP11-21	18p
10.	Loading Cylinder Spring	LG100-16-3	8p
11.	Loading Cylinder Washer		5p
12.	Rearsight Retaining Pin	LG100-16-5/9	8p
13.	Vertical Adjustment Screw	LG100-16-20	18p
14.	Horizontal Adjustment Spring	LG100-16-4/a	8p-
15.	Horizontal Adjustment Screw		10p
16.	Underlever Retaining Screw	LP11-16	25p
17.	Locking Screw	LG429-0-4	8p
18.	Loading Cylinder		195p
19.	Loading Chamber Stop	LP11-23	10p
20.	Underlever	LP11-7	325p
21.	Ball Catch	LP11-8	125p
22.	Spring to Ball Catch	LP11-9	15p
23.	Pin to Ball Catch	LG11-19	10p
24.	Underlever Pivot	LG11-130	38p
25.	Cocking Lever	LG100-2-7	25p
26.	Back Cap Pin	LG001-33(x2)	20p
27.	Trigger Pivots	LG422-2-8	15p
28.	Trigger Tension Spring	LG422-2-9	15p
29.	Trigger Adjustment Screw	LG-001-03	45p
30.	Trigger Block Assembly	LG-001-34	10p
31.	Trigger Spring	LG-001-35(x2)	25p
32.	Trigger Retainers		
33.	Trigger	LG-001-36	55p
34.	Piston Complete	LG429-24	220p
35.	Outer Mainspring	LP22-400	110p
36.	Inner Mainspring	LP14-400	90p
37.	Back Cap	LG-100-2-6	175p
38.	Butt	LG427-33	850p
39.	Fore End Screw	LG100-0-6	45p
40.	Fore End Washers	CM-1-10(x2)	22p
41.	Fore End Screw	LG100-0-6	45p
42.	Central Butt Screw	LG100-0-7	25p
43.	Trigger Guard	LP425-3-2	75p
44.	Trigger Guard Screw	B12-4-2	12p
45.	Butt Plate	F16-G11-V	60p
46.	Butt Pad	F16-G9	75p
47.	Butt Screws	B12-0-1(x2)	25p

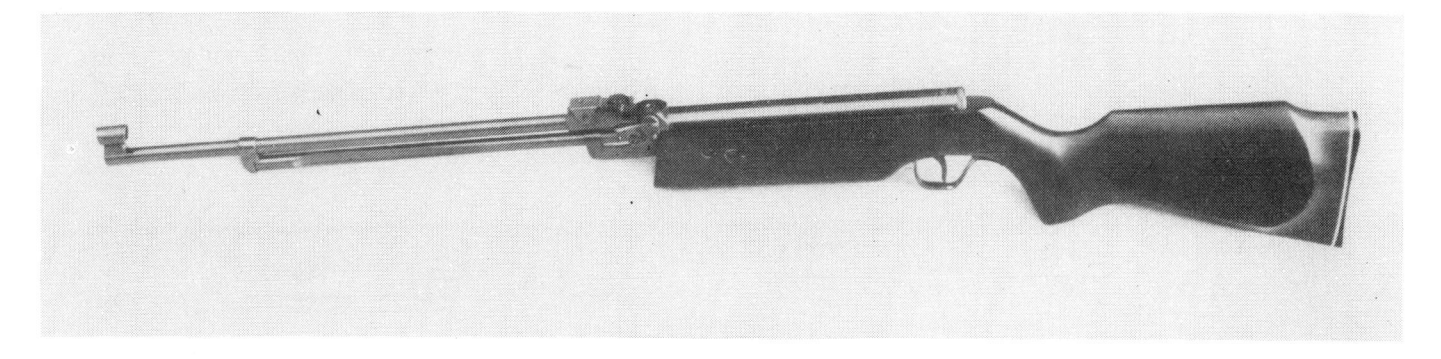

Relum Super Tornado (LG15)

MODEL Super Tornado (LG15).

MAKER Not known. Imported by Relum Ltd., Carlton Park Industrial Estate, Kelsole, Saxmundham, Suffolk.

DATE Introduced 1978 and took the place of the Tornado.

VALUATION £30—£60.
($45—$90).

DETAILS Improved model of the Tornado. Improvements being made to the fore and rearsights, cocking lever, trigger action and style of stock. 43 inches long. Foresight mounted on dovetail and protected by a hood. All metal rearsight which is fully adjustable. Under cocking lever is now one piece and is a lot easier to operate. L.H.S. of breech stamped "LG 15 MADE IN HUNGARY", also the serial number appears. Top of air chamber stamped "RELUM TORNADO" and grooved for telescopic sight. Grooves are 14 mm apart, Trigger adjustment is by way of small screw behind the trigger and small hole in the trigger guard. Well shaped stock with butt plate. The piston still retains the leather washer and the two coil springs, one inside the other, are also still used. Many parts are interchangeable with the old model Tornado. The end air chamber plug has a curled edging, this does not unscrew, but is held in place by a cross peg. Advertised weight 7 lbs 12 ozs. It would appear from the serial number that the manufacturers started from "0" again when they produced the LG15. For a review of the above see "Airgun World" July 1979. A B.S.A. Airsporter mainspring will fit the above and certainly improve the muzzle energy.

During the 1980s the above was imported into America by Precise International, 3 Chestnut Street, Suffern, NY 10901, U.S.A. and sold as the "Precise Minuteman Magnum" in .177, but advertised as the same length as the more usual .22. Advertised muzzle velocity 575 f.p.s., that makes me think that this must surely be .22 and not .177 as advertised.

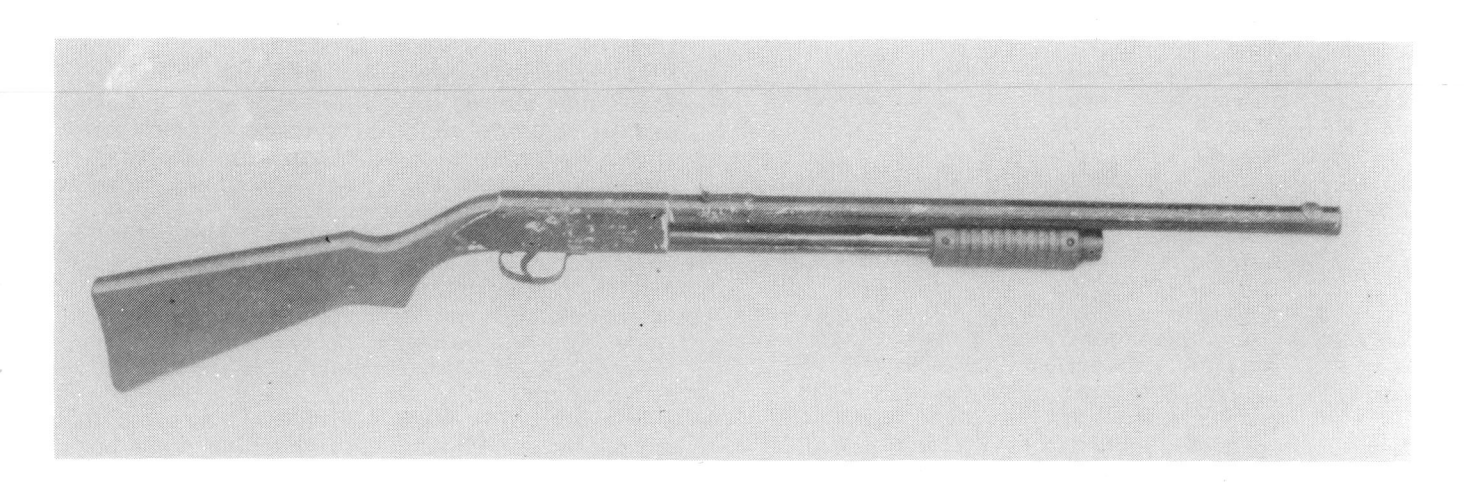

Remington Model 26 repeating air rifle

The Remington Model 26 repeating air rifle

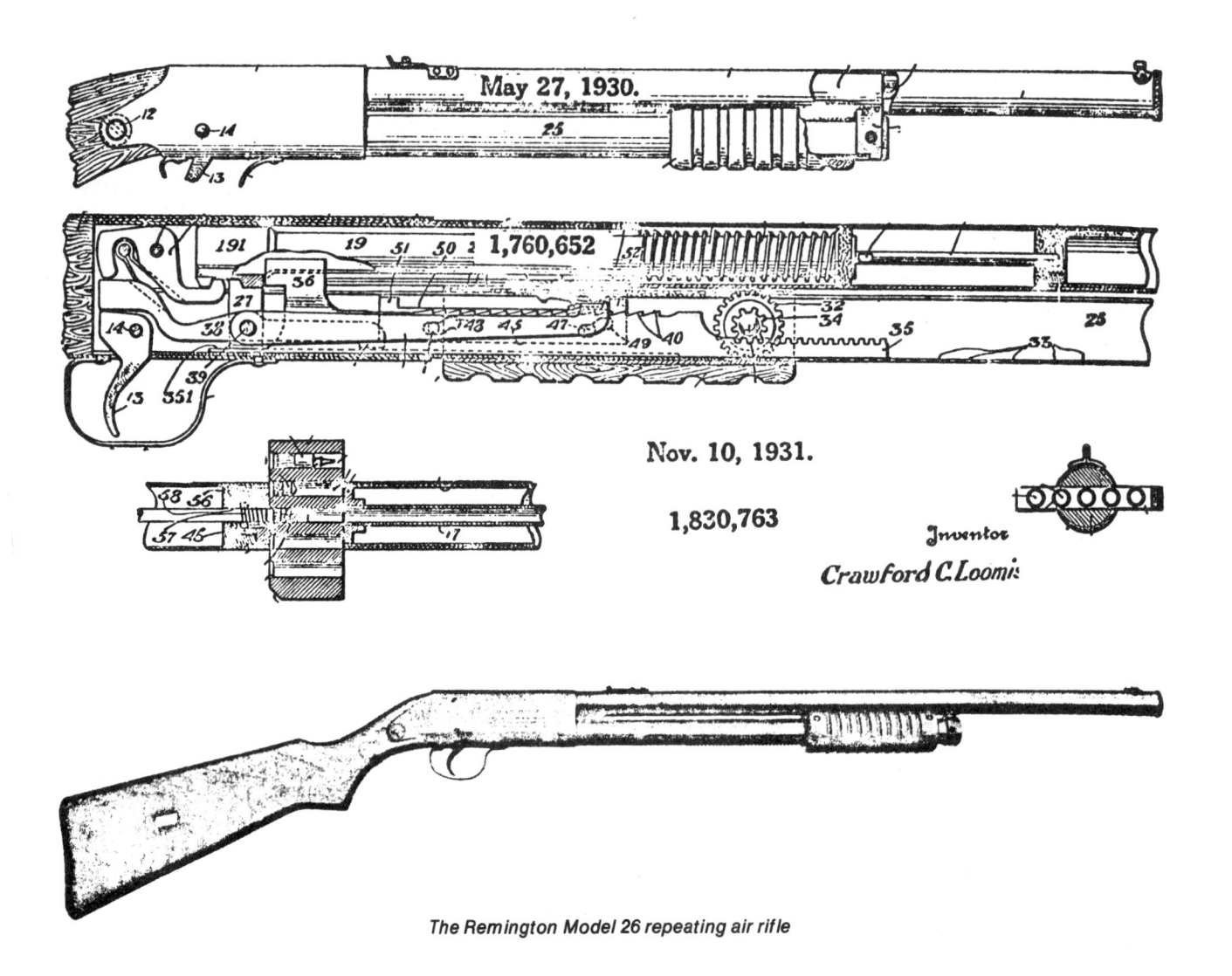

MODEL "Remington Air Rifle". Model 26 repeating air rifle.

MAKER Remington Arms Co. Inc., Arms Works, Ilion, N.Y., U.S.A.

DATE From mid-1928 to mid-1930. Production of around 20,000 only.

VALUATION A rare tinplate air rifle. £50 — £100. ($75 — $150).

DETAILS A surprising air rifle in that I never knew that Remington ever made a tinplate air rifle. 38 inches long. Black paint finish with wooden fore-end and simple parallel sided stock. Trombone repeating action that operates without mishap. Foresight brazed on to barrel whilst rearsight adjustable for windage and elevation. L.H.S. of body stamped.
   REMINGTON
      REG. U.S.PAT.OFF.
REMINGTON AIR RIFLE.
REMINGTON ARMS CO. INC. ARMS WORKS.
ILION, N.Y., MADE IN U.S.A. PATENTS PEND.
R.H.S. of body stamped
SAFETY FEATURE.
TO PULL TRIGGER, FORE-END MUST
BE IN EXTREME FORWARD POSITION.
ANY OTHER POSITION GUN IS SAFE.

Barrel tube screws out of the barrel body and has a parallel magazine tube running the length of the barrel. A very well made action that has proved faultless on the above example. The front face of the barrel is stamped "ZO". Barrel is smoothbore.

The development of the Model 26 began in 1927 by C. C. Loomis who also designed rifles, shotguns and pistols for Remington. There were five U.S. patents regarding the Model 26. Some of these were finally issued after the cessation of production. An unusual feature of above is the fact that the piston is cocked by a ratchet gear cog that rotates as the underside is pulled back. This also activates safety cams that prevent the action being fired whilst the gun is being cocked. The use of lead shot or BBs was recommended as the BB was forced fed past a crimp restriction that could bend or even break under the use of hard steel BBs. The stock is held to the action by one stock bolt, this gave way to a loose fit if abused. The manufacture of a quality tinplate with many parts just before the American depression soon tolled the end of the above model. For further details see "The American BB Gun" by Dunothan.

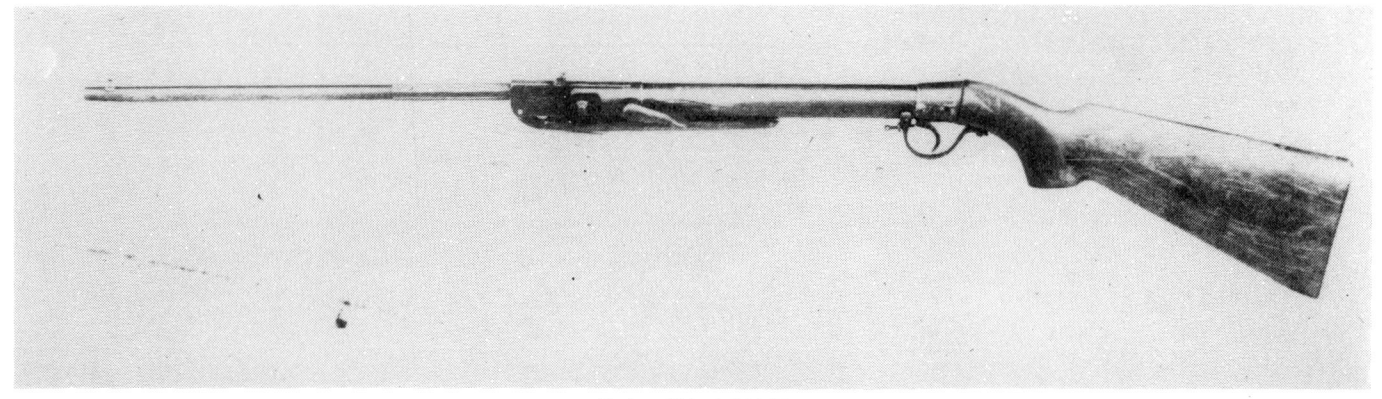

Roland Model 1927

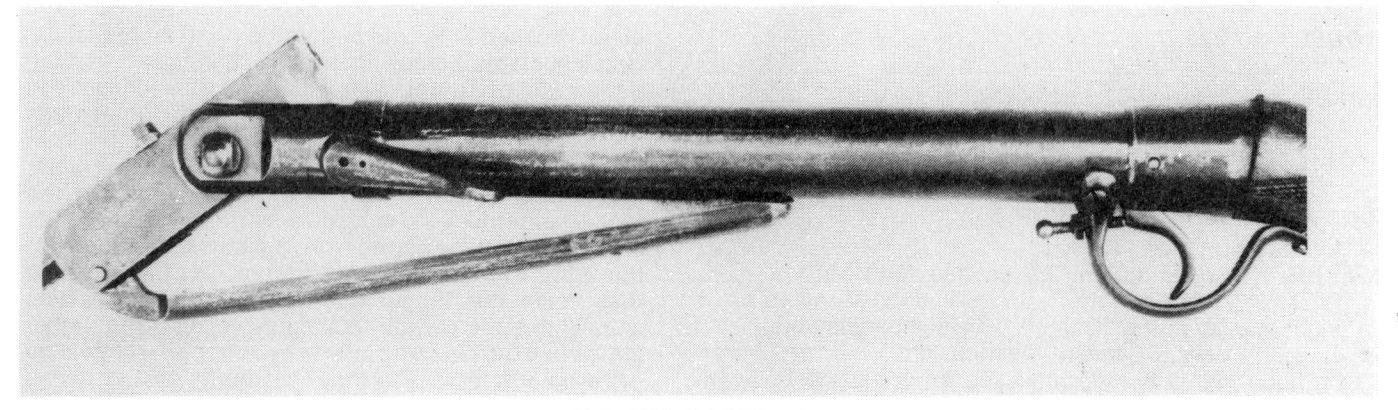

Roland Model 1927 action

MODEL Roland 1927.

MAKER Oscar Will (Wilheym Foss), Venuswaffenwerk, Zella-Mehlis (Thuringen), Germany. The above Jung Roland air rifle is identical to the Tell air rifles of the same period.

DATE The above style of air rifle with the side lift-up barrel release appeared as early as 1911 and was produced under various names right up until 1939.

VALUATION £40—£80. ($60—$120).

DETAILS Often mistaken for the Greener air rifle and often sold as such to "Green" collectors! 43¼ inches long with a 19 inch .22 rifled barrel. Barrel octagonal to round with serial number stamped on the underside. Foresight dovetail mounted, whilst the rearsight, identical to those fitted to Haenel air rifles, is also dovetail mounted. Top of barrel breech stamped "ROLAND 1927", would assume that this is the model number because at an earlier date have seen reference to the Roland Model 1909. The side barrel latch has two small holes drilled in it and is raised in order to release the barrel. Its angle of travel is about 90° whereas in the Greener air rifle it is 180°. Last two digits of serial number are stamped on various sundry parts. No other markings appear on the air rifle. Trigger adjustment through an improved style of trigger guard. Stock is still hand chequered with metal butt plate. About 1911 the above was sold in 5.7 mm calibre only with a Roland target kit. This was described as the Model 1909 and only sold complete with a bell target and pointed pellets, like the ordinary cat-slugs of that period but with a pointed head. This kit is best illustrated if the actual 1911 catalogue is quoted:

"The precision air rifle Roland Model 1909 is only supplied complete together with Roland Target. The construction is as follows; The Roland Target consists of a steel shield solidly mounted on a wooden coat of arms with mail rings from 1—12. On the rings their respective numbers have been marked all round so that each bullet (pellet), hitting the mark flattens on the target and stamps in automatically the number hit. The leaden bullet which adheres to the target is removed by the marksman with a bullet lifter. Thus the marksman can always prove his hit by means of his bullet (which has the ring number pressed into it when that number has been hit). When the bulls-eye 12 has been hit a bell rings. In shooting matches no list need be kept for every marksman delivers his bullets with numbers. The target is also suitable for hotel-keepers etc." (Oh Happy Days!).

The above "Roland"/Tell air rifle was also retailed by G. C. Bell & Sons of Glasgow as their "Club Air Gun for Match Shooting" available either blued or nickel plated, and in .22 or .177. Advertised weight 2.6 kilograms, 6¼ lbs. During the early 1930s the Midland Gun Company, Demon Gunworks, Bath Street, Birmingham sold it as the "Perfecta" for 50/-, i.e. £2.50, being sold in .177 only, and with a blued finish only. The foresight blade was tipped with German silver.

According to Smith the Jung Roland started life as being manufactured by Fredreich Langenham. It would appear that Roland air rifles also appeared after 1945 but with fully stocked actions. The above Roland also sold as the Model Tell 50. More confusion, according to "Waffenlexieon" by R. Mahrholdt, 1952, Jung Roland airguns were made by the Hubertus Metal Works, Sporting Arms Factory, Molln, Germany. I still think Oscar Will had something to do with Roland air rifles!

From a pre-war German catalogue dated somewhere between 1920 and 1940 there is a list of Roland air rifles with the following model numbers: 1909, 1910, 1912, and 1925, with a list of calibres that is very comprehensive, 5.4, 5.65, 5.7 and 5.75. Whether all the models were available in all the calibres listed is, I'm afraid, not quite clear. The Model 1927 is a late arrival as it was not listed.

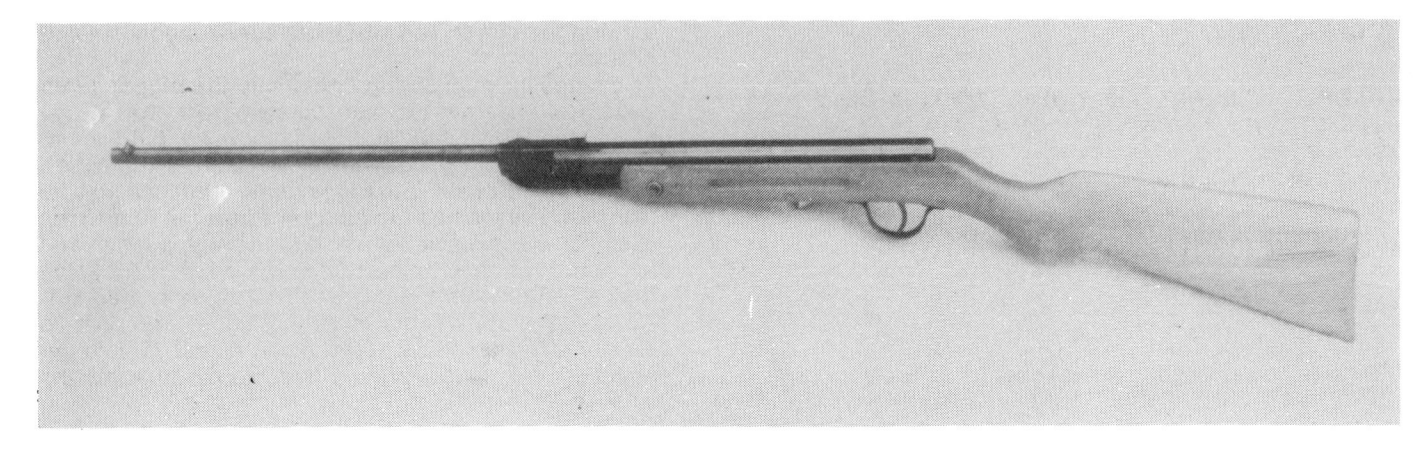

Slavia ZV3 air rifle

MODEL ZV3.

MAKER "Slavia" Czechoslovakia.

DATE Would assume 1960s.

VALUATION £20—£40. ($30—$60).

DETAILS Break action. 37¼ inches long with a 14¾ inch .177 rifled barrel. Unusual shaped pillar foresight, similar to the "Comet". Rearsight adjustable for elevation only. Originally the foresight was fitted with a hood. Serial number stamped on underside of barrel (021491). Top of air chamber stamped "ZV3 MADE IN CZECHOSLOVAKIA". Note that the Slavia air pistol is called ZVP. One piece stock without butt plate. Non-adjustable trigger. Prior to 1938 "Slavia" was the trade name of Antonin Vilimec who produced pistols in the town of Kdyne, Bohemia. In 1938 the factory was dissolved!

To change the mainspring first remove the two trigger guard wood screws, then the main bolt behind the trigger and the two stock screws at the front end. The action can now be parted from the stock. At the rear of the action there are two pins, first remove the lower pin that holds the trigger and trigger spring in place, usually this pin can be pushed out easily. The higher pin carries the tension of the mainspring so it should be removed with care. The inner trigger block and spring guide can now be slid out and the mainspring changed. Re-assemble in reverse.

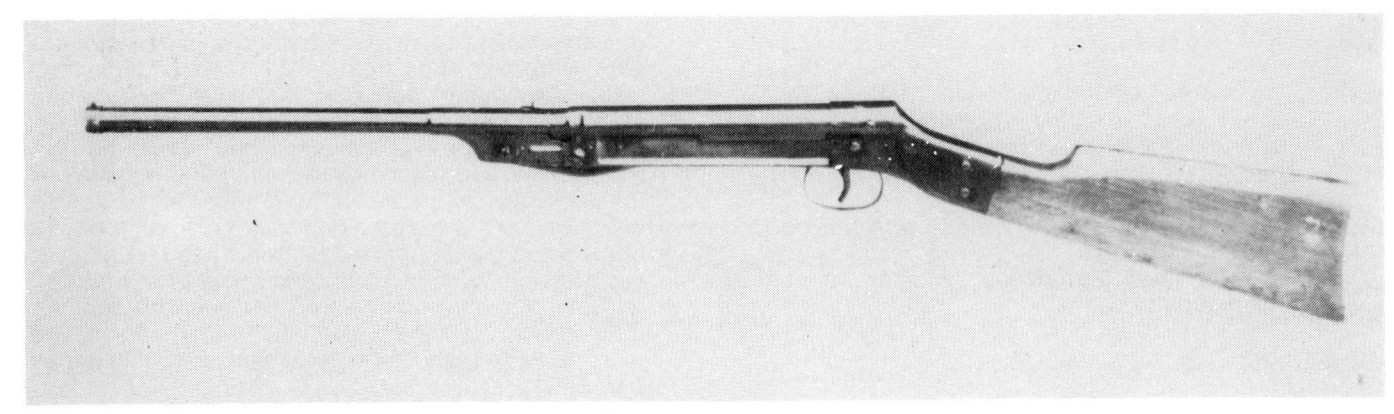

Stella Model 512

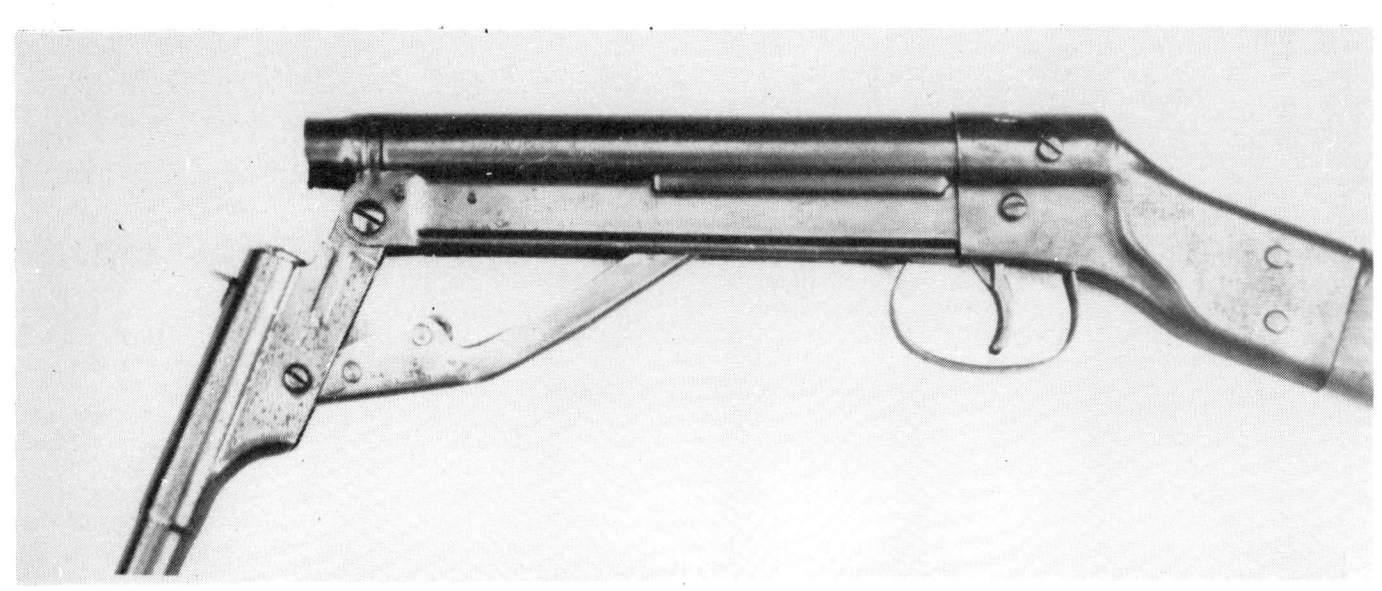

Stella Model 512 action — note cast iron trigger

MODEL 512.

MAKER "Stella" and marked "Made in Czechoslovakia". Almost identical model seen with "Slavia" trade name so might assume that "Stella" is an earlier version, see Slavia 612.

DATE Would assume 1950s to 1960s.

VALUATION £20—£30. ($30—$45).

DETAILS A tinplate break action air rifle very similar to the Diana Model 15, as a matter of fact parts will interchange. 32½ inches long (82 cms) with a 12 inch (30.5 cms) .177 smoothbore barrel. All parts are blued. Barrel has screw-in pillar foresight and a simple blade rearsight. The cocking lever incorporates the barrel latch and this clips on to the barrel pivot pin, although the actual design differs slightly from that on the Diana Model 15. Top of air chamber is stamped "STELLA 512 MADE IN CZECHOSLOVAKIA" the Stella has an arrow running through it. The stock has been roughly cut and finished.

To change the mainspring first unclip the trigger guard and then unscrew the two screws from the trigger block, this allows the trigger to float freely, but take no notice. You can now either tap or hammer the action away from the stock. The trigger and spring can now be removed. The mainspring guide is a bayonet fit into the chamber, place a screwdriver into the end, push in and turn and the spring guide should move out by pressure from the mainspring, if it doesn't it can be tapped out. The original mainspring may be about two inches shorter than that fitted to the Diana Model 15, take no notice as the longer spring will fit. Replacement is the reversal of the above.

Blocked barrels can be freed if jammed by lead pellets and matches by taking a thin steel rod, like a .22 cleaning rod and flattening the end and then honing into a sharp blade. You then introduce the rod into the barrel and ram it down into the blockage and turn slowly, repeat this and periodically take out the rod, turn barrel upside down and tap with wooden stock and allow debris to fall out.

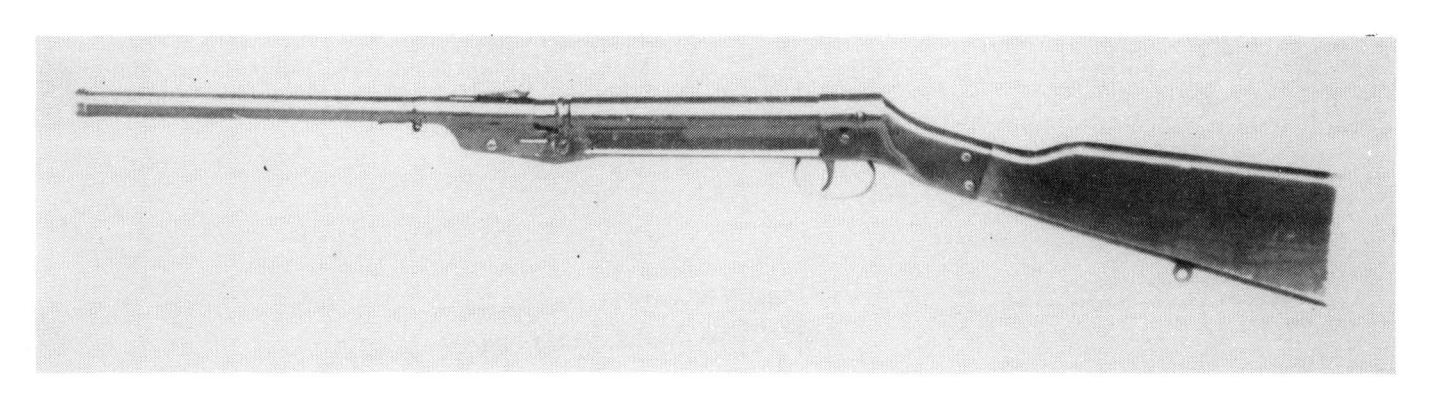

The Slavia 612

MODEL 612.

MAKER "Slavia" Czechoslovakia. "Slavia" was a trade name used by Antonin Vilimec, a gunmaker in Kdyne, Bohemia, although they were "dissolved" in 1938. The Slavia 612 is a 1950s and 1960s air rifle and has, what looks like a "Z" trademark and by a coincidence the three major arms producers are the following:
Zbrojovka Praga (Praga Arms Factory), Prague, Czechoslovakia.
Ceskoslovenska Zbrojovka Akciova Spolecnost (Czechoslovakian Arms Factory Ltd.), Brno, Moravia.
Ceska Zbrojovka Akciova Spolecnest (Czech Arms Factory Ltd.), Strakonice, Bohemia.

DATE 1950s and 1960s.

VALUATION £20—£30. ($30—$45).

DETAILS Almost the same as the Stella Model 512, except that the later Model 612 had a sheet metal trigger, machined stock whereas the Stella looked very much hand-made. 32½ inches long (82.5 cms) with a 12 inch (30.5 cms) .177 rifled barrel. The rifling is very wide and shallow and has about one turn only for its entire length, this has been the first Model 15 type air rifle I've seen with a rifled barrel. Simple fixed sights. Slings swivels are fitted, spot welded to underside of barrel and curtain rail eye-hook screwed into stock. A serial number stamped on the underside of the stock near the action. Top of air chamber is stamped with a "Z" and "U" logo and "SLAVIA 612 MADE IN CZECHOSLOVAKIA". Again, as with the Stella, many parts will interchange with the Diana Model 15 air rifle.

203

The Slavia 618

MODEL 618, 619 and 622.

MAKER "Slavia" of Czechoslovakia. Also seen for Relum on the air chamber.

DATE Would assume the 1970s.

VALUATION £20–£40. ($30–$60).

DETAILS Small sized moderately priced air rifle. 35¾ inches long with a 14⅛ inch rifled barrel in .177. All metal construction with deep blued finish. Fore and rearsights are dovetail mounted and was fitted with a foresight hood. Serial number, 442963, is stamped on side of breech. Air chamber has parallel grooves similar to B.S.F. airguns and is stamped "SLAVIA 618 — MADE IN CZECHOSLOVAKIA". Double pull trigger but lacks adjustment. A serial number may also appear stamped on the stock on the underside of the pistol grip. Some of these do not have a double pull trigger. The Model 619 in the deluxe version with "grained" stock, gold lettering, highly polished metal parts and fitted with a sling and sold in attractive box. The 622 is the .22 version of the 618 and boasted a muzzle velocity of 330 f.p.s. Nearly all smoothbore Model 618s have "H" at the end of the serial number whilst with a rifled barrel the serial number may have a "R" prefix and end with the letter "E". Slavia and Relum appear to be connected as some of these have been seen bearing both names.

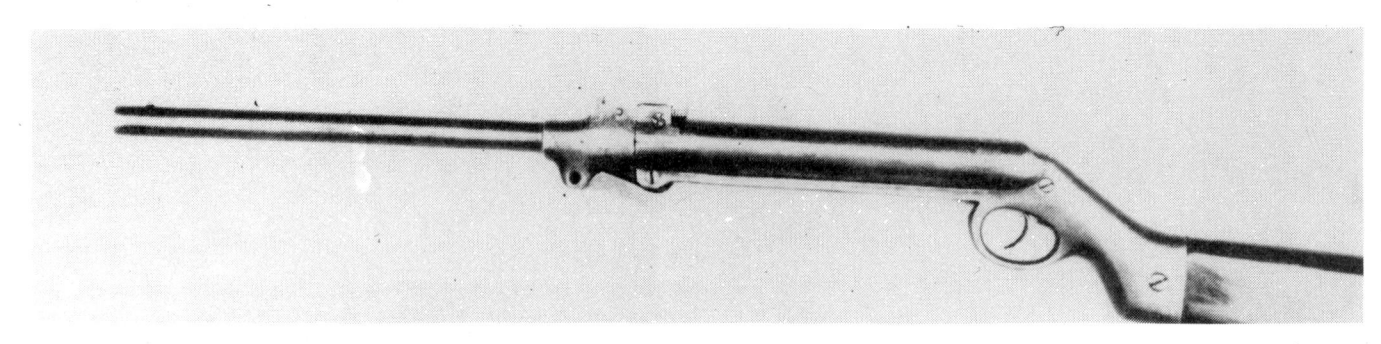

The "Speedy" air rifle

MODEL The "Speedy" air rifle.

MAKER Not known. Assumed to be German.

DATE Advertised 1927 in catalogue by G. C. Bell & Sons, Thistle Street, Glasgow. Price then 12/6.

VALUATION £30–£50. ($45–$75).

DETAILS 31½ inches long with 10¾ inch smoothbore barrel. Barrel has brass liner in what appears to be an outer hollow tube. This being brass with nickel plating. Serial number stamped on the breech face and on the opposing air transfer port face. Similar to the Gem air rifles. Gem type top "T" bar barrel latch with a tall rearsight set in groove just in front of barrel latch, missing on the above example. The cocking lever and butt plate also bear traces of nickel plating. Air chamber is separate tube clamped into place by the two halves of the outer parts of the air chamber and trigger housing. This also clamps the butt into place. One such example is featured in "Airgun World" January 1979. Serial number also appears on the underside of the "T" bar barrel latch. Advertised as having a nickel plated air chamber and available in .177 only.

Have seen three of the above with the following serial numbers: 3479, 6852, and 7046.

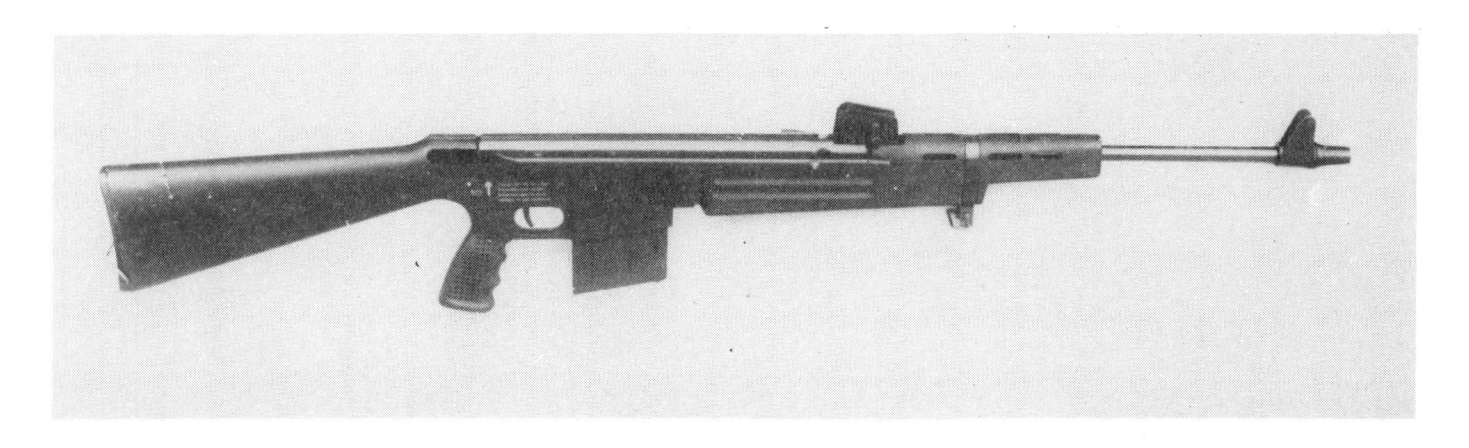

The Sussex Armoury "Jackal"

MODEL "Jackal". Also known as "Jackal Parabellum" Model 2000.

MAKER The Sussex Armoury, 34 North Street, Hailsham, Sussex. The Sussex Armoury stopped trading in 1982 and the range of air rifles were continued by the original manufacturers, N.S.P., Station Road Industrial Estate, Hailsham, East Sussex BN27 2ES.

DATE Introduced 1976. An improved model was introduced in 1979 as the Jackal .22 Hi-Power Model 2300.

VALUATION £40−£80.
($60−$120).

DETAILS The "Mean Machine". A British made military styled air rifle. All blued action with black military style A.B.S. stock. 45 inches long with an 18 inch barrel. Available in either .177 or .22. Advertised weight 7 lb 8 oz. Advertised muzzle velocity for .22 being 580 f.p.s. Plastic fore and rearsight. Serial number stamped just under rearsight on L.H.S. Stamped on top of air chamber "JACKAL". Grooved for telescopic sight. Action has anti-release rachet, but can be overcome as follows; when cocked take the strain of the mainspring and pull trigger with the other hand, the piston will then move forward a small distance until it meets the safety rachet. Now again take the strain of the mainspring and with the other hand press down the small lever that protrudes through a small slot near the cocking lever slot and when the small lever has been pressed down into the action the action can then slowly be returned to the unfired position. Always be prepared for the power of the mainspring. The dummy magazine is in actual fact a storage for pellets and has a sliding door for pouring pellets into it and out for loading. The stock is supplied with sling swivels. The rifled barrel has about 2½ twists of rifling. During 1977 a "Super Target Jackal" was available fitted with contoured wooden stock and match sights. Apparently the barrel is easily removable for changing or cleaning. There is a locking grub screw just under the rearsight on the R.H.S., and barrel unscrews. As the Jackal was only produced for three years it is well worth collecting for the future as it could well become a rarity. The barrel is stamped "SUSSEX ARMOURY HAILSHAM ENGLAND".

JACKAL 22/177 CALIBRE WEAPONS

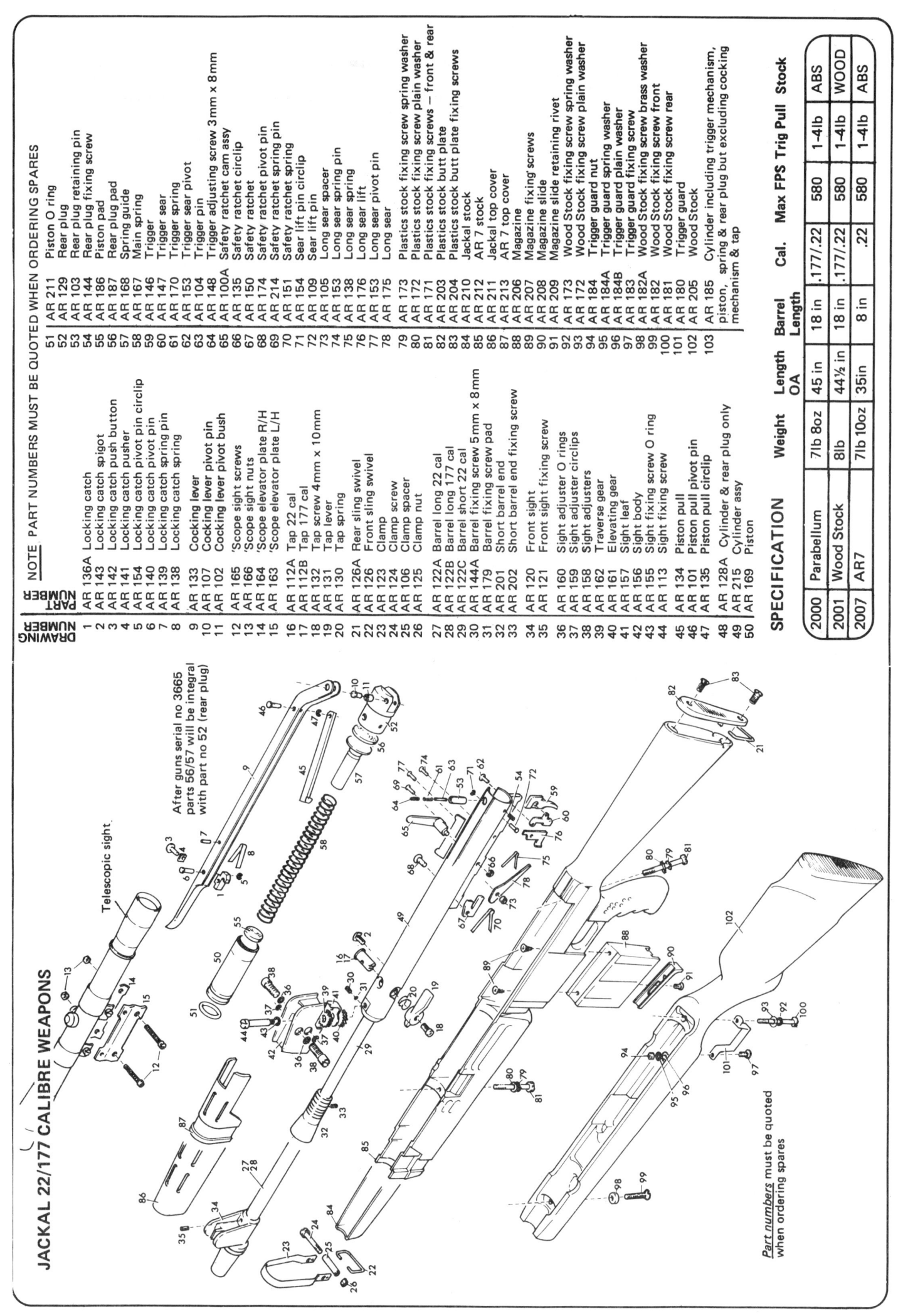

NOTE PART NUMBERS MUST BE QUOTED WHEN ORDERING SPARES

DRAWING NUMBER	PART NUMBER		DRAWING NUMBER	PART NUMBER	
1	AR 136A	Locking catch	51	AR 211	Piston O ring
2	AR 143	Locking catch spigot	52	AR 129	Rear plug
3	AR 142	Locking catch push button	53	AR 103	Rear plug retaining pin
4	AR 141	Locking catch pusher	54	AR 144	Rear plug fixing screw
5	AR 154	Locking catch pivot pin circlip	55	AR 186	Piston pad
6	AR 140	Locking catch pivot pin	56	AR 187	Rear plug pad
7	AR 139	Locking catch spring pin	57	AR 168	Spring guide
8	AR 138	Locking catch spring	58	AR 167	Main spring
9	AR 133	Cocking lever	59	AR 146	Trigger
10	AR 107	Cocking lever pivot pin	60	AR 147	Trigger spring
11	AR 102	Cocking lever pivot bush	61	AR 170	Trigger sear pivot
12	AR 165	Scope sight screws	62	AR 153	Trigger pin
13	AR 166	'Scope sight nuts	63	AR 104	Trigger sear spring
14	AR 164	'Scope elevator plate R/H	64	AR 148	Trigger adjusting screw 3mm x 8mm
15	AR 163	'Scope elevator plate L/H	65	AR 100A	Safety ratchet cam assy
16	AR 112A	Tap 22 cal	66	AR 135	Safety ratchet circlip
17	AR 112B	Tap 177 cal	67	AR 150	Safety ratchet
18	AR 132	Tap screw 4mm x 10mm	68	AR 174	Safety ratchet pivot pin
19	AR 131	Tap lever	69	AR 214	Safety ratchet spring pin
20	AR 130	Tap spring	70	AR 151	Safety ratchet spring
21	AR 126A	Rear sling swivel	71	AR 154	Sear lift pin circlip
22	AR 126	Front sling swivel	72	AR 109	Sear lift pin
23	AR 123	Clamp	73	AR 153	Long sear spacer
24	AR 124	Clamp screw	74	AR 105	Long sear spring pin
25	AR 106	Clamp spacer	75	AR 138	Long sear spring
26	AR 125	Clamp nut	76	AR 176	Long sear lift
27	AR 122A	Barrel long 22 cal	77	AR 153	Long sear pivot pin
28	AR 122B	Barrel long 177 cal	78	AR 175	Long sear
29	AR 122C	Barrel short 22 cal	79	AR 173	Plastics stock fixing screw spring washer
30	AR 144A	Barrel fixing screw 5mm x 8mm	80	AR 172	Plastics stock fixing screw plain washer
31	AR 179	Barrel fixing screw pad	81	AR 171	Plastics stock fixing screws – front & rear
32	AR 201	Short barrel end	82	AR 203	Plastics stock butt plate
33	AR 202	Short barrel end fixing screw	83	AR 204	Plastics stock butt plate fixing screws
34	AR 120	Front sight	84	AR 210	Jackal stock
35	AR 121	Front sight fixing screw	85	AR 212	AR 7 stock
36	AR 160	Sight adjuster O rings	86	AR 211	Jackal top cover
37	AR 159	Sight adjuster circlips	87	AR 213	AR 7 top cover
38	AR 158	Sight adjusters	88	AR 206	Magazine
39	AR 162	Traverse gear	89	AR 207	Magazine fixing screws
40	AR 161	Elevating gear	90	AR 208	Magazine slide
41	AR 157	Sight leaf	91	AR 209	Magazine slide retaining rivet
42	AR 156	Sight body	92	AR 173	Wood Stock fixing screw spring washer
43	AR 155	Sight fixing screw O ring	93	AR 172	Wood Stock fixing screw plain washer
44	AR 113	Sight fixing screw	94	AR 184	Trigger guard nut
45	AR 134	Piston pull	95	AR 184A	Trigger guard spring washer
46	AR 101	Piston pull pivot pin	96	AR 184B	Trigger guard plain washer
47	AR 135	Piston pull circlip	97	AR 183	Trigger guard fixing screw
48	AR 128A	Cylinder & rear plug only	98	AR 182A	Wood Stock fixing screw brass washer
49	AR 215	Cylinder assy	99	AR 182	Wood Stock fixing screw front
50	AR 169	Piston	100	AR 181	Wood Stock fixing screw rear
			101	AR 180	Trigger guard
			102	AR 205	Wood Stock
			103	AR 185	Cylinder including trigger mechanism, piston, spring & rear plug but excluding cocking mechanism & tap

SPECIFICATION

		Weight	Length OA	Barrel Length	Cal.	Max FPS	Trig Pull	Stock
2000	Parabellum	7lb 8oz	45 in	18 in	.177/.22	580	1-4lb	ABS
2001	Wood Stock	8lb	44½ in	18 in	.177/.22	580	1-4lb	WOOD
2007	AR7	7lb 10oz	35in	8 in	.22	580	1-4lb	ABS

Part numbers must be quoted when ordering spares

After guns serial no 3665 parts 56/57 will be integral with part no 52 (rear plug)

| Luftgewehre | Air-Guns | Rifles de aire comprimido | Fusils à air comprimé |

TELL — TELL

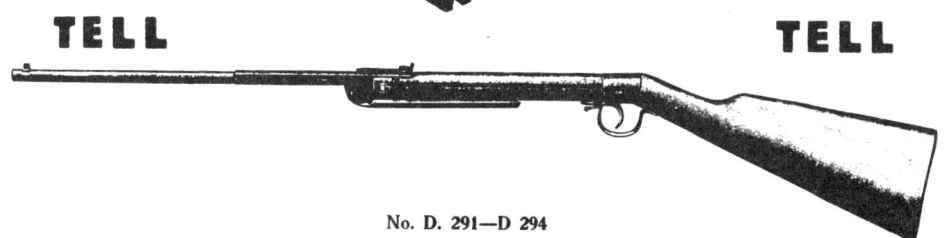

No. D. 291—D 294

	Glatt Liso	Smooth bore Lisse	Gezogen Rayado	Rifled Rayé				
No.	D 291	D 293	D 292	D 294	Schwarz brüniert, feiner polierter Schaft, Feder-Schraubvisier und Perlkorn, Länge 100 cm.	Black burnished, polished stock, spring rear sight, pearl front sight, length 100 cm.	Pavonado negro, culata pulida, alza de resorte, punto de mira de bola, largura 100 cm.	Bronzé noir, crosse polie, hausse à ressort, point de mire-perle, longueur 100 cm.
⌀	baugv	bauhm	baupo	bauru				
Cal.	4½ mm	5½ mm	4½ mm	5½ mm				
kg	2,600		2,600					
$	7.—	7.—	7.46	7.46				

Tell Model 1 air rifle (Wum Catalogue 1933)

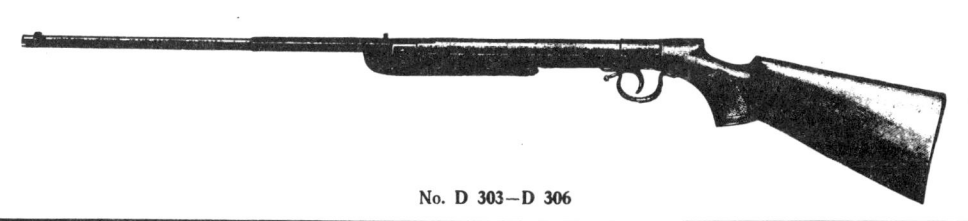

No. D 303—D 306

	Glatt Liso	Smooth bore Lisse	Gezogen Rayado	Rifled Rayé				
No.	D 303	D 305	D 304	D 306	Schwarz brüniert, feiner polierter Schaft mit englischem Pistolgriff, Feder-Schraubvisier und Perlkorn, Länge 100 cm.	Black burnished, polished stock, spring rear sight and pearl front sight, length 100 cm.	Pavonado negro, culata pulida, alza de resorte, punto de mira de bola, largura 100 cm.	Bronzé noir, crosse polie, hausse à ressort, point de mire-perle, longueur 100 cm.
⌀	bawog	bawus	bawyr	baxap				
Cal.	4½ mm	5½ mm	4½ mm	5½ mm				
kg	2,600		2.600					
$	7.92	7.92	8.40	8.40				

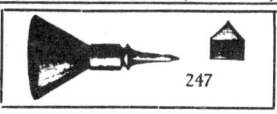

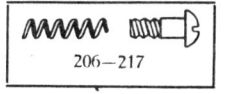

247 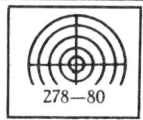   278—80   206—217

Tell Model 2 air rifle (Wum Catalogue 1933)

MODEL "Tell". Could be Model 1700/1700G.

MAKER Oscar Will, Venuswaffenwerk, Zella-Mehlis, Thuringen, Germany. This now makes about three addresses that I know of for Oscar Will. See Tell air pistol in "Airpistols" Edition.

DATE Above design appeared early 1910s and lasted until the early 1930s. The above example was rifled so would assume manufacture to be in the middle 1920s onwards as the first models might have been smoothbore.

VALUATION £40—£80. ($60—$120).

DETAILS 39⅝ inches long with a 17¾ inch .177 rifled barrel. Available in either .177 or .22. Round barrel with "FOREIGN" on the underside and a serial number, this matches the serial number also stamped on the underside of the air chamber. Blade foresight and long tangent rearsight both set in dovetails. Air chamber has standing figure of William Tell holding a rifle across his shoulders and an apple between his feet. The trademark has "41" stamped below it. Trigger adjustment by way of screw through trigger guard. Metal butt plate with "118" stamped in end of butt and on inside of butt plate. Advertised weight 2.6 kg. There was a deluxe version of the above sold with a pistol grip stock. When the above model first appeared it was available in .177 only. By the late 1920s the word "ORIGINAL" was placed in front of Tell in some of the catalogues it was also available in nickel plated. On the above example the barrel pivot could be unscrewed from the R.H.S., but only after a small grub screw had been removed. This grub locking screw is in the right hand barrel support and faced towards the barrel. This has to be removed before the pivot can be unscrewed. When barrel pivot is removed it will be noticed that running around the inside edge of the head is a series of holes, these engage with the point of the grub screw to prevent the barrel pivot screw becoming loose.

By the 1930s the above was sold in .177 and .22 smoothbore and rifled barrels. Advertised weight 2.6 kg. There were two models and they differed in the choice of either straight hand or pistol grip stocks, and the type of rearsights, either fixed "V" blade or long ramp type with adjuster wheel, as fitted to the pre-war Diana Model 5 target air pistol.

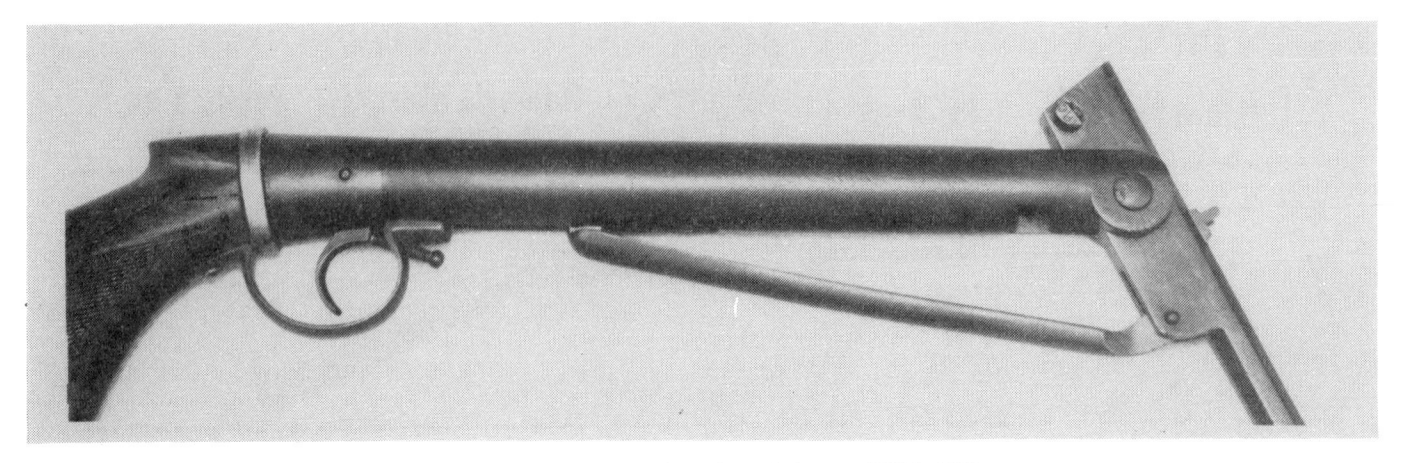

Tell air rifle with patent barrel catch. Patent 22202, 1905

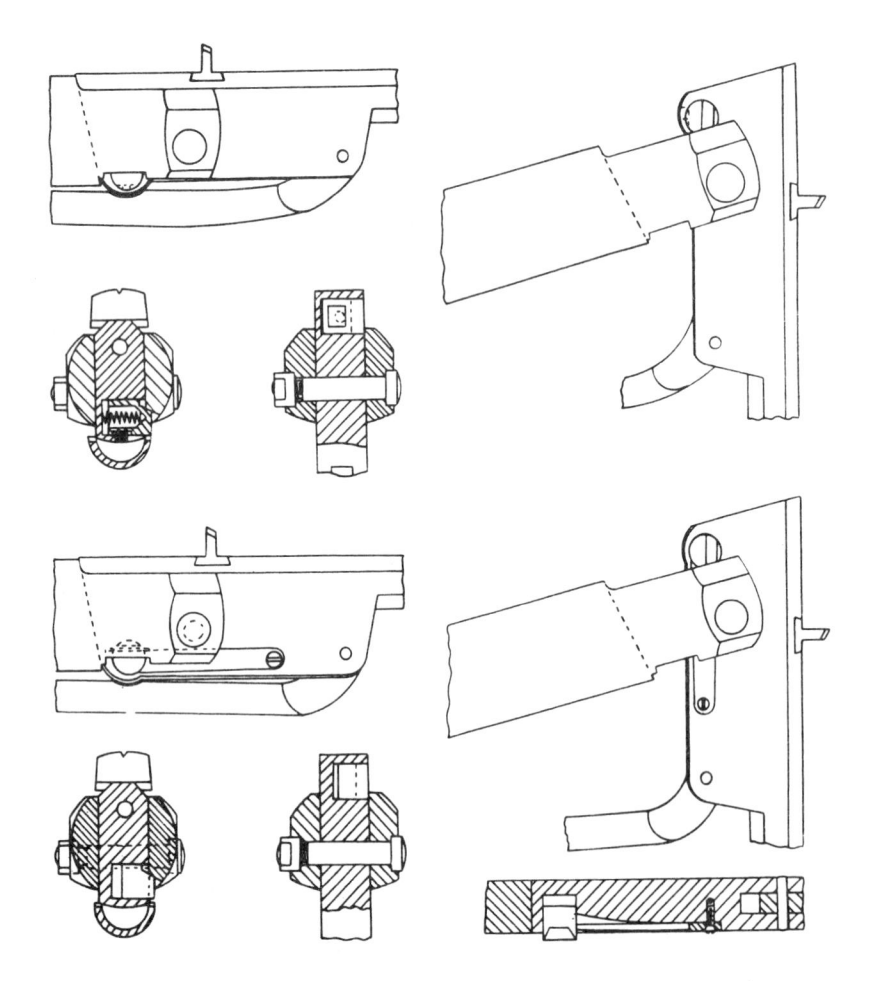

The two designs of patent number 2202 of 1905 by Oscar Will. the Tell air rifle mentioned in the text would appear to be of the upper design. Drawing by courtesy of "Guns Review"

MODEL A Tell break action air rifle.

MAKER Oscar Will, 390 Kleine Bahnhofstrasse, Zella St., Blassi, Thuringia, Germany. Address at time of patent, 1905.

DATE From around 1905 to 1939 in small numbers only. This style of barrel latch is not as common as the push-in button, pull-back rearsight, and the underside spring lever through the cocking lever.

VALUATION £40–£80. ($60–$120).

DETAILS The example seen was 38¾ inches long (99 cms) with a 17 inch (43.5 cms) .177 rifled barrel. Barrel was octagonal to round with "TELL" stamped in sloping capital letters between the sight and breech. Dovetail mounted sights with the rearsight having a wheel and blade and looking very like those fitted to Haenel air rifles. The air chamber has the rounded-downward drooping barrel support arms which are very similar to Haenel air rifles produced in the 1930s. Trigger adjustment by way of spherical headed screw through the trigger guard. The serial number, in this case 536, was stamped all over the place, barrel breech face, cocking lever, barrel latch plunger, air chamber, and on stock under butt plate. The one odd feature is the barrel catch. This is a spring loaded contoured button that protrudes from the lower part of the R.H.S. of the breech and engages with a cut-away in one of the barrel support arms. This design is patent number 22202 of 1905, see "Guns Review" July 1978. There were two variations, this one being the simpler of the two. They were introduced as an improvement on the push-in button type of that found on Millita air rifles of Langenham origins.

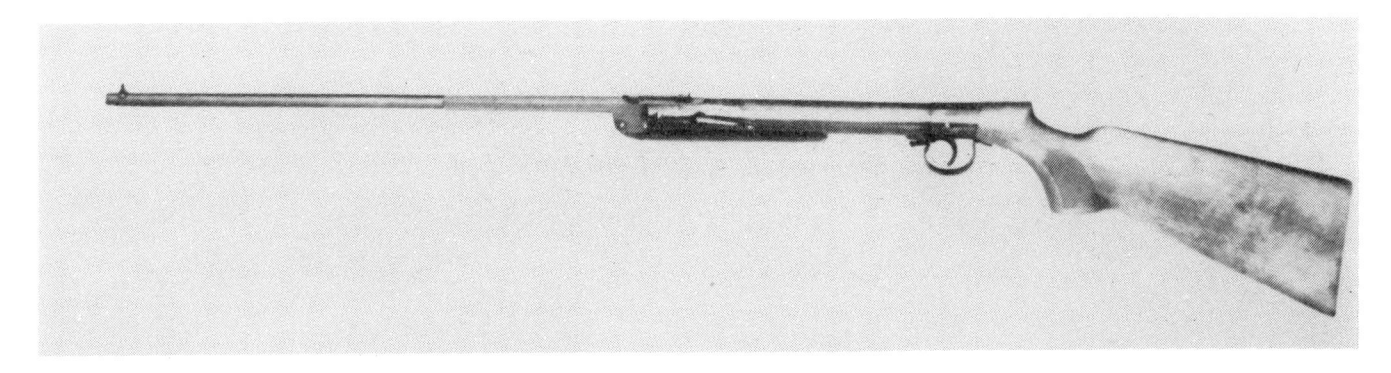

Tell side lever air rifle. Note extreme length of barrel

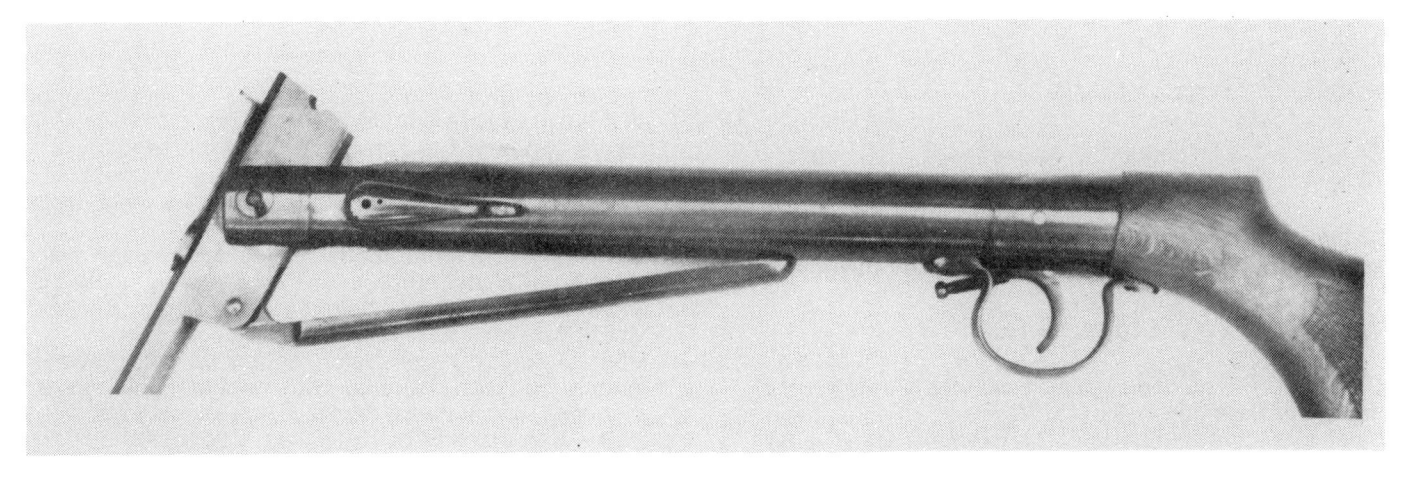

Tell air rifle

MODEL Tell Side Lever air rifle.

MAKER Oscar Will, Venuswaffenwerk, Zella-Mehlis, Thuringen, Germany.

DATE From around 1910 to 1939.

VALUATION £40—£80.
($60—$120).

DETAILS Another German side lever air rifle! This would appear to be of 1930s vintage. 43½ inches long (110 cm) with a 21¼ inch (54 cm) .177 rifled barrel. Barrel octagonal to round with "TELL" in scroll script on one of the barrel flats. Note change in style of the barrel support arms as opposed to those on the Roland and Precision models, they are identical to those on the Tell Models 1 and 2 air rifles. Trigger block is parallel sided and not truncated conical as on many Tell airguns. Stock has metal butt plate and is hand chequered. Trigger adjustment by way of spherical headed screw through the trigger guard. There is a small grub screw through one of the barrel support lugs, this has to be removed before the barrel pivot pins can be taken out.

The Wagria Model M58/M59

MODEL Wagria M58/M59.

MAKER Maschinen Appartebau, G.m.b.H., "Wagria", Ascherberg, Holstein, Germany.

DATE Very late 1940s to very early 1960s, would assume the 1950s to be the main period of production.

VALUATION £20—£40. ($30—$60).

DETAILS The one example seen was in a very sorry state, but have seen very few Wagria air rifles so have used it for the illustration. The example seen would appear to be the Model M58 because of the .177 barrel. The Model M59 had the .22 barrel. Almost 41 inches long with a 17¾ inch barrel. Foresight is dovetail mounted whilst the rearsight is made from cast alloy and is adjustable for elevation only. Each side of the barrel breech is stamped "WAGRIA" and on the L.H.S. "MADE IN GERMANY". The serial number, 31513, is stamped on the underside of the breech and on the underside of the air chamber. All in all it is a pretty basic break action air rifle.

Wagria appear to have made seven models as follows:

M50 — Would appear to have been the smallest and for junior use only. Would assume its calibre to have been in .177 only.

M55 — Again, a junior model. 39 inches long and available in .177 smoothbore only. Adjustable rearsight and double pull trigger. Weight about 4 lbs.

M56 — May be a .22 version of the M55.

M58 "Aero-Sport" — Same action as for previous models but manufactured with heavier components. 41 inches long and assumed to weigh about 6¾ lbs.

M59 — Same as M58 but fitted with a .22 barrel.

M60 or "160" or "Wagria-Rapid" — Barrel cocking repeater firing round lead balls. 4.45 mm calibre and having a ten-shot magazine. About 39 inches long and weighing about 5¼ lbs. They were common of German shooting ranges as powder guns were not allowed because they'd been naughty during the War!

M61 — Same as the M60 but fitted with a 50 shot magazine. Same calibre of 4.45 mm.

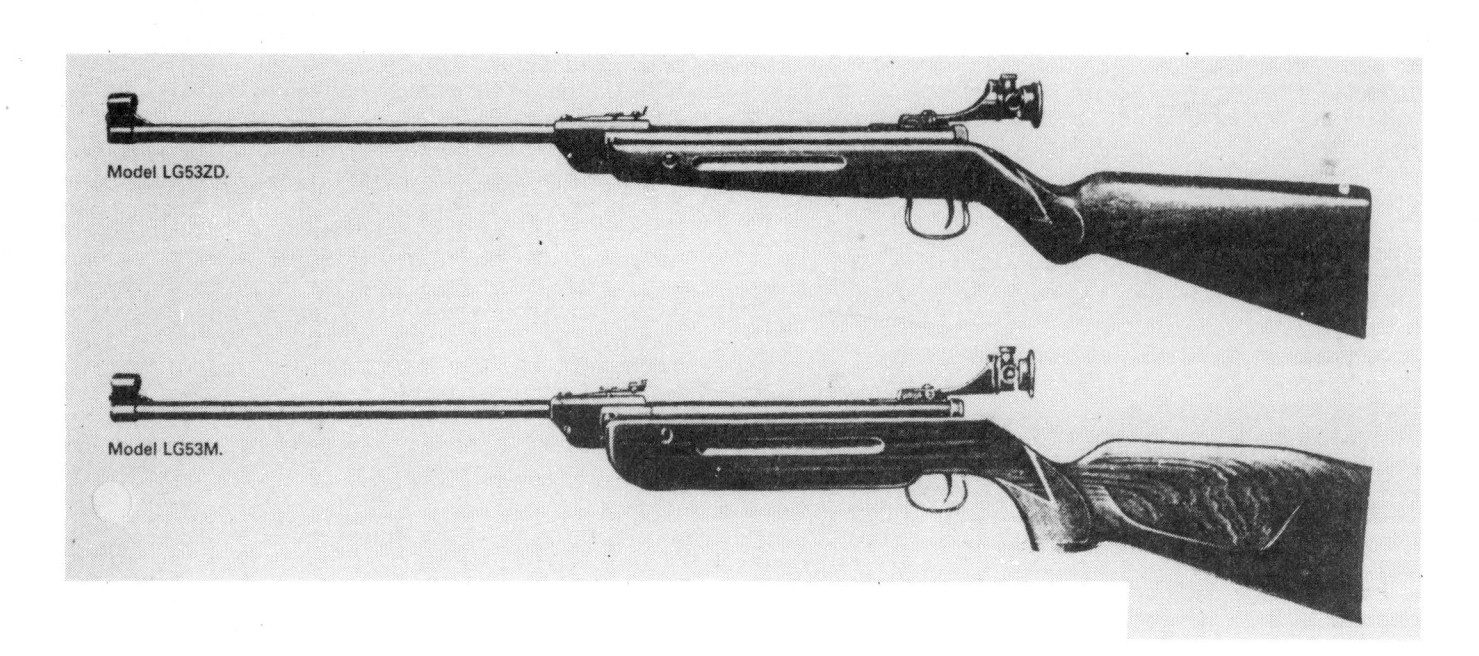

Walther Model LG53ZD and LG53M. (Courtesy of "Guns Review")

MODEL LG53 or LG53ZD.

MAKER Carl Walther, Sportswaffenfabrik, 79 Ulm-Donau, West Germany.

DATE 1953 to about 1966.

VALUATION £50—£150. ($75—$225).

DETAILS .177 recoiling target air rifle. 41¼ inches long with a 17¾ inch barrel. Hooded foresight with front screw for interchangeable foresight elements. Rearsight missing, but has been drilled and tapped should fitting one be necessary. Serial number 200910 stamped on L.H.S. of barrel breech and "MADE IN GERMANY". Top of air chamber marked "WALTHER LG Cal. 4.5 MOD 53 WALTHER'S PATENT". Walther aperture sight fitted to ramp as standard and supplied with the air rifle. The peepsight can only be removed by loosening locking screw and pushing the sight towards the barrel, to replace position sight in front of the ramp and then pull back towards the rear of the air rifle. There are three deep slots for positioning the aperture sight and care must be taken to only screw down the sight with these slots in line with the locking screw. Double linked cocking lever. Trigger adjuster behind the trigger. Hand chequered stock with black butt plate. All in all a very neat air rifle of high standard of finish. Advertised with a walnut stock. Advertised weight 5¾ lbs. Three foresight blades were available; post, roof, and bead. The same aperture sight was fitted to the Model LG55M. Advertised muzzle velocity 600 f.p.s. It would appear that the Model LG51Z was available at the same time as the above but sold with the rearsight fitted and without the aperture sight. There appears to have been a deluxe model called the LG53M (M for Marksman). All the above were fitted with a trigger lock that prevented firing when barrel was in open position.

The "Z" suffix stood for Zuge meaning grooves, i.e. a rifled barrel. The Model 53 was an improved version of the previous Model 51. The main improvement being in the sights. An optional adjustable trigger could be ordered for the Model 53.

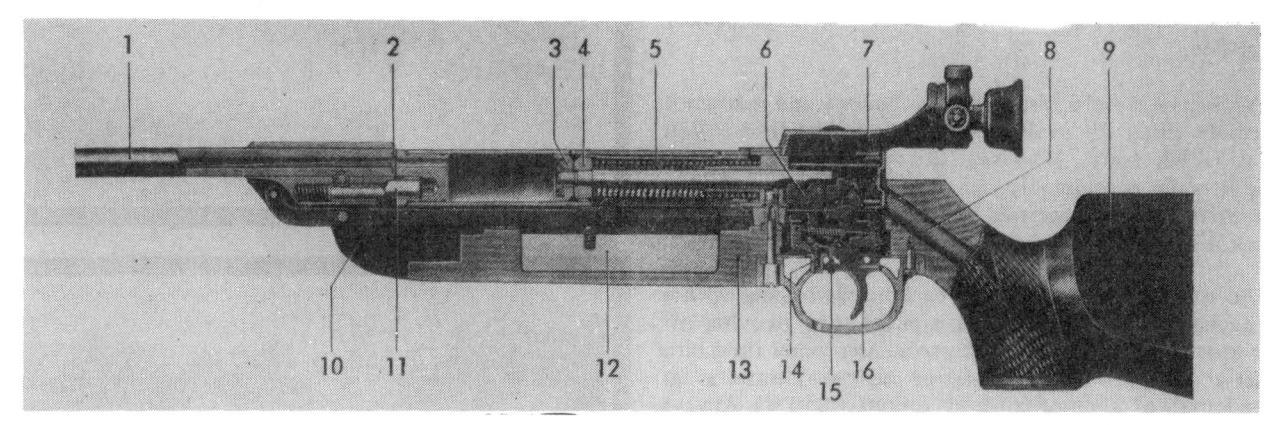

diagram for the Walther LG55

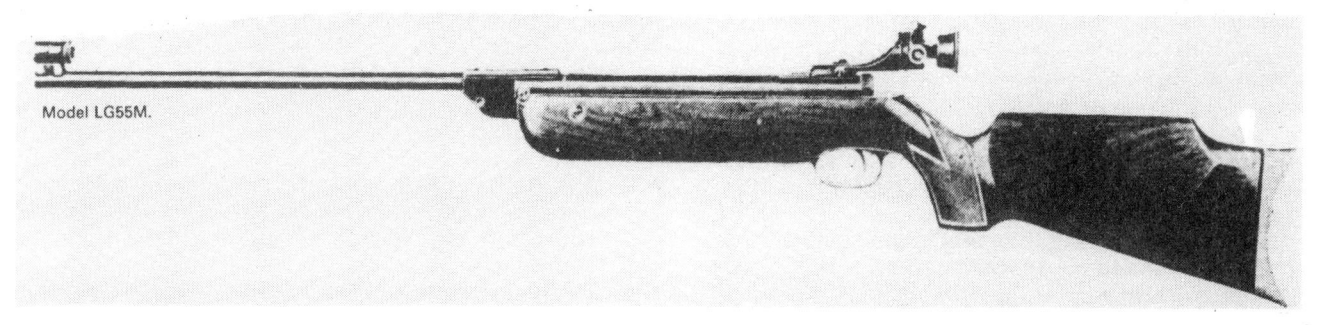

Walther Model 55. (Courtesy of "Guns Review")

MODEL 55.

DATE 1955 to 1967.

MAKER Carl Walther, Sportwaffen-Fabrik, Ulm, Donau, Germany.

VALUATION £100—£200. ($150—300).

DETAILS Walther's first rifle designed specially for the 10 metre target shooting of the German Shooting Association. This style of target shooting was not yet popular in Britain so the above model was not readily available. 41 inches long with a 17⅝ inch .177 rifled barrel. Above example has barrel weight tube. Foresight clamps into barrel and has interchangeable elements. The foresight must be removed before the weight tube can be taken off. Barrel breech is drilled and tapped for rearsight, but they were sold without the rearsight, an aperture sight was fitted in its place at the rear of the air chamber. Side of barrel breech stamped with "MADE IN GERMANY" whilst on other side the serial number. Top of air chamber stamped "WALTHER LG Cal.4.5 MOD 55 WALTHER'S PATENT". Rear of air chamber fitted with Walther peepsight. The stock is beautiful, full bodied hand chequered with cheek piece. The above is also called the Model 55M (M for Master). Advertised weight 9 lbs but with barrel weight 9 lb 10 oz. Stock made from either walnut or beech in the "Olympia" style. The Model 55 was also available with full Tyrolean stock and a double set trigger mechanism. The model changed very little during its period of production. During 1957 the leather washer was replaced by a synthetic piston washer. Also at a later date the peepsight ramp was altered from having grooves cut across it for placing the peepsight to a smooth surface. These aperture sights are currently fitted to the Feinwerkbau target air rifles. The Model 55 was not available in Britain but could be obtained from the importers on special order. The LG55 was replaced by the LGV. For further details of the history of Walther airguns see "Airgun World" May 1980, and April of the same year. Advertised velocity 550 f.p.s. In the early 1960s the availability situation changed and the Model 55 became more readily available to the public. The peepsight adjusts 5⅛ inch for each click of the adjuster screws at a range of 35 feet.

211

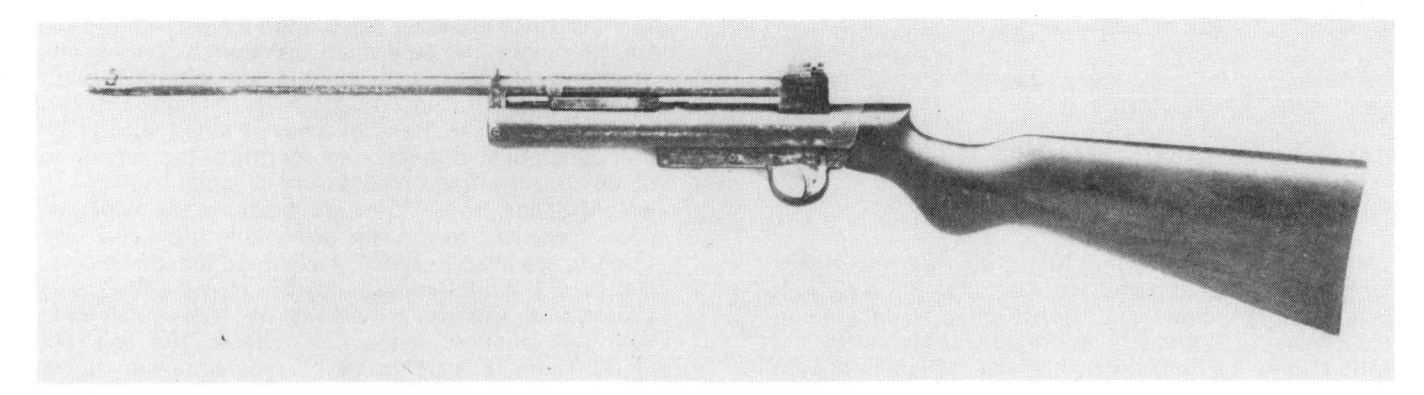

Webley Mk. I air rifle

MODEL   Mk. I.

MAKER   Webley & Scott.

DATE   Production 1926 to 1929.

VALUATION   Quite a rare air rifle hence the rather wide range of value from £150 up to £600. Their usual value is from £200 to £400 ($300—$600).

DETAILS   Serial number 718, 34 inches long. Barrel pivot support is stamped with calibre, above is .177 rifled. L.H.S. of trigger block stamped "WEBLEY AIR RIFLE MARK I" also has the winged pellet trademark. Fitted with safety button same as the pre-war air pistols. Interchangeable barrels in .22 and .177 only. Original price 72/6 and spare barrel 25/-. R.H.S. of the barrel port turret is stamped the patent markings for Great Britain, Belgium, France, Spain, Italy and Germany, whilst on the R.H.S. of trigger block is stamped the patent markings for Japan, Switzerland, Australia, U.S.A. and Canada. Serial number is also stamped on the R.H.S. Trigger adjustment is on the underside of the trigger block. Production was terminated on the introduction of the Webley Service Mk. II air rifle, although have seen advertisements for them both in the same catalogue. Smoothbore barrels were supplied to areas where rifled barrels are prohibited, i.e. Northern Ireland. Earlier models may have had the trigger adjustment at the front of the trigger block.

The following patent details appear in the same places as the Mk. I featured above. Stamped on R.H.S. of air port housing are the following:

"GT. BRITAIN PATENT No. 219872"
"BELGIUM BREVET No. 316878"
"FRANCE BREVÉTE No. 578498 S.G.D.G."
"SPAIN PATENT No. 89433"
"ITALY BREVETTATO No. 229158"
"GERMANY D.R.P. No. 414833"
and stamped on the R.H.S. of the trigger block:
"PATENTS GRANT"
"JAPAN PATENT No. 9186/24"
"SWITZERLAND PATENT No. +112976"
"AUSTRALIA PATENTED 21-12-23"
"U.S.A. PATENTED U.S.A. 7-7-25"
"CANADA PATENT 1925".

Interesting to note that the above patents are identical to those that appear on the Webley Mk. I air pistol 1925—1938.

Serial number of above Mk. I air rifle is 1434. Advertised weight 5¼ lb.

The Author is indebted to David Weeks for the following information. He has a boxed Webley Mk. I, serial number 48 and box measures 36¾ inches long, 6 inches wide and 1⅞ inches deep. Plain brown cardboard is used with:

THE "WEBLEY"
AIR   RIFLE
MARK   I

stamped on the top and printed in the bottom right-hand corner "WEBLEY & SCOTT LTD., BIRMINGHAM & LONDON." The inside of the box has no partitions.

Serial numbers seen for the Mk. I air rifle range from 583 up to 1421 with a change from the Birmingham and London address to just Birmingham occurring between numbers 721 and 1421.

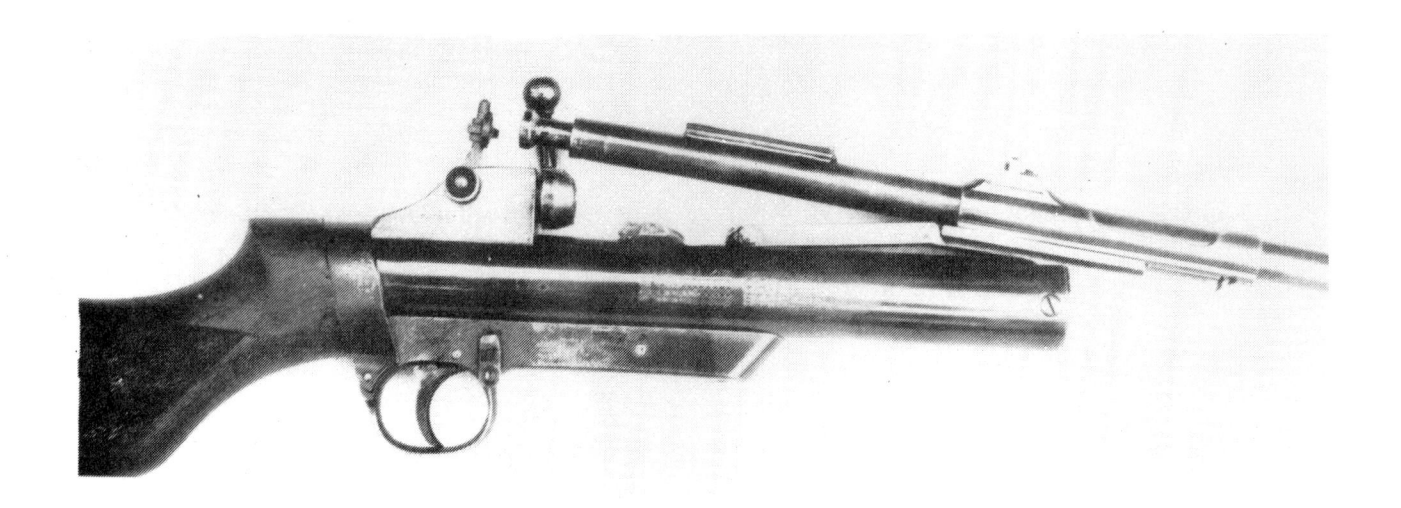

First Model Mk. II Service. R.H.S. of action. (No. S160)

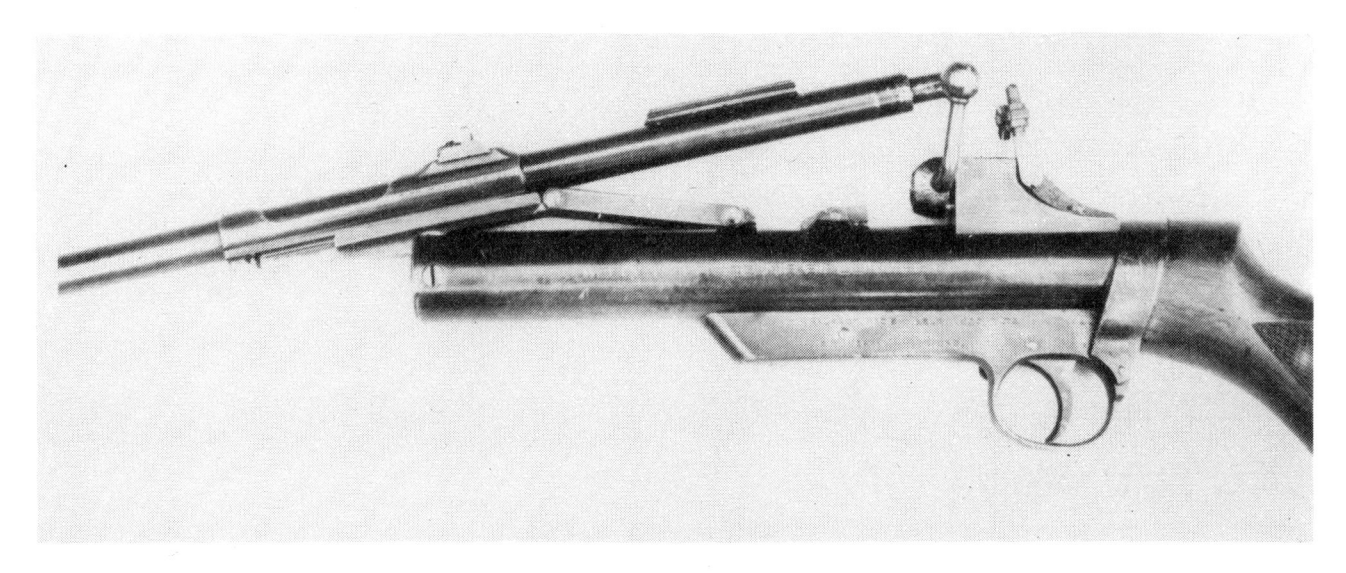

L.H.S. of Webley Mk. II Service. (No. S160)

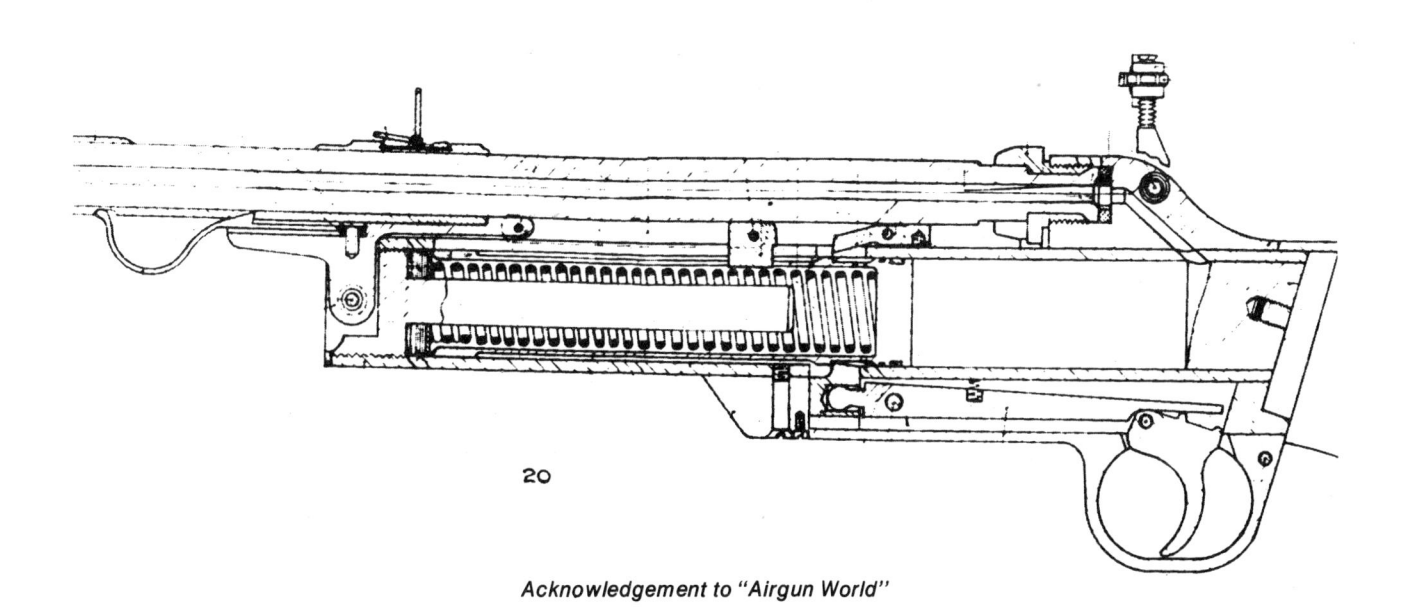

Acknowledgement to "Airgun World"

ACTION OF FIRST MODEL MK. II SERVICE AIR RIFLE

Note that the barrel breech sits into the action way past the bolt and the sear is in two parts, the rounded end of the sear arm rests inside the round section sear. The rearsight with two blades is commonly seen and the wavy spring on the underside of the barrel block in order to keep the barrel in place. The trigger has no tension spring so until the action is cocked this may slop about and look wrong, but it isn't.

This diagram also illustrates the patent 388547 of 1932. This was for the separate intercepting sear that sits on top of the air chamber. It is pushed out of engagement when the barrel is pressed down into the bolt for locking. Another patent shown in the above diagram is number 388548 again of 1932. This covered the dovetail mounted barrel and its quick removal, often too quick when well worn. This design was soon changed to the more stronger method on later models where the barrel actually slid into the breech block. For further details of the patents see "Guns Review" May 1980.

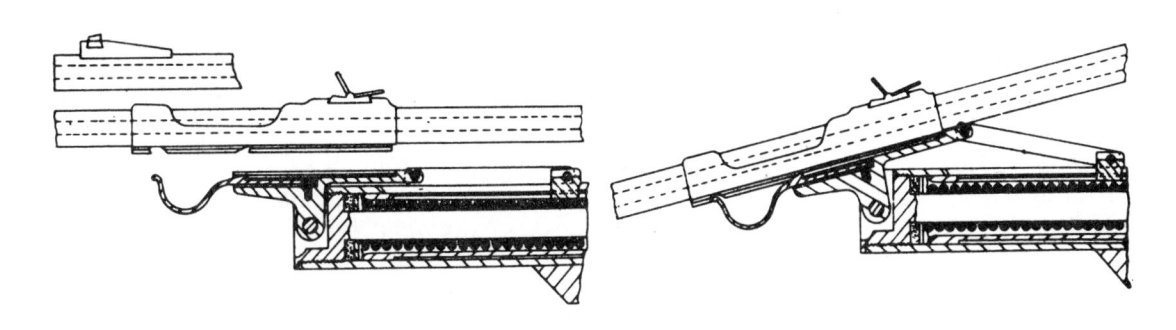

Patent 388548. (Acknowledgement to "Guns Review")

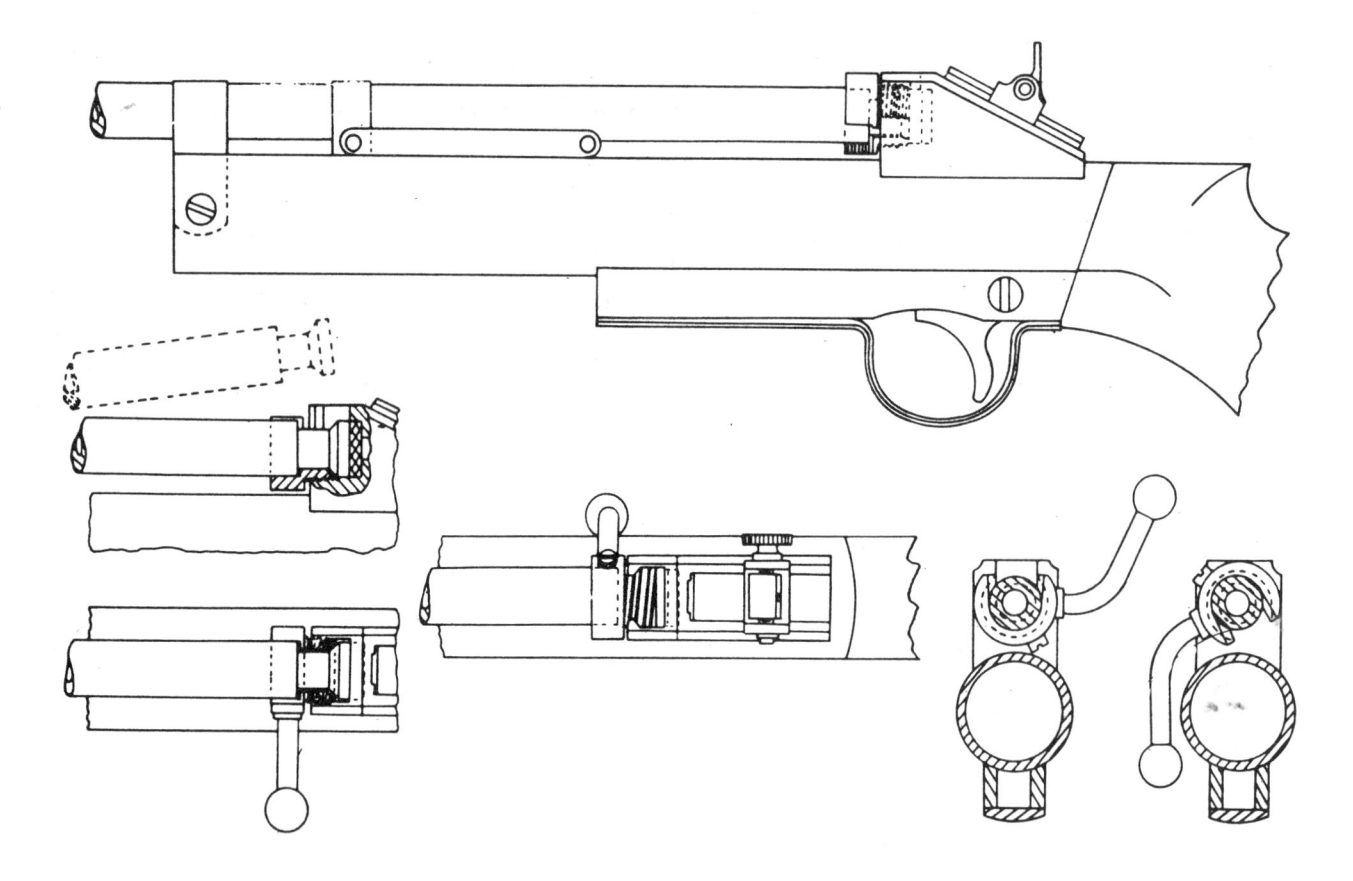

(144) Patent 371548 of 1931. Full Drawing. (Acknowledgement to "Guns Review")

Details of the original patent for the bolt action breech for the Mk. II Service air rifle. This probably dates the introduction as being 1931/1932. Note that the barrel mounting is very like that of the Mk. I air rifle, I have a recollection that I've seen one of these on my travels. This very first model must be very rare indeed. One small fault with this design is that unless the barrel mountings were very loose there was no allowance for the barrel breech face to be drawn against the seal ring of the transfer port when the bolt was rotated, unless of course the sealing ring was inside the bolt. For further details see "Guns Review" April 1980.

MODEL Mk. II Service First Model.

MAKER Webley & Scott Ltd., 81—91 Weaman Street, Birmingham. Address at time of manufacture.

DATE From the dates of the patents would assume date of manufacture to be from 1932 and from the Webley spares diagrams it would appear that production was 2,000 from 1932 to 1938, this being over six years, which averages out to around 330 per year. About half-way between 1932 and 1938 the breech block was altered from the dovetail rail mounted barrel to the more common separate breech block with push button barrel lock. From adverts this change would appear to have happened during 1935.

VALUATION £200—£400.
$300—$600.

DETAILS The first Model Mk. II Service is mainly distinguished by the dovetail mounted barrel that is one piece and the breech block. A long curved spring protruding outwards from the barrel mounting block holds that barrel mounting in place. This has to be pulled down in order to slide out the barrel. Basically a very weak design as when over powerfully cocking, the barrel can be pulled out of the dovetail rails. Side of barrel breech stamped "PATENT APPLIED FOR" and on other side ".22 CALIBRE" or .177. The rearsight is usually a twin leaf with one pivoted. The action has a safety catch and a "L" shaped peepsight. The breech bolt allows the barrel face to actually sit in the action of the action whilst on later models the breech face sits in the bolt, this means that the first model bolt is virtually in half and had a very coarse thread. The rest of the body lettering is the same as for other models. The sear on the first model is in two pieces, the sear arm and the sear tumbler that rides up and down in a circular hole, this will interchange with other models for the one piece sear. It is doubtful if this model was ever available in .25. The serial number should also appear stamped on the underside of the barrel support body.

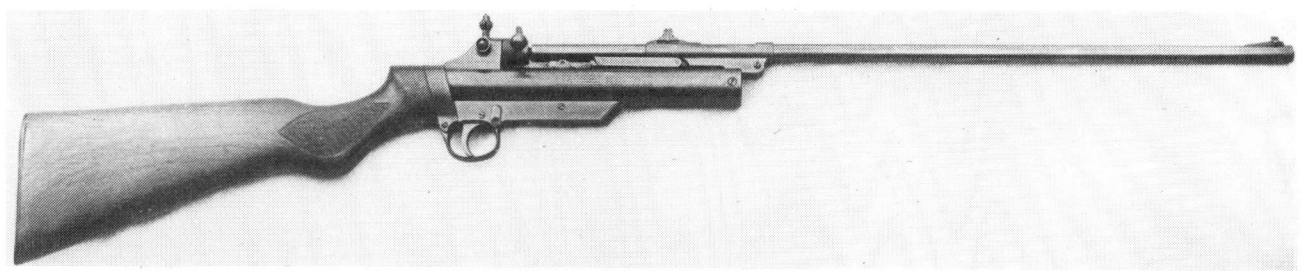

Webley Service Mk. II air rifle

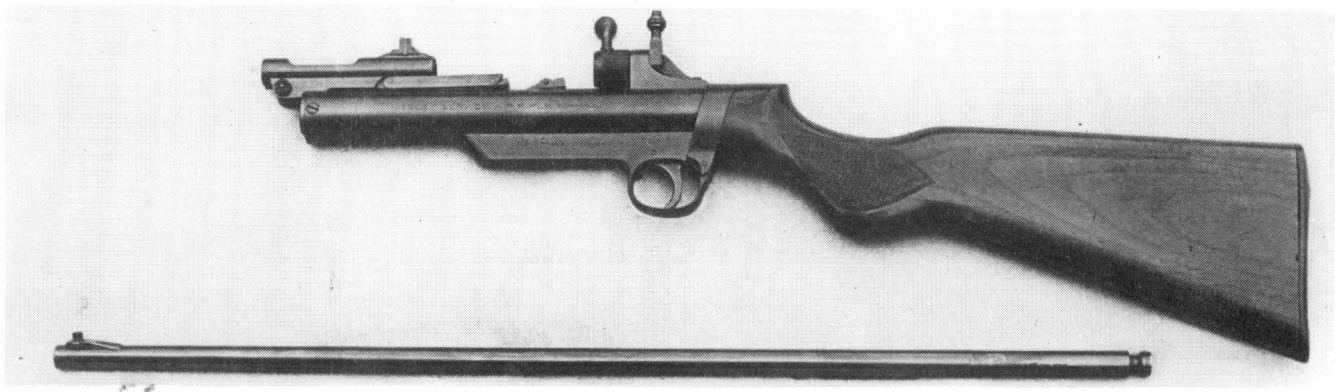

L.H.S. with barrel removed

R.H.S. with barrel removed

MODEL "Service Mk. II".

MAKER Webley & Scott.

DATE Production 1931/2—1946. First and Second series up to September 1938 and serial number S2000. Model illustrated was first advertised during 1935.

VALUATION £200—£400. ($300—$600). .22 and .177 barrels on their own usually sell for around £75 each ($113), whilst .25 barrels are hard to find less than £100 ($150).

DETAILS Serial number of above S1103, has .25 barrel only. 43¾ inches long with 25½ inch barrel. Has safety catch on R.H.S. of trigger action. Peepsight is of the "L" type, for illustration see page 38, Airgun World, February 1978. Stamped on L.H.S. of peepsight frame is "PATENT No. 371548" and on the air chamber, also on the L.H.S. is stamped
"GREAT BRITAIN PAT No 219872"
"U.S.A. PAT U.S.A. 7/7/25"
"SPAIN PAT No 89433"
"GERMANY D.R.P. No 414833
"CANADA PAT 1925".
On the R.H.S. of air chamber is stamped "WEBLEY SERVICE AIR RIFLE MARK II". The winged pellet trademark appears near the peepsight. Stamped on L.H.S. of trigger action is "MANUFACTURED BY WEBLEY & SCOTT LTD, BIRMINGHAM, ENGLAND". The .25 barrel is of the later type release and could have been altered at a later date than when it was manufactured. Push button barrel release and has "7507" stamped on the underside where the barrel slides into the barrel support. For further details of Service Mk. II air rifle see "Airgun World" February 1978.

Patent 371548 refers to the bolt action of retaining the barrel against the breech face and forming an air-tight seal. Further details see "Guns Review" April 1980.

Patent number 388547 refers to the intercepting sear that rests on top of the air chamber and is disengaged when the barrel has been replaced into the firing position. Patent dated 1932/33. See "Guns Review" May 1980.

There appears to be three main types of Service air rifle:
First Model: With "L" shaped peepsight, safety catch and dovetail mounted barrel with large forward facing leaf spring.
Second Model: Made until 1938 and would assume up to serial number S2000. This had "L" shaped peepsight, safety catch, but had the push button barrel release. Towards the end of this series the safety catch appears to have been left out.
Final Model: Centre frame peepsight, no safety catch, and the now normal push button barrel release. Final model started September 1938, number S2001 onwards. There are minor variations, but think that the above splits the Webley Mk. II Service into three major models.

The Second model was advertised during 1935 and was identical to that illustrated. The only difference being that it had no safety catch, otherwise it had the "L" shaped peepsight and usual barrel housing with side button for releasing the barrels for interchanging.

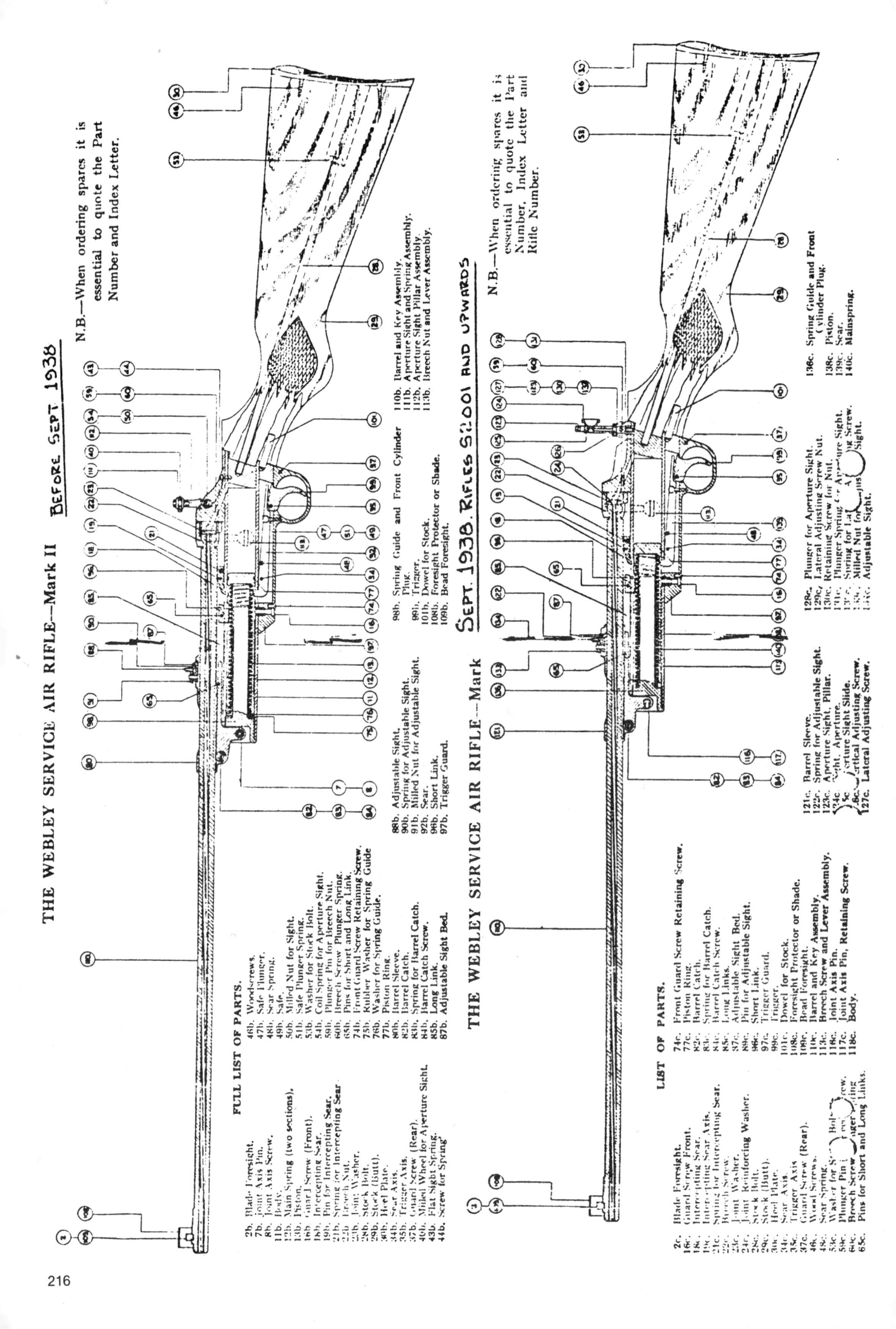

THE WEBLEY SERVICE AIR RIFLE—Mark II   Before Sept. 1938

N.B.—When ordering spares it is essential to quote the Part Number and Index Letter.

FULL LIST OF PARTS.

2b. Blade, Foresight.	46b. Woodscrews.	77b. Piston Ring.	110b. Barrel and Key Assembly.
7b. Joint Axis Pin.	47b. Safe Plunger.	80b. Barrel Sleeve.	111b. Aperture Sight and Spring Assembly.
8b. Joint Axis Screw.	48b. Sear Spring.	82b. Barrel Catch.	112b. Aperture Sight Pillar Assembly.
11b. Body.	49b. Safe.	83b. Spring for Barrel Catch.	113b. Breech Nut and Lever Assembly.
12b. Main Spring (two sections).	50b. Milled Nut for Sight.	84b. Barrel Catch Screw.	
13b. Piston.	51b. Safe Plunger Spring.	85b. Long Link.	
16b. Guard Screw (Front).	53b. Washer for Stock Bolt.	87b. Adjustable Sight Bed.	
18b. Intercepting Sear.	54b. Coil Spring for Aperture Sight.	88b. Adjustable Sight.	
19b. Pin for Intercepting Sear.	59b. Plunger Pin for Breech Nut.	90b. Spring for Adjustable Sight.	
21b. Spring for Intercepting Sear.	60b. Breech Screw Plunger Spring.	91b. Milled Nut for Adjustable Sight.	
22b. Breech Nut.	65b. Pins for Short and Long Link.	92b. Sear.	
23b. Joint Washer.	74b. Front Guard Screw Retaining Screw.	96b. Short Link.	
28b. Stock Bolt.	75b. Rubber Washer for Spring Guide.	97b. Trigger Guard.	
29b. Stock (Butt).	76b. Washer for Spring Guide.		
30b. Heel Plate.			
34b. Sear Axis.			
35b. Trigger Axis.			
37b. Guard Screw (Rear).			
40b. Milled Wheel for Aperture Sight.			
43b. Flat Sight Spring.			
44b. Screw for Spring.			

THE WEBLEY SERVICE AIR RIFLE—Mark   Sept. 1938. Rifles S2001 and upwards

N.B.—When ordering spares it is essential to quote the Part Number, Index Letter and Rifle Number.

LIST OF PARTS.

2c. Blade, Foresight.	37c. Guard Screw (Rear).	74c. Front Guard Screw Retaining Screw.	98c. Spring Guide and Front Cylinder Plug.
16c. Guard Screw Front.	46c. Woodscrews.	77c. Piston Ring.	99c. Trigger.
17c. Intercepting Sear.	48c. Sear Spring.	82c. Barrel Catch.	101c. Dowel for Stock.
18c. Intercepting Sear Axis.	53c. Plunger Pin.	83c. Spring for Barrel Catch.	108c. Foresight Protector or Shade.
21c. Spring for Intercepting Sear.	59c. Plunger Pin	84c. Barrel Catch Screw.	109c. Brad Foresight.
22c. Breech Screw.	65c. Breech Screw ...	85c. Long Links.	
25c. Joint Washer.		87c. Adjustable Sight Bed.	110c. Barrel and Key Assembly.
28c. Stock Bolt.		88c. Pin for Adjustable Sight.	113c. Breech Screw and Lever Assembly.
29c. Stock (Butt).		96c. Short Link.	116c. Joint Axis Pin.
30c. Heel Plate.		97c. Trigger Guard.	117c. Joint Axis Pin, Retaining Screw.
34c. Sear Axis.			118c. Body.
		121c. Barrel Sleeve.	128c. Plunger for Aperture Sight.
		123c. Spring for Adjustable Sight.	129c. Lateral Adjusting Screw Nut.
		123c. Aperture Sight, Pillar.	130c. Retaining Spring for Nut.
		124c. Sight, Aperture.	131c. Plunger Spring for Aperture Sight.
		125c. Aperture Sight Slide.	134c. Milled Nut for Lateral Adjusting Screw.
		126c. Vertical Adjusting Screw.	135c. Spring for Latch, Adjustable Sight.
		127c. Lateral Adjusting Screw.	136c. Spring Guide and Front Cylinder Plug.
			138c. Piston.
			139c. Sear.
			140c. Mainspring.

216

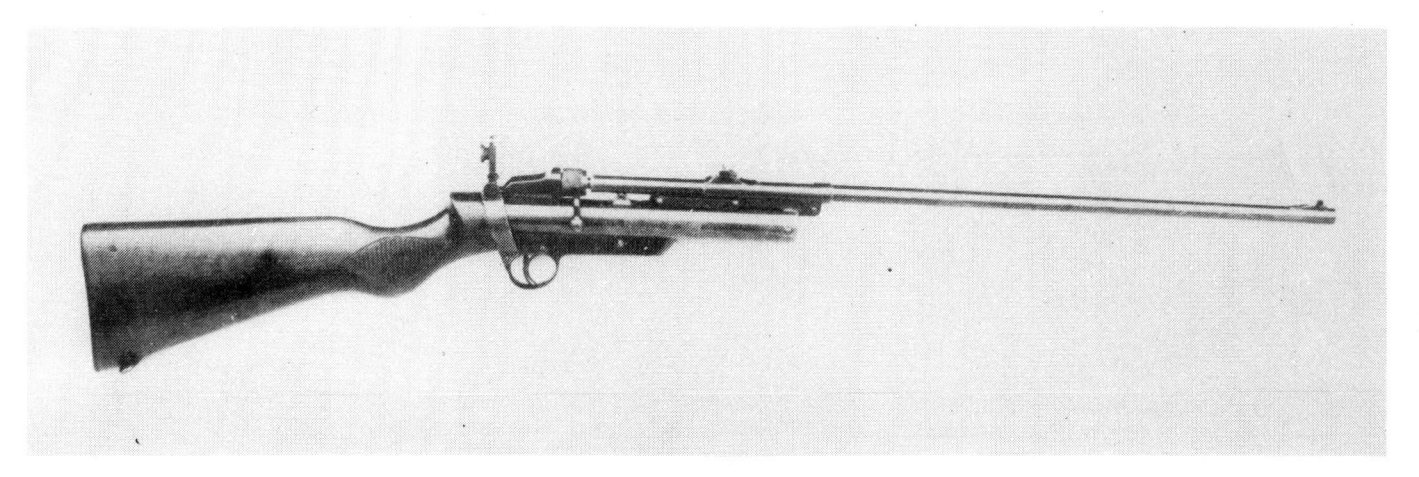

Webley Mk. II Service air rifle

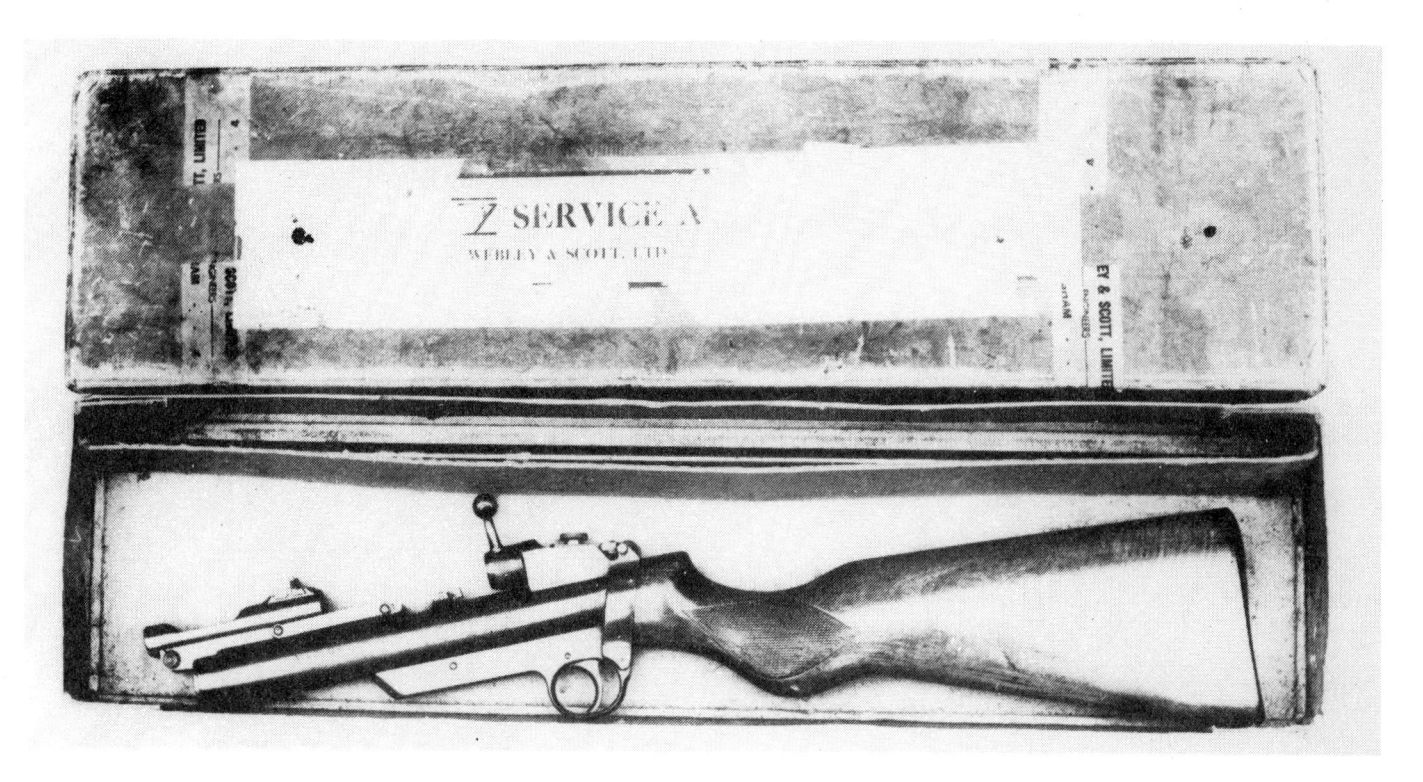

Webley Mk. II Service in original box. Note separate compartment for barrel

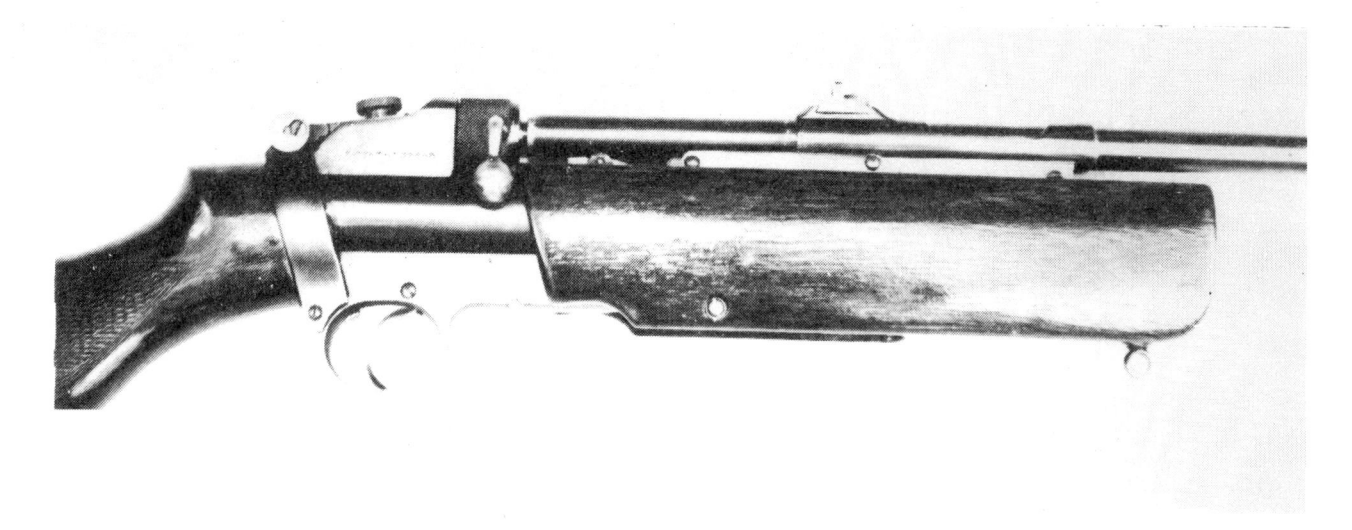

Webley Mk. II Service home-made fore-end. Note groove cut in underside of trigger action just in front of trigger guard, this aligns with screw in stock when fore-end is pushed on to chamber and action and stock cross screw is replaced. The fore-end totally encloses the chamber and action when in place

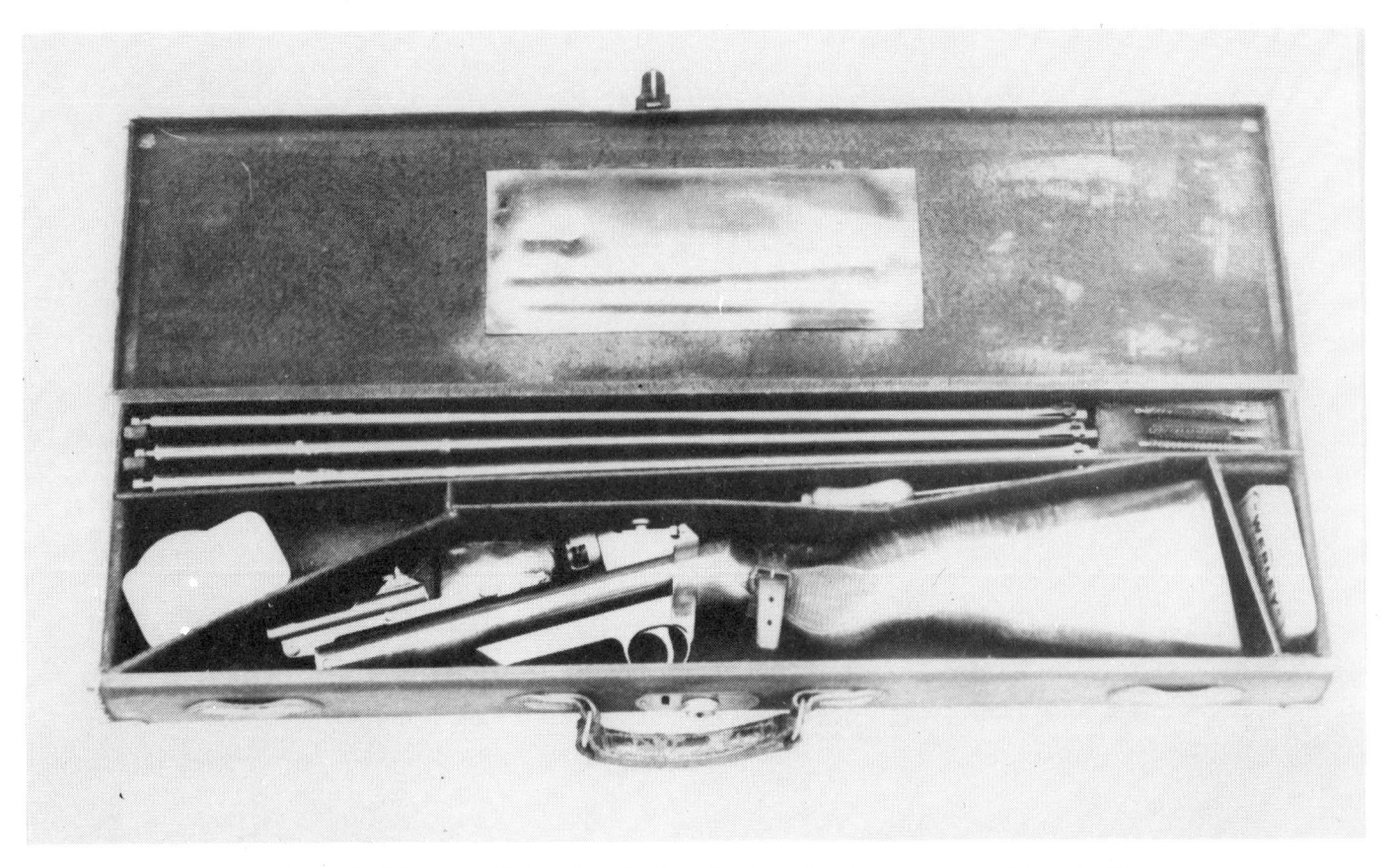

Cased Mk. II Service with three barrels. Note the three cleaning mops for each barrel calibre

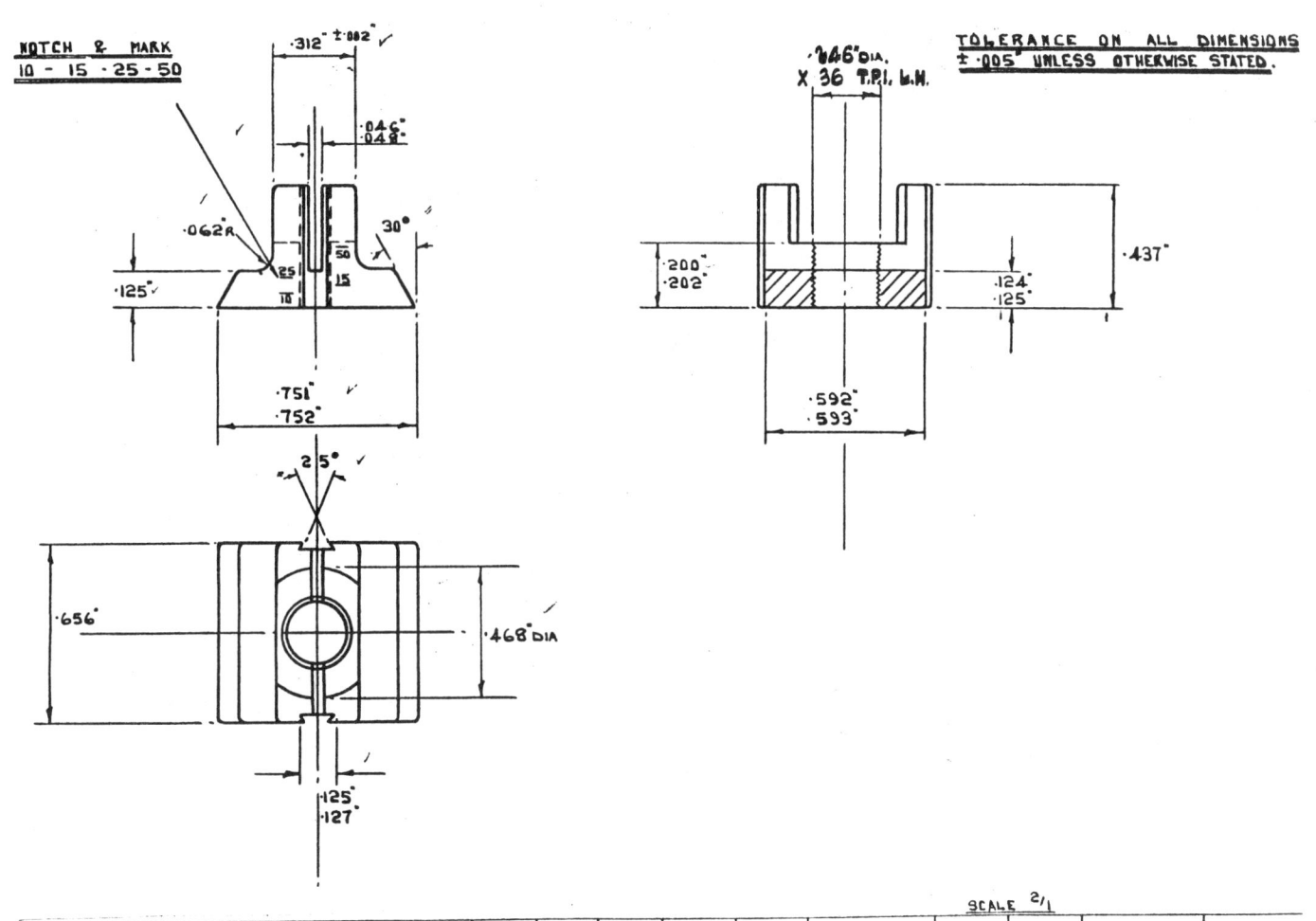

NOTCH & MARK
10 - 15 - 25 - 50

TOLERANCE ON ALL DIMENSIONS ± .005" UNLESS OTHERWISE STATED.

SCALE 2/1

THIS PRINT IS THE PROPERTY OF WEBLEY & SCOTT LTD WEAMAN STREET BIRMINGHAM	NAME	C.K.D		M.L.J.		MK II	AIR RIFLE					METAL
	DATE	21-2-38		13-8-40	1	ADJ. REAR	SIGHT	B.M.S.				COLOURED
	BY	DRAWN	CHECKED	TRACED	PASSED	QUAN	MODEL	UNIT	MATERIAL SPEC	SIZE	FORM	HEAT TREAT	FINISH
	MACHINE WHERE MARKED			'F'							
	GRIND do do			'G'		ADJUSTABLE SIGHT BED				147
	MACHINE ALL OVER			⊕		TITLE				PART NO

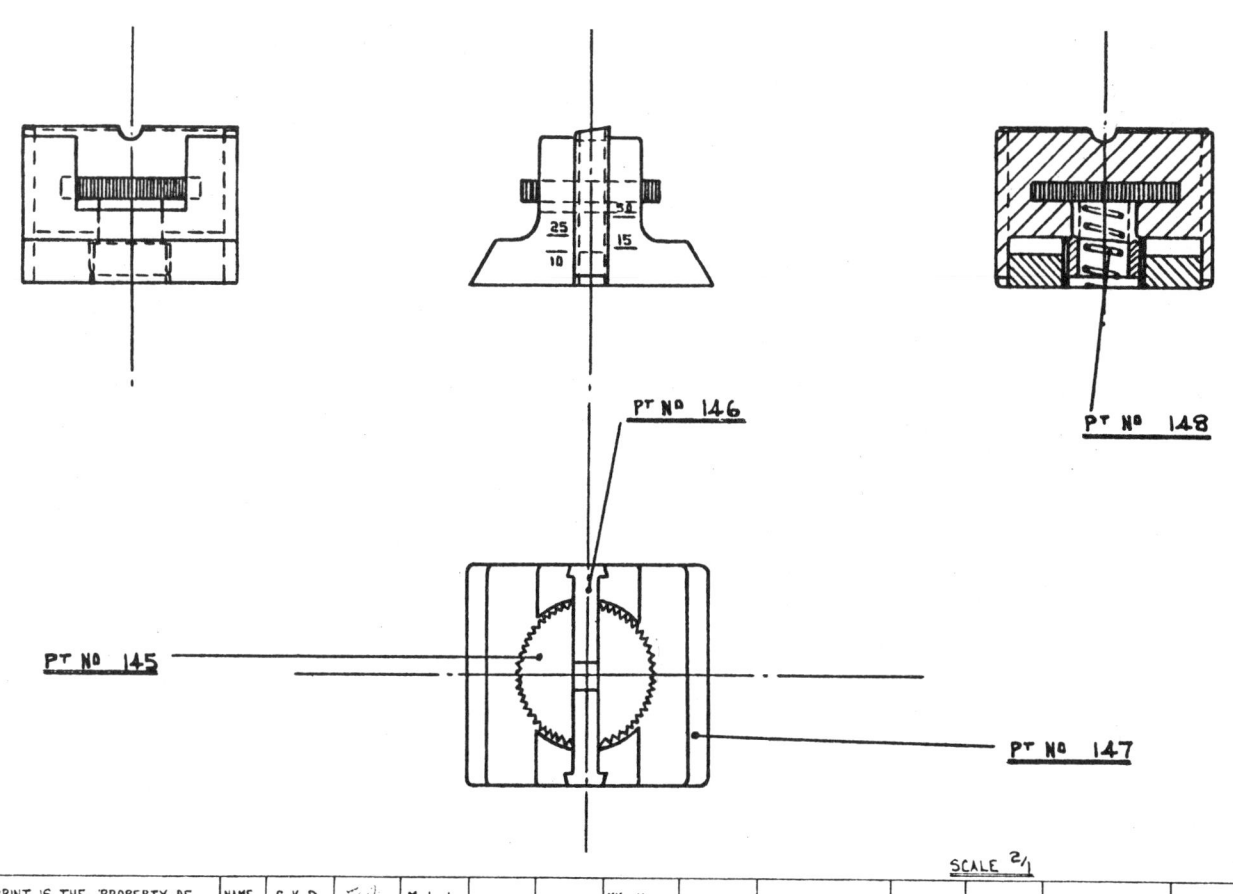

PT N⁰ 146

PT N⁰ 148

PT N⁰ 145

PT N⁰ 147

SCALE 2/1

THIS PRINT IS THE PROPERTY OF WEBLEY & SCOTT LTD WEAMAN STREET BIRMINGHAM	NAME	C.K.D.		M.L.J.		MK II AIR RIFLE						
	DATE	21-2-38		12-8-40								
	BY	DRAWN	CHECKED	TRACED	PASSED	QUAN	MODEL	UNIT	MATERIAL SPEC	SIZE	FORM	HEAT TREAT	FINISH
	MACHINE WHERE MARKED				'F'	ADJUSTABLE REAR SIGHT ASSY						144
	GRIND do. do.				'G'							
	MACHINE ALL OVER				⊕	TITLE						PART NO

·062 DIA

·235
·230
·200
·195
·170
·165

·085
·090

1/16 RAD

·032
·100

·25

SIGHT TO BE FILED

·250
·251

15°

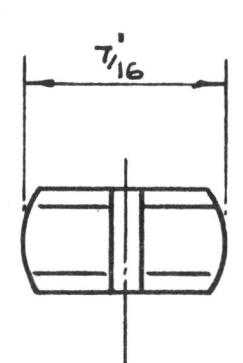

7/16

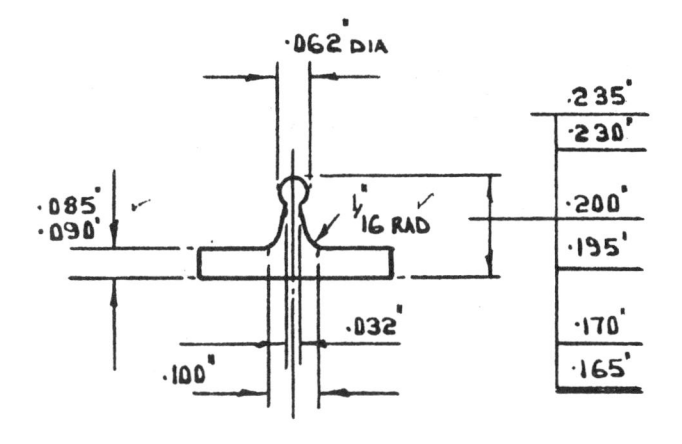

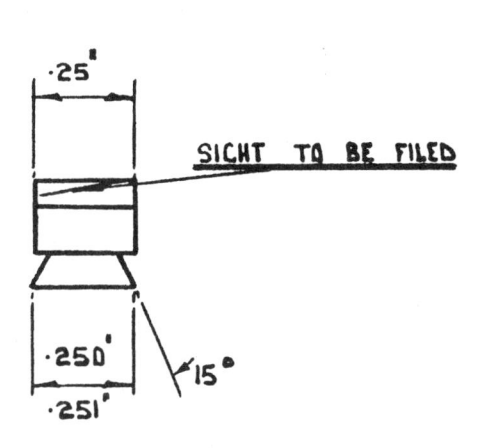

TOLERANCE TO ±·010 ON ALL FRACTIONAL DIMENSIONS UNLESS OTHERWISE STATED.

THIS PRINT IS THE PROPERTY OF WEBLEY & SCOTT LTD WEAMAN STREET BIRMINGHAM	NAME	L.H.		M.L.J.		MARK II AIR RIFLE	SELECTED MILD STEEL			BAR		METAL COLOUR
	DATE	14-3-38		21-8-40								
	BY	DRAWN	CHECKED	TRACED	PASSED	QUAN	MODEL	UNIT	MATERIAL SPEC	SIZE	FORM	HEAT TREAT	FINISH
	MACHINE WHERE MARKED				'F'	MRK II AIR RIFLE BEAD FORESIGHT						A.R.II/100
	GRIND do do				'G'							
	MACHINE ALL OVER				⊕	TITLE						PART NO

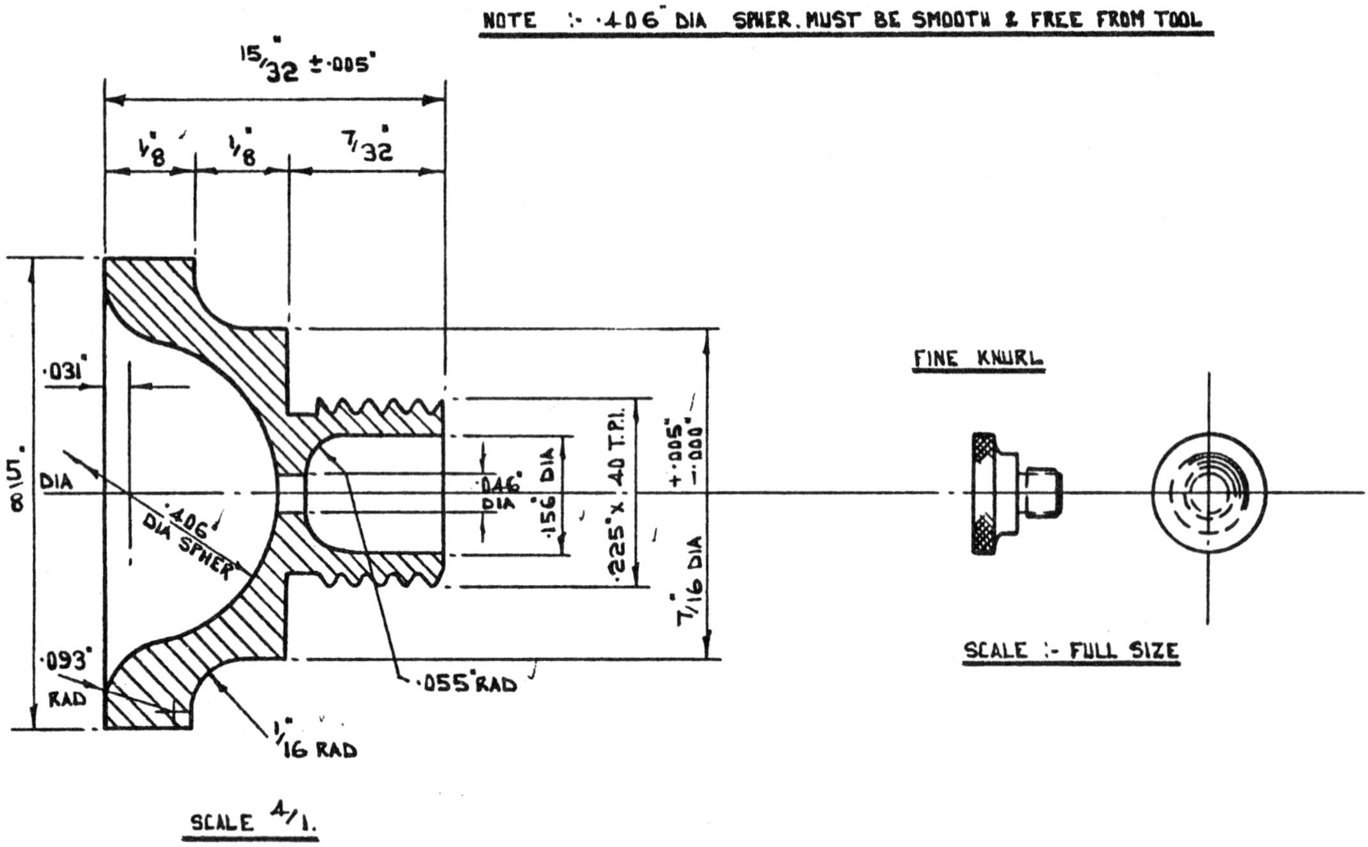

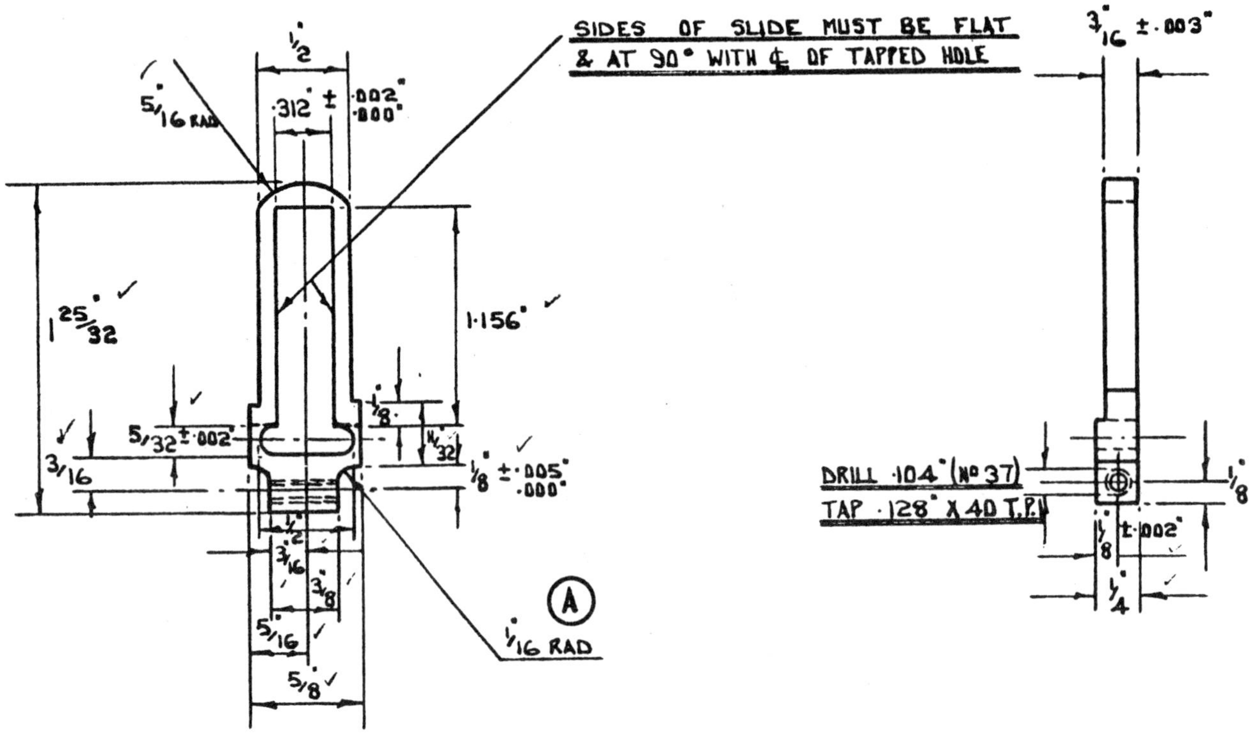

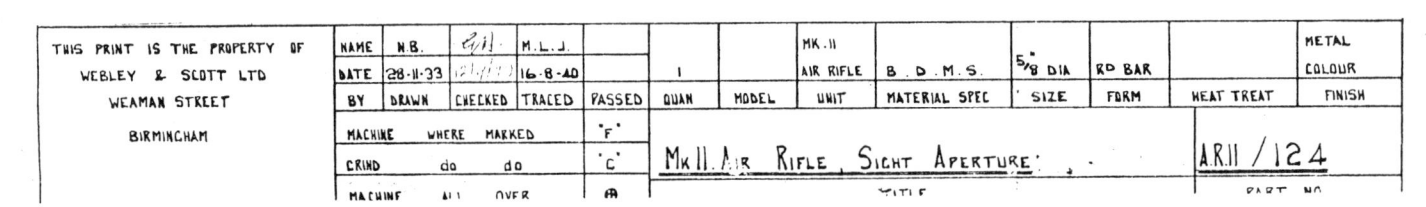

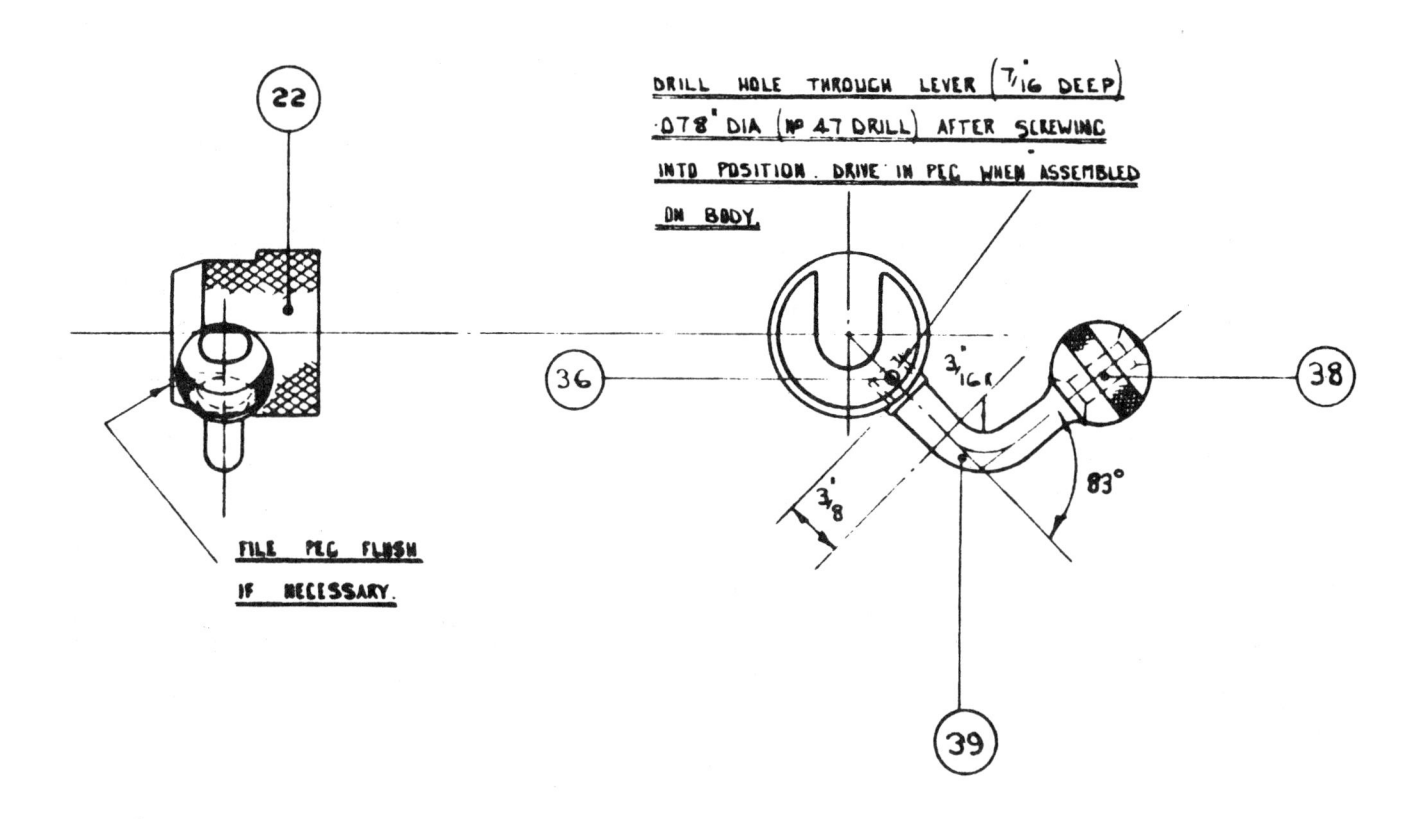

DRILL HOLE THROUGH LEVER (7/16 DEEP)
.078" DIA (Nº 47 DRILL) AFTER SCREWING
INTO POSITION. DRIVE IN PEG WHEN ASSEMBLED
ON BODY.

(22)

FILE PEG FLUSH IF NECESSARY.

(36) (38) (39)

3/16
3/8
83°

THIS PRINT IS THE PROPERTY OF WEBLEY & SCOTT LTD WEAMAN STREET BIRMINGHAM	NAME	B.C.	M.L.J.									
	DATE	19.7.33	23.8.40	•	1	AIR RIFLE	MK II					
	BY	DRAWN	CHECKED	TRACED	PASSED	QUAN	MODEL	UNIT	MATERIAL SPEC	SIZE	FORM	HEAT TREAT	FINISH
	MACHINE WHERE MARKED	'F'										
	GRIND do do	'G'		BREECH NUT ASSEMBLY				A.R.II / 113				
	MACHINE ALL OVER	⊕		TITLE				PART Nº				

KNURL

5/32
.312" DIA.
.187" +.001/-.000 DIA
1/4" DIA
1/16 CH.FR @ 45°
9/16" DIA. SPHERE

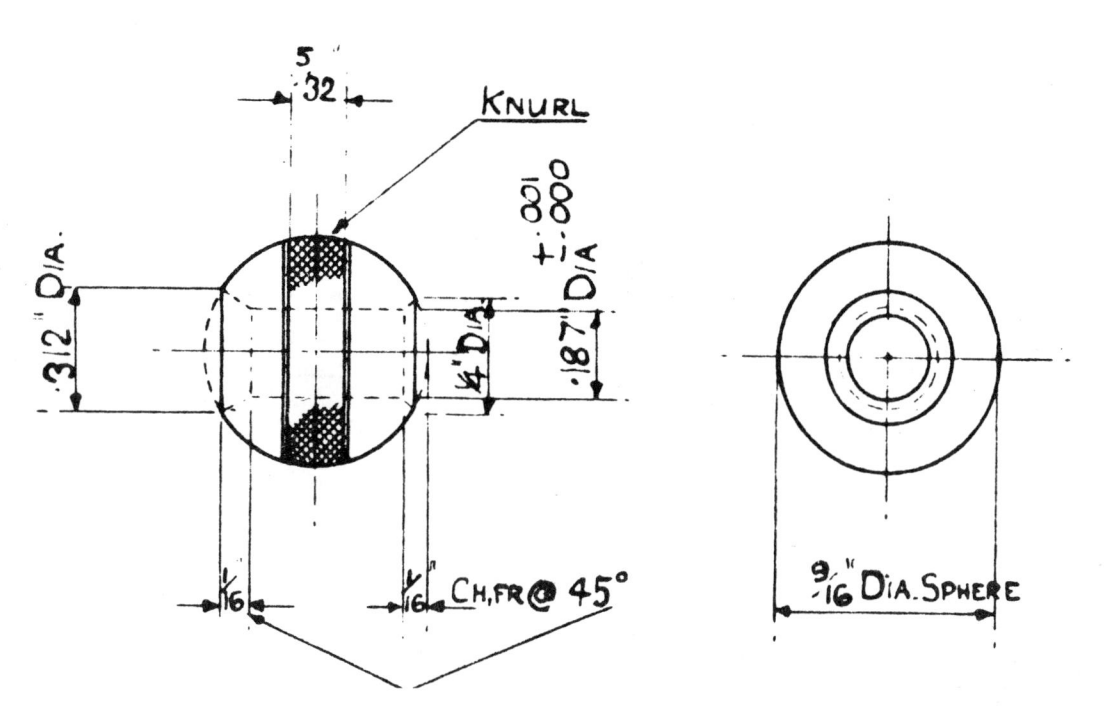

TOLERANCE ON ALL FRACTIONAL DIMENSIONS ± .010" UNLESS OTHERWISE STATED

SCALE 2-1

THIS PRINT IS THE PROPERTY OF WEBLEY & SCOTT LTD 81-91, WEAMAN STREET BIRMINGHAM AND MUST NOT BE SOLD TO ANY OTHER CONCERN	NAME	G.HIGGS	G.H			MRK.II AIR RIFLE	B.D. MILD STEEL	9/16	RD BAR		METAL COLOUR
	DATE	7-3-38	30-3-38								
	BY	DRAWN	CHECKED	TRACED	PASSED	QUAN	MODEL	UNIT	MATERIAL SPEC	SIZE	FORM	HEAT TREAT	FINISH
	MACHINE WHERE MARKED	'F'										
	GRIND DO DO	'G'		BALL FOR BREECH LEVER	MK.II AIR RIFLE			A.R.II /38				
	MACHINE ALL OVER	⊕		TITLE				PART Nº				

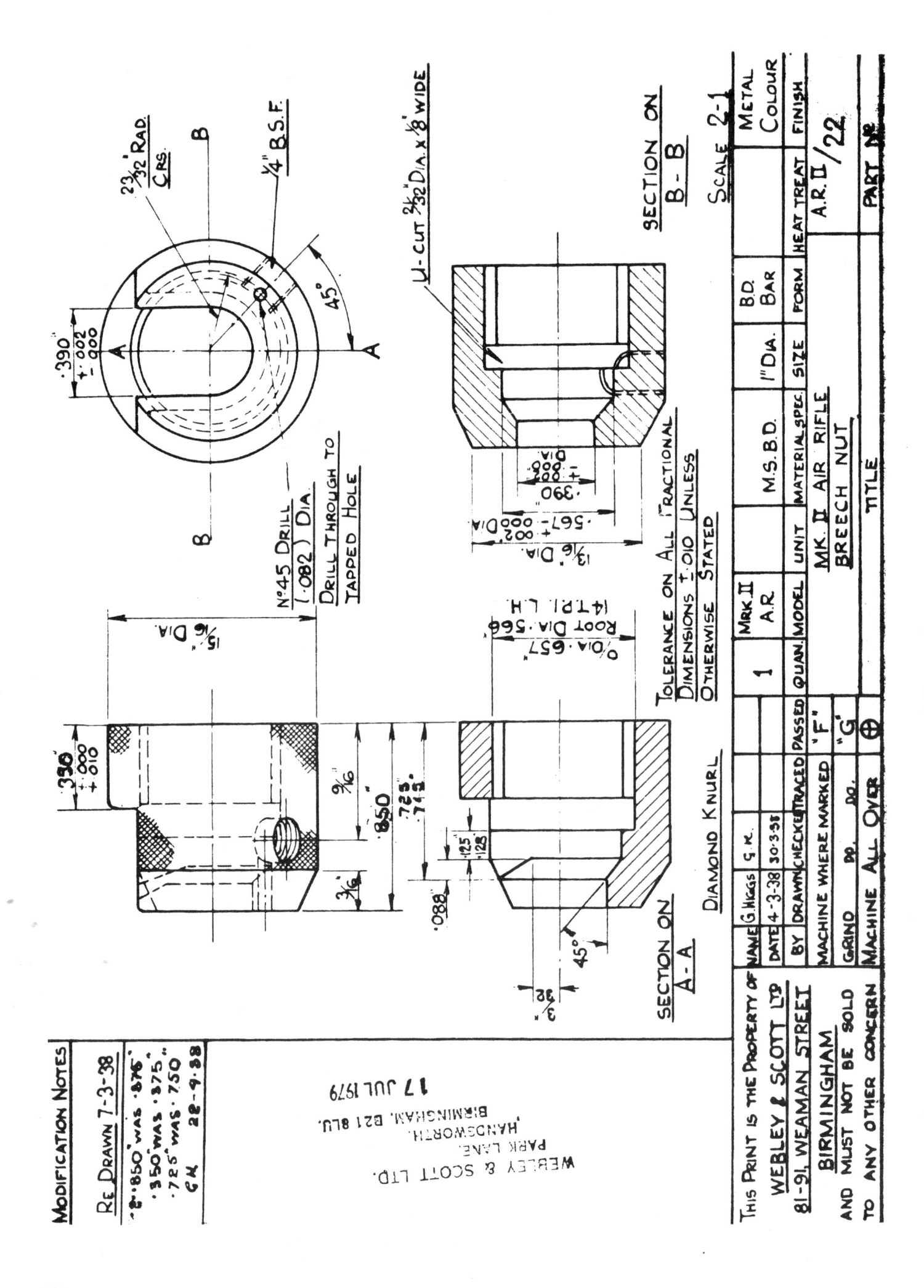

MK. II AIR RIFLE BREECH NUT

PART N° A.R.II/22

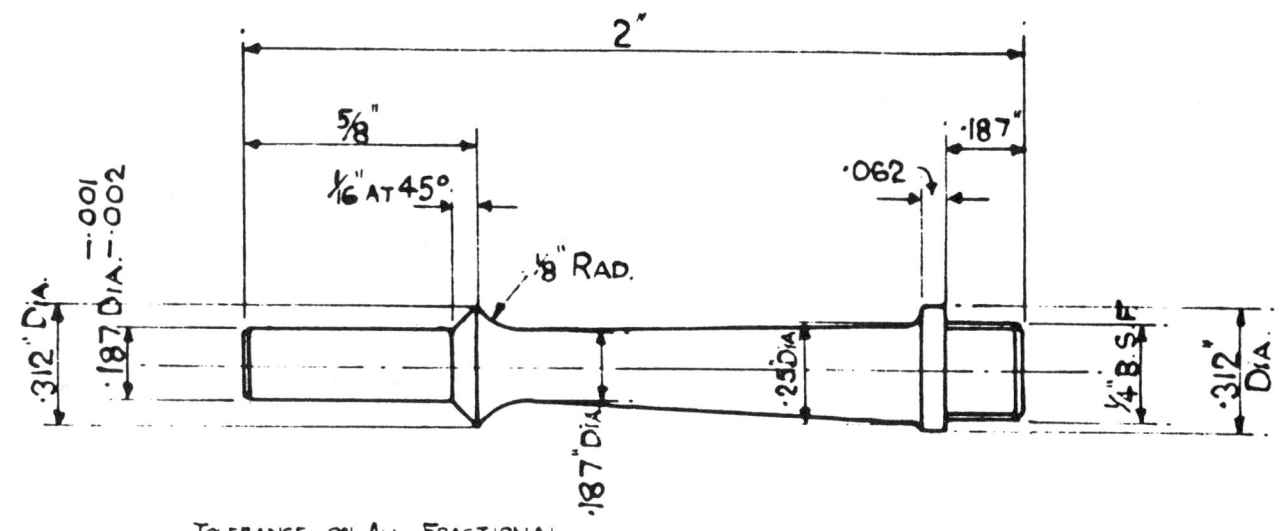

Breech Nut Lever / Adjustable Sight

Drawing 1: Breech Nut Lever

Dimensions:
- Overall length: 2"
- 5/8"
- .187"
- 1/16" AT 45°
- 1/8" RAD.
- .062"
- .312" DIA -.001/-.002
- .187" DIA
- .187" DIA
- .25 DIA
- 1/4 B.S.F.
- .312" DIA

TOLERANCE ON ALL FRACTIONAL DIMENSIONS ± .010" UNLESS OTHERWISE STATED

SCALE 2-1

THIS PRINT IS THE PROPERTY OF WEBLEY & SCOTT LTD 81-91, WEAMAN STREET BIRMINGHAM AND MUST NOT BE SOLD TO ANY OTHER CONCERN	NAME	G.HIGGS	G.H		1	MRK II AIR RIFLE		.45 CARBON STEEL		RD BAR		METAL COLOUR
	DATE	7-3-38	30-3-38									
	BY	DRAWN	CHECKED	TRACED	PASSED	QUAN	MODEL	UNIT	MATERIAL SPEC	SIZE	FORM	HEAT TREAT	FINISH
	MACHINE WHERE MARKED	"F"		MK. II AIR RIFLE BREECH NUT LEVER		A.R. II /39
	GRIND DO. DO.	"G"				
	MACHINE ALL OVER	⊕		TITLE		PART Nº

Drawing 2: Adjustable Sight

- .656"
- .437"
- .040 R
- .064 / .066
- .296 / .298
- .156 / .155
- .204 / .205
- .468"
- "U" SIGHT & ANGLE TO BE FILED
- .044 / .046
- .123 / .125
- 25° INC
- .5935 / .595

SCALE 2/1

THIS PRINT IS THE PROPERTY OF WEBLEY & SCOTT LTD WEAMAN STREET BIRMINGHAM	NAME	C.K.D.	G.H	M.L.J.		1	MK II AIR RIFLE ADJ. REAR SIGHT		M.S.				METAL COLOURED
	DATE	21-2-38	12/7/40	13-8-40									
	BY	DRAWN	CHECKED	TRACED	PASSED	QUAN	MODEL	UNIT	MATERIAL SPEC	SIZE	FORM	HEAT TREAT	FINISH
	MACHINE WHERE MARKED	"F"		ADJUSTABLE SIGHT		.146
	GRIND do do	"G"				
	MACHINE ALL OVER	⊕		TITLE		PART Nº

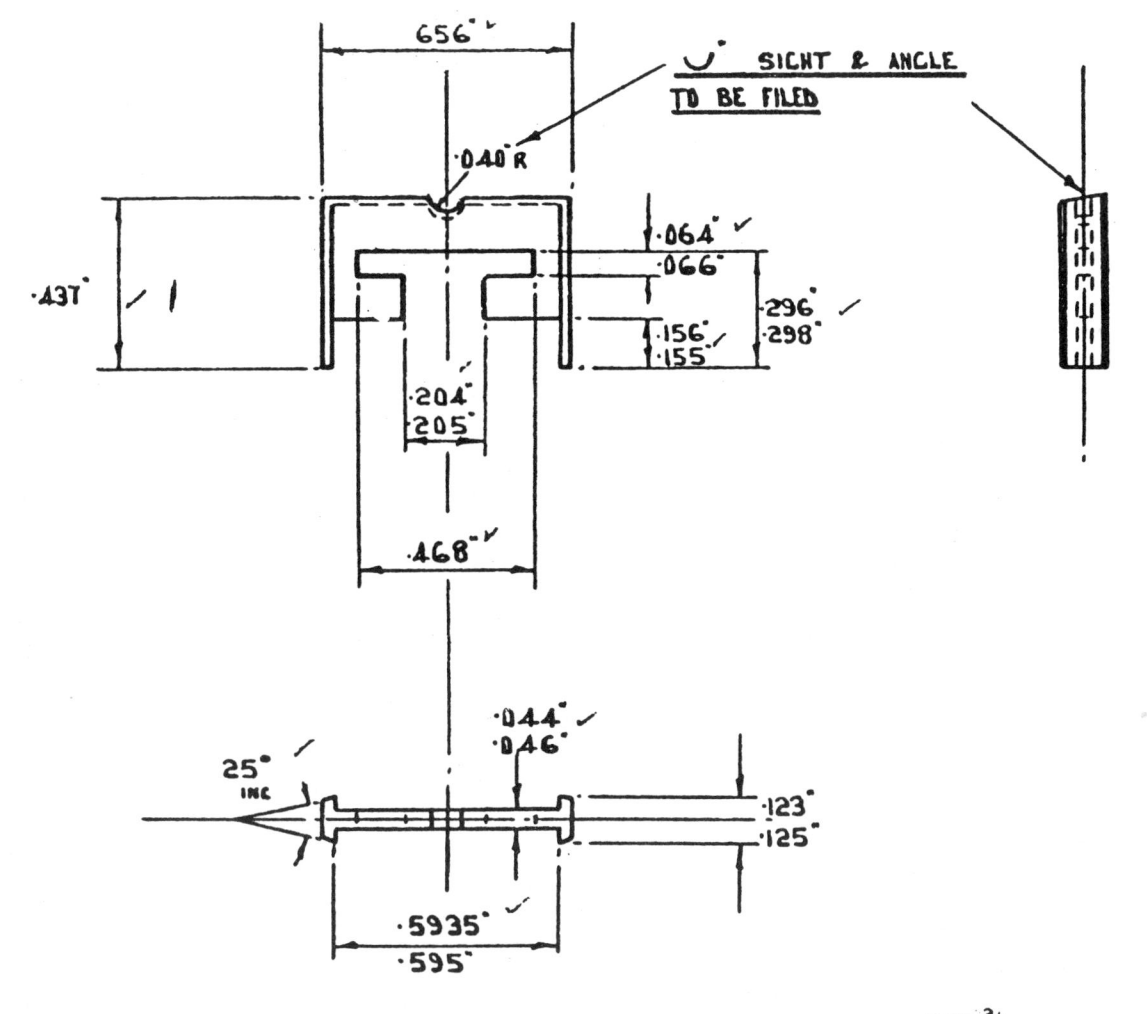

The WEBLEY SERVICE AIR RIFLE Mark II.

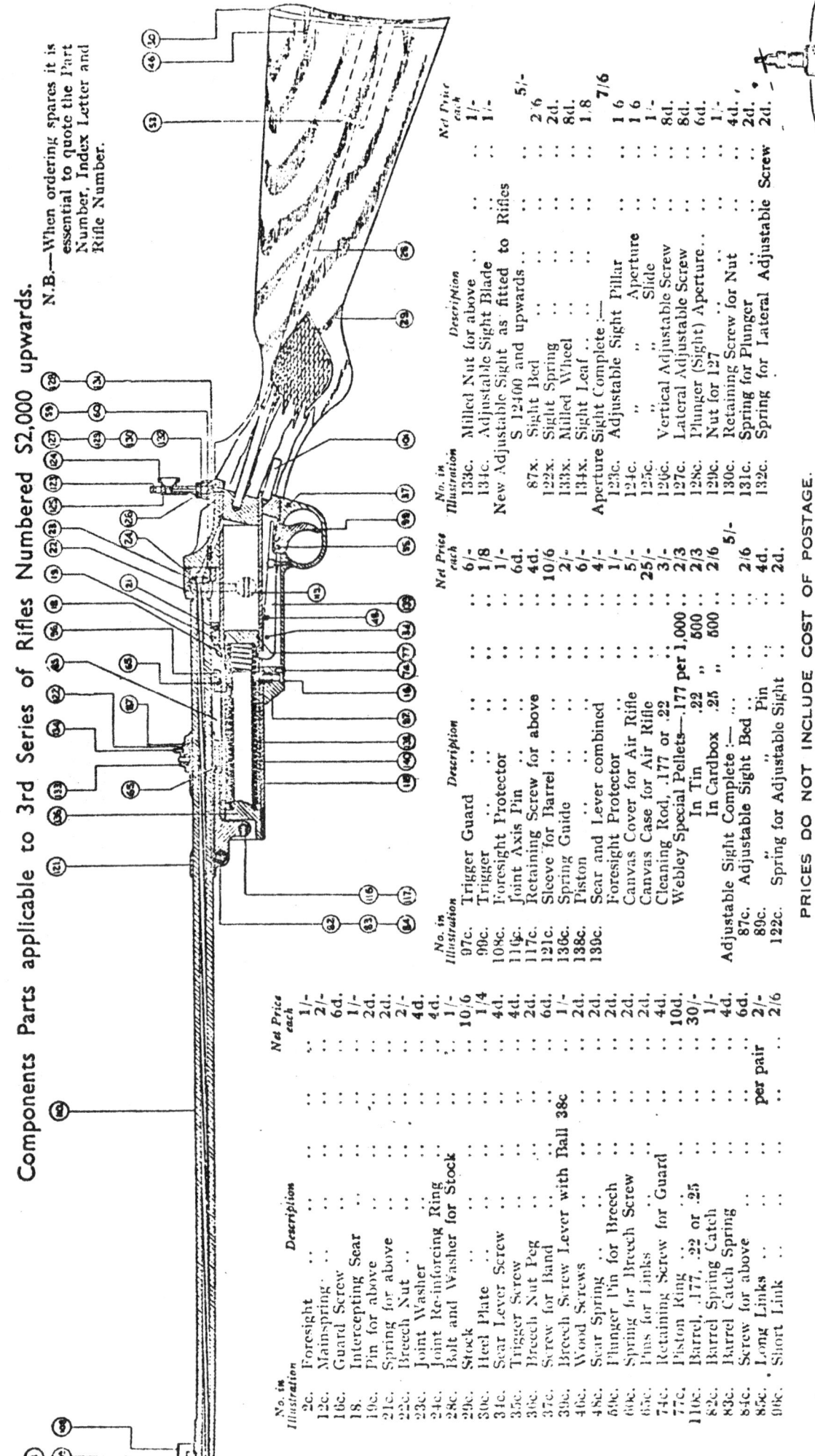

Components Parts applicable to 3rd Series of Rifles Numbered S2,000 upwards.

N.B.—When ordering spares it is essential to quote the Part Number, Index Letter and Rifle Number.

No. in Illustration	Description	Net Price each
2c.	Foresight	1/-
12c.	Mainspring	2/-
16c.	Guard Screw	6d.
18.	Intercepting Sear	1/-
19c.	Pin for above	2d.
21c.	Spring for above	2/-
22c.	Breech Nut	4d.
23c.	Joint Washer	4d.
24c.	Joint Re-inforcing Ring	..
28c.	Bolt and Washer for Stock	1/-
29c.	Stock	10/6
30c.	Heel Plate	1/4
31c.	Sear Lever Screw	4d.
33c.	Trigger Screw	4d.
35c.	Breech Nut Peg	2d.
37c.	Screw for Band	6d.
39c.	Breech Screw Lever with Ball 38c	1/-
46c.	Wood Screws	2d.
48c.	Sear Spring	2d.
59c.	Plunger Pin for Breech	2d.
60c.	Spring for Breech Screw	2d.
65c.	Pins for Links	2d.
74c.	Retaining Screw for Guard	4d.
77c.	Piston Ring	10d.
116c.	Barrel, .177, .22 or .25	30/-
82c.	Barrel Spring Catch	1/-
83c.	Barrel Catch Spring	4d.
85c.	Screw for above	6d.
86c.	Long Links ... per pair	2/-
90c.	Short Link	2/6

No. in Illustration	Description	Net Price each
97c.	Trigger Guard	6/-
99c.	Trigger	1/8
108c.	Foresight Protector	1/-
116c.	Joint Axis Pin	6d.
117c.	Retaining Screw for above	4d.
121c.	Sleeve for Barrel	10/6
136c.	Spring Guide	2/-
138c.	Piston	6/-
139c.	Sear and Lever combined	4/-
	Foresight Protector	1/-
	Canvas Cover for Air Rifle	5/-
	Canvas Case for Air Rifle	25/-
	Cleaning Rod, .177 or .22	3/-
	Webley Special Pellets—.177 per 1,000	2/3
	In Tin .22 " 500	2/3
	In Cardbox .25 " 500	2/6
	Adjustable Sight Complete :—	5/-
87c.	Adjustable Sight Bed	2/6
89c.	" " Pin	4d.
122c.	Spring for Adjustable Sight	2d.

No. in Illustration	Description	Net Price each
133c.	Milled Nut for above	6/-
131c.	Adjustable Sight Blade	1/8
	New Adjustable Sight as fitted to Rifles S 12400 and upwards	5/-
87x.	Sight Bed	2/6
122x.	Sight Spring	2d.
133x.	Milled Wheel	8d.
134x.	Sight Leaf	1/8
	Aperture Sight Complete :—	7/6
123c.	Adjustable Sight Pillar	1/6
124c.	" " Aperture	1/6
125c.	" " Slide	1/-
126c.	Vertical Adjustable Screw	8d.
127c.	Lateral Adjustable Screw	8d.
128c.	Plunger (Sight) Aperture	6d.
129c.	Nut for 127	1/-
130c.	Retaining Screw for Nut	4d.
131c.	Spring for Plunger	2d.
132c.	Spring for Lateral Adjustable Screw	2d.

PRICES DO NOT INCLUDE COST OF POSTAGE.

WEBLEY & SCOTT, LTD.
WEAMAN STREET, BIRMINGHAM, 4.

DOES your GUN SHOOT STRAIGHT? It's only as accurate as the pellet
WEBLEY Air Rifle & Air Pistol PELLETS

No. 2 Oil in Tin with Valve Spout, 1/-

MODEL Service Mk. II. (Third Series).

MAKER Webley & Scott.

DATE Production 1932—1946. Third series from September 1938 and serial number S2001.

VALUATION £200—£400.
($300—$600).

DETAILS The later type with no safety catch, improved push button barrel release, and "U" shaped improved peepsight that folds down into a recess at rear of air port passage way. Serial number of above S4501 stamped at rear of trigger guard, underside of barrel also stamped S4501. It appears that the original barrel has matching serial numbers. 25½ inch barrel, although have seen shortened barrels where a new bolt seal face has been cut and barrel moved along about half an inch in the push button support bracket. 41½ inches long. L.H.S. of port housing has winged pellet trademark, and on the L.H.S. of the air chamber is stamped "WEBLEY SERVICE AIR RIFLE MARK II". On the L.H.S. of the trigger block is stamped "MANUFACTURED BY WEBLEY & SCOTT LTD, BIRMINGHAM, ENGLAND". R.H.S. of port housing stamped "PATENT No. 371548". R.H.S. of air chamber stamped
"GREAT BRITAIN PAT No. 219872"
"U.S.A. PAT. U.S.A. 7/7/25"
"SPAIN PAT No. 89433"
"GERMANY D.R.P. No. 414833"
"CANADA PAT. 1925".
Advertised in 1935 as only being available in .22 or .177 only. Weight for .177 6 lb 10 oz, and for .22 6 lb 9 ozs, with velocities 550 f.p.s. for .22 and 600 for .177.
Have seen instruction booklet for the Webley Mk. II Service with "L" shaped pillar peepsight, safety catch, but fitted with push button barrel release, whilst the first model Mk. II had a large under leaf spring to hold barrel in position. Smoothbore barrels were available for countries where rifled barrels were prohibited. A canvas carrying bag with small handle was available for holding the airgun with barrels removed. A foresight protector was also available. The instruction booklet made no mention of the availability of a .25 barrel, could be that the .25 was a later addition. The .25 barrel was rarely advertised and could be that it was available mainly for the export market. Patent 219872 applied to the use of the barrel to cock the action. See "Guns Review" December 1979 for further details, whilst patent 371548 was for the turn bolt breech that pulled the barrel on to the breech end and thus formed an air-tight seal. See "Guns Review" April 1980. At a later date the support brackets for the intercepting sear were braised on to the air chamber and were more substantial than the previous variation. A fitted leather case was advertised by Webley's for the Mk. II air rifle. This had two straps and a brass lock and cost £3/0/0 in 1939. After production had ceased the replacement of mainsprings was made easier by returning the piston to Webley's who machined out the internal diameter to 55/64 inch in order that Webley Mk. III mainsprings could then be fitted. This service cost 6/- during the 1960s.

Trigger guards fitted with safety catches left over from the second series appear to have been used on Services with serial number in the early 2,000s. On air rifle number S2234 the hole for the safety latch had been threaded and a blank screwed in and finished off so as to be flush with rest of trigger block. The sear was also of the first series as the cut-out in the sear arm was present in order to engage the safety sear if it had been fitted. At a later date two numbers appear stamped on the underside of the barrel, one is the serial number whilst the other coincides with a number stamped on the barrel support block, these of course should match although they need not be the same numbers as the serial number.

The air seal on the piston was usually a phosphor-bronze piston ring working on the same principle as a car piston ring, but quite often pistons will be found with just a leather washer or even having both leather washer and piston ring, or even having two very thin rings in the gap usually reserved for one so that either ends are 180° to each other.

The serial number appears on the air chamber stamped between the support brackets for the trigger block. The "J" in a triangle as seen on some Webley air pistols has been stamped in the recess for the stock. Highest serial number seen is S13256.

Webley Junior air rifle

MODEL "Junior".

MAKER Webley & Scott Ltd., Birmingham, England.

DATE Very late 1940s or 1950. Production ceased late 1960s or 1970.

VALUATION £20—£40.
($30—$60).

DETAILS Smallest rifle made by Webley, or under contract for Webley by some other manufacturer. Tinplate construction. 36½ inches long with a 14½ inch .177 rifled brass liner barrel. Screw in bead foresight and wheel adjustable rearsight. Serial or batch number stamped on the underside of the barrel breech. All metal parts nicely blued in the true Webley tradition. Top of air chamber stamped "THE WEBLEY JUNIOR WEBLEY & SCOTT LTD BIRMINGHAM MADE IN ENGLAND". Advertised weight 3¼ lbs. When first produced they were available in smoothbore as well as rifled. The Junior could have been made by Millard Bros. of Scotland under licence for Webley as some parts will interchange. Advertised velocity 405 f.p.s. For its small size the Junior was given credit for fine accuracy due to machine rifled barrel and higher than normal power.

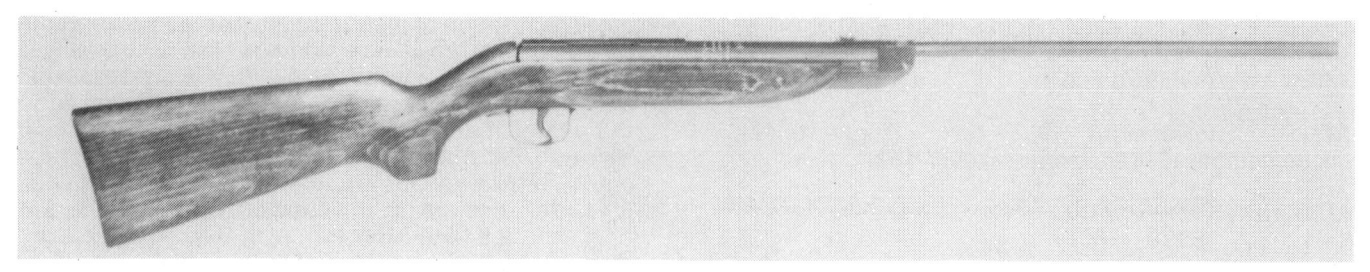

The Webley Ranger

INSTRUCTIONS FOR THE USE CARE AND MAINTENANCE OF THE WEBLEY RANGER AIR RIFLE

SHOOT WITH SAFETY

NEVER POINT A GUN AT ANYONE AND NEVER ALLOW ANYONE TO POINT A GUN AT YOU.

NEVER PICK UP A GUN, HAND IT TO ANYONE, OR ACCEPT A GUN FROM ANYONE, WITHOUT CHECKING TO SEE THAT IT IS NOT LOADED.

Your Ranger Air Rifle should give good service for many years if these simple instructions are followed:

1. **Trigger must not be pulled whilst barrel is in open position, otherwise it will fly back with considerable force causing damage. Do not fire the rifle unless there is a pellet in the barrel to take the shock of the piston thrust.**

2. Do not leave the rifle cocked when not in use. This reduces the life of the mainspring.

3. **Important** — When cocking the rifle there is no need to "break" it with a vicious jerk. Cock the rifle **gently** and you will hear a slight click when the sear engages.

4. **After cocking, make sure the barrel is properly seated before firing the rifle to avoid blowing out the breech washer and causing damage.**

5. After use, wipe the rifle with an oily rag to prevent rust. Webley Oil should be used (see next paragraph).

6. A few spots of Webley Oil applied through the hole in the air chamber will quickly restore any slight fall in velocity due to dry washer, but use oil very sparingly.

7. Sighting: Turn wheel to the left if you want the shots to go lower and to the right if you want them to go higher. The sight bed is set correctly, but if an adjustment becomes necessary, lightly tap the sight bed in the direction you want the shots to go, i.e. if the rifle is shooting to the right, and you want the shots to go left, tap the sight bed to left very slightly.

8. It is unlikely that it will be found necessary to fit a new mainspring except after very considerable use. It is preferable to have a spring fitted by your own gunsmith, but if this is not convenient, instructions to replace the mainspring are as follows:

   Remove the two front stock screws A40, washers A41, also stock and guard screw A38. Stock can then be detached from rifle.

   Remove trigger pivot screw A35 and trigger assembly.

   Push out body tube end cover A15.

   Remove mainspring locking piece A14 by inserting Tool No. T2098 and turning slightly to the left. Mainspring and guide can then be withdrawn.

   Fit guide into new mainspring and replace.

   Refit locking piece by means of tool, making sure that the lug engages into slot in body tube.

   Refit trigger assembly with screw A35.

   Fit trigger spring between the pip on the trigger and the lug on the end over A15.

   Refit stock.

   It is comparatively easy to carry out the above, provided you have the correct tool and a vice to hold the rifle. If not, the spring can be inserted by placing the rifle against a stop and using a piece of round wood, such as a file handle. Having pushed the locking piece A14 home so that the tang lines up with the slot in the body, push the tang into the slot with a screwdriver or other suitable tool.

9. For best results use Webley pellets which are carefully gauged to the rifling of your barrel.

10. A Webley target holder is a very useful extra and enables you to use your rifle with added safety.

11. A Webley Telescopic sight will give added enjoyment to your sport.

12. A new Webley Shooting Gallery is now available incorporating static and mobile targets, particularly produced for indoor shooting in the home.

WEBLEY & SCOTT LIMITED,
Park Lane, Handsworth,
Birmingham 21.

Printed in England
C87

A complete repair service is available for all Webley products

Component Parts of the Webley Ranger Air Rifle

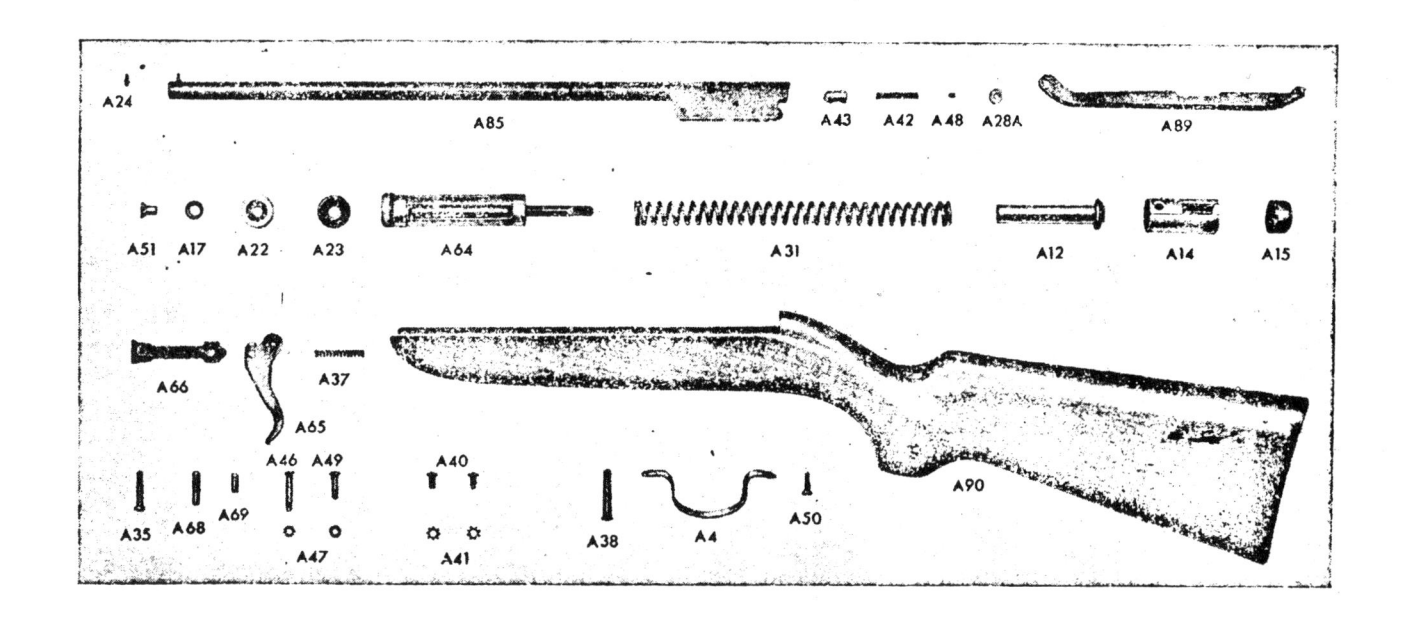

Your Ranger Air Rifle is fitted with a mounting plate on the body to accommodate the **Webley 415 Telescopic Sight.**

Spares should be ordered from the Dealer who supplied the Rifle and he will quote current prices.

Webley air rifle pellets and Webley oil in plastic containers should be used to give best performance.

Part No. in Illustration	Description	Part No. in Illustration	Description
A4	Trigger Guard	A42	Barrel Locking Plunger Spring
A12	Mainspring Guide	A43	Barrel Locking Plunger
A14	Mainspring Locking Piece	A46	Barrel Pivot Pin
A15	Body End Cover	A47	Lock Nut
A17	Piston Washer Support	A48	Barrel Locking Plunger Retaining Screw
A22	Piston Washer	A49	Loading Lever Pivot Pin
A23	Piston Backing Washer	A50	Trigger Guard Screw, Rear
A24	Foresight	A51	Piston Washer Screw
A28a	Barrel Joint Washer 3/16" thick	A64	Piston Assembly
A31	Mainspring	A65	Trigger with Sears Assembled
A35	Trigger Pivot Screw	A66	Sight Assembly
A37	Trigger Spring	A85	Barrel Assembly (Less Rearsight)
A38	Stock and Guard Screw	A89	Loading Lever
A40	Stock Screw	A90	Stock
A41	Washer	T2098	Tool for Replacing Mainspring

CODE LETTER IDENTIFICATION

As from January 1966 the Code Letter should be quoted on all orders for 'Ranger' Air Rifle parts. The Code Letter is stamped on the left hand side of the barrel, by the loading lever pivot pin.

For rifles marked **Code** Letter 'A' as list above.

For rifles marked **Code** Letter 'B' as list above except for loading lever A5.

For rifles marked **Code** Letter 'C' changes as for letters 'B' plus Barrel Pivot Pin A68 and Loading Lever Pivot Pin A69.

When ordering, it is essential to use **prefix** letter 'A', which indicates the model for which the component is required.

KEEP THIS LIST FOR FUTURE REFERENCE

WEBLEY & SCOTT LIMITED
Park Lane, Handsworth,
Birmingham 21.

A complete repair service is
available for all Webley products

MODEL Ranger.

DATE 1950 to 1970.

MAKER Webley & Scott Ltd., Birmingham, England.

VALUATION £20 – £40. ($30 – $60).

DETAILS Manufactured at the same time as the Webley "Junior" air rifle. The "Jaguar" air rifle was the follow-on from the "Ranger" when production ceased in 1970. 38¼ inches long with a 16 inch rifled barrel. Solid construction barrel and cocking lever. Webley tended to put too much into so little. Screw-in bead foresight and dovetail mounted rearsight adjustable for elevation only. Serial number stamped on underside of barrel breech. Slender air chamber stamped "THE WEBLEY RANGER — WEBLEY & SCOTT LTD — BIRMINGHAM — MADE IN ENGLAND", was also fitted with scope ramp spot welded on. Full length stock with seven grooves cut on either side of the fore-end. Available in .177 only. Advertised weight 3½ lbs. Appears to have been available rifled or smoothbore. Would assume that the "Ranger" sold in small numbers and survival rate must be pretty low. The scope ramp fitted was intended for the Webley 415 telescopic sight. From January 1966 a code letter was stamped on the L.H.S. of the barrel near the pivot pin, this indicated minor changes in the design; Code "A" was standard and made before minor changes took place. Code "B" denoted a change in the loading lever part A5, and Code "C" was as "B" plus changes in the barrel pivot pin A68 and the loading lever pivot pin A69. Early models were not fitted with a telescopic sight ramp.

Webley Jaguar

MODEL "Jaguar".

MAKER Webley & Scott Ltd., Birmingham, England.

DATE 1970 to late 1970s.

VALUATION £20 – £40. ($30 – $60).

DETAILS Appears to merge the "Junior" and "Ranger" models. The air chamber and barrel of the "Junior" and the stock from the "Ranger". The air chamber and barrel are identical to the British Diana Model 22 and it could be that these parts were made for Webley and assembled by them in Birmingham. 36½ inches long with a 14 inch rifled barrel. Tinplate construction. Serial number stamped under the barrel near pivot pin, unusual to have a serial number on a tinplate air rifle. Top of air chamber stamped "THE WEBLEY JAGUAR — WEBLEY & SCOTT LTD., BIRMINGHAM — MADE IN ENGLAND". Fitted with dumb-bell shaped telescopic sight ramp spot welded on in the true Webley style. Fore-end of stock grooved with seven lines and top of stock raised to be in line with rear of air chamber, these being characteristic with the design of the Mk. III. Double pull trigger but non-adjustable. Available in .177, but may have been sold in .22 as well when first introduced. Advertised weight 3 lb 12 oz. At a later date the stock became smooth and slightly longer to give an overall length of 39 inches. Spare parts may interchange with the Diana or Original Model 22. Other changes made towards the end of production was the fitting of a parallel sided scope ramp instead of the dumb-bell shaped variety and the dropping of the words "The Webley" in front of Jaguar on top of the air chamber. All spare parts will interchange with the Webley Junior air rifle.

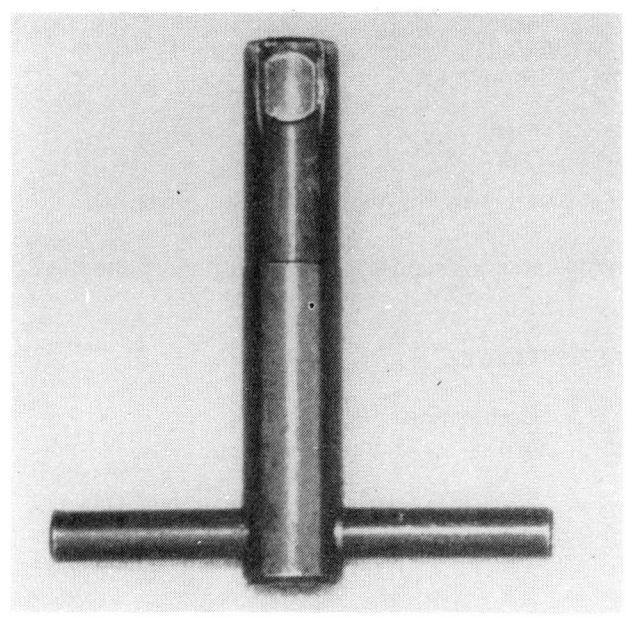

Webley Tool No. T2098

A bit of a puzzle this one but it does fit the piston of the Mk. II Service and has proved its worth in removing pistons. To remove the piston the tool is inserted into the air chamber and the raised portion at the end is placed into cocking lever slot in the piston. The piston is then drawn out of the air chamber. The puzzle is that the above has also been described as a mainspring inserter for the Webley Jaguar air rifle.

Shoot with safety

Other Webley Products
Double and single barrel Sporting Guns
Air Rifles and Air Pistols   Starting Pistols
Seat Sticks   Cleaning Accessories
Targets and Target Holders   Air Rifle Pellets
Cartridges and many other accessories for shooting

WEBLEY & SCOTT LIMITED
Park Lane, Handsworth,
Birmingham B21 8LU
Telephone: 021-553 3952/6

Parts List and Diagram of Parts
Spares should be ordered from the Dealer who supplied the rifle.

Part No.	DESCRIPTION OF PART	Part No.	DESCRIPTION OF PART
A65	TRIGGER WITH SEARS ASSEMBLED	A40	STOCK SCREW AND WASHER (A41)
A35	TRIGGER PIVOT SCREW	A50	GUARD SCREW, REAR
A37	TRIGGER SPRING	A4	TRIGGER GUARD
A62	BARREL ASSEMBLY (LESS REAR-SIGHT)	A5	LOADING LEVER
1367	BARREL JOINT WASHER	A49	LOADING LEVER PIVOT PIN
A42	BARREL LOADING PLUNGER SPRING	A31	MAINSPRING
A43	BARREL LOCKING PLUNGER	A12	SPRING GUIDE
A68	BARREL PIVOT PIN	A14	MAINSPRING LOCKING PIECE
A47	BARREL PIVOT PIN LOCK NUT	A24	FORESIGHT
	LOADING LEVER PIVOT LOCK NUT	A66	REAR SIGHT ASSEMBLY
A48	BARREL LOCKING PLUNGER RETAINING SCREW	A13	REAR SIGHT, LESS SCREW
*A7	BARREL LOCKING CATCH HOUSING	A25	REAR SIGHT ADJUSTING SCREW
*A44	BARREL LOCKING CATCH	A64	PISTON ASSEMBLY
*A45	BARREL LOCKING CATCH FIXING PIN	A17	PISTON WASHER SUPPORT
A15	BODY END COVER	A22	PISTON WASHER
	WEBLEY TELESCOPIC SIGHT	A23	PISTON BACKING WASHER
	3 MAGNIFICATIONS	A51	PISTON WASHER SCREW
A36	STOCK, PISTOL GRIP	*T2098	TOOL FOR REPLACING MAINSPRING
A38	STOCK AND GUARD SCREW		*WEBLEY OIL (IN PLASTIC CONTAINER WITH SPOUT)

*Items not illustrated.   When ordering, it is essential to use the prefix letter "A", which indicates the model for which the component is required.

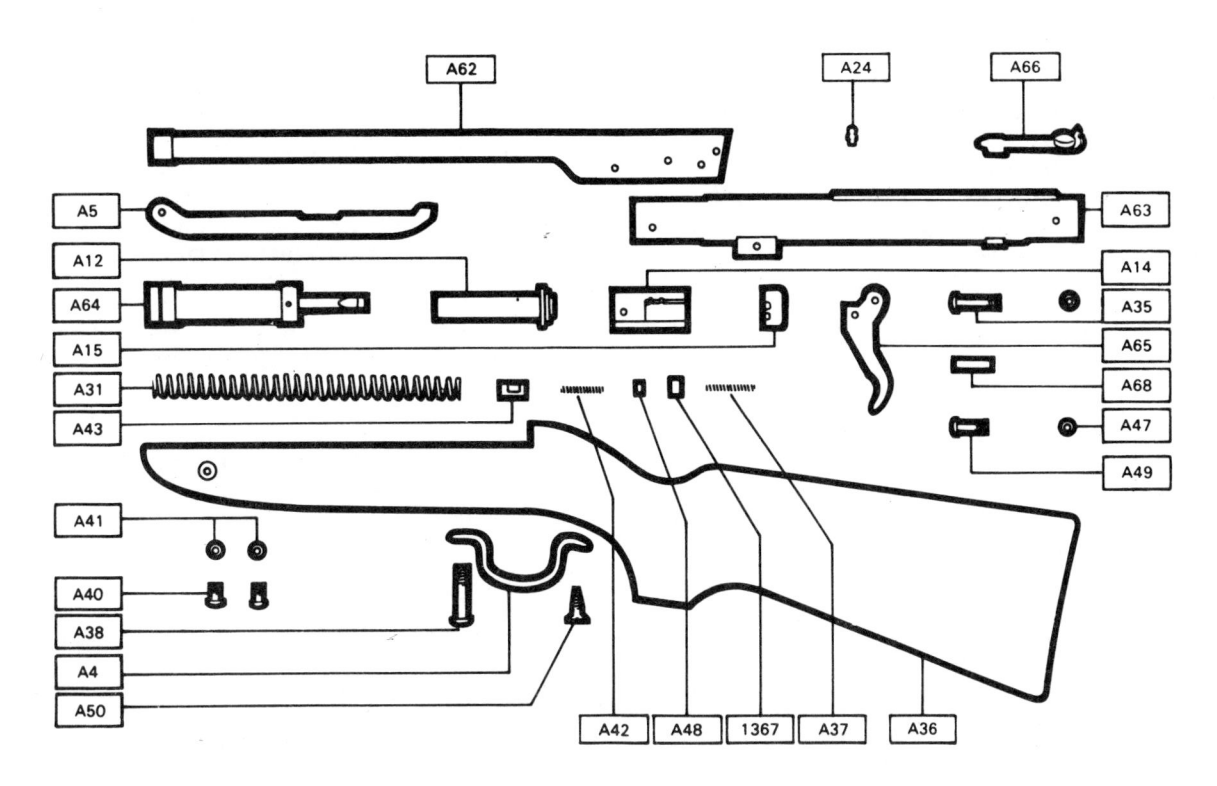

Component Parts of the Webley Falcon Air Rifle

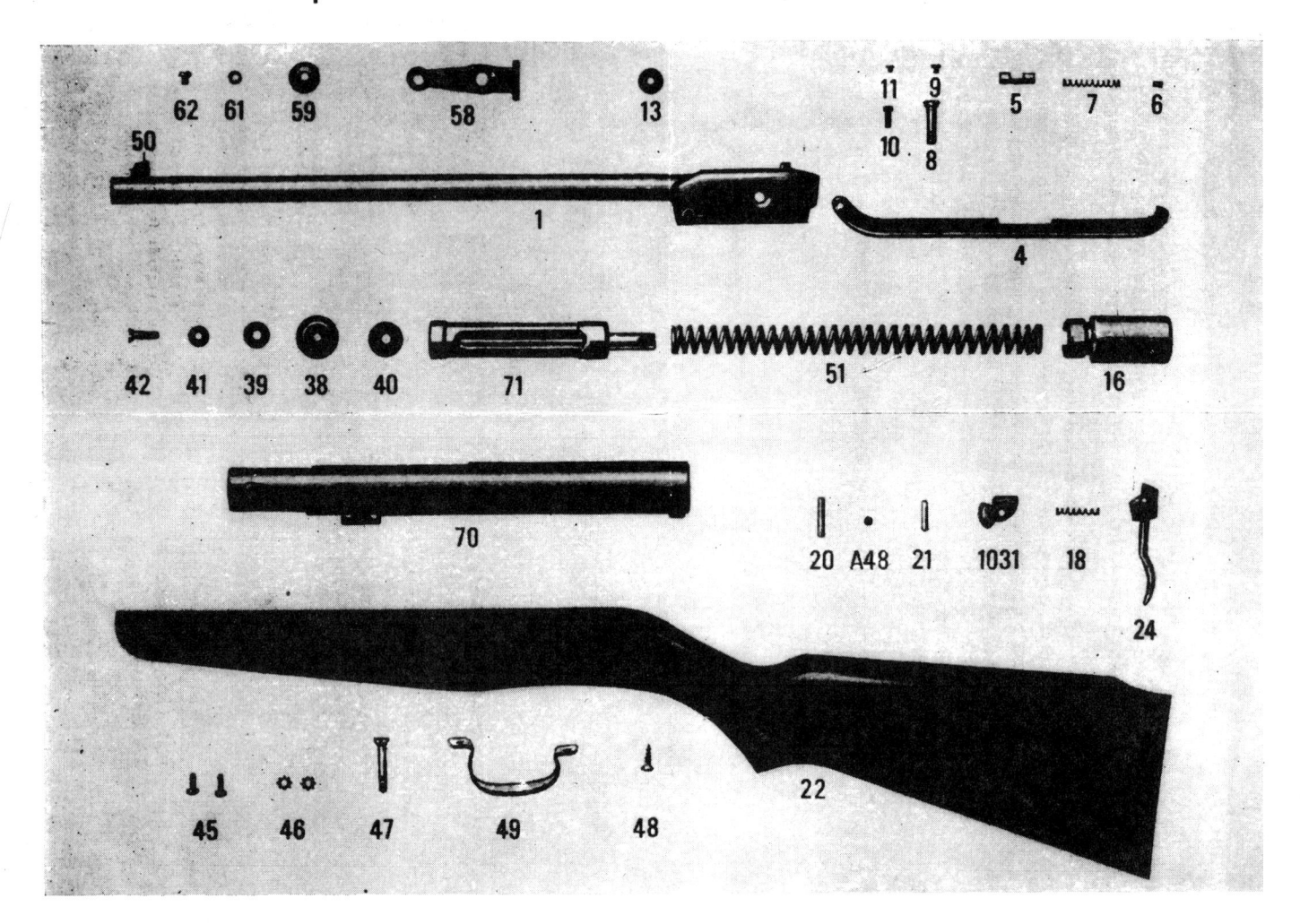

Old Type Rearsight (Not illustrated)

B52 Rear Sight Complete
B26 Rear Sight Spring
B28 Rear Sight Leaf
B29 Rear Sight Adjusting Spring
B30 Rear Sight Slide

PART No.	DESCRIPTION		PART No.	DESCRIPTION	
B1	Barrel Assembly (without sights)	P.T.	B58	Rear Sight Blade	
B5	Barrel Fixing Plunger		B59	Rear Sight Adjusting Nut	
B6	Barrel Fixing Plunger Retaining Screw		B60	Rear Sight Adjusting Screw	
B16	Trigger and Sear Housing		B61/62	Rear Sight Screw and Washer	
B7	Barrel Fixing Plunger Spring		B71	Piston Assembly	P.T.
B8	Barrel Joint Screw		B38	Piston Outer Washer	
B9	Barrel Joint Screw Retaining Screw		B39	Piston Inner Washer	
B13	Barrel Joint Washer		B40	Piston Inner Support	
B10	Loading Lever Joint Screw		B41	Piston Washer Plate	
B11	Loading Lever Joint Screw Retaining Screw		B42	Piston Washer Screw	
B4	Loading Lever	P.T.	B22	Stock	P.T.
B24	Trigger		B45/6	Stock Screw Front and Lock Washer	
B21	Trigger Axis Pin		B47	Stock and Guard Screw	
B49	Trigger Guard		B50	Foresight	
B48	Trigger Guard Screw Rear		B51	Mainspring	
1031	Sear			Webley Telescopic Sight	
B18	Sear Spring			Webley Oil (in plastic container with spout)	
B20	Sear Axis Pin		A48	Grub Screw	

Items marked P.T. are liable to Purchase Tax.

Spares should be ordered from the Dealer who supplied the Rifle and he will be pleased to quote at current prices

When ordering, it is essential to use the prefix letter "B", which indicates the model for which the component is required.

KEEP THIS LIST FOR FUTURE REFERENCE.

WEBLEY & SCOTT LTD.,
  Park Lane, Handsworth,
    Birmingham 21.

A complete repair service is available for all Webley products.

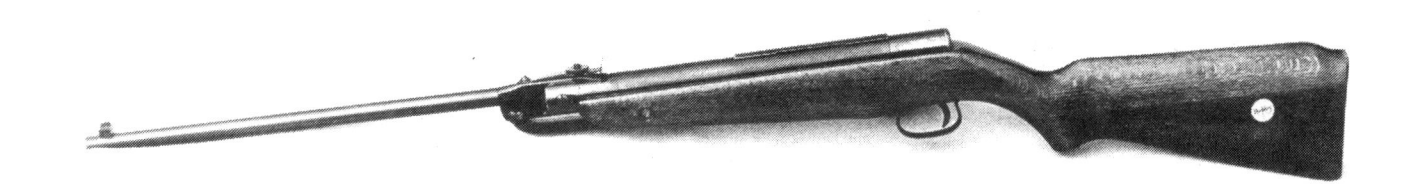

Webley "Falcon"

MODEL "Falcon".

MAKER Webley & Scott Ltd.

DATE 1960 to 1970.

VALUATION £30—£60.
($45—$90).

DETAILS Serial number of above 766. 41 inches long. Very well made. All metal. Webley name plate set in side of stock. Serial number stamped on underside of barrel breech so is covered by cocking arm when barrel is closed. Stamped on top of chamber "THE WEBLEY FALCON, WEBLEY & SCOTT LTD. BIRMINGHAM. MADE IN ENGLAND". Calibre of barrel is stamped on side of barrel breech. Fitted with plate for telescopic sight. Advertised in the 1960s with muzzle velocity 550 f.p.s. for .177 and 500 f.p.s. for .22. At a later date the medallion was no longer fitted to the stock. The foresight appears to be the same as fitted to the Webley Mk. III underlever. Advertised velocities, .177 — 550 f.p.s. and .22 — 450 f.p.s., whilst weight 6 lb. Before unscrewing the trigger block in order to replace the mainspring a small grub screw, part A48, must be removed first. The rearsight can also cause problems when being fitted, the reverse thread on the adjusting wheel and stud can be very tight, part number B59, first screw the stud into the adjuster wheel, it may be necessary to clamp the wheel, after the stud has been screwed well down into the wheel place the rearsight blade (B58) on to the stud and then screw it on to the top of the barrel in an anti-clockwise direction, then lastly replace the front screw and locking washer and tighten on.

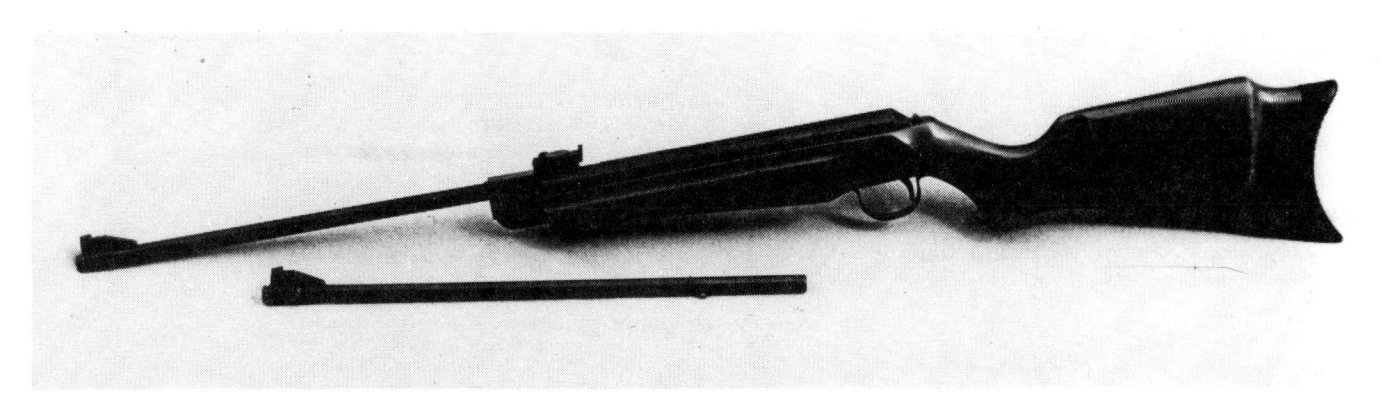

Webley "Hawk" Mk. I

MODEL "Hawk". Series I.

MAKER Webley & Scott Ltd.

DATE Series I 1971 to 1974.

VALUATION One barrel: £30—£60.
($45—$90).

DETAILS Interchangeable barrels. Locked in place by a rotating cam, coin operated. Very convenient. Automatic safety. 40 inches long. Surprisingly one of the best rifles in .177 that I've tested. Has a very stylish stock, but this was smoothed out when the Mk. II series was introduced. Serial number of above 13981 stamped on underside of barrel breech block, partly obscured by cocking lever. Stamped on side of air chamber "THE WEBLEY HAWK MADE IN ENGLAND" and on other side, "WEBLEY & SCOTT LTD., BIRMINGHAM". For a review of the above see "Guns Review" July 1971.
The cocking links will not interchange from the Mk. I to the Mk. II/III as the Mk. I is shorter than the other two.

Component Parts of the Webley Hawk Air Rifle

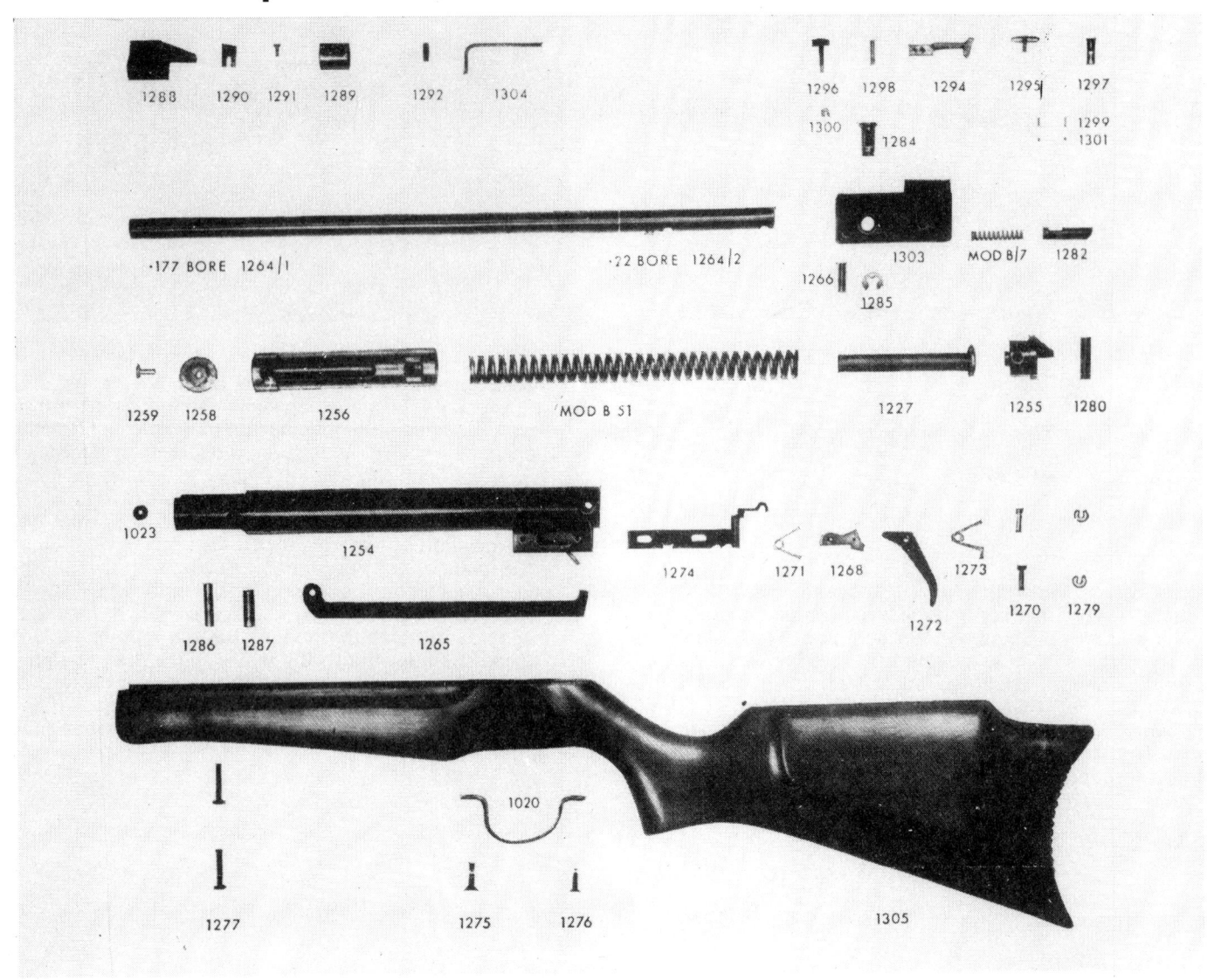

PART No.	DESCRIPTION OF PART		PART No.	DESCRIPTION OF PART
1227	Spring Guide Assembly		1280	Body End Plug Pin
1254	Body Tube Assembly		1282	Barrel Fixing Plunger
1255	Body End Plug		Mod B 7	Barrel Fixing Plunger Spring
1256	Piston Body		1284	Barrel Locking Key
1020	Trigger Guard		1285	Barrel Key Circlip
1258	Piston Washer		1286	Barrel Pivot
1259	Rivet		1287	Barrel Stop Pin
1260	Piston Assembly P.T.		1288	Foresight Ramp
Mod B 51	Mainspring		1289	Foresight Hood
1264/1 1264/2	Barrel Assembly P.T.		1290	Foresight Blade
			1291	Foresight Blade Screw
1265	Loading Lever P.T.		1292	Foresight Ramp Set Screw
1266	Loading Lever Axis Pin		1294	Rearsight Leaf
1267	Loading Lever Stop Pin		1295	Rearsight Vertical Screw
1268	Sear		1296	Rearsight Horizontal Screw
1270	Sear & Trigger Axis		1297	Rearsight Bar
1271	Sear Spring		1298	Rearsight Leaf Pivot
1272	Trigger		1299	Rearsight Click Spring
1273	Trigger Spring		1300	Rearsight Circlip
1274	Safe Slide		1301	Rearsight Ball
1275	Stock and Guard Screw		1023	Joint Washer
1276	Trigger Guard Woodscrew		1303	Rearsight Base and Barrel Housing Assembly
1277	Stock Screw Front		1304	Frontsight Socket Key
1279	Sear and Trigger Axis Clips		1305	Stock and Recoil Pad Assembly P.T.

Items marked P.T. are liable to Purchase Tax.

Spares should be ordered from the Dealer who supplied the Rifle and he will be pleased to quote at current prices.

KEEP THIS LIST FOR FUTURE REFERENCE

WEBLEY & SCOTT LTD.,
Park Lane, Handsworth,
Birmingham B21 8LU

A complete repair service is available for all Webley products

INSTRUCTIONS FOR THE CARE AND MAINTENANCE OF THE WEBLEY 'HAWK' AIR RIFLE

General Instructions

Your 'Hawk' Air Rifle will give good service for many years if these simple instructions are followed:

1. Do not fire the rifle without pellet in the barrel.
2. Do not leave the rifle cocked when not in use. This reduces the life of the mainspring.
3. **Important.** When cocking the rifle make sure the safe is pushed forward in the firing position, there is no need to break it with a vicious jerk. Tap the top of the barrel with your hand to open the spring lock, then cock the rifle gently as far as the barrel will go. Insert pellet and close barrel. The safe will go automatically when you cock the rifle, to fire, push the safe slide forward with your thumb.
4. After use, wipe the rifle with an oily rag to prevent rust. Webley oil should be used.
5. A few spots of Webley oil applied through the hole in the air chamber will quickly restore any slight fall in velocity due to a dry washer, but use oil sparingly.
6. The rifle is only as accurate as the pellet, for the accuracy and velocity claimed it is essential to use Webley special pellets. Do not be put off with a substitute.

To Assemble

7. The barrel is packed separately from the remainder of the rifle. To assemble, ascertain that the barrel locking key on the side of the spring lock is set to 'off'. A coin may be used to turn the key. Carefully insert the barrel as far as the barrel stop pin only.
8. Using the barrel as a lever, tap the barrel downwards to open the spring lock. Now insert barrel fully by sliding into block until it stops. Turn the key to the 'on' position. Do not use force. The key will turn in either direction — if resistance is met one way, turn the other. Close the spring lock.

To Change Barrel

9. Tap the top of the barrel to open the spring lock, turn the barrel key until the arrow points to 'off'. The barrel should then pull easily out of the block. Insert new barrel as directed in paragraphs 7 and 8 above.

To Adjust the Sights

10. **Rearsight.** VERTICAL: Turn the adjusting nut clockwise, to lower, anti-clockwise to raise.
    LATERAL: Turn the adjusting nut clockwise to shoot to the right. Anti-clockwise to shoot to the left.
11. **Frontsight.** The frontsight blade can be adjusted vertically or removed altogether by slackening the screw through the side of the block. The whole front sight assembly can be removed by undoing the grub screw through the top of the block with a socket screw key.

To Refit the Mainspring
(for servicing only)

12. Remove the front stock screws (1277) and front trigger guard screw. Stock can then be detached from rifle. The trigger, sear and safe slide will have to be removed. Do so in the following manner: Remove trigger axis pin circlip and pin, remove trigger and spring. Lever sear spring out of hole in sear, remove sear axis circlip and pin. The sear, spring and safe slide can now be removed from the rear of the bracket. Hold the gun upright with the rear body plug resting on a bench or table. Press down and push the pin out of the body end plug. The spring guide and spring can now be withdrawn.
13. Replace spring, spring guide, body end plug and pin, put both ends of sear spring into small hole in sear. Place on to safe slide and feed through bracket from the rear until holes line up. Replace pin and circlip. Unhook bottom limb of sear spring out of hole and let it flip down to bottom of bracket. Assemble trigger, spring, pin and circlip, make sure one end of trigger spring rests in the safe slide cut-out and the other end lies behind the trigger. Check action works, assemble to stock.

A complete repair service is available for all Webley products.

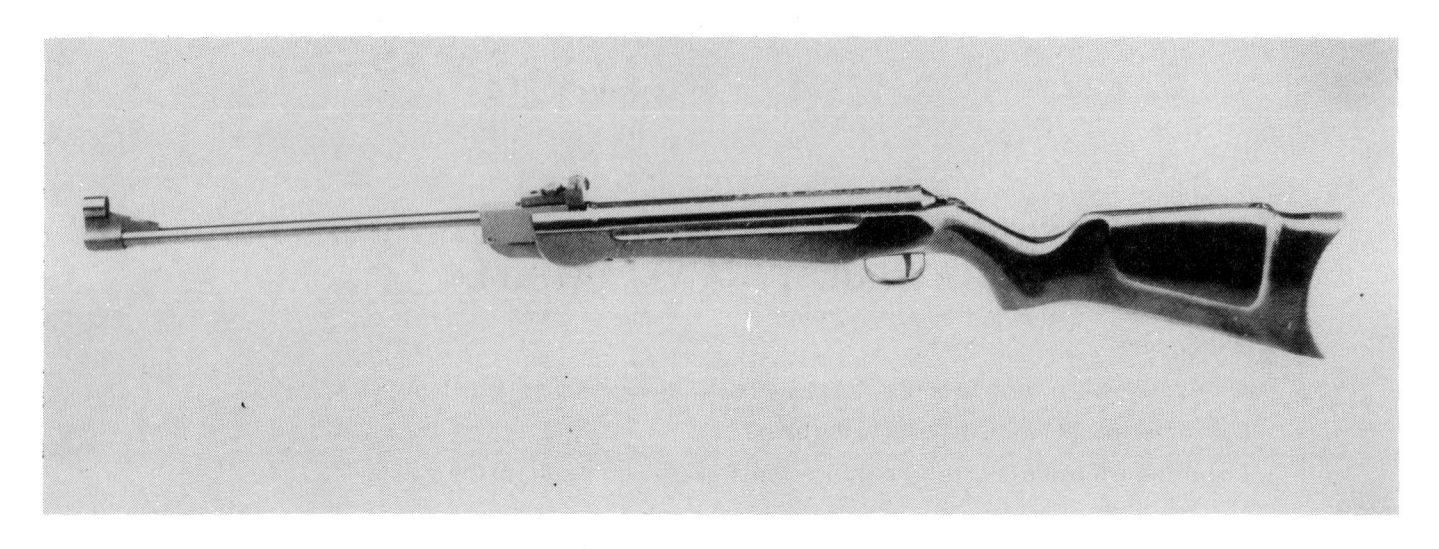

Webley Hawk Mk. II with Mk. I style stock

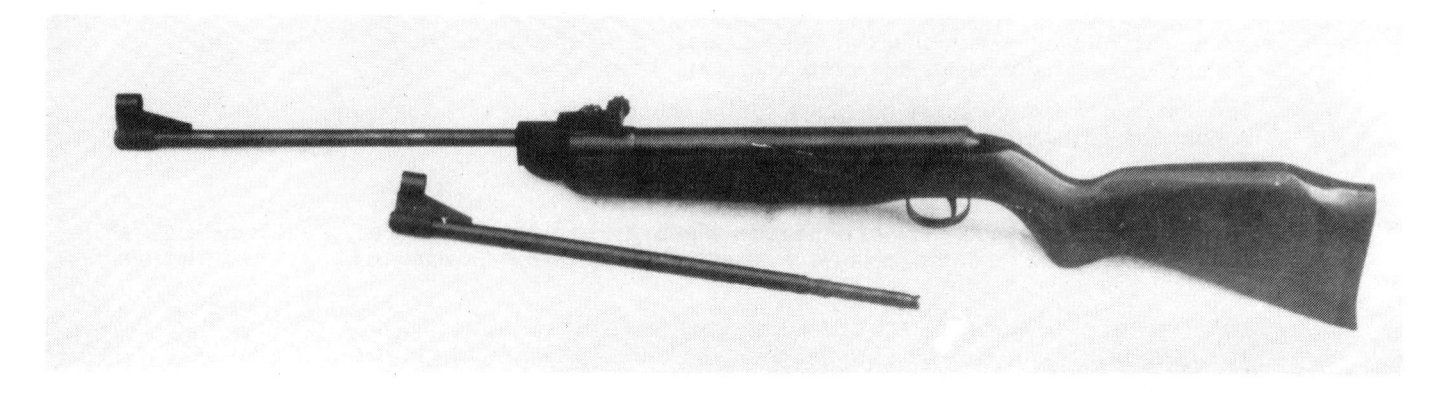

Webley Hawk Mk. II

MODEL Hawk Mk. II.

MAKER Webley & Scott.

DATE Introduced 1974 and superseded by the Hawk Series III in 1977.

VALUATION One barrel. £30—£60. ($45—$90).

DETAILS The interchangeable barrels screwed into the breech and are held in place by an Allen screw just in front of the rearsight. 41 inches long with 17 inch barrels. Top of each barrel is stamped with the calibre. Top of barrel breech stamped "WEBLEY & SCOTT LTD — BIRMINGHAM, ENGLAND". Serial number stamped on the underside of the barrel breech. On top of air chamber between the telescopic sight grooves is stamped "WEBLEY HAWK MK II". Stock has hard rubber recoil pad. Foresight can be removed by unscrewing the Allen screw, as can the rearsight. Trigger adjustment by way of Allen screw on top of the trigger block. Safety catch is automatic, but can be pushed back in when the air rifle is cocked in order to release the action instead of having to fire the airgun. The first Mk. IIs were advertised with the Mk. I style stock, at a later date the smoother style was introduced. The redesigned stock appeared in 1975. Advertised weight 6½ lb. Two telescopic sights were advertised for the above, Models 415 and 420. Advertised velocities .177 — 650 and for .22 — 550 f.p.s. Barrels should only be fitted with the breech open. Piston has two non-metallic piston rings. For a review see "Guns Review" June 1974. Care should be taken not to over tighten the grub screw on the foresight of any Webley Hawk air rifle. Export models sold in the U.S.A. would appear to be over the limit and were advertised as a "special top-power version". A limited number were given a highly polished and deeper blued finish, the trigger and safety were gold plated and the walnut stock was hand chequered to the fore-end and grip.

Shoot with safety

Other Webley Products
Double and single barrel Sporting Guns
Air Rifles and Air Pistols   Starting Pistols
Seat Sticks   Cleaning Accessories
Targets and Target Holders   Air Rifle Pellets
Cartridges and many other accessories for shooting

WEBLEY & SCOTT LIMITED

Park Lane, Handsworth,
Birmingham B21 8LU
Telephone: 021-553 3952/6

Parts List and Diagram of Parts
COMPONENT PARTS OF THE WEBLEY HAWK MARK II AIR RIFLE

PART No.	DESCRIPTION OF PART	No. OFF
1020	TRIGGER GUARD	1
1266	LOADING LEVER AXIS PIN	1
1267	LOADING LEVER STOP PIN	1
1270	SEAR TRIGGER & SAFE AXIS	3
1275	FRONT TRIGGER GUARD SCREW	1
1277	STOCK SCREW FRONT	2
1279	SEAR TRIGGER & SAFE AXIS CLIPS	3
1289	FORESIGHT HOOD	1
1367	JOINT WASHER	1
1433	BARREL HOUSING	1
1457	LOADING LEVER	1
1466	BARREL STOP PIN & BODY END PLUG PIN	2
1467	BARREL PIVOT	1
1469	BODY END PLUG	1
1471	PISTON	1
1472	BARREL FIXING PLUNGER	1
1473	PISTON RING	2
1474	BARREL FIXING PLUNGER SPRING	1
1476	.22 BARREL	1
1477	.177 BARREL	1
1487	SEAR	1
1488	TRIGGER ADJUSTING & FORESIGHT SCREW	2
1489	TRIGGER ADJUSTING SPRING	1

PART No.	DESCRIPTION OF PART	No. OFF
1490	TRIGGER	1
1557	BARREL LOCKING SCREW	1
1558	REARSIGHT BASE FIXING SCREW	2
1559	REARSIGHT BASE FIXING SCREW LOCKWASHER	2
1563	MAINSPRING	1
1568	BODY TUBE ASSEMBLY	1
1587	SAFE SLIDE	1
1588	REARSIGHT LEAF	1
1589	REARSIGHT BASE	1
1590	REARSIGHT VERTICAL SCREW	1
1591	REARSIGHT BLADE	1
1592	REARSIGHT HORIZONTAL SCREW	1
1593	SEAR SPRING	1
1594	TRIGGER GUARD WOODSCREW	1
1599	REARSIGHT LEAF SPRING	1
1600	REARSIGHT HORIZONTAL CLICK SPRING	1
1601	REARSIGHT CLICK BALL	1
1602	REARSIGHT HORIZONTAL SCREW PEG	1
1603	REARSIGHT LEAF FULCRUM PIN	1
1637	FORESIGHT	1
1639	STOCK & RECOIL PAD ASSEMBLY	1
1640	KEY & TAG ASSEMBLY	1

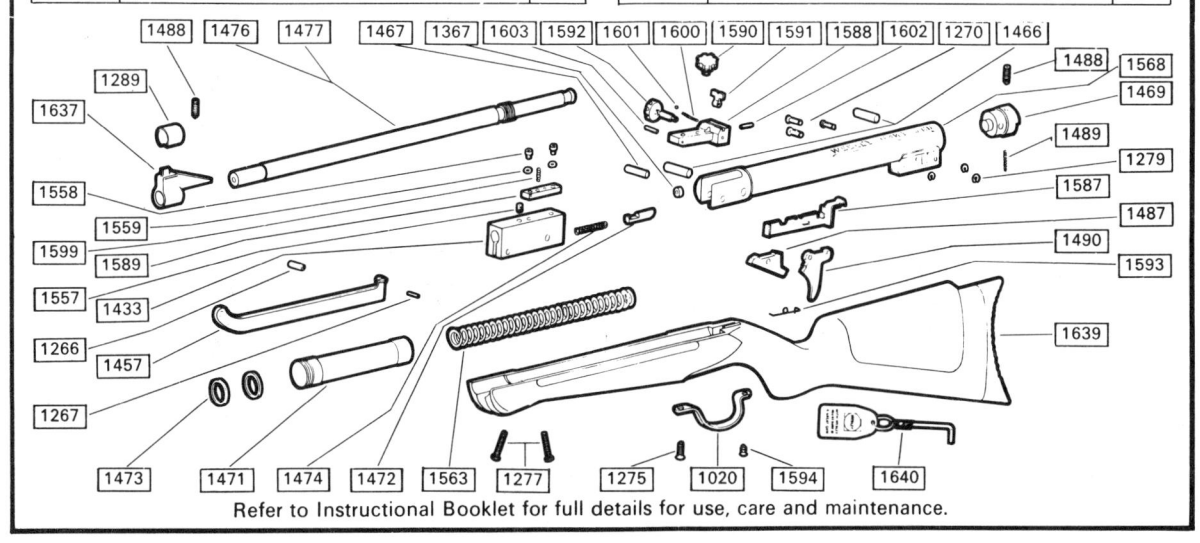

Refer to Instructional Booklet for full details for use, care and maintenance.

Specification

Velocity	.177 — 650 ft/sec
	.22 — 550 ft/sec
Weight approximately	6 lb 8 oz (2·95 kg)

Length overall	42¼" (107 cm)
Barrel length	17⅛" (43·5 cm)
Length between rear sight and foresight	16" (40·6 cm)

Fitting of interchangeable barrels

Rear sight

Adjustable trigger and safety catch

SPARE PARTS LIST FOR HAWK MK III AIR RIFLE

PART NO.	DESCRIPTION	NO. OFF
K4	BODY TUBE ASSEMBLY, NOT SUPPLIED AS A SPARE	
K9	JOINT WASHER	1
K13	PISTON RINGS	2
K14	PISTON	1
K15	MAINSPRING	1
K16	BODY END PLUG	1
K17	BODY STOP PIN & BODY END PLUG PIN	2
K21	BARREL PIVOT	1
K22	SEAR SPRING	1
K23	FORESIGHT HOOD	1
K24	TRIGGER	1
K25	FULCRUM PINS	3
K26	FULCRUM PIN CIRCLIPS	3
K27	TRIGGER ADJUSTING & FORESIGHT RETAINING SCREW	2
K28	SAFE SLIDE	1
K32	LOADING LEVER	1
K33	LOADING LEVER AXIS PIN	1
K34	LOADING LEVER STOP PIN	2
K44	BARREL & HOUSING ASSEMBLY ·177	1
K45	BARREL & HOUSING ASSEMBLY ·22	1
K46	BARREL FIXING PLUNGER	1
K47	BARREL FIXING PLUNGER SPRING	2
K48	BARREL PIVOT	1
K49	FORESIGHT	1
K55	FORESIGHT HOOD	1
K68	REARSIGHT LEAF	1
K69	REARSIGHT BLADE	3
K70	REARSIGHT HORIZONTAL SCREW	3
K71	REARSIGHT HORIZONTAL CLICK SPRING	2
K72	REARSIGHT HORIZONTAL CLICK BALL	1
K73	REARSIGHT HORIZONTAL SCREW PEG	1
K74	REARSIGHT BASE	1
K75	REARSIGHT LEAF FULCRUM PIN	1
K76	REARSIGHT VERTICAL SCREW	1
K77	REARSIGHT LEAF SPRING	1
K80	REARSIGHT BASE FIXING SCREWS	2
K81	REARSIGHT BASE FIXING SCREW LOCKWASHERS	2
K82	REARSIGHT ASSEMBLY COMPRISES K68, K69, K70, K71, K72, K73, K74, K75, K76, K77, K80 (2-OFF) & K81 (2-OFF)	1
K90	STOCK & RECOIL PAD ASSEMBLY	1
K91	TRIGGER GUARD	1
K92	TRIGGER GUARD WOOD SCREW	1
K93	STOCK & GUARD SCREW	1
K94	STOCK SCREWS FRONT	2
K97	SOCKET KEY	1
K101	SOCKET KEY & TAG ASSEMBLY	1

Webley Hawk Mk. III

MODEL "Hawk" Mk. III.

MAKER Webley & Scott.

DATE Introduced April 1977. No longer in production. Has been superseded by the Vulcan air rifle.

VALUATION £40−£80.
($60−$120).

DETAILS Does not have the interchangeable barrels as did the Hawk Mk. I and Mk. II. Telescopic sight grooves changed to 11.5 mm and deepened. "WEBLEY HAWK MK III" stamped on top of chamber. L.H.S. of barrel stamped with the calibre. Trigger adjustment is by way of the screw on top of the trigger block, similar to the B.S.A. Cadet Major. 41 inches long. Safety catch on L.H.S. of trigger block. Advertised muzzle velocities 650 f.p.s. for .177 and 550 f.p.s. for .22. Has the following improvements over the Hawk Mk. II, thickened and strengthened stock, re-styled safety catch, improved cocking lever, and telescopic sight mount grooves changed to 11½ mm. Advertised weight 6½ lbs.

The trigger mechanism can be tricky but the following procedure will help if you need to strip and replace parts:

Remove action from stock and by levering off the spring washers remove the trigger pin and pull out the trigger and spring. Now do the same with the front pin and remove, lastly remove the middle pin and slide out the sear, spring and finally the safety catch. To re-assemble slide in the safety from the rear and then introduce the sear with its wire spring into the underside of the trigger mechanism housing and fiddle them about until you can feed in the middle pin and replace spring washer, now pull the sear down and then insert the front pin and set with the washer, make sure that the sear is free to move downwards, finally insert the trigger and spring and replace the pin and washer. With a bit of luck it will work, but you never know with these Webley triggers.

Two quaint little habits about the Hawks that could cause some bother, are firstly, that if the front guard screw is either too long or screwed in too far it will foul with the sear and although the safety is off and the trigger pulled the thing will not go off! On the other hand, the second little thing that can go wrong is that when you push the safety forward the gun will fire without touching the trigger, when this happens you need either, or both, trigger and sear. The best way to enjoy Webley Hawks is to collect them, but not use them. Seriously though, as a safety precaution ALWAYS ease off the safety with the barrel pointed downwards, as there could always be the first time when the sear fails.

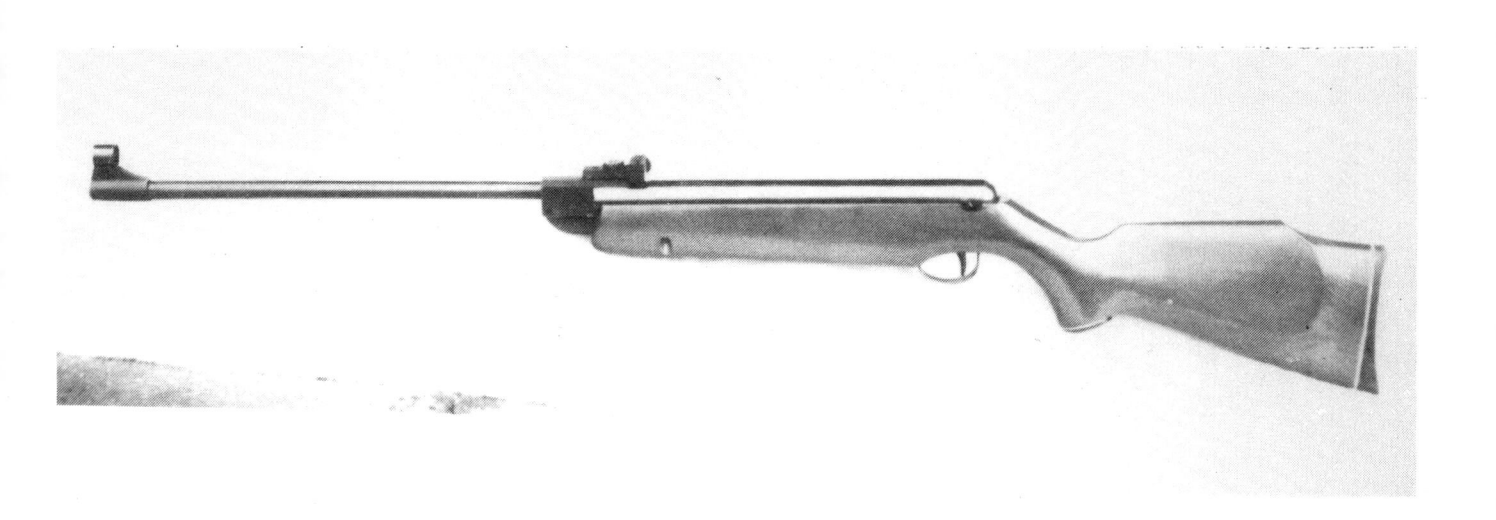

The Webley Vulcan Mk. II

SPARE PARTS LIST FOR THE NEW VULCAN AIR RIFLE

PART NO	DESCRIPTION	NO. OFF	PART NO	DESCRIPTION	NO. OFF	PART NO	DESCRIPTION	NO. OFF
V5	BODY TUBE ASSEMBLY, NOT SUPPLIED AS A SPARE		V26	FULCRUM PIN CIRCLIP	1	V71	REARSIGHT HORIZONTAL CLICK SPRING	3
V9	JOINT WASHER	1	V27	TRIGGER ADJUSTING SCREW	1	V72	REARSIGHT HORIZONTAL CLICK BALL	1
V10	PISTON SEAL	1	V29	SAFE SLIDE	1	V73	REARSIGHT HORIZONTAL SCREW PEG	1
V11	PISTON	1	V31	LOADING LEVER	1	V74	REARSIGHT BASE	1
V12	MAINSPRING	1	V33	LOADING LEVER AXIS PIN	1	V75	REARSIGHT LEAF FULCRUM PIN	1
V13	SPRING GUIDE	1	V34	LOADING LEVER STOP PIN	1	V76	REARSIGHT VERTICAL SCREW	1
V14	SPRING GUIDE RETAINING PIN	1	V40	BARREL AND HOUSING ASSEMBLY .177	1	V77	REARSIGHT LEAF SPRING	1
V15	BODY END PLUG	1	V41	BARREL AND HOUSING ASSEMBLY .22	1	V80	REARSIGHT BASE FIXING SCREW	2
V16	BODY END PLUG PIN	1	V46	BARREL FIXING PLUNGER	1	V81	REARSIGHT BASE FIXING SCREW LOCKWASHER	2
V17	BARREL STOP PIN	1	V47	BARREL FIXING PLUNGER SPRING	1	V82	REARSIGHT ASSEMBLY COMPLETE (NOT ILLUS.)	1
V18	CUSHIONING WASHER	1	V48	BARREL PIVOT	1	V88	STOCK	1
V20	SEAR	1	V50	FORESIGHT FIXING SCREW	1	V90	GUARD SCREW REAR	1
V21	SEAR FULCRUM PIN	1	V51	FORESIGHT	1	V91	TRIGGER GUARD	1
V22	SEAR SPRING	1	V55	FORESIGHT HOOD	1	V92	TRIGGER PLATE	1
V23	TRIGGER ADJUSTING SPRING	1	V68	REARSIGHT LEAF	1	V93	GUARD SCREW FRONT	1
V24	TRIGGER	1	V69	REARSIGHT BLADE	1	V94	STOCK SCREW FRONT	2
V25	FULCRUM PIN	2	V70	REARSIGHT HORIZONTAL SCREW	1	V97	SOCKET KEY	1

MODEL Vulcan. Mk. II Model.

MAKER Webley & Scott Ltd., Birmingham, England. During 1983 Webley moved to Frankley Industrial Park, Birmingham.

DATE Vulcan Mk. I 1979 to 1981.
Vulcan Mk. II 1981 onwards.

VALUATION £40–£80.
($60–$120).

DETAILS A powerful full-sized air rifle that also has the feel of quality. One of the English Rolls Royce airguns! 43½ inches long with a 19¼ inch rifled barrel available in .22 or .177. Diecast metal foresight whilst rearsight is the standard one fitted to all Webley products, almost! Side of breech has been bevelled and serrated and bears the maker's name and serial number. Solid and slightly wider than normal air chamber is grooved for telescopic sights. Trigger block is rounded at rear and also acts as a ramp stop as it stands slightly proud of the grooves. Trigger adjustment is by way of the Allen screw through the trigger block at top. Beautiful smooth stock very well finished. Manual safety catch on the side which can be ignored. Stock has no chequering, but the pistol grip and butt plate caps have white plastic liners which adds to the appearance. Advertised weight lies between 7½ to 7¾ lbs. The Vulcan boasts a double sealing arrangement that also lessens recoil from the rebounding of the piston after it has travelled down the air chamber. In most airguns the piston rebounds or bounces on the cushion of air at the end of the chamber, but in the Vulcan the piston continues to travel forward after the P.T.F.E. washer has reached the end of the chamber. During this extra journey a second rubber ring is compressed against the cylinder wall and acts as a brake on the piston and delays the rebound. Advertised velocity when new is 750 f.p.s. for .177 and 600 f.p.s. for .22. A deluxe version of the Vulcan is also available. A review of the above appears in "Airgun World" October 1982. The trigger mechanism appears to have been changed in some way because the instructions state "do not pull the trigger whilst cocking the gun".

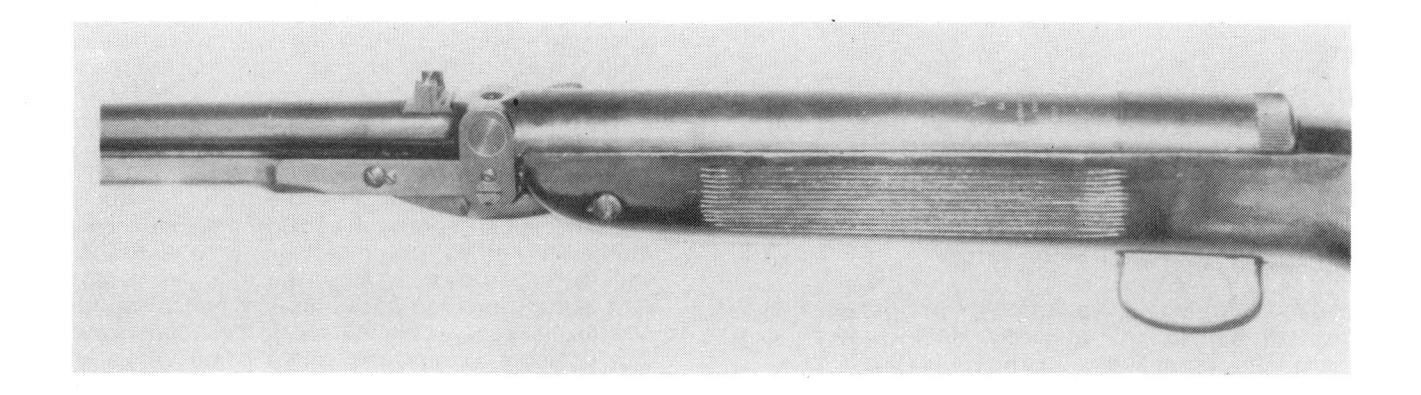

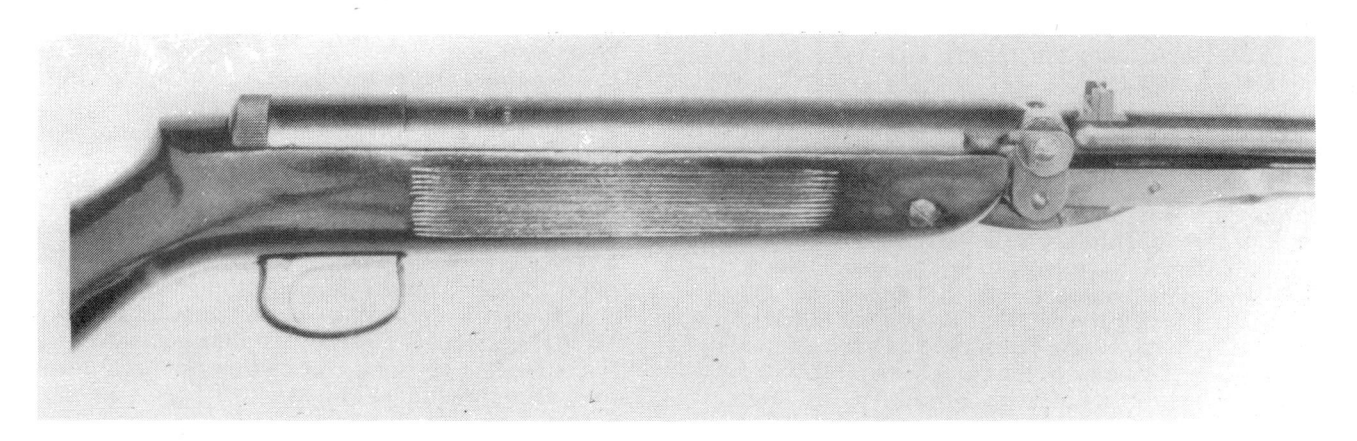

First pattern Webley Mk. III, 1947 to 1949

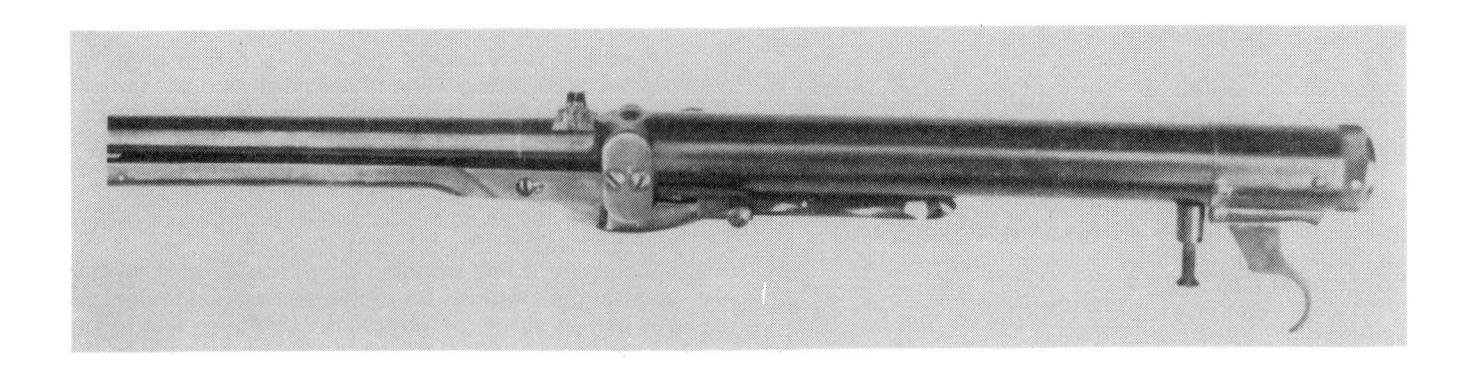

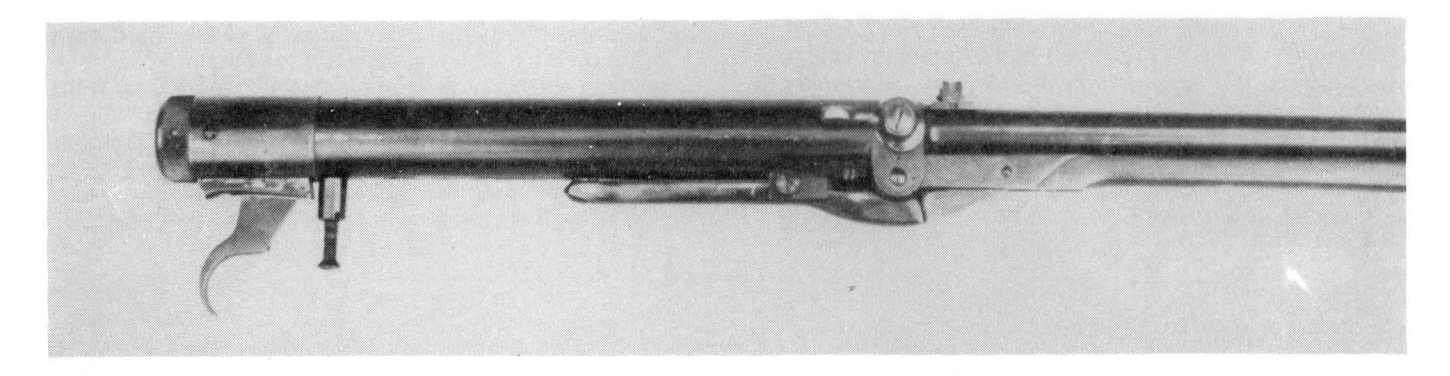

Webley Mk. III action, number 4325, showing first style trigger action and later style tap design

MODEL Mk. III First series and variations.

MAKER Webley & Scott Ltd., Birmingham, England.

DATE Advertised during 1946, but available 1947. The First series is assumed to have serial numbers from 1 to 2500 and date from 1947 to 1949, but it is not as simple as it first appears.

VALUATION £100—£200, £30a—£77a.
($150—$300, $45a—$116a).

DETAILS During the process of evolution creatures started off simple and gradually went through a process of increased complication until they specialised themselves into extinction, whereas with the Webley Mk. III it started off complicated and gradually simplified itself into extinction. It has often been said by airgun enthusiasts that if a limited edition of the Mk. III was reproduced they would buy no matter what the cost as to them it represents one of the finest air rifles ever produced.

Very few of the first series appear to exist and from a collector's point of view they rate highly and hence can command higher prices. Most of the characteristics follow the usual Webley style but over the years the basic design was altered and almost every part underwent some change and/or improvement.

The serial number is stamped in the usual place, although on the underside of the action it was stamped right inside the cocking lever pivot housing and almost cannot be seen. The serial number may also be stamped on the inside of the stock. The foresight is dovetail mounted and not soldered, as it is on later examples, the four corners of the sight are rounded and there are no side grooves for a sight hood. The rearsight is the same as that fitted to the later Webley Mk. II Service air rifles, centre screw adjustment with no little side grub screw for locking the blade. There are so many variations of the first model that this description applies to serial number 2002 fitted with a stock numbered 25209. The underlever cocking arm had extra machining to the edges to smooth them off near the cocking auxiliary link pivot, the auxiliary link by the way was slender and fitted very tightly to the underside of the air chamber, unlike on later models when it became quite thick and hung somewhat from the underside like a sagging ligament. The cocking lever pivot screw had a locking screw that fitted a half-moon cut away in the pivot screw head. This arrangement changed on later models. The tap arrangement must have been a headache as the tap relied on a conical fit into the body to align the loading bore with the barrel, so that with excessive wear the tap would gradually work itself into the conical depression and become out of line with the barrel, one way to correct this is to plate the tap with say copper to add a slight thickness to the tap and thus bring it out and back into line, hence you might see the odd copper coloured tap on the Webley travels. The chamber is stamped with the calibre near the loading port and at the rear of the chamber "THE WEBLEY MARK 3, WEBLEY & SCOTT LTD., BIRMINGHAM, MADE IN ENGLAND". The trigger block had a detachable serrated cup that was pinned into place. Now the trigger mechanism — the Achilles heal, apart from the tap. Along with the piston that had to have a very long piston centre rod to engage with the trigger mechanism was very troublesome and very prone to shearing off the inner tube and sear, hence another reason why they're so rare. The actual mechanism first appeared on pre-war German Diana air rifles and even on the first British Diana air rifles from Scotland, but they were not to gain popularity and after a very short period the mechanism was changed to the good old simplified system of either using just the trigger/sear as one unit or as two units as on the later Mk IIIs. The double pull trigger appeared on the pre-war Diana Models 45 and 27 for certain, and after the War have seen the Model 27 fitted with the same action. The action may be better explained by the original quote from a 1939 catalogue: "The weight force of the mainspring which in ordinary air rifles rest on the trigger, is transferred to a striker which when released by the trigger rushes forward and in turn released the mainspring in much the same way as hair triggers are operated. The (trigger) pull therefore can be very light and at the same time quite safe, a refinement that will be keenly appreciated by all keen air riflemen". So the identical mechanism was fitted to the first models of the Webley Mk. III, but it did not live happily ever after. The stock on 2002 with the number 25203 may not be the original stock, but as a point of interest the fore-end grooves numbered 13 on each side, at an earlier date these were originally 17.

Now it is assumed that the double pull trigger mechanism was used up to serial number 2500, so it is no surprise to find air rifle 4325 having the same trigger mechanism. The rest of the action was identical except for the following: The cocking lever was not smoothed off near the pivot screw as it is on the earlier model. The auxiliary cocking link was thicker. The tap design had been changed to the usual pattern with a backing plate.

It could be that the piston and trigger mechanism interchange and that some enterprising owner may have changed both so as to throw the above spanner, serial number 4325, into the "works".

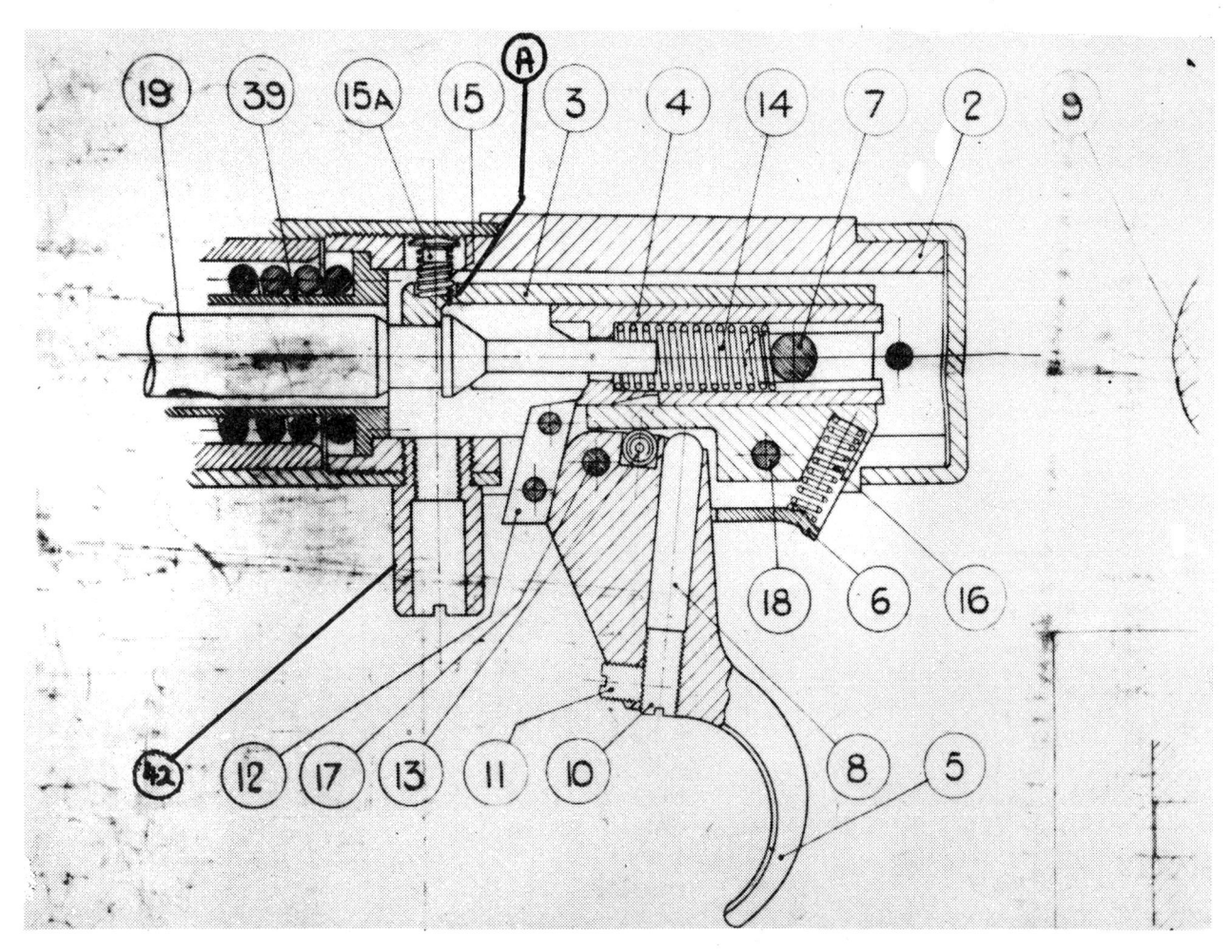

The first pattern double pull trigger mechanism. (Courtesy of Webley & Scott)

In order to change the mainspring and/or remove the trigger block first remove action from stock and then remove the stock locating plug, part number AR42, this has a reserve thread so is removed by screwing clockwise, now carefully turn the trigger block through 180 degrees and catch parts 15 and 15A as they fly through the hole left by the removal of the stock location plug. You can now carry on unscrewing the trigger block, but watch out for the mainspring tension taking over when you have run out of threads. The replacement is the reversal of the above, when half a turn from the trigger being fully screwed down parts 15 and 15A are introduced into the stock location plug hole and kept pushed down with a thin punch or screwdriver or whatever and kept down until the trigger is turned just enough then remove the screwdriver and carry on turning the trigger block fully into its home position. The trigger adjustment is by way of first loosening the locking screw, part 11, and then playing about with part 10. Screwing it in gives a long second trigger pull whilst screwing part 11 out gives a short second pull, it may be assumed that this adjustment has no effect on the sear to piston rod engagement. The sear engagement is set in the factory and should not be altered, although knowing some people adjustment can be made when you know how! Being a double pull in this case means that when cocking the action slowly you will, or should, hear two distinct clicks, the action will only engage on the second click and can be dry fired on the first click even though the sear has not engaged. The first click is made by the piston rod conical sear riding over the sear engagement on the outer casing, part 3, although why there should be a click when the trigger is pulled is at the moment beyond me. The second click occurs when the piston rod has pushed the inner tube, part 4, back and over the sear, part 12 and is now engaged. When the trigger is pulled the inner tube is released and pushed forward by part 14 and rides up the piston rod cone and pushes the outer tube up and out of the way. The main weak point of the system is the outer tube shearing at point A, it may be a good idea to fit the later type piston and trigger action if you wish to use the air rifle and keep the original aside for replacement to bring it back to its original condition should you wish to sell, in other words if you have one of these first trigger actions and it works then DON'T USE IT!

The loading tap was quite simple, but prone to wear out of alignment and shear off the thin squared section projection of the tap. The advertised trigger pull off was 2¼ lbs, overall length 43¼ inches with an 18½ inch barrel. Approximate weight was 6 lbs 13 ozs. It was first advertised in 1946, although not available until 1947. The standard model had straight grooving to the fore-end and a ribbed butt, whilst the deluxe model was hand chequered and fitted with a ribbed butt plate. By

1950 it was offered with either a birch or walnut stock. During 1953 the double pull trigger was still being advertised, but the stock was now available in walnut only. Further aids to dating the Mk. III may be made from the following:

1947 First model.
1948 Loading tap lever design changed to the curved type.
1949 Trigger mechanism changed, in May to be exact, to the two part trigger sear design which was used right up to the end. This was effected from gun number 2500, hence gun number 4325 still has the double pull trigger!
1957 Stock changed from the narrow and straight to the rounded bulbous shaped, this coincided with the corpulent happy days of the 1960s when someone said, "You've never had it so good."
1961 The rot sets in — Webley spot welded a scope rail on to the air chamber, these have a habit of lifting and falling off — moral is never use it!
1963 Enter the Supertarget — see separate section.
1965 The auxiliary loading lever changed in design and the loading tap lever became the straight variety. The foresight was now not only dovetail mounted but also soldered in place.
1966 During February the trigger and sear screws were replaced by pins, the stock and guard screws were replaced by standard round headed screws and the knurling was dropped from the trigger block. In April 1966 the trigger guard changed in shape. From June 1966 air rifles were given an "A" prefix to the serial number.

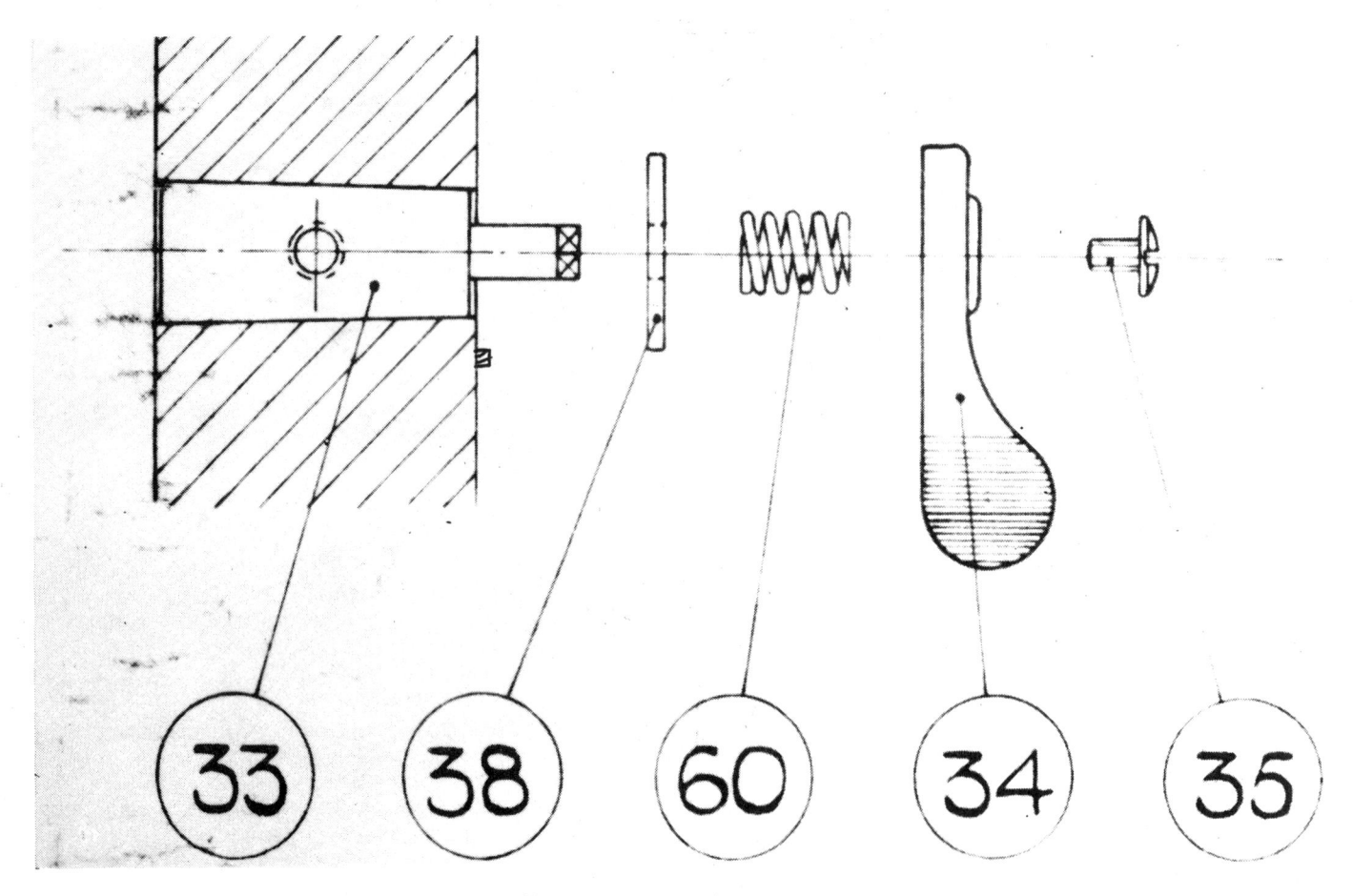

The first pattern loading tap. (Courtesy of Webley & Scott)

A peg protrudes from the body of the air rifle and goes through a hole cut in the outer rim of part 38, it then rests in a curved key-way cut in part 34 and this allows the tap lever to be rotated through 90 degrees only for opening and closing the tap for loading etc. Hence part number 38 does not rotate when the loading lever is turned.

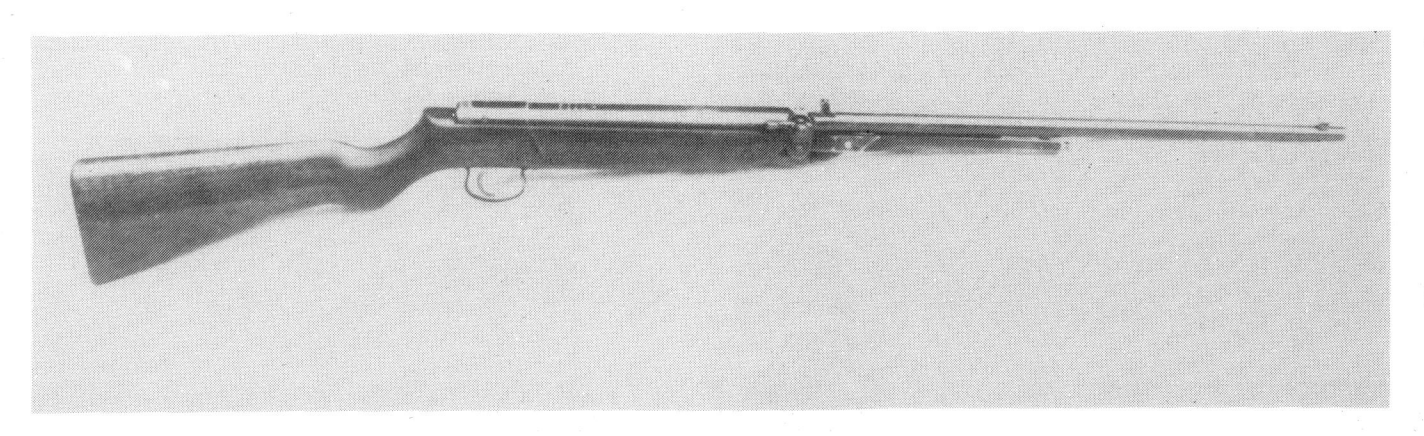

Webley Mk. III, 1949 to 1957 variation

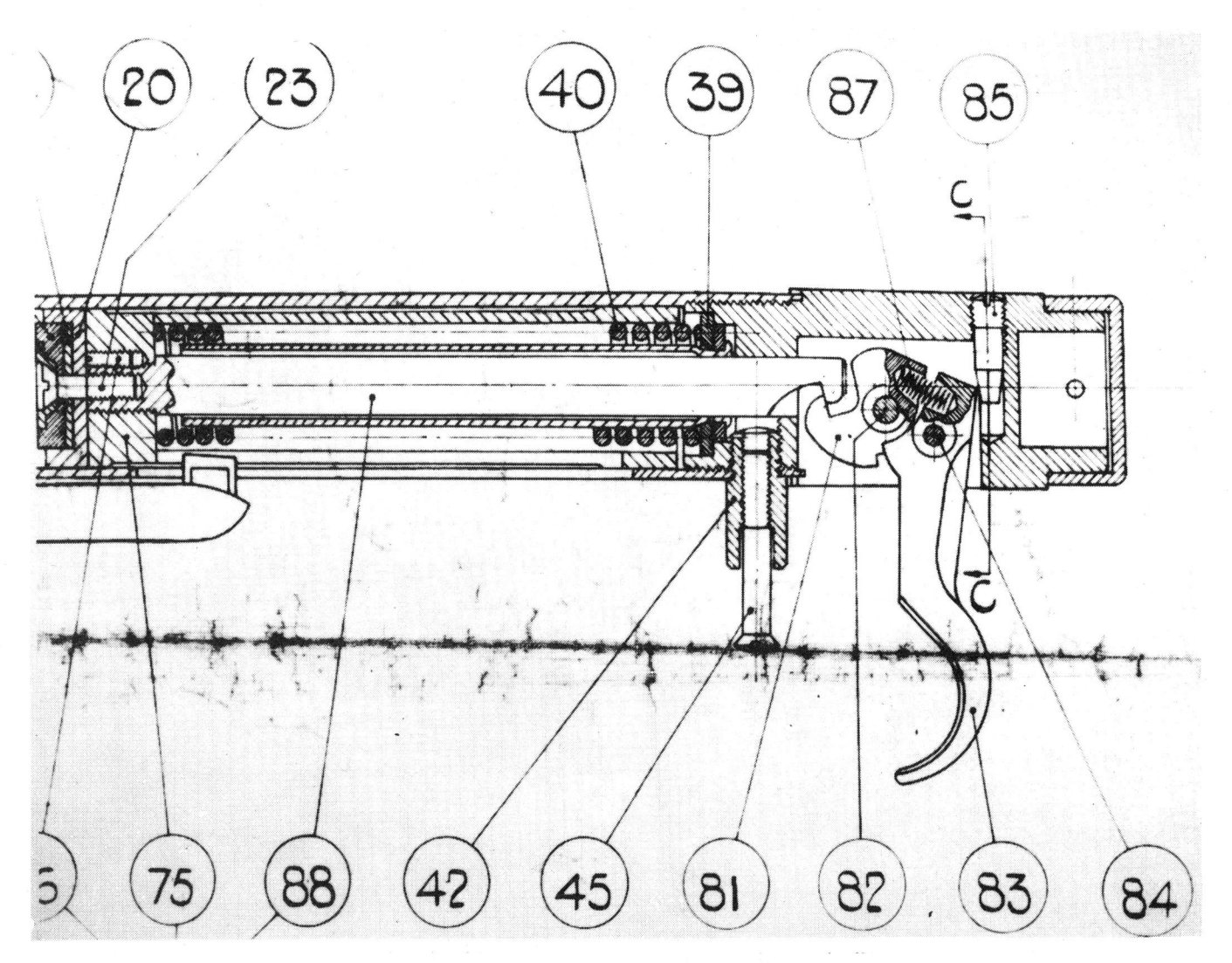

Trigger Mechanism, Second series and onwards, 1949 to 1975 with minor variation. (Courtesy of Webley & Scott Ltd.)

When removing the trigger and sear, remove trigger pin first and then take out trigger with spring, part numbers 83 and 87, then go for the sear, part number 81. When reassembling always start with the sear and then with the spring in place in the trigger rotate the sear until you can see the matching hole for the spring, then introduce the spring into the sear hole and move trigger up into the action and manoeuvre about until you can replace the trigger pin.

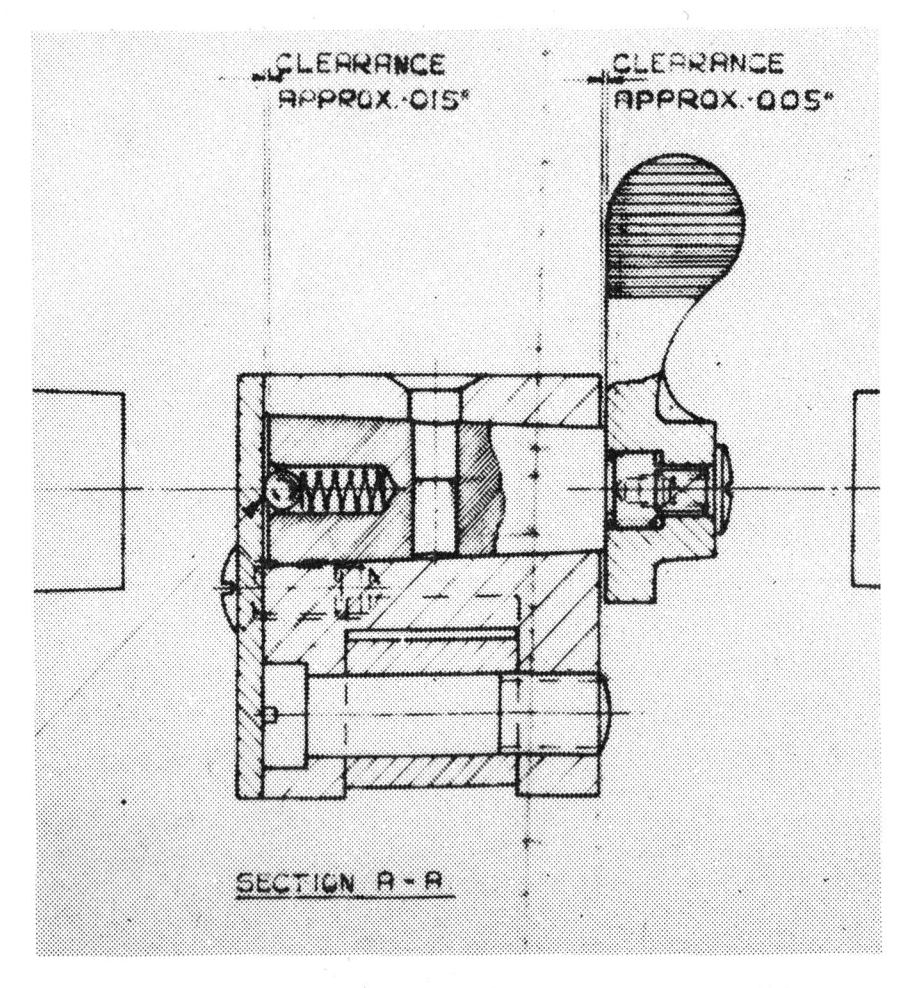

Second pattern tap loading design. (Courtesy of Webley & Scott Ltd.)

MODEL Mk. III. Series II from 2501 to 6000.

MAKER Webley & Scott Ltd., Park Lane, Handsworth, Birmingham 21. Address at time of manufacture.

DATE Mk. IIIs produced from 1947 to 1975. Above variation from 1949 to 1957. The Mk. III was advertised in 1946, but as yet the price was not fixed and delivery was not possible until 1947.

VALUATION £50—£150, £30a—£52a.
($75—$225, $45a—$78a).

DETAILS Serial numbers for the above model ran from 2501 onwards. This modification started in May 1949 and was brought about by the simplification of the trigger mechanism. The new bulbous stock was introduced during 1957. 42¾ inches long and available in either .22 or .177, serial numbers on cocking lever and underside of air chamber should always match. Machined curved style lever to loading tap. Not fitted with scope ramp, this ramp appeared during September 1961. Top of air chamber stamped "THE WEBLEY MARK 3 WEBLEY SCOTT LTD. BIRMINGHAM MADE IN ENGLAND". Trigger block had knurled end. Slender stock with grooving on each side of the fore-end. Small plastic medallion set in L.H.S. of stock bearing the message "WEBLEY REGD TRADE MARK" at a later date the wording was altered to just "WEBLEY". Notice distinct style of trigger guard and curved trigger. For the maintenance and stripping of the Mk. III see "Airgun World" February 1979. Advertised weight 6 lb 13 oz. The standard stock had the parallel grooves whilst the deluxe model was hand chequered and fitted with a ribbed heel plate. Two types of stocks were available, birch stock or walnut. It would appear that all the bulbous stocks were walnut. Care should be taken when removing the tap lever and it should not be levered off as this can break off the squared stud that fits into the lever, instead unscrew the two screws and remove the loading tap side plate, now loosen the tap lever screw and unscrew about two or three turns, finally give the now proud screw head a sharp tap and this will drive out the tap and loosen it from the lever.

AIR RIFLES AND PISTOLS SPARES
Webley Mark III Air Rifle

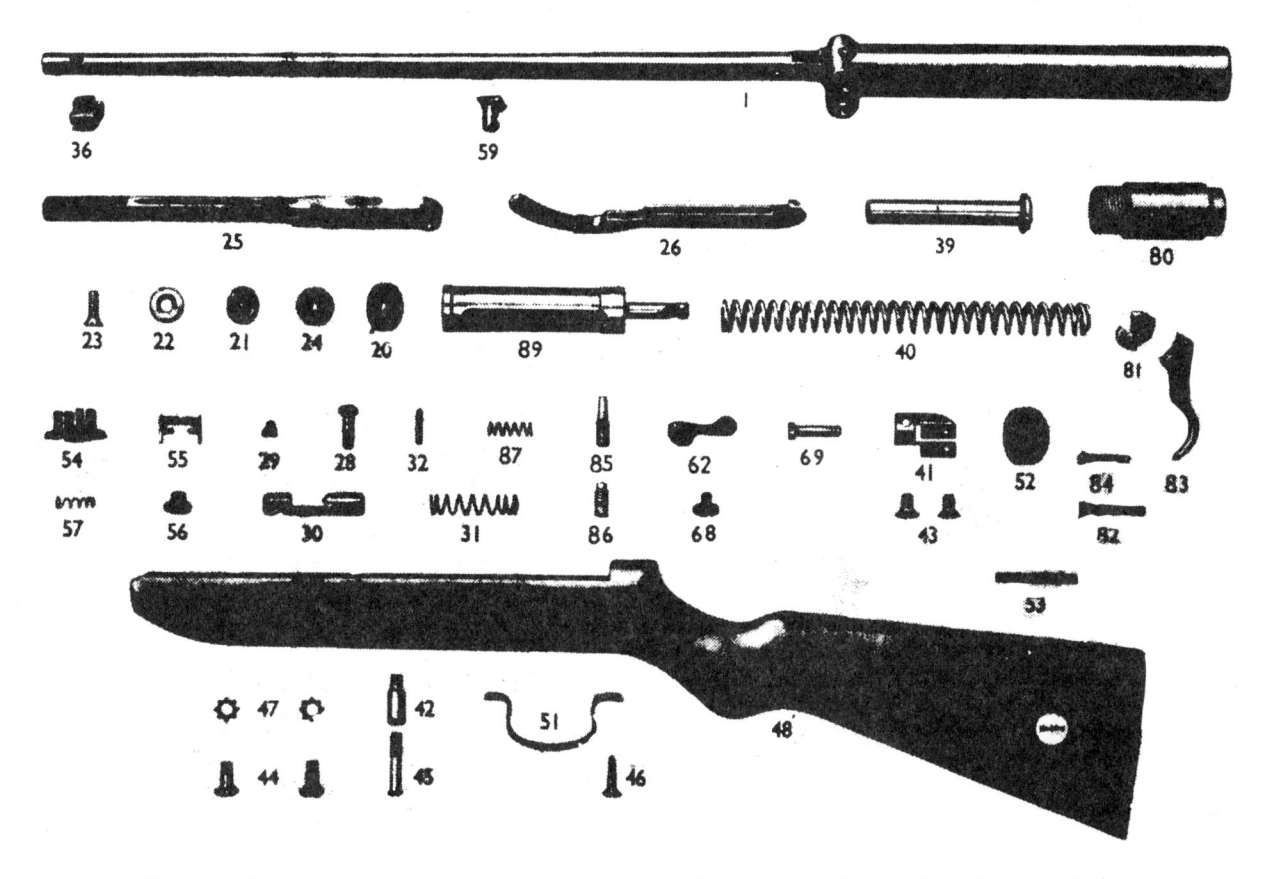

When ordering spares it is absolutely essential to quote the prefix AR, which is applicable to Mark III Air Rifle only, also the Rifle serial No., which is stamped on part No. AR.25.

POSTAGE ON SMALL PARTS OFTEN EXCEEDS COST OF PART.
PRICES INCLUDE POSTAGE.

Part No. in Illustration	Description	
AR.4	Inner Sear	6 6
AR.7	Sear Pivot Pin	1 -
AR.9	Sear Adjusting Screw	7d.
AR.10	Trigger Adjusting Screw	7d.
AR.11	Trigger Adjusting Locking Screw	6d. N.I. Series I and II Rifles only
AR.14	Sear Mainspring	7d.
AR.15	Sear Auxiliary Spring	9d.
AR.19	Piston (including Piston Rod and Keeper Screw)	18 -
AR.89	Piston (including Piston Rod and Keeper Screw)	16 -
AR.20	Piston Outer Washer	1 6
AR.21	Piston Inner Washer	1 -
AR.22	Piston Inner Washer Plate	5d.
AR.23	Piston Washer Screw	9d.
AR.24	Piston Washer Support	4d.
AR.25	Loading Lever	18 -
AR.26	Auxiliary Loading Lever	16 6
AR.27	Loading Lever Pivot Screw (N.I. Series I Rifles only)	1 3
AR.69	Loading Lever Pivot Screw	1 3
AR.28	Auxiliary Loading Lever Pivot Pin	1 2
AR.29	Pivot Pin Fixing Screw for AR.28	7d.
AR.30	Loading Lever Locking Plunger	4 -
AR.31	Loading Lever Plunger Spring	7d.
AR.32	Plunger Retaining Pin	7d.
AR.34	Loading Tap Lever	4 -
AR.35	Loading Tap Lever Screw	8d. N.I. Series I Rifles only
AR.36	Foresight Blade	3 3
AR.36a	Foresight Bead	3 9
AR.38	Loading Tap Washer (N.I. Series I Rifles only)	4d.
AR.39	Spring Guide	2/-
AR.40	Mainspring	4/6
AR.41	Stock Fixing Plate	2/3
AR.42	Stock Locating Plug	1/7
AR.43	Stock Fixing Plate Screw	9d.
AR.44	Stock Screws (Front)	1/2
AR.45	Stock and Guard Screw	1/3
AR.46	Guard Screw (Rear)	4d.
AR.47	Stock Screw Washers	3d.
AR.48W	Stock (Walnut)	
AR.51	Trigger Guard	3/-
AR.52	Tube End Cover	1/7
AR.53	End Cover Fixing Pin	7d.
AR.54	Back Sight Base	7/6
AR.55	Back Sight Leaf U	5/-
AR.55a	Back Sight Leaf V	5/-
AR.56	Back Sight Screw	1/7
AR.57	Back Sight Spring	7d.
AR.59	Locking Lever Catch	3/-
AR.60	Loading Tap Spring (N.I. Series I Rifles only)	4d.
AR.61	Trigger and Sear Assembly (N.I. Series I and II Rifles only)	16 6
AR.62	Loading Tap Lever	6/-
AR.64	Breech Block Side Plate	1/3
AR.65	Side Plate Screws	9d.
AR.66	Loading Tap Spring	5d.
AR.67	Ball for Spring AR.66	5d.
AR.68	Loading Tap Lever Screw	8d.
AR.81	Sear	5 3
AR.82	Sear Axis Pin	1 1
AR.83	Trigger	8 6
AR.84	Trigger Axis Pin	1 1
AR.85	Trigger Adjusting Screw	1 1
AR.86	Trigger Locking Screw	11d.
AR.87	Sear and Trigger Spring	7d.

THOMAS BLAND & SONS, 4-5 WILLIAM IV STREET, LONDON, W.C.2

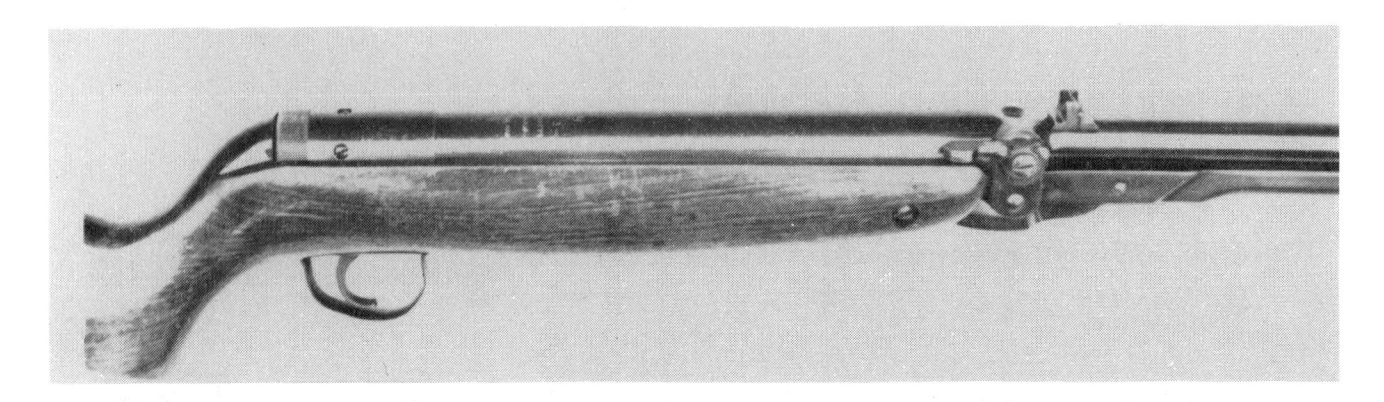

Webley Mk. III 1957 to 1961

MODEL Mk. III. Series III 6001 onwards.

MAKER Webley & Scott.

DATE Production of Mk. III 1946 to 1975, above variation 1957 to 1961.

VALUATION £50—£150, £30a—£52a.
($75—$225, $45a—$78a).

DETAILS In 1957 Webley fitted the more rounded style of stock and a telescopic sight ramp was fitted in 1961. 43 inches long. Flat style trigger guard. Rear of trigger block is serrated and the trade stamping is on the upper part of the air chamber and not on the trigger block as on later models. Serial number of above 22096. Stock has plastic Webley medallion on L.H.S. Trigger block has two screws, the one on top is the trigger adjustment, whilst the side screw appears to be the locking screw for the trigger adjustment. Advertised weight 6 lb 13 ozs. The third series of Webley Mk. IIIs appeared from serial number 6001 onwards. At a slight extra cost the above could be supplied fitted with swivel eyes for a carrying sling. The replacement of the sights is made easier by inserting the sights from the right as the airgun is held for firing. The Webley Mk. III piston washer will also fit the early model B.S.A. Airsporters. Highest serial number seen for the third Series is 35051. Although not listed in the spares diagram, the rearsight blade locking screw is part number AR78.

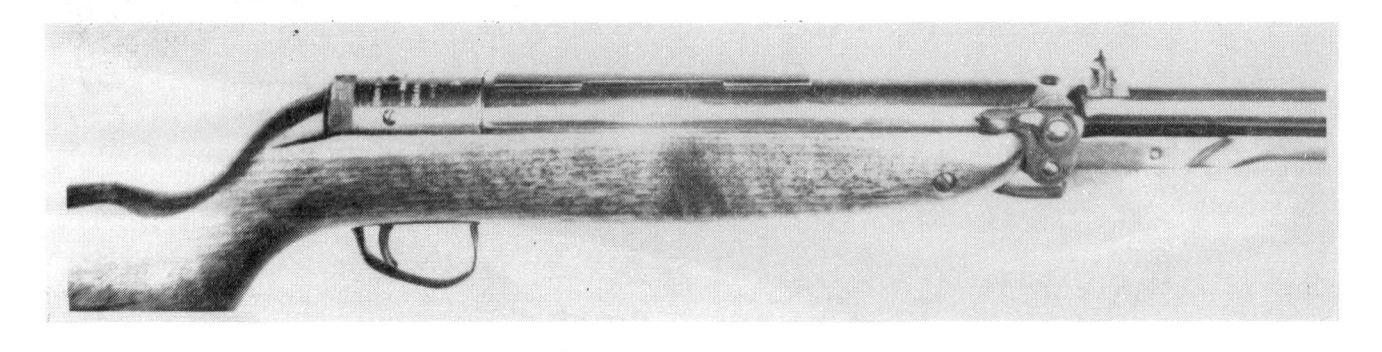

Webley Mk. III (1961 to 1964 variation)

MODEL Mk. III. Series 4 (1961 to 1964).

MAKER Webley & Scott.

DATE Production 1946 to 1975. Above example about 1961 to 1964.

VALUATION £50—£150, £30a—£52a.
($75—$225, $45a—$78a).

DETAILS Serial number of above 43511. Fitted with the dumbell shaped telescopic sight ramp. The trade stamps are on the trigger block, which has a serrated rear. 43 inches long. White plastic medallion set in stock. The loading lever cocking plunger, Part AR30, will act as a replacement for any of the pre-war B.S.A. underlevers with a similar push-button cocking lever. It sometimes happens that the lip will shear off these due to slapping back the lever against the barrel. Serial numbers seen for this series run from 42858 to 46289.

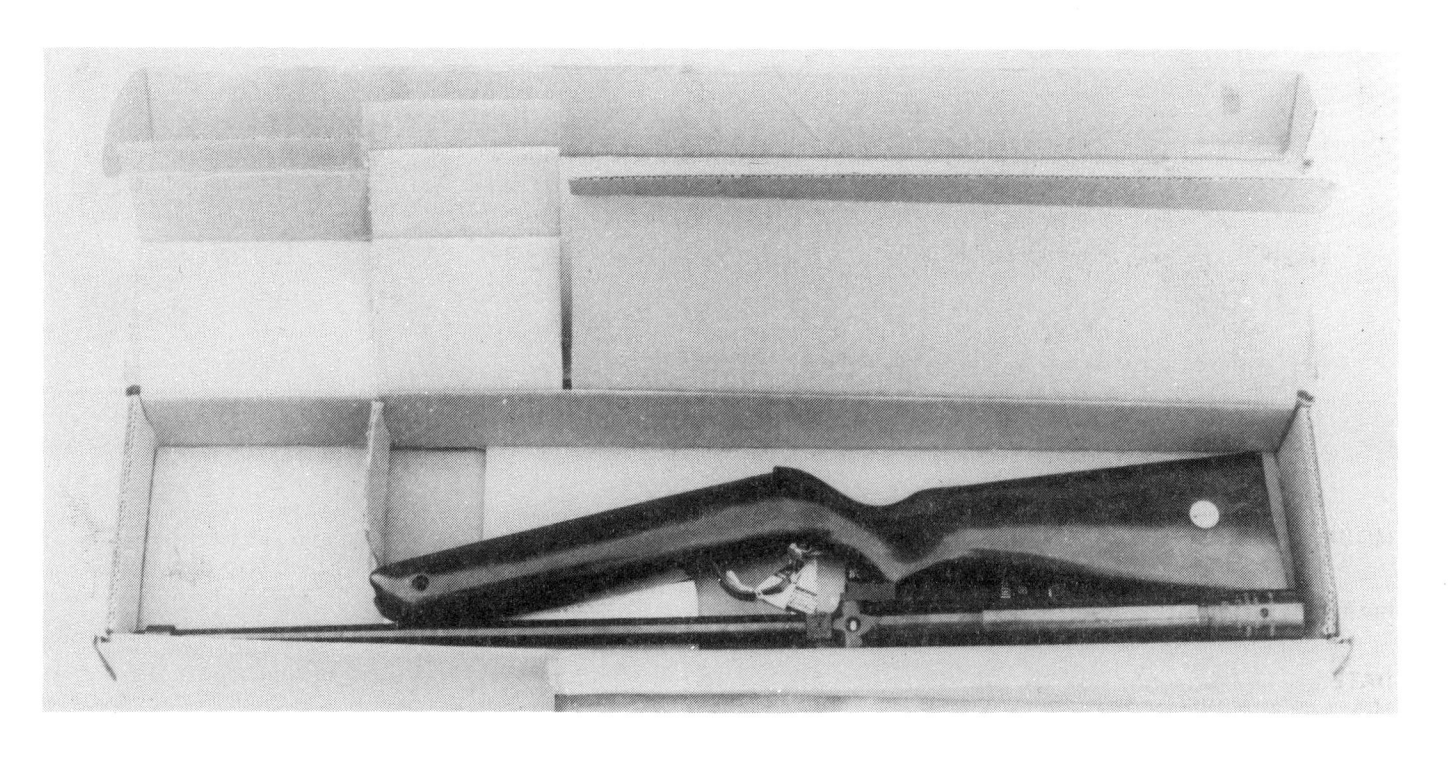

A boxed late Model Webley Mk. III

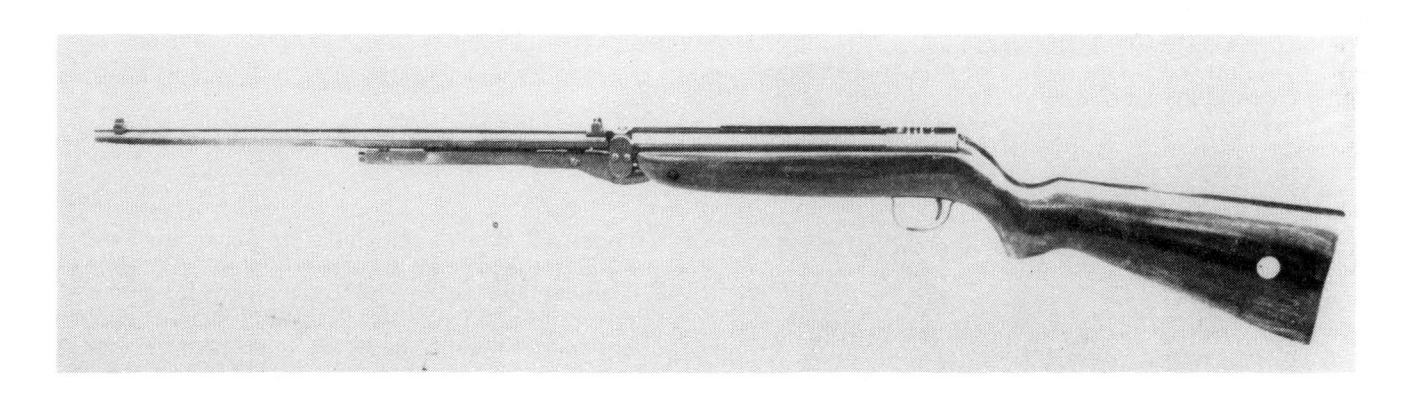

Webley Mk. III, late model

MODEL   Mk. III (late model).

MAKER   Webley & Scott Ltd.

DATE   Above 1946 to 1975. Above variant about 1964 to 1975.

VALUATION   £50—£150, £30a—£52a. ($75—$225, $45a—$78a).

DETAILS Introduced in 1947 and finished production 1975. Serial number of above is B8716, although have seen serial numbers with a "F" prefix. Very well made and should last a lifetime. 43 inches long, has a spot-welded telescopic sight ramp. Stamped on top of trigger block "THE WEBLEY MARK 3, WEBLEY & SCOTT LTD, BIRMINGHAM, MADE IN ENGLAND" and the calibre just behind the tap opening. Very similar to the pre-war B.S.A. underlevers. Serial number is stamped on the cocking lever and on the underside of the barrel near the cocking lever pivot pin, they should match. The stocks can be excellent, of all the airguns that I have seen, the finest stocks have been on Webley Mk. IIIs, the variety of patterned woods have surprised me, it is even worth considering collecting Webley Mk. IIIs for the stocks alone.

Advertised in 1968 with the following accuracy for five shots:
at 10 yards all shots in ⅜ bull —.177 and .22
at 40 yards all shots in 1¼ x 1¼ —.177
at 40 yards all shots in 1¾ x 1¾ —.22.
Advertised weight 6 lbs 14 ozs. See "Airgun World" February 1979 for stripping instructions for the Mk. III.
The Mk. III was sold stock and action separate in a plain brown cardboard box with fold-over partition formers to keep stock and action apart. Action was wrapped in brown oiled paper. It is to be noted that the loading tap is individually fitted and reamed to each air rifle so it is not recommended to change loading taps as this can lead to a loading tap out of line with the barrel and pellets being nicked or cut when they are fired. Apparently the foresight is permanently fixed, to remove rearsight, tap it from the right as the air rifle is held in the firing position. Telescopic sight ramp plates could be supplied with fixing screws if required or could be fitted by Webley's if the air rifle was returned. The sear is almost the same as that fitted to the pre-war B.S.A. Standard underlever and could act as a substitute.
The smoothbore version of the above will have an "S" stamped on the underside of the barrel near the cocking lever pivot and can only be seen when the cocking lever has been lowered.

Webley "Supertarget" fitted with Parke-Hale sights

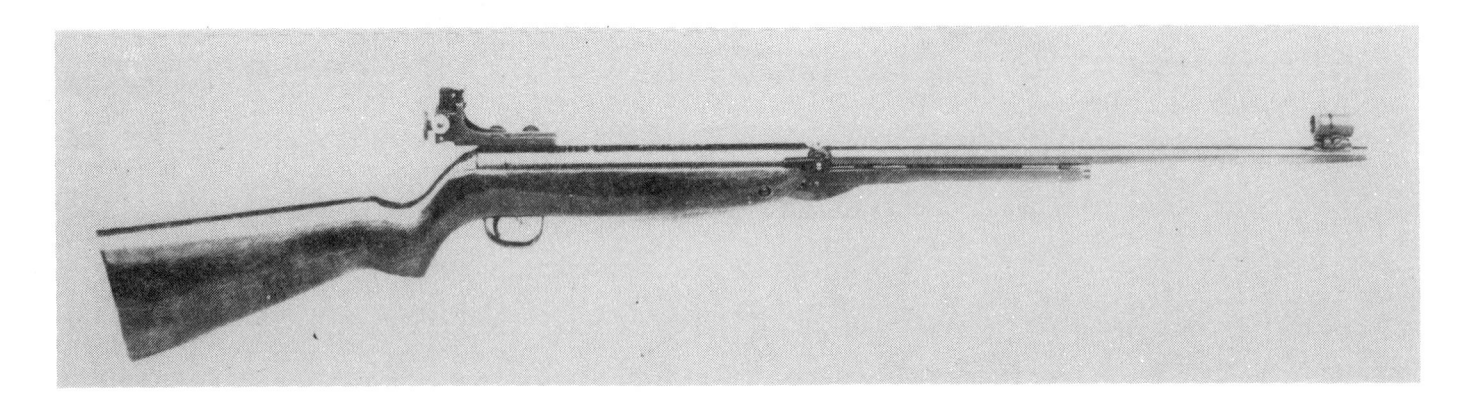

Webley Supertarget with Anschutz target sights

MODEL "Supertarget". Also referred to as the Model 2.

MAKER Webley & Scott.

DATE Introduced 1963, assume production finished around 1975.

VALUATION £100–£200. ($150–$300).

DETAILS Based on the .22 Mk. III. Serial number of above A4027, dated by Webley's as 23rd September 1967. Fitted with Parker-Hale rear peepsight PH17B and tunnel foresight FS22A. No rear blade sight at all. Has "SUPERTARGET" stamped on top of air chamber. Spare foresight blades in screw top cannister fitted to underside on pistol grip. Modified sometime in 1973 for Anschutz target sights. Weight of Supertarget varied from that of the Standard Mk. III. Weight of Standard model was 6 lb 14 oz, whilst the Supertarget weighed 9 lb 6 oz, these being advertised weights. For each click in adjustment of the PH17B peepsight for either windage or elevation will alter the point of impact about one tenth of an inch at 20 yards. To remove the foresight from the dovetail ramp first take out the sight element then unscrew Allen screw in the base of the sight, this is a locking screw. The sight can now be drifted out. The foresight is correctly fitted when the knurled ring is facing towards the rear.

Some of the above will be found without the "Supertarget" trade name, as on X44037. This was fitted with Parker-Hale target sights with no provision whatsoever for the rearsight, the usual trade markings were stamped on the trigger block. This could be an early example produced before it was called the "Supertarget". Serial numbers seen with Parker-Hale sights are A4027, A7171 and A8405. With Anschutz sights serial numbers seen were B5444, B5457 and B7028.

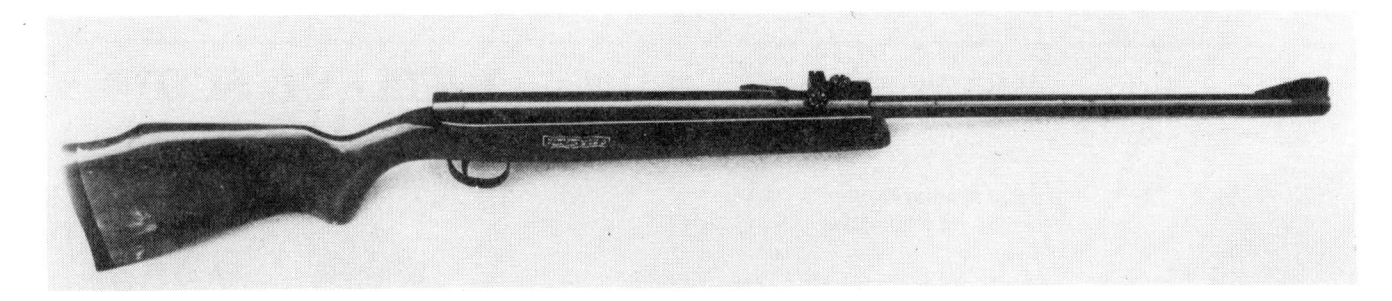

Webley "Osprey"

MODEL "Osprey".

MAKER Webley & Scott, Frankley Industrial Park, Birmingham.

DATE Current model. Introduced 1975.

VALUATION £40—£80.
($60—$120).

DETAILS Side lever cocking, but has a rather noisy action. 43 inches long. Plastic rearsight, foresight and tap port lever. Barrel heavy and wide which gives the impression of a slender air cylinder. Side safety catch. Unusual design for Webley's. Solid and heavy. Stamped "WEBLEY OSPREY" between telescopic mount grooves, "WEBLEY & SCOTT LTD BIRMINGHAM ENGLAND", and on other side of rearsight is stamped the calibre and serial number. Number of above 05018. Advertised velocities 650 — .177, and 550 — .22. The above is also available in a "Super-target" version. For a review of the Osprey see "Airgun World" December 1978. Advertised weight 7¾ lbs. Piston is fitted with two fibre rings. Although cocking lever has a safety ratchet it can be overrided in order to release that action should it be cocked and they do not wish to fire the air rifle. First pull back the cocking lever right back as though you are cocking the action, open tap, now take strain off mainspring with cocking lever with one hand and then pull trigger and allow lever to move slowly forward until it engages with the cocking lever safety ratchet, now the dangerous bit, keep the tension on the cocking lever and without moving it press down the pawl operating lever, part number 34, with it depressed slowly allow the cocking lever to move forward under tension of the mainspring and just before it comes to rest against the side of the air chamber remove your thumb (if you still have it!) Now close the tap. Having the tap open does act as some kind of safety buffer should things go wrong. Remember, all the way through this method NEVER release the cocking lever. Mainspring life for the Osprey should be very long as when not cocked it is barely under tension. This is known as being "over engineered".

The Webley Victor

MODEL Victor.

MAKER Webley & Scott Ltd., Park Lane, Handsworth, Birmingham. During 1983 the firm moved to the Frankley Industrial Park, Birmingham.

DATE 1981.

VALUATION £40—£80.
($60—$120).

DETAILS The junior version of the Vulcan. The same piston seal unit is used on the Victor as used on the Vulcan and is described as the "most efficient air rifles". This produces a junior size air rifle that is manufactured very close to the godly legal limit. Measuring just over 40 inches long with a 17¼ inch barrel in either .177 or .22. Advertised weight 7 lbs. Trigger is non-adjustable and has a pull of about 3½ lbs. Advertised muzzle velocities for .177 720 f.p.s. and for .22 being 580 f.p.s. so quite a powerful little air rifle. A review of the Victor appears in "Airgun World" February 1982.

Shoot with safety

Other Webley Products
Double and single barrel Sporting Guns
Air Rifles and Air Pistols   Starting Pistols
Seat Sticks   Cleaning Accessories   Target Changers
Targets and Target Holders   Air Rifle Pellets
Cartridges and many other accessories for shooting

WEBLEY & SCOTT LIMITED
Park Lane, Handsworth.
Birmingham B21 8LU
Telephone: 021-553 3952/6

Parts List and Diagram of Parts
COMPONENT PARTS OF THE WEBLEY OSPREY AIR RIFLE

PART No.	DESCRIPTION OF PART	No. OFF
12	PISTON	1
13	PISTON RINGS	2
14	DAMPING DISCS	2
15	MAINSPRING	1
16	BODY END PLUG	1
17	BODY END PLUG PIN	1
20	SAFE SLIDE	1
21	SEAR	1
22	SEAR SPRING	1
23	TRIGGER ADJUSTING SPRING	1
24	TRIGGER	1
25	FULCRUM PINS	5
26	FULCRUM PIN CIRCLIPS	5
27	TRIGGER ADJUSTING & RETAINING SCREW	3
31	PAWL	1
32	PAWL CANTILEVER SPRING	1
33	PAWL TENSIONING SPRING	1
34	PAWL OPERATING LEVER	1
35	PAWL OPERATING LEVER SPACER	1
39	LOADING LEVER	1
40	LOADING LEVER BOLT	1
41	LOADING LEVER BOLT SPRING	1
42	LOADING LEVER GRIP	1
43	LOADING LEVER BOLT PINS	4
44	AUXILIARY LEVER	1
45	AUXILIARY LEVER FULCRUM PIN	1
46	LOADING LEVER TENSIONING SPRING	1
47	LOADING LEVER FULCRUM PIN	1
48	LOADING LEVER FULCRUM PIN CIRCLIP	1
54	FORESIGHT	1
55	FORESIGHT HOOD	1
†59	LOADING TAP .177	1
†60	LOADING TAP .22	1

PART No.	DESCRIPTION OF PART	No. OFF
61	LOADING TAP SPRING	1
62	LOADING TAP LEVER	1
63	LOADING TAP LEVER SCREW	1
64	LOADING LEVER CATCH	1
65	LOADING LEVER CATCH WASHER	1
68	REARSIGHT LEAF	1
69	REARSIGHT BLADE	1
70	REARSIGHT HORIZONTAL SCREW	1
71	REARSIGHT HORIZONTAL CLICK SPRING	1
72	REARSIGHT HORIZONTAL CLICK BALL	1
73	REARSIGHT HORIZONTAL SCREW PEG	1
74	REARSIGHT BASE	1
75	REARSIGHT LEAF FULCRUM PIN	1
76	REARSIGHT VERTICAL SCREW	1
77	REARSIGHT LEAF SPRING	1
80	FIXING SCREW	3
81	FIXING SCREW LOCK WASHER	3
*83	BODY TUBE & BARREL ASSEMBLY .177	1
*84	BODY TUBE & BARREL ASSEMBLY .22	1
87	STOCK & RECOIL PAD ASSEMBLY	1
88	STOCK RECOIL DOWEL	1
89	STOCK FIXING SCREW FRONT	1
90	STOCK FIXING SCREW FRONT LOCKWASHER	1
91	TRIGGER GUARD	1
92	TRIGGER GUARD WOODSCREW	1
93	STOCK & GUARD SCREW	1
97	SOCKET KEY	1
101	SOCKET KEY RING TAG ASSEMBLY	1

†GUN MUST BE RETURNED TO DEALER FOR NEW TAP TO BE FITTED.
*NOT SUPPLIED AS A SPARE PART.

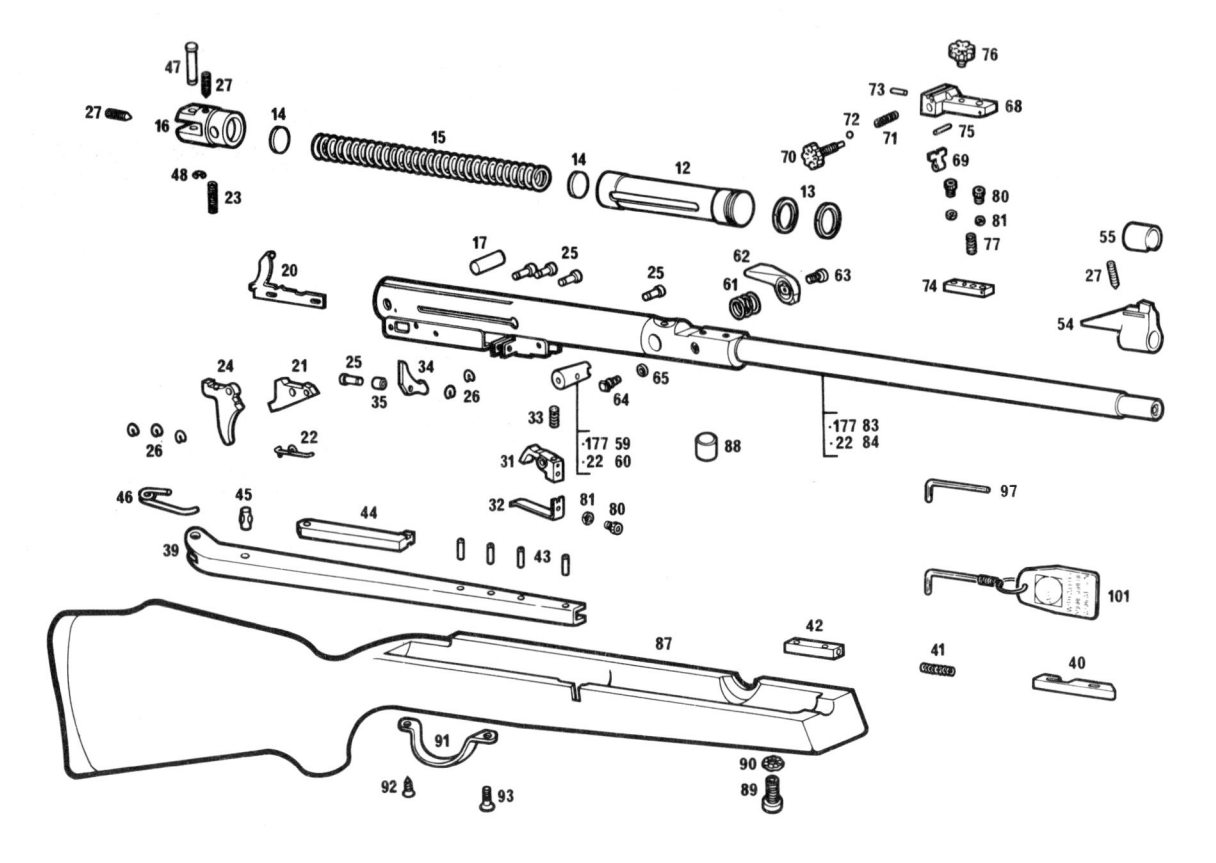

250

Weihrauch HW35 with deluxe stock and 22 inch barrel

MODEL HW35.

MAKER Hermann Weihrauch KG, D-8744 Mellrichstadt/Bayern, West Germany. Imported by Hull Cartridge Company, 58 De Grey Street, Hull, HU5 2SD.

DATE Introduced around 1957. An updated model, HW80 was introduced in 1981. See "Airgun World" June 1981 for review.

VALUATION £50—£100.
($75—$150).

DETAILS Quite a few variations exist of the above. It can be obtained with either a 19¾ inch or 22 inch barrel, choice of stocks and other accessories. Example examined had a 22 inch .22 rifled barrel with dovetail mounted foresight containing interchangeable sight elements. A sling swivel mount is clamped on to the barrel. Rearsight very similar to the LP53. On L.H.S. of breech is the barrel lock whicn is pulled forward to release the barrel. L.H.S. of breech stamped "HW35 MADE IN GERMANY KAL 5.5" whilst on the other side appears "WEIHRAUCH MELLRICHSTADT-BAY". Double linked cocking lever that clicks when cocking the action. Large diameter air chamber with 12 mm telescopic sight grooves. The serial number is stamped near the safety catch. Push button safety that can be pushed in to release the action when it has been cocked. Trigger adjustment behind the trigger. Above featured with deluxe stock. Before the War the Weihrauch factory was at Zella Mehlis. The above formed the basis for the "Barracuda" air rifle that fired an air/ether mixture. This was available in the U.S.A. during the late 1950s. During the middle 1960s the HW35 were imported by Edgar Bros., Vale Road, Woolton, Liverpool 25. It was advertised that the breech was slightly tapered so as to maintain a high air pressure whilst the pellet was travelling down the barrel, and the air left in the air chamber was used to lessen the recoil. Advertised weight with 19¾ inch barrel 8¼ lbs. During the late 1960s there were three models:

HW35 — Basic model. Length 45½ inches.
HW35L — Deluxe stock with sling swivels.
HW35E — 22 inch barrel. Chequered stock. Length 48 inches.

The above model appears to date from around the early 1970s. It was also imported by Optima Leisure Products, 75 Foxley Lane, Purley, Surrey CR2 3HP. During 1979 a thumb-hole stock was offered for the above, this aided the use by either left or right handed people. Available for the above is an aperture peepsight, a 4x32 telescopic sight, slings, cases etc. For a review see "Airgun World" October 1977. The HW35 is available in either .177 or .22. For stripping the HW35 see "Airgun World" November 1978. Up to serial number 754999 they have a 12 mm telescopic sight groove and from 755000 they have a 9 mm groove.

During August 1980, a consignment of the above were impounded by Customs & Excise and a selection were tested by the Forensic Laboratory. These were later advertised by the importers as being "well bedded in and all set to go" complete with Forensic Laboratory labels. The results of the tests proved that tne HW35E was within the limit of muzzle energy and the Senior Forensic Technician commented on the consistency of power and accuracy of the airguns tested. To remove action from stock, both trigger guard screws must be removed. Again, during August 1980 it was announced that three HW35s were gold plated and presented to the three directors of Hull Cartridge Company in recognition of the Company's success in selling the HW35 in Britain. See "Airgun World" August 1980 for further details. In December 1981, Optima Leisure Products advertised a "clickless" cocking lever and this modification was introduced with air rifle serial number 752000. This new addition does not interchange with existing air rifles so they introduced a modification for fitting to earlier models. Rifles made after 1977 were fitted with the push-in safety catch. It has been suggested that the HW35 originated from the re-designing of the HW50, one major element in the increase of power being the enlargement of the air chamber up to 13/16 inch. The barrel breech also has a very fine taper, even though it is rifled.

A review of the HW35 appears on "Sporting Air Rifle", November, 1985.

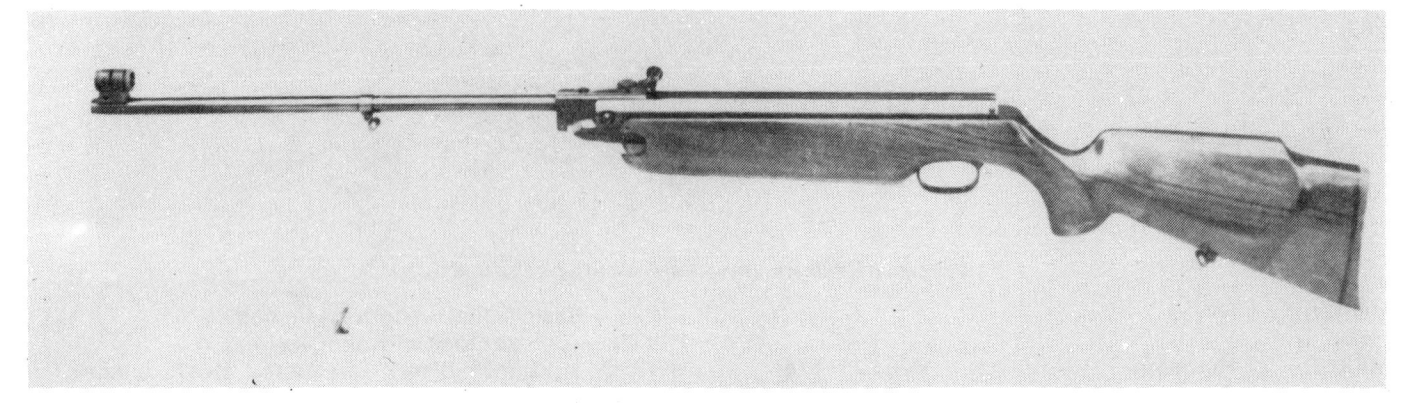

The Weihrauch HW35 "Vixen"

MODEL HW 35 "Vixen".

MAKER Hermann Weihrauch OHG, 8744 Mellrichstadt, Germany. The modification to vixen specification by Norman May.

DATE From about 1979 to 1981.

VALUATION £70—£150. ($105—$225).

DETAILS Besides the gold plated HW35s the Vixen must surely be the rarest variation of the HW35. 44½ inches long (130 cms) with a 19⅝ inch (50 cms) barrel. Tunnel foresight with interchangeable elements dovetail mounted whilst the rearsight is screw mounted and fully adjustable. Serial number on the underside of the barrel and on the L.H.S. of the breech block is stamped "HW35 — MADE IN GERMANY — KAL. 5.5", the breech lever is nickel plated. The other side of the block has "WEIHRAUCH — MELLRICHSTADT — BAY." and the word "VIXEN". Stock is hand chequered and fitted with butt plate and sling. The Vixen is golded-in. Most of the modification has been done internally to produce a Rolls Royce of Weihrauch air rifles. The main external features that distinguish the Vixen is the name on the breech block and the nickel plated barrel latch lever.

It took more than two years to research and perfect what goes into the Vixen and the final combination contains the following ingredients; the piston is sleeved on the inside so as to decrease its bore and thus produces a tighter fit on the spring and thus prevents buckling, a matching spring guide is also machined and each pair are fitted as a set and should not be mixed with other Vixens, if you find another! The chamber head is machined to fit the piston head and coated with a molybdenum compound and is thus lubricated for the life of the air rifle. The piston and guide are chrome plated and similarly coated. The mainspring is of Swedish steel and nickel alloy coated, although it is more prone to snap on initial fitting, if it lasts after the first few rounds it should then go on for at least three years and is likely to last even longer. The transfer port has also been altered for either .177 or .22, so that changing barrels is not recommended. The Vixen was sold complete with a fleecy lined gun bag bearing the Vixen logo.

During 1979 the Vixen was sold in three grades: Long barrelled 22 inch (56 cm) with a beech stock, this was the Standard Model that retailed for £123. Deluxe Model with a 19½ inch (49.5 cm) barrel and a walnut stock, cost £145. Export Model with the longer barrel and fitted with the "E" grade chequered stock, this final model sold for £157.

The Vixen mainspring is longer than the standard one fitted and refitting without the spring compressor is NOT recommended. One secret of the tight fitting mainspring is that on compression its diameter expands and it literally clamps itself into the piston and on to the spring guide, thus reduces very much any "twang" and piston bounce.

Using .177 hobby pellets the average velocity reading was 846 f.p.s. which equates to 11.6 ft lbs, whilst with .22 Hobby's the average velocity was 658 f.p.s. 11.4 ft lbs. When the air rifle is bedded in these figures only increase marginally to just under the legal limit judging by extensive tests by Norman May.

A review of the Vixen appears in "Airgun World" August 1979.

253

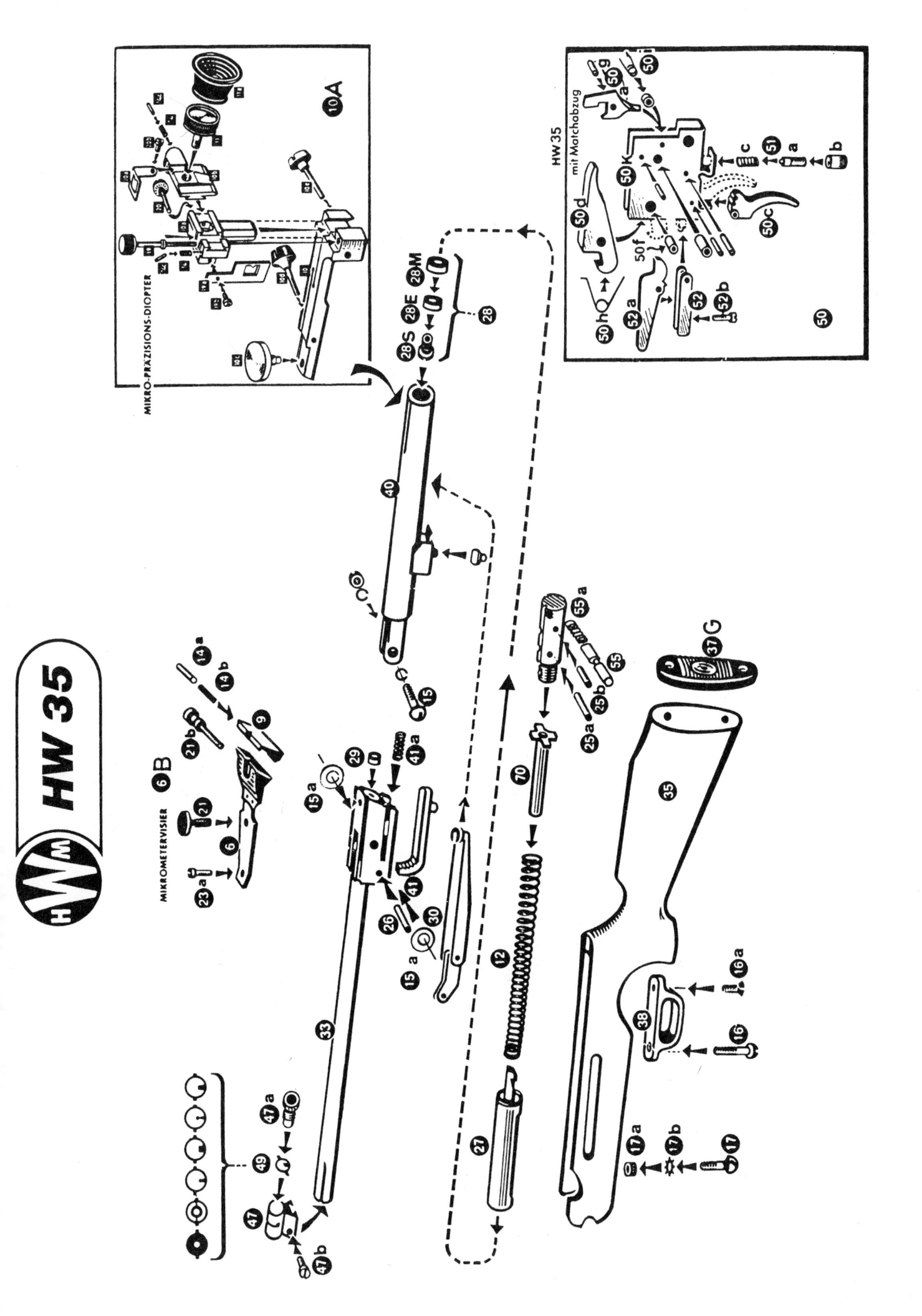

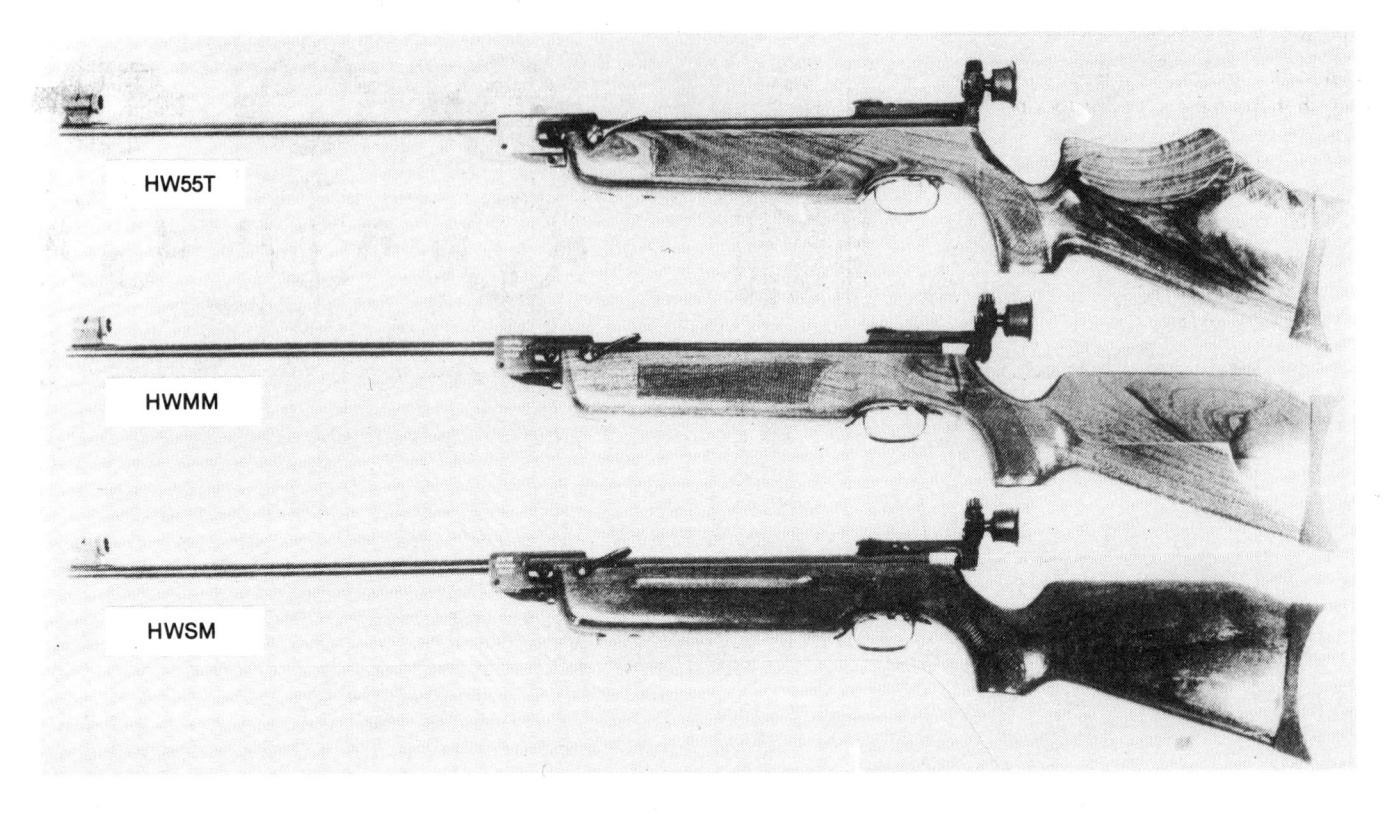

The three main varieties of HW55 available in the 1970s and 1980s

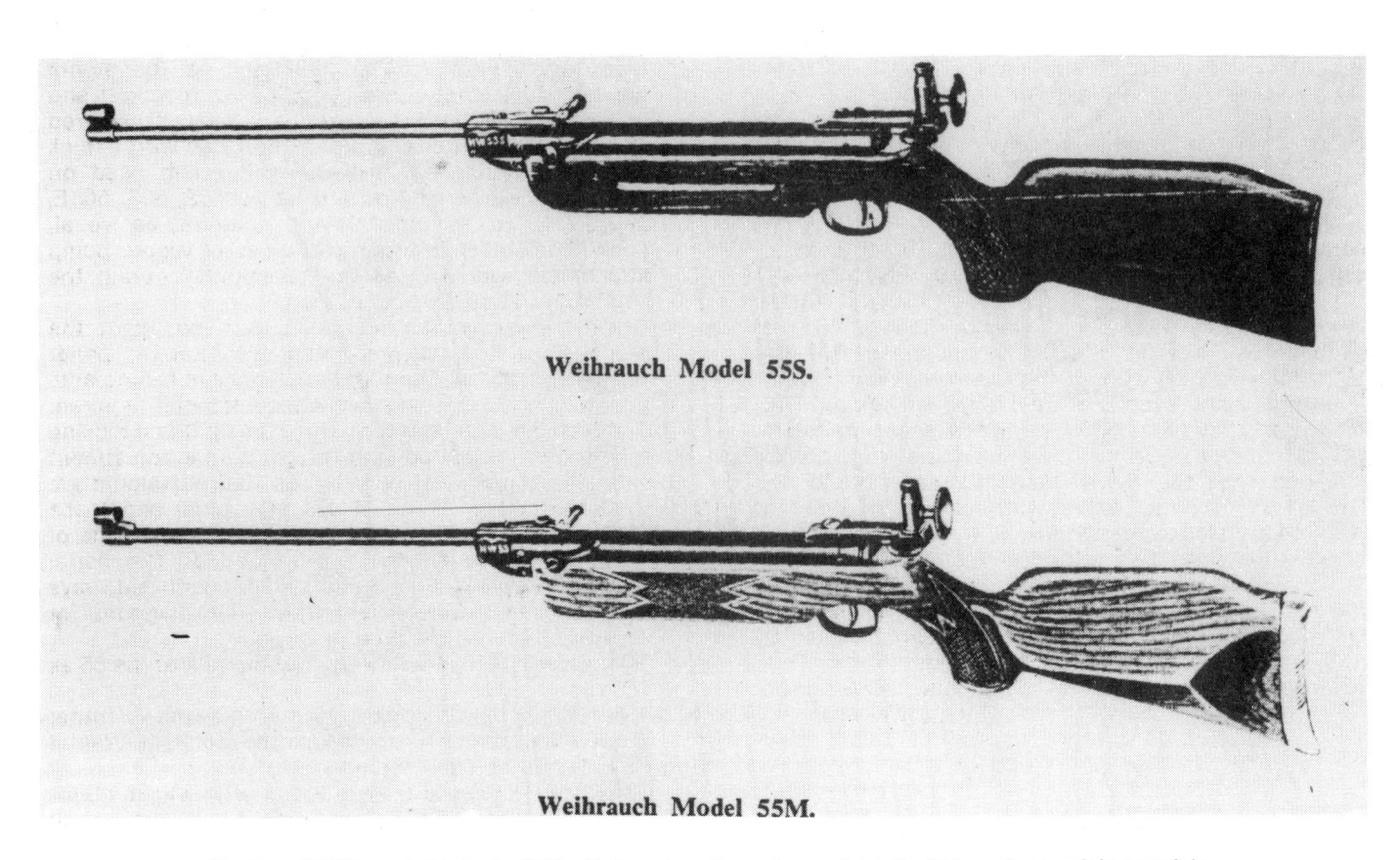

First two HW55s available in the 1950s. Note early pattern of peepsight, the fitting of open sight rearsight and the difference in stocks between the Standard and Match

Adjustable barrel locking

A uniform sighting line is ensured, shot after shot, by means of the locking lever (O).
The lock set-screw (R) when turned to the left, tighten the barrel lock. The hinge screw (S) prevents any loosening of the hinge.

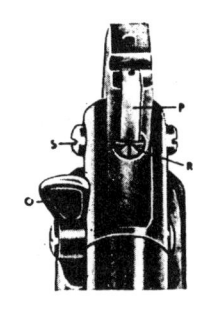

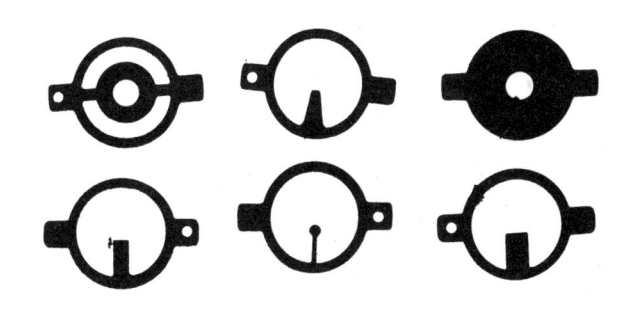

The barrel hinge and lock is fully adjustable

The six foresight elements supplied. (It used to be only four)

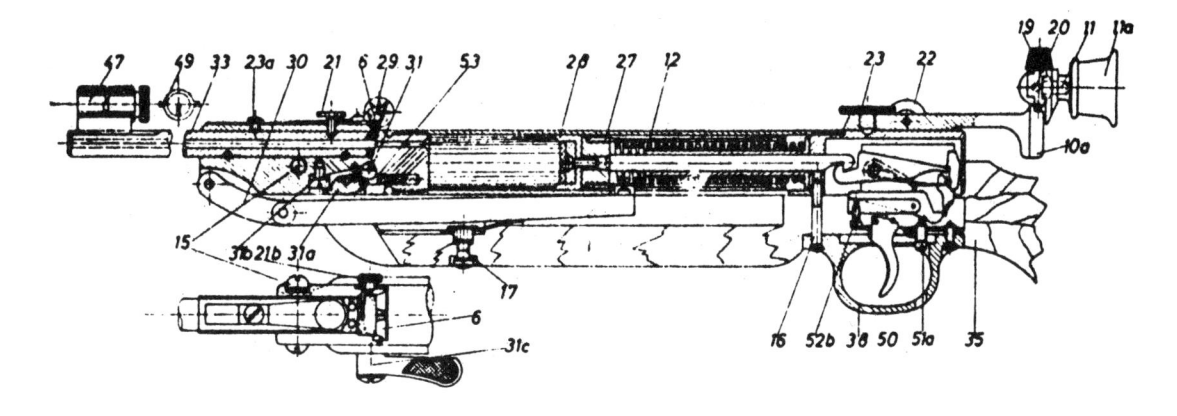

HW55 internals

MODEL HW55.

MAKER Hermann Weihrauch KG, D-8744 Mellricjstadt/Bayern, West Germany.

DATE Middle 1950s to present date.

VALUATION £100−£200. ($150−$300).

DETAILS A target air rifle with a difference. 43¼ inches long (100 cms) with an 18½ inch (47cms) .177 rifled barrel. Dovetail mounted foresight with interchangeable foresight elements. Usually six are supplied with the air rifle. From advertisements the Model 55 was sold without the rearsight, even though it is drilled and tapped should one be required. All metal parts have the deep blue that is associated with the Weihrauch quality. Side of barrel breech is stamped with the model name/number, "MADE IN GERMANY" and the calibre, which is only supplied in .177, there also appears the F-in pentagon which denotes the unrealistic level of muzzle energy allowed in Europe. The other side of the breech housing has the Weihrauch trade stamp with place of manufacture. On the underside is the last four digits of the serial number that is stamped on the trigger block. This could mean that each barrel is matched to the action for maximum accuracy. To release the barrel push the thumb lever forward through 90° and then break down the barrel for cocking, pull lever back when firing. The lever holds down the barrel against the transfer port face so fitting a new breech seal can be quite critical. The trigger adjustment is behind the trigger and reached through the guard. Each Model 55 is supplied with an aperture peepsight.

When they first appeared in the middle 1950s two models were available, Model 55S — Sporting stock and sights, this would appear to have the standard stock with a chequered grip and thin butt plate, and one single deep groove on the fore-end. The barrel was fitted with a rearsight as well as the peepsight. Advertised weight around 8 lbs. Approximate muzzle velocity rated at 500 f.p.s. Model 55M — Match stock and sights, a little confusing as the sights appear to be identical to the 55S, i.e. rearsight and peepsight. The stock, however, was finely chequered on the fore-end and on the grip and fitted with a thick rubber butt plate. The trigger mechanism used on both air rifles, as well on the Model 30S, 50S, 50SE, and 35, is the famous "Rekord" pattern, as we all know. The Model 55 fitted with an ether vapour pump attachment was sold as the "Barakuda" during the 1950s but was not very successful.

One of the major advantages advertised about the Model 55 is that the recoil happens after the pellet has left the barrel. The trigger mechanism has no anti-bear trap so can be released when cocked if required. The rearsight side screw on the peepsight is a locking nut for the vertical adjustment, so before adjustment this side screw must be released. Barrel weights are available in two sizes, 14 ozs (400 gms) and 2 lbs (900 gms). There was even a front stock weight of 14 ozs available for the heavy handed! The barrel locking design is fully adjustable for both sideways and upwards movement and wear. See diagrams for details.

By the early 1970s there were four models of the 55 as follows:

HW55SM — The standard model, this and all other models were sold without the middle rearsight. Walnut coloured stock. SM = "Standard Match".

HW55MM — Olympic style stock with slight cheek piece, chequered fore-end and grip, fitted with curved and ribbed deep rubbed butt plate. Stock now "first-class walnut". MM = "Master Match".

HW55F — Identical to the 55MM but having a "spring bolt locking".

HW55T — Fitted with a Tyrollian style stock made from walnut and fully chequered on fore-end and grip.

The Models 55MM and 55T were imported into this country for the first time during 1967 by the original distributors Edgar Brothers, Vale Road, Woolton,

Liverpool 25. Prices at that time being £35/11/0 and £38/12/0 respectively. By 1969 the muzzle velocity was quoted as 620 f.p.s., this equates to about 6¾ ft lbs, bearing in mind that this is a target air rifle with especially designed system that delays the recoil until after the pellet has left the barrel. It has been said that the pellet is propelled at the maximum volume of air and on leaving the barrel there is still air left in the chamber to bring the piston to a smooth and gentle halt. The alloy trigger can be adjusted from a pull of 4 ozs to 1 lb, and the adjuster screw has an outer locking ring. Another screw can be found by removing the trigger guard, this adjusts that distance that the trigger will travel on the first stage before it reaches the stage of releasing the sear. For cleaning the trigger mechanism it can be removed as one piece. By 1976 a new version was mentioned of the above design. The Model 55 has been described as the most accurate non-recoiless air rifle available.

For converting to field use remove the peepsight and replace the rearsight, finally change the mainspring for one from the HW50, this will increase the muzzle velocity.

Besides having a power system that brakes the piston by air pressure instead of allowing it to slam into the cylinder head, as on most airguns, the barrel has polygroove rifling with a breech taper 12 groove, right hand twist with one turn every 16½ inches. As the breech seal and washer are leather it is recommended that they are kept well lubricated.

A review of the 55 appears in "Guns Review" February 1970 and "Airgun World" April 1980.

Sometime during the middle to late 1970s a bi-pod rail was added to the fore-end.

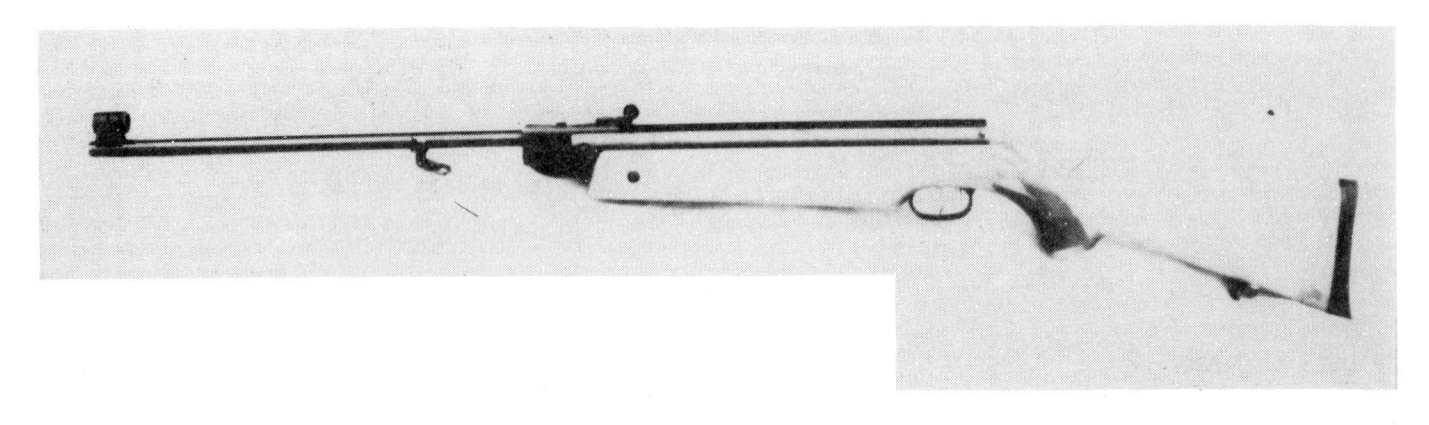

The Weihrauch HW80

MODEL   HW80.

MAKER   Herman Weihrauch KG, D-8744 Mellrichstadt/Bayern, West Germany.

DATE   1980 or 1981 onwards.

VALUATION   £50−£120. ($75−$180).

DETAILS   Introduced as a companion model to the HW35. Differs in three ways, no barrel latch, single piece cocking lever, and a new style piston head assembly. The HW80 is a full size hunting air rifle. 45¼ inches long with a 19⅝ inch barrel. Advertised weight 8 lbs 10 ozs. Has the same sights as the HW35. Very simple lettering stamped on this air rifle. Just the name and calibre, seems quite humble compared to the air rifle. Rolls Royce's are the same! Drain pipe sized air chamber is grooved for telescopic sights with two holes drilled between the grooves for mounting telesight stops. Trigger adjustment is behind the trigger. Very nice hardwood stock with hand chequering and rubber butt pad. Available in either .22 or .177. Advertised muzzle velocity for .177 being about 800 f.p.s. See "Airgun World" June 1981 for a review.

One small fault that can occur with the above is for the cocking lever and sliding shoe to wear and not be able to cock the action as the cocking length has decreased. This is often mistaken for the trigger action being at fault, but what is happening is that the underside of the barrel is coming to rest against either the two front screw lugs for the front stock screws, or against the stock groove for the cocking arm. A similar fault as experienced with Webley air pistols.

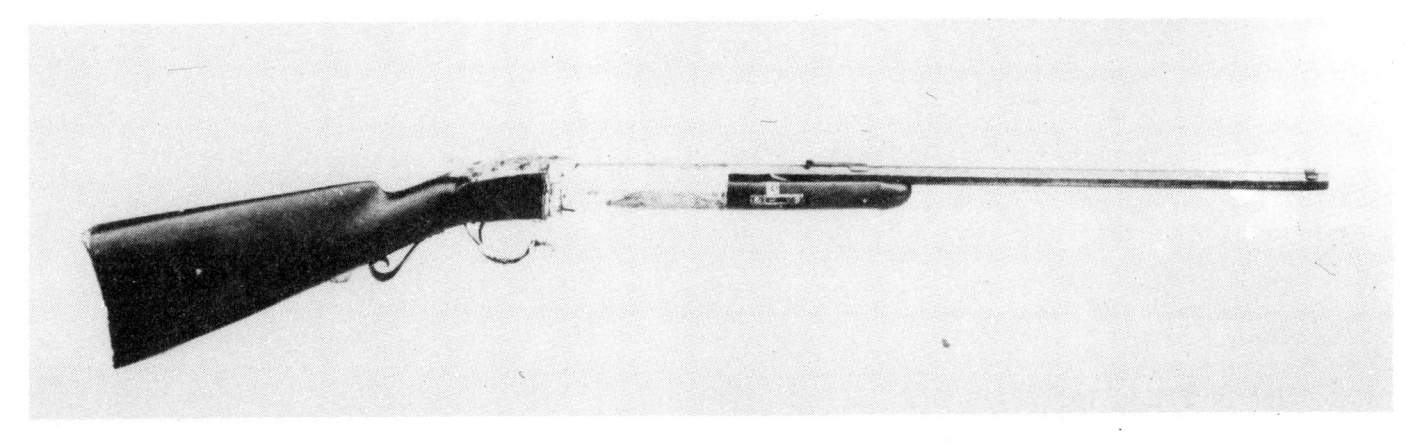

Oscar Will Bugelspanner target air rifle

MODEL Bugelspanner Target Air Rifle.

MAKER Oscar Will, Venuswaffenwerk, Zella St., Blasii, Germany.

DATE From as early as the middle 1800s to the middle 1950s, although this late date could be advertising of old stock.

VALUATION £150—£300. ($225—$450).

DETAILS 41 inches in length with a 20½ inch .25 smoothbore barrel. Octagonal barrel with foresight set in dovetail with screw on side for locking in position. Foresight blade tipped with German Silver. Rearsight is simple tangent blade for elevation only and is stamped "PAT.JAN 29,1901". Breech end has floral inlay. There is no breech seal, just metal to metal contact. Small wooden fore-end containing the barrel latch. The pressing down of small lever at side of barrel allows the barrel to spring up for loading. On underside of barrel stamped into the metal plate screwed to fore-end appears the monogram of Oscar Will. All the screw heads have radiating chisel work decoration. Air chamber and trigger block all bear traces of nickel plating, as do the trigger guard cocking lever and butt plate. They also have scroll and floral engraving. Unusual in the fact that the serial number is not visible. Trigger has adjustment screw behind. For the stripping of a Bugelspanner air rifle see "Airgun World" December 1979. The above style of trigger guard was referred to as the "spur guard trigger". Advertised weight 3 kg. Above style seen advertised 1911 to around 1953. Above was also available with a hair trigger. Later advertisements during 1920 to 1930s called it the "Original" Bugelspanner Luftgewehr. Rearsight on above does not appear to be original. Later models appear to have dropped the extended spur on the front of the trigger guard cocking lever. Have seen others with the serial number stamped under the barrel.

The serial number is also stamped under the barrel and cannot be seen unless the barrel is removed. To remove barrel a taper pin must be driven out from left to right as the air rifle is held pointing away from you, and replacing the pin from right to left and tapping it home as it is a tight fit. The barrel pivots on this pin. The above engraved model appears to be a deluxe version, the standard model was of course plainer, but still retained the nickel plated metal parts except for the barrel which was blued. By the 1930s it was sold in the following combinations: Standard model with smooth side stock; .25 smoothbore and .177 and .22 rifled. Same action as above with stock with cheek piece; .25 smoothbore, .177 and .22 rifled. Hair trigger action with deluxe stock; .25 smoothbore, .177 and .22 rifled.

OIL CANS

No. 1 OIL.
For use in Webley Air Pistol Mark I and Junior Model, and other Air Pistols and Rifles where piston is fitted with leather washers.

No. 2 OIL.
For use in Webley Air Rifles and Senior Air Pistols where Piston is fitted with piston ring.

"WEBLEY" OIL CAN
Available in two grades, see above. This style of tin with screw top tip and sold from around 1924 to 1939.

PELLETS

"BEATALL" PELLETS

Appeared during the middle 1930's and continued after W.W.2. From the appearance of the above tin lid would assume to above to be pre-war, dating from around 1933/5 to 1939 and maybe for a short period after, but more often found in paper packets after the war. Manufactured by Lanes Bros.

Sold in "boxes" of 500 (.177) and 1000 (.177) and in 500 only for .22. Lid colours were cream background with deep blue front ring with red background to the two semi-circular name panels with a red ring to outer and inner edge to the deep blue front panel.

B.S.A. "PYLARM" PELLETS

"Pylarm" pellets appeared during the late 1930's and were intended as a cheaper pellet than the Standard B.S.A. pellet that was available in rectangular boxes at the same time and earlier. Sold in .177 and .22 with lid labels as shown, the only difference being in the pellet size. Sold in tins of 500 and 1000 in .177 and in 500's for .22. Average weight of 10 .177 pellets was found to be 7.31 grains. After the W.W.2. the standard pellet name was dropped in favour of the "Pylarm" brand name. They were manufactured by Eley Bros.

Lid label is red centre bar and outer rim with yellow upper and lower segments. Printing in black.

"BULL DOG" AIR RIFLE PELLETS

Pre-war pellets but still referred to as slugs on other parts of the box. These were found with a German Tell air rifle. Although the packets boasted "perfect fit ensuring great force" the actual variation in size ranged from dropping straight through the barrel to sitting on top of the bore like some obese lead pellet. I also like the purely sexist reference to "all Boy's airguns" this being the same philosophy that is held in the Sahara desert in which a woman's hand must never be allowed to touch the udder of a camel otherwise it will turn the milk sour and the camel sterile! Bull dog brand pellets were manufactured by Lane Brothers, 45a New Church St., Bermondsey, London S.E., address at time of manufacture. Would date the above as 1910 to 1920s.

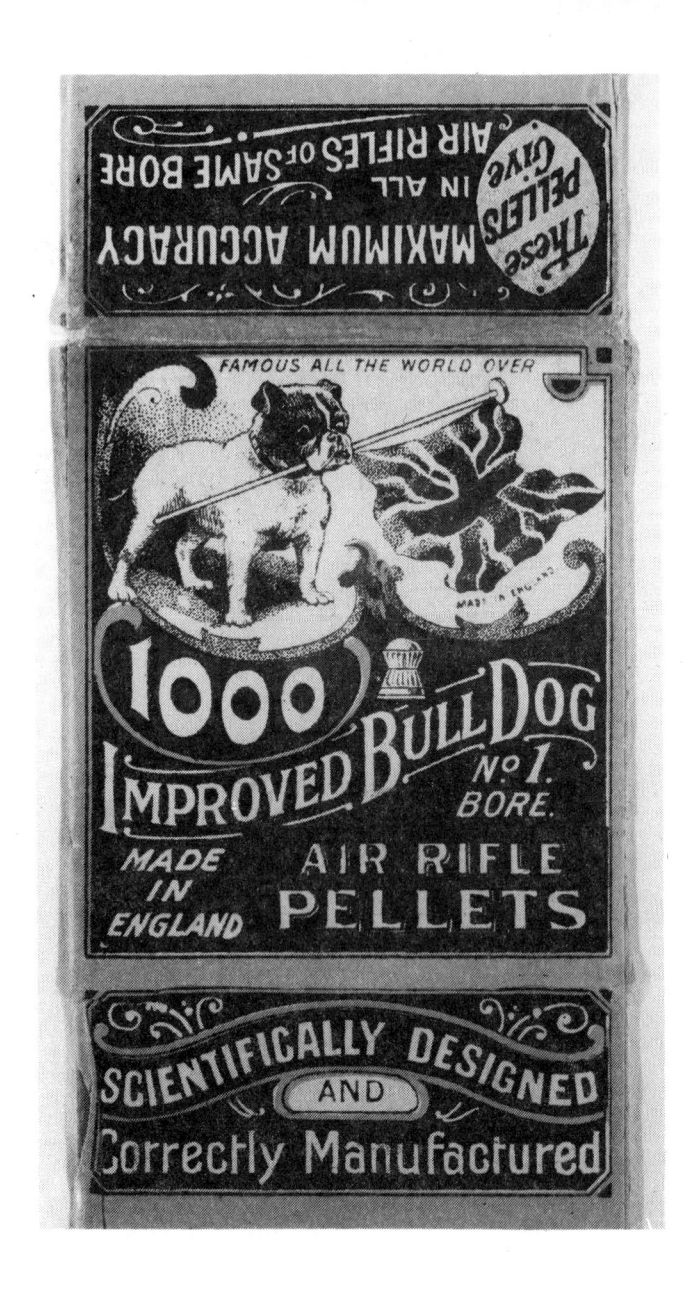

"IMPROVED" BULL DOG PELLETS

To date one of the most colourful and artistic box labels seen. Printed with four colours, red, white, blue and mustard. Bull dog pellets first appeared in the middle 1920s and were even around after the Second World War, although in different designed boxes. The above appear to have been produced up to 1939. With the same standard label they were available in the following sizes: .177 in 500s and 1,000s, and in 500s only for .22 and .25. Boxes of 1,000 .177 pellets measure 2¾ x 2¾ x 1½ inches.

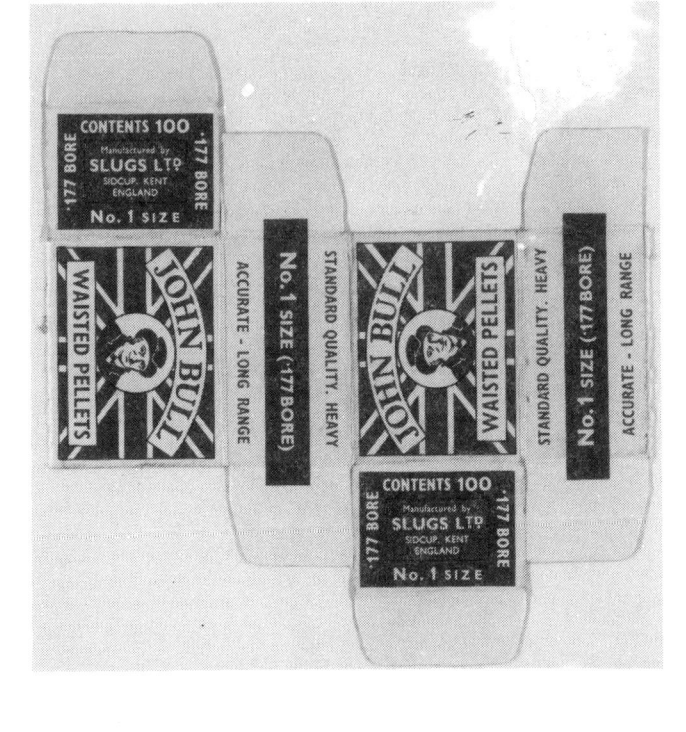

JOHN BULL WAISTED PELLETS

I associate these with cycle shops as as a child I used to buy John Bull cycle tyres and accessories so there may be some connection. Packets of 100 seen by the obvious firm of SLUGS Ltd., Sidcup, Kent, England. I would assume these to be available in the 1950s to early 1970s.

CAC WAISTED AIR RIFLE PELLETS

Pale green plastic box with hinged lid. Same design as Hyscore and advertised during the middle 1970s. Lid label shows a target shooter complete with ear protectors firing at a target, rather faint in the photograph, but the bulls eye can just be seen. These originally from New Zealand and were available during the 1980s.

262

CHAMPION SPECIAL 20 PELLETS
Average weight 10.54 grains, available in small numbers throughout the 1970's and 1980's although not readily available. Pellet on lid bore no resemblance to contents, usual round head with waist, ribbed and thick rear skirt. Lid with black printing with faded yellow background. This style of lid label also appeared for .22 (450) and for .25 (350).

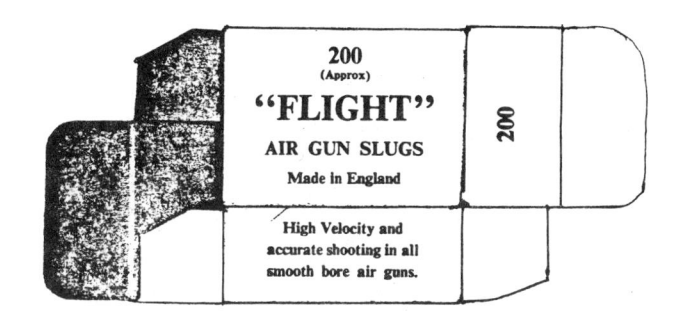

"FLIGHT" AIR GUN SLUGS
Black printing on white card boxes. Found in 200s, but no doubt other packets were available. Measures 2¾ x 1¼ x ¾ inches. Would assume these to date from the 1950s and 1960s. Note the good old "66" and "99" speech commas so rarely seen these days, also the awareness that these cup slugs were better in smoothbore airguns. Apart from the front, one side and one flap there is no other printing on the boxes.

HUSTLER AIRGUN PELLETS
Round cardboard container of approximately 250 .22 pellets, although the label refers to .177. Blue background label with purple pellets, three in number. The first as seen in the photograph bears the name and size of pellet, the second pellet shape has "Enjoy hours of straight shooting with Hustler 177 Air Gun Pellets. Precision made from the Highest Quality materials", the other pellet shape contains "Made in N.Z. by Sexton Engineering Ltd., Totara Ave., New Lynn, Auckland, N.Z." In the blue portion is the number of pellets, but in this case there is a white/blue stick-on label on the lid with the following "Approx 250 .22 Calibre".

DIANA DIABOLO PELLETS
These were found in a boxed pre-war German Diana tinplate air pistol, assumed Model 1. The first air pistol produced by Diana and cocked by a key that was placed on the nipple protruding from the end of the butt. The sample box of waisted pellets was brown in colour and made from a very coarse cardboard. The box opened in the same manner as a box of matches. Would assume that the above dates from the middle 1920s to the middle 1930s and was a sample packet.

263

"KOMET" PELLETS

Pale blue stick on label with darker blue printing. Pellets in tin look very much like Wasp. The ribbing only applies to the rear flange of the pellet and not to the underside of the head as shown on tin lid label.

KING AIRGUN SLUGS

Deep green packet with blue printing. Measures 1⅞ x 1¼ x ⅜ inches. The slug is of the domed head and hollow base with flat sides with four raised ribs. Usually referred to as "hollow slugs". Earliest advert seen for King slugs is during the middle 1920s and they were sold in .177 and .25 only. The .177s were offered in boxes of 100, 200, 500 and 1,000 whilst the .25 slugs were sold in 500s only. By the 1930s the .25 size appears to have been discontinued. By 1939 they would appear to have been renamed the "Queen" hollow slugs.

KING AIRGUN SLUGS

Bright deep yellow with black printing. Packets of 200 measure 1⅞ x 1¼ x ⅜ inches. Would assume same time period as above for packets of 100. The average weight of the "King" hollow slug is .36 grams or 5.55 grains. They were manufactured by Lanes Ltd.

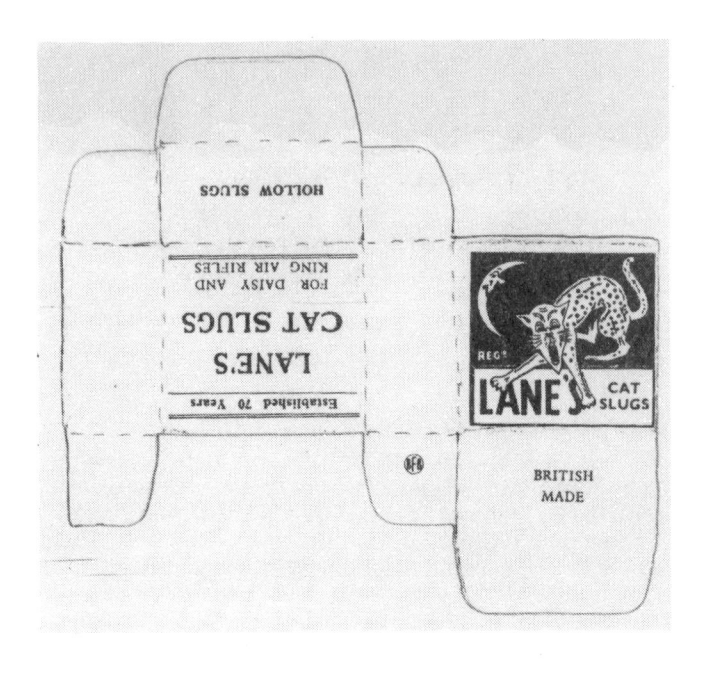

LANE'S CAT SLUGS

Black and white label on packets of 100 cup-shaped slugs. Intended for smoothbore airguns. Sold in boxes of 100 and 200 for .177 only. Appeared in the late 1930s and again just after 1945. During the middle 1950s they were also sold in packets of 500. Before 1939 they were sold in round tins with the same design on the lid.

LANE'S CAT SLUGS
Coarse cardboard outer measuring 1¾ x 1¼ x ⅝ inches. Average contents 200 simple cup slugs. Assumed age middle to late 1930's with a brief appearance after 1944. Average weight of the slugs is 6.95 grains. The design of the cat logo is from a different die as that which printed the later style of 100 packet.

LANE'S SPECIAL PELLETS
Tin of 500 "Special" pellets, enamelled lid in silver with black printing. Note unusual shape of pellet, being extremely long with a marked ribbed narrow waist. Edge of lid printed "MADE IN GREAT BRITAIN BY LANES LTD. SIDCUP KENT".

LANE'S TEMPERED DARTS .25
White cardboard box with yellow wrap around label. Above illustrations shown front and back printing with "Ask your Gunmaker for LANE'S PATENT "BANGO" BULLETS" on one side and on the other "Ask your Gunmaker for LANE'S PATENT MUSKETEER AIR RIFLE Price 35/-". Box measures 2 x 1½ x ⅝ inches. Average weight of each dart being 31.9 grains. Interesting to note that airgun ammunition was referred to as "bullets" and not as pellets. As the packet mentions the Musketeer it is safe to assume that these date from the same period, from around 1903 onwards. Before 1903 they were sold in lift up lid wallets as shown. These for the Lane's Ball Trigger Air Rifle (Gem style). It would appear that these darts were available in all three calibres. Address at time of manufacture being 45a, New Church Street, Bermondsey, London, SE. As regarding calibres, I'm not sure if .22 darts were available from this firm during this early period. For the early style of box see attached page from a 1902 catalogue.

LANE'S "TRIUMPH" PELLETS
The "Triumph" brand, also may have been referred to as the "Demon" Match Slugs, appeared during the late 1920's as the patent numbers on the tin lid are both dated from 1928, numbers being 308943/28 and 160/28. During the 1930's they were sold in boxes of 500 .177 for 10d, 1,000 .177 for 1/6 and in .22 (500) for 1/3. The tin above is the latter in .22. Pale green colour with black lettering. A very popular pellet in its day and "used by most of the air rifle clubs in the Birmingham area." Average weight of pellets as found in the tin was 17.2 grains. These appear to have ceased appearing after the W.W.2.

Details of the Patent 308943/28 may be found in "Guns Review", October, 1976. The tin was originally sealed with red canvas tape.

LANE'S AIR GUN AMMUNITION

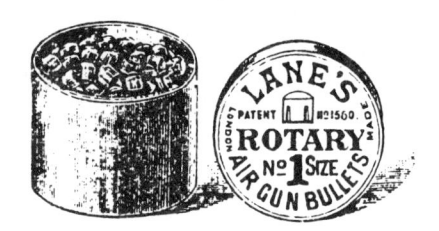

Lane's Patent "ROTARY" Bullets

Lane's "PERFECT" Bullets

Lane's "EXPANDED" Bullets

Lane's "MIDGET" Bullets

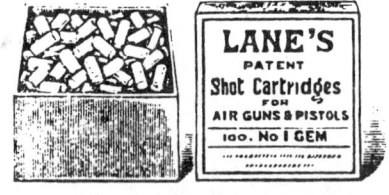

Lane's Patent Shot Cartridges

Lane's "TEMPERED" Darts

Lane's "B. B." PELLETS

ARE THE BEST

Write for Price List and Samples.

ADDRESS:

LANE BROTHERS,
45a, New Church Street, Bermondsey, London, S.E.

Telegrams: "Smokeless, London."   WHOLESALE ONLY.

Selection of Lane's Airgun Ammunition for 1902.

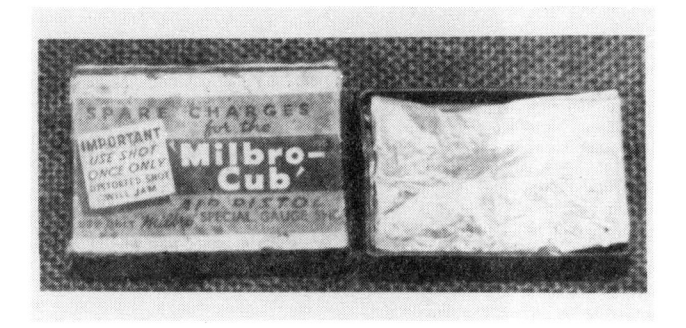

SPARE CHARGES FOR THE MILBRO CUB

Have rarely seen the word "charges" used in place of the more usual term for round shot. These charges for the Milbro Cub date from the late 1940s to early 1950s. The small buff coloured box with a red and yellow label opened and closed like a match box. Box measures 2¼ x 1½ x ¾ inches. The wording on the lid can quite clearly be read from the photograph, whilst on the underside is printed "NOMINAL QUANTITY 2000" there was also pencilled a price of 3/6 which equates to 17½p in foreign English money. From the box seen the contents would appear to be two packets of "special gauge shot" and they may have been spare washers for the rear breech of the Cub. This "special gauge shot" is 2.41 mm or 0.095 inches which is equivalent to number 7 shotgun pellet size.

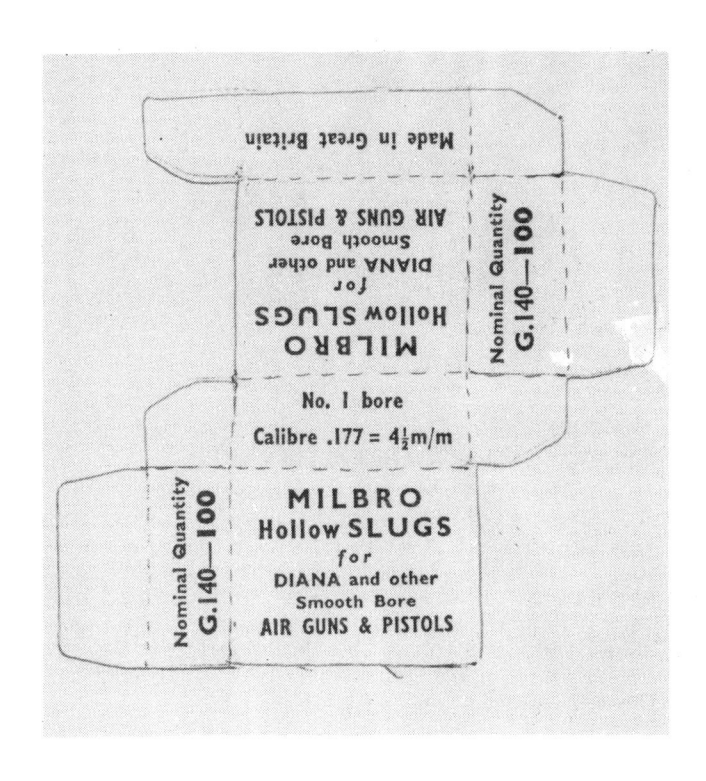

MILBRO HOLLOW SLUGS

Cup slugs for smoothbore airguns. Sold in packets of 100, 200 and 500. Labels have black writing on white background. Sold during the 1950s and 1960s and can still be found loitering at the back of many a shop pellet shelf. Available in .177 only. Boxes of 200 were coded G.142.

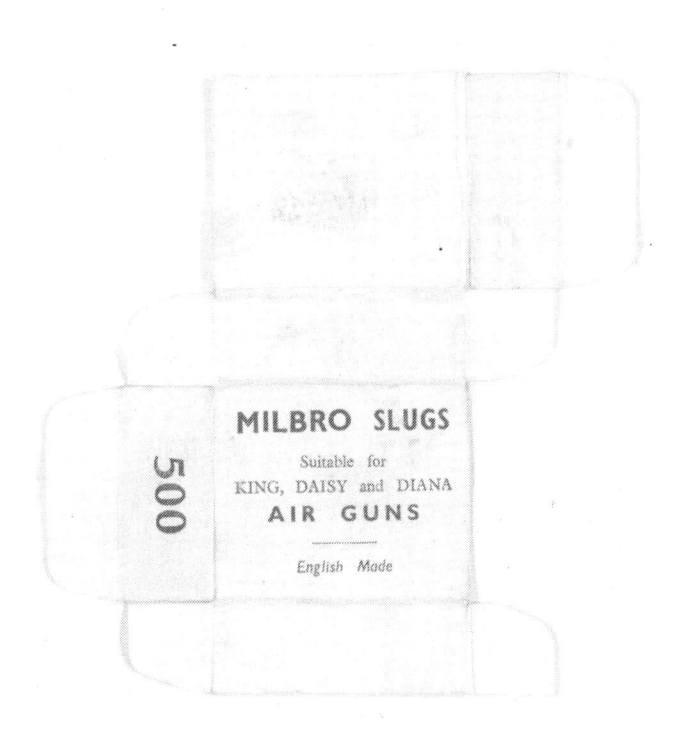

MILBRO SLUGS

Cup shaped slugs for smoothbore airguns. Seen in packs of 500, although may have also been sold in packs of 100 and 250. Black printing on white card. Very plain and printed on one side only so would assume these were the first to appear from Milbro. Suggested age being late 1940s to very early 1950s. Note that King and Daisy trade names appear first and King being a pre-1939 manufacturer so it was assumed by Milbro that there would be plenty of King air rifles still about.

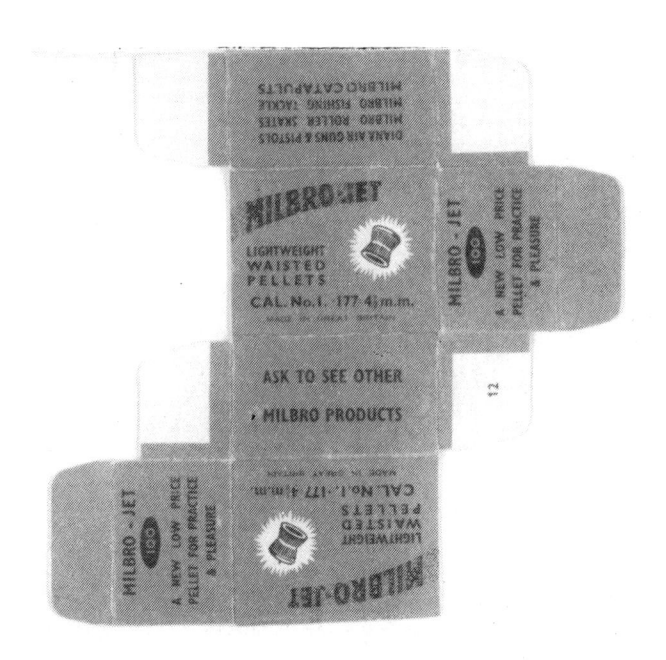

MILBRO JET LIGHTWEIGHT WAISTED PELLETS

Sold in boxes in both .177 and .22. Mustard coloured boxes with black printing and the pellet logo has a white background. Note the use of both Diana and Milbro trade names and the mention of the title Great Britain. They appear to have been sold during the 1960s and early 1970s. Advertisements claimed an extra 25 to 100 f.p.s. increase in velocity over other pellets. Pellet weights were 7.5 g for .177 and 14 g for .22. The .177s were sold in boxes of 100, 200 and 500 whilst the .22s were sold in 200 and 500 boxes only.

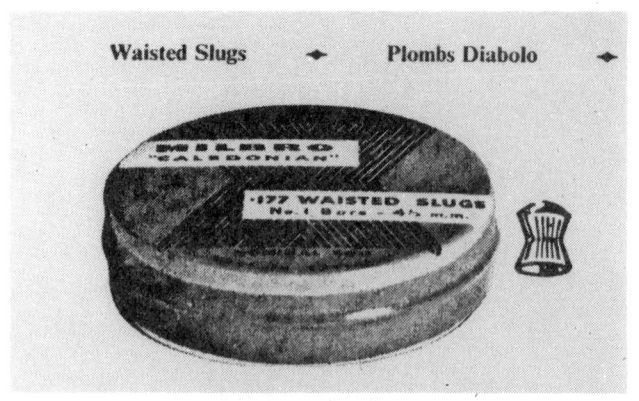

MILBRO "CALEDONIAN" PELLETS

As a coincidence one of their addresses in London was 467 Caledonian Road, London N.7. These were supplied for a short while in tins, but will mostly be found in boxes. Red coloured tin and sold in 100s, 200s and 500s for .177 and in 200s, 250s and 500s in .22. They were given away with the "Comet Shooting Set. Would assume the time span of the tinned variety to be from late 1950s to middle 1960s. Advertised pellet weight for the .177 was 8.5 g, and 14.5 g for the .22.

Simple tin of 100 .177 Milbro "Caledonian" Pellets.

THE "PRINCE" AIR GUN SLUGS

Post-war, and would assume 1950s to 1960s. The other associated names of "King" and "Queen" are pre-war, 1939. Simple printing black on white and seen in packets of 100, although it is safe to assume that they were sold in larger quantities. Straight sided slugs with a shallow domed head and hollow inside. "Prince" slugs were manufactured by Lanes Limited.

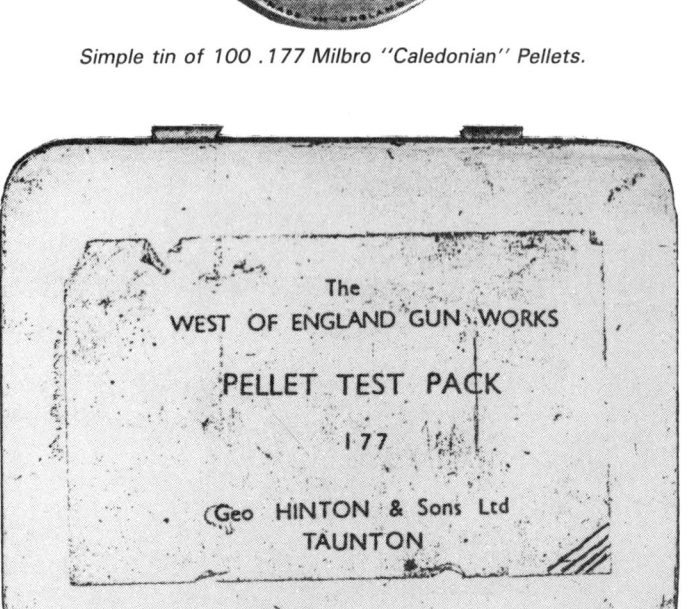

PELLET TEST PACK

White enamelled tin with black plastic insert with nine compartments each containing a sample selection of .177 pellets. A plan of contents was fixed to the inside of the lid as follows:

WASP	WEBLEY	H&N POINTED
MARKSMAN	MILBRO CALEDONIAN	H&N MATCH
BULLDOG	ELEY MATCH	(Label missing as this compartment was blank)

Would assume to above to date from the 1960's to 1970's.

RATTER PELLETS

A heavyweight pellet introduced 1983 specially designed for vermin shooting. Tins contained about 450 pellets. Manufactured by Lanes Limited, Faraday Way, St. Mary Cray, Orpington, Kent.

SILVA PELLETS

These originate from Australia and appear to date from the good old days of Dan Dare! Notice the futuristic shape of the projectile, almost as though they should contain little green men! Average weight being 5.24 grains, assumed to be made from a light lead alloy. Manufactured by Smith & Chesney, Makrickville, New South Wales, Australia. Assume to be 1950's to 1960's date. Found in the original brown paper envelope with red label.

It would appear that Australians wouldn't give a XXXX for their pellets either!

"TARGET" AIRGUN SLUGS

Post-war and would assume 1950s. Packets contained the usual cup shaped slugs with four raised ribs around the circumference of the skirt. I think they were called "Target" slugs because of this slight ribbing. Unusually brightly coloured box, being very deep blue with bright yellow printing. Boxes measure 1¾ x 1¼ x ⅝ inches.

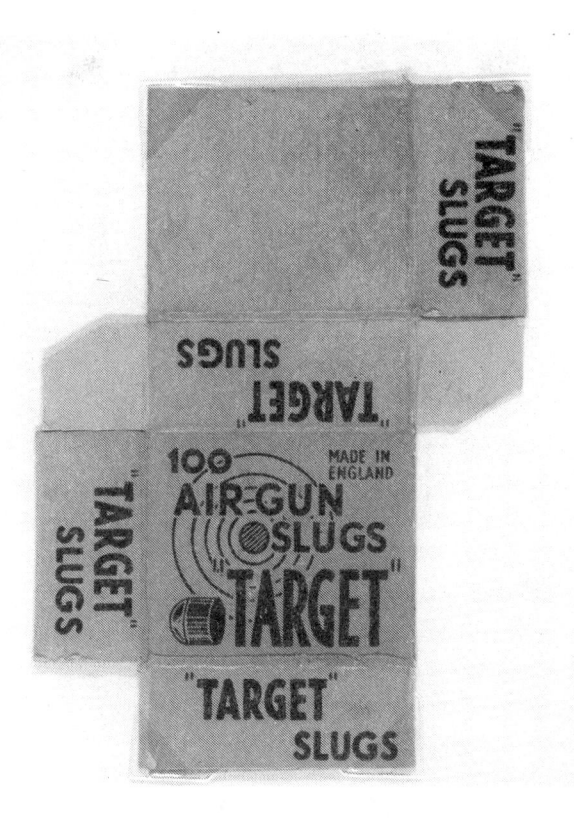

"SPITFIRE" .200 PELLETS

Marketed by Sussex Armoury, Hailsham, Sussex. Dates from around 1980 to 1983 when the firm stopped trading. From the style of tin would assume manufacture by Cammel of the Wirral. Label had outer blue border with red inner bull. Average weight of pellets 9.34 grains. Advertised as being made for the Jackal 2020 air rifle.

TARGET AIRGUN SLUGS

Packet of 100 that turned up in a Webley Junior air pistol box, 1950 to 1958 type, hence slightly confirming my belief that these are post-war. Pale green background with blue printing. Box measures 1½ x 1¼ x ⅝ inches.

"TARGET" AIRGUN SLUGS
Packets of 500 measure 2⅛ x 1¾ x ⅞ inches and are amber-yellow with bright red printing. Very colourful and pretty.

VIPER PELLETS
Lid label with yellow and red viper. Dating from the 1970's. Average weight of .22, pellet being 12.79 grains. Also available in .177 and .25.

WEBLEY SPECIAL PELLETS
Pale green label with black printing. Round tin which is not usual for Webley pellets. Would assume tins of .22 and .25 to be a different colour. Running around the edge of lid; "500 WEBLEY .177 SPECIAL PELLETS NO. 1 BORE FOR AIR PISTOLS & AIR RIFLES" and the flying winged pellet trademark as seen on the action of the Mk. II Service air rifle and on the brass medallion on the grip of the Mk. I air pistol. Very safe to assume that the above tin is dated from the middle 1920s.

"WEBLEY" .22 SPECIAL PELLETS
Orange tin with black printing. It would appear that the standard colour code of Webley's was orange for .22 and pale green for .177. Note that they were made for "Webley Air Pistols" and ONE "AIR RIFLE"! This style of tin appeared in 1924 and right up to the move from Weaman Street to Park Lane, Handsworth, Birmingham 21 in 1959. Clues to tin's age, must be pre-1958 as it has Weaman Street address, could be pre-war as Birmingham does not have a "4" area code and these appeared after the Second World War, hence would assume the age of the above tin to be between the middle 1920s, this being after they had stopped making the Mk. I air rifle, and up to 1939. Edge of tin bears the winged pellet trademark. The above tin would appear to be the first design as it appears on a spares list for the spring clip Webley Mk. I air pistol. This would tally with the introduction of the Mk. I air rifle which was about one to two years before the Mk. II Service. Hence the above tin is quite rare.

The above tin with identical lettering is also found coloured green for 1,000 .177 "Special Pellets". One of these tins contained a leaflet with the Birmingham 4 address.

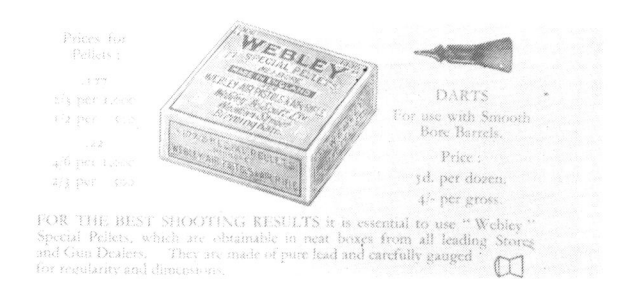

"WEBLEY" .22 SPECIAL PELLETS

Orange for .22 with black printing. Note that we now have "Air rifles" and the address is just Birmingham. From this I would suggest that the above tin dates from 1958 to the middle 1960s when the circular Webley logo appeared. Many of the above have been seen with over stickers bearing varying messages as to changes in contents, hence orange tins with .177 labels etc.

Average weight of ten pellets was 14.5 grains. (.22)

PACKETS OF 1,000 WEBLEY PELLETS

These first appeared about 1925 and were available right up to 1939. They were packed in cardboard boxes of 1,000 in either .22 or .177.

When they first appeared in the middle 1920s the wording on the packet lid was as follows:

"WEBLEY"
.177 Special Pellets.
(No. 1 BORE).
WEBLEY AIR PISTOL AND RIFLE PELLETS

WEBLEY & SCOTT LTD.,
WEAMAN STREET,
BIRMINGHAM.

Interesting to note that in the middle 1920s Webley were only manufacturing two airguns, the Mk. I air rifle and the Mk. I air pistol, hence the quote "Webley air pistol and rifle pellets" by the middle 1930s this statement became "WEBLEY AIR PISTOLS AND AIR RIFLE" because now we had the production of the Junior, Mk. I, Mk. II and Senior air pistols, but still only one air rifle, the Mk. II Service air rifle.

Green Tin for 1000 (.177) with over stamp temporary label for 500 (.22)

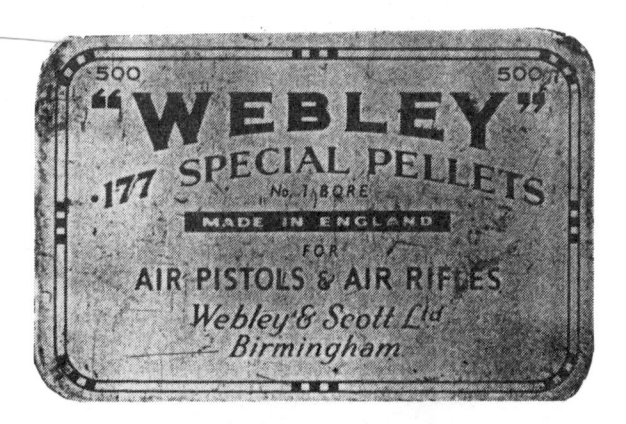

GREEN .177 (500) TIN OF WEBLEY PELLETS

1958 to middle 1960's period, measures 3 x 2 x ⅝ inches (British units). Labelling same as for .22 only smaller tin obviously for .177. Average weight of ten pellets 8.42 grains.

QUOTES AND CATALOGUES

Taken from a 1960s American gun catalogue. Only the Americans with their fine command of English could make such a statement: THIS DESIGN IS A MERGER OF TWO PATENTS — EACH OLDER THAN THE OTHER.

A 1983 reviewer of a gun catalogue ended a sentence with the sweeping statement: "ILLUSTRATED WITH ILLUSTRATIONS".

Taken from a letter regarding possession of arms for self protection, again American in origin: "WHEN A STRONG MAN ARMED KEEPETH HIS PALACE, HIS GOODS ARE IN PEACE" from the Bible, Chapter 11, verse 12, the Book according to Luke.

From a small booklet titled "The New Sport" the following quote is the last paragraph at the end of a little story about shooting B.S.A. air rifles in the home and garden! "AIR RIFLES SEEM TO ME JUST THE THING TO KEEP THE BOYS AT HOME, AND IF YOU'VE ANY DAUGHTERS, THEY'RE JUST THE THING TO BRING THE BOYS TO YOUR HOME". So watch out any girl who is reading this and your father has just bought you an air rifle!

A G. C. Bell & Sons Catalogue of 1925/6 contained a host of quotes that nowadays makes one's hair curl, even at the top and bottom of each page there was a quote that made one tingle with excitement such as: "GO AFTER HIM WITH A GUN"!!!!

A picture of a dead rat with all legs pointing skywards with the message "CONVICTED AND SHOT AT DAWN".

In 1926 rats were destroying £70,000,000 of foodstuffs each year so the youth of yesteryear were summonsed with the following message that even the R.S.P.C.A. would be up in arms about: "NOW BOYS, DON'T LET RATS OVER RUN THE WORLD, AND FOR FIFTY-TWO WEEKS EACH YEAR GO AT HIM WITH PISTOL, CATAPULT AND TRAP. EVERY BOY CAN HELP REDUCE THE RAT PLAGUE".

Now for parents and guardians of these little horrors hell bent on destroying it if it moves: "LORD ROBERTS SAID, 'EVERY BRITISHER SHOULD BE TAUGHT HOW TO HANDLE A RIFLE AND SHOOT STRAIGHT' (now comes the advertising!) SO IT RESTS WITH YOU (parent or guardian) TO DO YOUR DUTY TO YOUR YOUNGSTERS. PURCHASE YOUR BOY AN AIRGUN TO START WITH, AND WE CAN CHEERFULLY SAY (now this bit will really hurt!) THAT EVERY DOG, CAT, AND RAT THIS IS NOT BURIED WILL GIVE YOUR HOUSE A WIDE BERTH."

Another quote from the catalogue makes your chest swell with pride: "IN THE LADDER OF PATRIOTISM EVERY SHOT COUNTS". Now what does that mean?

TARGETS

THE IMPERIAL AUTOMATIC TARGET

MAKER Frederick Stanley Cox (of Britannia fame), 6 Freer Road, Handsworth, Birmingham, England.

DATE Seen advertised 1932—1933 so would assume late 1920s to middle 1930s, or even earlier.

VALUATION £20—£50. ($30—$75).

DETAILS They don't make targets like this any more! Cast iron and made to last lifetimes! Front measures 8 inches by 10 and weighs 14 lbs. Removable quarter inch thick face with three grooves cut around bull's eye. Cast in the front of the frame "IMPERIAL AUTOMATIC TARGET" and underneath the face "F. S. COX PATENTEE SOLE MAKER". Behind the face is a solid cast brass bell with "COX'S AUTOMATIC TARGET BELL" cast around the outer surface, as if there was any doubt as to its origin. Pivoting behind the target face is a projection that when struck falls back and hits another piece of metal that then strikes the bell, at the same time a figure five appears on either side of the target face. A piece of string is tied to the first metal strip and this string can be as long as the target is away from the shooter. To re-cock the action the string is pulled and the action is ready again. Originally the figure fives were painted red. Cost 30/- (£1.50 in 1933, the same price as a Webley Mk. I air pistol and 5/- (25p) dearer than a Warrior air pistol so the above target was very expensive, not only that it must have required a very substantial wall fixture in order to keep it in position! All in all "One hell of a target".

THE PARKER-HALE FOUR INCH TARGET HOLDER AND PELLET TRAP

Although advertised in Parker-Hale catalogues from around the late 1930s to 1955 a very similar pattern was sold as a B.S.A. target and pellet trap in 1939. The similarity is too close and it can be assumed that these were produced and sold to either B.S.A. or Parker-Hale with their names on the front just under the circular target card outer frame.

As can be seen the holder had a cast frame front and a rear that acted as the pellet trade, a simple yet strong target holder. It was packed in a box measuring 6½ inches (16.5 cms) square. Advertised weight was 2¼ lbs. It was listed as their part number A.R.T.7 and the cards as Number 52s. The B.S.A. price in 1939 was 6/6 (32½p) and in 1947 the price had risen to around 16/- (80p) including Purchase Tax.

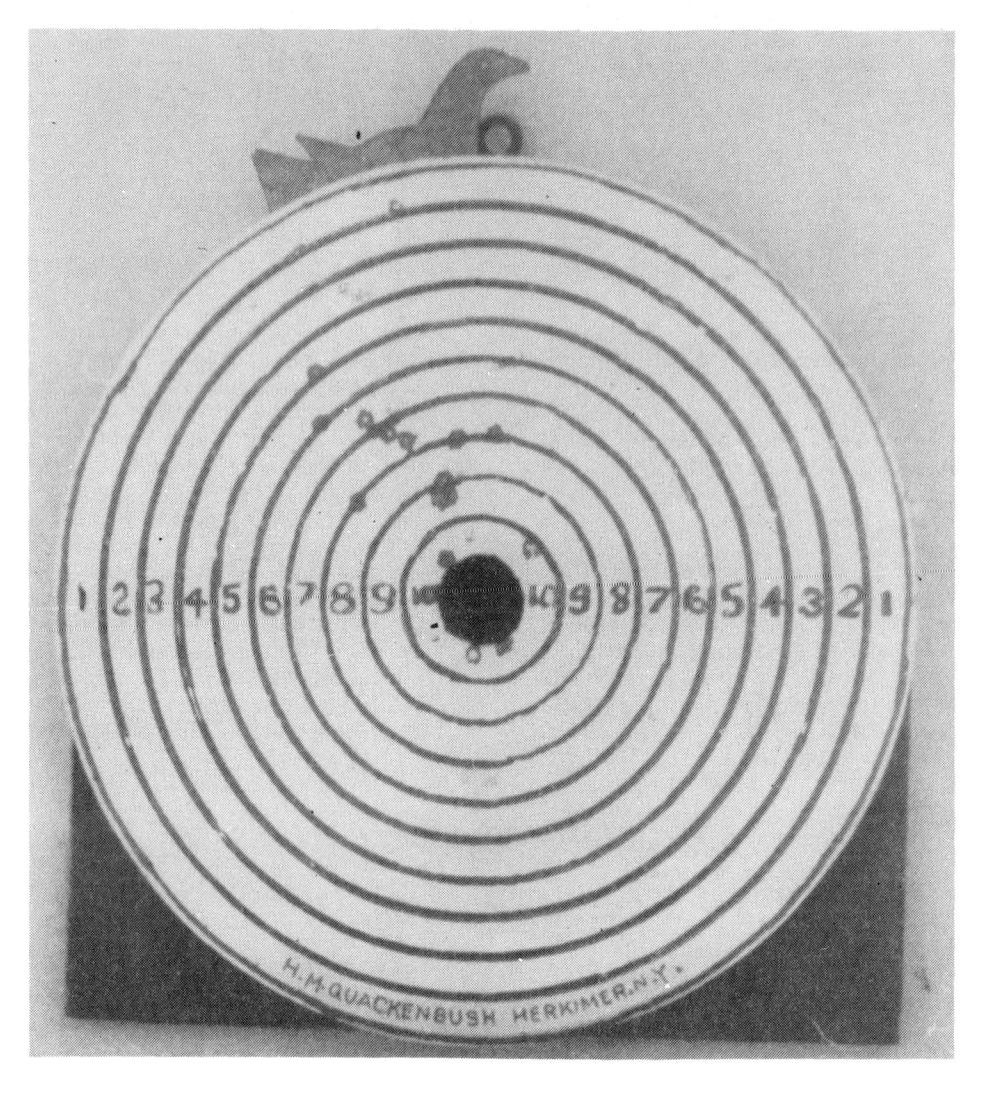

The cast iron Quackenbush bell target

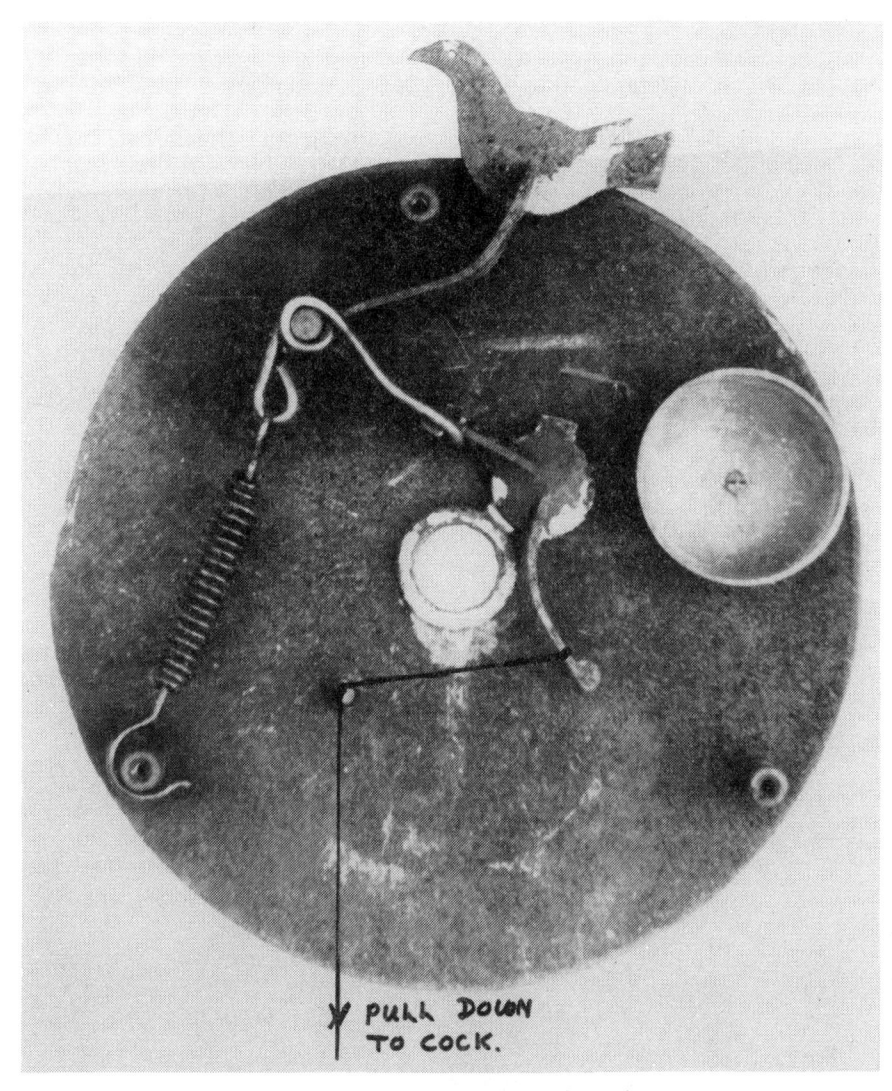

Reverse side of bell target in uncocked position

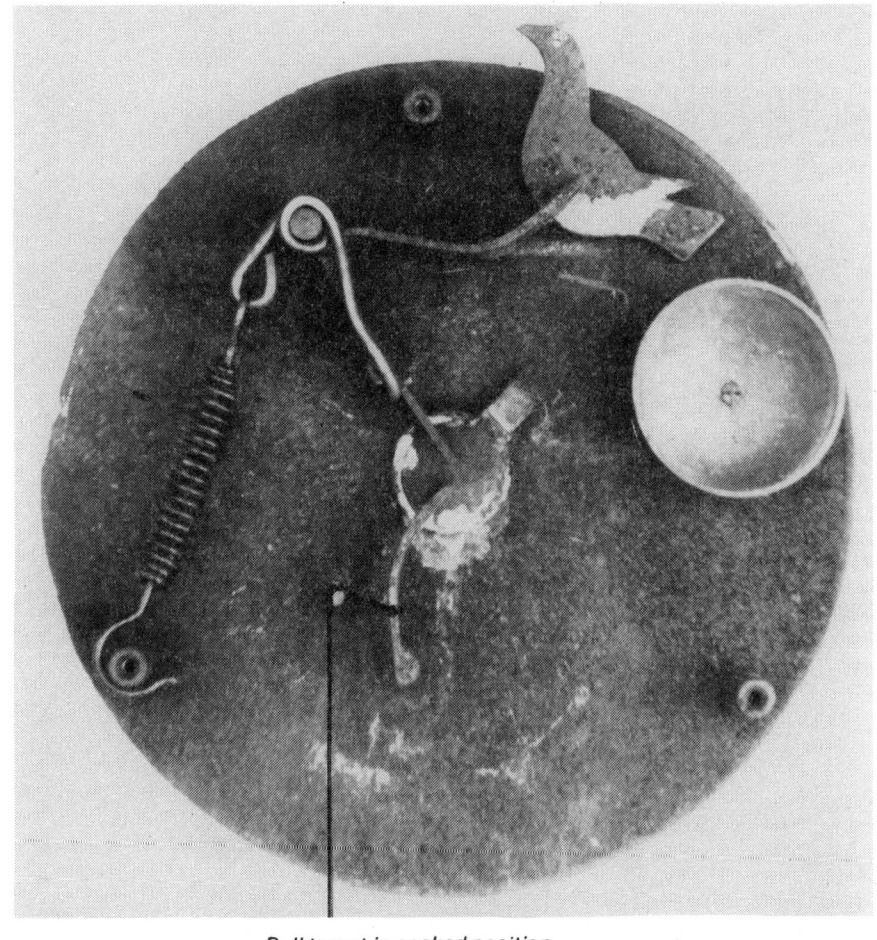

Bell target in cocked position

QUACKENBUSH BELL TARGET

Henry Marcus Quackenbush was born in 1847 and passed on during September 1933. The interest in producing airguns died with him. He started his own airgun business after working for the Remington Arms Co., Ilion, New York. He sighted his factory on the banks of the Mohawk River at Herkimer, New York, during 1871. During this period the Quackenbush Bell Target was manufactured.

Heavy cast iron circular target measuring 11¾ inch across with a 1¼ central hole for ringing the bell. The target face is split into ten rings each about ½ inch apart and labelled from 1 to 10 for scoring. Normally the target face would be coated with white non-drying paint and after each competitor the face would be wiped in order to erase the pellet marks, i.e. to "wipe the slate" clean. Cast in the outer ring towards the bottom "H. M. QUACKENBUSH, HERKIMER, N.Y." The whole target is fixed with three screws to a wooden backing plate that has a fixed hook at the top.

In the uncocked state the hen or chicken appears visible poking out of the top of the rim of the target face, but when the bell is cocked the hen is pulled down out of sight, only to pop up again when the black painted bull's eye has been struck. To cock the action the hen is pushed into the target, or a piece of string or wire is fixed as in the photograph and pulled down. When this is pulled down the centre bull is held in place by a lip of metal. As the bull is struck by a pellet the bull is pushed back and passed the edge of the lip and springs up thus ringing the bell and exposing the cock! Appears to work well with most airguns of moderate power upwards.

Any old target must be rare. A collector once turned up at an Arms Fair with a cast iron Chinese bell target and was offered from £15 up to £50 for it but he would not part with it. So can assume that this is about the right value of the above, somewhere between £15 and £50. ($23—$75).

TARGET HOLDERS & TARGETS

10 × 10 × 1 in. For use at 10 or 20 yards
Price: **13/6** net.

6½ × 6½ × 1 in. For use at 5 yards.
Price: **8/-** net.

Prices for TARGETS:
Large Size - **12/-** per 1,000
Small Size - **8/6** per 1,000

THE ABOVE TARGET HOLDERS have been specially designed for outdoor or indoor use, and are so arranged that the Pellets, after passing through the cardboard Targets, are trapped and caught.

Special WEBLEY Targets, suitable for the above, are obtainable from all principal Stores, Gun Dealers or Sports Depots.

WEBLEY TARGET HOLDERS

These were seen advertised from 1925 to the late 1930s. The first reference is in the Mk. I air rifle handbook and the last was in the Webley leaflet that also included the slant grip Senior, so one could say the date of availability was up to 1939. Their price did not alter during this period of time, almost 15 years which is quite an achievement. The circular portion that holds the target card would appear to be cast iron. Note the two sizes, the larger for 10 and 20 yard range whilst the smaller for 5 yards.